COMPENDIUM OF SCOTTISH SILVER II

Also by Rodney and Janice Dietert

Compendium of Scottish Silver (digital version)
The Edinburgh Goldsmiths I: Training, Marks, Output and Demographics

Compendium of Scottish Silver II

Rodney Dietert
Janice Dietert

Revised and expanded from the original Cornell University Digital Library project,
Compendium of Scottish Silver.

Major Photography Janice Dietert

Dietert Publications
Lansing, NY

Compendium of Scottish Silver II © 2007 by Rodney Dietert and Janice Dietert. All rights reserved. Printed in the United States of America. No part of this book may be used or reproduced in any manner whatsoever without written permission except in the case of brief quotations embodied in critical articles and reviews.

Cover Art by: David Kessler
　　　　http://www.flickr.com/photos/dkessler

Compendium of Scottish Silver II/

ISBN 978-0-6151-6304-8

Dietert Publications
Lansing, NY 14882

FRONT COVER PHOTO LEGEND

Front Cover Artwork by David Kessler.
For the town-associated marks, most were generously provided for use by Colin Fraser, FSA, Edinburgh and Lyon & Turnbull, Edinburgh.

The thistle imprint on the background is an outline of the 1763/64 Edinburgh standard mark.

The central thistle mug is 1701/02 Edward Penman, Edinburgh, provided courtesy of The Phoenix Collection.

Outer Circle Right Top to Bottom:
- Elgin, Saint
- Dundee, Crowned Heart in Shield
- Elgin, Cathedral
- Canongate, Stag's Head
- Banff, BANF
- Castle Douglas, Ruined Castle
- Cupar, Fleur de Lys
- Arbroath, Portcullis
- Elgin, Tree

Outer Circle Left Top to Bottom:
- Forres, Tower
- Dumfries, Foundered Anchor
- Edinburgh, Castle
- Aberdeen, Spurs (?)
- Aberdeen, Sunburst (or flower)
- Castle Douglas, Foundered Anchor
- Dumfries, Unicorn
- Aberdeen, Money Bag
- Dundee, Pot of Lilies

Inner Circle From Top Clockwise:
- Glasgow, Segmented Mark, Oak (with acorn and bird), Bell & Fish
- Greenock, Free Anchor
- Greenock, Sailing Ship
- Inverness, Camel
- Montrose, Rose (1790ca)
- Paisley, Rat Sagent
- Aberdeen, ABDN
- Perth, Double-headed Eagle
- Peterhead, PHD
- Peterhead, Foundered Anchor
- Aberdeen, Hand Holding Dagger
- Aberdeen, Spur
- Aberdeen, 3 Castle Turrets
- Wick, WICK
- Tain, TAIN
- Perth, Double-headed Eagle
- Glasgow, Tree/Fish/Acorn/Bell/Bird
- Montrose, Rose (1750 ca)
- Montrose, Rose (1820 ca)
- Leith, LEITH
- Inverness, INS
- Greenock, Tree

DEDICATION

To those who have crafted and will craft Scottish gold and silver wares.

ACKNOWLEDGEMENTS

The authors are deeply indebted to Henry Steuart Fothringham, Historian of the City of Edinburgh Incorporation of Goldsmiths, George Dalgleish, Principal Curator of Scottish History, National Museums of Scotland, and Colin Fraser of Lyon & Turnbull, Edinburgh, for their encouragement, sharing of notes, devotion of time, and direct assistance in the collection of data and images for this book. This book would not have been possible without their generous help. Mary Michel of The Incorporation of Goldsmiths, City of Edinburgh and Irene Mackay of the National Museums of Scotland, also provided much appreciated support. We express appreciation to Stephen Clarke and Jeanne Sloane of Christie's and Peter Waldron and John Culme of Sotheby's for allowing us access to a century of auction house records, lot descriptions and archival photographs. At Colonial Williamsburg, USA, John Hyman (Associate Curator) and John Davis, Head Curator, came to our assistance at key times. We also thank researchers Robert B Barker and Wynyard R T Wilkenson for their valuable suggestions. Anonymous collectors in Canada, Scotland and the U.S. were instrumental in this project by providing both details of their collections as well as photographs for use. Numerous silver dealers and related companies provided exceptional aid including: John H. Bourdon-Smith (J H Bourdon-Smith Ltd, London), James McConnaughy and Bard Langstaff of S.J. Shrubsole, Inc, Ben Goodwin (Goodwin's Antiques, Edinburgh), Edward Munves (James Robinson, Inc., NY), Nicholas Shaw (Nicholas Shaw Antiques), Alastair Dickenson (Alastair Dickenson Fine Silver), Brand Inglis, George Schrager (Schredds Antiques of Portobello), Jonathan Franks (I. Franks Antiques), Max Michalson (S J Phillips Ltd London), Frogworth Antiques, Asprey Ltd., London, AC Cooper Ltd. and Daniel Bexfield (Daniel Bexfield Antiques). We thank Professor Emeritus J. Robert Cooke, former Dean of Faculty of Cornell University for his support of the first digital version of the book that evolved into this expanded print version. Finally, we are most grateful to David Kessler, our favorite graphics artist, for his creative contributions.

Note: Any errors within the book are solely the responsibility of the authors and should not reflect on the generous individuals and organizations who aided us in this project.

TABLE OF CONTENTS

Guide to the Compendium	1
Abbreviations	2
Timeline of Earliest Form Appearance	3
Aids for Interpreting Scottish Hallmarks and Evaluating Scottish Silver	11
List of Plates	17
Baskets	21
Beakers	29
Bowls	35
Punch	37
Slop	45
Strawberry	47
Sugar	49
Boxes	73
Brooches, Medals and Badges	85
Candlesticks	93
Casters, Kitchen Peppers and Pepper Pots	107
Casters	108
Kitchen Peppers/Dredgers	121
Pepper Pots	122
Church Silver	125
Communion Cups and Beakers	127
Flagons and Basins	151
Lavers	152
Patens	155
Church Plates	157
Coffeepots and Chocolate Pots	159
Cream and Milk Containers	169
Cruets	193
Cups	197
Coconut Cups	198
Mazers	198
Tumbler Cups	199
Two-Handled Cups	203
Dinnerware	209
Dish Crosses and Dish Rings	211
Entrée Dishes	213
Epergnes	214
Jugs	214
Plates	219
Dinner/Table	220
Serving and Other Dishes	221
Tureens	221
Flatware	225
Fish Slices and Servers	227
Forks	233
Knives	241
Ladles	245
Marrow Spoons and Scoops	263
Skewers	269
Spoons	273
Sugar Tongs	325
Ink Pots and Ink Stands	333
Miscellaneous and Special Collections	337

Mugs... 355
        General Mugs...357
        Thistle Mugs/Cups...371
Mustard Pots... 385
Porringers and Bleeding Bowls..389
Quaichs... 393
Salts.. 409
Salvers.. 423
Sauceboats... 463
Strainers...471
Tankards... 477
Tazzas.. 487
Tea...493
        Caddies...495
        Kettles, Stands and Trays.. 501
        Teapots... 507
        Tea Services...563
Toast and Bannock Racks..571
Urns.. 575
Wine.. 581
        Coasters... 582
        Funnels... 584
        Funnels Stands... 587
        Goblets, Cups and Tasters... 589
        Labels... 593
Brief Glossary and Explanations... 601
Works Cited...611

GUIDE TO COMPENDIUM OF SCOTTISH SILVER II

Compendium of Scottish Silver II is an expanded, single-volume print version of the digital Compendium and contains more than 6,000 listings of extant Scottish silver. This new version updates the original work with the addition of 1,000 plus new listings, new photographs and a new section on hallmarks. Compendium II has many new provincial silver listings as well as the inclusion of more listings of 19th century silver. Compiled over a period of two decades via the resources of the Cornell University library system and through the generous assistance of numerous silver dealers, historians, collectors, museum curators and other experts, it is the most comprehensive catalog of Scottish silver published to date. It should prove to be a useful guide for researchers, dealers and collectors as well as an inspiration for those who appreciate the Scottish goldsmiths and marvel at their wares.

Silver items are listed by category (e.g. bowls) and subcategory (e.g. sugar bowls) in chronological order. For categories with only a few listings, they are likely to be found within the "Miscellaneous" section. In most cases, the listing is a verbatim extract from the museum catalog, auction record or magazine advertisement, etc. However, in several cases, the maker designation has been altered from an auction listing to reflect more recent advances in attributions (e.g. James Mitchell substituted for the Edinburgh mark, IM-figure-between and James Mitchelson substituted for attributions to John Main) or more recent concern over previous mark attributions (e.g. distinguishing between William Dempster's and William Davie's various punches). In many cases, there was no description of an item beyond a maker, year, and category. However, for some items (e.g. those currently in museums), the source listing itself may be used to obtain greater detail about a specific piece of interest.

When the same silver item was found in multiple sources, the sources were combined under one listing (e.g. multiple shops in sequence, or auctions and then museums, etc.). In cases where two or more items listed in different sources cannot be distinguished with certainty between them and may be the same piece, the first listing appears in normal text while the subsequent similar listings appear in italics. These may or may not be separate pieces and the user should be cautious. This is particularly a problem for Scottish provincial pieces that have incomplete descriptions and lack an annual date letter. Reference texts used in the compendium are abbreviated in the listing. Full bibliographic information follows at the end of the book for these sources. Journals and auctions are listed with as much information as was available. Even though the citations are as complete as possible, some may inevitably prove problematic (via errors in original transcription) or be difficult to pursue. We apologize in advance where this may be the case.

ABBREVIATIONS USED:

\# in an auction catalog = lot

\# in a book = the plate designation

" = inches

appx = appendix

ca = approximate

di = diameter

d = pennyweights (20 per troy ounce)

g or gm = grams

ht = height

mm = maker's mark

oz = troy ounces

p = page

vol = volume (of a journal or multi-volume text)

TIMELINE OF SCOTTISH SILVER FORMS: EARLIEST APPEARANCES

This timeline is offered solely as a guide based on current surviving pieces found in the database. These pieces are not necessarily the earliest actually produced. In a few cases entries are included and specified for pieces known to have existed in the past based on detailed records (e.g. patron accounts, etc.) even when the continued existence of the piece is uncertain. Certainly, earlier pieces may come to light in coming years. We hope this timeline will encourage a continued examination of Scottish silver style development and innovation. We have attempted to provide both Edinburgh and provincial examples whenever possible.

Pre-1500

Mazer—1320s ca---The Bute Mazer (unmarked bowl and boss 1320ca), mounts probably later

Probable Scottish Mace--- Faculty of Arts, University of St Andrews

16th Century

Cup with Maker's Mark---1530s ca---The Methune Cup, possible by John Vaitch

Marked Mazer---1520-50 The Watson Mazer possibly Adam Leis; 1550s-60s The St. Mary's Mazer Alexander Auchinleck, followed by the Tulloch and Galloway Mazers, James Gray, Canongate.

Scottish Crown---1540 reworking by John Mosman and Adam Leis of an earlier crown

Scottish Sceptre --- 1540 re-cast and augmented by Adam Leis, Edinburgh.

Marked Communion Cup---1563 Henry Thomsone, Edinburgh (originally a secular vessel)

Ewer---1565-67 James Cok I, Edinburgh

Seal-top Spoon ("The Cunningham") --- 1573ca William Cok, Edinburgh.

Disc-end Spoons --- 1579-81 George Heriot II, Edinburgh.

Baptismal Basin---1591 James Crawford, Edinburgh. (originally a secular vessel)

1600s and 1610s

Slip-top Spoon --- 1609-10ca, Gilbert Kirkwood, Edinburgh.

The Heriot Cup (Nautilus cup) --- 1611-13 Robert Dennistoun, Edinburgh.

Horse Racing Prize---1617ca The Lanark Bell maker Hugh Lindsay, deacon Robert Dennistoun

All-Silver Mazer (bowl-type)---1619ca Thomas Cleghorne I, Deacon James Dennistoun, Edinburgh. (Documentary evidence shows that all-silver mazers existed at least as early as 1573.) The other extant example is the St. Leonard's Mazer (16th-century, standing-type), University of St. Andrews.

City Mace (Edinburgh)---1617ca George Robertson I

1620s and 1630s

Wine Cup---1630ca Thomas Cleghorne I, Edinburgh

Coronation Items---1633ca Gold Ampulla, used at the Scottish Coronation of Charles I, unmarked.

Bread Plates (Trinity Church) --- 1633ca Thomas Kirkwood, Edinburgh.

Coconut Cup --- 1637-39 Andrew Dennistoun, Edinburgh.

1640s and 1650s

Wine Funnel—1640ca Adam Lamb, maker's mark only.

Sweetmeat Dish or Wine Taster --- 1646-48 Thomas Cleghorne I, Edinburgh.

Puritan Spoon---1649ca Alexander Scott (with spoon of 1648 of undesignated form)

Puritan Spoon --- 1651-53 or 1657-59 George Cleghorne, Edinburgh.

Court of Session Mace (dated) 1659-61—Edward Cleghorne I (Andrew Burrell Deacon)

1660s-1670s

Tankard (peg) ---1663-1681 by Edward Cleghorne I.

Quaich (fully marked)—1661-81 Edward Cleghorne I.

Set of Trefid spoons---1665-80 marks of Edward Cleghorne I and Alexander Reid (one maker, one deacon).

Trumpets—1669ca by Thomas Moncur, Glasgow. And 1675-80 ca Robert Brock.

Tazzas---1670s William Law, maker, Alexander Reid, deacon;
1670s ---Alexander Reid, maker and also as deacon; 1670s Alexander Scott.

Capstan Salt---1670ca Patrick Gairdyne, St. Andrews.

Dinner Plates---1671-73ca, Edinburgh, by Alexander Scott, deacon Edward Cleghorne (this based on documentary evidence only; the present whereabouts of these plates have not been traced.)

Ink-horn or Writing equipage ---1674ca Thomas Cleghorne, Edinburgh.

Two-Handled Porringer---1675-67 William Law (maker and deacon)

1680s

Gourd Cup --- 1680ca, Thomas Cleghorne II, Edinburgh

Two-handled Cup and Cover ---1682/83 Alexander Reid, Edinburgh.

Caster---1684/85 Thomas Yorstoun (apprentice to Edward Cleghorne I).

Flagon --- 1684/85 John Law, Edinburgh.

Tea Caddie --- 1685ca James Cockburn, Edinburgh.

Patch Box --- 1685/86 Robert Brock, Glasgow.

Tobacco Box --- 1685/86, by Robert Brock, Glasgow.

Pair of Tankards, "The Lyon Tankards" --- 1685/86 James Cockburn, Edinburgh.

Sanctus Bell—1686/87 Zaccharius Mellinus, Edinburgh.

Tumbler Cup—1680s Thomas Moncur (Glasgow); Robert Gardiner (Perth);
Tumbler Cup --- 1687/87 James Penman, Edinburgh.
Tumbler Cup --- 1694/95 James Luke, Glasgow.

Beaker (dated) ---1686/87 by James Penman, Pair Thistle shaped; two other provincial beakers likely earlier. Made as Communion Cups of Leslie.

Chalice, "The Forsyth Chalice" ---1688ca Zaccharias Mellinus, Edinburgh.

Saucepan --- 1688/89 George Scott, Edinburgh.

Bleeding Bowl ---1689/90 by James Penman, Edinburgh. Circular bowl, trefoil handle pierced with clovers.

1690s

Table Knives --- 1690ca, JS, Edinburgh.

Condiment or Child's Spoon ---1690ca George Yorstoun, Edinburgh.

Punch Bowl, "The Bruce Bowl" --- 1692/93 Robert Bruce, Edinburgh.

Chambersticks 1693/94---James Penman, Edinburgh.

Casters (set of three) --- 1693/94 Andrew Law, Edinburgh.

Thistle Mugs (pair) --- 1693/4 by James Cockburn
Thistle Mug ---1694/95 Andrew Law.

Dish Ring---1693/94 James Cockburn.

Individual Salt (circular)---1694/95 Robert Brock, Glasgow.
   Also Individual Salt--- 1710/11 William Ged, Edinburgh.

Two-handled Thistle Cup --- 1695/96 Edward Penman, Edinburgh.

Tablesticks (pair) --- 1695/96 James Penman, Edinburgh.

Tableforks—1698/99 Alexander Kincaid; same year Robert Bruce, Edinburgh Trefids, both originally large sets, and one by Thomas Cleghorne in the National Museums of Scotland.

Wall Sconces---1698/99 James Penman (Pair)

Monteith --- 1698/99 Colin McKenzie, Edinburgh.

Dog-nose spoon---1689/99 Edinburgh no maker's mark; 1695-1700 probably George Yorstoun Maker's mark only three times;

1700s

Tot Cup --- 1700ca Alexander Forbes, Edinburgh.

Marrow-Spoon---1700/01 Alexander Kincaid

Silver-mounted Mirror --- probably 1701 James Penman, Edinburgh.

Hanoverian Spoons --- 1702/03 Colin McKenzie, Edinburgh

Hanoverian Forks----1702/03 Colin McKenzie, Edinburgh

Jug --- 1701/02 Thomas Ker, Edinburgh.

Barber's Bowl and Ewer --- 1702/03 Thomas Ker, Edinburgh.

Child's Rattle --- 1703ca Robert Inglis, Edinburgh

Toilet Service "The Keir" --- 1703/04 Colin McKenzie, Edinburgh.

Casket --- 1705ca Thomas Ker, Edinburgh.

Hash Spoon --- 1705/06 John Luke Jr., Glasgow.

Officer's Badge (Incorporation of Surgeons)---1705-10ca Alexander Kincaid, Edinburgh.

Spout Cup --- 1707/08 Walter Scott, Edinburgh.

Seal Box --- 1709/10, by John Luke II, Glasgow.

Salvers --- 1709/10, maker not stated, Edinburgh (originally Hopetoun collection).

1710s

Pincushion, silver-mounted --- 1710ca Robert Bruce, Edinburgh.

Coffeepot---1713/14 Colin McKenzie (part of set)

Hot-milk Jug --- 1713/14 Colin McKenzie, Edinburgh.
    Also 1714/15 Mungo Yorstoun.

Teapot---1714/15 Colin McKenzie and Colin Campbell (both apprentices of James Penman).

Tea Caddy --- 1710ca, Johan Got-helf-Bilsings, Glasgow.

Teapot, apple-shaped --- 1715/16 Colin McKenzie

Silver Sword-Hilt --- 1715ca Henry Bethune, Edinburgh.

Flask--- 1716ca Alexander Kincaid, Edinburgh.

Teapot stand---1717/18 James Mitchelson., Edinburgh.

Sugar Bowl, octagonal --- 1717/18 by Henry Bethune and 1718/19 by William Aytoun.

Covered Sugar Bowl---1718/19 John Seatoun.

Strawberry Dish --- 1718/19 Henry Bethune, Edinburgh. And see 1725ca

Snuffer Stand---1719/20 Henry Bethune

Egg or Barrel-Shaped Teapot---1719/20 Henry Bethune (egg) and Colin McKenzie (barrel) (both James Penman apprentices).

1720s

Chocolate Pot --- 1720/21 Patrick Murray, Edinburgh.

Octagonal Teapot --- 1723/24 William Aytoun, Edinburgh.

Desert Spoons --- 1722/23 Kenneth McKenzie, Edinburgh.

Use of Wavy Border, Molded Edge, Bowls and Stands---1721/22 James Mitchelson-Private Collection UK, then 1723/24 James Ker; then 1725/26 James Ker (James Penman lineage).

Spirit Burner --- 1724/25 James Mitchelson, Edinburgh.

Strawberry Dish ---1725ca, by Robert Luke, Glasgow. (Edinburgh 1718-19)

Snuff Box --- Glasgow, 1725ca, Johan Got-helf-Bilsings, Glasgow.

Tea Kettle, Lamp and Stand---1725/26 James Mitchelson.

Snake-Handled Tea Urn---1723/24 William Aytoun, Edinburgh

Use of Curved Spout---1725/26 James Mitchelson (kettle) and Edward Penman (teapot) (apprentice of James Penman); 1726/27 James Tait

Three-Footed Sugar Bowl---1726/27 James Ker, Edinburgh

Pair of Branches for Candlesticks --- 1728/29 James Ker, Edinburgh.

Dry Mustard Pot --- 1729/30 William Aytoun, Edinburgh.

Square Salver --- 1729/30 maker's mark unclear, Edinburgh.

1730s

Dessert Knives --- 1730ca, unmarked, Edinburgh.

Bun Pepper --- 1730/31 William Aytoun, Edinburgh.

Double-Lipped Sauce Boats --- 1730/31 James Mitchelson, Edinburgh.

Punch Ladle --- 1733/34 William Aytoun, Edinburgh.

Cream boats---1733/34 James Ker and Ebenezer Oliphant, 1735/36 William Aytoun

Everted Rim Chased Sugar Bowls—1734/35 James Ker (four footed, part of set) (note also a 1734/35 James Tait bowl, three footed, rim flat everted shaped, but undecorated).

Urn Stand --- 1735/36 James Ker, Edinburgh.

Teaspoons, Scots fiddle pattern --- 1735ca (1731-1737) John Rollo, Edinburgh.

Kettle Set Equipped for Silver Table---1736/37 James Mitchelson

Taperstick --- 1736/37 James Ker, Edinburgh.

Gold Teapot --- 1736 James Ker, Edinburgh.

Cruet Frame --- 1736/37 William Marshall I, Edinburgh. Note this maker had an untimely death shorten his career.

Snuffer Tray --- 1736/37 Laurence Oliphant, Edinburgh.

Burgess-Ticket Box --- 1736/37 John Rollo, Edinburgh.

Gravy Boat --- 1737/38ca maker's mark RC, possibly Edinburgh.

Cake Basket---1739/40 James Ker; also 1740/41 by James Ker and 1740ca by James Ker

Punch Strainer --- probably late 1730s William Aytoun, Edinburgh.

1740s

Library Lamp --- 1740 William Aytoun Edinburgh (assay-master David Mitchell, Feb.-Sept.1740).

Traveling Canteen --- 1740/41 Ebenezer Oliphant. Edinburgh.

Inkstand---Robert Gordon

Use of Dolphin Handle---1743/44 WD (William Dempster or William Davie) on a cream boat.

Use of Artichoke Final---1743/44 William Aytoun; 1745-50 ca. James Glen (Glasgow).

Use of Bird Spout---1745-50 ca. James Glen (Glasgow) teapot.

Child's Rattle --- c.1745, by James Glen, Glasgow (earliest provincial)

Marine-Themed Hollowware—1747/48 WD (probably William Dempster) Cakebasket.

1750s

Tea Vases (pair) --- 1750ca James Glen Glasgow.

Use of Bird Finial---1753/54 Lothian & Robertson (kettle) and Robert Gordon (teapot).

Square Teapot---1753/54 Lothian & Robertson (Robertson trained by Edward Lothian).

Soup Tureen – 1756/57 James Welsh (trained by James Mitchell)

1760s

Pointed Old English Spoons --- 1763/64 Lothian & Robertson

Sugar Tongs---1760/61 by Alexander Aitchison I

1770s

Bannock or Toast Rack---1773/74 Patrick Robertson.

Servers/Fish Slices---1778/79 Peter Mathie server, 1780/81 WD probably William Davie Fish Slice

Onslow Pattern— 1767/68 Ker & Dempster; (also) 1776/77 WD script probably for William Davie or William Dempster, also one 1783-84 Alexander Gardner.

1780s

Wine Coaster---1781/82 WD for William Davie or William Dempster.

Wine Funnel Stand---1782/83 WD for either William Davie or William Dempster
ditto --- 1783-4 by W. & P. Cunningham.

Vase Shaped Sugar---1783/84 WD for William Davie or William Dempster.

Aids for Interpreting Scottish Hallmarks and Evaluating Scottish Silver

Scottish Silver *vs.* the Pretenders

Confusion over whether a piece of silver was made in Scotland is quite common. Most mis-categorization of non-Scottish silver as Scottish stems from certain similarities in one or more of the marks. For example, the town of Exeter also used a three-turreted castle as a mark. In this case, the central turret is not grounded as occurs with most examples of the Edinburgh castle mark. Nevertheless, Exeter pieces are quite frequently mislabeled as being Edinburgh silver. Another clue for proper identification is that the Exeter hallmarks on silver usually include a lion passant mark lacking on early Edinburgh silver.

The example below illustrates the Exeter hallmarks for the year 1815/16. Occasionally, this is erroneously attributed to Edinburgh 1799/800. For comparison, the assumed Edinburgh hallmarks using the same capital "T" date letter for 1799/1800 are shown below the Exeter marks. The Edinburgh hallmarks lack the Exeter lion standard mark and instead includes the thistle as the standard mark.

Exeter town mark (Courtesy of Frogworth Antiques)

Edinburgh town mark

A second major opportunity to mis-identify silver as Scottish is when Scottish-trained craftsmen practiced the trade in other parts of the world. Those Scottish trained goldsmiths often used thistle or other marks derived from their homeland. Hence, the presence of a thistle mark alone does not automatically prove that a piece was made in Scotland. This is particularly true if the item in question also carries other uncharacteristic marks for Scotland (e.g. animals normally dwelling in equatorial regions).

Finally, if a piece has a Scottish design element, it does not necessarily mean it was made in Scotland. In the 16th -19th centuries many major Scottish patrons had accounts not only in Scotland but also in London (in some cases even with Scottish-origin or trained London goldsmiths). Therefore, the appearance of a Scottish family's crest and motto on a piece of gold or silver is not sufficient to know for certain that the piece was crafted in Scotland. Other factors must be considered (hallmarks and or form). Later in the 19th and 20th centuries many English towns (e.g. Birmingham) produced Scottish symbol-themed (e.g. thistles) silver designed to be retailed in Scotland. This is commonly identified as Scottish in shops and sales but, in fact, it represents English silver made for the Scottish market.

Identifying the Maker

Assayed Edinburgh silver produced before 1681and the election of an assay master lacked a date letter, but it included the then current deacon's mark as the certification of the silver standard. When the marks were placed in a straight line, a majority of pieces have the maker's mark placed on the far left and the deacons' mark to the right of the castle town mark. But exceptions can exist. Therefore, knowledge of the terms of the deacons and acting deacons as well as the working periods of both the potential maker and deacon are helpful in identifying the marker *vs.* the assayer.

Below are the hallmarks from taken from a communion cup with marks of the maker, George Crawford (left of the town mark) and the Deacon, James Dennistoun.

(Courtesy of S. J. Phillips Ltd. London)

From 1681-1759 Edinburgh silver carried the mark of both the maker and the assay master (an elected post of The City of Edinburgh Incorporation of Goldsmiths). Assay masters and acting assay masters used their own makers' punches for marking certification of the silver standard of a given piece. Therefore, knowledge of the assay masters' terms of office is important in identifying the maker *vs.* the assay master and for dating some pieces where marks are lacking or rubbed.

In 1759, a thistle mark was adopted for Edinburgh assayed work. Therefore, the later 18th century Edinburgh silver would have only one maker's-like mark.

Note, in general, assay masters did not produce much of their own silver during their own term of office (e.g. silver by John Borthwick, James Penman, Edward Penman, or Hugh Gordon while serving as assay master). But there are examples where assay masters did assay their own work (e.g. Archibald Ure, Dougal Ged, and Edward Lothian).

Below is an example of Archibald Ure, Edinburgh, assaying his own work from 1731/32.

Ironically, some 19th century Scottish silver again presents another case where identification of the maker may be problematic due to the presence of two apparent maker's marks. In these cases, one mark is usually for the actual maker of the silver item and the second mark is the mark of a retailer (e.g. jewelry shop) of the maker's wares. The marks occur in addition to the town, standard and duty marks.

Edinburgh Work vs. Edinburgh-Assayed Silver

With the imposition of the duty tax on December 1, 1784, new silver produced in Scotland was supposed to be assayed at the Edinburgh assay office and the duty tax paid. In 1819, the Glasgow assay office opened and all silver produced in Glasgow and the general vicinity was assayed there with the duty collected. Hence until 1784, all silver with Edinburgh marks was produced and/or at least submitted for assay by Edinburgh freemen. In contrast, silver with Edinburgh assay marks falling between 1784 and 1819 could have been made anywhere in Scotland yet carry Edinburgh assay and duty marks. Silver from this period with maker's marks not found for Edinburgh was most likely produced elsewhere in Scotland. Provincial makers such as Robert Gray of Glasgow and Robert Keay of Perth are extensively represented among Edinburgh assayed silver from this period. From 1819 on Glasgow makers and those from the immediate area had silver assayed in Glasgow. Hence, silver from the Robert Gray shop appears with Glasgow hallmarks during the 1820s. However, much silver from Banff, Dumfries, Dundee, Montrose, Perth, Aberdeen makers continued to have Edinburgh assay marks.

Top Row: Marks for Alexander Gardner, Edinburgh 1796/97
Bottom Row: Marks for Robert Gray, Glasgow, on silver assayed 1797/98 in Edinburgh

When Missing Date Letters are the Norm

For reasons not clearly understood, a high percentage of Edinburgh marked silver produced between approximately 1790 and 1802 lacks a date letter. This is also the period during which provincial makers sent their silver to Edinburgh for assay and duty to be collected. The lack of a date letter during this interval is more the rule than the exception and, therefore, it is not considered as a negative for most valuation. In fact, if Edinburgh marked silver is found lacking a date letter, there is an excellent chance it was made between 1790 and 1802. Changes in the town, thistle and duty marks during this window can be used to help with more precise dating in the absence of a date letter.

Confusing Date Letter Cycles and Date Letters

While date letter cycles were designed to provide reasonably accurate dating to the precise 12 month cycle of the assay year, problems can still arise. One such case involves the Edinburgh date letter cycles spanning 1780 -1831. Because several capital *vs.* lower-case letters (e.g. C *vs.* c, O *vs.* o, P *vs.* p, S *vs.* s, U *vs.* u, V *vs.* v, W *vs.* w, X *vs.* x, Z *vs.* z) can be confused between these two cycles and some inverted letters may also look similar to each other (e.g.

lower-case q vs. b), dating may be off by one or more decades. Interestingly, when errors arise a majority of the dating errors specify the piece as earlier than its actual date of assay. These confounding letters can be correctly assessed if one examines the entire spectrum of shield cartouche shapes of the castle, thistle marks and letter marks for 1780/81-1831/32 and the duty marks for 1784/85-1831/32. For example, most shields used straight angled lines and a sharply pointed base until about 1820, while those falling later had a noticeable S curve ending in a rounded cup rather than a sharp point. Additionally, the castle itself changed significantly across the relevant years.

Below are examples of Edinburgh assayed hallmarks falling between 1789/90 and 1830/31. Note the hallmarks with the "c" date letter (in reality lower case c) is taken from a Matthew Craw quaich and can be shown to represent the year 1808/09 based both on shield shape and the presence of the duty mark. The alternative capital "C" hallmarks served for 1782/83, had different shield cartouche shapes and lacked a duty mark.

Patrick Robertson, Edinburgh, 1789/90

Alexander Gardner, Edinburgh 1796/97

Alexander Henderson, Edinburgh 1799/1800

Edinburgh assay, 1801/02

Robert Gray & Son, Glasgow, Edinburgh assay 1805/06

(Matthew Craw not shown) Edinburgh 1808/09

AE, Edinburgh 1830/31

Within other date letter cycles, there is also the potential for confusion particularly during the James Penman and Hugh Gordon terms as assay masters. However, in these cases the options usually fall only a few years apart and do not span a decade or more.

Design and Decoration of the Progressive Scottish Tea Service

In England a full tea service from the same year is relatively common. However, in Scotland, surviving tea services produced in the same year by the same maker are quite rare. Instead, pieces of a tea service were assembled one at a time by a family. It could sometimes take 20 years for a full service to be completely assembled. The style of the decoration changed over the interval. As a result, decoration of a service often reflected the style from which the last piece of the service was produced. If this were a London tea service, such a lag in style decoration would be considered a major negative for valuation. But with Scottish services, it is not as serious an issue. A prime example of this is found in the novel egg-shaped teapot and matching hot milk jug made by Henry Bethune in the Hyman Collection at Colonial Williamsburg. The pieces were clearly decorated in overlapping layers with the final layer reflecting the style of later acquisitions among the owners (the Foulis family).

Scottish Unmarked Covers and "Missing" Burners

Removable covers of casters, bowls, cups and urns were rarely marked in Scotland but were routinely marked in London. Lack of a hallmark on the cover of an 18th century Scottish caster or bowl is standard and not considered problematic. Additionally, burners for some items such as dish crosses were generally standard in 18th century England but optional (and frequently detachable) in Scotland. Hence, the lack of a burner with Scottish silver does not mean the item
is necessarily "missing" and that the piece is less than 100 percent of its original state. Instead, the piece may never have been equipped with a burner.

LIST OF PLATES

PLATES

1. Baskets. A 1761/62 cakebasket by W (star) D probably William Dempster, Edinburgh. Courtesy of a private collector, Photograph by Janice M. Dietert.

2. Beakers. Pair of 1768/69 beakers by Patrick Robertson, Edinburgh. Photograph courtesy of The Maple Swan Collection.

3. Bowls. Two distinctly different bowls-1726/27 three-footed lion's mask sugar bowl by James Ker, Edinburgh (left) and 1765ca covered sugar bowl by Milne & Campbell, Glasgow (right). Courtesy of The Phoenix Collection. Photograph by Janice M. Dietert.

4. Punch Bowls. A Presentation Punch Bowl 1820/21 by James McKay, Edinburgh. Photograph courtesy of J. H. Bourdon-Smith, London.

5. Slop Bowls. A three footed shallow Slop (or Sugar) Bowl, 1734/35 by James Tait, Edinburgh. Courtesy of The Phoenix Collection. Photograph by Janice M. Dietert.

6. Strawberry Bowls. A Strawberry Bowl/Dish 1730ca by George Cooper, Aberdeen. Photograph courtesy of The Maple Swan Collection.

7. Sugar Bowls. A Sugar Bowl 1750/51 by James Mitchell, Edinburgh. Courtesy of The Phoenix Collection. Photograph by Janice M Dietert.

8. Boxes. A Presentation Snuff Box 1798 by Alexander Gairdner, Edinburgh (top and bottom). Courtesy of The Phoenix Collection. Photograph by Janice M. Dietert.

9. Brooches, Badges and Medals. A School Medal 1851/52 by Peter Aiken, Glasgow (front and back). Courtesy of The Phoenix Collection. Photograph by Janice M. Dietert.

10. Candlesticks. A pair of Tablesticks 1745/46 by James Ker, Edinburgh. Courtesy of The Phoenix Collection. Photograph by Janice M. Dietert.

11. Casters. An Octagonal Caster made Fall of 1729 by James Ker (Edward Penman assayer), Edinburgh. Courtesy of The Phoenix Collection. Photograph by Janice M. Dietert.

12. Church Silver. A Communion Cup (1680s ca) by William Lindsay for the Church of Montrose. Photograph courtesy of The Maple Swan Collection.

13. Communion Cups. A Communion Cup 1658ca by Edward Cleghorne I, Edinburgh, for St. Leonard's Church, St. Andrews. Photograph courtesy of The Maple Swan Collection.

14. Patens. A Communion Paten 1650ca by Edward Cleghorne I, Edinburgh. Photograph courtesy of The Maple Swan Collection.

15. Plates. The Cruden Communion Bread Plate. Inscribed/dated 1691 for the church at Cruden Bay by GW, Aberdeen. Photograph courtesy of The Maple Swan Collection.

16. Coffeepots. An Edinburgh example 1759/60 by William Taylor. Courtesy of J.H. Bourdon-Smith, London.

17. Cream and Milk Containers. Group of three Edinburgh Cream Boats of different styles,

1744/45 Edward Lothian (left), 1752/53 Robert Gordon (center), 1741/42 James Weems (right). Courtesy of The Phoenix Collection. Photograph by Janice M. Dietert.

18. Cruets. 1792/93 an egg cruet with four cups by William Robertson, Edinburgh. Photograph courtesy of Schredds of Portobello, London (George Schrager, owner).

19. Cups. A Tumbler Cup 1717-19ca Edinburgh by Henry Bethune. Courtesy of The Phoenix Collection. Photograph by Janice M. Dietert.

20. Dinnerware. One of two Covered Entrée Dishes 1829/30 Marshall and Son, Edinburgh. Courtesy of a private collector. Photograph by Janice M. Dietert

21. Dish Crosses and Dish Rings. Top: A dish ring 1693/94 by James Cockburn. Photograph courtesy of A C Cooper Ltd, London and The Maple Swan Collection. Bottom: A Dish Cross 1767/68 by WD probably William Dempster, Edinburgh. Courtesy of The Phoenix Collection. Photograph by Janice M. Dietert.

22. Plates. One of a pair of Ashets (meat dishes) 1821/22 by George McHattie, Edinburgh. Courtesy of a private collector. Photograph by Janice M. Dietert.

23. Flatware. A Scots Fiddle Pattern Tea Straining Spoon 1730ca by William Aytoun, Edinburgh. Courtesy of a private collector. Photograph by Janice M. Dietert

24. Fish Slices. A Fish Slice 1807/08 by James Douglas, Edinburgh. Courtesy of The Phoenix Collection. Photograph by Janice M. Dietert.

25. Forks. A pair of Trefid Tableforks 1698/99 by Alexander Kincaid, Edinburgh. Courtesy of The Phoenix Collection. Photograph by Janice M. Dietert.

26. Knives. Two from a set of twelve 1786-90 Dessert Knives by Patrick Robertson, Edinburgh. Courtesy of a private collector. Photograph by Janice M. Dietert

27. Ladles. A pair of Dundee Sauce Ladles 1790ca by James Douglas. Courtesy of The Phoenix Collection. Photograph by Janice M. Dietert.

28. Marrow Spoons and Scoops. Four Marrow Scoops. 1747/48 by Dougal Ged, Edinburgh (top), 1840/41 Bone Marrow Club by WC, Edinburgh, made for Andrew Rutherford (2nd from the top), a twisted stem example 1815/16 by George McHattie, Edinburgh retailed by Heron (next to bottom), and a 1811/12 bulbous connection example by John Ziegler, Edinburgh (bottom). Courtesy of a private collector. Photograph by Janice M. Dietert.

29. Skewers. Top - A long skewer from a set of four 1820/21 by George Fenwick Center - a tiny skewer 1800 ca Inverness by Robert Naughton. Bottom - a leaf-decorated Skewer 1828/29 by Heron, Greenock, Glasgow assay. Courtesy of a private collector. Photograph by Janice M. Dietert

30. Spoons. Hash and Serving Spoons. From Top to Bottom: 1745 ca Hanoverian hash spoon by James Glen, Glasgow. 1703/04 Trefid Hanoverian pattern hash spoon by Colin McKenzie, Edinburgh. 1776/77 Onslow pattern hash spoon by WD, Edinburgh. 1789/90 Pointed Old English pattern hash spoon by Patrick Robertson, Edinburgh. 1865 ca Fiddle pattern serving spoon by John MacKay of Elgin. Photograph by Janice Dietert.

31. Tongs. Three Sugar Tongs. Left – 1790 ca by Peter Mathie, Edinburgh. Center - 1790ca James Erskine, Aberdeen. Right - 1800ca by PH, Paisley. Courtesy of The Phoenix Collection. Photograph by Janice M. Dietert.

32. Ink Pots and Inkstands. 1742/43 Inkstand with three members by Robert Gordon, Edinburgh. Photograph courtesy of George Dalgleish and the National Museums of Scotland.

33. Miscellaneous. Top left- a pair of Buckles Dundee 1780ca by William Scott. Center left – a Child's Rattle 1745 ca by James Glen of Glasgow. Bottom left - a pair of Spurs 1807/08 Edinburgh by James McKay. Right - cast top (unmarked but London made) of the Green Rod of Scotland. This top was made specifically for the Scottish coronation of George IV in 1821. All courtesy of a private collector. Photographs by Janice M. Dietert.

34. Mugs. A 1739/40 Edinburgh example by Patrick Murray III. Courtesy of The Phoenix Collection. Photograph by Janice M Dietert.

35. Mugs-General. An Edinburgh example 1734/35 by Dougal Ged. Courtesy of The Phoenix Collection. Photograph by Janice M. Dietert.

36. Mugs-Thistle. An Aberdeen example 1710ca by George Robertson. Photograph courtesy of The Maple Swan Collection.

37. Mustard Pots. 1841/42 Mustard Pot by James McKay, Edinburgh. Photograph courtesy of I. Franks Antique Silver, London Silver Vaults, London.

38. Porringers and Bleeding Bowls. A Bleeding Bowl 1749/50 by Dougal Ged, Edinburgh. Courtesy of The Phoenix Collection. Photograph by Janice M. Dietert.

39. Quaichs. An Edinburgh example 1808/09 by Matthew Craw. Courtesy of The Phoenix Collection. Photograph by Janice M. Dietert.

40. Salts. Two from a set of four Edinburgh human mask (possibly Jacobite) salts by Ebenezer Oliphant (1743/44). Courtesy of a private collector. Photograph by Janice M. Dietert.

41. Salvers. The Glasgow example of 1740ca is by Robert Luke. Courtesy of The Phoenix Collection. Photograph by Janice M. Dietert

42. Sauceboats. The 1763/64 Edinburgh example is by Alexander Gardner. Courtesy of The Phoenix Collection. Photograph by Janice M. Dietert.

43. Strainers and Squeezers. An oval Orange Strainer 1765ca by Adam Graham of Glasgow. Photograph courtesy of The Maple Swan Collection.

44. Tankards. An Edinburgh example of 1695/96 by Alexander Forbes. Photograph courtesy of S.J. Shrubsole, NY.

45. Tazzas. An Edinburgh example of 1698/99 by John Yorstoun. Courtesy of The Phoenix Collection. Photograph by Janice M. Dietert

46. Tea. Some components used in serving tea. A Sugar Bowl 1731/32 by Archibald Ure, a 1740/41 Cream Boat by James Mitchell, a 1739/40 Salver by James Mitchelson and examples of Scots Fiddle teaspoons by Ebenezer Oliphant, James Hewitt and WM. Courtesy of The Phoenix Collection. Photograph by Janice M. Dietert

47. Tea Caddies. The Edinburgh example is 1792/93 by William Robertson. Courtesy of a private collector. Photograph by Janice M. Dietert.

48. Tea Kettles, Stands and Trays. The Kettle and Stand is 1758/59 by WD probably William Dempster, Edinburgh. Courtesy of a private collector. Photograph by Janice M. Dietert.

49. Teapots. An Edinburgh example of 1735/36 by James Ker. Photograph courtesy of Asprey, Ltd. London.

50. Tea Service. An assembled Edinburgh Tea Service. Sugar 1730/31, Cream Boat 1735/36, and Salver 1740/41 all by William Aytoun, the teapot is 1734/35 by Hugh Penman. Courtesy of The Phoenix Collection. Photograph by Janice M. Dietert.

51. Toast and Bannock Racks. An Edinburgh example 1825/26, maker's mark obscured. Courtesy of the Phoenix Collection. Photograph by Janice M. Dietert.

52. Urns. An Ovoid Shaped Urn with Snake Handles 1738/39 by James Weems, Edinburgh. Courtesy of a private collector. Photograph by Janice M. Dietert.

53. Wine. A Wine Label, 1825/26 by JH, Edinburgh, Wine Funnel 1790 no maker's mark, Wine Funnel Stand, 1810ca James McKay, Edinburgh. All courtesy of The Phoenix Collection. Photographs by Janice M. Dietert.

54. Wine Cups and Goblets. 1807/08 Goblet by Robert Gray & Son, Glasgow (Edinburgh assay). Courtesy of J. H. Bourdon-Smith, London.

Baskets

Plate 1. A 1761/62 Cakebasket by W * D, probably William Dempster, Edinburgh. Courtesy of a private collector. Photograph by Janice M Dietert.

BASKETS

YEAR	MAKER	LOCATION	DESCRIPTION	SOURCE
	CAKE			
1739/40	James Ker assayer-David Mitchell	Edinburgh	Cake basket, possibly repaired, 12 ¾" long, 59 oz	S. J. Phillips, London 1991 Christie's October 23 1991 #94 Koopman, London early 1990s
1740/41	James Ker Assayer-Dougal Ged	Edinburgh	Cake basket, oval on pierced rim foot, everted sides pierced with formal ornament and with cast and applied shell scroll and mask border, center chased with border of fruit and foliage, swing handle rising from caryatid figures, Arms of Hope (Hopetoun), 13 ½" long, 66 oz	Christie's June 15, 1977 #118
1742/43	Robert Gordon	Edinburgh	Cake basket, engraved with arms of the Earl of Kintor, 14" long, 75.7oz	Gees, Clark Art Institute p184-185 #102
1745/46	James Ker Assayer Dougal Ged	Edinburgh	Cake basket, shaped oval, on spreading foot pierced with foliate scrolls, body pierced with crosses and scrolls, molded border with foliate scrolls and grotesque masks, shaped swing handle with female mask and foliate scroll terminals, base engraved with coat of arms in cartouche, handle engraved with a cipher and earl's coronet within a cartouche Arms of Hope (Hopetoun), 13" long, 61 oz	Christie's Glasgow March 1983, #80 Christie's London March 1992, #193 Shaw Collection National Museums of Scotland
1745 ca	James Ker	Edinburgh	Cake basket, no date letter	Baruch Collection catalog #333 1988 McKissick University of South Carolina, Columbia SC USA
1747/48	William Dempster	Edinburgh	Cake basket, Large scalloped seashell with dolphin feet and seahorse handle, earliest sale known from catalog, 58 oz	Country Life 1963, p 444 Sotheby's March 21, 1963 #161 Finlay 1991 #81 Christie's July 24, 1918 #121 National Museums of Scotland, 1963.34
1747/48	Robert Gordon	Edinburgh	Cake basket, Arms of Hume and others for Earls of Marchmount, swing handle with vacant cartouche, oval, pierced sides, applied rim with scrolls, spurne and female masks, claw feet, 15 ½" long, 75oz 13d	Sotheby's London November 1987, #71 Christie's July 17, 1946 #24
1747/48	*Robert Gordon Assayer Hugh Gordon*	*Edinburgh*	Cake basket, oval, on 4 claw feet, pierced with scrolls and crosses, with foliage, shell, scroll and female mask border, the foliage, mask and scroll handle with further applied scrolls and shells, 15 ½" long, 76oz	*Christie's March 28, 1984 #194* #71
1752/53	Ker & Dempster	Edinburgh	Cake basket, Pierced body, solid handle, contemporary Arms, 14 ¾" long, 50oz 13d	Jackson 2 volumes p 924, fig. 1234

YEAR	MAKER (continued)	LOCATION	DESCRIPTION	SOURCE
1753/54	Lothian & Robertson	Edinburgh	Cake basket, oval center with later armorial, sides pierced with leaf scrolls, saltires and flowerheads, border decorated with flowers – filled baskets and wheat sheaves, handle on master bracket supports, center with applied crested rococo cartouche, 14 ½" long, 58oz 10d	Sotheby's March 20, 1970, #85 Sotheby's London Nov 23, 2004 #72
1754/55	Patrick Robertson	Edinburgh	Cake basket, scrolled ball handle, 4 shell-footed legs with masks above scroll, diaper and scrolls, flange with shell and vintage mounts, 14" long	Los Angeles County Museum loan collection, Early Silver in California, Collection # 222
1755/56	Lothian & Robertson	Edinburgh	Cake basket, pierced leaf scrolls, foliage and saltires below a rococo border incorporating grape vines, handle on master bracket supports, vacant cartouche, ball and claw supports, 14" long, 56oz	Sotheby's London May 4, 2004 #102
1755/56	Lothian & Robertson	Edinburgh	Cake basket, no details	Connoisseur Magazine 1949, vol 123, p44 advertisement
1755/56	Dougal Ged	Edinburgh	Cake basket, well marked, 50.3oz	How of Edinburgh 1937 #111
1757/58	William Dempster	Edinburgh	Cake basket, for the 2nd Earl of Hopetoun, initial "H", under coronet, 15 ½" long, 66oz	Finlay 1991 #94 Christie's June 15, 1977 # 115 National Museums of Scotland MEQ 1204
1758/59	William Dempster	Edinburgh	Cake basket, possibly same as the one above, 13 ¾" long, 10 2/3" wide, 11 3/5" ht	Michael Rix Antiques Aberdeen Art Gallery and Museums (1995) #4230
1758/59	William Dempster	Edinburgh	Cake basket, mask and shell feet, border-chased shells, 13 ¾" long, 51oz 15d	Apollo January 1973, vol 97 p2 Bell of Aberdeen advertisement Christie's June 7, 1939 #41
1759/60	Lothian & Robertson	Edinburgh	Cake basket, shaped oval body, pierced in 4 panels of diaper work, border with shells and scrolls, swing handle, center engraved with "H" beneath an earl's coronet for the Earl of Hopetoun	National Museums of Scotland
1760/61	Not Available		Cake basket, gadrooned rim, shell at each end, 13 ½" long	Jackson 2 volumes p 926, # 1236
1761/62	William Dempster	Edinburgh	Cake basket, no details	Private Collection
1764/65	Robert Clark	Edinburgh	Cake basket, no details	Antiques Magazine 1965, p96

YEAR	MAKER	LOCATION	DESCRIPTION	SOURCE
1766/67	Patrick Robertson	Edinburgh	Cake basket, early recorded owner, Mackay and Chisholm	Cripps, p 151
1767/68	William Ker	Edinburgh	Cake basket, pierced sides, Arms of Dundas, 13 ¾" long, 37oz 12d	Sotheby's March 6, 1969 #113
1769/70	John Welsh	Edinburgh	Cake basket, 13" long, 43 oz	Country Life, November 16, 1964, vol. 136 p1388 advertisement
1770/71	Robert Clark	Edinburgh	Cake basket, no details	National Museums of Scotland
1771/72	William Davie	Edinburgh	Cake basket, pierced sides, 13 ½" wide, 25 oz	Sotheby's July 21, 1977 #169
1771/72	Patrick Robertson	Edinburgh	Cake basket, no details	National Museums of Scotland MEQ 662
1775/76	William Davie	Edinburgh	Cake basket, 13 ½" wide, 32oz 15d	Sotheby's June 14, 1984 #267
1775/76	*William Davie*	*Edinburgh*	*Cake basket, no details*	*Victoria & Albert Museum*
1778/79	Alexander Gardner	Edinburgh	Cake basket, sides formed by curved wire work bars overlaid on the inside with trailing flowers and foliage, rope rim, swing handle, 14" long, 26.8oz	Lyle Silver Review 1982 p 8 Sotheby's Hopetoun House November 12, 1979 #69
1783/84 ca	William Ker	Edinburgh	Cake basket, no details	Antiques Magazine 1970, vol 97
1785/86 ca	William Scott	Dundee	Cake basket, no details	Finlay 1991 #112
1789/90	W & P Cunningham I	Edinburgh	Cake basket, oblong with gadroon border interrupted with shells, on plain oblong base, 2 upturned handles	Scottish Art Review 1954 vol V p50 #1
1790/91	James Douglas or James Dempster	Edinburgh	Cake basket, boat form, pierced with mixed drapery and flower swags suspended from ribbon bows and Prince of Wales feathers, engraved with contemporary crest, 13 ¾" long, 28oz	Sotheby's NY USA 1995 #391
1794/95	W & P Cunningham I	Edinburgh	Cake basket, no details	Edward & Sons Glasgow Exhibition 1911 vol I, p 122 #64
1794/95	William Robertson	Edinburgh	Cake basket, no details	National Museums of Scotland MEQ 662
1796/97	W & P Cunningham I	Edinburgh	Cake basket, oval form, pierced with scrolling foliage, Arms of Richardson, 14" long, 28.6 oz	Nicholas Shaw Catalog 2004 p103
1796/97	W & P Cunningham I	Edinburgh	Cake basket, oval, pierced with swing handle, foliate decoration and on engraved crest, 14" long, 29oz	Gorringes LLP East Sussex, UK 2006 #1494

YEAR	MAKER	LOCATION	DESCRIPTION	SOURCE
1797/98	William Robertson	Edinburgh	Cake basket, no details	The Maple Swan Collection
1800/01	W & P Cunningham I	Edinburgh	Cake basket, navette-shaped on oval foot, with reeded borders, pierced below rim with a band of scrolling foliage and paterce, the swing handle chased with foliage and with a vacant cartouche, the center engraved with a crest, marked on the base, 14 ½" long, 26oz	Christie's London 2005 #159
1801/02	W & P Cunningham I	Edinburgh	Cake basket, no details	Christie's June 15, 1966 #130
1802/03	William Dempster	Edinburgh	Cake basket, oval, no details	National Museums of Scotland MEQ 1341
1805/06	Frances Howden	Edinburgh	Cake basket, engraved	Eldredge Auction December 1992 in Newtown Bee 1/8/93
1810 ca	W & P Cunningham I	Edinburgh	Cake basket, oval armorial engraved below a beaded border, skirt foot, swing handle with further beaded borders, Arms of Maconochie impaling Blair for Alexander Maconochie and Anna Blair, 13" wide, 33oz 4d	Sotheby's NY 1999 #436
1810 ca	Joseph Pearson	Dumfries	Cake basket, plain rounded oblong form, reeded border, spreading foot, wirework swing handle with central oblong cartouche, crested, marks "anchor, IP, stag's head, E", 11 7/8" long, 23oz	Christie's London 1999 #251
1812/13	George McHattie	Edinburgh	Cake basket, inscribed "From John Patterson, Esq....." 12 ¾" long, 33.9oz	Nicholas Shaw catalog, Winter 2000 p 75
1814/15	Not available	Edinburgh	Cake basket, rectangular with rounded corners and gadrooned edge, scallop shell corners, swing handle, 13" long, 31oz	Northeast Auctions Portsmouth, NH USA 2001 #360
1816/17	James McKay	Edinburgh	Cake basket, rectangular form with stepped sides and gadrooned border, plain molded swing handle, on a waisted conforming collet base, 12" X 10 3/8", 30oz 12d	Butterfields Auctioneers San Francisco, CA USA 1996 #5356
1819/20	Francis Howden	Edinburgh	Cake basket, circular, on four fluted feet with foliate scroll feet, a flat rim applied with a band of pierced scrolls, flowers and foliage, the swing handle with similar decoration against a matted ground, engraved with a crest in bowl of basket, marked on underside, 12 ½" di, 50oz	Christie's East NY, NY USA 2001 #250
1819/20	Robert Gray	Glasgow	Cake basket, circular on spreading foot, body chased and chased with flowers, 11 7/8" di., 36.9 oz	Nicholas Shaw Catalog, Winter 2000, p75
1822/23	Forrests (Retailer)	Edinburgh	Cake basket, plain oblong form on spreading foot with foliage and gadrooned border, swing handle with applied acanthus foliage motifs, crest and motto,	Christie's London 1999 #28

YEAR	MAKER (continued)	LOCATION	DESCRIPTION	SOURCE
			13" wide, 41oz	
1822/23	Forrests (Retailer)	Edinburgh	Cake basket, similarly as above, 13" long, 41.5oz	Christie's London 2002 #235
1826/27	Alexander Edmonstoun	Edinburgh	Cake basket, no details	The Scarlett Fox-Thieves Market Alexandria, VA 1994
1826/27	Francis Howden	Edinburgh	Cake basket, plain circular form, on four foliage and scroll feet, applied border cast and pierced with fruiting vines and scrolls, swing handle similarly chased, engraved coat-of-arms, 12 3/5" di, 50oz	Christie's London 1999 #73
1841/42	L? (possibly Leonard Urquhart)	Edinburgh	Cake basket or fruit basket, shallow circular form, lobed and embossed with flowers within a floral shell border, below a floral scrolled bail handle, engraved with a monogram, on a plain low pedestal foot, 14 1/3" di, 43.5oz	Cheffins Auction House, Cambridge, UK 27 June 2007, #280
1899/1900	James Aitchison	Edinburgh	Cake basket, no details, 10 ½" long	National Museums of Scotland 1968.37 +a,b
1902/03	Hamilton & Inches	Edinburgh	Cake basket, no details	National Museums of Scotland H.1994.1099
1929/30	RS	Glasgow	Cake basket or fruit basket, raised on four openwork thistle feet, body pierced with thistle design beneath an undulating rim, 11 ½" long, 27.3oz	Christie's Melbourne Australia, 2001 #284
DESSERT				
1858/59	Marshall & Sons	Edinburgh	Dessert basket, gilt, interwoven flowers, Arms of Campbell of Blythswood	Nicholas Shaw Catalog 2005, p101
SUGAR				
1786/87	Not Available	Edinburgh	Sugar basket, No details	The Maple Swan Collection
1790 ca	W & P Cunningham I	Edinburgh	Sugar basket, lacking date letter, neoclassical form, scalloped foot, bright cut borders, initials, reeded handles, sold with another item, 7 7/8" ht	Bonhams Sale 15120 Aug 22, 2007 #25
1790/91	W & P Cunningham I	Edinburgh	Sugar basket, oval octagonal form, wavy rim, threaded angular bale handle, paneled sides with bright cut border, engraved with crest of McLean, on elongated octagonal foot, 5 ½" long, 5.5oz	Lyon & Turnbull, Edinburgh UK The Murray Collection August 20, 2003, #173
1790/91	WR William Robertson or William Rynd	Edinburgh	Sugar basket, boat shaped outline with reeded edge, reeded swing handle, part of a service	Sotheby's Gleneagles August 31, 1992 #147 Private Collection

YEAR	MAKER	LOCATION	DESCRIPTION	SOURCE
1792/93	Alexander Gardner	Edinburgh	Sugar basket, boat shaped on oval foot, bright cut engraving, swing handle, vacant cartouche, 6 ¼" long, 8.9 oz	Nicholas Shaw Catalog Winter 2000 p73
1792/93	Robert Swan	Edinburgh	Sugar basket, oval with a swing handle	Private Collection
1795/96	GB	Edinburgh	Sugar basket, oval body, bright cut engraved with a band of grape vines below the reeded rim, swing handle, with creamer, 6" wide	Sotheby's Scone April 19, 1977 #54
1796/97	W & P Cunningham I	Edinburgh	Sugar basket set	Sotheby's November 29, 1973 #91
1796/97	Charles Bendy	Edinburgh	Sugar basket, oval on pedestal foot, crest and motto of Hutton, 6 ½" di, 9.9 oz	Nicholas Shaw Catalog 2004 p103
1797/98	Francis Howden	Edinburgh	Sugar basket, oval, swing handle, band of engraved decoration below rim, formed of alternating leaves and ovals, engraved initials "CK" in cartouche, 6 ¾" wide, 12oz 16d	JH Bourdon-Smith Catalog Private Collection
1798/99	W & P Cunningham I	Edinburgh	Sugar basket, boat shaped, bright cut, decorated 7 ¼" ht, 6 5/8" wide, 8.5 oz	Nicholas Shaw Catalog Winter 2002/03 p85
1798/99	W & P Cunningham I	Edinburgh	Sugar basket, parcel gilt work, bright cut engraved floral scrolls and baskets, 6 ¾" long	Gorringes LLP East Sussex, UK 2006 #1572
1814/15	George Fenwick	Edinburgh	Sugar basket or basin, two-handled, gilt-lined, molded oval with shell and gadrooned border and ball feet, the side bright cut engraved with baskets and foliage, 5 ¼" long, 11oz	Christie's London UK 2004 #136 and #623
SWEETMEAT				
1752/53	Ker & Dempster	Edinburgh	Sweetmeat basket, no details	National Museums of Scotland 1961.559
1758/59	William Dempster	Edinburgh	Sweetmeat basket, oval, pierced latticework sides and twisted swing handle, 5" long, 4oz 7d	Sotheby's NY USA 1997 #325
1766/67	Ker & Dempster	Edinburgh	Sweetmeat basket, no details	National Museums of Scotland 1943.265
1767/68	YR	Edinburgh	Sweetmeat basket, mm unclear and unattributed, no details	Jackson Marks p549 notes
1794/95	Francis Howden	Edinburgh	Sweetmeat basket, fluted bowl-shaped body, bright cut engraved with crossed foliate sprays enclosing vacant cartouches below a band of foliage at the lip, swing handle, on pedestal base conforming in outline, 6 ½", 8.8oz	Sotheby's Scone Palace April 23, 1979 #46

YEAR	MAKER	LOCATION	DESCRIPTION	SOURCE
1795/96	W & P Cunningham	Edinburgh	Sweetmeat basket, boat shaped, fluted, bright cut engraved with vacant ribbon tied roundels between leafy sprays and cornucopias, a further band of foliage and paterae at the rim, reeded swing handle, pedestal foot, 6" wide, 9.1oz	Sotheby's Gleneagles August 29, 1983 #494

Beakers

Plate 2. A pair of 1768/69 Beakers by Patrick Robertson, Edinburgh.
Courtesy of The Maple Swan Collection.

BEAKERS

YEAR	MAKER	LOCATION	DESCRIPTION	SOURCE
16th Century	Not available	Dundee	Beaker, gilt flowers and foliage, reeded ribs, Arms of Earls of Errol, 6 ¼" ht, 18oz 17d	Christie's November 24, 1919 #74
17th Century	Not available	Canongate	Beaker, stag's head mark (possibly), band of strap-work thistles, flowers, etc., molded foot, 7" ht, 12oz 5d	Christie's March 26, 1913 #130
1694/95	James Penman	Edinburgh	Beakers, pair, thistle-shaped beaker, no handle mid-rib girdle, 9oz 11d both (4oz 14d ea)	Christie's April 21, 1924 #223
1700/01	John Seatoun	Edinburgh	Beaker, thistle shaped, everted leaves, mid-rib girdle, flaring lip, base engraved with later initials, 3 ½" ht, 4oz 11d	Christie's April 24, 1956 #102
1737/38	James Ker	Edinburgh	Beakers, pair, no details	National Museums of Scotland K 2004.207 1 + 2
1738/39	James Ker	Edinburgh	Beakers, pair, tapered oval form, engraved with the Arms of Hay, Marquess of Tweedale, one with a molded rim to fit inside the other, 3 ¾" ht, 7oz both	Sotheby's Gleneagles August 29, 1978 #392
1740ca	Not available		Beaker, small cylindrical, slightly flaring lip, engraved with inscription "Culloden 16 Apr 1746", and later coat of arms and inscription "Major John Wilson-Barrells Regt", unmarked, 2 1/8" ht, 3oz	Christie's October 12, 1966 #97
1747/48	Dougal Ged	Edinburgh	Beaker, slightly bulbous body, flared lip, engraved with crest and motto "CALM", 2 ¾" ht, 4oz 17d	Sotheby's September 22, 1977 #195
1762/63	Not available	Edinburgh	Beaker, pair, tapering cylindrical shape, engraved with band of grapes and wheat within shell and scroll work near lip, crest and motto, mm unclear, 3 1/8" ht, 10.7oz	Sotheby's NY USA October 16, 1996 #264
1763/64	Lothian & Robertson	Edinburgh	Beakers, pair, tapering cylindrical with incised line near rim, engraved with script "F" initial, 3" ht, 3 ¼" di, 12 oz both	Mary Cooke Antiques, London UK 2007
1768/69	James Ker	Edinburgh	Beaker, plain, engraved "G" below rim, too late for this maker, 3" ht, 5.8 oz	JH Bourdon-Smith Catalog #43 August 2001 p 9
1768/69	Patrick Robertson	Edinburgh	Beakers, pair, decorated around rim, crest/motto Douglas "DOE OR DIE," 3" ht, 11oz 9d	Clayton Christie's Pictorial History p 228 #5 Christie's March 7, 1979
1768/69	Patrick Robertson	Edinburgh	Beakers, pair, crest/motto, "Promote Et Consulto," rims engraved with band of wheat ears and flowers, 3 ¼" ht, 14oz	Christie's July 6, 1988 #115

YEAR	MAKER	LOCATION	DESCRIPTION	SOURCE
1768/69	Patrick Robertson	Edinburgh	Beakers, pair, no details	The Maple Swan Collection
1770/71	William Dempster	Edinburgh	Beaker, no details	Bonhams London UK 2001 #164
1770/71	William Dempster or William Davie	Edinburgh	Beaker, straight sided tapering form, slightly flared lip, 2 ¾" ht, 3.4oz	Bonhams Sale 15120 Aug 22, 2007, #2
1773/74	James Hewitt	Edinburgh	Beakers, pair, like tall tumbler cups, tulip shaped, slightly tapering towards the top then straightening out at the rim, each engraved with a crest – a boar's head, beneath a motto "NON METUO" in a riband, probably for Hamilton, 3" ht, 8.3oz	Sotheby's Scone Palace April 19, 1977 #85
1774/75	Patrick Robertson	Edinburgh	Beakers pair, plain, narrow band of foliage, 3 ½" ht, 11oz 1d wt both (5oz 5 ea)	Christie's August 8, 1940 #39
1780ca	James McEwan	Glasgow	Beaker, plain, engraved motto "DEATH OR GLORY," 4oz 15d	Lyle Annual Review 1983 p 536 Christie's September 30, 1982 #130
1798/99	Francis Howden	Edinburgh	Beakers, pair, plain tapering cylindrical form, engraved with initials "WB/MN", 3 ¾" ht, 9.3oz both	Sotheby's Gleneagles August 29, 1978 #435
1781/82	William Davie or William Dempster	Edinburgh	Beaker, pair, with 2 bands of vine engraving and script "AD" monogram, 3 ¾" ht, 10.3 oz both	Nicholas Shaw Catalog Autumn 1999 p 55
1782/83	James Gilliland	Edinburgh	Beakers, pair of small beakers, no details	National Museums of Scotland MEQ 644-45 1961.1852-53
1790/91	Francis Howden	Edinburgh	Beaker, cylindrical form, engraved "CB" in an oval cartouche, 4 1/8" ht, 5.7 oz	Nicholas Shaw Catalog Winter 2000 p 72 Bonhams the Scottish Sale August 21, 2003 #21
1793/94	Alexander Gardner	Edinburgh	Beaker, no details	Sotheby's Gleneagles August 1987 #297
1793/94	William Robertson	Edinburgh	Beakers, double, barrel-shaped, gilt interior, 6 1/3" ht, 10.6oz	Christie's Geneva November 19, 1991 #28
1796/97	William Dempster	Edinburgh	Beakers, set of 3, with crest and motto	JH Bourdon-Smith, London 1994
1796/97	W & P Cunningham I	Edinburgh	Beakers, pair, straight tapering with flat bases, 3" ht, 6.6 oz both	S J Phillips Ltd London 2007
1799/1800	McHattie & Fenwick	Edinburgh	Beakers, pair, barrel form	National Museums of Scotland MEQ 1605

YEAR	MAKER	LOCATION	DESCRIPTION	SOURCE
1800 ca	James Douglas	Dundee	Beaker, tapering cylindrical shape, engraved "….To William Fairweather 1800"	Finlay 1991 #113
1800 ca	James Erskine	Aberdeen	Beakers, pair, horn with silver mounts, tapering cylindrical form, silver foot and rim partly scalloped and reeded, applied shield shaped plaque, engraved with crest, motto and initials "C. C." for Chalmers of Abderdeenshire, 6 ½" ht	Christie's Lanarkshire UK 1997 #306
1800/01	Francis Howden	Edinburgh	Beakers, pair, engraved band of foliate near rim with a vacant wreath contemporary inscription on base "To Mrs. Pitloh from Mr. Steele, 1801" referring to Gideon Steele, 3 ½" ht, 9oz both	eBay #1301296745 The Phoenix Collection Anonymous Collection
1805/06	Francis Howden	Edinburgh	Beakers, pair, plain, tapering, cylindrical form, later engraving, crest, 4 ½" ht, 14oz both (7oz each)	Christie's London October 1988 #90
1807/08	James McKay	Edinburgh	Beaker, straight-sided with crest and monogram, 3 ½" ht, 4.6 oz	Nicholas Shaw Catalog 2005 p 98
1810 ca	IA	Provincial	Beaker, silver-mounted horn, marked to rim "IA, b, thistle" slightly tapering form, applied shield with engraved initials applied scalloped rim inscribed to "John Leigh", 5" ht	Lyon & Turnbull Edinburgh UK May 25, 2006 #334
1827/28	F & S	Edinburgh	Beakers, pair, plain, tapering cylindrical form, 2 crests, motto of Weems	Sotheby's Gleneagles August 1988 #478 JH Bourdon-Smith, London 1992 James Robinson's, NY 1992
1833/34	James McKay	Edinburgh	Beaker, plain baluster on spreading support, 3" ht, 4oz 11d	Sotheby's NY USA 1999 #506
1834/35	Williams Marshall	Edinburgh	Beakers, pair, no details	The Maple Swan Collection
1841/42	M Bros?	Edinburgh	Beaker, cylindrical, no further details	Bonhams Leeds 2003 #87
1852/53	Robb & Whittet	Edinburgh	Beakers, pair, cylindrical with applied plain footrim and engraved reeded girdles, gilt interior, 3 3/8" ht	Christie's Lanarkshire UK 1997 #97
1861/62	MacKay & Chisholm	Edinburgh	Beaker, plain tapering cylindrical form, engraved key pattern borders, two vacant rope cartouches, gilt interior 2 2/3" di, 4oz	Lyon & Turnbull Edinburgh UK 2002 #454
1871/72	Hamilton & Inches	Edinburgh	Beakers pair, leaf engraving	National Museums of Scotland MEQ 1182-83 1976.29-30
1887/88	Hamilton & Inches	Edinburgh	Beaker, fluted, engraved with name, 5 ½" ht, 4.24oz	Crow's Auction Gallery, Dorking Surry, UK 2007 #220

YEAR	MAKER	LOCATION	DESCRIPTION	SOURCE
1897/98	Hamilton & Inches	Edinburgh	Beaker, cylindrical, no further details	Sotheby's NY USA Dec 16, 1998 #364
1895/96	W. M.	Edinburgh	Beakers, pair, thistle-shaped, whiskey beakers, 2 ½" ht, 3.5 oz	Nicholas Shaw Catalog Winter 2001 p 77
1920/21	Medlock & Craik	Inverness	Beaker, silver-mounted horn beaker, 3 5/8" ht	Nicholas Shaw Catalog Winter 2000, p85
1879/80	R & G Drummond (Retailer)	Glasgow	Beaker, cylindrical form, profusely chased with leaf scrolls and flowers, with further narrow bands above and below, in original fitted case	Bonhams London UK 2004 #411
1906/07	Mackay & Chisholm	Edinburgh	Beaker, spot hammered, applied Celtic scroll band interspersed with bosses, applied Celtic cross below, on a spreading circular foot, 4 2/3' ht, 8.5oz	Bonhams London UK 2007 #333

Bowls

Plate 3. Left – 1726/27 three footed lion's mask Sugar Bowl by James Ker, Edinburgh.
Right – 1765 ca covered Sugar Bowl by Milne & Campbell, Glasgow.
Courtesy of The Phoenix Collection. Photograph by Janice M Dietert.

Punch Bowls

Plate 4. A presentation Punch Bowl 1820/21 by James McKay, Edinburgh.
Courtesy of J H Bourdon-Smith, London.

YEAR	MAKER	LOCATION	DESCRIPTION	SOURCE
			BOWLS	
	PUNCH			
1692/93	Robert Bruce	Edinburgh	Punch bowl, The Bruce Bowl, plain, circular on slightly spreading rim foot, bowl almost straight, tucked in sides, narrow molded rim, engraved with arms, crest and motto "BONIS OMNIA BONA", 11" di, 43.8oz	Burlington Magazine 1937, vol 71 pp 278-31 Apollo July 1938 p 10-12 Clayton Dictionary p289 #413 How of Edinburgh Christie's November 27, 1957 Private Collection
1698/99	Colin McKenzie	Edinburgh	Monteith, Arms of Kinloch impaling Rocheid, decorated with shield shaped lobes, rim with 8 notches, 2 lion's masks and drop ring handles, 13 ¼" di, 70 oz	Christie's July 25, 1969 #134 Finlay 1991 #57 Shrubsole Huntley House Museum
1698/99	Colin McKenzie	Edinburgh	Monteith, the bowl with eight lobed panels on a stippled background, 14 1/8" di, 73.1oz	Private UK Collection
1700/01	Colin McKenzie	Edinburgh	Punch bowl, no details	Jackson Marks p544
1700/01	Colin McKenzie	Edinburgh	Monteith, bowl with oval lobed panels, central panel with a coat of arms, background stippled, rim with 9 notches with plain scalloped edge, plain domed and reeded foot	G E & R A Lee British Silver Monteith Bowls 1978 #126 Crichton Bros Ltd
1702/03	James Cockburn	Edinburgh	Monteith, shells, Arms of the Duke of Cumberland, defective (patched), plain, deep bowl on gadrooned foot, band of cut card foliage surrounding the bowl where it joins the foot, 8 shells on high points of rim, lions' masks and drop ring handles, crest and motto of George Johnson of Westerhall, 12 ½" di, 73oz	Christie's June 22, 1966 #175 Finlay 1991 #63 National Museums of Scotland MEQ 841
1702/03	Robert Inglis	Edinburgh	Monteith, no details	G E & R A Lee British Silver Monteiths 1978 #161
1702/03	Thomas Cleghorne III	Edinburgh	Punch bowl, on gadrooned foot, everted rim, also gadrooned with a rooster crest and motto above "VIRTUTE ET LABORE", 13 ½" di	Christie's NY USA October 5, 1983 #185 National Museums of Scotland MEQ 1572
1705/06	George Main	Edinburgh	Monteith, no details	G E & R A Lee British Silver Monteiths 1978 #200
1708/09	Alexander Kincaid	Edinburgh	Monteith, shallow bowl with everted rim, fitted with detachable rim with 9 plain reeded undulations, bowl engraved with a cipher, rim engraved with a	G E & R A Lee British Silver Monteiths 1978 #236 pl 1.42

YEAR	MAKER (continued)	LOCATION	DESCRIPTION ribanded motto "TOUR JOUR PREST"	SOURCE
1709/10	Charles Duncan	Edinburgh	Punch bowl, domed cover with similarly domed finial, crest and motto of Rutherford, 9" di, 50.5oz	Sotheby's March 16, 1937 #17 Peter Guille Antiques NY USA Wees, Clarke Art Institute p104 #46
1718/19	Colin Campbell	Edinburgh	Punch bowl, crest and motto	Sotheby's July 1968 #159 Apollo July 1968 vol 88 p 79
1719/20	William Ged	Edinburgh	Punch bowl, Royal Company of Archers, Queen's bodyguard in Scotland	Cripps p150 Finlay 1991 #63
Early 18th	Patrick Inglis	Canongate	Punch bowl, octagonal bowl	Finlay 1991 #104
1727/28	Henry Bethune	Edinburgh	Monteith, arms, crest, motto, coronet of Hope, 15 ¼" di, 174oz	Christie's NY USA 1999 #223 Christie's June 15, 1977 #126 Apollo 1933 vol 18 p156
1728/29	James Ker	Edinburgh	Punch bowl, plain, bowl chased all over with vertical flutes, rim with 8 notches, lion mask and drop ring handles, later applied crest and motto, 14 ¾" di, 78 oz	Christie's January or February 25, 1970 #24 Shrubsole Private Collection
1731/32	Kenneth McKenzie	Edinburgh	Punch bowl, shaped, applied reeded molding, 2 crests, everted, scalloped, 12 points, 9" di, 19oz	Shaw Collection Christie's Glasgow March 1983, #70 Sotheby's November 17, 1988 #100
1733/34	William Aytoun	Edinburgh	Monteith, rim, 7 ½" di	Christie's London 1992 #97
1739/40	Dougal Ged Assayer David Mitchell	Edinburgh	Punch bowl, circular on rim foot, flat chased below rim with shells and scrolls, crest and motto, "DEUM TIME" for Murray of Blackbarony, Pebblesshire, 9" di, 28oz	Phillips Edinburgh November 27, 2000 JH Bourdon-Smith Catalog Autumn 2000 Apollo March 2001 JH Bourdon-Smith advertisement
1746/47	James Ker Assayer Hugh Gordon	Edinburgh	Monteith, plain, circular, on domed spreading foot, with a reeded rib applied beneath the detachable shaped rim, rim with applied plain molding to the border, engraved with a cipher and earl's coronet within scrolling foliage and trellis work baroque cartouche, later monogram, cipher and coronet for John, 2nd Earl of Hopetoun (1704-1781), 11 3/8" di, 74oz	Shaw Collection Christie's Glasgow March 29, 1983 #89 British Silver Monteith Bowls, by Georgina E. Lee, 1978 #310

YEAR	MAKER (continued)	LOCATION	DESCRIPTION	SOURCE
				Scottish Art Review 1966 Vol IX #3 back cover
				How of Edinburgh advertisement Walter Willson Ltd
				Aberdeen Museums and Art Galleries
1750 ca	JW	Perth	Punch bowl, circular, fluted, on slightly spreading base, marks on base – double headed eagle of Perth, anchor, S, mm JW – 8 5/8" di, 29oz 5d	Phillips December 16, 1977
1750 ca	William Davie or William Dempster	Edinburgh	Punch bowl, George II, 12 ½" di	Lyle Silver Review 1982, p 17
1754/55	Lothian & Robertson	Edinburgh	Punch bowl, perfectly plain, with raised hemispherical body, 13 11/16" di, 9 3/8" ht, 69oz	Wees, Clark Art Institute p106-107 #49
1767 ca	Milne & Campbell	Glasgow	Punch bowl, flat chased decoration round the rim, presentation bowl, "The Owners of the ship Hector of Glasgow in a Testimony of gratitude to Robt Campbell of Dunie for his service in saving and protecting that ship when forced into Loch Castle in Distress in Novr 1767 Beg his Acceptance of this piece of plate, rococo cartouche with 3 masted sailing ship in difficulties, marks beneath the foot – mm, town mark "O" in square punch (which Mr. Henry Steuart Fothringham and Jackson know not the meaning of) – 10" di, 28.2oz	JH Bourdon-Smith London Autumn 1994
1770 ca	Milne & Campbell	Glasgow	Punch bowl, everted chased rim, inscribed	National Museums of Scotland H.1995.111
1771/72	Alexander Aitcheson	Edinburgh	Punch bowl, almost hemispherical scrolls and flower, swags, spreading feet, arms of MacDonell of Glengarry, 10 ½" di, 40oz 8d	Sotheby's Gleneagles/London August 1995 #157
1773/74	Patrick Robertson	Edinburgh	Punch bowl, George III, half spirally lobed shaped bowl, gadrooned rim, spreading circular base, 5 ½" di, 8oz	Neal's Auction, Nottingham March 2004, #52
1785/86	William Davie or William Dempster	Edinburgh	Punch bowl, perfectly plain bowl, on spreading rim foot, presented to John Boges by the Fives Club at Hamilton, 12 ½" di, 64oz	Sotheby's Gleneagles August 29, 1977 #195 Lyle Silver Review 1982 p18
1798/99	W & P Cunningham I	Edinburgh	Punch bowl, 6" ht, 32 oz	National Museums of Scotland 1972.82
1798/99	John McDonald	Edinburgh	Punch bowl, plain, Arms, crest and motto, and later Arms, 10 ¾" di, 42oz	Christie's July 15, 1975 #40

YEAR	MAKER	LOCATION	DESCRIPTION	SOURCE
1800/01	McHattie & Fenwick	Edinburgh	Punch bowl, inscribed to James Rose of Geddes, 12 ¼" di	Antiques Magazine February 1989 Shrubsole advertisement
1801/02	G & McC	Edinburgh	Punch bowl, plain hemispherical with bright cut rim, crested, reel shaped feet, 8" di, 14oz	Sotheby's NY USA 2004 #83
1805/06	McHattie & Fenwick	Edinburgh	Punch bowl, pair, band engraved, decorated, 10" di, 103 oz both (52oz ea)	Apollo 1979, vol 110 p 74 James Charles advertisement Christie's July 27, 1973 #8 Christie's July 5, 1967 #162
1807/08	Cunningham & Simpson	Edinburgh	Punch bowl, 11 ½" di, 47oz	Antiques Magazine 1966 p 94 Sotheby's June 4, 1981 #366 The Maple Swan Collection
1809/10	J F	Edinburgh	Punch bowl, mm unattributed, 9" di	Antiques Magazine 121 p 752 Shreve advertisement
1809/10	George Fenwick	Edinburgh	Punch bowl, inscribed from Renfrewshire volunteers, 11" di, 62oz 7d	Sotheby's February 28, 1974 #115
1810/11	James McKay	Edinburgh	Punch bowl, presented to Captain William Elliot, Esq. of Harwood, 10 ½" di, 55oz	JH Bourdon-Smith Catalog Autumn 2001 p 57
1810/11	John Ziegler	Edinburgh	Punch bowl, of the Incorporation of Trades of Edinburgh	National Museums of Scotland MEQ L1962.2
1810/11	Robert Gray & Son	Glasgow Edinburgh assay	Punch bowl, 11 ½" di	Holland Book p 216
1811 (or 1815)	W & P Cunningham II	Edinburgh	Punch bowl, no details	Antiques Magazine 1992 Jonathan Trace NY USA advertisement
1812/13	James McKay	Edinburgh	Punch bowls, pair, 11 ¾" di	Antiques Magazine 1930 vol 18 p 531 Wilson advertisement
1813/14	Robert Gray & Son	Glasgow Edinburgh assay	Punch bowl, 11 ½" di	Antiques Magazine 1982 p113

YEAR	MAKER	LOCATION	DESCRIPTION	SOURCE
1815/16	James McKay	Edinburgh	Punch bowl, prize from Highland Society of Scotland to Mr. George Bagrie, 9 ¾" di, 36oz	JH Bourdon-Smith Catalog Autumn 1996 #38 p53
1816/17	James McKay	Edinburgh	Punch bowl, George III, circular foot, dentil rim, plain circular bowl, engraved "Voted By the Highland Society of Scotland to Mr. Samuel Morton, Leith Walk, for having invented a Revolving Brake Harrow found to be effectual for the exterpation for weeds and pulverizing the ground 1816," 10 ½" ht, 9 ½" di, 34.4 oz	Bonhams Sale #10914, Lot #14 Nicholas Shaw Catalog 2005 p93
1819/20	James & William Howden	Edinburgh	Punch bowl, no details	National Museums of Scotland MEQ 38
1820/21	James McKay	Edinburgh	Punch bowl, presentation inscription "From the Highland Society of Scotland to Mr. Samuel Morton, Leith Walk for his invention dated 1816"	JH Bourdon-Smith London 2006
1821/22	James McKay	Edinburgh	Punch bowl, 10" di	Antiques Magazine 1999 p 292 Bell of Aberdeen advertisement
1823/24	Mitchell & Sons	Glasgow	Punch bowl, circular on spreading circular base, body chased with foliage, 10" di, 66oz (including ladle)	Christie's NY USA 1997 #254
1825/26	CB or RH	Edinburgh	Punch bowl, on pedestal foot	National Museums of Scotland MEQ 1593
1825/26	Phillip Grierson	Edinburgh	Punch bowl, not pictured	Holland Book p 216
1825/26	Winter	Edinburgh	Punch bowl, no details	Clayton p 288
1826/27	F & S	Edinburgh	Punch bowl, chased with cherubs above a plain cartouche, 10 3/8"di, 41oz	Nicholas Shaw Catalog Winter 2000 p76
1826/27	George McHattie	Edinburgh	Punch bowl, 11 ½" di, 44oz	Christie's London July 14, 1993 #19
1829/30	James McKay	Edinburgh	Punch bowl, chased	JH Bourdon-Smith Catalog 1994
1831/32	Robert Gray & Son	Glasgow	Punch bowl, 10" di	Apollo July 1975 vol 101 p86
1832/33	James McKay	Edinburgh	Punch bowl, chased with leaves and flowers, engraved "To John Kinton, Esq., Surgeon....."	National Museums of Scotland K.2004.57
1832/33	Robert Gray	Glasgow	Punch bowl, 10" di, 36oz 14d	Lyle Annual Review 1980 p 572 Sotheby's

YEAR	MAKER	LOCATION	DESCRIPTION	SOURCE
1833/34	William Marshall	Edinburgh	Punch bowl, no details	Sotheby's Hopetoun House May 1990 #81
1834/35	James McKay	Edinburgh	Punch bowl, no details	National Museums of Scotland MEQ 747
1835/36	J & W Marshall	Edinburgh	Punch bowl, domed foot, circular bowl, engraved with floral garlands and 2 oval cartouches, one depicting a crest beneath which is "John Scott Finnart, 1837", the other engraved "Presented to Mr. John Scott, in gratitude for his spirited exertions in saving the Cargo of the Jean & Peggy, stranded 1785, 12 ½" di, 61 oz	Bonhams Sale 10914 lot #13
1835/36	Leonard Urquehart	Edinburgh	Punch bowl, chased with hunting and racing scenes, floral scrolls, spreading foot, 9" di, 29oz	Skinner, Inc, Boston, MA USA 1991 #134
1838/39	WC	Edinburgh	Punch bowl, on domed foot, the body with a series of scrolled cartouches enclosing floral sprays, 6" ht, 11 2/3" di, 48oz	Bonhams Sale 1512 Aug 22, 2007 #30
1889/90	Sorley	Glasgow	Punch bowl, circular, chased with flowers, half fluted on pedestal foot, 9 1/8" di, 26.5oz	Nicholas Shaw Catalog Winter 2000 p92
1893/94	Hamilton & Inches	Edinburgh	Punch bowl, crest and motto "PATIENTIA VINCIT" 9" di, 5 ½" ht, 25 oz	Heritage Galleries, Dallas TX Sale 600 May 2004 #18022
1897/98	David Crichton	Edinburgh	Punch bowl, circular with two spatulate and loop handles on a domed foot, Arms of Sir William Ogilvy – Dalgleish", 17 ¾"di, 34.4oz	Nicholas Shaw Catalog 2004 p105
SERVING				
1814/15	JWH	Edinburgh	Bowl, serving, oval paneled body and gadrooned border, 28 1/2" di, 4 ½" ht	Pook & Pook Inc, Downingtown, PA USA 2004, #77
1893/94	Hamilton & Inches	Edinburgh	Bowl, partly fluted, hemispherical form, inscribed, 8 ¼"di, 20oz	Bonhams Solihuss, West Midlands, UK 2004 #360
1896/97	R & W Soley	Glasgow	Bowls, set of three, one larger and a pair, circular on stepped and domed foot, lower body chased with acanthus, two lion's mask ring handles, largest 12"di, 92oz 10d all	Christie's London UK 2006 #117
1897/98	Hamilton & Inches	Edinburgh	Bowl, rose, ovoid, chased with band of grotesque masks flanked by cornucopia and floral scrolls, rim pierced with conforming decoration, 12" long, 61oz 7d	Sotheby's London UK 2004 #372f
1897/98	Hamilton & Inches	Edinburgh	Bowl, quatrefoil-shaped, lobed sides, on four ball feet, 7 7/8" di, 12oz	Bonhams London UK 2005 #468

YEAR	MAKER	LOCATION	DESCRIPTION	SOURCE
1903/04	Brook & Son	Edinburgh	Bowls, pair, lobed circular form, heavily embossed scroll floral and beaded decoration, each with four flying scroll feet modeled as mythical beasts, 8 ½" di, 20z both	Pook & Pook, Inc Downingtown, PA USA 2004 #77
1923/24	MacKay & Chisholm	Edinburgh	Bowls, rose, two acanthus leaf handles, sides with applied girdles, presentation inscription below, spreading circular foot, 14 ½" across handles, 56oz	Bonhams London UK 2006 #206
1934/35	Hamilton & Inches	Edinburgh	Bowl, rim decorated with Celtic motifs, 20oz	Gorringes LLP East Sussex, UK 2006 #1487

Slop Bowls

Plate 5. A 1734/35 three footed shallow Slop Bowl by James Tait, Edinburgh. Courtesy of The Phoenix Collection. Photograph by Janice M Dietert.

YEAR	MAKER	LOCATION	DESCRIPTION	SOURCE
	SLOP			
1730 ca	George Cooper	Aberdeen	Slop bowl, circular with scalloped upright rim on pedestal foot, 3 ¾" di, 4.1oz	Noble Collection Nicholas Shaw Catalog 2004 p98
1733/34	William Aytoun	Edinburgh	Slop bowl, everted scalloped, later Arms/Supporters, baron's coronet above, 6" di, 7oz 17d	Sotheby's November 11, 1982 #16
1734/35	James Tait	Edinburgh	Slop bowl, or sugar, everted lip, plain, on 3 pad feet, crest, partially rubbed crowned leopard's head, erased initial below "AH", 2 ½" ht, 5 ¼" di	JH Bourdon-Smith London 1993 The Phoenix Collection
1735 ca	Alexander Forbes	Aberdeen	Slop bowl, bombe form, everted, scalloped rim, on 3 trefoil and paw feet, initials, 3 1/8" di, 7oz	Delieb p78-79
1735-40	Alexander Forbes	Aberdeen	*Slop bowl, scalloped edge, flat-cased with flowers, shells and trellis work, on 3 paw feet, pad supports, 6" di, 29oz*	*Sotheby's London March 6, 2004* #254
1814/15	Robert Gray & Son	Glasgow Edinburgh assay	Bowl, identified as a waste bowl, squat circular on gadrooned circular foot, shoulder with anthemion band, part of a service	Christie's NY USA 2005 #172

Strawberry Bowls

Plate 6. A Strawberry Bowl/Dish 1730 ca by George Cooper, Aberdeen. Courtesy of The Maple Swan Collection.

YEAR	MAKER	LOCATION	DESCRIPTION	SOURCE
STRAWBERRY				
1717/18	Mungo Yorstoun	Edinburgh	Strawberry bowl, fluted, circular form on rim foot, crest and motto, initials "MM", 8 5/8"di, 19 oz	Bonhams Edinburgh August 2003 #64
1718/19	Henry Bethune	Edinburgh	Strawberry dish, circular fluted on rim foot, center engraved with crest and motto	Christie's South Kensington October 30, 1990 #106
1718/19	William Aytoun	Edinburgh	Strawberry dish, The Haig Dish, with later initials of Sarah Robertson, 11.4oz	How's Notes on Antique Silver 1941 vol I, p20
1719/20	William Ged	Edinburgh	Strawberry dish, circular, fluted in 16 segments	How's Notes on Antique Silver 1941 vol I, p12
1723/24	William Aytoun	Edinburgh	Strawberry bowl, The Haig Bowl, with Latin inscription, 12.6oz	How of Edinburgh 1937 #90
1727/28	David Mitchell Assayer – Edward Penman	Edinburgh	Strawberry bowl, no details	Koopman 1993 (International Antiques Show NYC)
1730 ca	George Cooper	Aberdeen	Strawberry bowl, engraved with crest and motto, script initials "IC", sides fluted into 16 panels below shaped rim, ring foot, 7 ½" di, 10oz 16d	Sotheby's November 29, 1984 #287 The Maple Swan Collection
1731/32	William Aytoun	Edinburgh	Strawberry bowl, circular, fluted, on rim foot, flat chased, 12 panels of foliage with molded scalloped rim of 12 points, 8 ½" di, 12oz	Christie's Edinburgh June 6, 1995 #340

Sugar Bowls

Plate 7. A Sugar Bowl 1750/51 by James Mitchell, Edinburgh.
Courtesy of The Phoenix Collection. Photograph by Janice M Dietert.

YEAR	MAKER	LOCATION	DESCRIPTION	SOURCE
SUGAR				
1717/18	Henry Bethune	Edinburgh	Sugar bowl, octagonal	National Museums of Scotland MEQ 1346
1718/19	William Aytoun	Edinburgh	Sugar bowl, octagonal box/bowl, set with coffee pot and cream jug, later initials, script "SR", 4 3/8" ht, 15oz 8d	Sotheby's October 22, 1970 #213 Brett p194 #814
1718/19	John Seatoun	Edinburgh	Sugar bowl, cup on rim, cover missing	JH Bourdon-Smith London 1993
1718/19	John Seatoun	Edinburgh	Sugar bowl, covered bowl, foot on rim, with cover also with a rim foot on top, 3 5/8" di, 8oz 3d	Christie's November 29, 1972 #108 How's Notes on Antique Silver 1944, vol 4 p9
1718/19	John Seatoun	Edinburgh	Sugar bowl, covered, foot and cover on rims, cylindrical with rounded base, 3 ½" di, 8oz 10d, possibly same as one above.	Sotheby's NY USA April 15, 1998 #313
1718/19	Colin Campbell	Edinburgh	Sugar bowl, plain, circular, almost hemispherical but with everted lip, engraved with contemporary arms of Hathorn of Over- Aires (Wigton) quartering Stewart of Phisgill, with mottos in riband above and below, on rim foot, 7 ½" di	Sotheby's July 4, 1968 #159 Walter Willson Private Collection
1718/19	William Aytoun	Edinburgh	Sugar bowl, without its cover, also sometimes called a beaker, plain, circular nearly straight sided body, tucked in on splayed rim foot, engraved with a crest and motto, 3 ¾" di, 3 1/8" ht, 6.5oz	Christie's Scotland November 11, 1987 #55
1719/20	James Mitchelson	Edinburgh	Sugar bowl, with lid, plain, circular, spreading bowl on spreading foot, narrow molded rim, cover with similar rim foot, bird crest, engraved, 4 ½" di, 10oz 19d	Christie's December 13, 1967 Wilson and Sharp Noble collection
1719/20	Henry Bethune	Edinburgh	Sugar bowl, plain, engraved with a widow's lozenge, split rim, 6" di, 10oz	Apollo March 1971 vol 93 p2 Bell of Aberdeen advertisement
1719/20	Not available	Edinburgh	Sugar bowl, cup on rim with footed (rim) top, 8oz 5d	How's Notes on Antique Silver 1944 # 5
1720 ca	Edward Penman	Edinburgh	Sugar bowl, covered sugar on molded foot, rim on cover	Sotheby's London Picture Files
1721/22	James Mitchelson	Edinburgh	Sugar bowl, everted wavy bordered rim, molded edge	Muirhead Moffat & Co Private Collection UK
1723 ca	Not available	Edinburgh	Sugar bowl, plain, circular sugar bowl, probably an Alexander Edmonstoun bowl, 6 oz 3d	Christie's May 4, 1949 #83 Christie's London October 12, 1966

YEAR	MAKER (continued)	LOCATION	DESCRIPTION	SOURCE
				How of Edinburgh
1723/24	William Aytoun	Edinburgh	Sugar bowl, plain, hemispherical on spreading foot, later crest and motto, 4 ½" di, 6oz 2d	Christie's February 27, 1974 Clayton Christie's Book p152 #3
1723/24	William Aytoun	Edinburgh	Sugar bowl, cover missing, later engraved, crest and initials "AS," gilt, 4 7/8" di, 6oz	Christie's Edinburgh February 1, 1991 #245
1723/24	William Aytoun	Edinburgh	Sugar bowl, plain, molded foot, 4 ¾" di, 6oz 18d	Christie's October 13, 1954 #84 Christie's January 12, 1954 #165 Thomas Lumley Ltd
1723/24	Alexander Edmonstoun	Edinburgh	Sugar bowl, plain on spread rim foot, just short of hemispherical, 4 ½" di, 6oz 3d	Christie's Glasgow March 1983 #92 How's Notes on Antique silver 1944, vol 4, p9 Shaw Collection
1723/24	James Ker	Edinburgh	Sugar bowl, circular, with scalloped rim and accompanying helmet creamer	Wilson & Sharp Glasgow Exhibition 1911 vol I, p108 #22
1724/25	James Ker	Edinburgh	Sugar bowl, covered, on pedestal, marked on bowl and cover, double domed top, ball finial, 5" ht, 13oz	Scottish Art Review 1964 vol IX #3 back cover How of Edinburgh Shaw Collection Finlay 1991 #73 Christie's Glasgow March 1983 #93 National Museums of Scotland MEQ 1561 1983
1724/25	Thomas Mitchell	Edinburgh	Sugar basin, octagonal, no details	Jackson Marks p546 notes Crichton Bros
1725 ca	Robert Luke	Glasgow	Sugar bowl and cover, oval, baluster finial, shaped outline, 4" long, 11oz 10d	Christie's March 19, 1934 #141 How of Edinburgh Collection Gardner Collection Connoisseur Magazine 1934 vol 93 p347
1725/26	William Aytoun	Edinburgh	Sugar bowl, The Annandale Bowl, with crest of Johnston, Marquess of Annandale, with an accompanying stand	How of Edinburgh 1937 #92 Private Collection UK

YEAR	MAKER	LOCATION	DESCRIPTION	SOURCE
1726/27	James Ker	Edinburgh	Sugar bowl, circular bowl on 3 lion mask knees with lion paw feet, slightly everted corded rim, coat of arms, crest and motto of Kelso, approximately 5 ¾" di, scratch wt 11oz 12d,	Art Institute of Chicago Christie's East NY October 15, 1996 #354 Shrubsole, 1996 The Phoenix Collection
1727/28	James Tait	Edinburgh	Sugar bowl, covered sugar on spreading foot, engraved border bayonet fitting cover, engraved monogram, with stand to match, both body near the mouth and the lid have a band of formalized foliage in compartments, 4"di, 12 oz 12d total	Christie's Glasgow March 1983, #88 Christie's March 31, 1971 #81 Metropolitan Museum of Art #133ab 1983 Christie's March 5, 1971 #81 How of Edinburgh Collection
1727/28	James Tait	Edinburgh	*Sugar bowl, covered, circular, engraved with a wreath enclosing the initials "AM", detachable cover, body with one band of foliage near the mouth, 4" ht*	*Scottish Art Review 1971 vol XIII, #2 back cover* *How of Edinburgh advertisement*
1727/28	James Ker	Edinburgh	Sugar bowl, part of a set, circular, molded edge, 12 points on raised foot, everted, scalloped, part of a 4 piece set, possibly with crest	Apollo 1934 vol 20 p25 Wilson & Sharp advertisement Finlay 1991 #134 How's Notes on Antique Silver 1941 vol I, p23
1727/28	David Mitchell	Edinburgh	Sugar bowl, everted chased rim (later),	Apollo March 1962 vol53 p69 National Museums of Scotland
1727/28	William Aytoun Assayer – Edward Penman	Edinburgh	Sugar bowl, everted wavy border, molded edge, crest (3 arrows) and motto of Leyboum or Poplar, 8 ½" di, 19oz 5d	Christie's February 27, 1971 #160
1727/28	James Mitchelson	Edinburgh	Sugar bowl, shaped flat rim, with stand, wavy border, molded edge	Park Lane Exhibition 1929 #69
1728/29	Henry Bethune	Edinburgh	Sugar bowl, everted rim, wavy border, molded edge, 4oz 10d	Christie's Scottish Picture Files July 10-11, 1984 #376 Negative #252239
1728/29	Henry Bethune	Edinburgh	*Sugar bowl, everted rim, wavy border, molded edge, 5 1/8" di*	*Christie's South Kensington November 10, 1998 #86*
1728/29	Henry Bethune	Edinburgh	Sugar bowl, covered, spherical body, double crested below monograms, detachable cover with a baluster finial, on spreading foot, 4 ¾" di, 9.5oz	Sotheby's October 31, 1974 #42

YEAR	MAKER	LOCATION	DESCRIPTION	SOURCE
1728/29	Not available	Edinburgh	Sugar bowl, small, plain, no everted rim	Antiques Magazine February vol 107 Bell of Aberdeen advertisement
1728/29	James Ker	Edinburgh	Sugar bowl, plain, circular rim foot, slight spreading sides, 6 ¾" di, 9oz 18d	Apollo March 1942 vol 35, # 7 Bell of Aberdeen advertisement Christie's May 21, 1952
1728/29	James Mitchelson	Edinburgh	Sugar bowl, everted, molded edge, initials on bottom, 10 points	Hyman Collection - Colonial Williamsburg 1994
1728/29	James Mitchelson	Edinburgh	Sugar bowl, circular, wavy border, molded edge, 10 points, 5 3/8" di, 7.4oz	Nicholas Shaw Catalog 2004 p100
1728/29	Edward Penman	Edinburgh	Sugar bowl, lacking its detachable cover, on circular stepped base with 2 crests side by side under ribanded mottos, with a matching teapot	Christie's December 14, 1972 #109 Koopman London
1729/30	James Ker	Edinburgh	Sugar bowl, cupping bowl with shell handle	Connoisseur Magazine 1934 vol 93 p347
1729/30	William Aytoun	Edinburgh	Sugar bowl, plain, circular, on spreading foot, shaped narrow molded border, 8 points, 5 ½" di, 7oz	Christie's Edinburgh April 29, 1992 Private Collection
1729/30	Henry Bethune	Edinburgh	Sugar bowl, on molded foot, with everted wavy border and molded rim, engraved with a crest, 5 ½" di, 7.8oz	Christie's London December 20, 1972 #179 JH Bourdon-Smith London
1729/30	Ker & Dempster Assayer Archibald Ure	Edinburgh	Sugar bowl with everted shaped rim, sold with like teapot stand, note that date is too early for these makers	Christie's London UK 2005 #476 JH Bourdon-Smith Catalog Spring 2007 #47 p15
1730 ca	George Cooper	Aberdeen	Sugar bowl, plain circular, on spreading rim foot, 5oz 3d	Christie's July 3, 1984 #123
1730 ca	George Cooper	Aberdeen	Sugar bowl cover, circular, plain, 3 worn marks – e, GC, 3 castles, 3oz	Phillips Edinburgh October 22, 1982 #36
1730ca	George Cooper	Aberdeen	Sugar bowl, with cover, set	Connoisseur Magazine 1955 vol 135 p 90
1730 ca	George Cooper	Aberdeen	Sugar bowl, plain circular bowl, brass wire rim, 4 ¼" di, 5oz 4d	Christie's January 24, 1901 #61 Christie's June 18, 1912 #472

YEAR	MAKER	LOCATION	DESCRIPTION	SOURCE
1730 ca	Alexander Forbes	Aberdeen	Sugar basin, no details	National Museums of Scotland L1980.5
1730 ca	Robert Luke	Glasgow	Sugar bowl, circular, later engraved with initials below a coronet, shaped molded rim, on circular foot, 5" di, 6oz 11d	Sotheby's Sept 23, 1973 #3
1730 ca	Robert Luke	Glasgow	Sugar bowl, on 4 bifurcated scroll feet, winged cherub's masks above, shaped molded rim chased below with shells, masks and drapery festoons, 4 ½" di, 7oz 2d	Christie's April 12, 1967 #44
1730 ca	George Cooper	Aberdeen	Sugar bowl, plain circular form, stepped spreading foot, engraved with initials "GR/CF", 3 marks on base – GC, 3 towers, gothic e – 4 ¼" di, 4.5oz	Phillips Edinburgh August 24, 2001 # Nicholas Shaw Catalog Winter 2000 p68
1730ca	Robert Luke	Glasgow	Sugar bowl, waved reeded rim, on pedestal base, 4 ¾" di, 6oz 14d	Sotheby's Scone April 23-24, 1975 #86
1730/31	William Aytoun	Edinburgh	Sugar bowl, everted scalloped molded rim, 10 points, scratch wt 9:8 on bottom	Asprey (London) 1992 The Phoenix Collection
1731/32	Archibald Ure	Edinburgh	Sugar bowl, plain molded rim not everted, crest of three turreted castle, 4 ¾" di	Sotheby's January 22, 1970 #168 C J Vander Antiques Antiques Magazine February 1987 Shrubsole advertisement The Phoenix Collection
1731/32	James Ker	Edinburgh	Sugar bowl, with wavy border and molded rim on tall pedestal foot, crest and motto, 9 points	The Maple Swan Collection
1731/32	William Aytoun	Edinburgh	Sugar bowl, everted scalloped, wavy border, molded edge, crest, 8oz 5d	Christie's May 3, 1961 #161 Thomas Lumley Ltd Sotheby's December 14, 1967 #107 How of Edinburgh National Museums of Scotland MEQ 1983.25
1731/32	William Aytoun	Edinburgh	Sugar bowl, everted scalloped molded edge, crest and motto, "Suum Cuique?", 4" di, 3" ht, 8oz 16d	Connoisseur Magazine July 1961 How of Edinburgh advertisement
1731/32	James Ker	Edinburgh	Sugar bowl, covered, no details	National Museums of Scotland MEQ L1980.7

YEAR	MAKER	LOCATION	DESCRIPTION	SOURCE
1731/32	Henry Bethune	Edinburgh	Sugar bowl, everted scalloped wavy border, molded rim, crest and motto, 8 points, 6" di, 7oz 8d	Sotheby's Gleneagles August 29, 1978 #396 Lyle Silver Review 1982 p16
1732/33	William Aytoun	Edinburgh	Sugar bowl, everted, scalloped, molded edge, foot like 1733 service, 8 points on rim, 5 ½" di, 6oz 6d	Christie's June 23, 1971 #72
1732/33	William Aytoun	Edinburgh	Sugar bowl, everted rim, wavy border, 6" di, 7oz 10d	Christie's Feb 20, 1935 #116 Christie's Dec 20, 1937 #86
1732/33	William Aytoun	Edinburgh	Sugar bowl, wavy border, molded edge on cup-type foot, probably 8 points	Connoisseur Magazine February 1939 p107-109 How of Edinburgh Collection
1732/33	William Aytoun	Edinburgh	Sugar bowl, wavy border, molded edge, 8 points, on spreading stepped foot, 5 ½" di, 6.8oz	Sotheby's Oct 31, 1974 #82
1732/33	James Mitchelson	Edinburgh	Sugar bowl, everted rim, wavy border, molded edge, 5 ¼" di, 7oz 3d	Christie's April 5, 1950 #103 How of Edinburgh Collection Connoisseur Magazine 1950 vol 126 p 151
1733/34	William Aytoun	Edinburgh	Sugar bowl, hemispherical plain bowl, below a slightly everted wavy rim, on reeded spreading foot, 7 ½" di, 14oz	Sotheby's Nov 11, 1993 #446
1733/34	William Aytoun	Edinburgh	Sugar bowl, circular with everted shaped and molded scalloped rim, 10 points, engraved with slightly later coat of arms all below a baron's coronet, arms of Evans quartering Stafford impaling Noel for George Evans 3rd Baron Carbery, in catalog by Christie's, 6" di, 7.8oz	Baron Carbery Sotheby's Nov 11, 1982 #16
1733/34	William Aytoun	Edinburgh	Sugar bowl, everted wavy border, scalloped rim with molded edge, 9 points, together with stand, Arms of Menzies impaling Campbell, with a similar stand	Sotheby's London Nov 11, 1982 #16 Connoisseur Magazine 1954 vol 133 p66 How of Edinburgh advertisement Clayton Dictionary p42 #43
1733/34	William Aytoun	Edinburgh	Sugar bowl, wavy border, everted scalloped rim, molded edge, part of the Girdwood Tea Service, 9 points	Connoisseur Magazine 1934 vol 93 p131 Christie's Dec 13, 1967 Finlay 1991 #73
1733/34	William Aytoun	Edinburgh	Sugar bowl, serrated non everted edge, low broad foot, 7 ½"di, 14oz	Christie's London July 1992 #97 Sotheby's November 11, 1993

YEAR	MAKER (continued)	LOCATION	DESCRIPTION	SOURCE #446
1733/34	Alexander Kincade	Edinburgh	Sugar bowl, everted, wavy beaded edge, 8 points, crest and motto of Durham, 5 ¾" di	Christie's April 24, 1968 #94 Asprey London 1994 Exhibition
1734/35	Not available	Edinburgh	Sugar bowl, compressed circular, shaped everted rim is flat chased with scrolls, fruit and foliage, on 3 hoof feet issuing from trefoils, 5 ¼ " di, 6oz	Sotheby's June 29-30, 1989 #149
1734/35	Dougal Ged	Edinburgh	Sugar bowl, circular, everted, chased, 5 ½"di , 7oz	Sotheby's January 26, 1967 #146 Sotheby's March 23, 1994 Connoisseur Magazine 193? vol 98 p241 How of Edinburgh 1937 #99
1734/35	James Ker	Edinburgh	Sugar bowl, everted on 4 pad feet-set, light chasing, crest, motto, coronet of Hope, part of a service	Christie's June 16, 1977 #121 Clayton Dictionary p419 #650 National Museums of Scotland MEQ 1209 1977.8
1734/35	Not available	Edinburgh	Sugar bowl, wavy border, molded edge, spiral fluting inside, 12 points on bowl edge, 12 fluted sections inside, 7 ½" di	Shreve, Crump & Low advertisement probably from the 1940s
1734/35	William Aytoun	Edinburgh	Sugar bowl, no details	Sotheby's February 2, 1961 #90
1735 ca	Johan Got-helf-Bilsings	Glasgow	Sugar bowl, almost hemispherical body, plain, flattened wavy rim, chased with leaf and shell motifs on matted ground, base with initials, on molded spreading foot, 6 ½" di, 10oz 14d	Sotheby's August 27-28 1970 #110
1735 ca	Patrick Gordon	Banff	Sugar bowl, everted scalloped molded edge, crest and motto of Duff, with cream jug, 5 ¼" di	Finlay 1991 #120 Scotland Art Academy 1939 #969 Noble collection Nicholas Shaw Catalog 2004 p108 Glasgow Empire Exhibition 1938 #913 National Museums of Scotland K2004.208.1
1735 ca	Not available	Edinburgh	Sugar bowl, everted scroll, plain	Waldron #912
1735 ca	Not available	Edinburgh	Sugar bowl, covered ball shape, 2 crests	Waldron #913

YEAR	MAKER	LOCATION	DESCRIPTION	SOURCE
1735 ca	George Cooper	Aberdeen	Sugar bowl, circular bowl on pedestal foot, engraved script "GR" above "CF" on side, 4 1/8" di, 4.7oz	Nicholas Shaw Catalog Winter 2000 p68
1735/36	William Aytoun Assayer – Archibald Ure	Edinburgh	Sugar bowl, wavy border, bowl misdated as 1748, 8 points on rim, 5 ½" di	Christie's London June 23, 1971 #72 Negative #730829
1735/36	Edward Lothian	Edinburgh	Sugar bowl, Chippendale edge, pedestal foot	JH Bourdon-Smith Catalog Autumn 2005 #46 p 26
1736/37	Dougal Ged	Edinburgh	Sugar bowl, with 2 leaf capped handles, Earl of Moray	Finlay 1991 #70
1737/38	Archibald Ure	Edinburgh	Sugar bowl, circular on molded foot, everted rim chased with a band of flowers, shells and diaper work, 6" di, 9.7oz	Christie's June 18, 1969 #189 Simon Kaye Antiques Christie's June 2, 1976 #157
1737/38	James Ker	Edinburgh	Sugar bowl, everted scalloped wavy border, molded edge, on spreading foot, 10 points, 6 ¼" di, 8oz 10d	Christie's Glasgow Sale, March 1983 Lot #71 Shaw Collection
1737/38	Archibald Ure	Edinburgh	Sugar bowl, slightly everted, crude edge chasing, 6" di, 10 oz	Apollo April 1982 vol 95 p219 Bell of Aberdeen advertisement
1737/38	*Archibald Ure*	*Edinburgh*	*Sugar bowl, slightly everted rim with chased band*	*National Museums of Scotland MEQ 1164 1976.11*
1737/38	William Aytoun	Edinburgh	Sugar bowl, everted rim, chased shells and flowers, on 3 feet, 5 ½" di	Scotland Art Academy Exhibition 1939 #912 Milne-Davidson Collection
1737/38	Hugh Penman	Edinburgh	Sugar bowl, circular on 3 hoof feet, everted chased rims, 5 ½" di, 5oz 12d	Christie's December 14, 1938 #32 Hearst Collection
1737/38	William Aytoun	Edinburgh	Sugar bowl, hemispherical bowl, everted rim, flat chased with the usual decoration, on 3 hoof feet, issuing from trefoils, 5 1/8" di, 8oz	JH Bourdon-Smith Catalog Spring 1983
1738/39	James Ker	Edinburgh	Sugar bowl, circular on 3 scroll and hoof feet, plain body with rounded sides, shaped everted rim, chased with flowers, foliage and shells, engraved with initials, 5" di, 7.3oz	Christie's May 26, 1971 #145
1739/40	Edward Lothian Assayer David Mitchell	Edinburgh	Sugar bowl, plain, hemispherical, everted lip, chased with flowers, diaper, shell and foliate motifs, on spreading foot, 6" di, 6.6oz	Sotheby's March 19, 1964 #75 Sotheby's April 30, 1985 #

YEAR	MAKER	LOCATION	DESCRIPTION	SOURCE
1739/40	Charles Blair	Edinburgh	Sugar bowl, circular, everted rim, chased, 5 ¼" di, 8oz 13d	Christie's July 12, 1940 #73
1739/40	Edward Lothian	Edinburgh	Sugar bowl, shaped rim, chased flowers and shells, with later crest, 6oz 13d	Christie's July 14, 1961 #153
1739/40	James Ker	Edinburgh	Sugar bowl, everted, chased, on 3 paw feet, part of a 4 piece service	Christie's April 27, 1949 #81
1739/40	HB conjoined Henry Bethune	Edinburgh	Sugar bowl, everted rim, wavy border, molded edges on 3 feet, large body low to the ground	Sotheby's Sale W03765 Olympia March 6, 2003 #254
1740 ca	Attributed Colin Allan More likely Charles Allan, Jamaica	Attributed Aberdeen (Jamaica)	Sugar bowl, circular, on 3 paw feet with lions' masks above, chased with floral swags on matted ground, molded lip, engraved with initials "TM", provenance Christie's March 11, 1953 #96, 4 ½" di, 14oz, see research of Robert B Barker	Christie's March 29, 1983 #31
1740 ca	Attributed Colin Allan More likely Charles Alan, Jamaica	Attributed Aberdeen (Jamaica)	Sugar bowl, circular, on 3 paw feet with lions' masks above, chased with flower heads and foliage on matted ground, plain molded rim, mm CA struck 3X's, 4.3/8" di, 14oz, see research of Robert B Barker	Christie's Scotland November 14, 1985 #293
1740 ca	Colin Allan	Aberdeen	Sugar bowl, 2 handled, body with spiral flutes, crest and motto "LOVE IN GLORY"	Christie's London Scottish Picture File sent for auction in 1952 but returned
1740 ca	Not available		Sugar bowl, coconut shaped, cover and cream jug, each on 3 hoof feet, silver calyx to the bowl chased with flowers and similarly chased rims, triple leaf finial	Christie's November 11, 1964 #62
1740 ca	Robert Luke	Glasgow	Sugar bowl, with cover, oval bombe body, on spreading foot, molded rim, domed cover, baluster finial, 4 ½" long, 11oz	Christie's NY USA October 27, 1986 #562
1740 ca	Robert Luke	Glasgow	Sugar bowl, winged, masks and cherubs along rim, bowl on 4 truncated scrolled feet, masks and drapery, 4 ½" di, 7oz 2d	Christie's April 12, 1967 #44 How of Edinburgh Collection
1740/41	Hugh Penman	Edinburgh	Sugar bowl, circular, everted rim, chased, on 3 hoof feet, 5 ½" di, 5oz 12d	Christie's December 14, 1938 #32 Hearst Collection
1742/43	James Clark	Edinburgh	Sugar bowl, everted rim, on stepped domed foot, chased, part of a 3 piece tea service	Christie's July 5, 1967 #172 Preston Ltd Antiques advertisement
1742/43	Edward Lothian	Edinburgh	Sugar bowl, everted rim, chased, part of a 3 piece service, crested 5 ¼" di	Sotheby's March 18, 1962 #12
1742/43	Edward Lothian	Edinburgh	Sugar bowl, everted chased rim, engraved crest and motto, mixed service with creamer 1744 by AC.	Geoffrey J Munro Sotheby's London June 18, 1987 #251

YEAR	MAKER (continued)	LOCATION	DESCRIPTION	SOURCE
1743/44	William Aytoun	Edinburgh	Sugar bowl, everted, chased like the 1727 Mitchell bowl	Apollo March 1951 vol 53 p 69 National Museums of Scotland
1743 ca	James Glen	Glasgow	Sugar bowl, circular, on 3 paw feet, sides chased with flowers, scrolls and wave ornament, similarly decorated shaped rim, 5" di, 8oz 11d	Christie's January 26, 1972 #103
1743/44	Robert Hope	Edinburgh	Sugar bowl, everted rim, chased flowers and scrolls, 6oz 16d	Christie's December 17, 1930 #25
1743/44	William Davie or William Dempster	Edinburgh	Sugar bowl, everted, chased, on 3 paw feet, part of a set, crest and motto of Curie	Antiques Magazine vol 88 #410 Shrubsole Apollo January 1974 vol 99 p43
1743/44	William Dempster or William Davie	Edinburgh	Sugar bowl, on 3 paw feet, trefid attachments, very broad everted and chased shaped rim, part of a mixed set with 1739 James Mitchelson teapot and 1743 dolphin handled Dempster or Davie cream boat	Asprey advertisement Spink Ltd
1743/44	James Ker	Edinburgh	Sugar bowl, everted rim, chased, on 3 cabriole legs with paw feet, part of a set, "AE" for the Erskine family	Christie's June 22, 1960 #14 Clayton Dictionary p421 #617
1743/44	James Ker	Edinburgh	Sugar bowl, circular, everted rim, chased, on 3 cabriole legs with paw feet, trefid knees, 6oz 19d	Apollo 1933 vol 17 p13 How of Edinburgh advertisement
1743/44	Edward Lothian	Edinburgh	Sugar bowl, no details	National Museums of Scotland 1957.253
1743/44	John Welsh	Edinburgh	Sugar bowl, no details	National Museums of Scotland 1947.363
1743/44	Charles Dickson II	Edinburgh	Sugar bowl, circular, on pedestal foot, everted shaped and chased rim, script initials "CS" underneath	Hyman Collection - Colonial Williamsburg Antiques Magazine June 1996 pp845-856
1744/45	Ebenezer Oliphant	Edinburgh	Sugar bowl, plain, bulbous body, everted chased rim, foliate and scroll flat chasing, 3 cast applied feet as lions' paws, 5 ½" di, 6.6oz	Spencer Marks Antiques F237 East Walpole, MA USA
1745 ca	James Glen	Glasgow	Sugar bowl, everted, chased on large molded rim feet, Arms of Dennistoun, 8 7/8" di, 14oz	Christie's Glasgow March 1983, #46

YEAR	MAKER	LOCATION	DESCRIPTION	SOURCE
1745/46	James Ker	Edinburgh	Sugar bowl, no details	National Museums of Scotland MEQ L 1983.26
1745/46	James Ker	Edinburgh	Sugar bowl, with a cream boat, no details	The Maple Swan Collection
1746 ca	Edward Lothian (or William Davie)	Edinburgh	Sugar bowl, everted, chased, combined with a 3 piece service, crest and motto of Curle, part of a 3 piece tea service	Sotheby's March 18, 1962 #12 Connoisseur Magazine October 1968
1746/47	Edward Lothian	Edinburgh	Sugar bowl, circular, chased, everted wavy rim, engraved with a crest, a hand holding a nautical instrument, motto "SEDULITATE", 5 ½" di, 8oz 5d	Scottish Art Review 1966 vol IX, #4 back cover How of Edinburgh advertisement Private Collection
1746/47	William Aytoun Assayer Hugh Gordon	Edinburgh	Sugar Bowl, flat shaped circular border chased with flowers, leaves and shells, on 3 feet headed by trefoils, 5" di, 7oz 13d	Sotheby's February 26. 1976 #139
1746/47	James Ker Assayer Hugh Gordon	Edinburgh	Sugar bowl, on 3 foliate and paw feet, plain body of squat circular form, engraved with crest, shaped everted rim engraved with flower heads and foliage, crest of Bogle,	Christie's March 27, 1984 #269
1746/47	Edward Lothian Assayer Hugh Gordon	Edinburgh	Sugar bowl, plain, on molded foot, flat everted rim chased with a band of foliage, flowers and wave ornament, engraved with crest and motto, 5 5/8" di, 7oz 17d	Sotheby's March 25, 1981 #167
1746/47	James Ker	Edinburgh	Sugar bowl, everted, chased rim, on 3 paw feet, part of 3 piece service	Sotheby's NY June 10-12, 1980 #433
1746/47	William Aytoun	Edinburgh	Sugar bowl, everted, chased, on 3 pad feet, 5" di, 7oz 13d	Sotheby's February 28, 1976 #139
1747/48	Robert Low	Edinburgh	Sugar bowl, everted, chased pedestal, crest of Princess Elizabeth Duchess of Edinburgh	Queen's Collection pl. 9
1748/49	James Mitchell	Edinburgh	Sugar bowl, on 3 paw feet, trefid attachments, everted and chased rim, 5 3/8" di	Christie's London July 25, 1973 #175 Negative #744575 Stock #650 VT JH Bourdon-Smith London
1748/49	James Mitchell Assayer Hugh Gordon	Edinburgh	Sugar bowl, plain circular, on 3 scroll and paw feet, shaped rim chased with band of flowers, wave ornament and scrolls, IM figure between mark not attributed in ad, 5 3/8" di, 6oz 15d	Christie's July 25, 1975 #175

YEAR	MAKER	LOCATION	DESCRIPTION	SOURCE
1748/49	Robert Low Assayer Hugh Gordon (continued)	Edinburgh	Sugar bowl, shallow circular body, everted wavy lip, engraved with scrolls and foliage, on 3 claw feet, underside with initials "RMM", 5"di, 7oz 12d	Sotheby's Hopetoun House, April 29, 1987 #69 JH Bourdon-Smith Catalog Spring 1987 #19 Sotheby's London auction
1748/49	Charles Dickson II	Edinburgh	Sugar bowl, everted, chased, on 3 paw feet, 5" di	Ticher Irish Silver Book p52 a,b
1748/49	IC or IE	Edinburgh	Sugar bowl, everted rim, chased, on pedestal foot, body later chased	Jack Simmons London 1995 Antiques Magazine
1748/49	James Mitchell Assayer – Hugh Gordon	Edinburgh	Sugar bowl, wavy rim, flat, chased with flowers, 5 ½" di, 21oz 10d	Sotheby's London December 18, 2004 #286
1749/50	Hugh Gordon	Edinburgh	Sugar bowl, tapering, molded, circular, on knurled stylized paw feet, shaped rim, 5" di, 7.25oz	Christie's South Kensington December 8, 1993 #337
1750 ca	Colin Allan	Aberdeen	Sugar bowl, on 3 paw feet, lions heads above mm only, initials "TM" on front, chased on ref. with lid, 4 ½" di, 11oz	Christie's Glasgow March 1983 #31 Christie's October 22, 1952 #116 Christie's March 11, 1953 #96
1750 ca	Colin Allan	Aberdeen	Sugar bowl, plain, on 3 feet, 4" di, 5oz 19d	Lyle Silver Review 1982 p16
1750/51	James Mitchell	Edinburgh	Sugar bowl, everted rim, chased, pedestal foot, 5 ¼" di, 8oz	JH Bourdon-Smith London 1993 The Phoenix Collection
1753/54	Lothian & Robertson	Edinburgh	Sugar bowl, everted chased rim, pedestal foot, tree crest crown above, inverted pear shaped body, stepped domed foot, 9oz 8d	Ticher Irish Silver Book p28-29 Holland Book p221 Christie's March 24, 1914 #68 Ashburton Collection
1757/58	James Welsh	Edinburgh	Sugar bowl, everted, chased, 4 ¾" di, 9oz 9d	Sotheby's June 26, 1975 #161
1758-70	William Dempster	Edinburgh	Sugar bowl, part of a tea service of varying dates	Scottish Art Review 1953 vol IV, #4 Bell of Aberdeen advertisement
1759/60	Lothian & Robertson	Edinburgh	Sugar bowl, part of a set, no details	National Museums of Scotland MEQ 605 1961.1675
1760/61	William Dempster	Edinburgh	Sugar bowl, inverted pear shape on a spreading foot, side chased with floral swags, gadrooned border, 4 ¾" di, 9.5oz	Christie's London UK 2004 #614

YEAR	MAKER	LOCATION	DESCRIPTION	SOURCE
1760/61	J Mc	Edinburgh	Sugar bowl, everted, rim inverted, pear shaped body, 5 ¾" di, 7oz 12d	Christie's June 25, 1968 #33
1760 ca	Colin Allan	Aberdeen	Sugar bowl, slightly everted, waved rim with gadrooning, on 3 paw feet	Sotheby's NY August 1987 #285
1761/62	Lothian & Robertson	Edinburgh	Sugar bowl, inverted, pear shaped, everted rim, chased	Mary Cooke Antiques London 1995 Connoisseur Magazine 1934 vol 93 p347
1761/62	*Lothian & Robertson*	*Edinburgh*	*Sugar bowl, inverted pear shape, everted notched rim, engraved with initials, McKenzie family provenance, 3 ¼" ht, 8.6oz*	*Christie's NY USA 1999 #315* *Nicholas Shaw Catalog Winter 2000 p71* *Bonhams The Scottish Sale August 21, 2003 #22*
1761/62	William Dempster	Edinburgh	Sugar bowl, inverted pear shape on a circular foot, everted notched plain rim, band of chased flowers on body, 4 5/8" di, 7.8oz	Nicholas Shaw Catalog Winter 2001 p72
1761/62	William Dempster	Edinburgh	Sugar bowl, with chased flowers, script "M"	National Museums of Scotland MEQ 715
1762/63	Patrick Robertson	Edinburgh	Sugar bowl, 2 handled, inverted pear shaped body, everted rim, capped tall handles, 8" over handles, 10oz	Antiques Magazine Bell of Aberdeen advertisement
1764/65	James Welsh	Edinburgh	Sugar bowl, plain shape, cover missing, on a simple low foot, initial script "F" below coronet, 4 ¾" di	Apollo April 1973 vol 97 p2 Bell of Aberdeen advertisement
1765 ca	Adam Graham	Glasgow	Sugar bowl, inverted, pear shaped, molded foot, 4 ¼" di, 6oz 15d	Christie's March 2, 1965 #105
1765 ca	*Adam Graham*	*Glasgow*	*Sugar bowl, inverted, pear shaped, chased, 4 ½" di*	*Sotheby's NY October 1991 #366*
1765 ca	*Adam Graham*	*Glasgow*	*Sugar bowl, no details*	*National Museums of Scotland MEQ 1962.1026*
1765/66	Ker & Dempster	Edinburgh	Sugar bowl, on a pedestal, part of a service	Antiques Magazine 1956 vol 69
1766/67	Patrick Robertson	Edinburgh	Sugar bowl, small cup on rim, slightly everted	Jonathan Trace NY USA James Robinson NY USA 1993
1767 ca	Milne & Campbell	Glasgow	Sugar bowl, covered sugar, inverted pear shape, chased band body, shaped top with leaves, pineapple finial, 6" ht	Goodwin's Antiques November 1995 The Phoenix Collection

YEAR	MAKER	LOCATION	DESCRIPTION	SOURCE
1767 ca	Not available	Edinburgh	Sugar bowl, part of a service	Antiques Magazine 1951 vol 60 Bell of Aberdeen advertisement
1767/68	Ker & Dempster	Edinburgh	Sugar bowl, part of a service, circular inverted pear shaped body, everted chased rim, chased body, on a raised foot	Apollo 1951 vol 53 p11 Bell of Aberdeen advertisement
1767/68	TA (over struck date letter)	Edinburgh	Sugar bowl, oval, everted, chased, inverted pear shaped body, crest of Murray Earls of Mansfield, 5 1/3" di	Christie's December 19, 1988 #215
1767/68	Alexander Gardner	Edinburgh	Sugar bowl, plain, molded lip, engraved inscription "A present from Miss Arnots...."	Christie's January 31, 1945 #60
1767/68	Alexander Gardner	Edinburgh	Sugar bowl, plain bowl, on low foot, 6 ½" di, 12oz 15d	Sotheby's Gleneagles August 29, 1978 #432 Lyle Silver Review 1982 p16
1767/68	*Alexander Gardner*	*Edinburgh*	*Sugar bowl, plain, with molded rim, 6 3/8" di, 12.8oz*	*Connoisseur Magazine 1947 vol 23 p119-120 Asprey London advertisement*
1767/68	Benjamin Tait	Edinburgh	Sugar bowl, inverted pear shape on circular foot, chased fruit and flowers, initials "EJF" on side, 4 ½" di, 7.9oz	Nicholas Shaw Catalog Winter 2000 p71
1767/68	Benjamin Tait	Edinburgh	Sugar bowl, inverted pear shaped body, on stepped molded pedestal foot, slightly everted rim, broad band of chasing with foliage decoration around the upper body, 3 ¾" di, 8oz	Gorringes Auction Lewes England, March 16, 2006 #1920
1767/68	Patrick Robertson	Edinburgh	Sugar bowl, chased	JH Bourdon-Smith London 1993
1768/69	John Robertson	Edinburgh	Sugar bowl, no details	The Maple Swan Collection
1770 ca	Milne & Campbell	Glasgow	Sugar bowl, everted, chased, inverted pear shape, matched service	Connoisseur Magazine 1954 vol 133 p6 Bell of Aberdeen advertisement
1770 ca	Milne & Campbell	Glasgow	Sugar bowl, covered, chased decoration	National Museums of Scotland MEQ 1057
1770/71	Adam Graham	Glasgow	Sugar bowl, plain, circular, slightly turned out lip, engraved initials "AGAP"	Private Collection
1771/72	James Welsh	Edinburgh	Sugar bowl, Castle Grant	Cripps Book p 151 Connoisseur Magazine 1941-42 vol 108 p136
1772/73	WD script	Edinburgh	Sugar bowl, engraved script initials "AIR"	National Museums of Scotland

YEAR	MAKER	LOCATION	DESCRIPTION	SOURCE MEQ 901
	William Dempster or William Davie			
1773/74	James Welsh	Edinburgh	Sugar bowl, oval, everted chased rim	JH Bourdon-Smith London 1995
1773/74	William Davie	Edinburgh	Sugar bowl, plain, oval, slightly everted lip, applied gadrooning on the inside, on oval domed gadrooned foot, crest – knight on horseback, 2 ¾" ht	Bonhams the Scottish Sale August 21, 2003 #17
1773/74	Patrick Robertson	Edinburgh	Sugar bowl, part-fluted ogee form with gadrooned border and cast oval foot, 5 1/8" di, 7.75oz	Christie's London UK 2003 #420
1776 ca	Milne & Campbell	Glasgow	Sugar bowl, chased, with lid	Apollo October 1980 vol 92 p2 Bell of Aberdeen advertisement
1776/77	William Davie	Edinburgh	Sugar bowl, small, chased band, flaring lip, script "WC", 3 3/8" di	Christie's NY April 1989 #457
1776-80	William Davie	Edinburgh	Sugar bowl, oval, everted rim, gadrooned borders, 6" di, 9oz 14d	Sotheby's November 2, 1991 #120
1777/78	James Hewitt	Edinburgh	Sugar bowl, covered, oval	Connoisseur Magazine 1934 vol 94 p138
1780 ca	John Robertson	Canongate	Sugar bowl, chased with swing handle	Finlay 1991 #120
1782/83	James Gilliland	Edinburgh	Sugar bowl, vase shaped on spreading circular foot, engraved, crest and motto of Thomson, initials "MWF", 4 7/8" di, 9.9 oz	Nicholas Shaw Catalog Winter 2000 p71
1782/83	*James Gilliland*	*Edinburgh*	*Sugar bowl, vase shaped on spreading circular base, crest, motto and initials, part of mixed service*	*Christie's Lanarkshire UK 1998 #61*
1783/84	William Davie	Edinburgh	Sugar bowl, bowl is goblet like, on a foot with a tall pedestal, part of a service	Country Life May or June 1968 vol 143
1783/84	Not available	Edinburgh	Sugar bowl, hemispherical body, beaded edge, all over bright cut engraving, ribbon swags supporting 2 blank cartouches, on a stepped circular foot, 5 3/8" di, 4 1/8" ht, 9oz	Lyon & Turnbull The Murray Collection August 20, 2003 #174
1785/86	James McEwan	Glasgow	Sugar bowl, no details	Antiques Magazine vol 100 p464 Bell of Aberdeen advertisement
1788/89	Patrick Robertson	Edinburgh	Sugar basin, deep, on trumpet foot, light band of decoration below reeded rim, engraved with an angel, a Maltese cross in her coiffe, holding a shield charged with arms. An engrailed bend charged with 3 buckles between a seeded rose and a buck's head, 5 ¼" di, 8oz 4d	Private Collection

YEAR	MAKER	LOCATION	DESCRIPTION	SOURCE
1789 ca	W & P Cunningham I	Edinburgh	Sugar bowl, part of a service	Christie's May 1-2, 1991 #236
1789/90	Not Available	Edinburgh	Sugar bowl, part of a service	Country Life July 16, 1964 vol 136 p184 Provenance Hughes
1789/90	Patrick Robertson	Edinburgh	Sugar bowl, part of a service	National Museums of Scotland MEQ 674
1790 ca	Alexander Stewart, Jr	Inverness	Sugar bowl, part of a service	Connoisseur Magazine 1934 vol 93 p347
1790/91	W & P Cunningham I	Edinburgh	Sugar bowl, part of a service	Christie's March 2, 1966 #170
1791/92	William Robertson	Edinburgh	Sugar bowl, part of a service	Finlay 1991 #98 Country Life February 13, 1964 vol 135 p31
1792/93	Robert Swan	Edinburgh	Sugar bowl, oval sugar basket, swing handle, 6 ½" across, 11oz	Private Collection
1793/94	Francis Howden	Edinburgh	Sugar bowl, no details	National Museums of Scotland MEQ 136 1940.383
1795/96	Not available	Edinburgh	Sugar bowl, part of a service	Antiques Magazine vol 38 p50 Shreve advertisement
1795/96	G & M	Edinburgh	Sugar bowl, part of a service	Christie's July 12, 1989 #127
1795 ca	John Keith	Banff	Sugar bowl, not pictured	Connoisseur Magazine 1934 vol 93 p347
1795/96	G & M	Edinburgh	Sugar bowl, part of a 3 piece service	Christie's July 12, 1989
1798/99	James McKay	Edinburgh	Sugar bowl, no details	National Museums of Scotland MEQ 877
1800 ca	John Keith	Banff	Sugar bowl, goblet shaped, swing handle	JH Bourdon-Smith Catalog 1994
1800 ca	J Heron	Greenock	Sugar bowl, plain on rim, pedestal foot, 5 ¼" di, 7oz	Connoisseur Magazine 1952 vol 130 p11 Asprey advertisement
1800/01	W & P Cunningham I	Edinburgh	Sugar bowl, part of a service	Antiques Magazine 1958 vol 71

YEAR	MAKER	LOCATION	DESCRIPTION	SOURCE
1802/03	W & P Cunningham I	Edinburgh	Sugar bowl, oval, part fluted foot, creek key motif on shoulder, gilt interior with crest, motto and initials, part of a service	Christie's London UK 2000 #369
1802/03	Francis Howden	Edinburgh	Sugar bowl, fluted, part of a service	Christie's November 30, 1938 #23
1802/03	Francis Howden	Edinburgh	Sugar bowl, monogram in foliate, part of a service	Christie's November 9, 1966 #30
1802/03	Not available		Sugar bowl, part of a set, inscription given to the Royal Company of Archers	Christie's November 19, 1919 #42
1804/05	Alexander Spence	Edinburgh	Sugar bowl, part of a service	Antiques Magazine vol 41 p 295 Bell of Aberdeen advertisement
1804/05	Morehead & Arthur Assayed Edinburgh	Glasgow	Sugar bowl, 2 handled, plain reeding	Silver Plus, Inc 1993
1804/05	W & P Cunningham I	Edinburgh	Sugar bowl, two handled open, with foliate engraving inscribed "Presented by the 3rd troop of E. L. Y. C., to Francis Walker, Esq./ Their Captain 1805", 8" long, 8.4oz	Eldred's Auction Gallery, East Dennis, MA USA June 28, 2007 #123
1806/07	George McHattie	Edinburgh	Sugar bowl, rectangular, waisted bulbous body, two handles on four ball feet, part of a service	New Orleans Auction Galleries 2003 #60
1806/07	W & P Cunningham I	Edinburgh	Sugar bowl, part of a service, Arms of Kincraigie	Sotheby's Hopetoun House April 26, 1988 #76
1807/08	Cunningham & Simpson	Edinburgh	Sugar bowl, octagonal, everted, beaded edge, with Arms, 8" di, 18oz 8d	Sotheby's December 4, 1975 #198
1807/08	Cunningham & Simpson	Edinburgh	Sugar bowl, not pictured	Antiques Magazine vol 66, p 94
1807/08	Cunningham & Simpson	Edinburgh	Sugar bowl, tub shaped, 9" di	Sotheby's April 19, 1973 #110
1808/09	James McKay	Edinburgh	Sugar bowl, part of a service	Apollo 1974 vol 100, p17
1808/09	James McKay	Edinburgh	Sugar bowl, no details	The Maple Swan Collection
1808/09	RK overstrike	Perth	Sugar bowl, part of a service	Sotheby's Hopetoun House April 1989 #42
1808/09	Francis Howden	Edinburgh	Sugar bowl, part of a service	Antiques Magazine vol 46 p120

YEAR	MAKER	LOCATION	DESCRIPTION	SOURCE
1808/09	Dick & McPherson	Edinburgh	Sugar bowl, oblong with two handles on 4 ball feet, bright cut engraving, 4 3/8" ht, 9.1 oz	Nicholas Shaw Catalog Winter 2002/03 p88
1808/09	Cunningham & Simpson	Edinburgh	Sugar bowl, no details	National Museums of Scotland 1945.38
1809/10	George Fenwick	Edinburgh	Sugar bowl, initial "H", part of a 3 piece service	Sotheby's February 26, 1976 #38
1809/10	James McKay	Edinburgh	Sugar bowl, circular with chased band around rim, crest and motto, "In Deo Fides" and initial "F", 5 ½" di, 11.5oz	Nicholas Shaw Catalog Winter 2000 p71
1809/10	*James McKay*	*Edinburgh*	*Sugar bowl, part of a service*	*Apollo 1967 vol 85 p 87*
1810/11	George Fenwick	Edinburgh	Sugar bowl, bombe shape, initial "H", crest of Hay, part of a 3 piece service	Christie's Edinburgh May 1-2, 1991 #246
1811/12	George Fenwick	Edinburgh	Sugar bowl, part of a service	Lyle Annual Review 1983 p 615
1811/12	Francis Howden	Edinburgh	Sugar bowl, plain, crest and motto of Fullerton of Westwood, 6 ½" di, 17.3oz	JH Bourdon-Smith Catalog Autumn 1997 #39 p31
1811/12	James McKay	Edinburgh	Sugar bowl, part of a service	Sotheby's Hopetoun House May 1990 #86
1812/13	James McKay	Edinburgh	Sugar bowl, part of a service	Antiques Magazine vol 115 #328 Shreve advertisement
1813/14	George Fenwick	Edinburgh	Sugar bowl, plain, on a rim foot, crest and motto of Gordon, 5 ¼" di, 10oz	Christie's Glasgow March 1983 #67
1814/15	James McKay	Edinburgh	Sugar bowl, part of a service, 2 handled, on ball feet, fluted body, oblong shape	Apollo 1934 vol 19 Bell of Aberdeen advertisement
1814/15	George Fenwick	Edinburgh	Sugar bowl, oblong bellied form, tongue and dart border, two handles, on ball feet, part of a service	Bonham London UK 2006 #291
1815/16	George Fenwick	Edinburgh	Sugar bowl, pair, 7" di, 30oz 12d total (15oz 6d ea)	Christie's May 11, 1938 #60 Connoisseur Magazine February 1939 p2 Crichton Brothers advertisement
1817/18	James McKay	Edinburgh	Sugar bowl, part of a service	National Museums of Scotland MEQ 634

YEAR	MAKER	LOCATION	DESCRIPTION	SOURCE
1817/18	James McKay	Edinburgh	Sugar bowl, circular with part fluting and foliate scroll handles, 5 2/3" id	Christie's London UK 1997 #30
1818/19	James McKay	Edinburgh	Sugar bowl, compressed form with part fluting, shell and leaf motif border, engraved with a crest, part of a service	Christie's London UK 2001 #183
1818/19	James McKay	Edinburgh	Sugar bowl, circular fluted body with gadrooned rim and two rising leaf-capped handles, 7 ½" di	Christie's Melbourne Australia 2001 #473
1818/19	John Heron Assay Edinburgh	Greenock	Sugar bowl, oval, 8" di	Lyle Annual Review 1983 p542 Sotheby's
1818/19	James McKay	Edinburgh	Sugar bowl, part of a service	Sotheby's Gleneagles vol 90 p29
1819 ca	John McDonald	Edinburgh	Sugar bowl, part of a service	Antiques Magazine 1959 vol 76 Shreve advertisement
1820 ca	Edward Livingston	Dundee	Sugar bowl, part of a service	Finlay 1991 #111
1820 ca	James McKay	Edinburgh	Sugar bowl, part of a service	National Museums of Scotland MEQ 1312
1820/21	Alexander Edmonstoun	Edinburgh	Sugar bowl, part of a service	Sotheby's Picture File "AE"
1820/21	Not available		Sugar bowl, part of a service	Connoisseur Magazine 1952 vol 130 p24
1821/22	George McHattie	Edinburgh	Sugar bowl, squat circular form semi-fluted with gadrooned border, acanthus clasped handles, stepped circular pedestal foot, part of a service	Lyon & Turnbull Edinburgh UK May 25, 2006 #343
1823/24	James McKay	Edinburgh	Sugar bowl, part of a service	Apollo April-June 1968 vol 87 p106
1824/25	James McKay	Edinburgh	Sugar bowl, part of a service	Sotheby's Gleneagles August 1987 #305
1825 ca	Not available	Edinburgh	Sugar bowl, part of a service	Apollo August 1967 vol 86 p2 Bell of Aberdeen advertisement
1825 ca	Charles Murray	Perth	Sugar bowl, bowl with creamer	Christie's Edinburgh May 1-2, 1991 #304
1825/26	James McKay	Edinburgh	Sugar bowl, part of a service	Sotheby's Hopetoun House April 1988 #77

YEAR	MAKER	LOCATION	DESCRIPTION	SOURCE
1825/26	James McKay	Edinburgh	Sugar bowl, circular with chased foliate base, gilt interior, chased cartouche with engraved crest, chased body, 6 ¼" ht, 16oz 10d	Christie's NY USA 2003 #285 Provenance Edward S Whitney
1826/27	Alexander Edmonstoun	Edinburgh	Sugar bowl, part of a service	Sotheby's Hopetoun House April 1988 #81
1829/30	James McKay	Edinburgh	Sugar bowl, part of a service	Sotheby's Hopetoun House April 1988 #83
1830/31	James McKay	Edinburgh	Sugar bowl, compressed globular form with a foliate scroll motif rim, on a spreading foot, gilt interior	Christie's London UK 2001 #107
1832 ca	William Marshall	Edinburgh	Sugar bowl, part of a service	Sotheby's Gleneagles August 1988 #483
1832/33	Elder & Co	Edinburgh	Sugar bowl, part of a 3 piece service	Sotheby's Gleneagles August 1977 #29
1833/34	Marshall & Sons	Edinburgh	Sugar bowl, no details	National Museums of Scotland MEQ 541
1834/35	Elder & Co	Edinburgh	Sugar bowl, part of a 3 piece service	Sotheby's Gleneagles August 27, 1990 #101
1834/35	James McKay	Edinburgh	Sugar bowl, William IV, circular form, everted wavy rim, 2 scroll handles, 3 ¾" di, 13.5oz	Bonhams Sale 10914 #7
1835/36	Lawrence Urquhart	Edinburgh	Sugar bowl, not pictured	Warman Price Guide 27th ed, p585
1835/36	Elder & Co	Edinburgh	Sugar bowl, part of a 4 piece coffee service	Christie's April 23, 1983 #92
1837/38	James Mc Kay	Edinburgh	Sugar bowl, baluster shaped, circular foot, decorated with swirling flutes, scrolling foliage and flowers, monogram, part of a service	Christie's London UK 2005 #331
1837/38	Leonard Urquhart	Edinburgh	Sugar bowl, vermeil interior, repoussed floral boughs, engraved with a "B" initial, part of a service	Du Mouchelles, Detroit, MI USA 2002 #1025
1838/39	James McKay	Edinburgh	Sugar bowl, pair, one slightly larger, chased	JH Bourdon-Smith London 1994
1838/39	AM over striking mm	Edinburgh	Sugar bowl, part of a 3 piece service	Sotheby's August 28, 1969 #86
1838/39	James McKay	Edinburgh	Sugar bowl, gilt interior, baluster shaped on circular foot, chased scrolling flowers, cartouche, part of a service	Christie's NY USA 2004 #984

YEAR	MAKER	LOCATION	DESCRIPTION	SOURCE
1840/41	Robb & Whittet	Edinburgh	Sugar bowl, circular waisted form, upper body chased with band of scrolls, rocaille and floral sprays, on four tab feet, gilt interior, part of a service	Christie's London UK 2003 #406
1842/43	MacKay & Chisolm	Edinburgh	Sugar bowl, part of a service	Lyle Annual Review 1993
1842/43	James & William Marshall	Edinburgh	Sugar bowl, circular, everted wavy rim, on pedestal foot, engraved body and rim, 6 ½" di, 10.2 oz	Nicholas Shaw Catalog 2005 p105
1843/44	James McKay	Edinburgh	Sugar bowl, shell form on wavy fluted foot, 4 ½" di, 8.3 oz	Nicholas Shaw Catalog Winter 2002/03 p 86
1843/44	D. C. Raitt	Edinburgh assay	Sugar bowl, two handled with leaf scrolls, sides chased with leaf scrolls and flowers, "C" scroll cartouches, spreading circular foot	Bonhams London UK 2004 #382
1844/45	James McKay	Edinburgh	Sugar bowl, part of a service	Lyle Annual Review 1993
1847/48	James & William Marshall	Edinburgh	Sugar bowl, earlier style, 5 ¾" di, 7.5 oz	JH Bourdon-Smith Catalog Autumn 1991, #34 p47
1847/48	J & W Marshall	Edinburgh	Sugar bowl, circular	JH Bourdon-Smith Catalog 1993
1852/53	GCS	Edinburgh	Sugar bowl, baluster form, chased with flowers, part of a service	Christie's NY USA 2005 #249
1853/54	James McKay	Edinburgh	Sugar bowl with shaped rim, embossed decoration and three feet, 5 ½" di	Christie's London UK 1998 #171
1859/60	J E Vernon	Edinburgh	Sugar bowl, 2 handled, chased, 7" di, 11oz	Fellow & Sons Auction, June 2003 Lot #9
1860/61	Marshall & Son	Edinburgh	Sugar bowl, heavily chased, crest and motto, "SPEM FORTUNA ALIT" for Kinnear, 5 7/8" di, 10.4 oz	Nicholas Shaw Catalog Winter 2001 p78
1862/63	Crichton	Edinburgh	Sugar bowl, heavily decorated, winged figures on handles, engraved script "B"	National Museums of Scotland MEQ 955
1870ca	William Marshall	Edinburgh	Sugar bowl, hemispherical, inscribed "From Anne to Grand Mama" below rim	Christie's London UK 1999 #38
1875/76	W Marshall & Co	Edinburgh	Sugar bowl, on a pedestal, engraved, bead decoration, monogrammed "C.A.M.", 5" di	Payne & Son Ltd, Oxford 2005 Ref 4/70
1875/76	Marshall & Son	Edinburgh	Sugar bowl, engraved foliate scroll rim, sides chased among reversed flutes, monogrammed scroll cartouche, three cast leaf scroll supports, 6" di, 9oz	Bonhams London UK 2005 #340
1875/76	Mackay, Cunningham & Co	Edinburgh	Sugar bowl, Golf Trophy bowl, chased with leaves and thistles	National Museums of Scotland MEQ 139

YEAR	MAKER	LOCATION	DESCRIPTION	SOURCE
1876/77	John Crichton	Edinburgh	Sugar bowl, serpent handles, body chased with panels with crowing rooster on a barrel, insect amid plants, butterfly amid foliage, with French import mark, part of a service	Christie's NY USA 1998 #292
1885/86	JR	Glasgow	Sugar bowl, bombe form, engraved with foliate scroll and flower motif, gadrooned rim, two leaf capped reeded handles, on three mask and paw feet, gilt interior, part of a service	Christie's London UK 2001 #114
1886/87	William Marshall	Edinburgh	Sugar bowl, standing bowl, no details	National Museums of Scotland MEQ 855
1888/89	Hamilton & Inches	Edinburgh	Sugar bowl, part-chased with rising foliage and spreading foot, with later initials and date "1926-1945", 5 ¾" di, 11oz	Christie's London UK 2004 #598
1899/1900 Or 1900/01	Hamilton & Inches	Edinburgh	Sugar bowl, no details	National Museums of Scotland MEQ 904 1968.466
1912/13	J Weir	Glasgow	Sugar bowl, hand hammered, 4 ¾" di, 6.5 oz	Nicholas Shaw Catalog Winter 2002/3 p89
1975/76	Malcolm Appleby	Edinburgh	Sugar bowl, 2 ½" di	National Museums of Scotland 1977.240

Boxes

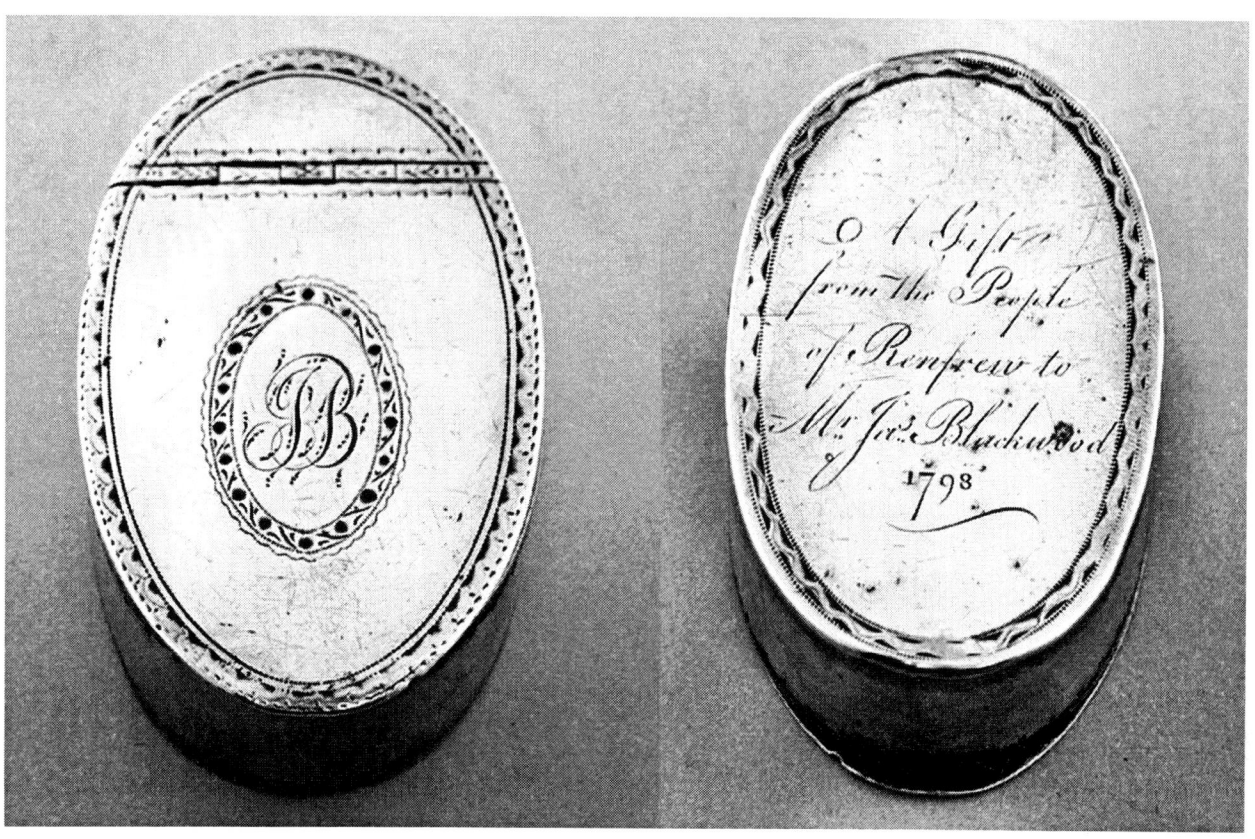

Plate 8. A presentation Snuff Box 1798 by Alexander Gardner, Edinburgh. Courtesy of The Phoenix Collection. Photograph by Janice M Dietert.

YEAR	MAKER	LOCATION	DESCRIPTION	SOURCE
			BOXES	
1604 ca	George Cunningham	Canongate	Seal case, The Montrose Box, arms of the Earl of Montrose	National Museums of Scotland LH 419.1
1640 ca	Thomas Kirkwood	Edinburgh	Seal box, mm only TK, lid engraved with the Arms of Great Britain marshaled for use in Scotland	Clayton Dictionary p340 #505
1685 ca	Robert Brock	Glasgow	Tobacco box, engraved with arms and initials block "IR"	Finlay 1991 #59 National Museums of Scotland MEQ 1556 1983
1695/96	Thomas Ker	Edinburgh	Seal case	National Museums of Scotland 1961 V4 AB
1695 ca	William Clerk	Glasgow	Patch box	Finlay 1991 #45
1700/01	John Luke	Glasgow	Seal box, Glasgow University	National Museums of Scotland MEQ 1036
1705/06 ca	Thomas Ker	Edinburgh	Toilet casket on 4 ball feet, cipher for the Earl of Hopetoun, 9 ¾" long, 47oz	How of Edinburgh Christie's Glasgow March 1983 #103 Shaw Collection National Museums of Scotland MEQ 1566 1963
1710 ca	George Cooper	Aberdeen	Snuff mull, mm only, initials "AP"	Shaw Collection Christie's Glasgow March 1983 #32
1718/19	William Aytoun	Edinburgh	Sugar box/bowl, (see description under bowls)	Sotheby's October 22, 1870 #213 Brett, p 194 #814
1730 ca	George Cooper	Aberdeen	Silver snuff mull, mm only, vase shaped	Goodwin Antiques Edinburgh 1993
1730 ca	George Cooper	Aberdeen	Snuff mull, vase shaped, engraved Arms	National Museums of Scotland NQ 454
1735 ca	Charles Dickson I or Charles Duncan	Edinburgh	Toilet boxes, pair, mm only, plain circular form, gilt interiors, later script initials probably "JS LC", 2 "di, 1.8oz	Woolley & Wallis April 20, 2005 #881

74

YEAR	MAKER	LOCATION	DESCRIPTION	SOURCE
1736/37	John Rollo	Edinburgh	Burgess Ticket Box, lid with central raised oval panel, with arms of city of Edinburgh, corners engraved shell like motif and scrolling acanthus foliage, thread border with alternating beads and ovolos, base plain, presented to Sir John Barnard on the occasion of his being given the freedom of Edinburgh, inside is the original Burgess ticket dated 8 June 1737, 10" wide, 31oz	Clayton's Dictionary p 341 #506 Sotheby's March 6, 1958 #135 National Museums of Scotland 1958.237c
1740 ca	Not available	Tain	Capstan form snuff mull chased with large relief, 2 ½" long, 3 oz	Nicholas Shaw Catalog 2004 p 97
1740 ca	*Hugh Ross*	*Tain*	*Capstan form, all silver snuff mull*	*Christie's Lanarkshire UK 1998 #97*
1746 ca	James Mitchelson	Edinburgh	Snuff mull, engraved with the Arms of Simon Lord Lovat, and Castle Downe, 2 3/8" ht	Clayton Dictionary p362 #531 Christie's July 8 1964 #105
1746-58	JL	Glasgow	Vinaigrette box, chased borders 1 ½" wide, mm JL between 2 fleur-de-lys, inner lid plated 1825 ca	Sotheby's May 24, 1970 #65
1750 ca	R A		Snuff mull	Sotheby's Gleneagles August 1991 # 43
1750 ca	Not available	Unknown	Snuff box, cylindrical standing form, the sides part chased with flowerheads and scroll work cover, with later initials, 2 1/8" ht, unmarked	Christie's London UK 2006 #1405
1760 ca	Colin Allan	Aberdeen	Snuff mull, all silver, of upright straight sided form, chased with shell and scroll border, hinged lid with shell detail surmounting engraved foliate initials, within a leaf surround, 2" ht, 2.1 oz	Bonhams Sale 15120 Aug 22, 2007 #137
1760 ca	R N	Inverness	Cowrie box	Luddington p 87
1760 ca	David Warnock	Glasgow	Snuff mull, baluster form, applied girdle, lid initialed "JM"	Sotheby's Gleneagles August 31, 1982 #44
1760 ca	James Gilliland	Edinburgh	Snuff mull, oblong, inverted pear shape, chased	National Museums of Scotland NQ 406 1963
1767/68	John Clark	Edinburgh	Sugar box, to accompany earlier William Aytoun tea caddies, square with straight sides and molded borders, with slightly raised stepped cover	Christie's March 22, 1978 National Museums of Scotland MEQ 1257
1770 ca	Craw & Hill	Canongate	Snuff box, circular, engraved "J. WD", 2 2/8" wide, 3.2 oz	Nicholas Shaw Catalog 2004 p 93

YEAR	MAKER	LOCATION	DESCRIPTION	SOURCE
1770 ca	James Hewitt	Edinburgh	Freedom box for Trinity House	National Museums of Scotland H.1994 1096
1774/75	Alexander Aitchison & Son	Edinburgh	Snuff box, no details	National Museums of Scotland NQ 436
1776/77	Alexander Gardner	Edinburgh	Bougie box, reticulated cylindrical body, plain S-scroll handle, pull off domed cover, 2 7/8" ht, 3oz	Woolley & Wallis Salisbury, UK April 24, 2007 #821
1780 ca	Patrick Robertson	Edinburgh	Snuff box, gold, circular	National Museums of Scotland H 1993.568
1780 ca	Not available		Snuff box, ovoid section, Arms in rococo cartouche, "Adam Taitt Crieff"	Christie's March 28, 1962 #77
1780/81 ca	Not available	Edinburgh	Cowrie box	Luddington p87
1784/85	William Davie or William Dempster	Edinburgh	Snuff box, cowrie shell, silver mounts and hinged lid, borders with bright cut motifs, 4 ½" long	Sotheby's Gleneagles August 29, 1978 #358
1785/86	Robert Bowman	Edinburgh	Snuff box, pointed, oval, no details	National Museums of Scotland NQ 420
1789 ca	JW	Glasgow	Snuff box, standing, oval section, lid inscribed with the monogram "LMcL", base inscribed "From the Inverary Lodge to the Revd. Mr. MacLahlan, their chaplain, 1789"	Private Collection
1790/91	George Christie	Edinburgh	Snuff box, no details	National Museums of Scotland NQ 221
1793/94	Alexander Gardner	Edinburgh	Dumfries Freedom Box	National Museums of Scotland H 1990.10
1795 ca	William Robertson	Edinburgh	Snuff mull, cowrie shell with moss agate set, 3 ¾" long	Nicholas Shaw Catalog Winter 2000 p80
1795 ca	William Robertson	Edinburgh	Snuff box, rectangular, with chamfered corners, flush hinged lid, bright cut engraved with a drapery cartouche enclosing initials "A M" and inscribed "To Mrs. Derbyshire" further inscribed "GARDE CECI POUR VOTRE AMIE", possibly a gift from Robert Burns to Miss Ann Masterson, 3" wide	Sotheby's Gleneagles August 29, 1973 #163
1795/96	William Robertson	Edinburgh	Snuff box, gold	Antiques Magazine 1996 p 697 Shrubsole

YEAR	MAKER	LOCATION	DESCRIPTION	SOURCE
1796/97	William Auld	Edinburgh	Presentation box, gold	Apollo May 1972 vol 95 p 49
1798 ca	Alexander Gardner	Edinburgh	Snuff box, oval, bright cut and engraved with the presentation "A gift from the people of Renfrew to Mr. John Blackwood 1798", a script "B" in an oval cartouche on the front, 2 3/8" long	Hobart House, CT USA 1991 The Phoenix Collection
1799 ca	WC	Greenock	Snuff box, presented by the Greenock Florists Society to Mr. L. McLachlane, 3" long, 3oz	Christie's London UK 2002 #232
1800 ca	Francis Howden	Edinburgh	Snuff box, oval, part hinged lid, engraved with leaf motifs ad a central initial, base engraved, "James Dickson; Hawick", 3 ¼" long, 2.5 oz	Christie's London UK 2001 #119
1800 ca	Alexander Gardner & Co	Edinburgh	Snuff box, navette form, gilt interior, crest and arms of Grant, presented to Captain James Grant by his Western Abernath Company of Volunteers in 1802, 4 3/4" long, 6 oz	Christie's London UK 2006 #319
1800 ca	John Lyall	Ayr	Snuff mounted oak, rectangular from piece of Old Brig of Ayr as inscribed, 3 ½" long	Christie's Lanarkshire UK 1997 #13
1800 ca	Not available	Edinburgh	Presentation box	Waldron Price Guide, p 81
1800 ca	William Ritchie	Perth	Cowrie box, with the initials "JH	JH Bourdon-Smith Catalog 1991 p 26 #34
1800 ca	J C	Aberdeen	Silver patch box inscribed with piece of Prince Charlie's Tartan	National Museums of Scotland MEQ 569
1800 ca	J Pirie	Aberdeen	Cowrie shell snuff mull engraved "WD"	Nicholas Shaw Catalog Winter 2000 p 88
1800 ca	JR		Cowrie shell snuff mull, inscribed "1846 Robert Hay….."	Nicholas Shaw Catalog Winter 2001 p76
1800 ca	William Ritchie	Perth	Cowrie mull with plough and initials "WM"	JH Bourdon-Smith Catalog, Autumn 1991, #34, p 26
1810 ca	WR (Possibly William Robertson)	Edinburgh	Snuff box, no details	Christie's East NY USA 1999, #110
1810 ca	James Erskine	Aberdeen	Tobacco box, the cover fluted around a minutely engraved rhyme	Sotheby's London UK Sept 2, 1998 #492

YEAR	MAKER	LOCATION	DESCRIPTION	SOURCE
1810 ca	James Erskine	Aberdeen	Snuff box, oblong, bright cut decoration, hinged lid, engraved with initials "JC" and the base "John Cameron", 2 3/8" long	The Morris Collection Christie's Scotland July 3, 1984 #100 Christie's Lanarkshire UK 1998 #87
1807/08	John Ziegler	Edinburgh	Snuff box, rectangular with rounded corners, plain, gilt interior, 3 1/8" X 2" X ¾"	eBay #110143348511 July 2007
1808/09	Robert Keay	Perth Edinburgh assay	Snuff box, presentation, plain oblong with incurved sides and integral hinge, gilt interior, presented to "Mr James Wilson by his Perth Evening Class pupils on 2 Feb 1813", 3" long	Christie's London UK 1997 #75
1808/09	P Cunningham & Sons	Edinburgh	Snuff box, bright cut engraved, rounded oblong form, wavy borders around sides, pattern of opposing crescents and floral motif, gilt interior, initialed "JW", 2 ½" long, 2oz	Woolley & Wallis Salisbury UK April 24, 2007 #605
1810 ca	DS		Vinaigrette with inlaid agate	Nicholas Shaw Catalog Winter 2000 p88
1810 ca	William Law	Dundee	Vinaigrette, oblong with rounded corners, grille engraved with a thistle and rose motif	Asprey Small Collectible Catalog 1990 p58 #191 back cover
1810 ca	RW	Possibly Scottish	Silver mounted tortoise shell lid with floral and scroll motifs, initials in a central cartouche, gilt interior, 3 1/8" long	Christie's London UK 2000 #388
1811/12	Francis Howden	Edinburgh	Seal box, affixed to an extract of a Minute of the Incorporation of Goldsmiths	National Museums of Scotland MEQ 1583 1984
1813/14	James McKay	Edinburgh	Box, double lidded	The Maple Swan Collection
1813/14	John Hay & Richard Haxton	Edinburgh	Freedom box for Trinity House	Sotheby's London November 11, 1993 #179 National Museums of Scotland H.1994.1096
1813/14	DS	Edinburgh	Snuff box, silver, oblong, presented to David Paton	National Museums of Scotland NQ 457 1965.2017
1815 ca	John McDonald	Edinburgh	Snuff mull, cowrie shell, engraved "To John Telfer from his grandfather"	Nicholas Shaw Catalog Winter 2000 p 80
1817/18	R. P.	Edinburgh assay	Snuff box, 3 1/8" long	Bonhams London UK 2001 #26

YEAR	MAKER	LOCATION	DESCRIPTION	SOURCE
1817/18	John Hay	Leith	Snuff box, with carnelian panel, rectangular, chased with thistles, 3 ¼" long	Sotheby's NY USA, Feb 13, 2001 #47
1819/20	Robert Gray & Son	Glasgow	Snuff box, oval shell with silver hinged engraved lid	Leslie Hindman Auctioneers Chicago, IL USA 1998 #321
1820 ca	J R	Perth	Snuff box, mm 3x, cowrie shell, engraved with inscribed ode to snuff	Shrubsole, NY 1993
1820 ca	George Elder	Banff	Snuff box, mounted mother of pearl	Shrubsole, NY 1993
1820 ca	George Booth	Aberdeen	Seal box, no details	National Museums of Scotland MEQ 1187
1820 ca	Richard Haxton	Edinburgh	Nutmeg grater, oval, lid set with red carnelian agate, interior fitted with original iron grater, ring at other end, mm only	Private Collection
1820 ca	Richard Haxton	Edinburgh	Vinaigrette, oblong with rounded corners, lid set with red carnelian agate, short chain with a ring, mm only	Private Collection
1820 ca	Possibly John Sid	Possibly Perth	Snuff box, rectangular, inscribed "Wm Myles", 3" long	Sotheby's NY USA 1997 #53
1820/21	George Fenwick	Edinburgh	Snuff box, plain rectangular form, lid engraved with a crest and motto, 2 ¾" long, 2.7 oz	Bonhams Sale 10914, #27
1821/22	George McHattie	Edinburgh	Snuff box, plain oblong, cover with crest and motto, front with inscription, gilt interior, 3 ¼" long	Christie's Lanarkshire UK 1998 #89
1822 ca	TM	Perth	Snuff box, rectangular, made for Peter Christie Merchant, with crest and initials, 3" long	JH Bourdon-Smith Catalog Autumn 1991 p26 #34
1822/23	John Blackwood Caw	Edinburgh	Snuff box, lid decorated with a view of Nelson's Column in Edinburgh within floral border, 3" long	Gorringers LLP, Lewes 2001 #1967
1823/24	A E	Edinburgh	Snuff box, silver,	Scarlet Fox, Alexandria VA, 1994
1824/25	Richard Haxton I	Edinburgh	Table snuff box, oblong, silver, gilt interior, concave sides, chamfered base and lid, lid with decorated thumb-piece and engraved with crest and inscription "Presented to Wm. Walker to Mr. David. Stocks As a token of Respect for his attention as one of the Trustees to the interest of the Family of my Brother in Law the late Mr James Marr," fully marked in the lid, mm ex's inside the bottom	Private Collection

YEAR	MAKER	LOCATION	DESCRIPTION	SOURCE
1824/25	IG	Edinburgh	Snuff box, gold, rectangular	National Museums of Scotland MEQ 1526 1982
1824/25	RH (Probably Richard Haxton)	Edinburgh	Snuff box, plain oblong form with beveled cover, large floral thumbpiece and concave sides, gilt interior, mm 4xs only, 3 7/8" long, 6.5 oz	Woolley & Wallis Salisbury UK April 24, 2007 #829
1825/26	James McKay	Edinburgh	Snuff box, 18ct gold, rectangular, bombe side, chased with various classical buildings, cover applied at later date with rose diamond set, initials "DH", interior of lid inscribed "Presented to Robert Steuart Esqr. Of Alderston, by the members of the East Lothian Club as a mark of Gratitude and Respect for his service as their Secretary, 1826," 3 3/8" X 2 3/8", 4oz 18d	Private Collection
1825 ca	James Nasmyth	Edinburgh	Snuff box, plain, silver, no details	National Museums of Scotland MEQ 453
1828 ca	John Austin	Perth	Snuff mull, cowrie shell, engraved "To Robert Fife Blairington....." 3 ¼" long	Nicholas Shaw Catalog 2005 p99 JH Bourdon-Smith Catalog Autumn 1991 p 26 #34
1836/37	James Nasmyth	Edinburgh	Snuff box, rectangular, no details	National Museums of Scotland NQ 437
1828/29	John Argo	Banff	Snuff box, cowrie shell	JH Bourdon-Smith Catalog p26 #34
1831/32	James Nasmyth	Edinburgh	Snuff box, oblong with engine-turned panels, hinged lid with cast scroll thumbpiece, gilt interior	Christie's Lanarkshire UK 1997 #18
1832/33	John Blackwood Caw	Edinburgh	Snuff box, rectangular, sides stamped with flowers and foliage, lid stamped with Scottish figural scene, 2 7/8" long	Sotheby's London UK Oct 22, 1998 #301
1832/33	James Nasmyth	Edinburgh	Snuff box, plain, oblong, engine turned, concave sides, gilt interior, lid with scroll and flower thumb-piece, engraved with initials "AP", 3 1/8" wide, 3 oz	Private Collection
1833/34	James Nasmyth	Edinburgh	Snuff box, lid embossed and chased with flowers, scrolling leaves and acorns against a textured ground, bombe sides and base, engine turned, 3 ½" long	Gorringes LLP, East Sussex UK 2006 #1618
1834/35	James Nasmyth	Edinburgh	Snuff box, circular, all-over decoration of scrolls and foliage on matted ground, center of lid and base each with a cartouche, lid with crest of a stag's head, latter vacant, gilt interior, small scratched initials, interior of lid scratched "1068", 2 ¼" di, 2 oz 17d	Private Collection Sotheby's Edinburgh April 29, 1992

YEAR	MAKER	LOCATION	DESCRIPTION	SOURCE
1834/35	CHF	Edinburgh	Vinaigrette, 1 ½" long	National Museums of Scotland 1976.631
1834/35	AGW	Edinburgh	Snuff box, gold, presented to William Hay	S. J. Phillips London 2006 #22381
1834/35	James McKay	Edinburgh	Gold box	Christie's London October 1988 #362
1834/35	A. G. Wighton	Edinburgh	Snuff box, gold, rectangular engine turned, presented to William Hay, Esq. by the inhabitants of Dunse, dated 1835	S. J. Phillips Ltd, ref #22381
1835 ca	RH (Possibly Richard Haxton)	Probably Edinburgh	Patch box, circular, the base inset with a moss agate panel (cracked), the cover with an ivory plaque incised and stained with a crest and motto of Patterson, Bart. of Bannockburn, Stirlingshire, 2 ¾" di	Christie's Lanarskshire UK 1997 #11
1836/37	J. Asherheim	Edinburgh	Snuff box, rectangular with incurved sides, cover set with agate, with a crest and motto, 3 ½" long	Christie's NY, USA 2004 #894
1836/37	James Nasmyth & Co	Edinburgh	Vinaigrette, oblong form, engine turned formed as a snuff box, fitted to the interior with a smaller vinaigrette with pierced foliate grill, presentation inscription on the lid, 3 1/3" long, 3 oz	Bonhams Sale 15120 Aug 22, 2007 #52
1837/38	James Nasmyth	Edinburgh	Snuff box, early Victorian, rectangular, engraved "Presented to Mr James Miller from the workers of Pleasance Bank Mill, Dundee, 13 July 1839", 3 3/8" X 2", 4 oz	Private Collection
1839/40	James Nasmyth & Co	Edinburgh	Snuff box, rectangular form with scroll engraving	Gorringes LLP, East Sussex UK 2003 #1124
1840/41	James Nasmyth & Co	Edinburgh	Snuff box, oblong with engine turned lozenge pattern, cover engraved "R. Scotland ALLOA", 4" wide, 3 oz	Christie's London UK 2007 #115
1840/41	James Nasmyth & Co	Edinburgh	Snuff box, oblong, hinged lid engraved with the monogram " JH" in oblong reserve, presented to Mr. James Henderson on the 9th July 1850 by the Rifle Club, gilt interior, 2 3/4" X 1 ¾"	Christie's Lanarskshire UK 1998 #88
1841/42	James Nasmyth & Co	Edinburgh	Snuff box with racing scene, 3 7/8" long	JH Bourdon-Smith Catalog Autumn 1991 p26 #34
1841/42	James Nasmyth & Co	Edinburgh	Card case, scrolling foliate and engine turned design, monogrammed cartouche, 3 ¾" X 2 2/3"	eBay #110118845072 2007

YEAR	MAKER	LOCATION	DESCRIPTION	SOURCE
1846/47	James MacKay	Edinburgh	Snuff box, silver with a hardstone, rectangular with cut corners, mounts of flowers and foliate scrolls, 5 ¼" long	Sotheby's London UK, Oct 22, 1998 #301
1848/49	James Nasmyth	Edinburgh	Victorian snuff box, rectangular form, engine turned, floral thumbpiece, 3 1/8" long, 3.9 oz	Bonhams Sale 10914, #30
1858/59	George Carstairs	Edinburgh	Silver case (toothpick?), engine turned decoration, 2 ½" X 1", .9 oz	The Phoenix Collection
1858/59	John Crichton	Edinburgh	Snuff box, silver, mother-of-pearl, plaque of Leda and her children, with set stones, gilt interior, inscribed as being remounted in 1859 and belonging to George Hutton Wilkinson, Harperley Park	Christie's NY USA 2006 #61
1865/66	MacKay & Chisholm	Edinburgh	Silver-mounted hoof snuff box, cover engraved with a border of fruiting vines, rim engraved with leafy band, center plain, gilt interior, 2 ¾" long	Bonhams London UK 2003 #254
1866/67	George Carstairs	Edinburgh	Snuff box, oval, lid engraved with presentation to W. Graham, Esq. dated 1866, 4" long	Gorringes LLP East Sussex, UK 2006 #1367
1868 ca	John Russell	Glasgow	Freedom box, rectangular, from Campbeltown, Argyll, presented to John Douglas Sutherland Campbell, Marquis of Lorne, 1868, silver gilt, 5 5/8" X 3 ½" X 2"	Asprey Small Collectibles Catalog 1990 p3 #6
1870 ca	Jonathan Pears Hutton	Edinburgh	Decorative box on 4 ball feet	National Museums of Scotland MEQ 1242 1977.41
1876/77	D M	Edinburgh	Card case, with woman's picture on the front, (possibly a mate to the following one?)	National Museums of Scotland MEQ 1328
1876/77	David McGregor	Perth Edinburgh assay	Box, depicting the Hon. Mrs. Graham after her portrait by Thomas Gainsborough engraved on the front, the back with engraved scenes of Perth with bridge and river, 3.9" X 2.75"	JH Bourdon-Smith Catalog Spring 2007 #47 p55
1880 ca	George Jamieson	Aberdeen	Vinaigrette, silver and agate, panel with granite lid with rock crystal, 2 ¼" ht, 3.9 oz	Nicholas Shaw Catalog Winter 2001 p78
1888/89	James Aitchison	Glasgow	Silver-gilt casket, rectangular with batswing fluted borders, chased with profuse foliage, two motto scrolls for the family of Jardin or Jardine, on four partially-pierced scroll-embellished bracket feet, 17"X14"X5", 187oz gross	Christie's London UK 2007 #1431
1889/90	Marshall & Son	Edinburgh	Freedom box for the City of Edinburgh for Henry Morton Stanley Esq., in original leather box with burgess ticket, 10 7/8" long, 50 oz gross	Christie's London UK 2002 #105
1893 ca	Medlock	Inverness	Ram's horn snuff, silver mounted, presented by Captain Grant	Nicholas Shaw Catalog 2005 p 206

YEAR	MAKER	LOCATION	DESCRIPTION	SOURCE
1899 ca	Ferguson & MacBean	Inverness	Ram's horn snuff, silver mounted with citrine, presented to Colin Chisholm, Esq., 3 ½" long, 2.9oz	Nicholas Shaw Catalog Winter 2001 p78
1899/1900	Robert & William Sorely	Glasgow	Cigarette box, spot hammered with cedar lining, cover and sides inset with 18th and 19th century coins, 8 ¼" long	Christie's London UK 2004 #127
1910/11	Robert & William Sorely	Glasgow	Cigar box, presentation, rectangular, presented to John Charles Cunningham by the Unionist Party of Renfrew county, 9 ¾" long	Christie's East, NY USA 2001 #329
1916/17	D & C Edwards	Glasgow	Presentation casket for Ninian Bannatyne Steward, 10 7/8" long, 48.8 oz	Nicholas Shaw Catalog Winter 2000 p 81

Brooches, Badges and Medals

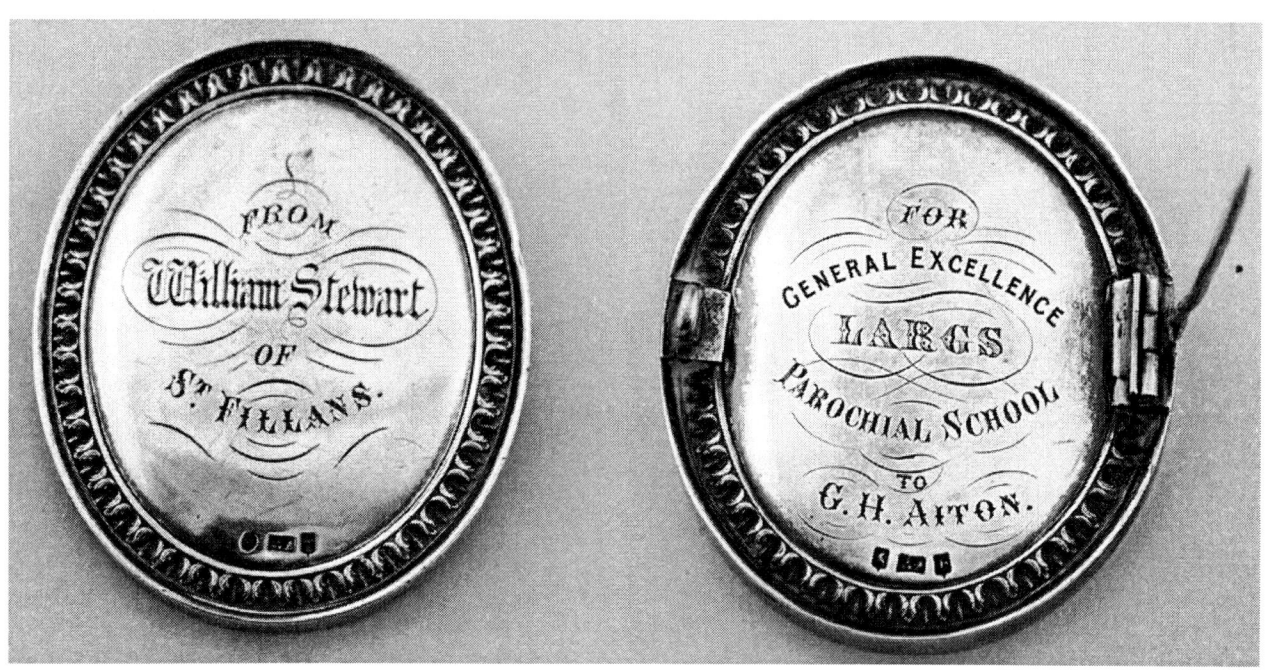

Plate 9. A School Medal 1851/52 by Peter Aiken, Glasgow (front and back).
Courtesy of The Phoenix Collection. Photograph by Janice M Dietert.

BROOCHES, BADGES AND MEDALS

YEAR	MAKER	LOCATION	DESCRIPTION	SOURCE
1633 ca	Nicholas Briot	Edinburgh	Medal celebrating the Scottish coronation of Charles I, signed by Briot at the Edinburgh mint	Several extant in the National Museums of Scotland Private Collection
1705 ca	Alexander Kincaid	Edinburgh	Officer's badge, oval cloak badge of the Officer of the Incorporation of Surgeons of Edinburgh, figures and motifs in high relief, mm only, perhaps the finest of all Edinburgh trade officer badges	Royal College of Surgeons Edinburgh
1709/10	John Seatoun	Edinburgh	Plaid Brooch, no details	Jackson Marks p545
1725/26	James Tait	Edinburgh	Armorial Badge of the Incorporation of Goldsmiths	National Museums of Scotland MEQ L1998.11
1727 ca	Not available	Edinburgh	Brooch, no details	Christie's NY October 1988 #369
1750 ca	Thomas Borthwick	Inverness	Brooch, round, no details	National Museums of Scotland NGA 61
1760 ca	Colin Allan	Aberdeen	Silver heart brooch	National Museums of Scotland NGA 292
1783 dated	Not available not marked	Edinburgh	Fellowship medal, oval, for the Royal Society of Edinburgh, engraved on the reverse with a Presentation inscription "ROYAL/SOCIETY/EDINBURGH, INSTITUTED/1783" to "ANDw DUNCAN M.D./1783" 1 1/8" X 1 7/16", .5oz,	Private Collection
1783 dated	Not available not marked	Edinburgh	Fellowship medal, oval, for the Royal Society of Edinburgh, engraved on the reverse side with a Presentation inscription "ROYAL/SOCIETY/EDINBURGH, INSTITUTED/1783" to "JAS. GREGORY M.D.'1783" 1 1/8" X 1 7/16", .5 oz	Private Collection
1783 dated	Not available not marked	Edinburgh	Fellowship medal, oval, for the Royal Society of Edinburgh, engraved on the reverse side with a Presentation inscription "ROYAL/SOCIETY/EDINBURGH, INSTITUTED/1783" to "ALEXANDER HAMILTON, M.D./1783" 1 1/8" X 1 7/16", .5 oz	Private Collection
1783 dated	Not available not marked	Edinburgh	Fellowship medal, oval, for the Royal Society of Edinburgh, engraved on the reverse side with a Presentation inscription "ROYAL/SOCIETY/EDINBURGH, INSTITUTED/1783" to "JOHN ROGERSON M.D./1783", 1 1/8" X 1 7/16", .5oz	Private Collection
1790 ca	Patrick Robertson	Edinburgh	Silver club medal, oval, neoclassical, ribbon-tied scroll mount, engraved "Helter-Skelter..." and on the other side "Rost. Campbell, original member", with crest and motto, 3 ½"	Christie's Lanarkshire UK 1997 #7

YEAR	MAKER	LOCATION	DESCRIPTION	SOURCE
1790 ca	George Christie	Edinburgh	Deputy Lieutenant's Badge	National Museums of Scotland NC 381
1796/97	William Robertson	Edinburgh	Silver badge, no details	National Museums of Scotland K.1999.1450
1799 dated	Not available	Edinburgh	Fellowship medal, oval, for the Royal Society of Edinburgh, engraved on the reverse side with a Presentation inscription "ROYAL/SOCIETY/EDINBURGH, INSTITUTED/1783" to "Wm BLIZARD ESQ/F.R.S./1799", 1 1/8" X 1 7/16", .5 oz	Private Collection
1811/12	James McKay	Edinburgh	Medal from Highland Society of Scotland to David Call	National Museums of Scotland H.1986.62
1814/15	W & P Cunningham II	Edinburgh	Medal from Benjamin McKay's Latin Academy	National Museums of Scotland
1817/18	J M	Edinburgh	Silver medal Mr. Andrew's English School	National Museums of Scotland 19882.290
1818/19	A Mossman	Edinburgh	Silver prize medal of Mr. Scott's Writing School	National Museums of Scotland 1968.499
1821/22	R M	Edinburgh	Medal, engraved "VIVANT VERITAS"	National Museums of Scotland H.1958.1966
1824/25	James McKay	Edinburgh	Medal, Highland and Agricultural Society of Scotland	National Museums of Scotland H.1947.94
1824 dated	Not available	Edinburgh	Fellowship medal, oval, for the Royal Society of Edinburgh, engraved on the reverse side with a Presentation inscription "ROYAL/SOCIETY/EDINBURGH, INSTITUTED/1783" to "WILLm MUIR/1824" 1 1/8" X 1 7/16", .5oz	Private Collection
1824 dated	Not available	Edinburgh	Fellowship medal, oval, for the Royal Society of Edinburgh, engraved on the reverse side with a Presentation inscription "ROYAL/SOCIETY/EDINBURGH, INSTITUTED/1783" to "W.H. PLAYFIAR/1824" 1 1/8" X 1 7/16", .5oz	Private Collection
1824 dated	Not available	Edinburgh	Fellowship medal, oval, for the Royal Society of Edinburgh, engraved on the reverse side with a Presentation inscription "ROYAL/SOCIETY/EDINBURGH, INSTITUTED/1783" to "WmWOOD ESQ/PRES.ROY.COLL.SURG./1824" 1 1/8" x 1 7/16", .5oz	Private Collection
1825/26	Marshall & Sons	Edinburgh	Bar brooches	National Museums of Scotland NAB 67

YEAR	MAKER	LOCATION	DESCRIPTION	SOURCE
1826/27	James McKay	Edinburgh	Medal, Highland Society of Scotland to Mr. John Young 1826	Nicholas Shaw Catalog Winter 2000 p87
1827 dated	James McKay	Edinburgh	Medal as above to Mr. John Young 1827	Nicholas Shaw Catalog Winter 2000 p87
1827/28	AE (probably Alexander Edmonstoun)	Edinburgh	Silver Fireman's medal, circular with a central leaf motif, crest and a suspension ring, presented to John Rood, Fireman dated August 1828	Christie's London UK 2005 #438
1830 ca	C J & S	Aberdeen	Double heart brooch	National Museums of Scotland NDG 92
1830 dated	Not available	Edinburgh	Circular medal, attachment to be worn from a broad ribbon, obverse engraved with winged and skated Mercury holding a banner with the words "OCIOR EURO," reverse with inscription "Edinburgh Skating Club/W. D. Gillon, 29th December 1830"	Private Collection
1831 dated	James McKay	Edinburgh	Oval medal, engraved on the obverse with a plough in a field, reverse with inscription "Given by the Highland Society to James Ross, 1831"	Private Collection
1831 dated	William Marshall	Edinburgh	1st prize medal, circular, Macdonald Prize, awarded to John Young in 1831, obverse Depicting MacDonald arms, reverse showing Arms of Edinburgh Academy in full relief, whole set in silver-gilt rim with ring and mount, 2" di	Private Collection
1835/36	C & C		Prize medal, Roslin Gymnastic Club won by Thomas Dods	National Museums of Scotland M.1981.59
1835/36	James McKay	Edinburgh	Brooch, silver gilt, presented to the Marquess of Breadalbane	National Museums of Scotland MEQ 1514
1836/37	MM obscured	Edinburgh	Plaid brooch, Sutherland Highlander's, 3 ¾" di	Nicholas Shaw Catalog Winter 2001 p83
1838/39	James McKay	Edinburgh	Medal, Highland and Agricultural Society of Scotland	National Museums of Scotland H.1986.82
1839/40	James McKay	Edinburgh	Silver prize medal Dalkeith Gymnastic Games	National Museums of Scotland M.1982.20
1839/40	William Marshall	Edinburgh	Bar brooches	National Museums of Scotland NAB 67

YEAR	MAKER	LOCATION	DESCRIPTION	SOURCE
1839/40	Peter Aiken	Glasgow	Brooch, round, no details	National Museums of Scotland NGB 115
1840 ca	J L	Edinburgh	Silver Prize class medal	National Museums of Scotland M.1982.18
1840 ca	W M	Edinburgh	Crowned double heart brooch	National Museums of Scotland NAB 49
1840 ca	W M	Edinburgh	Double heart brooch	National Museums of Scotland NAB 39
1840 ca	W M	Edinburgh	Crowned heart brooch	National Museums of Scotland NAB 129
1840 ca	W M	Edinburgh	Heart brooch, silver and enamel	National Museums of Scotland NAB 130
1840/41	J M	Edinburgh	Silver medal Dalkeith Gymnastic Games	National Museums of Scotland M.1982.19
1840/41	W M	Edinburgh	Crowned heart brooch	National Museums of Scotland NAB 54
1844/45	R McG		Curling medal	National Museums of Scotland M.1959.935
1851/52	Peter Aiken	Glasgow	Medal, engraved "from William Stewart of St. Finian" on reverse "For general Excellent Parochial School to G. H. Aiton", 2 ½ di	The Phoenix Collection
1855/56	James Nasmyth & CO	Edinburgh	Gold medal of Edinburgh Royal High School	National Museums of Scotland 1981.118
1874/75	Aitchison	Edinburgh	Prize medal Edinburgh School of Medicine	National Museums of Scotland M.1975.322
1877/78	J W	Aberdeen	Prize medal "Spey Avon & Fidochside Farmers Club 1877"	National Museums of Scotland M.1976.222
1878/79	J D Davison	Glasgow	Silver agricultural prize medal, circular from the Stirling Agricultural Society to Mr. J. Scoular	Christie's London UK 1999 #63
1882/83	R S	Glasgow	Medal, Auchengray Agricultural Society Presented to Gavin Black, Esq., 2 5/8" di	Nicholas Shaw Catalog Winter 2000 p87

YEAR	MAKER	LOCATION	DESCRIPTION	SOURCE
1884/86	A Mossman & Co	Edinburgh	Medal of the Royal High School of Edinburgh	National Museums of Scotland M.1984.17
1883/84	John Robertson & Son	Edinburgh	Gold medal, Scottish Twenty Club 1883	National Museums of Scotland M1980.292
1887/88	Robert Yale	Aberdeen	Prize medal "Central Banffshire Farmers Club 1887"	National Museums of Scotland M.1976.220
1889 Dated	David McGregor	Perth	Scottish Horticultural Association gold medal, presented to Mr. William Rushtou	Sotheby's NY USA 1999 #399
1891/92	R & HB Kirkwood	Edinburgh	Plaid brooch, for the Cameron Highlanders, with thistle border and sphinx center	Gorringes LLP, East Sussex UK 2006 #1691
1892/93	R & HB Kirkwood	Edinburgh	Plaid brooch, for Officer of the Seaforth Highlanders	Christie's London UK 1987 #180
1894/95	Hamilton & Inches	Edinburgh	Brooch, formed as a conifer and fir cone spray, 5 ¼" long	Sotheby's Edinburgh UK 1993 #26
1895/96	William Reid Christie	Inverness	Gold football medal, 9ct, engraved "N. S. F. A., 1895-96, won by Clack FC"	Lyon & Turnbull Edinburgh UK 2006 #362
1895/96	Mackay & Chisolm	Edinburgh	Prize medals, 2, of the Scottish Pipers Society	National Museums of Scotland M.1984.12-13
1900 ca	M C		Heart brooch, large, silver	National Museums of Scotland NC 1337
1900 ca	M Rettie & Sons	Aberdeen	Double heart brooch	National Museums of Scotland. NGB 68
1900 ca	M Rettie & Sons	Aberdeen	Silver brooch, round	National Museums of Scotland NGB 87
1900 ca	M Rettie & Sons	Aberdeen	Crowned double heart brooch	National Museums of Scotland NGB 126
1904/05	F R & Co Ld	Edinburgh	Medal, Edinburgh Society of Musicians 1904	National Museums of Scotland M.1982.116
1908/09	JB & S		Gold medal of Scottish National Exhibition – 1908	National Museums of Scotland 1980.289

YEAR	MAKER	LOCATION	DESCRIPTION	SOURCE
1912/13	Henry Tatton	Edinburgh	Plaid and Citrine Brooch in Case, 3 ¼" di	Nicholas Shaw Catalog Winter 2005 p104
1918/19	Wilson & Sharp	Edinburgh	Celtic cross pendant	National Museums of Scotland NF 37 1960.2941
1931/32	Kirkwood & Son	Edinburgh	Prize medal Highlands Agricultural Society of Scotland 1931	National Museums of Scotland MEQ 1972.126

Candlesticks

Plate 10. A pair of Tablesticks 1745/46 by James Ker, Edinburgh.
Courtesy of The Phoenix Collection. Photograph by Janice M Dietert.

YEAR	MAKER	LOCATION	DESCRIPTION	SOURCE
			CANDLESTICKS	
1693/94	James Penman	Edinburgh	Chambersticks, pair, octagonal bases with raised gadrooned edges, simple loop finger grips with thumb caps	Finlay 1991 #54 Noble Collection National Museums of Scotland MEQ 1473.1-2
1895/96	James Penman	Edinburgh	Candlesticks, pair	Private Collection UK
1897/98	Patrick Murray I	Edinburgh	Candlesticks, pair, one fully marked, the other mm only, on molded octagonal bases, the faceted baluster stems knopped and banded, faceted campana shaped sconces with detachable nozzles, 7 ¾" ht, 39.6oz	Sotheby's July 24, 1980 #236
1698/99	James Penman	Edinburgh	Wall sconces, pair, originally Earl of Hopetoun, shaped upright oval	Finlay 1991 #56 Sotheby's June 25, 1953 #153 Sotheby's London UK 2006 #130 National Museums of Scotland
1699/1770	Robert Inglis	Edinburgh	Candlestick, pair	Antiques Magazine vol 103
1699/1770	Mungo Yorstoun	Edinburgh	Candlesticks, pair, cast, square welled bases with cut corners rising to triple knopped stems and banded sconces, sconces stamped "9" and "10", scratch weights 11:12 and 12:2, 6 ½" ht, 23.1oz	Sotheby's June 24, 1953 # 117 Sotheby's February 5, 1987 #53
1700/01	Thomas Ker	Edinburgh	Candlesticks, set of 4, gadrooned base, baluster stems, crest and motto of Hope, 7" ht, 69oz	Christie's June 15, 1977 #135 Clayton Dictionary p60 #75 Linlithgow Collection
1700/01	Alexander Kincaid	Edinburgh	Candlesticks, pair, the square stepped bases welled and with cut corners, rising to knopped baluster stems and reeded sconces, 6 ¾" ht, 27.8oz	How's Notes on Antique Silver 1941 vol I p22
1702/03	Patrick Murray I	Edinburgh	Candlesticks, pair, no details	Hutchinson Exhibition
1703/04	Alexander Forbes	Edinburgh	Candlesticks, pair, octagonal baluster shape, on square bases with cut corners, reeded and knopped baluster stems rising from faceted sconces, crest, 6.9" ht, 28oz	Clayton Christie's Book p108 #5 Christie's November 29, 1967 #144
1703/04	Colin McKenzie	Edinburgh	Candlesticks, pair, no details	Glasgow Exhibition 1911 vol I, p120 #30
1706/07	Colin McKenzie	Edinburgh	Chambersticks, pair, plain square pans, 4 ball feet, initials underneath, 3 3/8" sq, 13oz 3d	Christie's May 3, 1984 #57

YEAR	MAKER	LOCATION	DESCRIPTION	SOURCE
1707/08	John Seatoun	Edinburgh	Candlesticks, set of 4, not pictured	Finlay 1991 p 137 Connoisseur Magazine 1934 vol 93 p134
1707/08	John Seatoun	Edinburgh	Candlesticks, set of 4, no details	National Museums of Scotland 1943.279 a-c
1707/08	Thomas Ker	Edinburgh	Candlesticks, pair, no details	Connoisseur Magazine 1953 vol 131 p16 advertisement
1708/09	Robert Bruce	Edinburgh	Candlesticks, pair, circular molded, each on a sunken base shouldered with 16 facets, the baluster stem and vase-shaped socket also faceted, crest and motto of Carmichael, 7 ½" ht, 27 oz	Christie's Glasgow March 1983 #99 Shaw Collection Koopman Antiques
1709/10	Mungo Yorstoun	Edinburgh	Candlesticks, pair, octagonal, 6 ½" ht, base 4" across	Antiques Magazine vol 47 p 252 N Bloom & Son Ltd advertisement
1709/10	James Mitchelson	Edinburgh	Candlesticks, pair, coat of arms	Asprey London 1993
1709/10	Colin McKenzie	Edinburgh	Chambersticks, pair, engraved with earl's coronet above a Capital B, two C's and hearts and the word "Remember", 4 ½" di, 14oz	JH Bourdon-Smith Catalog Autumn 2001 #43 p12 Sotheby's October 29, 1959 #73 Spink London Phillips Edinburgh August 24, 2001 #560
1709/10	Colin McKenzie	Edinburgh	Candlesticks, pair, octagonal, knopped baluster stems leading to spool shaped scones, 6" ht, 28.6oz	Sotheby's Gleneagles August 25, 1977 #163
1709/10	Henry Bethune	Edinburgh	Candlesticks, pair, on molded octagonal bases, with sunk circular centers and octagonal stems, one with mm only, 6 ¾" ht, 23.2oz	Christie's February 16, 1960 #121
1709/10	John Seatoun	Edinburgh	Candlesticks, set of 4, no details	Girdwood Collection Glasgow Exhibition 1911, vol I, p120 #42
1710 ca	Edward Penman Assayer marks	Edinburgh	Chambersticks, pair, circular on bun supports, later heart crest below motto "TRUE TO THE END", ring handles, earl's coronet, 4" di, 14oz 16d	Sotheby's London UK April 28, 1999 #184
1710/11	Patrick Turnbull	Edinburgh	Candlesticks, pair, cast, with cut corner bases, 6 ¾" ht, 30oz	JH Bourdon-Smith Catalog Autumn 2000
1710/11	Colin McKenzie	Edinburgh	Tablesticks, pair, with crest and motto of Farquharson, 6 ¾" ht, 40oz 3d	Sotheby's March 3, 1938 #114 Sotheby's November 11, 1949

YEAR	MAKER (continued)	LOCATION	DESCRIPTION	SOURCE #98
				Connoisseur Magazine 1950 vol 125 p 68
1710/11	Colin McKenzie	Edinburgh	Tablesticks, set of 4, with later branches by James Ker 1728/29, octagonal bases with partly octagonal baluster stems and vase shaped sockets, bases with a cartouche containing a sun in splendor and a motto, 6 5/8" ht 78oz all	Finley 1991 #79 Sotheby's June 25, 1953 #154 Christie's March 24, 1982 Connoisseur Magazine 1953 vol 132 p200 Clayton Christie's Book p144 #1
1711/12	John Seatoun	Edinburgh	Chambersticks, pair, one with worn mm, circular with molded border and rising scroll handle, reeded socket with control band, crest of Hamilton, 19oz	Christie's March 24, 1982, #76
1711/12	David Mitchell	Edinburgh	Candlestick, pair, octagonal, crest of Hamilton, 6 ¾" ht, 28 oz	Christie's London May 1993 #115
1712/13	Alexander Forbes	Edinburgh	Candlesticks, not pictured	Cripps p 149
1714/15	Colin McKenzie	Edinburgh	Chambersticks, octagonal, on 4 bun feet, capped ring handle, crest and motto of Stirling, 7oz 8d	Christie's March 24, 1982 #75
1714/15	Patrick Turnbull	Edinburgh	Candlesticks, set of 4, on stepped square bases with canted corner, knopped octagonal baluster, marked on bases, 7" ht	Christie's NY USA October 1988 #41
1716/17	Edward Penman	Edinburgh	Tablesticks, pair, octagonal bases and nozzles, engraved with "H/AF/AH", 6 ½" ht,	Christie's Picture Book April 27, 1973 #144 Christie's June 22, 1960 #93 Christie's Negative #260203 Nicholas Shaw Catalog 2005 p86
1718/19	Colin McKenzie	Edinburgh	Chamberstick, no details	National Museums of Scotland MEQ 1158
1720/21	James Mitchelson	Edinburgh	Candlesticks, pair, octagonal stepped bases rising to knopped baluster stems, spool sconces, bases with a crest, 6 ½" ht	Apollo September 1972 vol 96 Antiques Magazine vol 102
1725/26	James Tait	Edinburgh	Candlesticks, set of 4, crest and motto of Haigh or Haig, 7" ht, 59oz	Finley 1991 #129 Christie's June 24, 1981 #66
1726/27	James Ker	Edinburgh	Chambersticks, pair, no details	Sotheby's November 16, 1965 #151

YEAR	MAKER	LOCATION	DESCRIPTION	SOURCE
1728/29	James Ker	Edinburgh	Candlesticks, pair, with fluted baluster stems, molded sconces and octagonal bases, with re-entrant corners, crest	Sotheby's July 19, 1958 #130 Simon Kaye Antiques
1728/29	James Ker	Edinburgh	Branches of candlesticks, pair, presently with 1710 McKenzie candlesticks but possibly made for 1728 Ker candlesticks	Sotheby's June 25, 1953
1728/29	James Ker	Edinburgh	Chambersticks, pair, circular, plain with molded rims, octagonal molded sconces, flat section handles pierced with a hole for suspension, undersides with crest, 8 ½" ht, 19.2oz	Sotheby's December 16, 1965
1730/31 And 1732/33	James Mitchelson	Edinburgh	Candlesticks, set of 8, 4 each year, no details	Private Collection UK
1731 & 48	William Aytoun and William Dempster	Edinburgh	Candlesticks, matched, no details	Antiques Magazine vol 82 p 580
1733/34	James Ker	Edinburgh	Chambersticks, set of 4, circular with molded borders, capped flying scroll handles, crest and motto underneath, date and assayer wrong, 36oz	Christie's March 26, 1969 #97 Clayton Christie's Book p 108
1733/34	James Ker	Edinburgh	Candlestick, circular banded nozzle on a square tapering baluster stem, square dished base with re-entrant corners, crest of the Order of the Thistle (with "Ls") and a later crest for the Earl of Carlisle	Lyon & Turnbull, Edinburgh UK The Murray Collection August 20, 2003 #198
1734/35	Alexander Kincaid	Edinburgh	Tapersticks, pair, no details	National Museums of Scotland MEQ1055-56 1971.277-278
1734/35	William Aytoun	Edinburgh	Single chamberstick, marked base and pan, 4 7/8" di, 8oz 6d	Sotheby's April 5, 1982 #409 or #209
1735/36	John Rollo	Edinburgh	Candlesticks, set of 4, no details	Connoisseur Magazine 1950 vol 126 p 152
1736/37	James Ker	Edinburgh	Taperstick, no details	Antiques Magazine vol 127 p 1274 Hobart House advertisement
1736/37	James Ker	Edinburgh	Taperstick, on square base, incurved corners, baluster stem with detachable nozzle, with initial "H" and a coronet, perhaps for Hopetoun?, 4 3/8" ht, 4.2oz	Christie's June 15, 1977 #120
1737/38	James Mitchelson	Edinburgh	Candlesticks, set of 4 candlesticks of small size, fluted baluster stems, square bases with incurved angles, with identical crests, 6" ht, 51.5oz all	Sotheby's January 14, 1965 #168 Sussex Goldsmiths

YEAR	MAKER	LOCATION	DESCRIPTION	SOURCE
1739/40	James Ker Assayer Archibald Ure	Edinburgh	Chambersticks, a pair, each on plain circular base, molded rim, spool shaped socket and semi ring, flying scroll handle with plain thumb piece fitted with socket for a missing dowser	Christie's Glasgow July 12, 1983 #200 Christie's Edinburgh April 27, 1988 #60
1739/40	William Aytoun Assayer David Mitchell	Edinburgh	Chambersticks, a pair, plain, circular, plain molded border, detachable nozzles, 17.2oz	Christie's June 15, 1977 #119
1740 ca	James Ker	Edinburgh	Chambersticks, crest and motto, 8oz	Lyle Annual Review 1994 p488
1740/41	Hugh Penman	Edinburgh	Candlesticks, pair, each on shaped fluted base, rising to faceted knopped stem, with banded spool form sconces, one side of each base with crest and motto for Coutts, family of Thomas Coutts distinguished banker, 6 ½" ht, 24.5oz	Sotheby's March 14, 1996 #151 Christie's NY USA October 20, 1999 #313
1745 ca	Ker & Dempster Assayer Hugh Gordon	Edinburgh	Candlesticks, pair, cast sticks with hexafoil bases with shells, inner border of roses, fluted baluster stems, spool shaped sockets, shell decorated nozzles, 8 ½"	Lyon & Turnbull February 20, 2004
1745 ca	James Ker Assayer Hugh Gordon	Edinburgh	Candlesticks, set of 4, on shaped square bases, with sunken centers, with faceted baluster stems and vase-shaped sockets, each engraved with a cipher and earl's coronet, 6 7/8" ht, 51oz all	Christie's June 21, 1978
1745 ca	James Ker	Edinburgh	Candlesticks, pair, shaped square base, cast and chased with scrolls, shells and scale work, each with baluster stem and spool shaped socket, 8" ht, 37oz all	Christie's July 8, 1987
1745/46	James Ker	Edinburgh	Candlesticks, pair, shaped square bases, no nozzles, rococo decoration, 8" ht	Lorentz Antiques Toronto 1991 The Phoenix Collection
1745/46	James Ker	Edinburgh	Candlesticks, set of 4, cipher and earl's coronet, 6.9" ht, 51 oz	Christie's June 21, 1978 #104
1747/48	Ker & Dempster over striking John Café	Edinburgh	Candlesticks, set of 4, each on shaped square base, cast with shells at the angles, baluster stems, vase shaped sockets, detachable nozzles, 9 ¼" ht, 68oz all	Christie's London July 11, 1990 #170
1747/48 & 1759/60	William Dempster	Edinburgh	Candlesticks, pair, with branches and sticks, 59 ½" long, 101oz	Christie's London November 10, 1993 #201
1748/49	Edward Lothian	Edinburgh	Candlesticks, pair, square bases with canted corners	Connoisseur Magazine 1939 vol 103 p14 Edward and Son advertisement

YEAR	MAKER	LOCATION	DESCRIPTION	SOURCE
1748/49	William Aytoun	Edinburgh	Candlesticks, set of 4, shaped bases	Finley 1991 #79
1749/50	Edward Lothian 1 pair, Ker & Dempster 2nd pair Assayer Hugh Gordon	Edinburgh	Candlesticks, 2 pairs, fluted baluster stems, on shaped square crested bases, chased at the angles with shell motifs, detachable nozzles, 8 ½" ht,	Sotheby's December 3, 1964 #118
1749/50	William Aytoun Assayer Hugh Gordon	Edinburgh	Chambersticks, pair, circular pans, engraved with same crests between coronets and mottos, campana shaped sconces, flying scroll handles, molded rims, 5 ½" di, 16oz 12d both	Sotheby's June 24, 1973 #154 Shrubsole
1749/50	Ebenezer Oliphant Assayer Hugh Gordon	Edinburgh	Tablesticks, set of 4, engraved with crest, motto and coronet, crest of Maxell, Earl of Nithsdale, (Note: the same sticks possibly listed for Edward Lothian), 7 ¾" ht, 66oz all	Sotheby's September 1, 1998 #558 JH Bourdon-Smith
1749/50	William Aytoun	Edinburgh	Chambersticks, pair, crest, motto and coronet, 5 ½" di, 16oz 12d	Sotheby's June 21, 1973 #154
1749/50	*William Aytoun Assayer Hugh Gordon*	*Edinburgh*	*Candlesticks, pair, plain circular pans, engraved at later date with crest of Torphichen, molded rims, bell shaped sconces, simple scroll handles, 16oz 12d both*	*Sotheby's December 1, 1966 #173*
1749/50	Edward Lothian	Edinburgh	Candlesticks, pair, stepped shaped square bases with a crest and motto, below the knopped flared stems and banded spool shaped sconces, with possible late multifoil nozzles, crest and motto of John Horburgh of that Ilk, 7 ¼" ht, 36.5oz	Sotheby's Gleneagles August 29, 1983 #505
1749/50	*Edward Lothian*	*Edinburgh*	*Candlesticks, set of 4, shaped square bases with shells and corners, shaped knopped baluster stems rising to sconces, the sconces with central applied rib, with possible late multifoil nozzles, coronet, crest and motto of William Maxwell, Earl of Nithdale, (Note: the same sticks possibly listed for Ebenezer Oliphant),*	*Sotheby's Gleneagles September 1, 1998 #558*
1750 ca	Colin Allan	Aberdeen	Candlesticks, pair	Finley 1991 #109
1750/51	Dougal Ged	Edinburgh	Candlesticks, pair, no details	National Museums of Scotland 1961.556-57
1750/51	Dougal Ged	Edinburgh	Candlesticks, set of 4, 6 ¾" ht, 51.8oz all	The Breadalbane Collection Sale 1935 #70
1751/52	Ebenezer Oliphant	Edinburgh	Candlesticks, pair, on shaped square bases, the corners with figural portraits, crest and motto of Moore, Muir and Mure, 9 ¼" ht, 43.1oz	Nicholas Shaw Catalog Winter 2000, p69

YEAR	MAKER	LOCATION	DESCRIPTION	SOURCE
1752/23	James Mitchell	Edinburgh	Candlesticks, pair, brass form, crest and motto, 7 ½" ht, 33oz	Christie's NY USA October 1996 #205
1753/54	Lothian & Robertson	Edinburgh	Chambersticks, pair, plain, circular, 5 ½" di, 16oz 14d	Private Collection
1754/55	Lothian & Robertson	Edinburgh	Candlesticks, pair, no details	National Museums of Scotland 1957.364 a
1754/55	Robert Gordon	Edinburgh	Chambersticks, pair, no details	The Maple Swan Collection
1755/56	Alexander Gardner	Edinburgh	Candlesticks, pair, on shaped square bases, with detachable nozzles, crest and motto of Robertson, 7 7/8" ht, 33.2oz	Nicholas Shaw Catalog Winter 2000 p69
1756/57	Ker & Dempster	Edinburgh	Candlesticks, pair, shaped square bases with concave sides, faceted corners applied with cartouches, fluted and counter fluted columns, 13 ½" ht, 50oz	Antiques Magazine vol 75 Scottish Art Review vol VII p37 #2 Bell of Aberdeen advertisement
1757/58	Robert Gordon	Edinburgh	Candlesticks, set of 4, octagonal domed base, fluted column stems with Corinthian capital socket, detachable nozzles with gadrooned borders, initials "IP", sold with matching pair 1763/74	Christie's London UK 1998 393
1757/58	William Davie or William Dempster	Edinburgh	Candlesticks, pair, cast hexafoil with original nozzles	Antiques Magazine vol 102 National Museums of Scotland MEQ 879-80
1757/58	William Davie or William Dempster	Edinburgh	Candlesticks, pair, rococo design, on shaped square bases	S J Phillips Ltd London UK of London, #24400 2005
1758/59	James Gilliland	Edinburgh	Candlesticks, set of 4, quatrefoil base with shell capped corners, knopped column, vase shaped sockets, and square wax pans, crested, 8 ½" ht	Bonhams Sale 15120 Aug 22, 2007 #16
1758/59	William Davie or William Dempster	Edinburgh	Candlesticks, set of 4, rococo design	Sotheby's April 1968 #104
1758/59	William Davie or William Dempster	Edinburgh	Candlesticks, set of 4, columnar stems, with domed crested shaped square bases, crest – lion rampant facing dexter, 13 ½" ht, 99oz 19d	Sotheby's Scone April 1979 #95
1758/59	William Davie or William Dempster	Edinburgh	Candlesticks, set of 4, 9" ht, 77oz 16d	Sotheby's July 10, 1990 #366
1758/59	William Davie or William Dempster	Edinburgh	Candlesticks, set of 4, no details	The Maple Swan Collection

YEAR	MAKER	LOCATION	DESCRIPTION	SOURCE
1758/59	Robert Gordon	Edinburgh	Candlesticks, pair, octagonal bases rising to shaped knopped fluted and counter fluted columns, false Corinthian capitals, detachable nozzles, gadroon borders, crest and motto, 13 ½" ht, 57oz 12d	Sotheby's at Blair Castle September 1980 #100 Lyle Silver Review 1982 p567
1758/59	Robert Gordon	Edinburgh	Chambersticks, pair	The Maple Swan Collection
1758/59	William Dempster	Edinburgh	Candlesticks, pair, hexafoil with original nozzles, 8" ht (measured without the nozzles), 37oz 10d	Private Collection
1759/60	William Dempster	Edinburgh	Candlesticks, see 1747 entry, crest	Christie's November 10, 1993 #201
1759/60	Robert Gordon	Edinburgh	Candlesticks, pair	Lorentz Antiques Toronto Canada 1994
1759/60	Lothian & Robertson	Edinburgh	Candlesticks, pair, shaped square bases, sticks with concave sides, flat cut corners, gadrooned collar rims, swirled fluting, 12 ½" ht	Finlay 1991 #94 Apollo March 1969 vol 89 p2
1759/60	*Lothian & Robertson*	*Edinburgh*	*Candlesticks, columnar, pair*	*National Museums of Scotland MEQ 1060-61 1971.282-283*
1760/61	Dougal Ged Overstriking William Dempster	Edinburgh	Candlesticks, pair, shaped octafoil stepped base with band of gadrooning, columnar stem with a Corinthian capital, base with arms, crest and motto, Arms of City of Edinburgh, crest for Maxwell of Springkell, Dumfries (with plated branches), 13 ½" ht	Christie's NY USA 2000 #220
1760/61	William Dempster	Edinburgh	Candlesticks, set of 4, hexafoil with original nozzles, each stick and nozzle engraved with contemporary crest of Coutts, either for James Coutts, 2nd of Hallgreen or for his near kinsman Alexander Coutts, Usher of the White Rod, 8 ¾" ht, 75oz 10d	Private Collection
1761/62	Lothian & Robertson	Edinburgh	Candlesticks, pair, square bases, crest and motto, 10 ½" ht, 50 oz 4d	Sotheby's October 11, 1979 #214
1761/62	Lothian & Robertson	Edinburgh	Candlesticks, set of 4, square bases rim decorated, loaded, columnar stems, Corinthian capitals, ovolo borders, detachable nozzles, 12 ½" ht	Sotheby's Hopetoun House November 13, 1978 #71
1761/62	*Lothian & Robertson*	*Edinburgh*	*Candlesticks, pair, possibly same as preceding, slight dished square bases with crest and motto, knopped hexagonal stems banded capripana shaped sconce and detachable nozzles, gadroon borders on edges, en suite with set of 4 by Robert Gordon 1762/63*	*Sotheby's Scone Palace April 1977 #99*
1761/62	William Dempster	Edinburgh	Candlesticks, set of 4, shaped square bases, knopped and faceted stems and detachable nozzles, decorated with shell motifs, one nozzle by William Cafe, London, the remainder unmarked, 9" ht, 64.8oz	Sotheby's Gleneagles August 29, 1978 #391

YEAR	MAKER	LOCATION	DESCRIPTION	SOURCE
1761/62	William Dempster	Edinburgh	Candlesticks, pair, square bases chased with bold lobes and shells below columnar stems, stiff leaf sconces and detachable gadroon bordered nozzles, loaded, 12 ¾" ht	Sotheby's Gleneagles August 31, 1992 #160
1761/62	*William Dempster*	*Edinburgh*	*Candlesticks, pair, no details, possibly same as above*	*Edward & Sons Glasgow Exhibition 1911, vol I, p120 #41*
1762/63	Robert Gordon	Edinburgh	Candlesticks, set of 8, Crest of Dundas	Christie's NY October 1988 #414
1762/63	Robert Gordon	Edinburgh	Candlesticks, set of 4, crest and motto, 10 ½" ht, 104 oz	Sotheby's Scone Palace April 19, 1977 #98
1762/63	*Robert Gordon*	*Edinburgh*	*Candlestick, one of the above set of 4*	*Sotheby's Scone Palace April 23, 1979 #81*
1763/34	William Dempster	Edinburgh	Candlesticks, set of 4, no details	National Museums of Scotland 1955.77 a-c
1763/64	Alexander Gardner	Edinburgh	Candlesticks, set of 4, crest and motto, 9 ¾" ht, 80oz	Antiques Magazine January 1967 Christie's April 26, 1966 #108
1763/34	Alexander Gardner	Edinburgh	Candlesticks, set of 4, shaped square bases with shells at corners, fluted knopped stem, spool-form socket, shaped square nozzle, base with engraved crest and motto of Hay of Alderston, Co., Haddington, Scotland, 7" ht, 69oz 10 d	Christie's NY USA 1999 #311
1763/34	Robert Gordon	Edinburgh	Candlesticks, pair, matching the set of 4 by Gordon of 1757/58	Christie's London UK 1998 #93
1764/65	Ker & Dempster	Edinburgh	Candlesticks, set of 4, square bases, crest below on earl's coronet, chased bands of shell motifs above the gadroon borders, columnar stems, open work Corinthian capitals, detachable nozzles, marks on 2 sticks covered by loading, 15 ½" ht	Sotheby's Gleneagles August 28, 1975 #63a
1764/65	Alexander Gardner	Edinburgh	Chamberstick, with gadrooned shaped border and looped handle, crest – boar's head and motto "FORWARD OURS" for Seatoun of Touch, 5 ½" across, 92oz	JH Bourdon-Smith Catalog London 1992
1767/68	James Gilliland	Edinburgh	Candlesticks, pair, no details	Christie's NY USA 1984 #32
1768/69	William Davie or William Dempster	Edinburgh	Candlesticks, set of 4, shaped square bases decorated with shells at the angles, triple knopped stems scored with vertical lines, spool shaped sconces, detachable nozzles, 9" ht, 64oz	Sotheby's Blair Castle September 12, 1980 #43 Sotheby's Gleneagles August 29, 1983 #500

102

YEAR	MAKER	LOCATION	DESCRIPTION	SOURCE
1768/69	David Marshall	Edinburgh	Candlestick, may be part of a pair or a set, Corinthian column and capital, severe stepped base with 2 courses of gadroon molding	Geoffrey Wills: Candlesticks 1974 p72
1769/70	William Davie or William Dempster	Edinburgh	Candlesticks, pair, no details	The Maple Swan Collection
1770 ca	Milne & Campbell	Glasgow	Candelabra, pair, no details	National Museums of Scotland K.1999.264 (1-4)
1771/72	William Davie or William Dempster	Edinburgh	Candlesticks, pair, mid century form, 9 ¼" ht, 36oz 6d	Sotheby's London October 19, 1972 #166
Sotheby's Gleneagles August 25, 1997 #137
1771/72	*William Davie or William Dempster*	*Edinburgh*	*Candlesticks, pair, cast, crest of Dundas, part of the previous set, 9" ht, 36oz*	*JH Bourdon-Smith Catalog Autumn 1997, #39 p 58*
1772/73	Not available	Edinburgh	Candlesticks, set of 8, no details	Antiques Magazine vol 50 p202
1772/73	Patrick Robertson	Edinburgh	Candlestick, set of 6, columnar, on square gadrooned bases, 111oz	Linlithgow Collection
Christie's London June 15, 1977 #101
Negative #787169 Stock #241YL
JH Bourdon-Smith London
1778/79	Possibly James Hewitt	Edinburgh	Candlesticks, pair, shaped and stepped square bases with shells at corners, knopped stem, spool form scone, 9 3/8" ht, 35oz	Christie's London UK 2003 #424
1780 ca	Possibly Robert Gray	Possibly Glasgow	Chamberstick, heart shaped, loop handle, starburst-type decoration, 6 1/" wide, 3.2oz	Ritchies Toronto CN 2007 #1090
1786/87	Patrick Robertson	Edinburgh	Candlesticks, set of 6, square base, coronet, initial "H", 6" ht, 111 oz	Christie's June 15, 1977 #101
1786/87	Patrick Robertson	Edinburgh	Chambersticks, pair, 5 ½" di, 25.1oz	Lyle Silver Review 1982 p34
1786/87	David Marshall	Edinburgh	Candlesticks, set of 4, Corinthian with case, 12" ht	Sotheby's October 21, 1971 #1
1793/94	William Robertson	Edinburgh	Chambersticks, pair, circular form, vase shaped sconces with threaded rings, crest, conical snuffers with same crest, dished circular base, fluted shoulders, threaded rim	Lyon & Turnbull August 20, 2003 #196
National Museums of Scotland MEQ 897

YEAR	MAKER	LOCATION	DESCRIPTION	SOURCE
1789/90	I B	Provincial Edinburgh assay	Chamberstick, plain galleried pan, short socket for candle	Finlay 1991 #83 Private Collection
1801/02	John McDonald	Edinburgh	Chambersticks, George III, gadrooned circular base, provision to take a storm shade and conical snuffer, crested, engraved with an order and motto, "Honestae Gloria Fax Mentes," 4 ¾" di, 6.5oz	Nicholas Shaw Antiques 2005 Woolley & Wallis January 26, 2005 #430
1801/02	John McDonald	Edinburgh	Chamberstick, no details	National Museums of Scotland MEQ 1224
1809/10	R Gray & Son	Glasgow Assay Edinburgh	Chamberstick, no details	Sotheby's Gleneagles August 1988 #472
1814/15	Not available		Candlesticks, set of 8, no details	Antiques Magazine vol 48 p61
1814/15	George Fenwick	Edinburgh	Column sticks, pair, Arms of Ferguson of Pitfour, also marked "GF Tobago", crest and motto "VIRTUTE", 9 ½" ht, 39oz	Nicholas Shaw Catalog Winter 2002/03 p87 National Museums of Scotland K2003.2526
1814/15	WP Possibly William Peat	Edinburgh	Chambersticks, pair, circular form, scroll gadrooned borders, molded part lobed sconces, detachable nozzles, leaf capped scroll handles, 4 " wide, 22oz	Lyon & Turnbull, Edinburgh UK 2003 #310
1815 ca	Alexander McLeod	Inverness	Candlesticks, pair, no details	Lyle Silver Review 1982 p143
1817/18	James McKay	Edinburgh	Taperstick, circular with gadrooned borders, snuffer lacking, handled damaged, 1 5/8" ht, 2 ¾" di, 2.2oz	Bonhams Sale 10914, #25
1818/19	Robert Gray & Son	Glasgow	Chamberstick, no details	National Museums of Scotland MEQ 1066 1972.259
1825 ca	Alexander Cameron	Dundee	Candlesticks, pair, no details	Finlay 1991 #112
1835/36	Elder & Co	Edinburgh	Chambersticks, 38oz 1d	Sotheby's November 8, 1973 #162
1876/77	Hamilton & Inches	Edinburgh	Candlesticks, pair with quatrefoil bases, 7 ½" ht, 25oz	JH Bourdon-Smith Catalog Autumn 1997 #39 p58
1893/94	Hamilton & Inches	Edinburgh	Candlesticks, pair, 9 ½" ht	Bonhams London UK 2002 #397

YEAR	MAKER	LOCATION	DESCRIPTION	SOURCE
1895/96	James Crichton & Co	Edinburgh	Candlesticks, set of 4, in 17th century style with wide square bases and stop-fluted stems, 8", 73oz	Sotheby's NY USA 1996 #204
1900/01	Hamilton & Inches	Edinburgh	Candlesticks, pair of Adam-style candlesticks	National Museums of Scotland MEQ 947-948 1969.683-84
1904/05	Robert & William Sorley	Glasgow	Candlesticks, pair, 9" ht	Christie's NY USA 1999 #396
1910 ca	Frazer, Ferguson & McBean	Inverness	Candlestick, silver-mounted deer hoof on a pink granite circular base, with vase-shaped socket and fixed nozzle, 11" ht	Christie's London UK 1999 #5

Casters, Kitchen Peppers and Pepperpots

Plate 11. An octagonal Caster wrought Fall of 1729 by James Ker, Edinburgh. Courtesy of The Phoenix Collection. Photograph by Janice M Dietert.

CASTERS, KITCHEN PEPPERS/DREDGERS AND PEPPER POTS

YEAR	MAKER	LOCATION	DESCRIPTION	SOURCE
	CASTERS			
1684/85	Thomas Yorstoun	Edinburgh	Lighthouse castor, top with pierced quatrefoils, body with script initials "JJ/AM" date letter needs verification	Glasgow Empire Exhibition 1938 #11, #24 Sotheby's April 23, 1993 #302
1686/87	James Cockburn	Edinburgh	Lighthouse caster, initialed "IS/SM" above a reeded girdle and dome foot, the bayonet lock cover pierced below cutcard work, baluster finial, 7" ht, 7oz 14d	Sotheby's NY USA 1996 #164
1690/91	James Penman	Edinburgh	Cylindrical sugar caster, cut card work, domed cover plume, engraved with "MS 1691", 7 1/3" ht	Apollo December 1948 p 148 Scottish Art Academy Exhibit 1939 #938 J. Cathcart-White Collection National Museums of Scotland 1943.259
1693/94	Andrew Law	Edinburgh	Casters, set of 3, cylindrical bodies, finely engraved above reeded girdles, foliate cut-card work on spreading bases, Arms of Ramsey impaling another, lighthouse form, 7 ¾" & 6" ht, 22oz	Sotheby's December 2, 1965 or 66 #200 Christie's June 24 1987 #71 Holland p 34 Clayton Dictionary p73 #99
1694/95	Thomas Ker	Edinburgh	Caster, plain, cylindrical, fluted top, gadrooned foot, 5 ½" ht, 4oz 14d	Christie's June 8, 1908 #67
1694/95	George Yorstoun	Edinburgh	Sugar caster, cylindrical dome cover, bayonet joint, spreading base, 7.1" ht	Finlay 1991 #51 Scottish Art Academy Exhibit 1939 #938 J. Cathcart-White Collection National Museums of Scotland 1961.593
1697/98	John Seatoun	Edinburgh	Caster, bulbous base, gadrooned cover and border, 8.9" ht	Park Lane Exhibit 1929 #254 Earl of Strathmore Collection
1697/98	Colin McKenzie	Edinburgh	Caster, pear shaped, gadrooned foot, cut card work, fluted finial, gilt, 10oz 17d	Christie's May 5, 1920 #23
1697/98	Robert Bruce	Edinburgh	Caster, cylindrical, gadrooned foot, cover overlapping sleeve, 7 ¾" ht, 11oz 8d	Christie's April 22, 1953 #104
1699/1700	Colin McKenzie	Edinburgh	Caster, rib around the center, gadrooned foot, crest and motto, 6"ht, 5oz 15 d	Christie's July 10, 1945 #34

YEAR	MAKER	LOCATION	DESCRIPTION	SOURCE
1700/01	Walter Scott	Edinburgh	Sugar caster, gadrooned base, cut-card work on top and bottom of base, finely pierced top, armorials of Thomson of Charleston, crest and motto, 9 7/16" ht, 16.2oz	Brand Inglis, Ltd 1987 Acorn, Boston Museum of Fine Art pp327-328 #25
1702/03	James Penman	Edinburgh	Set of 3 casters, gadrooned base, bulbous body, Arms of Earl of Strathmore, 8 ¼" ht, 6 ½" ht, 30oz 13d	Christie's December 8, 1948 #131 Scottish Art Academy Exhibit 1939 #918 Seaford House Exhibit 1929 #551 Park Lane Exhibit 1929 #254 Connoisseur Magazine 1949 vol 123 p 66
1702/03	Colin McKenzie	Edinburgh	Caster, cone shaped, cut card work, gadrooned finial, 6oz 7d	Christie's Dec 18, 1928 #39
1702/03	Colin McKenzie	Edinburgh	Caster, plain, gadrooned foot, 6oz	Christie's Nov 26, 1908 #32
1702/03	George Scott Jr	Edinburgh	Casters, set of 3, 8 ½" ht and 6" ht, 32oz 16d, probably same as below	Christie's June 18, 1951 #151 Connoisseur Magazine 1951 vol 128 p131
1702/03	*George Scott Jr*	*Edinburgh*	*Casters, set of 3, cylindrical, gadrooned base, reeded girdle, engraved with initials "WG" above "JL", 8" ht, 5 7/8" ht, 31oz*	*Christie's Feb 5-10, 1987 #55 Noble Collection Nicholas Shaw Catalog 2005 p85*
1702/03	Robert Bruce Assayer – James Penman	Edinburgh	Casters, pair, cylindrical, on gadrooned foot, slight baluster girdle, detachable cover with molded and gadrooned ribs, cover pierced with trefoils and scrolls, one cover with inner sleeve, crest and motto "JE RENJE PLUS" possibly for Erskine, 5 ½" ht, 11.2oz	Christie's Dublin May 10, 1976 #445 Sotheby's Hopetoun House April 1988 #62 JH Bourdon-Smith Catalog Spring 1998
1703/04	John Seatoun and I (T) H	Edinburgh	Casters, set of 3, octagonal, cut card work at the shoulders, the tallest by "IH" or "TH", the others by John Seatoun	Finlay 1991 #79 Sotheby's April 22, 1942 #63 Sotheby's Dec 3, 1953 #332 Christie's June 1921 #326 Lockett Collection
1703/04	John Seatoun	Edinburgh	Caster, octagonal, each mark on a different facet of the octagon, gadrooned spreading foot, domed cover with gadrooned flange, cut-card work on top, later crest of Campbell, 7 ½" ht, 9oz	Sotheby's July 14, 1966 #194 Shaw Collection Christie's Glasgow March 1983 #96 National Museums of Scotland MEQ 1563 1983

YEAR	MAKER	LOCATION	DESCRIPTION	SOURCE
1706/07	Colin McKenzie	Edinburgh	Caster, 10 ¾" ht	Connoisseur Magazine January 1959
1706/07	Colin McKenzie	Edinburgh	Caster, pair, pear shaped, 3 bands of fluting, acorn finial, 7" ht, 12oz 8d	Christie's March 19, 1934 #144 Gardner Collection
1706/07	*Colin McKenzie*	*Edinburgh*	*Caster, pair*	*Connoisseur Magazine 1934 vol 93 p348*
1706/07	Patrick Murray I	Edinburgh	Casters, set of 3, baluster bodies engraved below the girdle with crest, covers with slip-lock joints, 2 pierced in a diaper design, the third blind, acorn finials on molded rim feet, 8" ht and 5 ¾" ht, 25.3oz	Sotheby's April 3, 1958 #164 Country Life August 1959 p133 Sotheby's April 23, 1993 #301
1707/08	Walter Scott Assayer – James Penman	Edinburgh	Caster, circular foot, molded mid-rib, 8 ½" ht, 11oz	Christie's November 9, 1949 #131
1708/09	Colin McKenzie	Edinburgh	Casters, pair, straight cylinders tapering toward the top, covers pierced with different diaper patterns, acorn finial, molded rim foot, 6 ¾" ht, 15.2oz	Christie's or Sotheby's Feb 24, 1966 #35
1708/09	Walter Scott	Edinburgh	Baluster caster with molded girdle, engraved with a monogram, 8 ½" ht, 11.6oz	Nicholas Shaw Catalog Winter 2000 p67
1708/09	Thomas Cleghorne III	Edinburgh	Casters, set of 3, baluster form, on domed circular foot, crest, high domed pierced cover with girdle, acorn finial, 8 5/8" ht and 7" ht, 25oz	Christie's Edinburgh Nov11, 1987 #59
1709/10	Robert Bruce	Edinburgh	Caster, pear shaped, rib around body, pierced cover, 8" ht, 11oz 8d	Christie's May 3, 1961 #83 Thomas Lumley, Ltd
1710/11	Henry Bethune	Edinburgh	Sugar casters, set of 3, plain, pear shaped, on stepped spreading foot, acorn finial, later engraved with a crest and Bath motto within a laurel wreath surround, engraved "SD/ RDP/ IP", 7 7/8" ht and 6 1/8" ht, 22oz 1d	S. J. Phillips Inc 1991 Tessier's London 1994 Shaw Collection Christie's Glasgow March 1983 #94 Christie's October 23, 1957 #153 National Museums of Scotland H.1994.742
1710/11	Robert Bruce	Edinburgh	Caster, cylindrical, on domed spreading foot, molded applied girdle on body and base of pierced domed cover, baluster finial, engraved "Mary Hay Lady Randerstone elder 1710", 7 5/8", 30oz	Shaw Collection Christie's Glasgow March 29, 1983 #102 National Museums of Scotland MEQ 1562

YEAR	MAKER	LOCATION	DESCRIPTION	SOURCE
1712/13	James Tait	Edinburgh	Crest, plain, pear shaped, baluster finial, crest, 7 ½" ht, 7oz 9d	Christie's April 19, 1961 #126
1712/13	*James Tait*	*Edinburgh*	*Blind caster, with crest and motto*	*National Museums of Scotland MEQ 1111 1974.419*
1713/14	Patrick Turnbull	Edinburgh	Casters, set of 3, plain, octagonal	National Museums of Scotland MEQ L1983.18-20
1714/15	Mungo Yorstoun	Edinburgh	Casters, octagonal, no girdle, part of a mixed set of 3 smaller, crest and motto "Live but Dreid", cover pierced and lightly engraved, 7 ½"	Sotheby's July 4, 1968 #89 Simon Kaye Antiques
1714/15	Mungo Yorstoun	Edinburgh	Caster, baluster form, with molded lip, on spreading stepped foot, applied reeded shoulder girdle, crest and motto of the Earl of Lindsay, 7 ½" ht, 7.9oz	Sotheby's Gleneagles August 29, 1994 #141
1714/25	James Inglis	Edinburgh	Casters, set of 3, octagonal, pear shaped	Connoisseur Magazine 1927 vol 305 p 46
1715/16	Edward Penman	Edinburgh	Caster, octagonal vase form, engraved with crest and motto, cover pierced with urns and foliage, molded borders, cover fitted with later detachable inner lid, 6 ½" ht, 5oz 10d	Sotheby's NY USA 2005 #289
1715/16	Not available	Edinburgh	Caster, octagonal vase form, with reeded foot, shoulder girdle and rim, detachable cover with plain broad applied girdle and pierced stylized sprays, faceted baluster finial, crest and motto, 6 3/8" ht, 5.1oz	Clayton Christie's Book p161 #5 Christie's London January 29, 1969
1716/17	John Seatoun	Edinburgh	Casters, pair, octagonal, rib faceted, ball finial, 7" ht, 13oz 9d	Christie's March 29, 1939 #69
1716/17	Mungo Yorstoun	Edinburgh	Caster, octagonal, pear shaped, top unmarked	JH Bourdon-Smith London 1994
1716/17	Patrick Murray I	Edinburgh	Caster, octagonal, pear shaped, 11oz	Country Life June 11, 1964 vol 135 p1545 advertisement
1716/17	Patrick Murray I	Edinburgh	Casters, set of 3, octagonal, double molded rib, baluster reeded finial, engraved with the Arms of the City of Edinburgh, 8"ht and 6 ½" ht, 30oz	Christie's June 15, 1977 #129
1717/18	Edward Penman	Edinburgh	Caster, octagonal, pear shaped body, 8" ht	Scottish Art Academy Exhibit 1939 #946 Stirling-Maxwell Collection
1718/19	James Mitchelson	Edinburgh	Caster, octagonal vase form, reeded base, shoulder trim, cover pierced in sections, faceted finial	Scottish Art Review vol XIV #4 1975 How of Edinburgh advertisement on back cover

YEAR	MAKER	LOCATION	DESCRIPTION	SOURCE
1718/19	Patrick Turnbull	Edinburgh	Caster, octagonal vase form, on stepped spreading foot, molded shoulder, girdle and rim, pierced cover with plain girdle, faceted baluster finial, 7" ht, 7.3oz	Sotheby's Gleneagles August 1988 #448
1718/19	Patrick Murray I	Edinburgh	Caster, octagonal, baluster form, 7 ½" ht, 11oz	JH Bourdon-Smith Catalog Autumn 2000
1719/20	Colin Campbell	Edinburgh	Caster, octagonal vase form, on stepped domed foot, molded shoulder girdle and rim, cover pierced with stylized leaf-filled roundels, faceted vase finial, 6 ¼" ht, 8oz	Sotheby's Hopetoun House April 29, 1987 #71
1721/22	Alexander Kincaid	Edinburgh	Caster, octagonal vase form, on molded stepped foot, reeded molded shoulder girdle and lip, cover pierced with engraved scrolls, initial "B"	JH Bourdon-Smith Catalog #33 p11 Sotheby's Hopetoun House May 1990
1720 ca	Not available Assayer-Edward Penman	Edinburgh	Caster, octagonal, crest and motto, 6 1/3" ht, 5oz 2d	Christie's January 29, 1959 #127
1722/23	William Aytoun	Edinburgh	Caster, plain octagonal with ribbing, octagonal baluster finial, 7 ¼" ht, 10oz 10d	Christie's June 7, 1939 #44
1723/24	Alexander Edmonstoun I	Edinburgh	Casters, set of 3, octagonal form, molded reeded foot, shoulder girdle and rim, covers with applied girdle, crest and motto, 7 ½" ht and 6 ¾" ht, 33.4oz	How's Notes on Antique Silver vol I, p22 1941
1724/25	James Mitchelson	Edinburgh	Muffineer caster, plain bellied rib, collet foot	Art Treasures Exhibit 1932 #542 How of Edinburgh Collection
1725 ca	George Robertson	Aberdeen	Caster, The Urquhart Sugar Caster, engraved with crest of Urquhart, motto "PER MARE ET TERRAS", pierced domed lid, acorn finial, 6 ½" ht, 8oz	JH Bourdon-Smith Catalog Spring 1985 Aberdeen Museums and Galleries ABDAG001380
1726/27	James Mitchelson	Edinburgh	Caster, no details	National Museums of Scotland 1933.57
1726/27	Edward Penman	Edinburgh	Caster, pear shaped, largest of mixed set of 3, different makers, crest and motto "Live but Dreid"	Sotheby's July 4, 1968 #69
1726/27	James Tait	Edinburgh	Caster, octagonal, later chased with stiff leafage above the foot and scrolling foliage below the cover, 5 ¾" ht, 5oz	Sotheby's Scone Palace April 14, 1980 #81

YEAR	MAKER	LOCATION	DESCRIPTION	SOURCE
1727/28	James Ker	Edinburgh	Casters, set of 3, octagonal, crest and motto "SUN TE TESTE", 8" ht and 7" ht, 28oz 15d	Sotheby's April 12, 1945 #44 Christie's auction
1727/28	William Aytoun	Edinburgh	Casters, set of 3, octagonal, 7 ¾" ht and 6 ½" ht, 25oz 14d	Christie's May 15, 1911 #33 Christie's July 16, 1913 #61 Christie's April 24, 1942 #4
1728/29	Edward Penman	Edinburgh	Casters, set of 3, plain octagonal vase form, worn crest of a stag, motto "CUBUE NE PULIS" 8" ht and 6 ½" ht, 34oz	Christie's June 23, 1976 #114 National Museums of Scotland L410Y, Ya, Yb
1728/29	James Ker	Edinburgh	Casters, pear shaped, no girdle, smaller pair of a mixed set of 3, crest and motto "Live but Dreid", 7 ½" ht	Sotheby's July 4, 1968 #89 Simon Kaye Antiques
1728/29	James Mitchelson	Edinburgh	Casters, set of 3, plain, octagonal	National Museums of Scotland MEQ 1983.15
1729/30	James Ker Assayer – Edward Penman	Edinburgh	Caster, octagonal, molded reeded shoulder girdle, faceted vase finial crest and motto "Kind heart" for Duff of Banffshire, 8 3/8" ht, 13.8oz	Christie's October 31, 1984 #153 Antiques Magazine February 1987 Shrubsole advertisement The Phoenix Collection
1729/30	William Aytoun Assayer – Alexander Ure	Edinburgh	Caster, vase shaped, engraved with initial "AR" below the applied girdle, domed cover, pierced panels of trellis work and foliage, bell finial, base with bands of reeding, initial "N" underneath, 8 ½" ht, 10oz	Sotheby's Gleneagles August 1991 #213
1729/30	Not Available	Edinburgh	Casters, pair, plain pear shaped, on circular molded foot, body with girdle, one cover pierced, one blind, one unmarked, engrave with initials, 5 ½" ht, 10.3oz	Christie's March 31, 1971 #78
1729/30	William Aytoun	Edinburgh	Dry mustard caster, pear shaped, bun top, crest and motto of Cunningham, 4 1/8"ht, 3oz 15d	Christie's Glasgow March 1983 #79
1729/30	William Aytoun	Edinburgh	Dry mustard caster, crest and motto of Dick, 4 ¼" ht, 3.6oz	Noble Collection Nicholas Shaw Catalog 2005 p 89
1730 ca	James Ker	Edinburgh	Casters, set of 3, vasiform, pierced tops on two, crest and motto	L. Fletcher-Silver #88 p52 in Edinburgh Corporation Museum
1730 ca	Robert Luke	Glasgow	Caster, plain, pear shaped, on spreading foot, applied reeded girdle, associated domed detachable cover, engraved with crest of Lathom, marks rubbed, cover unmarked, 4 1/8" ht, 4oz	Christie's Gleneagles November 21, 1990 #37

YEAR	MAKER	LOCATION	DESCRIPTION	SOURCE
1730 ca	Robert Luke	Glasgow	Caster, pear shaped, possibly with the wrong lot number and same as above, no details	*Christie's Edinburgh November 21, 1990 #35*
1730 ca	Robert Luke	Glasgow	*Caster, plain, pear shaped, on spreading foot, with reeded applied band, bun top, engraved with crest of Latham, cover possibly associated, mm 2X's, date letter indistinct, cover unmarked, 4" ht, 4oz 10d*	*Christie's March 29, 1983 #49 Shaw Collection Christie's Scotland November 14, 1985 #276*
1730/31	James Ker Assayer-Archibald Ure	Edinburgh	Caster, octagonal form, cover, engraved panels with later pierced band, applied girdle, crest and motto of Colquhoun "That Ilk and Luss" Dumbartonshire, 7 ½" ht 10oz 15d	Sotheby's Gleneagles August 29, 1995 #170
1731/32	James Ker	Edinburgh	Caster, octagonal, applied girdle, acorn finial, later coat of arms for Fuller and initial "F", 9" ht, 15oz 18d	Sotheby's December 1, 1966 #124 Christie's May 16, 1979 #87 Sotheby's Hopetoun House November 13, 1978 #95 Antiques Magazine v116, p 1049 Shrubsole advertisement
1732/33	James Ker	Edinburgh	Casters, set of 3, Arms of Dennistoun	Apollo October 1990 p26
1732/33	*James Ker*	*Edinburgh*	*Casters, set of 3, no details*	*Connoisseur Magazine 1941 vol 107 p230*
1732/33	James Ker	Edinburgh	Casters, set of 3, pierced tops 7 ½" ht and 6 ½" ht (two)	Huntley House Museum, Edinburgh HH348670
1732/33	James Ker	Edinburgh	Mustard casters, pair, no details	National Museums of Scotland MEQ 32-33
1735 ca	John Rollo	Edinburgh	Caster, octagonal baluster form, with contemporary arms, possibly of Hamilton, high domed pierced cover, with bayonet fitting, 7 5/8" ht, 11oz	Phillips Edinburgh August 24, 2001 #558
1736/37	Dougal Ged	Edinburgh	Casters, set of 3, one blind, plain vase shaped body, on spreading foot, domed lid with alternating panels of diaper work and scroll work, 7 ½" ht and 6 ¼" ht, 21.9oz	Sotheby's Scone Palace April 13, 1976 #123 National Museums of Scotland MEQ 1168-70 1976.15-17
1736/37	Archibald Ure	Edinburgh	Caster, vase shaped, body with later crest, chased with flowering foliage on a matted ground, cover pierced with leaf and lattice work panels below ball finial, 7 ¼" ht, 7.7oz	Sotheby's March 14, 1974 #188
1736/37	Dougal Ged	Edinburgh	Casters, pair, plain vase shaped bodies, on spreading feet, with domed	Sotheby's April 13, 1976 #123

YEAR	MAKER (continued)	LOCATION	DESCRIPTION	SOURCE
1738/39	James Ker	Edinburgh	covers, decorated with diaper and scroll work, larger one pierced, smaller one blind, 7 ½" and 6 ¼" ht, 21.9oz both	Christie's May 30, 1904 #75
1738/39	James Ker	Edinburgh	Caster, only the lower part	Sotheby's Gleneagles August 29, 1983 #506
1738/39	James Ker	Edinburgh	Caster, baluster, lobed and ribbed below the molded girdle, on spreading base, cover pierced with alternating panels of diaper work, flower heads and stylized foliage, bell shaped finial, 8" ht, 10oz	Christie's NY USA 2005 #452
1738/39	James Ker	Edinburgh	Caster, baluster form on circular foot with fluted lower body, cover pierced with alternating floral draper and floral urn panels, baluster finial, neck engraved with crest and motto, 7 ½" ht, 7oz 10d	Sotheby's March 27, 1984
1739/40	Not available Assayer Archibald Ure	Edinburgh	Caster, vase shaped, shoulder with applied girdle, on spreading base, cover pierced and engraved with alternate panels of diaper work and stylized foliage, bell shaped finial, crest a bent arm holding a scimitar, and motto "Dread God", 5 ¾" ht, 5.1oz	Guthrie p96 #278 JH Bourdon-Smith London 1994
1740 ca	Alexander Johnson	Dundee	Caster, pair, vase-shaped, crested, marked AI twice, K, Dundee town mark	
1740ca	Robert Luke	Glasgow	Caster, vase shaped, blind slip on cover, engraved with alternate panels of diaper work and floral motifs radiating from baluster finial, 5 ¾" ht, 4oz 17d	Sotheby's February 22, 1968 #167
1740/41	James Hally	Edinburgh	Sugar caster, no details	National Museums of Scotland 1943.257
1740/41	Not available	Edinburgh	Caster, inverted pear form, on spreading circular foot, baluster finial, later chased with rococo flowers and foliage, with ribbon floral swags, 7.3oz	Christie's March 2, 1987 #203
1740/41	William Davie or William Dempster	Edinburgh	Caster, baluster body with molded girdle, spreading foot, detachable domed cover pierced with alternating panels of diaper work and scroll below the bell finial, inner sleeve, 6 ½" ht, 6.6oz	Sotheby's Gleneagles August 30, 1982 #495
1741/42	James Mitchelson Assayer – Dougal Ged	Edinburgh	Casters, set of 3, baluster, pierced covers, plain, misdated in the catalog, 6 ¾" ht, 5 ¼" ht, 14oz	Christie's NY October 15, 1966 #266
1741/42	James Ker	Edinburgh	Caster, baluster body with reeded girdle at the shoulder, detachable cover pierced in alternating panels of saltires and scrolling foliage below a baluster finial, 6 ¼" ht, 5.1oz	Sotheby's Gleneagles August 25, 1997 #158
1741/42	Dougal Ged	Edinburgh	Caster, blind, baluster body	National Museums of Scotland MEQ 896 1967.654

YEAR	MAKER	LOCATION	DESCRIPTION	SOURCE
1741/42	Dougal Ged	Edinburgh	Casters, vase shaped, on molded foot, girdle, blind cover engraved with foliage, baluster finial, 5 ½" ht, 5oz	Christie's January 30, 1963
1741/42	James Mitchell	Edinburgh	Casters, pair, no details	Christie's June 30, 1963
1741/42	James Mitchell	Edinburgh	Casters, set of 3, vase shaped baluster, on circular molded base, high domed pierced cover, baluster finial, misdated in catalog as 1742/43, 6 ¾" ht and 5 ½" ht, 14oz	Christie's East NY USA October 15, 1996 #266
1744/45	Charles Dickson II	Edinburgh	Caster, vase shaped, acorn finial, pierced cover, on circular foot, with crest and motto, 5" ht, 4.4oz	Sotheby's October 31, 1963 #137 Christie's December 20, 1974 #192 Christie's September 23, 1987 #5
1745 ca	Alexander Johnston	Dundee	Casters, 2 almost matching, vase shaped bodies, engraved with later identical crests, pierced covers, acorn finials, on rim feet, 6 ½" ht, 13oz 11d, possibly same as 1740 ca examples	Sotheby's November 20, 1958
1745 ca	James Glen	Glasgow	Caster, two, inverted pear shaped, molded at shoulder above initials, spreading base, blind cover, spirally fluted between bands of flat chased shells, diaper and other motifs, bell finial, 6 ¼" ht, 7oz 1d	Sotheby's April 4-5 1982
1745 ca	James Glen	Glasgow	Caster, for pepper or dry mustard, baluster form, domed cover chased with flute, foliage and diaper work, engraved with initials, cover unmarked, 6" ht, 7oz	Christie's November 23, 1983 #143
1746/47	Ebenezer Oliphant	Edinburgh	Sugar castor, no details	Hayden p227 National Museums of Scotland 1898.248
1746/47	Hugh Gordon	Edinburgh	Caster, vase shaped body, on spreading foot, detachable cover with 6 panels alternately scroll engraved and diaper pierced, 6" ht, 4oz 7d	Sotheby's Gleneagles August 19, 1996 #125
1746/47	Ebenezer Oliphant Assayer Hugh Gordon	Edinburgh	Casters, set of 3, plain baluster bodies, on spreading feet, covers well pierced in alternating panels, 2 pierced and one engraved to match blind, urn finials, 7 7/8" ht and 6 5/8" ht, 20.5oz all	Lyon & Turnbull August 20, 2003 #199 The Murray Collection
1746/47	Not available	Edinburgh	Caster, no details	Apollo May 1947 v70
1746/47	Hugh Gordon	Edinburgh	Caster, 7 ¼" ht	Apollo February 1967 vol 85 p2 Bell of Aberdeen advertisement
1747/48	Not available Assayer Hugh	Edinburgh	Caster, vase shaped, chased with bands of flower clusters and shell motifs, cover with alternately pierced and scroll engraved panels, mm over struck,	Sotheby's January 29, 1970 #112 Sotheby's July 23, 1970 #196

YEAR	MAKER	LOCATION	DESCRIPTION	SOURCE
	Gordon		6 ½" ht, 6oz 14d	
1748/49	Hugh Gordon	Edinburgh	Sugar caster, inverted pear shape, on spreading circular foot, unmarked top with baluster finial, body engraved with crest and motto, 5 ½" ht	Christie's South Kensington August 3, 1981 #325
1748/49	James Gilliland	Edinburgh	Set of 3 casters, no details	How's Notes on Antique Silver vol I, p21 1941 Connoisseur Magazine 1934 vol 93 p347
1748/49	Robert Gordon	Edinburgh	Caster, no details	William Walter London 1994
1749/50	Not available Assayer Hugh Gordon	Edinburgh	Casters, pair, vase shaped, each engraved above applied molded girdles with crests and mottos, pierced and engraved covers, urn-shaped finials, on spreading bases, 5 ¾" ht, 7oz 15d	Sotheby's May 15, 1969 #4
1752/53	Ker & Dempster	Edinburgh	Caster, pear shaped, on circular foot, cover pierced with circles, with a crest, 5 ½" ht, 3.3oz	Christie's June 20, 1973 #12
1753/54	Hugh Gordon	Edinburgh	Casters, set of 3, part of a cruet, baluster form	Sotheby's Gleneagles August 29, 1974 #112
1754/55	William Davie or William Dempster	Edinburgh	Caster, mm in plain rectangle in script initials, no details	Jackson Marks p548
1755/56	Alexander Gardner	Edinburgh	Casters, set of 3, baluster form, each engraved with an anchor crest and motto beneath a coronet, 21oz	How's Notes on Antique Silver vol I, p21, 1941 How of Edinburgh 1837 #111
1756/57	Not available	Edinburgh	Caster, baluster, later chased scroll and floral decoration, mm poorly struck, 7" ht, 5.6oz	Sotheby's June 6, 1998 #177
1756/57	IM in an engrailed rectangle James McKenzie I or James Mitchelson	Edinburgh	Casters, pair, said to be by James McKenzie I, plain, pear shaped bodies, covers pierced with trellis or scrolling leaf panels below acorn finials, one caster engraved but blind, 5 1/8" ht, 7oz	Sotheby's May 9-11, 1989 #137
1756/57	Robert Gordon	Edinburgh	Caster, no details	Antiques Magazine 1977 112
1757/58	James Gilliland	Edinburgh	Muffineer, no details	National Museums of Scotland MEQ 858 1966.1005
1757/58	William Taylor over striking another	Edinburgh	Caster, on spreading circular foot, high domed cover with baluster finial, sold with another smaller en suite, 6 5/8" ht, 10oz both	Christie's June 24, 1986 #344

YEAR	MAKER	LOCATION	DESCRIPTION	SOURCE
1758/59	Not available	Edinburgh	Caster, *plain*, pear shaped, on circular foot, covered pierced with flowers and scrolls, bell shaped finial, 7 ½" ht, 8.5oz	Christie's October 29, 1975 #131
1758/59	Benjamin Coutts	Edinburgh	Caster, baluster form, cover with simple foliate piercing, urn finial, molded rim foot, 6 ¼" ht, 5.2oz	Sotheby's June 24, 1965 #33
1758/59	*Benjamin Coutts*	*Edinburgh*	*Caster, molded borders, cover pierced in alternating panels below acorn finial, spreading foot, 6" ht, 5.2oz*	*Sotheby's April 10-11, 1978 #87*
1758/59	WD probably William Dempster	Edinburgh	Casters, pair, pear shaped, each on molded foot, pierced cover, baluster finial, coronet and initials, 7" ht, 13.6oz	February 4, 1967 #183
1758/59	WD probably William Dempster	*Edinburgh*	Caster, plain, vase shaped, circular molded foot, pierced cover, baluster finial, 8" ht, 9.6oz	Christie's June 3, 1959
1758/59	WD probably William Dempster	Edinburgh	Caster, vase shaped, on molded foot, cover *pierced* with spiral bands of rosettes and scrolls, baluster finial, 6 ½" ht, 6.2oz	Christie's November 11, 1959 #67
1758/59	WD probably William Dempster	Edinburgh	Caster, vase shaped, reeded at waist, otherwise plain, cover pierced in a foliate design, urn finial, molded rim foot, 7 ¼" ht, 7.3oz	Sotheby's July 12, 1962 #135 Sotheby's November 8, 1962 #149 Simon Kaye Antiques
1758/59	Hugh Gordon	Edinburgh	Caster, baluster form, detachable domed cover, baluster finial, reeded borders, 5 3/8" ht, 3.5oz	Phillips Edinburgh August 24, 2001 #551
1760 ca	Hugh Gordon	Edinburgh	Casters, a matched pair, baluster form, spreading foot, pierced dome covers, baluster finials, *crest of double headed eagle and motto of Loudon, mm only*, 6 ½" ht, 9oz	Phillips Edinburgh November 27, 2000 #320
1760 ca	John Welsh	Edinburgh	Caster, inverted pear shape, chased with foliage, 5 ¾" ht	*Christie's March 22, 1982 #23*
1760 ca	Lothian & Robertson	Edinburgh	Sander, no details	National Museums of Scotland
1760 ca	Adam Graham	Glasgow	Caster, 8" ht	Apollo August 1967 vol 86 p2 Bell of Aberdeen
1760/61	Patrick Robertson	Edinburgh	Sugar caster, no details	JH Bourdon-Smith London 1996
1760/61	*Patrick Robertson*	*Edinburgh*	*Caster, baluster form, molded girdle, vase shaped finial, crest of Hastings, 7 ½" ht, 7oz*	*Nicholas Shaw Catalog Winter 2000 p72*

YEAR	MAKER	LOCATION	DESCRIPTION	SOURCE
1760/61	*Patrick Robertson*	*Edinburgh*	*Caster, baluster form, acorn finial, body engraved with a crest, 7 ¼" ht, 6oz*	*Christie's Scotland August 23, 1996 #80*
1760/61	MK conjoined Probably James McKenzie I	Edinburgh	Caster, baluster form with bell-shaped finial, cover unmarked, 7" ht, 5.75 oz	Christie's London UK 2006 #235
1761/62	William Taylor	Edinburgh	Caster, initials above a girdle, detachable cover pierced in panels, urn finial	Sotheby's Hopetoun House November 12, 1979 #54
1762/63	Not available	Edinburgh	Caster, plain, baluster with pierced top, 7 ½" ht	I. Frank Antiques London 2006 #e8373
1763/64	Lothian & Robertson	Edinburgh	Casters, set of 3, baluster, cover with acorn finials, 16.3oz all	Phillips London August 2, 1991 #139
1765 ca	Adam Graham	Glasgow	Caster, cover pierced with flowers and foliate motifs, with crest, 5 3/8" ht, 3.5oz	Christie's October 22, 1969 #50
1765/66	Not available	Edinburgh	Caster, reeded at waist, pierced cover, urn finial, 6 ¾" ht, 5.5oz	Sotheby's May 10, 1973 #80
1765/66	Patrick Robertson	Edinburgh	Caster, no details	Christie's NY October 1988 #330
1766/67	Patrick Robertson	Edinburgh	Caster, chased, repaired, 8 ¼" ht	Sotheby's NY Oct 27, 1982 #356
1766/67	Patrick Robertson	Edinburgh	Caster, vase shaped, on spreading foot, chased with spiral flutes, applied on shoulder with reeded band, raised cover pierced with scrolling foliage, baluster finial, 7 1/8" ht, 6oz 14d	Christie's July 27, 1977 #263 Christie's December 14, 1977 #129
1766/67	Patrick Robertson	Edinburgh	Caster, baluster form, chased with swirling flutes, pierced dome cover, baluster finial, cover unmarked, 8" ht, 8.5oz	Christie's February 7, 1983 #208
1766/67	William Ker	Edinburgh	Caster, inverted pear shape, molded at shoulder, on spreading foot, cover pierced and engraved with swirl panels featuring floral sprays, bell-shaped finial, 5 ½" ht, 3oz 12d	Sotheby's June 29-30 1981 #109
1766/67	Patrick Robertson	Edinburgh	Casters, set of 3, inverted pear shape, chased with spiral fluting, engraved with crest of Mitchelson,	Christie's January 17, 1977 #98 Christie's March 7, 1977 #64
1766/67	Gilliland and Ker	Edinburgh	Casters, set of 3	Private Collection 2005
1770/71	William Davie or William Dempster	Edinburgh	Casters, set of 3, one blind, baluster bodies chased with restrained festoons, 2 covers pierced with wavy then foliate motifs, baluster finials, spreading domed	Sotheby's Gleneagles August 29, 1978 #412

YEAR	MAKER (continued)	LOCATION	DESCRIPTION	SOURCE
1771/72	Not available	Edinburgh	feet, 7" ht, 5 ¾" ht, 14.3oz	Sotheby's Melbourne AU May 2, 2004 #203
1775 ca	Milne & Campbell	Glasgow	Casters, pair, baluster form, knopped finial, spreading foot, pierced top	JH Bourdon-Smith London 1992
1775/76	Alexander Gardner	Edinburgh	Casters, set of 2, one large, one small, chased	Connoisseur Magazine 1932 vol 90 p65
1778/79	Patrick Cunningham	Edinburgh	Casters, set of 3	National Museums of Scotland 1939.142
1783/84	Not available	Edinburgh	Caster, sugar, no details	Scottish Art Review vol VIII, p33 #2 1961 Muirhead Moffat advertisement
1795/96	Not available	Provincial	Casters, pair, baluster form with reeded shoulders and rims, detachable baluster covers	Hughes p63
1813/14	WP	Edinburgh	Caster, no details	Sotheby's Melbourne AU May 2, 2005 #534
1814/15	Not available	Edinburgh	Caster, vase form, 3 ½" ht, 4oz 1d	Christie's Lanarkshire UK 1998 #54
1819/20	George McHattie	Edinburgh	Pepper caster, stylized thistle shape, gilt interior, domed detachable cover, crest of Stirling, probably of Keir, Perthshire, 4" ht, 4oz	Christie's Melbourne AU 2005 #351
1830/31	Adam Elder	Edinburgh	Pepper caster, 3.3.oz	National Museums of Scotland MEQ 857
1831/32	W P Cunningham	Edinburgh	Caster, pierced in 18th century style	Nicholas Shaw Catalog 2005 p99
1893/94	Ferguson & McBean	Inverness Edinburgh assay	Pepper castor, 3 5/8" ht, 2.4oz	Christie's London UK 2001 #101
1893/94	Ferguson & McBean	Inverness Edinburgh Assay	Casters, pair, silver-mounted wood, baluster wood body with carved Celtic knot motifs, spreading foot with silver rim, pierced silver cap, 7 ½" ht	Christie's London UK 2006 #1663
1899/1900	Dunningham & Co	Aberdeen Edinburgh Assay	Caster, silver-mounted wood, baluster wood body with Celtic motifs, silver foot mount and silver bun top with beaded rim, 6 ½" ht	Christie's London UK 1999 #55
			Caster, silver-mounted horn, lighthouse form with tapering cylindrical horn body, plain silver rim, simply pierced high-domed cover with ball finial, 10" ht	

YEAR	MAKER	LOCATION	DESCRIPTION	SOURCE
1904/05	Hamilton & Inches	Edinburgh	Caster, sugar, octagonal baluster form with pierced and engraved cover and acorn finial	Christie's Lanarkshire UK 1997 #595
1915/16	Hamilton & Inches	Edinburgh	Casters, pair of novelty peppers, modeled as artillery, cylindrical form with screw fitting bases, engraved bands to simulate fuse caps, 3 1/3" ht	Bonhams London UK 2005 377
KITCHEN PEPPERS/ DREDGERS				
1708/09	Not available	Edinburgh	Kitchen pepper/dredger with handle	Connoisseur Magazine 1943 vol 112 p68
1723/24	John Seatoun	Edinburgh	Kitchen pepper/dredger, cylindrical, domed cover, scroll handle, 2 ¾" ht	Scottish Art Academy Exhibit 1939 #428
1730 ca	Patrick Scott	Banff	Kitchen pepper/dredger, cylindrical, domed cover, scroll handle, 3" ht	Scottish Art Academy Exhibit 1939 #418
1750 ca	James Ker	Edinburgh	Kitchen pepper pot, scroll handle, crested within a collar, catalog confusing in description, 2 ¾" ht, 1.8oz	Sotheby's Gleneagles August 29, 1983 #498
1750 ca	James Welsh	Edinburgh	Kitchen pepper pot, mm only, cylindrical, crested, with scroll handle and molded borders, flat detachable cover with turret dispenser, 2 ¾" ht, 2oz	Sotheby's Gleneagles September 1, 1981 #439
1750 ca	Lothian & Robertson	Edinburgh	Kitchen pepper, cylindrical, on molded rim foot, with ring handle, raised cover pierced with scrolls, 2 ¼" ht, 2oz	Christie's February 17, 1977 #107 Thomas Lumley, Ltd Sotheby's NY USA April 23, 1983 #296
1750 ca	James Ker	Edinburgh	Kitchen pepper pot, scroll handle, crested within a collar, catalog confusing in description, 2 ¾" ht, 1.8oz	Sotheby's Gleneagles August 29, 1983 #498
1756/57	Patrick Robertson	Edinburgh	Kitchen pepper pot, presumably, catalog description confusing, crested with a motto, 2 ¼" ht, 1.4oz	Sotheby's Gleneagles August 29, 1983 #499
1760/61	James Hewitt	Edinburgh	Kitchen pepper/dredger, cylindrical, domed cover, ring handle, 2 ¼" ht	Scottish Art Academy Exhibit 1939 #425 Milne-Davidson Collection
1790ca	William Robertson	Edinburgh	Kitchen pepper, plain drum shaped with side handle, engrave with a crest, 2 ¾" ht, 2.5oz	Christie's London UK 2004 #595

YEAR	MAKER	LOCATION	DESCRIPTION	SOURCE
PEPPER POTS				
1730 ca	Robert Luke	Glasgow	Pepper caster, plain, pear shaped, on spreading foot, girdle, detachable bun top, crest of Lathom, 4" ht, 4.5oz	Shaw Collection Christie's Glasgow March 29, 1983 #49
1730/31	William Aytoun	Edinburgh	Bun pepper pot, baluster body with molded girdle, otherwise plain, bun top, on circular foot, 4 ½" ht, 3.8oz	Sotheby's March 25, 1965 #135
1730/31	*William Aytoun*	*Edinburgh*	*Bun pepper pot, baluster form, with molded edge to the joined body, on stepped foot, 4" ht, 4oz*	*Lyon & Turnbull The Murray Collection August 28, 2003 #176*
1730/31	William Aytoun	Edinburgh	Bun pepper pot, baluster body, on circular molded base, applied girdle, partly pierced and detachable low domed cover, 5" ht (sold as part of a lot)	Christie's NY USA October 16-17, 1995 #426
1740 ca	William Gilchrist	Edinburgh	Spice pot, mm only, circular with cover, plain, engraved with crest of a fish over the initial "V", 2 7/8" ht, 1.6oz	Phillips Edinburgh October 22, 1982 #163
1741/42	Robert Gordon	Edinburgh	Pepper pot, plain, vase shaped, on circular foot, rib about body and rim, pierced bun shaped cover, bell shaped finial, 4 ½" ht, 3.5oz	Christie's Scotland Nov 25-27, 1997 #112
1753/54	James Gilliland	Edinburgh	Pepper box, Sir Home	Cripps p 150
1760 ca	Not available	Edinburgh	Pepper pot, no detail	The Maple Swan Collection
1760/61	Patrick Robertson	Edinburgh	Pepper pot, no details	The Maple Swan Collection
1760/61	William Dempster	Edinburgh	Pepper pot, no details	The Maple Swan Collection
1760/61	Lothian & Robertson	Edinburgh	Pepper pot, no details	The Maple Swan Collection
1760/61	Lothian & Robertson	Edinburgh	Pepper pot, no details	The Maple Swan Collection
1760/61	Ker & Dempster	Edinburgh	Pepper pot, no details	The Maple Swan Collection
1760/61	Not available	Edinburgh	Pepper pot, no details	The Maple Swan Collection
1761/62	John Clark	Edinburgh	Kitchen pepper pot, cylindrical with ring handle, narrow sleeve on the cover with pierced thimble-like top, 2 ¾" ht, 2oz	Sotheby's Gleneagles August 29, 1983 #496
1761/62	William Taylor & Ker	Edinburgh	Pepper caster, no details	Jackson Marks p548 notes

YEAR	MAKER	LOCATION	DESCRIPTION	SOURCE
1766/67	Ker over striking another	Edinburgh	Pepper caster, plain vase shape, reeded molding at mid section, high domed cover pierced and engraved with flowerheads and foliage, acorn finial, mm over struck by that of Ker, 5 1/3" ht, 3.5oz	Christie's Glasgow January 31, 1984 #165
1772/73	Alexander Gardner	Edinburgh	Kitchen pepper pot, cylindrical form, with a loop handle, 2 ½" ht, 2oz	Sotheby's Gleneagles September 1, 1981 #440
1775/76	Patrick Robertson	Edinburgh	Pepper pot, no details	The Maple Swan Collection
1780/81	William Taylor	Edinburgh	Pepper pot, no details	The Maple Swan Collection
1781/82	Patrick Robertson	Edinburgh	Pepper pot, no details	The Maple Swan Collection
1781/82	J & W McKenzie	Edinburgh	Kitchen pepper pot, cylindrical form, loop handle	Phillips London May 27, 1994 #227
1785 ca	*I & WM*	*Edinburgh*	*Pepper cruet, probably James and William McKenzie*	*Sotheby's April 23, 1993 #296*
1790 ca	Robert Keay I	Perth	Pepper caster, no details	National Museums of Scotland MEQ 442
1800 ca	Robert Keay I	Perth	Pepper pot	The Maple Swan Collection
1800 ca	Francis Howden	Edinburgh	Pepper pot, no details	Dundee Museums and Art Galleries 1964-144
1817/18	George Fenwick	Edinburgh	Pepper pot, vase-shaped, 3 3/8" ht, 2oz 1d	Private Collection
1820 ca	Alexander Cameron	Dundee	Pepper pot, no details	The Maple Swan Collection
1825/26	James McKay	Edinburgh	Pepper pot, no details	The Maple Swan Collection
1831/32	William Cuningham	Edinburgh	Pepper pot, of baluster form, on circular foot, with knop finial, 3 ½", 2.4oz	Bonhams Sale 15120 Aug 22, 2007 #24
1890/91	R & H. B. Kirkwood	Edinburgh	Pepperettes, pair, or sand casters, 2" ht, 3.4oz	JH Bourdon-Smith Catalog Autumn 2005, #46, p19

Church Silver

Plate 12. A Communion Cup 1680s ca by William Lindsay for the Church of Montrose.
Photograph courtesy of The Maple Swan Collection.

Communion Cups

Plate 13. A Communion Cup 1658 ca by Edward Cleghorne I, Edinburgh, for
St. Leonard's Church, St. Andrew's
Courtesy of The Maple Swan Collection.

YEAR	MAKER	LOCATION	DESCRIPTION	SOURCE
			CHURCH SILVER	
	COMMUNION CUPS			
1563 dated	Henry Thomson Deacon James Cok I	Edinburgh	Communion cup, for the Kirk Session of Fogue	Finlay 1991 #23 Antiques Magazine vol 56 p272
1585/86	John Mosman Deacon John Mosman	Edinburgh	Communion cups, pair, for the Kirk Session of Roseneath	Holland p205 Finlay 1991 #23
1596-1600	Hugh Lindsay Assayer – David Heriot	Edinburgh	Communion cups, pair, engraved "For the Kirk of Currie 1657", 6 ½" di	Jackson Marks p408 National Museums of Scotland L436.1
1608-10	Gilbert Kirkwood Deacon Robert Dennistoun	Edinburgh	Communion beakers, pair, donated by Lady Marion Douglas, Kirk Session of Arbirlot, 5 3/16" ht	Burns pp 293-294
1611-13	George Crawford Deacon David Palmer	Edinburgh	Communion cups, pair, one engraved with the name of each Parish, Kirk Session of Fala and Soutra (which later merged)	Burns p260
1615-17	George Robertson I Deacon George Crawford	Edinburgh	Communion cup, Kirk Session of Dumfermline	National Museums of Scotland H.1996.206
1617-19	Gilbert Kirkwood	Edinburgh	Communion cups, pair, Kirk Session of Dalry, 7 3/16" ht	Burns p 263
1617-19	Gilbert Kirkwood	Edinburgh	Communion cups, pair, Kirk Session of Glencairn, 7 ¾" ht	Burns p276
1617-19	Gilbert Kirkwood	Edinburgh	Communion cups, pair, Kirk Session of Cambuslang, 7 ¾" ht	Burns p 268
1617-19	Gilbert Kirkwood	Edinburgh	Communion cups, pair, Kirk Session of Carstairs, 7" ht	Burns p 266
1617-19	Gilbert Kirkwood	Edinburgh	Communion cups, Kirk Session of Kirkwall, 9 ½" ht	Burns pp 269-270
1617-19	Gilbert Kirkwood	Edinburgh	Communion cup, Kirk Session of Fyvie, 7 5/8" ht	Burns pp 267-268
1617-19	Gilbert Kirkwood	Edinburgh	Communion cups, pair, Kirk Session of Penpont, 8 ¼" ht	Burns p269
1617-19	George Crawford Deacon John Lindsay	Edinburgh	Communion cups, pair, Kirk Session of Cawdor, 7 7/8" ht	Burns pp261-262
1617-19	John Lindsay maker and Deacon	Edinburgh	Communion cups, pair, Kirk Session of Closeburn, 7 7/16" ht	Burns p275

YEAR	MAKER	LOCATION	DESCRIPTION	SOURCE
1617-19	George Robertson I Deacon John Lindsay	Edinburgh	Communion cup, pair, Kirk Session of Holywood, 5 5/16" ht	Burns p263
1617-19	George Robertson I Deacon John Lindsay	Edinburgh	Communion cup, pair, Kirk Session of Dumfries	Jackson Marks p541
1617-19	George Robertson I	Edinburgh	Communion cups, pair, Kirk Session of Coulter	Burns p 275
1617-19	Thomas Thomson Deacon John Lindsay	Edinburgh	Communion cups, pair, Kirk Session of Middlebie, 7 13/16" ht	Burns p266
1617-19	George Crawford Deacon John Lindsay	Edinburgh	Communion cups, pair, Kirk Session of Penicuik	Burns Appx VI p638
1617-19	Thomas Thomson Deacon John Lindsay	Edinburgh	Communion cups, Kirk Session of Ecclefechan	Jackson Marks p541
1617-19	George Crawford	Edinburgh	Communion cup, no details	Jackson Marks p541
1617-19	Gilbert Kirkwood	Edinburgh	Communion cups, pair, Balmaghie parish church	Finlay 1881 #28 Burns p265 National Museums of Scotland KJ L1979.9-10
1617-19	Thomas Cleghorne I Assayer – John Lindsay	Edinburgh	Communion cup, Currie Kirk session	National Museums of Scotland L.463
1619-21	Gilbert Kirkwood Deacon James Dennistoun	Edinburgh	Communion cups, pair, Kirk Session of Straiton	Jackson Marks p541
1619-21	Gilbert Kirkwood Deacon James Dennistoun	Edinburgh	Communion cups, pair, Kirk Session of Blantyre, 7 ½" ht	Burns p268
1619-21	George Crawford	Edinburgh	Communion cups, 4, Kirk Session of Inveresk, 8 5/8" ht	Burns pp212-213
1621-23	George Robertson I	Edinburgh	Communion cups, 2 separate pairs, for the Kirk Session Town Church, 7 ¾" ht	Burns p196-197 St. Andrews
1621-23	Gilbert Kirkwood	Edinburgh	Communion cups, pair, Kirk Session of Inchture	1st and 2nd Lord Kinnaird, Burns p 275

YEAR	MAKER	LOCATION	DESCRIPTION	SOURCE
1621-23	Gilbert Kirkwood	Edinburgh	The Dalrymple Hay Cup, initialed "S/TH" and "D/MH" for the Hays used both as a communion cup and a baptismal basin in successive generations of the Dalrymple Hays	Sir Thomas Hays Burns p262
1621-23	George Robertson I	Edinburgh	Communion beaker, first secular and later donated to the church in 1630, Kirk Session of Methlick, 5 7/8" ht	Burns pp 296-297
1623-25	George Crawford	Edinburgh	Communion cup, Kirk Session of Beith, 8 1/16" ht	Burns p 263
1623-25	Gilbert Kirkwood	Edinburgh	Communion cup, presented to the church later in 1636, Kirk Session of Aberchirder	Burns p208
1623-25	Gilbert Kirkwood	Edinburgh	Communion cups, 2, engraved and dated with different years, 1618 and 1645, Kirk Session of Carnwarth, 6 11/16" ht	Burns pp 209-210
1623-25	Gilbert Kirkwood	Edinburgh	Communion cups, pair, Kirk Session of Tynron, 7 7/8" ht	Burns p269
1630 ca	William Anderson	Aberdeen	The Fintray Communion Cup, for Fintray Parish Church, possibly the earliest known marked piece of Aberdeen silver, the piece mis-ascribed in Jackson to Alexander Reid of Edinburgh	Jackson Marks p541
1631 ca	Robert Gairdyne	Dundee	Communion cups, pair, engraved inscription dated 1631, Kirk Session of Brechin	Burns illustrated p 382
1633 ca	Thomas Kirkwood	Edinburgh	Communion cup, presented in 1633, Kirk Session of Inverkeithny, 7 ½" ht	Burns p208
1633 ca	Thomas Cleghorne I	Edinburgh	Communion cups, pair, Greyfriars	National Museums of Scotland L.1950.20-21
1633-35	Thomas Kirkwood Deacon George Crawford	Edinburgh	Communion cup, Kirk Session of Aberchirder, 7 9/16" ht	Burns p208
1633-35	Adam Lamb Deacon George Crawford	Edinburgh	Communion cup, Kirk Session of Greyfriars, 8 ¼" ht	Burns pp 232-233
1634 ca	Robert Gairdyne	Dundee	Communion cups, pair, engraved below rim "FOR KILSPINDIE AND RAIT 1634" and the initials "M/DW", Kirk Session of Kilspindie	Burns illustrated p 383 On loan to Perth City Art Gallery & Museum
1635-37	Thomas Kirkwood	Edinburgh	Communion cup, Kirk Session of Inverkeithny, 7 ½" ht	Burns p209

YEAR	MAKER	LOCATION	DESCRIPTION	SOURCE
1636 ca	Alexander Lindsay	Dundee	Communion cups, Kirk Session of Kettins, 7 3/8" ht, 4 ½" di bowl	Jackson Marks 1989 p599 Burns p384
1636 ca	Alexander Lindsay	Dundee	Communion cups, Kirk Session of Belhevie, 7 5/16" ht, 3 7/8" di bowl	Jackson Marks 1989 p599 Burns p 384-385
1637-39	John Scott (Maker and Deacon)	Edinburgh	Communion cups, either a pair or 4, Kirk Session of South Leith	Jackson Marks p542
1637-39	John Wardlaw Deacon John Scott	Edinburgh	Communion cup, engraved at the lip "For the Kirk of Newbatl", on baluster stem, a plain quatrefoil die stamped collet above the domed foot, Kirk Session of Newbattle, 7" ht, 19.8oz	Sotheby's London UK June 5, 1997 #48 Sotheby's London UK June 7, 2005 #133
1637-39 or 1646-48	Adam Lamb Deacon John Scott	Edinburgh	Communion cups, pair, Kirk Session of Paisley Abbey, 9 ¼" ht	Burns pp 270-272
1638/39	George Crawford	Edinburgh	Communion cup, date engraved is 1638, Kirk Session of Arbuthnot, 10 ½" ht	Burns pp 272-274
1640-42	Patrick Borthwick	Edinburgh	Communion cups, pair, Kirk Session of Tollbooth, 8 13/16" ht	Burns p234
1640-42	John Scott Acting Deacon John Fraser	Edinburgh	Communion cups, pair, Kirk Session of Canongate,	Jackson Marks p542
1640-42	John Scott Acting Deacon John Fraser	Edinburgh	Communion cups, pair, Kirk Session of St. Giles, Edinburgh, 10 1/16" ht	Jackson Marks p542
1640-42	John Scott	Edinburgh	Communion cups, pair, Kirk Session of Kinghorn, 7 11/16"	Burns pp277-278
1640-42	John Scott Acting Deacon John Fraser	Edinburgh	Communion cups, pair, Kirk Session of South Leith, 9" ht	Jackson Marks p542
1640-42	Nicoll Trotter Acting Deacon John Fraser	Edinburgh	Communion cups, Kirk Session of Tollbooth, Edinburgh	Burns p215
1642 ca	Robert Gairdyne	Dundee	Communion cup, single cup with wide shallow bowl on slender stem, made in Edinburgh 1637-39 by John Fraser, deacon John Scott, Kirk Session of Monifeith, 7 ¾" ht, 2" depth of bowl, 6 ¾" di bowl, 4 5/16" di foot	Burns illustrated pp 385-389

YEAR	MAKER	LOCATION	DESCRIPTION	SOURCE
1642 ca	Walter Melville	Aberdeen	Communion beaker, beautifully engraved to match the earlier Ellon cup made in Amsterdam in 1634, Kirk Session of Ellon, 7 1/8" ht, 3 1/2" di rim, 3 1/4" di foot	Burns pp 427-428
1642-44	Patrick Borthwick	Edinburgh	Communion cups, pair, Northwest Parish	National Museums of Scotland 1979.4-5
1643 dated	Nicol Trotter	Edinburgh	Communion cups, pair, Northwest Parish, dated 1643	National Museums of Scotland KJ L1979.6-7
1643-48	Robert Gairdyne	Dundee	Communion cups, pair, Kirk Session of Brechin, engraved inscriptions on cups each include a different date 1643 and 1648, donor of earlier cup was Mr. Alexander Bisset, donor of later cup was Mr. William Rait, successive ministers of the parish, Mr. Rait became Principal of King's College, Aberdeen,	Burns illustrated p 382-383
1644/45	John Wardlaw	Edinburgh	Communion cups, pair	National Museums of Scotland KJ L.1950.22-23
1644-46	Patrick Borthwick Deacon Adam Lamb (continued)	Edinburgh	Communion cups, pair of a set of 4 cups, Kirk Session of Haddington, 9 1/4" ht	Sotheby's London UK Nov 30, 1972 #113 S J Phillips Ltd London UK Ltd, London UK Burns p234
1644-46	Patrick Borthwick Deacon Adam Lamb	Edinburgh	Communion cups, pair of a set of 4 cups, Kirk Session of Haddington 9 1/4" ht	Sotheby's London November 30, 1972 #114 S J Phillips Ltd London UK Burns p234
1644-46	George Cleghorne Deacon Adam Lamb	Edinburgh	Communion cup, broad bowl, knopped stem, strong pedestal base, one of 4 cups made for the Kirk of Newbattle, Kirk Session of Newbattle, 7" ht, 17.7 oz	Sotheby's June 5, 1997 #147
1644-46	Thomas Cleghorne Deacon Adam Lamb	Edinburgh	Communion cup, Kirk Session of Newbattle, 7 1/2" ht 19.3oz	Sotheby's June 5, 1997 #? Sotheby's November 6, 1997 #?
1644-46	Andrew Dennistoun Deacon Adam Lamb	Edinburgh	Communion cup, Kirk Session of Newbattle, 7" ht, 18oz	Jackson Marks p542
1645/46	Patrick Borthwick	Edinburgh	Communion cups, pair	Brett p124
1645 ca	Patrick Borthwick	Edinburgh	Communion cups, 2 pairs	Apollo November 1972 vol 96 p164

132

YEAR	MAKER	LOCATION	DESCRIPTION	SOURCE
1645 ca	*Patrick Borthwick Deacon Adam Lamb*	*Edinburgh*	*Communion cup, band resembling ermine around exterior edge of rim, hexagonal shaped stem, engraved on bowl "For the Kirke of Hadingtoune 1645", 9 ¼" ht, 8 3/16" di rim*	*Museum of Fine Art, Boston USA 1973.172*
1646-48	John Scott	Edinburgh	Communion cups, pair, Carsphairn, cups engraved with the date 1647, 8" ht, Kirk Session of Carsphairn	Burns p276
1648-50	Alexander Scott	Edinburgh	Communion beakers, pair, Kirk Session of Biggar, 6 ½" ht	Burns pp303-304
1649 ca	Thomas Moncur	Edinburgh	Communion beaker, "For the Church at Kearn" inscribed on the base, part of the communion plate at Kearn, Aberdeenshire, 6" ht	Nova Scotia Museum, vol 6, #3 Spring 1981 p16 "The Occasional"
1649-50	Thomas Scott Deacon George Cleghorne	Edinburgh	Communion cup, Kirk Session of Dalmellington, 7 ¾" ht	Burns p274
1651-53 or 1657-59	Robert Gibson Deacon James Fairbairn	Edinburgh	Communion cups, 3, Kirk Session of Dalkeith, 7 ½" ht,	Burns p214
1651-53 or 1657-59	John Wardlaw Deacon James Fairbairn	Edinburgh	Communion cups, Kirk Session of Dunbar	Jackson Marks p542
1651-53	Patrick Borthwick Deacon James Fairbairn	Edinburgh	Communion cup, Kirk Session of Dalkeith, 7 ½" ht	Burns p274
1655/57	James Symontoun	Edinburgh	Communion cups, pair, Kirk Session of Keir, 8 3/16" ht	Burns p214
1657 ca	George Robertson II	Edinburgh	Communion cups, pair, Walston church	National Museums of Scotland H.1992.1890
1657-59	Edward Cleghorne I	Edinburgh	Communion cups, pair, Kirk Session of Dalgety, 7" ht	Burns p214
1657-59	Alexander Scott	Edinburgh	Communion cup, Kirk Session of the Town Church, St. Andrews, 9 1/8" ht	Burns pp 197-198
1657-59	John Wardlaw	Edinburgh	Communion cups, 4, Kirk Session of Dunbar, dated 1657, 8 1/8" ht	Burns p226
1658/59	Edward Cleghorne I	Edinburgh	Communion cup, the St. Leonard's Kirk Cup	The Maple Swan Collection
1659	*Edward Cleghorne I Deacon James*	*Edinburgh*	*Communion cup, plain deep bowl, foot chased with a band of egg and dart, baluster stem, inscribed "St. Leonard's Kirk 1659", Kirk Session of St.*	*Christie's Scotland November 19-20, 1986 #298*

YEAR	MAKER *Fairbairn*	LOCATION	DESCRIPTION Andrews, 7 5/8" ht, 13oz	SOURCE
1659-61	Edward Cleghorne I Deacon James Fairbairn	Edinburgh	Communion cup, Kirk Session of Abercorn, 8 1/16" ht	Burns p225
1659-61	Edward Cleghorne I	Edinburgh	Communion cup, Kirk Session of Bo'ness, 7 7/8" ht	Burns p226
1660 ca	Robert Gairdyne	Dundee	Communion cups, pair, Kirk Session of Kilspindie	Perth City Art Gallery and Museum
1661-63	Patrick Borthwick	Edinburgh	Communion cups, pair, with the arms of the donor George Trotter of Charterhall, Kirk Session of Fogo, 8 15/16" ht	Burns pp280-281
1663-65 or 1671-73 or 1679-81	Alexander Scott Deacon Edward Cleghorne I	Edinburgh	Communion cup, Kirk Session of Linlithgow, 8 3/8" ht	Burns pp 237-238
1663-84	Edward Cleghorne I Deacon Patrick Borthwick	Edinburgh	Quaich used as a Communion cup, Kirk Session of Alvah, may also be listed under quaichs, 6 3/8" ht	Burns p401
1665-67	AL Deacon James Symontoun	Edinburgh	Communion cup, Kirk Session of Wemyss, said to be by Andrew Law but too early	Jackson Marks p543
1665-67	AL Deacon James Symontoun	Edinburgh	Communion cup, (not entirely clear that it's a communion cup), said to be by Andrew Law but too early	Glasgow Exhibition 1911
1665-67	William Law	Edinburgh	Communion cups, pair, Kirk Session of Glencorse	Burns pp278-279
1665-67	William Law	Edinburgh	Communion cups, pair, presentation inscription dated 1773, arms of the donor Sir William Purves of Woodhouselee, Bt., Kirk Session of Mid-Calder, 7 7/16" ht	Burns p228
1667-69	Alexander Scott	Edinburgh	Communion cups, 4, Kirk Session of Cupar	Burns Appx. VI, p635
1667 dated	Thomas Lindsay II	Dundee	Communion beakers, pair, St Vigeans, 5 3/16" ht, 3 7/16" di lip	Jackson Marks 1989 p599 Burns p297-298
1669-71	Alexander Scott Deacon Alexander Reid	Edinburgh	Communion cups beaker-shaped, presented in 1676, Kirk Session of Arbroath, 5 ¼" ht	Burns p 298-299

YEAR	MAKER	LOCATION	DESCRIPTION	SOURCE
1669-71	William Law	Edinburgh	Communion cup, presentation date of 1670, Deacon's mark obscured by a repair, Kirk Session of Saltoun	Burns pp 220-221
1671 ca	William Lindsay	Montrose	Communion cup, 8 ¾" ht, 5 3/16" di bowl, 4 1/8" depth bowl, 4 ¾" di foot, Kirk Session of Forfar	Burns p 396
1671 ca	Patrick Gairdyne	St Andrews	Communion cups, pair, Kirk Session of Saint Andrews, 7" ht, 8" di bowl, 5 11/16" di foot	Burns p 198-9
1671-78	Alexander Galloway	Aberdeen Possibly	Communion beakers, pair, decorated with a series of birds, Kirk Session of Turriff	Burns p295
1671-73	William Law	Edinburgh	Communion cup, inscription dated 1673, Kirk Session of North Leith, 7 7/8" ht	Burns p227, illustrated opposite p216
1674/75	James Cockburn Deacon Alexander Reid	Edinburgh	Communion cup, Kirk Session of Lingformacus, 9 13/16" ht	Burns p286
1674-76	Alexander Reid	Edinburgh	Communion cups, pair, arms of the donor David Scrymgeour of Bowhill, Kirk Session of Auctherderran	Burns pp281-283
1675ca	George Rolland	Edinburgh	Communion cup, mm only, inscription dated 1671, note Rolland was not free until 1675 so possibly a different maker, Kirk Session of Kennoway, 9 5/8" ht	Burns pp314-316
1675-77	William Law	Edinburgh	Communion cups, pair, mm only so date assumed, Kirk Session of Aberlady, 9 ¾" ht	Burns p287
1675-77	William Law	Edinburgh	Communion cups, pair, donation inscription dated 1677, mm only, Kirk Session of Kilwinning, 7" ht	Burns pp316-317
1676 ca	Alexander Reid	Edinburgh	Communion cups, pair, cups altered with only the mm readable, presentation inscription dated 1676, Kirk Session of Muiravonside, 9 ½" ht	Burns p286
1676 ca	Not available	Montrose	Communion cups, pair, engraved, FOR THE CHURCH GLAMIS 1676", bowl is engraved with the arms of the Earl of Strathmore & Kinghorne (d. 1695), the shield surmounted by the earl's coronet, arms between wing-like plumes, date 1676 below the plumes, Kirk Session of Glamis	Burns p 396
1677-79	William Law Deacon Alexander Reid	Edinburgh	Communion cups, pair, Kirk Session of Ballingry, 9 ½" ht	Burns pp 283-284

YEAR	MAKER	LOCATION	DESCRIPTION	SOURCE
1669-71	William Law	Edinburgh	Communion cup, presentation date of 1670, Deacon's mark obscured by a repair, Kirk Session of Saltoun	Burns pp 220-221
1671 ca	William Lindsay	Montrose	Communion cup, 8 ¾" ht, 5 3/16" di bowl, 4 1/8" depth bowl, 4 ¾" di foot, Kirk Session of Forfar	Burns p 396
1671 ca	Patrick Gairdyne	St Andrews	Communion cups, pair, Kirk Session of Saint Andrews, 7" ht, 8" di bowl, 5 11/16" di foot	Burns p 198-9
1671-78	Alexander Galloway	Aberdeen Possibly	Communion beakers, pair, decorated with a series of birds, Kirk Session of Turriff	Burns p295
1671-73	William Law	Edinburgh	Communion cup, inscription dated 1673, Kirk Session of North Leith, 7 7/8" ht	Burns p227, illustrated opposite p216
1674/75	James Cockburn Deacon Alexander Reid	Edinburgh	Communion cup, Kirk Session of Lingformacus, 9 13/16" ht	Burns p286
1674-76	Alexander Reid	Edinburgh	Communion cups, pair, arms of the donor David Scrymgeour of Bowhill, Kirk Session of Auctherderran	Burns pp281-283
1675ca	George Rolland	Edinburgh	Communion cup, mm only, inscription dated 1671, note Rolland was not free until 1675 so possibly a different maker, Kirk Session of Kennoway, 9 5/8" ht	Burns pp314-316
1675-77	William Law	Edinburgh	Communion cups, pair, mm only so date assumed, Kirk Session of Aberlady, 9 ¾" ht	Burns p287
1675-77	William Law	Edinburgh	Communion cups, pair, donation inscription dated 1677, mm only, Kirk Session of Kilwinning, 7" ht	Burns pp316-317
1676 ca	Alexander Reid	Edinburgh	Communion cups, pair, cups altered with only the mm readable, presentation inscription dated 1676, Kirk Session of Muiravonside, 9 ¼" ht	Burns p286
1676 ca	Not available	Montrose	Communion cups, pair, engraved, FOR THE CHURCH GLAMIS 1676", bowl is engraved with the arms of the Earl of Strathmore & Kinghorne (d. 1695), the shield surmounted by the earl's coronet, arms between wing-like plumes, date 1676 below the plumes, Kirk Session of Glamis	Burns p 396
1677-79	William Law Deacon Alexander Reid	Edinburgh	Communion cups, pair, Kirk Session of Ballingry, 9 ¼" ht	Burns pp 283-284

YEAR	MAKER	LOCATION	DESCRIPTION	SOURCE
1682 ca	William Lindsay	Montrose	Communion cups, pair, Kirk Session of Fordoun, presentation inscription dated 1682, 7 ½" ht, 4 7/8" di bowl	Burns p398
1682/83	Not available	Edinburgh	Communion cups, pair, ordered and completed in May 1683, Kirk Session of Wittingham	Burns p322
1682/83	James Penman	Edinburgh	Communion cups, pair, Kirk Session of Ratho, 8 1/8" ht	Burns pp238-240
1682/83	Mrs. William Law	Edinburgh	Communion cup, Kirk Session of Culross, 8 9/16" ht	Jackson Marks p 543 Burns pp228-229
1683 ca	William Lindsay	Montrose	Communion cups, pair, presentation inscription dated 1683, Kirk Session of Aberlemno, 7 ½" ht, 4 11/16" di bowl	Burns p 399
1683 ca	William Lindsay	Montrose	Communion cups, pair, presentation inscription dated 1683, Kirk Session of Laurencekirk, 7 15/16" ht, 5 1/16" di bowl	Burns pp 399-400
1683/84	Thomas Yorstoun	Edinburgh	Communion cup, Kirk Session of Pebbles 8 ¾" ht	Jackson Marks p543 Burns pp317-319
1683/84	John Borthwick	Edinburgh	Communion cups, pair, cups were not in assay master's account, hence they may have been marked off the books, Kirk Session of Kingsbarns, 8 7/8" ht	Burns p317
1683/84	John Law	Edinburgh	Communion cups, 4, given by John Douglas of Raynie in 1682 and possibly paid for then, Kirk Session of Kirkcaldy, 8 9/16" ht	Burns p289
1683/84	William Law	Edinburgh	Communion cups, pair, Kirk Session of Yester, 8 13/16" ht	Burns p289
1683/84	James Penman	Edinburgh	Communion cups, pair, Kirk Session of Meigle, 7 1/8" ht	Burns pp 289-290
1685/86	James Penman	Edinburgh	Communion cups, pair, from the French Church in Edinburgh	National Museums of Scotland IL.2003.46
1685/86	*James Penman*	*Edinburgh*	*Communion cups, pair, 8 ¾" ht, 34oz 3d*	*Sotheby's November 6, 1969 #191*
1685/86	James Penman	Edinburgh	Communion cups, Kirk Session of Pittenweem	Jackson Marks p543
1685/86	James Cockburn	Edinburgh	Communion cups, pair, Kirk Session of Auchtermuchty, 8 3/16" ht	Burns p320
1685/86	James Cockburn	Edinburgh	Communion cup, Kirk Session Rosemarkie, 8" ht	Burns pp320-322
1685/86	James Penman	Edinburgh	Communion cups, pair, presentation inscription is dated 1679, Kirk Session of Ceres	Burns p319

YEAR	MAKER	LOCATION	DESCRIPTION	SOURCE
1685/86	James Penman	Edinburgh	Communion cups, gifted in 1685, Kirk Session of St Ninian's, Stirling, 7 13/16" ht	Burns pp226-227
1686 ca	James Cockburn	Edinburgh	Communion cup, date letter not present only year of 1686 indicated, Kirk Session of Cockpen, 6 ¾" ht	Burns pp221-222
1686/87	James Penman	Edinburgh	Communion Cups, Kirk Session of Dunblane, 6 13/16" ht	*Jackson Marks p 543* Burns p231
1686/87	James Penman	Edinburgh	Communion beakers, pair, beaker form, applied molded foot, Kirk Session of Drumblade, 6 3/16" ht	Burns pp299-300
1686/87	James Penman	Edinburgh	Communion cups, pair, *beaker form* with flared rims, finely engraved with vine leaves and bunches of grapes, inscribed "the blood…*1688*", *Kirk Session of Leslie*	Aberdeen City Art Gallery and Museum
1687 ca	Robert Gairdyne	Perth	Communion cup, pair, bowl of bucket form, similar to those of the church of Innerpeffray and Kinnoull, inscription below the rim reads "GIFTED BY THE INHABITANTS OF COWPAR IN ANGWS FOR THE COMMNION SERVICE ANNO 1687", Kirk Session of Coupar-Angus, 7" ht, 4 5/16" di bowl, 3 1/8" depth bowl, 4" di foot	Burns illustrated p 394
1687	Robert Gairdyne	Perth	Communion cups, pair, Kirk Session of Innerpeffray, dated	How of Edinburgh Private Collection UK
1687/88	James Cockburn	Edinburgh	Communion cups, *for the Kirk Session of Sprouton*	Jackson Marks p 543
1687/88	James Penman	Edinburgh	Communion cups, pair, Kirk Session of Redgorton, 8 ½" ht	Burns p320
1688 ca	William Lindsay	Edinburgh	Communion cup, Montrose church, (Note: this may be the same or a mate to the prior Lindsay cup)	Clayton Christie's Book p183 #16 Christie's Glasgow July 7, 1984
1688	*James Penman*	*Edinburgh*	*Communion beakers, pair, each engraved "…for the use of the church in the Eucharist by William Watson, Leslie, 1688", for the Leslie church*	*Aberdeen Museums and Galleries* ABDAG011115
1688/89	Zaccharias Mellinus	Edinburgh	Communion chalice, The Forsyth Chalice, see also patens, *for use in the Catholic service*	Finlay 1991 p55 National Museums of Scotland IL2003.47.9
1689/90	James Cockburn	Edinburgh	Communion cups, pair, Kirk Session of Benholm, 7 7/8" ht	Burns p322
1689/90	William Scott	Edinburgh	Communion cup, Kirk Session of Temple, 6 11/16" ht	Jackson Marks p544 Burns p279-280

YEAR	MAKER	LOCATION	DESCRIPTION	SOURCE
1690 ca	Robert Gairdyne	Perth	Communion cup, lamb and flag mark for Perth, Kirk Session of Muthill, 7 3/8" ht, 4 ½" di bowl, 3 ½" depth bowl, 4 1/8" di foot	Burns pp 384-5
1690/91	James Cockburn	Edinburgh	Communion cups, Kirk Session of Bothkennar	Jackson Marks p544 Burns pp 330-331
1691 ca	George Walker	Aberdeen	Communion cups, Kirk Session of Monymusk	Jackson Marks 1989
1691/92	James Law	Edinburgh	Communion cup, for Falkland gift of Hays	Cripps p149
1691/92	James Cockburn	Edinburgh	Communion cups, pair, Kirk Session of Crawford	Burns Appx VI, p635
1691/92	Robert Inglis	Edinburgh	Communion cups, pair, larger of 2 pairs, Kirk Session of Hawick, 8 3/8" ht	Burns p323
1691/92	Robert Inglis	Edinburgh	Communion cups, pair, smaller of 2 pairs, Kirk Session of Hawick, 7 3/8" ht	Burns p323
1692 ca	William Scott I	Banff	Communion beakers, pair, underside of base inscribed "M/I * D/1692", initials are those of Mr. John Dunbar, minister of the parish from 1676-1716, Kirk Session of Cullen, 5 ¾" ht, 3 15/16" di lip, 3 1/6" di foot, 3/8" ht foot	Burns p 301
1692/93	Robert Inglis	Edinburgh	Communion cups, set of 4, goblet form with round knopped stem, Kirk Session of Lasswade, 9 1/8" ht	Burns p245
1692/93	Robert Inglis	Edinburgh	Communion cups, pair, this pair matches the pair made the following year for the same church by the same maker, Kirk Session of Prestonkirk	Burns Appx VI, p630
1692/93	Robert Inglis	Edinburgh	Communion cups, Kirk Session of Bothkennar, 8" ht	Jackson Marks p544 Burns 330
1693/94	Robert Inglis	Edinburgh	Communion cups, pair, these match the pair made the preceding year for the same church by the same maker, Kirk Session of Prestonkirk	Burns Appx. VI, p630
1693/94	Alexander Forbes	Edinburgh	Trinity College Kirk, engraved "For the North East Paroche"	National Museums of Scotland L.1987.8
1693/94	John Seatoun	Edinburgh	Communion cup, pair, Kirk Session of Kirriemuir, 6 5/16" ht	Jackson Marks p544 Burns pp279-280
1694 ca	George Walker	Aberdeen	Communion beakers, set of 4, from the Church of Auchreddy, 4 3/16" ht, 3 ½" di lip, 2 9/16' di foot, Kirk Session of Longside	Burns p 296 Aberdeen Museums and Galleries ABDAG0011129 on loan from the Kirk Session of the Parish of New Deer

YEAR	MAKER	LOCATION	DESCRIPTION	SOURCE
1894/95	James Penman	Edinburgh	Communion cup, Kirk Session of Abercorn, 8" ht	Burns p225
1895/96	Alexander Forbes	Edinburgh	Communion cups, pair, one cup for Borthwick, 7 ¾" ht	Jackson Marks p544 Burns p334
1695/96	Thomas Cleghorne	Edinburgh	Communion cups, pair, 9 13/16", Cleghorne paid June 29, 1696, Kirk Session of Prestonpans	Cripps p149 Burns pp423-325
1696 ca	James Cockburn	Edinburgh	Communion cups, pair, Kirk Session of Pittinain, 8 ½" ht	Burns p331
1696 ca	George Ziegler	Canongate	Communion cups, pair, Kirk Session of Bolton, cups possibly renewed	Burns p 367 Jackson Marks p954 National Museums of Scotland
1696/97	Robert Brock	Glasgow	Communion cup, engraved with the date 1897, Kirk Session of Hamilton	Jackson Marks p568
1697 ca	George Walker	Aberdeen	Communion cups, pair, Kirk Session of Fintry	Jackson Marks p583
1697/98	George Ziegler	Canongate	Communion cups, pair, for the Bolton parish, East Lothian, dated 1698	National Museums of Scotland KJ 318
1697/98	Thomas Ker	Edinburgh	Communion cups, pair, Kirk Session of Tynninghame now Whitekirk, 9 5/16" ht	Burns p327
1698 ca	Not available	Banff	Communion beakers, pair, inscribed as being given in 1698, bears the Banff town mark, Kirk Session of Cullen	Burns p 305
1698/99	John Luke	Glasgow	Communion cups, Kirk Session of Rutherglen	Burns p372
1698/99	Thomas Ker	Edinburgh	Communion cup from Trinity College Kirk	Jackson Marks p544 Finlay 1991 #55 National Museums of Scotland MEQ L1987.7
1699 ca	Not available mm rubbed	Inverness	Communion cup, Kirk Session of Kiltearne, 8 5/16" ht, 4 5/16" di bowl, 4 5/16" di foot	Burns illustrated p 391
1699/1700	Robert Brock	Glasgow	Communion cup, Kirk Session of St. Martin's	Burns p 370
1699/1700	Robert Inglis	Edinburgh	Communion cups, pair, goblet form with broad round-knopped stem, Kirk Session of Athelstaneford, 8" ht	Burns p245
1699/1700	Robert Brock	Glasgow	Communion cups, pair, Kirk Session of Strathblane	Jackson Marks p568

YEAR	MAKER	LOCATION	DESCRIPTION	SOURCE
1700 ca	George Walker	Aberdeen	Communion cups, Kirk Session of Longside	Jackson Marks
1700/01	Colin McKenzie	Edinburgh	Communion cups, Kirk Session of Dalserf	Jackson Marks p544, Burns pp331-332
1701/02	James Penman Maker and Assayer	Edinburgh	Communion cups, pair, Kirk Session of Dunning, 8 ¼" ht	Burns pp325-326
1701/02	John Luke II	Glasgow	Communion cups, pair, Kirk Session of Renfrew	Jackson Marks p568
1701/02	George Scott	Edinburgh	Communion cups, pair, Kirk Session of Gargunnock, 8 5/16" ht	Burns p325
1701/02	Thomas Cleghorne Assayer – James Penman	Edinburgh	Communion cup, no details	Untemeyer p167
1701/02	George Scott	Edinburgh	Communion cup, Kirk Session of New North Kirk	Cripps p149
1702ca	David Dunlop	Canongate	Communion cups, pair, Kirk Session of West Linton	Burns p 368
1702/03	Thomas Ker	Edinburgh	Communion cups, Kirk Session of Carlaverock, 7 3/8" ht, 23.7oz	Untermeyer Collection, Metropolitan Museum of Art, NY USA
1702/03	James Seatoun	Edinburgh	Communion cup, Kirk Session of Pittenweem	Cripps p149
1702	David Dunlop	Canongate	Communion cups, pair, dated 1702, Kirk Session of West Linton, 6 9/16" ht	Burns p 368
1702/03	Robert Bruce	Edinburgh	Communion cups, pair, Kirk Session of Rhynd, 9 5/8" ht	Burns pp362-363
1703 ca	George Walker	Aberdeen	Communion beakers, 4, bequeathed in part by Alexander Galloway, deceased former goldsmith in Aberdeen, Kirk Session of Longside, 6 9/16" ht, 4 3/8" di lip, ½" ht foot, 2 7/8" di foot	Burns p 305
1703/04	W I	Edinburgh	Communion cup, Kirk Session of New North Kirk	Cripps p149
1703/04	George Scott	Edinburgh	Communion cup, Kirk Session of New North Kirk	Cripps p149
1703/04	Robert Inglis	Edinburgh	Communion cup, Kirk Session of West St. Giles, Edinburgh, 8 5/16" ht	Burns p241
1703/04	Robert Inglis	Edinburgh	Communion cups, pair, Kirk Session of Lesmahagow, 10 1/16" ht	Burns pp247-248
1703/04	Thomas Cleghorne III	Edinburgh	Communion cups, pair, Kirk Session of Mertoun, 8 7/16" ht	Burns p328

YEAR	MAKER	LOCATION	DESCRIPTION	SOURCE
1703/04	George Walker	Aberdeen	Communion beakers, pair, for the Nigg Church	Aberdeen Museums and Galleries ABDAG001037 acquired in 1974 Burns pp332-333
1704/05	Thomas Ker	Edinburgh	Communion cups, pair, Kirk Session of Clackmannan, 8 13/16" ht	Burns p332
1704/05	Alexander Kincaid	Edinburgh	Communion cups, pair, foot and stem separated by a curved over hood, Kirk Session of Carmichael, 9 7/16" ht	
1704/05	William Law	Edinburgh	Communion cups, pair, Kirk Session of Fossoway, 9 1/8" ht	Burns p248
1704/05	Robert Bruce	Edinburgh	Communion cups pair, Kirk Session of Anworth, 9 3/16" ht	Burns p363
1704/05	Thomas Cumming	Glasgow	Communion cups, pair, dated 1704, Kirk Session of Kilpatrick	Jackson Marks p568
1704/05	Thomas Ker	Edinburgh	Communion cups, Kirk Session of St Michaels Dumfries, 8 5/8" ht	Cripps p149 Burns pp 333-334
1705/06	James Tait	Edinburgh	Communion cups, Kirk Session of Rattray	Jackson Marks p545 Burns Appx VI p636
1705/06	Colin McKenzie	Edinburgh	Communion cups, pair, Kirk Session of Strathaven	Burns Appx VI, p636
1706/07	Robert Inglis	Edinburgh	Communion cups, pair, Kirk Session of Balfron, 9 ¾" ht	Burns p249
1706/07	John Seatoun	Edinburgh	Communion cups, pair, goblet form with baluster stem, Kirk Session of Dunbarny, 9 ¼" ht	Burns p246
1707/08	Robert Bruce	Edinburgh	Communion cups, pair, Kirk Session of Monimail, 7 13/16" ht	Burns pp326-327
1707/08	Robert Inglis	Edinburgh	Communion cups, pair, Kirk Session of Whitekirk, 9 3/16" ht	Burns p249
1707/08	Walter Scott	Edinburgh	Communion cups, 4, given by retiring minister Reverend Tomas Wilkie, engraved date 1708, Kirk Session of Lady Yester's Kirk, 9 ¼" ht	Burns pp336-337
1707/08	William Ged	Edinburgh	Communion cups, Kirk Session of Crieff	Jackson Marks p545 Burns p336
1707/08	John Penman Jr	Edinburgh	Communion cups, inscribed "gifted 1709", Kirk Session of Broughton	Jackson Marks p545 Burns p336
1707/08	Robert Inglis	Edinburgh	Communion cup, Cromdale church Morayshire	Cripps p149
1708 ca	James/John Luke	Glasgow	Communion cups, 4, Kirk Session of Greenock,	Burns p 371-2

142

YEAR	MAKER	LOCATION	DESCRIPTION	SOURCE
1708 ca	James/John Luke	Glasgow	Communion cups, Kirk Session of Rutherglen	Burns p 372
1708 ca	William McLean	Inverness	Communion cup, presentation inscription to the "Church of Inneralin", dated 1708, Kirk Session of Inverallan	Burns p 392-3
1708/09	Mungo Yorstoun	Edinburgh	Communion cups, pair, Eddleston church, 9"ht	Cripps p149 Burns p355
1708/09	Robert Ker	Edinburgh	Communion cups, pair, donor Mr. James Guthrie, Irongray church, 8 ½" ht	Cripps p149 Burns p335
1708/09	Henry Bethune	Edinburgh	Communion cups, pair, Kirk Session of Kirkliston, 9 ½" ht	Burns pp242-244
1708/09	John Seatoun	Edinburgh	Communion cup, Kirk Session of St. Cyrus, 4 5/16" ht	Burns pp250-251
1709 ca	James/John Luke	Glasgow	Communion cups, pair, Kirk Session of Barony	Burns p 372
1709 ca	James/John Luke	Glasgow	Communion cup, 4, Kirk Session of Kilmarnock	Burns p 372-3
1710 ca	David Dunlop	Canongate	Communion cups, pair, sources and location unknown	Existence probable
1710/11	William Ged	Edinburgh	Communion cups, pair, cups acquired by the Parish in 1711, Kirk Session of Leuchars	Burns pp 225-2226
1710/11	Colin McKenzie	Edinburgh	Communion cups, pair, Kirk Session of Dirlton, 9 1/8" ht	Burns p363
1710/11	James Mitchelson	Edinburgh	Communion cups, one for Borthwick, no details	Jackson Marks p545
1711/12	Patrick Turnbull	Edinburgh	Communion cups, one for Penningham	Jackson Marks p545
1713/14	Alexander Kincaid	Edinburgh	Communion cups, 4, Kirk Session of Rothesay, 11 3/8" ht	Burns p359 and Appx VI p636
1714/15	Colin McKenzie	Edinburgh	Communion cups, pair, Kirk Session of Maybole, 9 1/8" ht	Burns p364
1714/15	Mungo Yorstoun	Edinburgh	Communion cups, Kirk Session of Maryton, Montrose	Jackson Marks p545 Glasgow Exhibition 1911
1715 ca	John Walker	Aberdeen	Communion cups, pair, Kirk Session of Marykirk	Burns p 636
1717/18	Patrick Turnbull	Edinburgh	Communion cups, pair, Kirk Session of Legerwood, 9 ¼" ht	Cripps p149 Burns p358

YEAR	MAKER	LOCATION	DESCRIPTION	SOURCE
1717/18	John Seatoun	Edinburgh	Communion cups, pair, Kirk Session of Corstorphine	Cripps p149 Burns pp231-232
1717/18	Robert Inglis	Edinburgh	Communion cup, Kirk Session of Beath, 8 ¼" ht	Burns p256
1717/18	Robert Inglis	Edinburgh	Communion cups, pair, Kirk Session of Errol, 8 5/16" ht	Burns p256
1717/18	Patrick Turnbull	Edinburgh	Communion cups, pair, Kirk Session of Westruther, 9 3/16" ht	Burns pp358-359
1718/19	Robert Inglis	Edinburgh	Communion cups pair, Kirk Session of Galashiels, 8 7/16" ht	Burns pp256-257
1719/20	Mungo Yorstoun	Edinburgh	Communion cups, pair, bell shaped body, engraved "Bought for the Kirk Session of Direlton 1720", 9" ht, 35.6oz	Sotheby's October 31, 1974 #145
1719/20	Henry Bethune	Edinburgh	Communion chalice, probably originally a Communion cup, bell shaped, probably later engraved with "HIS" and a cross motif within a sunburst, 18.6oz	Phillips Edinburgh September 20, 1985 #240 Phillips April 18, 1984 #171
1720 ca	Patrick Scott	Banff	Communion beakers, pair, Kirk Session of Cullen	Burns p 302
1720 ca	William Scott II	Banff	Communion beakers, pair, engraved with the arms of the donor, William Leslie of Birdsbank, Kirk Session of Cullen, 5 ¾" ht, 4" di lip, 3 1/16" di foot, 3/8" ht foot	Burns p 300-01
1720 ca	Patrick Scott	Banff	Communion Beaker, molded foot rim, gently flaring body, engraved with inscription "Dedicated to the Church of Boyndie by James Ogilvie of Culphin 1720", marks - mm 2X's, heart shaped punch, BANFF, 5 ¾" ht, 11.9oz	Bonhams August 21-23, 2003 #131
1720/21	IB	Glasgow	Communion cups, pair, Kirk Session of Douglas	Burns p 374
1720 ca	William Scott II	Banff	Communion beakers, pair, presentation inscription dated 1625, bear the arms of the donor, George Ogilvie, Kirk Session of Cullen, 5 5/8" ht, 4 1/8" di lip, 3 1/16" di foot, 9/16" ht foot	Burns p 302
1720/21	James Inglis	Edinburgh	Communion cups, pair, Kirk Session of Pencaitland	Jackson Marks p546
1721 ca	Robert Luke	Glasgow	Communion cups, pair, Kirk Session of New Kilpatrick	Burns p 373
1721/22	Henry Bethune	Edinburgh	Communion cups, pair, Kirk Session of Kelso, 7 ¾" ht	Burns pp253-254
1721/22	Charles Duncan	Edinburgh	Communion cups, pair, presented to the Parish by Reverend Daniels McKay in 1723, Kirk Session of Jedburgh, 10 1/16" ht	Burns p337 illustrated opposite p356

YEAR	MAKER	LOCATION	DESCRIPTION	SOURCE
1722/23	Charles Duncan or Charles Dickson	Edinburgh	Communion cups, Kirk Session of Ayr, dated 1722	Cripps p150
1722/23	Colin Campbell	Edinburgh	Communion cups, Kirk Session of Kinnaird	Jackson Marks p546 Burns p338
1723/24	Colin Campbell	Edinburgh	Communion cups, pair, similar to the Kinnaird cups by the same maker one year earlier, Kirk Session of Danziel, 8 3/16" ht	Burns p338
1724 ca	Simon McKenzie	Inverness	Communion cups, pair, Kirk Session of Forres, 9" ht, 5 ¼" di bowl, 4 ¼" di foot, 4 ½" depth bowl	Burns illustrated p 391-2
1724 dated	Simon McKenzie	Inverness	*The Forres Communion cups, pair, beaker shaped bowls, trumpet shaped stems with central knops, spreading domed feet, flared rims, engraved below flared lips with "GIVEN BY JOHN NICOLSON WRITER IN EDNR TO THE KIRK OF FORRESS ANNO 1643 AND REPAIRD ~: ANNO 1724 BY YE ANNUAL RENTS OF MORTIFICATIONS LEFT BY THE DONATOR TO THIS BURGH",*	Sotheby's Gleneagles August 30, 1973 #71 Silver Lyon, Ltd Private Collection UK Museum
1724/25	Henry Bethune	Edinburgh	Communion chalices, pair, with later covers, from Lord Doune, 8 3/8" ht	National Museums of Scotland L455.7-10
1725 ca	Robert Luke	Glasgow	Communion cups, pair, Kirk Session of Bonhill	Burns p 373-4
1725/26 or 24/25	David Mitchell	Edinburgh	Communion cups, pair, Kirk Session of Moneydie	Burns Appx VI p636
1725 ca	Patrick Gordon	Banff	Communion cup, Kirk Session of Auchterless	Jackson Marks p591
1726/27	Henry Bethune	Edinburgh	Communion cups, pair, dated 1726, Kirk Session of Forteviot, 10 3/8" ht	Burns p252 and Appx VI p635
1726-30 ca	Alexander Smith	Dundee	Communion cup, Kirk Session of Dundee	Jackson Marks p599 On loan to the Dundee Museum and Art Galleries 1074-1040
1727 ca	John Walker	Aberdeen	Communion cups, Kirk Session of Alford	Jackson Marks p583
1727 ca	John Walker	Aberdeen	Communion cups, Kirk Session of Dyke	Jackson Marks p583
1727/28	Henry Bethune	Edinburgh	Communion cup, no details	Jackson Marks p546
1728 ca	Simon McKenzie	Inverness	Communion cups, pair, The Sutherland Cups, each on domed circular foot with flanged base, spool shaped stem, broad plain knop, plain bucket shaped bowl, everted lip, engraved with crest, motto and coronet, crest is that of Countess of Sutherland, 3 marks -MK conjoined, INS, O - 8" ht, 34oz	St. Andrew's Church of Scotland, Golspie

YEAR	MAKER	LOCATION	DESCRIPTION	SOURCE
1728 ca	Johan Got-helf-Bilsings	Glasgow	Communion cups, pair Kirk Session of Douglas	Jackson Marks p569
1728 ca	Alexander Forbes	Aberdeen	Communion cups, pair, engraved with the date 1728, Kirk Session of Logie-Pert	Burns p 636
1728 ca	William Livingston	Elgin	Communion cup, engraved "These cups were gifted to the parish of Kundurkass by Margaret and Christian Lesslies of Akenwall 1728", Kirk Session of Boharm	Burns pp 381 & 635
1728 ca	William Livingston	Elgin	Communion cup, engraved "These cups were gifted to the parish of Kundurkass by Margaret and Christian Lesslies of Akenwall 1728", Kirk Session of Dumbarton	Burns p 380
1728/29	James Anderson	Edinburgh	Communion cups, pair, flared rims, inverted bell-shaped bowls, girdle, maker's father was the Clerk of this church at the time so nepotism may have factored into this contract, Kirk Session of Falkirk, 9" ht	Burns pp339-340
1728/29	Alexander Edmonstoun	Edinburgh	Communion cup, Anstruther church, Easter	Cripps p150 Burns p359
1729 ca	John Walker	Aberdeen	Communion beakers, pair, Kirk Session of Dykes, 5 9/16" ht, 4 ½" di lip, 3 1/8" di foot, 5/8" ht foot	Burns p 306-307
1729/30	Not available	Edinburgh	Communion cups, pair, Kirk Session of Dolphinton, 8 ¼" ht	Burns p339
1729/30	Charles Blair	Edinburgh	Communion cups, pair, Kirk Session of Morebattle, 8 3/16" ht, 28plus oz	Burns pp257-258
1730 ca	James Anderson	Edinburgh	Communion cups, 4, date letter obliterated but maker had a short career in Edinburgh, Kirk Session of Melrose	Burns p340
1730 ca	Robert Luke	Glasgow	Communion cups, pair, Kirk Session of Dunlop	Burns p 635
1730/31	Charles Blair	Edinburgh	Communion cups for Morebattle, originally made in 1655 and remade by Charles Blair in 1730	Glasgow Exhibition 1911 vol I, p103 #14
1731 ca	Alexander Forbes	Aberdeen	Communion cups, Kirk Session of Marycoulter, 9 5/16" ht, 5 1/8" di bowl	Jackson Marksp583
1731 ca	IB	Glasgow	Communion cups, pair, Kirk Session of Dumbarton	Burns p 374-5
1731 ca	*Johan Got-helf-Bilsings*	Glasgow	*Communion cups, pair, Kirk Session of Dumbarton*	*Jackson Marks p569*

YEAR	MAKER	LOCATION	DESCRIPTION	SOURCE
1731/32	Hugh Gordon	Edinburgh	Communion cup, Kirk Session of Kilsyth	Jackson Marks p547 Burns p547
1731/32	James Tait	Edinburgh	Communion cups, pair, Kirk Session of Crichton, 8 5/8"ht	Cripps p149 Burns p360
1732/33	James Ker	Edinburgh	Communion cups, pair, refashioned from earlier cups, Kirk Session of Montrose, 8 13/16" ht	Burns pp340-342
1733	Charles Dickson I or Charles Duncan	Dundee	Communion cups, Kirk Session of Dundee	Jackson Marks p600 On loan to the Dundee Museums and Art Galleries 1974-1038-39
1733/34	James Mitchelson	Edinburgh	Communion cup, Kirk Session of Birsy and Harray	Jackson Marks p547 Burns p343
1733/34	James Mitchelson	Edinburgh	Communion cup, Kirk Session of Panbride	Cripps p150
1733/34	James Ker Assayer – Archibald Ure	Edinburgh	Communion cups, pair, Kirk Session of Auchinleck, 8 7/8" ht	Cripps p150 Burns pp 342-343
1733/34	William Aytoun	Edinburgh	Communion cup, Kirk Session of Kilrinney	Cripps p150
1734 ca	Robert Luke	Glasgow	Communion cups, Kirk Session of Barony Church, Glasgow	Jackson Marks p569
1734/35	Kenneth McKenzie	Edinburgh	Communion cups, pair, Kirk Session of Fowlis Wester, 10" ht	Burns pp360-361
1735/36	Hugh Penman	Edinburgh	Communion cups, pair, Kirk Session of Dunino, 8 13/16" ht	Burns pp253-254
1735/36	John Rollo	Edinburgh	Communion cups, for the Parish of Stow	Jackson Marks p547 Burns pp254-255
1736/37	Hugh Penman	Edinburgh	Communion cup, Kirk Session of Kinross	Jackson Marks p547 Cripps p150 Burns pp343-344
1738 ca	Robert Luke	Glasgow	Communion cups, 6, only recorded straight set of 6 communion cups in the possession of the Church of Scotland, they are mentioned in the Kirk Session Records, 3 Nov 1738, cost 34 pounds 5 shillings, donor Mr. Nimmo, Kirk Session of Fenwick, 8 11/16" ht, 4 7/8" di lip, 4 ½" di foot	Burns p 377
1741/42	William Aytoun Assayer Dougal Ged	Edinburgh	Communion cup, Kirk Session of Newburgh, 8 13/16" ht	Cripps p150 Burns p361

YEAR	MAKER	LOCATION	DESCRIPTION	SOURCE
1741/42	Lawrence Oliphant Assayer – Dougal Ged	Edinburgh	Communion cups, 4, Kirk Session of Alloa, 8 ½" ht	Cripps p150 Burns p329
1742 ca	Alexander Johnston	Dundee	Communion cup, Kirk Session of Oathlaw	Kirk Session of Oathlaw
1742/43	Robert Gordon	Edinburgh	Communion cups, for the Parish of Auldearn, 6 1/8" ht	Jackson Marks p547 Burns p306
1742/43	Robert Gordon	Edinburgh	Communion beaker, dated 1744, Auldearn	Cripps Book, p 150
1743/44	Edward Lothian	Edinburgh	Communion cups, pair, inscription says bought in 1744, Kirk Session of Kemback, 10 1/16" ht	Cripps p150 Burns pp 345-346
1743/44	Edward Lothian	Edinburgh	Communion cups, for the Parish of Kirkcudbright, 8 11/16" ht	Jackson Marks p547 Cripps p150 Burns p347
1745 ca	Alexander Forbes	Aberdeen	Communion beakers, pair, Kirk Session of Crimond	Burns p303
1748/49	Robert Gordon	Edinburgh	Communion cups, pair, with the arms of Mansfield, Kirk Session of Ruthwell, 7 ½" ht	Burns p347
1750 ca	James Abercrombie	Aberdeen	Communion beakers, pair, given to St. Clement's Church in 1798	Aberdeen Museums and Galleries ABDAG008612
1750 ca	Thomas Johnston	Montrose	Communion cups, pair, Kirk Session of Marykirk, 7 11/16" ht, 4 3/8" di bowl	Burns p400
1750/51	Alexander Campbell	Edinburgh	Communion cups, pair, Envershoolan parish church	National Museums of Scotland KJ 236.237
1751/52	Robert Low	Edinburgh	Communion cups, pair, Kirk Session of Tongue, 8 5/8" ht	Burns p365
1752 ca	James Glen	Glasgow	Communion cups, pair, Kirk Session of Bothwell	Burns p 377-78
1755/56	Lothian & Robertson	Edinburgh	Communion cups, pair or 4, Kirk Session of The Tron, 10 ½" ht	Burns pp347-348
1755/56	IM in a rectangle James Mitchelson or James McKenzie I	Edinburgh	Communion cups, pair, Kirk Session of Old Cumnock, 8 ¾" ht	Burns p346
1756	James Glen	Glasgow	Communion cups, pair, dated 1756, Lockwinnock Parish Church	National Museums of Scotland KJ 233-234 1977.1-2

YEAR	MAKER	LOCATION	DESCRIPTION	SOURCE
1756/57	James Glen	Glasgow	Communion cups, pair, Lochwinnock parish church	National Museums of Scotland KJ 233-234 1977.1-2
1758-59 or 59-60	Lothian & Robertson	Edinburgh	Communion cups, pair, with Latin inscription, Kirk Session of Murroes	Burns p348
1758/59	Lothian & Robertson	Edinburgh	Communion cups, pair, Kirk Session of New Abbey, 9 ¾" ht	Burns p349
1759/60	James Gilliland	Edinburgh	Communion cups, pair, Kirk Session of Lesmahagow	Burns p247
1760 ca	Milne & Campbell	Glasgow	Communion cups, pair, Kirk Session of Inverary	Burns p 346
1760 ca	John Steven	Dundee	Communion cup, no details	Dundee Museums and Art Galleries 1974-1044
1760 ca	James Gilliland or Alexander Gardner	Edinburgh	Communion cup, on circular molded foot, with knopped stem, broad bowl with molded rib and reeded rim, engraved "Associate Congregation Hawick, 1769", said to be made by J Gardner, but more likely either James Gilliland or Alexander Gardner, Kirk Session of Hawick, 9 ¼" ht	Christie's May 14, 1963 #53
1760 ca	David Warnock	Glasgow	Communion cups, pair, For St. George's Tron Parish church, Glasgow	National Museums of Scotland H.1993.632-633
1760 ca	David Warnock	Glasgow	Communion cups, set of 4, slightly everted lips, tapering baluster stems and circular bases, 8 ¼" ht, 66.5oz both	Breadalbane Collection Sale 1935 #363
1760 ca	Adam Graham	Glasgow	Communion cups, pair, Kirk Session of Aberfoyle	Burns p 635
1760/61	Alexander Aitcheson	Edinburgh	Communion cup, Kirk Session of Langton	Cripps p150
1762/63	John Welsh	Edinburgh	Communion cups, for the Parish of Liberton	Jackson Marks p549
1762/63	James Gilliland	Edinburgh	Communion cup, Kirk Session of Gordon	Cripps p150
1763 ca	William Craw	Canongate	Communion cups, engraved under foot "Mr. Moir Mint", parish of Auchtertool, 8 ¾" ht, 4 ½" di bowl	Jackson Marks p954
1763/64	Alexander Gardner	Edinburgh	Communion cups, pair, ecclesiastical inscriptions removed, baluster stems, bowls slightly caulked and flared, 9 7/8" ht, 37oz 15d wt	Sotheby's Scone Palace April 23, 1979 #89 Private Collection
1764 ca	Colin Allan	Aberdeen	Communion beakers, pair, presentation inscription reads "This Communion cup was left in Legacie to the Kirk Session of Keig by Peter Garioch of	Burns p 307

YEAR	MAKER (continued)	LOCATION	DESCRIPTION	SOURCE
			Tulloch, Esq', who Died May 6th 1764", Kirk Session of Keig	
1765 ca	James Wildgoose	Aberdeen	Communion cups, East Church in Aberdeen	Jackson Marks p588
1765 ca	Bayne & Napier	Glasgow	Communion cups, pair, Kirk Session of St Quivox	Burns p 378-9
1766/67	Alexander Gardner	Edinburgh	2 Communion cups from St. Paul's and St. George's Episcopal Church, Edinburgh	National Museums of Scotland KJ 218-219 1975.267-268
1770 ca	James Gordon	Aberdeen	Communion cups, Kirk Session of New Machar	Jackson Marks p583 Burns p 308-309 One beaker from the group on loan to Aberdeen Museums and Galleries ABDAG011113
1770 ca	Colin Allan	Aberdeen	Communion beaker, given to the church by Alexander Thompson, NS New Machar	Aberdeen Museums and Galleries ABDAG011114
1770 ca	James Gordon	Aberdeen	Communion cups, pair, engraved with date 1770, Kirk Session of Kemnay	Burns p 636
1771 ca	James Gordon	Aberdeen	Communion cups, pair, engraved with date 1771, Kirk Session of Kemnay	Burns p 636
1772 ca	James Gordon	Aberdeen	Communion cups, pair, engraved with date 1772, Kirk Session of Kennethmont	Burns p 636
1773/74	William Davie or William Dempster	Edinburgh	Communion cups, for the Parish of Lanark	Jackson Marks p549
1775 ca	James Law	Aberdeen	Communion beakers, pair, Kirk Session of Foveran	Burns p 308
1778 ca	James Law	Aberdeen	Communion beakers, pair, Kirk Session of Birnie, 5 13/15" ht, 4 ¾" di lip, 2 13/16" di foot, 9/16" ht foot	Burns p 307
1779 ca	James Gordon	Aberdeen	Communion beaker, Kirk Session of New Machar	Burns p 308-9
1789 ca	William Scott	Dundee	Communion cups, Kirk Session of Oathlaw, 6 ½" ht, 4 3/8" di bowl, 3 3/16" di foot	Burns pp 390, 636
1792 ca	W & P Cunningham I	Edinburgh	Communion cups, pair, inscribed "Relief Church Campbell's Street 1792", 9 ¼" ht, 30oz	Scottish Art Review vol VII 1959 p37 #2 Bell of Aberdeen
1796/97	George Christie	Edinburgh	Communion cups, pair, Kirk Session of Fortingall	Jackson Marks p549

YEAR	MAKER	LOCATION	DESCRIPTION	SOURCE
1797/98	W & P Cunningham I	Edinburgh	Communion cup, Kirk Session of Tullieallan	Jackson Marks p549
1799 ca	John Ewen	Aberdeen	Communion beakers, pair, purchased from John Ewen but actual maker unknown, Kirk Session of New Bourtie	Burns p 309-10
1799/1800	W & P Cunningham I	Edinburgh	Communion cups, Kirk Session of Symington and Dunlop	Jackson Marks p549
1811/12	Patrick Cunningham & Sons	Edinburgh	Communion cups, pair from St. Paul's and St. George's Episcopal church, Edinburgh	National Museums of Scotland KJ 221-222
1811	Peter Lambert	Aberdeen	Communion beakers, pair, from St. Clement's Church	Aberdeen Museums and Galleries ABDAG008611
1825 ca	George Elder	Banff	Communion beakers, pair, Kirk Session of New Rhynie	Burns p 309
1841	GB & S Probably George Booth & Son	Aberdeen	Communion beakers, pair, from St. Clement's Church	Aberdeen Museums and Galleries ABDAG008613
1877	Not available	Dundee	Communion cups, pair, for St. Clements Parish Church	Dundee Museums and Art Galleries 1974-449
1880/81	George & Michael Crichton	Edinburgh	Communion cups, pair from St. Paul's and St. George's Episcopal Church, Edinburgh	National Museums of Scotland KJ 225-228
FLAGONS				
1684/85	John Law	Edinburgh	Flagon, no details	Glasgow Exhibition 1911 Jackson Marks p543
1724/25	Henry Bethune	Edinburgh	Communion flagons, pair, from Lord Doune, 11" ht	National Museums of Scotland L.455.11-12
1765/66	Gilliland & Ker	Edinburgh	Flagons, cylindrical, molded band around center, engraved "St. Peter's Chapel Montrose," 12 ¾" ht, 120oz	Christie's November 21, 1973 #60
1835/36	James McKay	Edinburgh	Flagons, pair, urn shaped with slender necks, raised and everted spout, domed lid, with flower finial, double scroll handle, domed foot, with 6 lobes below a gadrooned knop, 15 3/8" ht, 4 ¾" di base	Royal Ontario Museum, Toronto CA, 960.121.a-b
1862/63	John Pears Hutton Also carries marks CR & S	Edinburgh	Flagon, chased cherubs on the body, 2 cherubs on the lid, John Pears Hutton not likely to have been the maker since he was only 18 at the time, 13 3/8" ht	Huntley House Museum, Edinburgh HH894/33

YEAR	MAKER	LOCATION	DESCRIPTION	SOURCE
	Charles Robb & Son			
1877/78	Marshall & Sons	Edinburgh	Communion flagons, pair, silver-gilt, St. Mary's Episcopal Church, England	National Museums of Scotland KJ 210-211
1880/81	George & Michael Crichton	Edinburgh	Flagon, from St. Paul's and St. George's Episcopal Church, Edinburgh	National Museums of Scotland KJ 224
	LAVERS AND BASINS			
1592/93	David Gilbert Deacon William Cok	Edinburgh	Baptismal basin for St. John's Kirk, Perth	Jackson Marks p541 Finlay 1991 #25 Perth City Art Gallery and Museum
1621/22	George Crawford	Edinburgh	Lavers, set of 3, on spreading feet, chased with leaf scrolls	S. J. Phillips Ltd. London #15105
1633-35	Thomas Kirkwood Deacon George Crawford	Edinburgh	Baptismal basin, Trinity College Kirk	Finlay 1991 #26 National Museums of Scotland L.1987.9
1643 dated	Nicholas Jorgensen	Canongate	The Forgue Communion Basin	Burns p207
1649 ca	Andrew Burrell	Edinburgh	Baptismal basin, Greyfriars	National Museums of Scotland L.1989.9
1665-67	William Law	Edinburgh	Baptismal basin for North Leith	Jackson Marks p543 Burns p531
1674 dated	Edward Cleghorne I	Edinburgh	Baptismal laver and basin, Kirk Session of Canongate, laver 9 ¼" ht, basin 15 13/16" di	Burns p518
1681 dated	Edward Cleghorne I	Edinburgh	Baptismal laver and basin, Kirk Session of Newbattle, laver 10" ht, basin 15" di	Burns p523
1682/83 or 1694/95	AL Possibly Andrew Law (if later date)	Edinburgh	Baptismal laver and basin, Kirk Session of The Tron	Burns p520
1693/94	James Cockburn	Edinburgh	Laver and basin for the parish of Meigle, Perthshire	Private Collection UK

YEAR	MAKER	LOCATION	DESCRIPTION	SOURCE
1696/97	Walter Scott	Edinburgh	Baptismal laver from Trinity College Kirk	National Museums of Scotland IL.2001.66.6
1700/01	George Scott	Edinburgh	Baptismal laver and basin, Kirk Session of St Cutbert's Edinburgh, laver 8 13/16" ht, basin 13 ¼" di	Burns p525
1701/02	*Walter Scott*	*Edinburgh*	*Baptismal laver from Trinity College Kirk, y same as the one dated 1696/97 and in the National Museums of Scotland, but misdated*	Trinity College Kirk
1704/05	Mungo Yorstoun	Edinburgh	Baptismal laver and basin, donation inscription from Sir Alexander Erskine of Cambo dated 1705, Kirk Session of Kingsbarns, laver 9 5/16" ht, basin 15" di	Burns p526
1707/08	Mungo Yorstoun	Edinburgh	Baptismal laver and basin, Baptismal laver and basin, donated by Mary Erskine, Kirk Session of West St Giles Edinburgh, laver 12" ht, basin 17" di	Burns p528
1707 ca	Walter Scott	Edinburgh	Incense burner, Holyrood	National Museums of Scotland L.1987.10
1707/08	Walter Scott	Edinburgh	Baptismal Laver, Greyfriars	National Museums of Scotland IL.2003.66.5 Jackson Marks p545
1712/13	Charles Duncan	Edinburgh	Baptismal laver and basin, Kirk Session of Crail	Burns p528
1756/57	Robert Gordon	Edinburgh	Baptismal laver and basin, laver with no lid and leaf capped scroll handle, molded girdle, Kirk Session of Bothwell, laver 6 ¾" ht, basin 12 ½" di	Burns pp528-529
1775/76	Ebenezer Oliphant	Edinburgh	Baptismal basin, Parish of Kirkcaldy	Jackson Marks p547

Patens

Plate 14. A Communion Paten 1650 ca by Edward Cleghorne I, Edinburgh.
Courtesy of The Maple Swan Collection.

YEAR	MAKER PATENS	LOCATION	DESCRIPTION	SOURCE
1600 ca	Not clear	Provincial	Paten, plain, stepped rim, spool shaped feet, marks – mm EA 2X's, thistle – 4 ½" di, 2oz 17d	Sotheby's June 12, 1980 #125
1650 ca	Edward Cleghorne I	Edinburgh	Communion paten	The Maple Swan Collection
1688/89	Zaccharias Mellinus	Edinburgh	Paten for the Forsyth Chalice	Finlay 1991 #55
1700 ca	Robert Luke	Glasgow	Pedestal bowl and cover, plain, stepped cover, wood finial, on molded foot, 4 ½" di,	Sotheby's May 29, 1958 #153
1745 ca	Alexander Johnston	Dundee	Paten, with some apparent damage, subsequent repair	Bonhams Scottish Sale August 2005
1759/60	James Weems	Edinburgh	1st paten from St. Paul's and St. George's Episcopal Church, Edinburgh	National Museums of Scotland KJ.220 1975.269
1759/60	James Weems	Edinburgh	2nd paten from St. Paul's and St. George's Episcopal Church, Edinburgh	National Museums of Scotland KJ.217 1975.266
1766/67	Gilliland and Ker	Edinburgh	Oblong paten, St. Peter's Episcopal Church at Montrose, engraved in the center	National Museums of Scotland KJ.212 1974
1811/12	Patrick Cunningham & Sons	Edinburgh	Paten from St. Paul's and St. George's Episcopal Church, Edinburgh	National Museums of Scotland KJ 220 1975.269

Church Plates

Plate 15. The Cruden Communion Bread Plate, inscribed 1691 for the church at Cruden Bay by GW, Aberdeen.
Courtesy of The Maple Swan Collection.

YEAR	MAKER	LOCATION	DESCRIPTION	SOURCE
	CHURCH PLATES			
1633 ca	Thomas Kirkwood Deacon George Crawford	Edinburgh	Bread plates, pair, for Trinity Church, Edinburgh, 20 ½" di	Finlay 1991 #27 Burns p224
1635-37	George Robertson I	Edinburgh	Communion bread plate, Duffus Church Morayshire	National Museums of Scotland H.1996.206
1691 ca	GW	Aberdeen	Bread plate of Cruden, tazza like with gadrooned border on rim, inscription in center	The Maple Swan Collection
1717/18	Charles Duncan	Edinburgh	Bread plates for the parish of North Leith, mistakenly ascribed to Charles Dickson I	Kirk Session of North Leith Jackson Marks p545
1882	George Jamieson & Sons	Aberdeen	Alms plate, St. Paul's Church Aberdeen, reworked from an 18th Century plate	National Museums of Scotland L.1976.11

Coffee Pots and Chocolate Pots

Plate 16. A Coffeepot 1759/60 by William Taylor, Edinburgh.
Courtesy of J H Bourdon-Smith, London.

COFFEEPOTS AND CHOCOLATE POTS

YEAR	MAKER	LOCATION	DESCRIPTION	SOURCE
	COFFEEPOTS			
1713/14	Colin McKenzie	Edinburgh	Coffeepot, plain, tapering, octagonal, domed cover, curved spout, wooden handle, crest and motto, arms of Baillie, with a cream jug	Antiques Magazine October 1949 vol 56 Scottish Art Academy Exhibit 1939 #895 Lady Binning Collection Finlay 1991 #73 National Museums of Scotland MEQ 899 Dalgleish & Maxwell, The Lovable Craft, 1987 Fig 29
1718/19	Henry Bethune	Edinburgh	Coffeepot, octagonal, domed cover	Christie's March 15, 1906 #21
1720/21	William Aytoun	Edinburgh	Coffeepot, part of a 3 piece coffee service, pot of octagonal tapering form, long faceted curved spout with capped beak, on octagonal molded rim foot, faceted domed lid, baluster finial, double scroll wooden handle, later monogram "SR"	Sotheby's October 22, 1970 #213 Brett p197 #814
1731/32	Alexander Kincaid	Edinburgh	Coffeepot, plain, cylindrical, matted, fluted top, fluted spout, ball finial, 10 ½" ht, 25oz 10d gross wt	Christie's Dec 19, 1956 #133 Sotheby's Jan 10, 1963 Sotheby's Nov 17, 1966 #257 Simon Kaye Antiques National Museums of Scotland MEQ 1340 1980.69
1740/41	James Ker	Edinburgh	Coffeepot, baluster form, chased above and below with scrolls, flowers and foliage, on 4 legs with lion's masks, paw feet, plain curved spout, wooden scroll handle, stepped domed lid, bun and button finial, engraved with unicorn crest below motto, possibly for Stewart of Appin, or of Ardsheal, 32oz	How's Notes on Antique Silver 1941 vol I, p23 Connoisseur Magazine 1939 p 107-09 How of Edinburgh Collection and advertisement Apollo vol 17 advertisement
1741/42	William Aytoun	Edinburgh	Coffeepot, tapering cylindrical body, chased with shells and scroll motifs, with a crest, 10" ht	Bonham Sept 26, 1975 #654
1741/42	Edward Lothian	Edinburgh	Coffeepot, no details	Antiques Magazine 1969 vol 95 p586 Bell of Aberdeen advertisement
1741/42	*Edward Lothian*	*Edinburgh*	*Coffeepot, no details*	*Sotheby's NY Feb 1985 #219*

YEAR	MAKER	LOCATION	DESCRIPTION	SOURCE
1741/42	Ebenezer Oliphant	Edinburgh	Coffeepot, tapering cylindrical body, on molded rim foot, with curved spout, hinged domed lid, baluster finial, chased with bands of fruit, scrolls, scale work, rococo ornamentation, with a monogram, 10" ht, 30oz	Christie's September 28, 1994
1743/44	Robert Hope	Edinburgh	Coffeepot, no details	Jackson Marks p547
1744/45	WD William Dempster or William Davie	Edinburgh	Coffeepot, stated to be a chocolate pot and by Drummond, plain, on spreading rim foot, stepped domed lid, baluster finial, long plain tapering gently curving spout, 9 ¼" ht, 21oz	Christie's May 16, 1979 #84
1746/47	Edward Lothian	Edinburgh	Coffeepot, excellent marks and condition, no details	How of Edinburgh 1937 #98
1749/50	Ebenezer Oliphant Assayer Hugh Gordon	Edinburgh	Coffeepot, plain tapering form, chased with floral and "C" scroll border, slightly domed hinged lid, spout capped with dolphin/sea monster, terminating in scrollwork, on spread circular base, cone finial, 10 ¾" ht, 30oz 10d	Bonhams Knightsbridge, February 22, 1994 #235 Sotheby's London August 20, 1995 #159 Sotheby's Gleneagles August 28, 1995 #159 Sotheby's London July 11, 1996 #175
1749/50	Ebenezer Oliphant Assayer Hugh Gordon	Edinburgh	Coffeepot, tapered cylindrical body, tucked in base, plain except for a chased floral band at the neck and rococo ornament around handle sockets, curved spout terminating in grotesque dolphin mask, pineapple finial, 10 ½" ht, 31oz, *possibly same as above*	Sotheby's January 14, 1965 #170
1749/50	Ebenezer Oliphant	Edinburgh	Coffeepot, bird's head spout, chased flowers and scrolls, pineapple finial, 10 ¾" ht, 25oz 5d	Christie's November 18, 1936 #47
1749/50	JH Probably James Hill	Edinburgh	Coffeepot, tapering cylindrical body, plain except for foliate and floral chasing around the neck and base, artichoke finial, 10" ht, 26oz	Mary Cooke Antiques April 1993
1750/51	Edward Lothian	Edinburgh	Coffeepot, similar to Alexander Kincaid 1731/32, but with no decoration, wooden handle, tucked in base, bell finial	Finlay 1991 #82
1753/54	Robert Low	Edinburgh	Coffeepot, no details	Christie's London 1988 p62
1753/54	James Weems	Edinburgh	Coffeepot, straight sided, rococo chased with shells, flowers and leaves, 12 ¼" ht, 33.6oz	Nicholas Shaw Catalog Winter 2001 p70
1753/54	Robert Low	Edinburgh	Coffeepot, on molded circular foot, leaf capped curved spout, hinged dome lid, bud finial, chased with scrolls and rococo ornament, 9 ¾" ht, 29oz	Christie's October 14, 1987 #196 Unsold
1753/54	Robert Low	Edinburgh	Coffeepot, on molded circular foot, leaf capped curved spout, hinged domed lid, bud finial, chased with scrolls and rococo ornament, 8 ¾" ht, 16.4oz	Christie's March 9, 1988 #172

YEAR	MAKER	LOCATION	DESCRIPTION	SOURCE
1753/54	*Robert Low*	*Edinburgh*	*Coffeepot, no details*	*Exhibition of Scottish Silver, Edinburgh 1948, p12 #147 Sir Charles D Hope - Dunbar*
1753/54	Ker & Dempster	Edinburgh	Coffeepot, tapering cylindrical body, plain, on circular molded foot, foliage capped curved spout, domed lid, bud finial, with a monogram, 10 ½" ht	Christie's Oct 27, 1971 #172
1754/55	Ker & Dempster	Edinburgh	Coffeepot, no details	Edward & Sons, Glasgow Exhibition 1911 Vol I p109 #36
1754/55	Robert Low	Edinburgh	Coffeepot, tapering, cylindrical, tucked-in base, chased with original scrolls, flowers, foliage and scale-work, engraved with crest of an armed forearm beribboned at the elbow, embowed sinister, issuing from a cloud and carrying a spear, insulated silver handle not original, 10 ¼" ht, 32oz 10d	Private Collection
1754/55	*Robert Low*	*Edinburgh*	*Coffeepot, cylindrical, tapering, chased scrolls, flowers and fruits, crest, cone finial, 10 ¼" ht, 33.2oz*	*Antiques Magazine 1954 vol 89 Christie's January 24, 1964 #171*
1755 ca	Colin Allan	Aberdeen	Coffeepot, no details	Finlay 1991 #110
1756/57	James Gilliland	Edinburgh	Coffeepot, tapering cylindrical body, rounded on the base on a rim foot, chased with 2 bands of shells, scrolls and flower sprays, swan neck spout, leaf-capped double scroll handle, 10 ¼" ht, 33oz	Sotheby's November 28, 1963 #105
1756/57	Ker & Dempster	Edinburgh	Coffeepot, no details	Sotheby's NY USA April 12, 1994 #292
1756/57	Lothian & Robertson	Edinburgh	Coffeepot, plain tapering body, spreading rim base, domed lid with acorn finial, 9 ½" ht, 28.3oz	Phillips Glasgow June 30, 1988 #355
1756/57	Robert Low	Edinburgh	Coffeepot, tapering body, chased with broad bands of shell work, scrolls and flowers incorporating 2 vacant cartouches, tucked in on molded foot, decorated spout and lid with leafy finial, 10" ht	Sotheby's April 23, 1970 #113
1758/59	James Welsh	Edinburgh	Coffeepot, no details	Jackson Marks p 548
1758/59	William Dempster or William Davie	Edinburgh	Coffeepot, pear shaped body, repoussed and chased with fruit, flowers, scrolls and other motifs, domed lid with leaf spray finial, short high spout on a spreading foot, 11" ht, 37.5oz	Sotheby's Gleneagles April 23, 1976 #33
1759/60	Lothian & Robertson	Edinburgh	Coffeepot, pear shaped body with repousse work, chased with scrolls, flowers and shell work, with carved grotesque mask spout, domed cover with flower and scroll finial	Lyle Annual Review 1983 p565 Christie's December 9, 1981, #86

YEAR	MAKER	LOCATION	DESCRIPTION	SOURCE
1759/60	Lothian & Robertson	Edinburgh	Coffeepot, no details	National Museums of Scotland MEQ 698 1964.1836
1759/60	William Taylor	Edinburgh	Coffeepot, rococo decorated, 10 ½" ht, 31oz	JH Bourdon-Smith Catalog Autumn 2002 #44 p 18
1760 ca	Colin Allan	Aberdeen	Coffeepot, scratch weight on base 26:13	Aberdeen Museums and Galleries ABDAG001008
1760/61	Lothian & Robertson	Edinburgh	Coffeepot, domed like with cast fruiting branch, spout ending in an animal head, crest and motto of Graham, 10 ½" ht, 34.8oz	Sotheby's April 3, 1958 #160 Antiques Magazine 1958 vol 74 Lyon & Turnbull The Murray Collection August 20, 2003 #200 Nicholas Shaw Catalog Winter 2004 p100
1760/61	John Robertson	Edinburgh	Coffeepot, straight sided, chased with flowers and foliage, artichoke finial, wooden handle, 10 ¼" ht, 32oz	Nicholas Shaw Catalog Winter 2002/03 p83
1760/61	John Robertson	Edinburgh	Coffeepot, tapering cylindrical form with chased floral, foliate, and scroll decoration, stepped foot, domed lid, acanthus or artichoke finial, acanthus capped silver handle and spout, initials "JC", crest and motto "IF I CAN" for Colquhoun of Killermont, Dumbartonshire, 10" ht, 30oz	Bonhams The Scottish Sale August 21, 2003 #27
1760 ca	Milne & Campbell	Glasgow	Coffeepot, pear shaped, fruit and scroll chasing, wood handle, crest of an eagle pierced with an arrow, 9 ½" ht, 31.9oz	JH Bourdon-Smith Catalog Autumn 2005 #46 p26
1760 ca	Adam Graham	Glasgow	Coffeepot, 10 1/8" ht, 30 oz	Christie's Glasgow March 1983 #47
1760 ca	John Cruikshank	Elgin	Coffeepot, with stand	Finlay 1991 #119
1761/62	Alexander Gardner	Edinburgh	Coffeepot, straight sided, tapering form with tucked in base, domed lid with pineapple finial, scroll mounted leaf-capped curved spout, coat of arms, motto "PROCEDAMUS IN PACE" for Montgomery, 9 ¾" ht, 31oz	Nicholas Shaw Catalog Winter 2001 p73 Bonhams The Scottish Sale August 21, 2003 #26
1762/63	Adam Graham	Edinburgh	Coffeepot, rococo style, flowers, finial, 12 ¼" ht	Clayton Dictionary p97 #138 Scottish Art Academy Exhibit 1939 #954 Stuart-Stevenson Collection
1762/63	WD Probably William	Edinburgh	Coffeepot, tapering cylindrical body, chased above and below with floral swags and leaves, scrolls and flower heads, domed lid, bud finial, wood	Sotheby's Gleneagles August 31-September 1, 1987 #290

YEAR	MAKER Dempster	LOCATION	DESCRIPTION handle, later crested, 10" ht, 28oz all	SOURCE
1763/64	Ker & Dempster	Edinburgh	Coffeepot, baluster body, extensively chased with fruit, flowers and ornaments, short high spout, domed lid with bird finial, spreading base, wooden double scroll capped handle, 11 ½" ht, 35.8oz	Sotheby's Gleneagles August 29, 1978 #442
1765 ca	Adam Graham	Glasgow	Coffeepot, on circular molded foot, chased with fruit, shells, scrolls and foliage, curved spout, domed lid, beaded cone finial, 9 7/8" ht, 30.9oz	Christie's April 26, 1977 #81
1765 ca	Adam Graham	Glasgow	Coffeepot, baluster form, decorated with 2 bands of chased scrolls, flowers and foliage, dome lid with latticed acorn finial, curved scrolled spout capped and supported with foliage, wooden scroll handle, 10 1/8" ht, 30oz	Shaw Collection Christie's Glasgow March 29, 1983 #47
1765/66	Ker & Dempster	Edinburgh	Coffeepot, covered in rococo decoration, coat of arms in rococo cartouche, lid with a bird finial, 34oz	Scottish Art Review vol V, 1954, p40 #1
1765/66	*Ker & Dempster*	*Edinburgh*	*Coffeepot, bird finial, arms of Buchanan of Lanark, 11 ¼" ht, 35oz*	*Sotheby's January 10, 1963 #173 JH Bourdon-Smith London*
1765/66	*Ker & Dempster*	*Edinburgh*	*Coffeepot, no details*	*National Museums of Scotland MEQ 637 1963.640*
1766/67	Alexander Gardner	Edinburgh	Coffeepot, tapering circular form, scroll handle, leaf capped spout, domed hinged lid, cone finial, whole on raised circular foot, engraved with coat of arms of Ramsay, kin of the Earls of Dalhousie, 10" ht, 32oz	Bonhams March 6, 2001 #162
1767/68	Not available	Edinburgh	Coffeepot, baluster shaped, engraved with monogram and crest, underneath with an inscription dated 1769, repousse and chased with scrolls, flowers, foliage, and shell ornament, wood handle and hinged lid, decorated to match the body, bud finial, on molded rim foot, 10 ½" ht, 29oz 11d	Sotheby's July 23, 1959 #94
1769/70	Patrick Robertson	Edinburgh	Coffeepot, large, elongated inverted pear form, rococo decoration, on plain circular foot, wooden handle	Hayden p229 National Museums of Scotland Jackson Marks p549 Apollo May 1947 p68 National Museums of Scotland 1986.51
1775 ca	James Wildgoose	Aberdeen	Coffeepot, pear shaped, flowers, wavy bands, 11 ½" ht	Finlay 1991 #110 Scottish Art Academy Exhibit 1939

YEAR	MAKER	LOCATION	DESCRIPTION	SOURCE
1775/76	James Hewitt	Edinburgh	Coffeepot, urn shaped on pedestal foot, beaded and acanthus rims, chased and domed hinged lid, bird finial, wood scroll handle, engraved crest and motto, 12 ¼" ht, 34oz gross	Christie's NY USA 2003 #254
1776/77	Patrick Robertson	Edinburgh	Coffeepot, no details	Dundee Museums and Art Galleries 1978-636
1782/83	Robert Bowman	Edinburgh	Coffeepot, silver gilt vase-shaped, body with applied festoons pendant from ribbons and 2 oval disks, one initialed "LJS", curved spout, loop handle, both with bird's heads	Sotheby's Hopetoun House November 10, 1980 #58 Finlay 1991 #101
1792/93	Not available	Edinburgh	Coffeepot, no details, 118 oz	Bruun Rasmussen Veile, Denmark 2007 "838
1797/98	W & P Cunningham I	Edinburgh	Coffeepot, on hexagonal base, engraved leaf decoration, hinged lid with pineapple finial, 9" ht	Mallam Oxford UK 2007 #187
1805/06	Francis Howden	Edinburgh	Coffeepot, no details	National Museums of Scotland MEQ 1199 1976.46
1809/10	James McKay	Edinburgh	Coffeepot, baluster shape, half fluted, crest – an arrow pointing downward, 10 ¾" ht, 35oz	Nicholas Shaw Catalog Winter 2000 p80
1810/11	Francis Howden	Edinburgh	Coffeepot on stand, squat ovoid form with domed cover and ball finial, serpentine spout, angular handle, gadrooned rims, full armorials, removable two part infuser, stand on 3 reeded paw feet, 12 ¼", 41oz all	Skinner Inc, Boston MA USA #19
1813/14	Robert Gray & Son	Glasgow Edinburgh assay	Coffeepot with stand and burner, part of a 4 piece tea and coffee service	Sotheby's NY USA 1998 #544
1816/17	M & R	Glasgow Edinburgh assay	Coffeepot, part fluted, part of a mixed assembled service, 7 ¼" ht	Christies London UK 2006 #1685
1819/20	W & P Cunningham II	Edinburgh	Coffeepot, no details	National Museums of Scotland MEQ 1178
1819/20	James McKay	Edinburgh	Coffeepot, no details	National Museums of Scotland MEQ 1316
1819/20	WH	Edinburgh	Coffeepot, baluster form, body chased with scrolling foliage, crest and motto of Torrance or Turnbull, wooden scroll handle, 28.5oz	Bonhams sale 15120 Aug 22, 2007 #22

YEAR	MAKER	LOCATION	DESCRIPTION	SOURCE
1820/21	George McHattie	Edinburgh	Coffeepot, partly fluted, pear-shaped, on spreading circular foot, gadrooned rim, acanthus foliage finial to partly fluted domed cover, engraved crest of a spread eagle beneath a viscount's coronet (supposed to be for George Boyle, 4th Earl of Glasgow (1765-1843), but presumable someone else), retailer's mark "Morton" for Robert Morton, small repair at base of spout, 10" ht, 28oz	Private Collection Christie's Edinburgh April 29, 1992
1822/23	James McKay	Edinburgh	Coffeepot, tapering cylindrical form engraved with full armorials with a crest and motto, pedestal foot, bud finial, 10 ¾", 25oz	Sotheby's NY USA 1995 #35
1823/24	James Howden & Co	Edinburgh	Coffeepot, no details	The Maple Swan Collection
1824/25	James McKay	Edinburgh	Coffeepot, no details	National Museums of Scotland MEQ 688
1825/26	Robert Gray & Son	Glasgow	Coffeepot, of baluster form on circular domed foot, chased on the sides with two panels of C-scrolls, foliage and rocaille, carved leaf-capped spout, domed cover, pineapple finial, leaf-capped scroll handle, 11 ½" ht, 30oz gross	Christie's East NY USA 2001 #349
1826/27	William Marshall & Son	Edinburgh	Coffeepot, baluster form, crest below motto "CAVE ADSUM", chased, melon finial, 10" ht, 27oz 14d	Sotheby's NY USA 1999 #429
1827/28	James McKay	Edinburgh	Coffeepot, baluster on a flattened circular base, lower body chased with C-scrolls, flowers and foliage and scale-crest on both sides, wood handle, domed cover, artichoke finial, 33oz gross	Christie's East NY USA 2000 #226
1830/31	James McKay	Edinburgh	Coffeepot, elaborately chased with floral motif on stippled background, 9 ¼" ht, 9 ½" over handle	Cincinnati Art Museum 1978.414
1831/32	Elder & Co	Edinburgh	Coffeepot, no details	Sotheby's Gleneagles August 1987 #305
1832/33	Leonard Urquhart	Edinburgh	Coffeepot, embossed with foliage and spiral gadroons, crested below motto "DILIGENTIA FIT UBERTAS", 13" ht, 39oz 16d	Sotheby's London UK 2004 #221 Christie's London UK 2006 #1686
1833/34	Daniel Sutherland	Glasgow	Coffeepot, no details	Sotheby's Hopetoun House May 1990 #80
1836/37	James McKay	Edinburgh	Coffeepot, inverted pear form, on a spreading foot, center cartouche with full armorials, 32oz Gross	Christie's London UK 2001 #218
1837/38	James McKay	Edinburgh	Coffeepot, baluster form, shaped circular foot, 12 ¼" ht	Christie's London UK 2005 #331
1837/38	James McKay	Edinburgh	Coffeepot, ovoid form, ornately chased, engraved crest both sides, leaf capped scroll handle, domed cover and finial on raised scroll feet, 9 ¼" ht,	Joel, South Yarra AU 2007 #825

YEAR	MAKER (continued)	LOCATION	DESCRIPTION	SOURCE
			39.62 oz	
1837/38	J & W Marshall	Edinburgh	Coffeepot, chased	JH Bourdon-Smith London 1993
1840/41	Marshall & Sons	Edinburgh	Coffeepot, no details	National Museums of Scotland MEQ 816
1846/47	William Marshall & Sons	Edinburgh	Coffeepot, part of a 4 piece service, butterfly decoration, 11" ht	Huntley House Museum Edinburgh HH2809/65
1847/48	J & W Marshall	Edinburgh	Coffeepot, designed by David Ramsay Hay	National Museums of Scotland 1986.151
1852/53	WCS	Edinburgh	Coffeepot, baluster form, chased with flowers, monogrammed, part of a service	Christie's NY USA 2005 #249
1866/67	EM	Edinburgh	Coffeepot, heavily embossed, sold with a matching teapot	Lyon & Turnbull, Edinburgh UK 2003 #232
1881/82	William Marshal (probably)	Edinburgh	Coffeepot, on a stylized garland foot, ivory-insulated handle, crest, sold with a matching teapot, 11" ht	Christie's London UK 2006 #1745
1900/01	Hamilton & Inches	Edinburgh	Coffeepot, with a lamp	National Museums of Scotland MEQ 1171 1976.18
1986/87	Adrian Hope	Edinburgh	Coffeepot, with straight sides	National Museums of Scotland MEQ 1602a & b
1990	Adrian Hope	Edinburgh	Coffeepot, no details	Aberdeen Museums and Galleries ABDAG008802
COFFEE SERVICE				
1718/20	William Aytoun	Edinburgh	Coffee service, octagonal, 3 pieces, 56.9oz	Brett p194 #814 Sotheby's October 22, 1970 #213
1782/83	William Cunningham I	Edinburgh	Coffee service, 3 pieces	Antiques Magazine vol 76 p252
CHOCOLATE POTS				
1720 ca	Robert Bruce	Edinburgh	Chocolate pot, no details	Dundee Museums and Art Galleries, 1978-2061
1720/21	Patrick Murray	Edinburgh	Chocolate pot, Selkirk race prize, engraved with the Selkirk Arms	Bell of Aberdeen

YEAR	MAKER (continued)	LOCATION	DESCRIPTION	SOURCE
				Grantully Castle Antiques National Museums of Scotland MEQ 1065
1734/35	Edward Lothian	Edinburgh	Chocolate pot, no details	Antiques Magazine vol 50 p 303 Bell of Aberdeen advertisement
1760 ca	Milne & Campbell	Glasgow	Chocolate pot, baluster form chased with knuckled ribs and foliate scrolls, sliding finial topped by a spread-winged bird, 10" ht, 32oz 15d	Sotheby's NY USA April 16, 2005 #265
1765 ca	Adam Graham	Glasgow	Chocolate pot, no details	Aberdeen Museums and Galleries ABDAG001243

Cream & Milk Containers

Plate 17. Group of 3 Edinburgh Cream Boats of different styles.
Left – 1744/45 Edward Lothian; Center – 1752/53 Robert Gordon;
Right – 1741/42 James Weems
Courtesy of The Phoenix Collection. Photograph by Janice M Dietert.

CREAM AND MILK CONTAINERS

YEAR	MAKER	LOCATION	DESCRIPTION	SOURCE
1713/14	Colin McKenzie	Edinburgh	Hot milk jug, covered, octagonal baluster form, wooden double scroll handle, coat of arms of Baillie with coffee pot	Finlay 1991 #73 Sotheby's November 30, 1967 How of Edinburgh
1714/15	Mungo Yorstoun	Edinburgh	Cream jug, upright, pitcher form, molded faceted spout with tear drop at the base, molded rim, bold scrolling handle, on spreading foot, 4 ½" ht, 7.8oz	Clayton Christie's Book p82 #2 Christie's 1902 Christie's July 5, 1972 Sotheby's Hopetoun House November 13, 1978 #77 S J Phillips Ltd London UK Ltd London UK National Museums of Scotland MEQ 1294 1978.81
1717/18	Not available	Edinburgh	Hot milk jug, covered, baluster body, on spreading rather flat foot, double scroll silver handle, domed lid, acorn finial, rim is continuous, spout has drop at bottom, full coat of arms opposite handle	Country Life January 14, 1965 p74 illus article by G. Bernard Hughes
1718/19	William Aytoun	Edinburgh	Creamer, pitcher type, octagonal, upright, small spout, silver scroll handle, with coffee pot and sugar box, 4 ¾" ht, 10oz	Sotheby's October 23, 1970 #213 Brett #814
1718/19	Not available	Edinburgh	Covered hot milk jug, no details	Connoisseur Magazine 1935 vol 96 p56
1719/20	Colin McKenzie	Edinburgh	Cream jug, pitcher form, short spout, single scroll handle, later initials on the bottom, 4 ½" ht, 5oz 7d	Antiques Magazine December 1982 vol 122, p1155 Shrubsole advertisement Ivory Collection Glasgow Empire Exhibition #41, pl. 19 Sotheby's Gleneagles August 28, 1969 #137 Sotheby's Blair Castle September 12, 1980 #163 Sotheby's June 29-30 #148 Sotheby's February 18, 1982 #157
1719/20	James Mitchelson	Edinburgh	Cream jug, upright, pitcher type, plain double scroll handle, short molded curved spout with continuous rim	Clayton Christie's Book, p152 #4 Christie's February 27, 1974 #84
1719/20	Mungo Yorstoun	Edinburgh	Cream jug, upright, 4 3/8" ht, 7oz 10d	Finlay pl #80

YEAR	MAKER (continued)	LOCATION	DESCRIPTION	SOURCE
1719/20	Mungo Yorstoun	Edinburgh	*Cream jug, no details*	Asprey Collection, November 1993, #13 Holland p221
1719/20	Mungo Yorstoun	Edinburgh	*Cream jug, baluster shape*	*Glasgow Empire Exhibition*
1722/23	Henry Bethune	Edinburgh	Hot milk jug, tall, ovoid/egg shaped, matches teapot of the same year, later chased with fruits, shells, and scale work, crest and motto of Foulis of Ravelston	*Antiques Magazine June 1996* p844 *Hyman Collection - Colonial Williamsburg* G1994-192
1723/24	Kenneth McKenzie	Edinburgh	Cream jug, upright, no details	Connoisseur Magazine 1954 vol 133, p6 Sotheby's London November 26, 1953
1723/24	Kenneth McKenzie	Edinburgh	Cream jug, baluster form, with arms, crest and motto of Penderleith of Blyth, scratch weight 7=2, 4 ½" ht, 7oz (possibly same as above)	Sotheby's NY USA 2000 #414
1723/24	James Ker	Edinburgh	Cream jug, helmet shaped, wavy border, with a sugar bowl	Wilson & Sharp *Glasgow Empire Exhibition 1911*, vol I, p108 #22
1725 ca	Robert Luke	Glasgow	Cream boat, oval, flared and waved rim, lip chased with shells, foliate scrolls and scale work, leaf capped double scroll handle, on 3 faceted supports, 6" di, 5oz 16d	Sotheby's May 11, 1967 #63 How of Edinburgh
1725 ca	Robert Luke	Glasgow	Cream jug, baluster body, molded foot, double scroll handle, 4 ½" ht, 2 3/8" di at base, 2 1/8" di at mouth	McKissick Museum, University of South Carolina, Columbia, SC USA 1.219
1725/26	Henry Bethune	Edinburgh	Covered hot milk jug, 4 ½" ht, 9.2oz	Connoisseur Magazine 1952 vol 128 p201 Phillips January 28, 1977 #180 Shrubsole 50 years catalog *Hyman Collection - Colonial Williamsburg* G1994-173
1725/26	Robert Luke	Glasgow	Cream boat, no details	Apollo May 1967, vol 85 p 96

YEAR	MAKER	LOCATION	DESCRIPTION	SOURCE
1725/26	William Aytoun	Edinburgh	Cream jug, of plain baluster shape on a stepped spreading foot, short upscroll spout, reeded rim, C-scroll handle, 3 1/3" ht (to top of handle), 8.3oz	S. J. Phillips Ltd, 2007 #31536
1727/28	James Ker	Edinburgh	Hot milk jug, covered, near spherical form, on molded spreading foot, molded V-shaped lip, silver scroll handle, lid with spherical finial, engraved around mouth and on rim of lid with bands of conventional decoration, 4 ¾" ht, 10oz	Breadalbane Collection Connoisseur Magazine 1953 Christie's March 7, 1962 #112 Shaw Collection Christie's Glasgow March 1983 #87 Metropolitan Museum of NYC AC#1983.24
1727/28	James Ker	Edinburgh	Cream jug, helmet shaped, molded edge, on oval foot, body flares out and up to the scalloped mouth with a small spout, molded drop below, straight then scroll-shaped handle, girdle high on body, part of the Johnson 4 piece tea service, 5 ½" long, 2 7/8" wide	How's Notes on Antiques Silver vol I, 1941 p23 Finlay 1991 #134 Brooklyn Museum 63.95.2
1727/28	James Mitchelson	Edinburgh	Cream jug, upright baluster form, 4" ht	Sotheby's auction
1727/28	Alexander Kincaid	Edinburgh	Milk jug, covered, on 3 hoof feet, wooden handle, acorn finial, hinged lid, engraved initial "H"	Fogg Art Museum, Harvard University 1949.114.111 Hutchinson Collection
1728/29	James Ker	Edinburgh	Hot milk jug, covered, near spherical body, on spreading reeded molded foot, engraved around mouth and on lid with a narrow band of masks, scrolls and strap work, short curved lip, silver plain capped, single scroll handle, domed lid with applied hinge, bun and button finial 4" ht, 6oz	Christie's July 10-11, 1984 #378
1729/30	James Ker Assayer Edward Penman	Edinburgh	Hot milk jug, covered, plain spherical body, short v-shaped spout, applied hinged lid, urn finial, simple plain capped silver scroll handle, on stepped spreading base, 4" ht, 6.7oz	Sotheby's December 2, 1980 #227 Lyon & Turnbull February 20, 2004 #255
1730 ca	James Tait	Edinburgh	Hot milk jug, covered, mm only, spherical on circular molded foot, short spout, ball finial to the cover, wooden handle, 5 ¼" ht, 9.5oz	Christie's February 13, 1957 Sotheby's London June 9, 1994 #310
1730 ca	Robert Luke	Glasgow	Cream boat, oval, lip and everted rim flat chased with foliage, flower heads, and a shell, double scroll handle, on 3 hoof feet, 6"	Sotheby's Gleneagles August 31, 1981 #453
1730 ca	Robert Luke	Glasgow	Cream boat, on 3 hoof feet, scroll handle, everted rim, engraved with shell and scrolling foliage, 5oz 2d	Christie's December 19, 1979 #163
1730 ca	Robert Luke	Glasgow	Cream boat, plain oval shape, on 3 fleur-de-lys and paw feet, shaped everted	Christie's Edinburgh June 6, 1995

YEAR	MAKER (continued)	LOCATION	DESCRIPTION	SOURCE #339
1730 ca	George Cooper	Aberdeen	rim, chased with flower heads, scale work, and shells, scroll handle, gilt interior, engraved with crest, mm slightly rubbed, 7 ¼" wide, 8oz Cream jug, on a pedestal, tall silver handle, short spout, baluster body, from the Kirkhill Tea Service of 5 pieces, crest and motto of the Gordon family	Connoisseur Magazine 1955, vol 135 p90 How of Edinburgh advertisement Aberdeen Museums and Galleries ABDAG008503 Purchased in 1986
1730/31	James Anderson	Edinburgh	Milk jug, no details	Jackson Marks p 547
1730/31	William Aytoun	Edinburgh	Hot milk jug, covered, spherical body, silver handle, ball and button finial, on tall stem, tall spout, like other 1730 Aytoun example except broader area of decoration, scrolls, leaves, and matting, no juxtaposed v's or arrows	Country Life August 1959 pp130-133 article with photos
1730/31	William Aytoun	Edinburgh	Milk jug, spherical shaped, bell and button finial, on tall stem, silver double scroll handle, opposing V's as a band decoration surrounding lid/body junction, tall spout, decoration is simpler and earlier than other Aytoun example	Christie's Scottish Picture Files 1952 National Museums of Scotland 1953 125
1730/31	William Aytoun	Edinburgh	Cream jug, helmet shaped, broad girdle, engraved with crest and motto in a riband	National Museums of Scotland MEQ 1327
1732/33	James Michelson	Edinburgh	Cream jug, helmet shaped, flying scroll handle, applied reeded girdle, 4 1/8" ht, 5.5oz	Connoisseur Magazine 1941 vol 107, p230 Bonhams Knightbridge February 22, 1994 #234
1732/33	William Aytoun	Edinburgh	Cream jug, helmet shaped, broad girdle on upper body	Ivory collection Glasgow Empire Exhibition 1938 illus pl 19 #54
1733/34	James Ker	Edinburgh	Cream boat, everted rim engraved with lattice work, flowers and foliage, a shell at the lip with leaf capped double scroll handle, on 3 hoof feet, headed by trefoils 6 1/4"' long, 6oz	Sotheby's March 14, 1974 #195
1733/34	James Ker	Edinburgh	Cream boat, on hoof feet, with leaf capped double scroll handle, shaped everted rim engraved arabesques, underside with an initial, 6" long, 5.8oz	Christie's South Kensington May 16, 1989 #35
1733/34	William Aytoun	Edinburgh	Cream jug, helmet shaped part of the Girdwood Tea Service	Connoisseur Magazine 1934, vol93 p131 Finlay 1991 #74

YEAR	MAKER	LOCATION	DESCRIPTION	SOURCE
1734/35	James Ker	Edinburgh	Hot milk jug, covered, on 4 feet, part of the Hopetoun Tea Service, 5 5/8" ht	Clayton Dictionary p419 #650 Linlithgow Collection National Museums of Scotland MEQ 1208 1977.7
1735 ca	William Aytoun	Edinburgh	Cream boat, shallow oval body, projecting wavy rim, long lip, chased with flowers, shells, and leafage, double scroll handle, on 3 hoof feet, sold with matching sauce boat dated 1828, 14.1oz both	Sotheby's July 28, 1960 #183 How of Edinburgh
1735 ca	Patrick Gordon	Banff	Cream jug, upright, sparrow beak spout, crest of Duff, (with a sugar bowl), 4 ½" ht	Noble Collection Glasgow Empire Exhibition 1938, #913 Finlay 1991 #120 Nicholas Shaw Catalog 2004 p108 National Museums of Scotland K.2004.208.2
1735 ca	James Mitchelson	Edinburgh	Cream jug, oval helmet shaped, plain, engraved initials, 4 3/8" ht, 5.3oz	Phillips ? Edinburgh May 17, 1991 #81
1735 ca	George Cooper	Aberdeen	Cream jug, upright, pear shaped, on pad feet, silver double scroll handle, part of a mixed Aberdeen Tea Service	Queen's Silver p66, #10
1735/36	William Aytoun	Edinburgh	Cream boat, everted chased rim and spout, 3 pad feet with trefid knees, leaf capped double scroll silver handle, 6 ¾" long	JH Bourdon-Smith London 1993 The Phoenix Collection
1735/36	Edward Lothian	Edinburgh	Covered hot milk jug, spherical body, silver double scroll handle, ball and button finial, tall spout, mixed decoration in narrow band near mouth with scrolls and diaper work, 8oz	Holland p 121 Noble Collection Christie's December 13, 1967 #23 Wilson & Sharp
1736/37	James Ker	Edinburgh	Cream boat, everted rim, chased paw feet, initial script "M", conjoined under crown, low body, uplifted spout, 7 ½" ht	Ticher Irish Silver p26 Shrubsole
1737/38	Edward Lothian	Edinburgh	Cream boat, on 3 scroll feet, issuing from trefoils, shaped borders chased with flowers, scrolls and shells, with leaf capped double scroll handle, with initials "DMD" or DDM, 6.5oz	Christie's July 10-11, 1984 #377 Christie's November 10, 1998 #87 Christie's London Negative #25239
1737/38	R C	Edinburgh	Cream boat, possibly Edinburgh, said to carry date letter and mm only, oval body with crest of Lord Borthwick, his baron's coronet above, his motto "QUI	Sotheby's Gleneagles August 31 September 1, 1987 #288

YEAR	MAKER (continued)	LOCATION	DESCRIPTION	SOURCE
			CONDUCIT" below, shaped wavy rim, on 3 hoof feet, issuing from shell headed legs, leaf capped flying scroll handle, 5 ½" long, 3.5oz	
1738/39	James Ker	Edinburgh	Cream boat, on paw feet, trefid lobed legs, everted chased rim, leaf scroll handle, 6oz 15d	Christie's Glasgow March 1983 #77 Shaw Collection Koopman, London UK
1739/40	James Mitchelson	Edinburgh	Cream boat, everted rim, chased, on 3 hoof feet, leaf capped double scroll handle, 6 ½" long, 7.7oz	Sotheby's Gleneagles August 29, 1978 #437 Lyle Silver Review 1982, p45
1739/40	James Mitchelson	Edinburgh	Cream boat, on 3 hoof feet, with scrolls above, shaped rim flat chased with flowers, shells and foliage, double scroll handle, 5.7oz	Christie's December 20, 1974 #193
1739/40	James Ker	Edinburgh	Cream boat, part of a 4 piece service, silver handle, short spout, chased rim and spout, paw feet and trefid knees	Connoisseur Magazine 1933, vol 91 p342 Christie's April 27, 1949 #81 Christie's London Negative #157597
1740ca	James Glen	Glasgow	Cream boat, oval, plain body, on 3 paw feet, headed by comma motifs, waved lip, leaf capped double scroll handle, underside with initials, 6", 6oz	Sotheby's August 26, 1972 # 71
1740 ca	John Baillie	Inverness	Cream jug, pear shaped, on spreading foot, with v-shaped spout, scroll handle, provenance Shaw Collection, #43, 2oz 10d	Christie's July 3, 1984 #161 Christie's March 29, 1983 #43 Shaw Sale Aberdeen Museums and Galleries ABDAG01365 purchased in 1984
1740 ca	Ebenezer Oliphant	Edinburgh	Cream boat, everted rim, lip chased, double scroll handle, on 3 hoof feet with voluted trefid cabriole legs	Scottish Art Review vol VIII 1961 p35 #2 Bell of Aberdeen
1740 ca	Colin Mitchell	Canongate	Cream boat, everted plain rim, plain lip, leaf capped double scroll handle, on 3 hoof feet, body later chased	National Museums of Scotland MEQ 1143 P.1975
1740 ca	John Baillie	Inverness	Hot milk jug, ovoid, with cover, on 3 hoof feet, v-shaped spout with molded drop, engraved around the border and cover with band of stylized foliage, baluster finial, scroll handle, engraved with later initials "CM", marks – IB, UB, Sl...I, H - 5" ht, 12oz	Christie's July 3, 1984 #163 Christie's March 29, 1983 #41 Clayton Christie's p183 #17

YEAR	MAKER	LOCATION	DESCRIPTION	SOURCE
1740 ca	Robert Luke	Glasgow	Cream boat, on 3 paw feet, trefid attachments, chased everted rim and spout, capped double scroll silver handle, 7" long, 8.7oz	Sotheby's NY USA April 25-26, 1978 #770
1740 ca	John Baillie	Banff	Cream jug, upright, tall baluster body, on molded foot, narrow v spout, silver double scroll handle	Shaw Collection Christie's Glasgow March 1983 #43
1740/41	James Mitchell	Edinburgh	Cream boat, everted chased rim, on 3 paw feet, 7 3/8" long, 7oz	James Robinson NY 1989 The Phoenix Collection
1740/41	Dougal Ged Assayer Dougal Ged	Edinburgh	Cream boat, oval form, everted wavy rim, decorated with shells, scrolls and flowers, on 3 hoof feet, with leaf capped handle, 7 ¼" long, 7.2oz	Sotheby's March 24, 1966 # N Bloom Antiques
1740/41	James Mitchelson	Edinburgh	Cream boat, shaped everted rim and lip, flat chased with rococo ornament, gilt interior, leaf capped double scroll handle, on 3 paw feet, headed by trefoil, 6 ½" long, 4.5oz	Sotheby's NY USA April 23, 1993 #294
1740/41	Lawrence Oliphant	Edinburgh	Cream boat on 3 voluted cabriole legs, 7.3oz	How's Notes on Antiques Silver vol i, 1941 p22
1740/41	Edward Lothian Assayer Dougal Ged	Edinburgh	Cream boat, on 3 hoof feet with trefid knees, chased everted rim and spout, leaf capped double scroll silver handle, 6 ¾" long, 5oz	Sotheby's NY USA October 3-4, 1974 #305
1741/42	James Weems Assayer Dougal Ged	Edinburgh	Cream boat, broad everted plain shaped rim, on 3 paw feet, with trefid attachments, script "W" on bottom, 7 5/8" across	Shrubsole NY 1993 The Phoenix Collection
1741/42	Ebenezer Oliphant Assayer Dougal Ged	Edinburgh	Cream boat, everted chased rim, on paw feet	William Walter Ltd, London 1991
1741/42	Lawrence Oliphant	Edinburgh	Cream boat, everted chased rim, on 3 paw feet, 7.3oz	How of Edinburgh 1937 #97 Connoisseur Magazine February 1939, p107-109 How of Edinburgh advertisement
1741/42	Edward Lothian	Edinburgh	Cream boat, on 3 applied hoof feet, shaped everted rim chased with arabesques, leaf capped double scroll handle 7 ¼" long, 6oz	Christie's October 18, 1982 #209 Christie's February 18, 1985 #73 Christie's April 1, 1985 #47 Christie's South Kensington November 28, 1989 #442 Christie's Glasgow November 21, 1990 #39
1741/42	Ebenezer Oliphant	Edinburgh	Cream boat, on 3 paw feet, leaf capped double scroll handle, everted rim, lip chased with scrolls, foliage and rococo ornament, 2 sets of initials, 8" long,	Christie's May 18, 1988 #66 Christie's South Kensington May

YEAR	MAKER (continued)	LOCATION	DESCRIPTION	SOURCE
			6.5oz	18, 1990 #387 Christie's October 2, 1990
1742/43	Robert Low	Edinburgh	Cream boat, plain oval body, inner rim and lip chased with shell, scroll and floral designs, scroll handle, on 3 paw feet, 6 ¾" long, 5.5oz	Sotheby's July 23, 1959 How of Edinburgh
1742/43	George Forbes	Edinburgh	Cream boat, on 3 paw feet, shaped everted rim, lip chased with shells and foliage, double scroll handle, crest and monogram, 6.6oz	Christie's March 26, 1958
1742/43	IC Probably James Campbell	Edinburgh	Cream boat, part of a 3 piece tea service, on 3 hoof feet, acanthus double scroll handle, everted chased rim	Christie's July 18, 1963 Christie's July 5, 1967 #172 De Havilland Antiques Apollo vol 88 October 1968 p54
1742/43	James Clark	Edinburgh	Cream boat, everted chased rim, on pad feet, leaf capped double scroll handle, initials script "F" or "T" in a circle	Apollo October 1968 vol 88 p54 Christie's July 5, 1967 #172
1742/43	Edward Lothian	Edinburgh	Cream boat, chased everted rim and spout, on 3 paw feet, leaf capped double scroll handle, 7.6oz	Apollo vol 17 1933 pXIII
1743 ca	Robert Luke	Glasgow	Cream boat, plain body, everted rim, v-shaped spout, double scroll handle, 3 paw feet, 7" from lip to handle, 8oz 15 d	JH Bourdon-Smith Catalog Spring 1973
1743/44	William Davie or William Dempster	Edinburgh	Cream boat, everted chased rim, flying dolphin handle, part of a mixed set of 3 pieces	Apollo January 1974 vol 99 p43 Asprey advertisement Spink advertisement
1743/44	James Ker	Edinburgh	Cream boat, everted chased rim, on 3 paw feet, initials "AE", part of a 3 piece tea service	Clayton Dictionary p42 #651
1743/44	William Aytoun	Edinburgh	Cream boat, on 3 feet, everted rim chased with crest	National Museums of Scotland MEQ 814
1743/44	Edward Lothian	Edinburgh	Cream jug, pear shaped, on circular foot, molded lip, double scroll handle, body engraved with a cipher and a border of shells and scrolls, 3 7/8" ht, 6.2oz	Christie's July 26, 1960
1743/44	HP Probably Hugh Penman	Edinburgh	Cream boat, chased on the flared and wavy lip with flower heads, leaves and scrolls, leaf capped double scroll handle, 3 paw feet, 6 ½" long, 5.5oz	Sotheby's December 15, 1966 #46 N. Boom & Son Ltd Christie's July 26, 1972 #155
1743/44	*Hugh Penman*	*Edinburgh*	*Cream boat, no details*	*Holland p 221*

YEAR	MAKER	LOCATION	DESCRIPTION	SOURCE
1743/44	Robert Gordon	Edinburgh	Cream boat, no details	Dundee Museums and Art Galleries 1964-27
1744/45	William Dempster or William Davie Assayer Hugh Gordon	Edinburgh	Cream boat, everted chased rim, on 3 paw feet, capped double scroll handle	Christie's London July 25, 1973 #177 JH Bourdon-Smith London Christie's London Negative #744575 JH Bourdon-Smith Catalog Autumn 2002 p21 #44
1744/45	Edward Lothian	Edinburgh	Cream boat, everted chased rim, on 3 hoof feet, with trefid attachments, 6 ½" long	The Phoenix Collection
1744/45	William Dempster or William Davie	Edinburgh	Cream jug, covered, upright, on 3 scroll and pad feet, u-shaped lower half of body with band of leafy chased decoration, also on outside of almost flat lid, cone or artichoke finial, leaf capped double scroll handle	Finlay 1991 #80
1744/45	Edward Lothian	Edinburgh	Cream jug, upright, on 3 cabriole and pad feet, u-shaped lower body, double scroll silver handle, part of a 3 piece service	Sotheby's May 3, 1962 #12
1744/45	William Dempster or William Davie	Edinburgh	Cream boat, oval, on 3 scroll and paw feet issuing from scrolled volutes, capped double scroll handle, shaped rim chased with flowers and scrolls, 6 ¾" long, 7.2 oz	Christie's July 25, 1973 #177
1744/45	AG	Edinburgh	Cream jug, sold with a teapot and bowl by Edward Lothian	Sotheby's May 3 #12 Simon Kaye Antiques Sotheby's June 18, 1987 #251
1744/45	James Ker	Edinburgh	Cream boat, everted shaped rim and lip chased with flowers foliage and shell motifs, on 3 paw feet issuing from volutes, crest and motto of Duncan, 6 ¾" long, 7.2oz	Brett #818 Sotheby's March 14, 1974 or 1984 #195 JH Bourdon-Smith Catalog 1974 JH Bourdon-Smith Catalog autumn 2002 p21
1745 ca	James Glen	Glasgow	Cream boat, plain oval, on 3 stylized fleur-de-lis and paw feet, shaped everted rim chased with flower heads and foliated scrolls, leap capped flying scroll handles, later gilt interior, engraved with later crest, long marked to the base, crest of Stuart, 6 ½" long, 5oz	Christie's Scotland November 25-27, 1997
1745 ca	James Glen	Glasgow	Cream boat, on 3 paw feet, leaf capped double scroll silver handle, chased everted rim	Finlay 1991 #107 Glasgow Art Gallery and Museum

YEAR	MAKER	LOCATION	DESCRIPTION	SOURCE
1745 ca	James Glen	Glasgow	Cream boat, oval, on 3 paw feet headed by comma motifs, wavy lip, leaf capped double scroll handle, underside initialed, 6" long, 6oz	Sotheby's August 24, 1972 #71
1745 ca	James Glen	Glasgow	Cream boat, no details, 7.1oz	How of Edinburgh 1937 #101
1745 ca	A D	Aberdeen	Cream jug, baluster body, raised on hoof feet headed by trefoils, 2 unidentified marks A. D. in a shaped shield and a bird's head, 4 ½" ht, 5oz 10d	Sotheby's October 31, 1974
1745 ca	James Glen	Glasgow	Cream jug, baluster form, quite plain, double scroll leaf capped handle, 3 ½" ht, 3oz 10d	Sotheby's July 21, 1966
1745 ca	James Glen	Glasgow	Cream boat, leaf capped scroll handle, everted edge, on paw feet, 7" from lip to back of handle, 7.25oz	JH Bourdon-Smith Catalog Spring 1981
1745 ca	Not available	Edinburgh	Cream boat, oval, everted shaped chased rim, 3 semi cabriole legs with paw feet, dolphin flying handle	Brand Inglis 1980 p137 #152
1745/46	Robert Gordon	Edinburgh	Cream boat, everted chased rim, dolphin handle	Country Life 1963 p444
1745/46	James Ker	Edinburgh	Cream boat with bowl	The Maple Swan Collection
1745/46	William Dempster	Edinburgh	Cream jug, no details	National Museums of Scotland 1962.730
1746/47	William Aytoun	Edinburgh	Cream boat, everted chased rim, on paw feet, set, leaf capped double scroll handle, swan or pelican crest, 8"	Ticher Irish Silver p27 Holland p18 Hyman Collection - Colonial Williamsburg G1995-11
1746/47	Hugh Penman	Edinburgh	Cream boat, no details	The Maple Swan Collection
1746/47	Edward Lothian	Edinburgh	Cream boat, everted chased rim, on pad feet, double scroll handle, crest and motto of Curle, part of a service	Antiques Magazine vol 86 p410 Shrubsole advertisement
1746/47	James Welsh Assayer Hugh Gordon	Edinburgh	Cream boat, George II, on 3 scroll and paw feet, shaped everted rim chased with flowers, foliage and scrolls, double scroll handle, 7oz	Christie's October 16, 1968 #79
1746/47	WD possibly William Davie, Assayer Hugh Gordon	Edinburgh	Cream boat, on 3 foliate and paw feet, otherwise plain body engraved with crest and motto, everted rim chased with foliage, flying scroll handle formed as a dolphin, motto "For…DEFENSE", crest of a ram's head	Christie's Scotland November 14, 1985 #312
1746/47	James Ker	Edinburgh	Cream boat, on 3 paw feet, leaf capped reverse scroll handle everted lip	Christie's March 27, 1984 #269

YEAR	MAKER Assayer Hugh Gordon	LOCATION	DESCRIPTION	SOURCE
1746/47	Robert Gordon	Edinburgh	Cream boat with dolphin handle, 7 ¼"	Noble Collection National Museums of Scotland A.1981.306
1746/47	Robert Gordon	Edinburgh	Cream boats, pair, dolphin-handled cream boats, on lion paw feet, everted chased rims, crest of Udney "All my hope is in God", 9" long, 25.3oz total	Nicholas Shaw Catalog 2001 p70
1746/47	James Ker	Edinburgh	Cream boat, on 3 paw feet, trefid attachments, leaf capped double scroll handle, chased everted rim and spout, part of a 3 piece service	Sotheby's NY USA June 10-11, 1980 #433
1747/48	Robert Low	Edinburgh	Cream boat, on pad feet, chased rim, no spout, crest of Princess Elizabeth as Duchess of Edinburgh	Grimwade The Queen's Silver # 9
1747/48	Robert Gordon	Edinburgh	Cream boat, on large paw feet, leaf capped handle, chased rim, 8 ½"	Apollo April 1972 vol 95 p2 Bell of Aberdeen Sotheby's July 4, 1966 #157
1748/49	Ker & Dempster	Edinburgh	Cream boat on 3 hoof feet, scroll handle 4 5/8" wide, 4.9 oz	Nicholas Shaw Catalog 2005 p92
1748/49	*Ker & Dempster*	*Edinburgh*	*Cream boat of sauceboat, helmet shaped on 3 hoof feet, scroll handle, 4.9oz*	*Bonhams sale 15120 Aug 22, 2007 #5*
1749/50	Ebenezer Oliphant	Edinburgh	Cream boat or sauce boat, oval, everted shaped chased rim, on paw feet, flying dolphin or monster-headed handle, initial "L", other side crest and motto "EX BELLO QUIES", 8" long, 10oz	Sotheby's Gleneagles August 25, 1997 #151
1750 ca	James Glen	Glasgow	Cream boat, mm twice, on 3 voluted cabriole paw feet, everted plain border, leaf capped double scroll handle, 6oz 5d	Christie's Glasgow March 1983 #50 Shaw collection
1750 ca	Colin Allan	Aberdeen	Cream jug, baluster form	Christie's London July 1992 #100
1750 ca	Colin Allan	Aberdeen	Milk pot, small, covered, no details	Private Collection UK
1750 ca	James Glen	Glasgow	Cream jug, no details	National Museums of Scotland MEQ 30
1751/52	Edward Lothian	Edinburgh	Cream boat, chased everted wavy rim, lip also engraved and chased, 7 ¼" long, 6oz 5d	Private Collection

YEAR	MAKER	LOCATION	DESCRIPTION	SOURCE
1751/52	IM in a rectangle James McKenzie I or James Mitchelson	Edinburgh	Cream jug, no details	National Museums of Scotland 1952.1290
1752/53	Robert Gordon	Edinburgh	Cream boat or sauce boat, shaped rim with leaf and scroll chasing, on 3 scroll pad feet with shell attachments, dolphin handle, 6 3/4" long	The Phoenix Collection
1752/53	John Welsh	Edinburgh	Cream boat, on 3 shell and hoof feet, chased with a band of foliage, shaped everted rim	Christie's Glasgow June 11, 1991 #170
1753/54	Lothian & Robertson	Edinburgh	Cream boat, inverted pear shaped body, on 3 paw feet, furry attachments, intertwined snake handle, crest and motto 5" long, 4.7oz	Munro Collection Wark, Huntington Library #155
1753/54	Robert Low	Edinburgh	Creamboat or sauce boat, chased rim, double scroll handle, shell feet, crest of a lion rampant grasping a sword, motto "PAR VALUER", 8" long	Metropolitan Museum of NYC USA AC#13.42.70
1754/55	Hugh Gordon	Edinburgh	Cream boat, listed as a sauce boat, shallow body of shaped outline, on 3 shell and scroll feet, wavy rim and a flying scroll handle, 8oz	Christie's December 5, 1962
1754/55	Lothian & Robertson	Edinburgh	Cream boat, listed as a sauce boat, gadrooned and molded rim, on gadrooned and rising foot, elaborate serpent and scroll handle, body later chased with rococo flowers and scrolling foliate swags, vacant rococo cartouche, 6" long, 6.3oz	Christie's South Kensington November 28, 1989 #245 Christie's Edinburgh November 21, 1990 #40
1755/56	William Gilchrist	Edinburgh	Cream boat, on 3 paw feet, everted chased rim, flying handle, 7 ½" long, 9oz	Sotheby's March 23, 1993 #125
1758/59	Lothian & Robertson	Edinburgh	Cream boat or sauce boat, part of a mixed 3 piece service, heavy leaf capped double scroll silver handle, chased rim and spout, 7.7oz	Christie's London March 26, 1980 Christie's Negative #941051 AP784
1759/60	Not available	Edinburgh	Cream boat, plain oval body, flying scroll handle, 3 hoof feet, 5 ¼" long, 4.1oz	Sotheby's November 1962 #97 Simon Kaye Antiques
1760 ca	Colin Allan	Aberdeen	Mask milk jug, upright, on pedestal, applied swags, capped double scroll silver handle, gadrooning around the top	Lorentz Antiques Toronto Canada 1993
1760 ca	Colin Allan	Aberdeen	Cream Jug with sugar on 3 pad feet	Sotheby's August 1987 #285
1760 ca	Ker & Dempster	Edinburgh	Milk jug, on pedestal foot, possibly chased with cluster of flowers, sold with sugar bowl of 1748/49 same maker, 4 ½" ht, 15.1oz with bowl	Sotheby's November 11, 1971 #111 Koopman London
1760 ca	Milne & Campbell	Glasgow	Cream boat, oval, plain, on 3 hoof feet, shaped everted rim, leaf-capped flying scroll handle, engraved on side with initial "M", 6" long, 5oz	Christie's Edinburgh April 29, 1992

YEAR	MAKER (continued)	LOCATION	DESCRIPTION	SOURCE Private Collection
1760 ca	CK (continued)	Canongate	Cream boat, on 3 hoof feet, everted plain rim and spout, double scroll handle, body later chased all over with heavy floral decoration	Christie's December 20, 1974 Negative #759494 Stock #184 WY
1760/61	Lothian & Robertson	Edinburgh	Cream boat, no details	National Museums of Scotland MEQ 606 1961.1676
1760/61	Lothian & Robertson	Edinburgh	Cream jug, baluster body, 2 crests, chased with floral sprays and flutes, leaf capped double scroll handle, 3 shell feet headed by masks, 5 ¾" ht, 7.8oz	Sotheby's Scone Palace April 13, 1976 #128
1761/62	Lothian & Robertson	Edinburgh	Cream boat, inverted pyri form shape, everted notched rim, engraved script "CM", 7 ¼" long, 7.3oz	Christie's NY USA 1999 #315 Bonhams The Scottish Sale August 21, 2003 #23 Nicholas Shaw Catalog Winter 2004 p92
1762/63	Lothian & Robertson	Edinburgh	Cream boat, flying handle (repaired), leaf edging,	James Robinson, NY USA 1990
1762/63	Lothian & Robertson	Edinburgh	Cream jug, upright, pear shaped body, molded lip, leaf capped double scroll silver handle, 5" ht, 7.5oz	Shaw Collection Christie's Glasgow March 1983 #78
1762/63	Lothian & Robertson	Edinburgh	Cream boat or sauce boat, on 3 hoof feet, leaf capped scroll handle, scroll rim, 8" long, 6oz	Shrubsole NY USA 1981 E4087
1762/63	Alexander Gardner	Edinburgh	Cream boat, on 3 hoof feet, chased band of flowers and scrolls, double scroll handle, 4.9oz	Christie's November 1969 #34 Christie's March 23, 1970 Simon Kaye Antiques
1763/64	Alexander Gardner	Edinburgh	Cream jug, with an earlier pot in a case, upright, pear shaped body, swirled bands of floral decoration and flutes, double scroll handle	Christie's London October 1988 #154
1765 ca	Robert Clark & James Hill	Edinburgh	Cream boat, oval, leaf capped flying scroll handle, on 3 hoof feet, crest, motto, and coronet, 4 ½" long, 3.6oz	Sotheby's November 11, 1971, #79
1765/66	Ker & Dempster	Edinburgh	Cream boat, part of a service, no details	Antiques Magazine 1956, 65
1765/66	John Welsh	Edinburgh	Cream boat, no details	National Museums of Scotland MEQ 852 1966.999

YEAR	MAKER	LOCATION	DESCRIPTION	SOURCE
1767/68	Ker & Dempster	Edinburgh	Cream boat, on 3 hoof feet, slightly everted rim, crest and motto of Douglas, 7" long, 6.4oz	Nicholas Shaw Catalog Winter 2002/03 p93
1767/68	Ker & Dempster	Edinburgh	Cream jug, upright, inverted pear shaped body, stepped foot, upswept spout, chased around the upper body, part of a 3 piece tea service	Apollo vol 53 1951 pXI
1769/70	William Taylor	Edinburgh	Cream boat, chased wavy rim, damage to rim, 6 ½" long, 6oz 3d	Private Collection Sotheby's Gleneagles August 27, 1990
1770 ca	Milne & Campbell	Glasgow	Cream boat, no details	Connoisseur Magazine 1954 vol 133 p6 Bell of Aberdeen advertisement
1770 ca	Not available		Cream boat, part of a service	Antiques Magazine 1951 vol 60 Bell of Aberdeen advertisement
1770/71	William Dempster or William Davie	Edinburgh	Cream jug, flying handle, part of a 3 piece serve dating 1758-1770	Scottish Art Review vol IV 1953 #4 Bell of Aberdeen advertisement
1771/72	James Welsh	Edinburgh	Cream boat, no details	Connoisseur Magazine 1941-42 vol 180, p138
1773/74	Patrick Robertson	Edinburgh	Cream boat, no details	Connoisseur Magazine 1934 vol 94 p66
1775 ca	James McEwan	Glasgow	Cream boat, part of a 3 piece service, no details	Private Collection
1779/80	James Hewitt	Edinburgh	Cream boat, inverted pear shape, everted notched rim, acanthus capped scroll handle, 7" long, 5.3oz	Bonhams Sale 10914, #12 Nicholas Shaw Catalog Winter 2004 p92
1779/80	*James Hewitt*	*Edinburgh*	*Cream boat, squat pear shape, molded oval leaf-shaped everted border, leaf-capped scroll handle, 7" wide, 5oz*	*Christie's Lanarkshire UK 1997 #57*
1780ca	James Glen	Aberdeen	Cream jug, vase-shaped on spreading circular base with rim foot, engrave ribbon-tied husk festoons with initials "LGG", sold with a matching sugar basin	Christie's London UK 1999 #19
1782/83	James Gilliland	Edinburgh	Cream jug, helmet-shaped, circular base, beaded rim, engraved with neo-classical ribbon-tied floral garland, oval cartouche with crest, motto and initials, part of a mixed service	Christie's Lanarkshire UK 1998 #61

YEAR	MAKER	LOCATION	DESCRIPTION	SOURCE
1783/84	William Davie or William Dempster	Edinburgh	Cream boat, part of a service, no details	Country Life Magazine May/June 1968 vol 143
1784/85	W & P Cunningham I	Edinburgh	Cream jug, covered, helmet shaped, bright cut engraving, circular pedestal foot, double scroll handle, fully marked on outside of foot, initials "S.G.W.", 7" ht, 7.2oz	Sotheby's Gleneagles August 29, 1978 #431 Sotheby's Blair Castle September 12, 1980 #57 Private Collection
1785 ca	Robert Anderson	Inverness	Cream jug, upright, body and foot with fluted panels, snake handle	Finlay 1991 #116
1785/86	Not available	Edinburgh	Cream jug, helmet form with a beaded rim and handle, raised conforming foot, with duty mark incuse, 6" ht, 5oz	Christie's London UK 2001 #122
1789/80	Not available		Cream boat, part of a service, no details	Country Life Magazine July 1954 vol 16, p184
1789/91	W & P Cunningham I	Edinburgh	Cream boat, part of a 4 piece service, no details	Christie's May 1, 2001 #236
1790 ca	Alexander Stewart Jr	Inverness	Cream boat, part of a service, no details	Connoisseur Magazine 1934 vol 93 p347
1790 ca	W & P Cunningham I	Edinburgh	Cream jug, lacking date letter, neo-classical form, scalloped foot, bright cut border of scrolling foliage, reeded handle, engraved initial, 7" ht, sold with another	Bonhams Sale 15120 Aug 22, 2007 #25
1790/91	William Robertson or William Rynd	Edinburgh	Cream jug, upright, with loop handle, on spreading oval base, crest and motto in an oval, part of a 4 piece tea service	Sotheby's Gleneagles August 1992 #147 Private Collection
1791/92	W & P Cunningham I	Edinburgh	Cream jug, helmet shaped, 10 sided, loop handle, bright cut decoration	Firestone and Parsons, Boston 1992
1791/92	William Robertson	Edinburgh	Cream jug, part of a service, no details	Finlay 1991 #98 Country Life Magazine February 13, 1964 vol 135 p 31
1793/94	Not available	Edinburgh	Cream boat, on feet, tall, Adam style, 3oz 15d	Christie's Glasgow March 1983 #73 Shaw Collection
1793/94	ID James Douglas	Edinburgh	Creamer, part of a set, Adam style, attributed to James Dempster but more likely James Douglas	William Walter Ltd, London 1994

YEAR	MAKER	LOCATION	DESCRIPTION	SOURCE
1794/95	Alexander Spence	Edinburgh	Cream jug, engraved with a vacant drapery cartouche within bright-cut leaves, and wigglework bands, initialed "N" on underside, part of a service	Sotheby's NY USA 1998 #542
1795 ca	Not available		Creamer, part of a service, no details	Antiques Magazine vol 38 p50 Shreves advertisement
1795/96	George Bain	Edinburgh	Cream boat, helmet shaped body, bright cut engraving, high loop handle, square pedestal base, with sugar basket, 6 ½" ht	Sotheby's Scone April 19, 1977 #54
1795 ca	James Douglas	Edinburgh	Cream boat, no details	William Walter Ltd, 1991
1795 ca	William Byres	Banff	Cream jug, upright, sparrow beak, no details	Country Life, May 7, 1987 vol 181 #112-113
1795/96	G & M	Edinburgh assay	Cream boat, part of a 3 piece service, no details	Christie's July 12, 1989
1795/96	Alexander Spence	Edinburgh	Cream jug, helmet shaped, bright cut and wriggle worked drapery cartouche with later crest and motto, reeded loop handle, oval pedestal base	Sotheby's Gleneagles September 1, 1981 #444
1796/97	William Robertson	Edinburgh	Cream boat, Adam style, part of a service, no detail	William Walter Ltd, London 1994
1796/97	W & P Cunningham I	Edinburgh	Cream jug, part of a service, no detail	Sotheby's November 29, 1973 #91 Christie's March 25, 1981
1796/97	W & P Cunningham I	Edinburgh	Cream jug, round topped handle, oval base, 3 3/8" di, 6" ht	Huntley House Museum Edinburgh
1796/97	Alexander Gardner	Edinburgh	Cream boat, oval outline, concave fluting, bright cut, part of a 4 pieced mixed tea service	N & I Franklin Private Collection
1796/97	Charles Bendy	Edinburgh	Cream jug, helmet shaped, on square foot, crest and motto of Hutton, 6 ¼", 6.1oz	Nicholas Shaw Catalog 2004 p103
1797/98	W & P Cunningham I	Edinburgh	Cream jug, vase shaped, bright cut, body fluted into panels, 2 foliate cartouches, reeded handle, oval spreading base, 5 ¾" ht, 4.8oz	Sotheby's Gleneagles August 27, 1979 #205
1798/99	James McKay	Edinburgh	Milk jug, no details	National Museums of Scotland MEQ 635
1800 ca	W & P Cunningham I	Edinburgh	Cream jug, oval form on spread oval foot, bright cut engraved, vacant cartouche either side, loop handle, no date letter	Bonhams London 2006 #292

YEAR	MAKER	LOCATION	DESCRIPTION	SOURCE
1800/01	W & P Cunningham I	Edinburgh	Cream boat, part of a service, no details	Antiques Magazine 1957 vol 71
1800/01	W & P Cunningham I	Edinburgh	Cream jug, helmet shaped, chased with a frieze of flowers, 6" ht, 6.5oz	Nicholas Shaw Catalog Winter 2002/03 p85
1800/01	McHattie & Fenwick	Edinburgh	Cream jug, square top handle, oval, oblong base, with a sugar bowl, 5 5/8" X 3 ¼" X 5 1/8" ht	Huntley House Museum Edinburgh HH3488/70
1800/01	W & P Cunningham I	Edinburgh	Cream jug, of oval section with a part fluted foot, Greek key motif shoulder, gadrooned rim, gilt interior, crest, motto and initials, part of a service	Christie's London UK 2000 #369
1802/03	Francis Howden	Edinburgh	Cream jug, upright, flat on the bottom, 3 girdles applied to the upper body, squared off handle, part of a 3 piece tea service	Scottish Art Review vol VIII 1961 p33 #2 Glasgow firm advertisement
1802/03	*Francis Howden*	*Edinburgh*	*Cream jug, bright cut engraved with paneled center, gilt interior, part of a service*	*Christie's London UK 2006 #1684*
1804/05	Alexander Spence	Edinburgh	Cream jug, part of a 4 piece service, rectangular, with bright cut decoration	Antiques Magazine vol 41, p295 Bell of Aberdeen
1806/07	W & P Cunningham I	Edinburgh	Cream boat, part of a 3 piece service, Arms of Kincragie	Sotheby's Hopetoun House April 26, 1988 #76
1806/07	George McHattie	Edinburgh	Milk jug, bright cut, engraved body on 4 ball feet, crest and motto of Sandeman of Perth, 4 ½" ht, 6.8oz	Nicholas Shaw Catalog Winter 2002/3 p86
1806/07	George McHattie	Edinburgh	Creamer, rectangular waisted bulbous body, on four ball feet, part of a service	New Orleans Auction Galleries 2003 #60
1806/07	W M	Edinburgh	Cream jug, plain oblong form with thread mount	Christie's London 2001 #180
1807/08	George McHattie	Edinburgh	Milk jug, on 4 ball feet, crest and motto of Sandman of Perth, bright cut decoration, 4 ½" ht, 6.76oz	Nicholas Shaw Antiques 2004
1807/08	James McKay	Edinburgh	Cream boat, part of a service, no details	Apollo 1974 vol 100 p17 Holmes advertisement
1807/08	Robert Gray & Son	Glasgow Edinburgh assay	Cream jug, circular shape with half reeded body, part of a service	Rosebury's London UK 2007 #665
1807/08	IM	Edinburgh	Cream jug, shaped handle, foliate embossing, part of a service	Jacobs & Hunt Hampshire 2007 #210

YEAR	MAKER	LOCATION	DESCRIPTION	SOURCE
1808/09	Francis Howden	Edinburgh	Cream boat, part of a service, no details	Antiques Magazine vol 46, #20
1808/09	R K (over struck)	Perth Edinburgh assay	Cream boat, part of a service, no details	Sotheby's Hopetoun House April 1989 #42
1808/09	Cunningham & Simpson	Edinburgh	Cream jug, no details	National Museums of Scotland 1945.39
1808/09	Dirk & McPherson	Edinburgh	Milk jug on 4 ball feet, 4" ht, 6.6oz	Nicholas Shaw Catalog Winter 2002/03 p88
1809/10	James McKay	Edinburgh	Cream boat, part of a service, no details	Apollo 1967 vol 85, p 87
1809/10	George Fenwick	Edinburgh	Cream boat, part of a 3 piece service, on bun feet, initial "H"	Sotheby's February 26, 1976 #38
1809/10	George Fenwick	Edinburgh	Milk jug, no details	National Museums of Scotland MEQ 1608
1809/10	George Fenwick	Edinburgh	Cream jug, rectangular, squared off handle, full coat of arms below a coronet, motto below "THROUGH"	Sotheby's Gleneagles August 1988 #473
1809/10	George McHattie	Edinburgh	Cream jug with angular handle, part of a service	Pook & Pook, Downingtown, PA USA 2004 #624
1810 ca	Newlands and Grierson	Glasgow	Cream jug, ovalled rectangular form, gilt interior, on 4 ball feet, part of a 3 piece service	Sotheby's Gleneagles August 24, 1997 #122
1810/11	George Fenwick	Edinburgh	Cream boat, part of a service, no details	Christie's Edinburgh May 1, 1991 #246
1811/12	George Fenwick	Edinburgh	Cream boat, part of a service, no details	Lyle Annual Review 1983 p 615
1811/12	James McKay	Edinburgh	Cream boat, part of a service, no details	Sotheby's Hopetoun House May 1990 #86
1812/13	MM (indistinct)	Edinburgh	Cream jug, ovoid shape on a circular foot, flat scroll handle, crest and motto "SAND CRAINTE", 6 ¼" ht, 6.5oz	Christie's London UK 2003 #419
1812/13	James McKay	Edinburgh	Cream boat, part of a service, no details	Antiques Magazine vol 115, p 1328 Shreve advertisement

YEAR	MAKER	LOCATION	DESCRIPTION	SOURCE
1814/15	Robert Gray & Son	Glasgow Edinburgh assay	Cream jug, squat form, gadrooned circular foot, shoulder with anthemion band, part of a service	Christie's NY USA 2005 #172
1814/15	Robert Gray & Son	Glasgow Edinburgh assay	Cream jug, Greek revival manner of circular form, chased and embossed with bands of anthemion and stylized foliage within fluted borders, part of a service, possibly the same as above	Christie's NY USA 1999 #80
1814/15	W & P Cunningham II	Edinburgh	Cream Jug, engraved to Mr. James Paterson as a historical award	National Museums of Scotland K.2004.205
1814/15	James McKay	Edinburgh	Cream jug, on 4 ball feet, gadrooned band, part of 3 piece service	Apollo 1934 pIV Bell of Aberdeen advertisement
1814/15	George Fenwick	Edinburgh	Cream jug, oblong bellied form, tongue and dart border, engraved band of fruiting vines, lobed lower body, ball feet, part of a service	Bonhams London UK 2006
1816-19	James McDonald	Edinburgh	Cream boat, part of a service, no details	Antiques Magazine 1959 vol 76 Shreve advertisement
1817/18	James McKay	Edinburgh	Milk jug, no details	National Museums of Scotland MEQ 635
1817/18	James McKay	Edinburgh	Cream jug, pear shaped, armorials, engraved foliate scroll motifs, sold with an 1815/16 teapot	Christie's London UK 2001 #107
1818/19	James McKay	Edinburgh	Cream jug, compressed form with part fluting, shell and leaf motif border, crest, part of a service	Christie's London UK 2001 #183
1818/19	James McKay	Edinburgh	Cream boat, part of a service, no details	Sotheby's Gleneagles 1990
1819/20	James McKay	Edinburgh	Cream boat, part of a service, no details	Sotheby's Gleneagles 1990
1819/20	W & P Cunningham II	Edinburgh	Cream jug, oval fluted body, leaf capped scroll handled, gadrooned rim, scrolled cartouche, part of a 3 piece service, 3" ht	Fogg Art Museum Harvard University, 1848.49 Leverette House
1820 ca	William Jamieson	Aberdeen	Cream jug, marked WJ, A,B,D,WJ, no details	Aberdeen Museums and Galleries ABDAG003152
1820 ca	Alexander Cameron	Dundee	Cream jug/boat, no detail	Dundee Museums and Art Galleries, 1986-114

YEAR	MAKER	LOCATION	DESCRIPTION	SOURCE
1820 ca	Robert Anderson	Inverness	Cream jug, paneled body, snake handle, crest and motto	National Museums of Scotland MEQ 1591 1985
1820 ca	Edward Livingstone	Dundee	Cream boat, part of a service, no details	Finlay 1991 #111
1820 ca	James McKay	Edinburgh	Milk jug, no details	National Museums of Scotland MEQ 1311
1820/21	Not available		Cream boat, part of a service, no details	Connoisseur Magazine 1952 vol 130 p 24
1820/21	Alexander Edmonstoun	Edinburgh	Cream boat, part of a 3 piece service, no details	Sotheby's File Photo
1820/21	W & P Cunningham II	Edinburgh	Cream boat, no details	National Museums of Scotland MEQ 1323
1820/21	CB	Edinburgh	Cream jug, circular with partly fluted body, elaborate shell and foliate scroll rim, part of a service	Christie's East NY USA 1998 #52
1821/22	George McHattie	Edinburgh	Milk jug, squat circular form, semi-fluted with gadrooned border, acanthus clasped handle, stepped circular pedestal foot, part of a service	Lyon & Turnbull Edinburgh UK May 25, 2006 #343
1823/24	James McKay	Edinburgh	Cream boat, part of a service, no details	Apollo April–June 1968 vol87 p106
1824/25	James McKay	Edinburgh	Cream boat, part of a 3 piece service, no details	Sotheby's Gleneagles August 1987 #305
1825/26	George Beech	Edinburgh	Cream boat, part of a service, no details	Christie's NY June 28, 1989
1825/26	James McKay	Edinburgh	Cream boat, part of a service, no details	Sotheby's Hopetoun House April 1988 #77
1825/27	Not available		Cream boat, part of a service, no details	Apollo August 1967 vol 86 p2 Bell of Aberdeen advertisement
1825 ca	Charles Murray	Perth	Cream boat, with a bowl, no details	Christie's Edinburgh May 1, 1991 #304
1826/27	Alexander Edmonstoun	Edinburgh	Cream boat, part of a service, no details	Sotheby's Hopetoun House April 1988 #81

YEAR	MAKER	LOCATION	DESCRIPTION	SOURCE
1827/28	Robert Gray & Sons	Glasgow	Cream jug, gadrooned foot and rim	National Museums of Scotland MEQ 854
1828/29	Robert Keay II	Perth Edinburgh assay	Cream jug, part of a 3 piece service, no details	National Museums of Scotland MEQ 949-951 1969
1828/29	James McKay	Edinburgh	Cream jug, squat form, scroll handle, on anthemion scroll feet, 6 ½" ht	Gorringes LLP East Sussex UK 2006 #1609
1829/30	James McKay	Edinburgh	Cream boat, part of a service, no details	Sotheby's Hopetoun House April 1988 #83
1829/30	James McKay	Edinburgh	Hot milk jug, 6" ht	JH Bourdon-Smith Catalog #34 p47
1832/33	Elder & Co	Edinburgh	Cream boat, part of a 3 piece service, no details	Sotheby's Gleneagles August 29, 1977
1832/33	William Marshall	Edinburgh	Cream boat, part of a service, no details	Sotheby's Gleneagles August 1988 #484
1834/35	Elder & Co	Edinburgh	Cream boat, part of a 3 piece service, no details	Sotheby's Gleneagles August 27, 1990 #101
1835/36	Elder & C0	Edinburgh	Cream boat, part of a 4 piece service, no details	Christie's November 23, 1983 #92
1835/36	Elder & Co	Edinburgh	Cream jug, no details	Bonhams London UK 2001 #73
1835/36	William Whitecross	Aberdeen Edinburgh assay	Cream jug, plain circular compressed form, gilt interior, part of a mixed service	Christie's London UK 2002 #226
1837/38	James McKay	Edinburgh	Cream jug, helmet-shaped, with contemporary initial "C", part of a service	Christie's Lanarkshire UK 1998 #62
1838/39	Leonard Urquhart	Edinburgh	Cream jug, semi-fluted inverted pear form on a spreading circular foot, chased with scrolls and foliage, gilt interior, part of a service	Christie's London UK 2004 #119
1838/39	James McKay	Edinburgh	Creamer, baluster on circular foot, repossed body, gilt interior, part of a service	Christie's NY USA 2004 #984
1838/39	A M (over struck) Adam Mossman	Edinburgh	Cream boat, part of a 3 piece service, no details	Sotheby's August 28, 1959 #86

YEAR	MAKER	LOCATION	DESCRIPTION	SOURCE
1839/40	Robert Keay II	Perth Edinburgh assay	Cream jug, no details	Dundee Museums and Art Galleries 1962-701-2
1840/41	Robb & Whittet	Edinburgh	Cream jug of circular waisted form, chased, on four tab feet, gilt interior, part of a service	Christie's London UK 2003 #406
1842/43	Robert Keay II	Perth Edinburgh assay	Cream jug, part of a 3 piece service, no details	National Museums of Scotland MEQ 736-738 1964
1842/43	McKay & Chisolm	Edinburgh	Cream boat, part of a service, no details	Lyle Annual Review 1983
1844/45	James McKay	Edinburgh	Cream boat, part of a service, no details	Lyle Annual Review 1983
1846/47	William Marshall & Sons	Edinburgh	Cream jug, octagonal, butterfly decoration, part of a 4 piece service, 4 3/8" X 3 1/8" X 5 5/8" ht	Huntley House Museum Edinburgh HH2809/65
1849/50	Walker Crichton	Edinburgh	Cream jug, globular on spreading foot, gilt interior, part of a service	Christie's London UK 2006 #1687
1852/53	WCS	Edinburgh	Cream jug, baluster form, chased with flowers, monogrammed, part of a service	Christie's NY USA 2005 #249
1872/73	McKay & Cunningham	Edinburgh	Cream pail with gothic script inscription, 9oz	JH Bourdon-Smith Catalog Autumn 1993 #36 p40
1874/75	Pollack and Meldrum	Edinburgh	Cream jug, no details, part of a 3 piece service, 4 5/8" X 3 5/8"di X 7 3/8" ht	Huntley House Museum Edinburgh HH1666/56
1876/77	Hamilton & Inches	Edinburgh	Cream jug, decorated with signs of the Zodiac, part of a service	Christie's NY USA 2002 #656
1876/77	John Crichton	Edinburgh	Cream jug, faceted oblong, serpent handle, beaded rim, repousse panels, singing rooster, insect amid plants, butterfly amid flowers and foliage, with French import mark, part of a service,	Christie's NY USA 1998 #292
1885/86	JR	Glasgow	Cream jug, bombe form, gadrooned rim, reeded handle, engraved foliate motifs, gilt interior, part of a service	Christie's London UK 2001 #114
1896/97	Not available	Glasgow	Cream jug, chased with scenes from Sir Walter Scott's "Lay of the Last Minstrel", part of a 3 piece service, 4 1/8" X 6 ½"	Huntley House Museum Edinburgh LR 36/60
1905/06	Hamilton & Inches	Edinburgh	Cream jug, circular form, hammered finish, line of domed bosses around the rim	Christie's London UK 2002 #195

YEAR
1992/93

MAKER
Adrian Hope

LOCATION
Edinburgh

DESCRIPTION
Creamer, no details

SOURCE
Aberdeen Museums and Galleries ABDAG008803

Cruets

Plate 18. An Egg Cruet with 4 cups 1792/93 by William Robertson, Edinburgh. Photograph courtesy of Schredds of Portobello, London (George Schrager, owner).

YEAR	MAKER	LOCATION	DESCRIPTION	SOURCE
			CRUETS	
1736/37	William Marshall I	Edinburgh	Warwick cruet frame, cinquefoil base supporting the ring bottle holders and central handle, also applied with later initial and crested oval shield, vase shaped castors each applied with a girdle at the shoulder, covers pierced with alternate panels of stylized foliage and diaper work, later cut glass bottles with silver mounts, 8" ht, 32.4oz (of weighable silver)	Sotheby's November 16-17, 1981 #411
1736ca	Not available	Edinburgh	*Warwick cruet*	*Lyle Annual Review 1983 p568* Sotheby's sales
1740/41	Hugh Gordon	Edinburgh	Warwick cruet frame, cinquefoil, base plate and bottle rings connected by leaf wrapped brackets above shell pad supports, armorial engraved rococo cartouches, central scroll ring handle with turned stem, bottles and casters missing, 10 ½" ht, 35.9 oz	Sotheby's Gleneagles August 31, 1999 #512
1745 ca	James Glen	Glasgow	Oil and vinegar cruet frame, on 4 shell and scroll feet, applied with a vacant cartouche, double scroll handle, 2 silver mounted glass bottles, 7 3/8" long, 13oz 5d	Christie's May 18, 1977 Christie's July 27, 1977
1748/49	Edward Lothian Assayer Hugh Gordon	Edinburgh	Cruet frame, with 3 casters and pair of silver mounted cut glass oil and vinegar bottles, frame with ring holders, central baluster screw on handle and shell supports, rococo cartouches enclosing an engraved coat of arms on one side, 3 vase shaped casters engraved with identical crests and mottos repeated on caps, marked on stand and caster bases, 9 ¼" ht, 68oz 2d all	Sotheby's August 26, 1972 #78
1750 ca	James Ker	Edinburgh	Cruet set, 3 casters, repairs to caster covers, 2 bottles, mm only 4x, 10" ht	Christie's NY April 12, 1988 #219
1750 ca	Ker & Dempster	Edinburgh	Cruet frame, on four shell feet, cartouche with crest, ring handle, composite later set of cut glass bottles with silver mounts, 10 ¼" ht, 28oz frame	Christie's Lanarkshire UK 1997 #575
1751/52	Hugh Gordon	Edinburgh	Cruet, set of 3 casters	Antiques Magazine 1959 vol 76
1752/53	James Mitchell	Edinburgh	Cruet frame, cinquefoil design, with central handle (London 1750ca), 6 bottle rings, applied with a crested floral and rococo decorated plaque, on 4 scroll and shell supports, with silver capped cut glass bottle, crest of Blair or Scott, 12" ht, 45.5oz	Sotheby's Gleneagles, August 29, 1974 #112 Sotheby's Scone Palace April 19, 1977 #94
1753/54	William Aytoun	Edinburgh	Cruet set, no details	Antiques Magazine July vol 66
1753/54	Robert Gordon	Edinburgh	Cruet set, no details	Antiques Magazine 1960

YEAR	MAKER	LOCATION	DESCRIPTION	SOURCE
1753/54	Hugh Gordon	Edinburgh	Quinquefoil cruet frame with 3 casters and 2 bottles, 10 ¼" ht, 40oz (minus the bottles)	Sotheby's Gleneagles August 29, 1974 #112
1753/54	Ker & Dempster	Edinburgh	Cruet frame, cinquefoil shape, central baluster handle, scroll and shell supports, no bottle or casters, with applied cartouche with a crest. 10 ½" ht, 26.8oz	Sotheby's June 24, 1965 #29 How of Edinburgh National Museums of Scotland MEQ 818 1965.1889
1754/55	Ker & Dempster	Edinburgh	Cruet frame, on 4 shell feet, molded bottle rings, flower and scroll cartouche at one side, central ring handle, later glass bottles, 3 with silver covers, with crest, motto and coronet, 29oz	Christie's February 23, 1972 #79
1754/55	Dougal Ged	Edinburgh	Cruet frame, stand on 4 leaf capped shell feet, applied rococo cartouche, detachable baluster handle, with 3 inverted pear casters with pierced domed covers and baluster finials, 2 silver mounted cut glass bottles, cartouche with coat of arms of Stirling, casters with later monograms within mottos, bottle mounts with crest and motto, 10 ¼" ht, 52oz	Christie's May 3, 1995 #65
1755 ca	Ker & Dempster Assayer Hugh Gordon	Edinburgh	Cruet stand, on 4 shell feet, cinquefoil frame with asymmetric scrolled cartouche, engraved with a crest, central support surmounted by a scrolled ring handle, composite set of 5 later cut glass and silver mounted bottles, 10 ¼", 28oz	Christie's Glasgow May 13, 1997
1755/56	Robert Gordon	Edinburgh	Cruet frame on 4 shell feet, baluster stem with scroll handle, plain asymmetric cartouche, fitted with 2 cut glass bottles, casters missing, 9 ½" ht, 27oz	Christie's Glasgow March 27, 1984 #255 Christie's Glasgow November 15, 1984 #192
1757/58	Robert Gordon	Edinburgh	Cruet frame, with a crested escutcheon, ring holders, central handle and shell supports, casters of baluster form, 2 glass bottles with unmarked silver mounts, 41.5oz	Sotheby's July 18, 1963 #342 Simon Kaye Antiques
1757/58	Robert Gordon	Edinburgh	Warwick cruet, on raised shell feet, central baluster handle, three baluster casters, two glass bottles, cartouche with crest and motto, 9" ht, 41.5oz. note: possibly the same as above in spite of date difference	Shrubsole London UK 1963 Christies NY USA 2000 #232
1760 ca	Milne & Campbell	Glasgow	Cruet set, stand with 3 casters and 2 bottles, vacant cartouche, on shell feet	The Maple Swan Collection
1761/62	James Welsh	Edinburgh	Cruet set, no details	National Museums of Scotland MEQ 617 1962.1025
1761/62	WD Probably William Dempster	Edinburgh	Cruet frame, on 4 scroll and shell feet, gadrooned borders, 2 vase shaped crested casters by Samuel Wood, London, over striking that of William Dempster of Edinburgh (or could it be Dempster over striking Wood), with later	Christie's July 11, 1979 #219

YEAR	MAKER (continued)	LOCATION	DESCRIPTION	SOURCE
			silver mounted glass bottles, 55oz	
1762/63	Robert Gordon	Edinburgh	Cruet frame, no casters or bottles, quinquefoil with asymmetrical cartouche with armorials on 4 open work shell feet, 10 ½", 30oz	Sotheby's Gleneagles August 27, 1979 # 204
1763/64	Ker & Dempster and William Dempster	Edinburgh	Cruet frame, cinquefoil, on shell feet, 3 casters, 2 bottles, 2 of the casters by William Dempster, rococo cartouche with arms on frame, 10 ½" ht, 34.3oz	Sotheby's October 28, 1976
1765 ca	Adam Graham	Glasgow	Cruet frame, sexfoil shaped base plate and bottle rings joined by 4 shell-footed scroll supports, central turned ring handle, vacant cartouche, 7 ¾" ht, 14.1oz (without bottles)	Sotheby's Blair Castle September 12, 1980 #40 Christie's June 24, 1986 #164
1765 ca	Milne & Campbell	Glasgow	Cruet frame, for 2 bottles with 2 original silver mounted glass bottles, escutcheon engraved with initials "APC"	Private Collection
1778/79	William Davie or William Dempster	Edinburgh	Cruet frame, boat shaped, with oil and vinegar	National Museums of Scotland MEQ 898
1792/93	William Robertson	Edinburgh	Four cup egg cruet, with cups, plain quatrefoil frame, central loop handle, cups with crest of McCadam, with similar loose cups (2 extra)	Christie's London UK 2004 #618 Schredds of Portobello, London
1810/11	James McKay	Edinburgh	Egg cruet, no details	National Museums of Scotland MEQ 1130
1819/20	James McKay	Edinburgh	Egg cruet stand, 4 gilt lined cups, center handle, circular base, 7 5/8" ht, 7" across the cups	Huntley House Museum Edinburgh HH1292/51
1832/33	George Paton	Edinburgh	Egg cruet with 6 cups	National Museums of Scotland MEQ 1064
1881/82	L A	Edinburgh	Cruet set, 3 piece	The Maple Swan Collection

Cups

Plate 19. A Tumbler Cup 1717-19 ca by Henry Bethune, Edinburgh. Courtesy of The Phoenix Collection. Photograph by Janice M Dietert.

YEAR	MAKER	LOCATION	DESCRIPTION	SOURCE
			CUPS	
	COCONUT			
1600 ca	Thomas Lindsay	Dundee	Coconut cup, no details	Private Collection UK
1637-39	Andrew Dennistoun	Edinburgh	Coconut cup, no details	Finlay 1991 #33
1640 ca	Robert Gairdyne II	Dundee	Coconut cup, no details	Private Collection UK
1655 ca	Robert Banks	Canongate	Coconut cup, The Tulloch Coconut Cup	Location unknown
1660 ca	Patrick Gairdyne	St Andrews	Coconut cup with 2 silver handles on a low foot	Private Collection UK
1670 ca	Not available	Provincial	Coconut cup, nut held by 3 hinged straps, engraved scalloped edges, slightly flared lip with corded girdle, repeated on trumpet foot, marked on base only with M crowned, 5 ¾" ht,	Sotheby's May 17, 1973 #178
1690 ca	Matthew Colquhoun	Ayr	Coconut cup, silver mounted, on circular turned wood foot and baluster stem, silver mounts with engraved and scalloped rims, engraved with initials, marks – mm 5X's – 4 ¼" ht	Christie's February 9, 1972 #138
1690 ca	William Scott I	Banff	Coconut cup, four marks, mm 2X's	Private Collection UK
1695 ca	William Scott Elder	Banff	Coconut cup, with silver mounts	Aberdeen Museums and Galleries ABDAG001038
1711 dated	Not available		Coconut cup, dated 1711, mounted, 3 vertical silver spines to a silver rim, initials "MMD" on rim and "RMD" opposite rim, 4" ht, 3 ¼" di	Royal Ontario Museum, Toronto Canada 928.44
1720 ca	William McLean	Inverness	Coconut cup, gift to Provost Duff, no further details	National Museums of Scotland 1952.48
1791/92	Alexander Gardner	Edinburgh	Coconut cup, silver mounted, on octagonal base and stem, coat-of-arms, crest and motto above, palm trees and monogram "MC" beneath, gilt interior, 7 ½" ht	Christie's NY USA 2007 #141
1800/01	W & P Cunningham I	Edinburgh	Coconut cup, silver mounted, plain trumpet foot, engraved band of zig-zag motifs, silver mounted rim, engraved "Patrick George Moncrieff", 6 ¼" ht	Christie's London UK 2002 #201
	MAZERS			
1320 ca	Not available		The Bute Mazer, arms of John Fitzgilbert and others, probably partly Scottish, bowl and boss 1320 ca, mounts probably later	Finlay 1991 #9 National Museums of Scotland

YEAR	MAKER	LOCATION	DESCRIPTION	SOURCE
1520-50	Not available A fleur-de-lis mark	Edinburgh	The Watson Mazer, possibly partly Scottish, mm unascribed	Finlay 1991 #18
1557 ca	James Gray	Canongate	The Tulloch Mazer	Private Collection UK
1561/62	Alexander Auchinleck	Edinburgh	The St. Mary's Mazer, plain rim and a plain trumpet foot	Finlay 1991 p19 St Mary's College, University of Aberdeen
1569 ca	James Gray	Canongate	The Galloway Mazer	Clayton's Dictionary p245 #353 National Museums of Scotland MEQ 148 1954.691
1576 ca	John Mosman Acting Deacon Adam Craig	Edinburgh	The Fergusson Mazer	How of Edinburgh W. Randolph Herst Collection S J Phillips Ltd London UK Ltd London UK London Finlay 1991 p19, 22
1580 ca	RL	Edinburgh	Mazer, no details	Apollo August 1977 vol 100, p97
1591 ca (or earlier)	James Cok III Deacon George Heriott II	Edinburgh	The Craigievar Mazer, note maker probably James Cok III or possibly James Crawford	Finlay 1991 #21 Private Collection UK On loan to National Museums of Scotland as QL 1987.12
1619-21	Thomas Cleghorne I Deacon James Dennistoun	Edinburgh	Mazer, all silver bowl, with dentine mid-rib, originally with traces of cloth under the teeth, many sources state the maker as James Dennistoun dated 1617 but he was Deacon at the time	Finlay 1991 #32 Sotheby's London June 1987 #199 Holland p209 Asprey London 1992 Private Collection
TUMBLER CUPS				
1680 ca	Thomas Moncur	Glasgow	Tumbler cup, tapering, large, circular form, slightly spreading sides, engraved with arms and initials "W.C.M." within crossed plumes mantling Arms of Crockett, 2 5/8" ht, 4" dl, 5.6oz	Park Lane Exhibition 1929 #668 Provenance of Sir Godfrey Christie's March 26, 1958 #162 Christie's May 17, 1927 #116 Thomas Lumley Ltd Noble Collection Nicholas Shaw Catalog 2004 p93

YEAR	MAKER	LOCATION	DESCRIPTION	SOURCE
1680 ca	Robert Gardiner	Perth	Tumbler cup, plain form, engraved with initials "IW MA", 2 ½" ht, 5oz 9d	Clayton Christie's p 183 #18 Christie's July 3, 1984 #190
1687/88	James Penman	Edinburgh	Tumbler cup, plain, 3 ½" di	Art Treasure Exhibition 1932 #487 How of Edinburgh Collection Scottish Art Academy Exhibit 1939 #483 Noble Collection Christie's December 10, 1908 #89
1692/93	Thomas Cleghorne	Edinburgh	Tumbler cups, pair, slightly everted lip, 3 ½" di, 9oz 9d both (4oz 14d ea)	Christie's July 26, 1933 #68 How of Edinburgh Collection
1692/93	Thomas Cleghorne	Edinburgh	Tumbler cup, everted lip, engraved initials, 2 ½" ht, 4oz , possibly related to above pair	Sotheby's Gleneagles August 1991 Christie's October 24, 1990 #222
1692/93	Robert Inglis	Edinburgh	Tumbler cups, pair, with crest of a stag and motto "SI DUES QUIS CONTRA"	Sotheby's November 3, 1949 #101
1694/95	James Luke	Glasgow	Tumbler cup, apparent split repair, engraved script "JB", carrying the prototype mark for James Luke, 2 ½" ht, 3 1/3" di, 5oz 10d	Christie's July 17, 1963 #137 Christie's auction 1963 Connoisseur 1964
1694/95	James Luke	Glasgow	*Tumbler cup, 5oz 5d*	*How of Edinburgh Exhibition 1992*
1694/95	James Luke	Glasgow	*Tumbler cup, marks - IL in a wavy edged punch, town mark, IL repeated, date letter O - initials "JB" to the right of the mark, 2 ½" ht*	*Clayton's Dictionary p448 #703*
1700/01	John Luke II	Glasgow	Tumbler cup, engraved with the initials "MWGJB" on the front, 2 ¾" ht, 5.6oz	Christie's London UK 2004 #98 Nicholas Shaw Catalog 2005 p87
1702/03	Robert Inglis	Edinburgh	Tumbler cup, slightly everted lip, initials, 2 ¾" ht	Christie's April 24, 1964 #95
1705 ca	Robert Inglis	Edinburgh	Tumbler cup, initials "RS", 2 ¾" ht, 7oz 10d	Christie's July 5, 1972 #10
1717-19	Henry Bethune (continued)	Edinburgh	Tumbler cup, everted lip, crest and motto, gilt interior, apparently no date letter but assayer for 1717-19 time period, crest and motto "JUVANT ASPERA FORTES" for Steuart of Allenton	Goodwin's Antiques 1992 The Phoenix Collection

YEAR	MAKER	LOCATION	DESCRIPTION	SOURCE
1720 ca	Simon McKenzie	Inverness	Tumbler cup, "MK" mark, 2 1/6" ht	Scottish Art Academy Exhibit 1939 #447 Provenance Major HN Robertson
1740 ca	Dougal Ged	Edinburgh	Tumbler cup, marks very rubbed, 3 1/3" di, 5.5 oz	Christie's Edinburgh November 21-22, 1988 #294
1743/44	James Clark	Edinburgh	Tumbler cup, no details	Antiques Magazine 122 p584 Argentum advertisement
1743/44	James Ker & William Aytoun	Edinburgh	Tumbler cups, 2 matching cups, each with slightly everted lip, on by Ker 1743/44, the other by Aytoun with an indistinct date letter, 2 ½" ht, 11.3oz	Christie's October 13, 1987 #193
1743/44	Edward Lothian	Edinburgh	Tumbler cup, plain, circular with slightly flared rim, 2 ½" ht, 5.6oz	Sotheby's April 30, 1985 #125
1743/44	Ebenezer Oliphant	Edinburgh	Tumbler cup, slightly everted lip, tucked in base, narrow band of bright cup decoration near lip, crest in an oval within drapery mantling and crossed foliate sprays, 3 ¾" ht, 5.9oz	Sotheby's September 25, 1973 #5
1745 ca	James Glen	Glasgow	Tumbler cups, pair, plain no everting	Goodwin's Antiques Edinburgh, 1995
1747/48	Dougal Ged	Edinburgh	Tumbler cup, with crest and motto "Calm", 2 ¾" ht, 4oz 17d	Sotheby's September 22, 1977
1747/48	*Dougal Ged*	*Edinburgh*	*Tumbler cup, everted lip*	*Lyle Annual Review 1981*
1753/54	Dougal Ged	Edinburgh	Tumbler cup, slightly everted lip, tucked in base, engraved with initials "JW" and "KS" in script, 3" ht, 3.8oz	Sotheby's October 29, 1970
1759/60	Not available	Edinburgh	Tumbler cup, shaped outline, gilt interior, mm indistinct, 3 ¾" di, 5.2oz	Christie's December 20, 1974 #187
1759/60	John Robertson	Edinburgh	Tumbler cup, sold with another matching one 1766/67 by Alexander Aitchison, slightly waisted bell shaped form, on tucked in base, monogrammed and dated, 3" ht, 9.4oz both	Sotheby's June 20, 1963 #127 Simon Kaye Antiques
1759/60	John Robertson	Edinburgh	Tumbler cup, no details	National Museums of Scotland MEQ 796
1761/62	John Clark	Edinburgh	Tumbler cup, slightly everted rim and tucked in base, initials in script "JW" and "KS" for John Wilson and Katherine Stevenson, 2 ½" ht, 3.8oz	Sotheby's December 10, 1970 #277
1762/63	William Dempster or William Davie	Edinburgh	Tumbler cup, flat chased rococo floral pattern, cartouche with crest, 2 ¾" ht, 4" di	Sotheby's March 11, 1971 #128 Art Institute of Chicago 41.485 N.A. 15593 R 7481

YEAR	MAKER	LOCATION	DESCRIPTION	SOURCE
1762/63	Lothian & Robertson	Edinburgh	Tumbler cups, pair, slightly tapering bodies, rococo borders of scrolls, wheat ears and bunches of grapes, later crest and motto, 3"ht, 11.4oz	Sotheby's Edinburgh April 28, 1992 #102
1763/64	William Davie or William Dempster	Edinburgh	Tumbler cup, body slightly tapering toward the top, with slightly everted rim, with a crest (pelican in piety) below the motto "CELESTES....", 2 ¾" ht, 4.6oz	Sotheby's Gleneagles September 1, 1981 #454
1764/65	Ker & Dempster	Edinburgh	Tumbler cups, pair, slightly everted lip, chased with a band of leaves and flower heads, 8oz both	Christie's London November 10, 1993
1765/66	Ker & Dempster	Edinburgh	Tumbler cups, pair, no details	JH Bourdon-Smith London Apollo 1993
1765/66	*Ker & Dempster*	*Edinburgh*	*Tumbler cups, pair chased band, everted lip, 2 ½" ht, 8oz wt*	*Christie's November 1993, #180*
1766/67	Alexander Aitchison I	Edinburgh	Tumbler cups, pair, engraved script initials "DNIP 1755"	National Museums of Scotland MEQ 797
1766/67	Ker	Edinburgh	Tumbler cups, pair, with the initials "PG" on the bottom	National Museums of Scotland MEQ 1166-67 1976.13-14
1767/68	William Dempster or William Davie	Edinburgh	Tumbler cups, everted rim, engraved with crest and moot "We are Saved by Faith"	Hyman Collection - Colonial Williamsburg L1999-80
1769/70	William Dempster or William Davie	Edinburgh	Tumbler cup, no details	JH Bourdon-Smith London 1992
1772/73	William Davie or William Dempster	Edinburgh	Tumbler cups, pair, no details	The Maple Swan Collection
1773/74	James Hewitt	Edinburgh	Tumbler cups or beakers, pair, with crest and motto of Hamilton, 3" ht, 8oz 6d	Sotheby's Scone April 19, 1977 #85
1776/77	William Davie or William Dempster	Edinburgh	Tumbler cup, slightly everted lip, engraved initials "WC", 3 1/3" di, 4oz 10d	Christie's NY April 18, 1989 #457
1800 ca	Alexander Ziegler	Edinburgh	Tumbler cups, pair, slightly waisted, plain bodies, flared rims, each engraved with the initial "P", 3" di, 8.7oz	Noble Collection Sotheby's Gleneagles September 1, 1998 #546 JH Bourdon-Smith London
1800 ca	W & P Cunningham I	Edinburgh	Tumbler cup, no details	Dundee Museums and Art Galleries 1963-739-1

YEAR	MAKER	LOCATION	DESCRIPTION	SOURCE
1802/03	McHattie & Fenwick	Edinburgh	Tumbler cup, covered on a spreading circular foot, presented to Walter Riddell, 13 ½" ht, 39.7 oz	Nicholas Shaw Catalog Winter 2000 p79
1802/03	T & E	Edinburgh assay	Tumbler cup, covered, bright cut, engraved, presented to Mr. John Burns 18 April 1803	Nicholas Shaw Catalog Winter 2000 p79
1815/16	W & P Cunningham II	Edinburgh	Tumbler cup, no details	JH Bourdon-Smith London 1992
1819/20	George McHattie	Edinburgh	Tumbler cup, no details	Hancock & Co, London UK 1992
1996/97	William Kirk	Edinburgh	Tumbler cup, pair, no details	Aberdeen Museums and Galleries ABDAG011058
TWO-HANDLED				
1682/83	Alexander Reid	Edinburgh	Two handled cup, covered, very ornate with chased leaves near base, chased decoration on cover, large pinecone finial	Finlay 1991 #60 National Museums of Scotland H.MEQ1467
1693/94	James Penman	Edinburgh	Two handled cup, covered, 2 strap handles, each topped by a knop, contemporary cipher "JMC", Arms of Campbell of Netherplace, Ayreshire, 7 ¾" ht, 28oz 4d	Hyman Collection - Colonial Williamsburg 1992 Sotheby's October 11, 1979 #215 Sotheby's Hopetoun House, November 13, 1978 #63 Christie's July 14, 1954 #154 Finlay 1991 #60
1694/95	John Seatoun	Edinburgh	Two handle cup, engraved on either side of a cylindrical body with armorials, initials and dates at later periods, 2 scroll handles, flat later chased cover, turned finial, on rim foot, 6 ½" ht, 17.5oz	Sotheby's November 15, 1962 #31 Jessop Antiques
1695/96	James Penman	Edinburgh	Two handled thistle cup, reeded girdle, applied lobes, 2 cast plain capped scroll handles, base with initials, 3 ½" ht, 7.4oz	Grantully Castle Antiques Sotheby's April 28, 1977 #190
1696/97	James Cockburn	Edinburgh	Two handled thistle cups, pair, plain, uncapped cast scroll handles, bodies initialed above applied girdle "AM/SD", 3 ¼" ht, 13.6oz	Christie's March 18, 1959
1707/08	William Scott	Edinburgh	Two handled cup, covered, The Hopetoun Spout Cup, with 2 single scroll handles, circular molded foot, plain body, stud thumb piece, arms of the city of Edinburgh, domed cover, acorn finial	Finlay 1991 #65 Clayton Dictionary p284 #572 Earl of Hopetoun Christie's London June 15, 1977 #137 National Museums of Scotland MEQ 1206 a-b, 1977.5 a*b

YEAR	MAKER	LOCATION	DESCRIPTION	SOURCE
1708/09	John Seatoun	Edinburgh	Two handled cup, covered, 8" ht, 35oz 9d	Sotheby's Hopetoun House April 1988 #67
1709/10	John Seatoun	Edinburgh	Two handled cup, Arms of Baillie of Jerviswood, crest and motto	Sotheby's November 30, 1967 #109 *Burlington Magazine* December 1970 vol 112, p50 How of Edinburgh National Museums of Scotland H.1991.2 1-2
1715 ca	William MacLean	Inverness	Two handled cup, miniature, on reeded rim foot, *with reeded band applied around body*, scroll handles, engrave with conjoined initials "DML", dated 1715, 2" ht, 2oz 10d	Christie's July 3, 1984 #164 Christie's July 12, 1983 #194 Clayton Dictionary p173 #9
1720 ca	Simon McKenzie	Inverness	Two handled thistle cup, girdle, initials "DML"	National Museums of Scotland 1580 1980
1724/25	Charles Blair	Edinburgh	Two handled cup, with spout, body engraved opposite spout with full armorials for George Innes, writer in Edinburgh, 9 7/8" ht, 55oz	Private Collection UK
1725 ca	Robert Luke	Glasgow	Two handled cup, circular, 2 scrolled handles, plain, engraved with 2 coats of arms, motto, 4 marks – RL, tree, RL, S – 4 ¾" ht, 20.9 oz	Phillips Edinburgh May 22, 1987 #87
1725 ca	Robert Luke	Glasgow	Two handled cup, no cover, plain, straight sided with tucked in base, on reeded rim foot, 2 leaf capped scroll handles, contemporary Arms of Orr, 7 ¾" ht, 10oz	*Scottish Art Review* vol XIII 1972 #4 back cover How of Edinburgh advertisement
1725 ca	Robert Cruickshank	Old Aberdeen	Two handled cup, covered, marks - RC, OABD, C, Huntly Race Prize	Private Collection UK
1727	Colin Mitchell	Canongate	Two handled cups, pair, vase shaped, engraved *with presentation inscription* "The Gift of Mrs E Crompton/to/C Smithson/June 20th 1727" and "The Gift of/Mrs E Crompton/to/M Rose/June 20th 1727", 3 ¾" ht, 13.34oz	Sotheby's December 1, 1982 #59 Phillips Edinburgh May 22, 1987 Sotheby's July 29, 1990 #309
1730 ca	Robert Luke	Glasgow	Two handled cup, on spreading base, slightly everted body, acanthus capped scroll handles, engrave on one side with contemporary coat of arms of John *Orr of Barrowfield and Cam,lachie*, on the other with later arms of Mackenzie impaling Gordon, 4 5/8" ht, 20oz , possibly related to previous ones	Christie's November 21-22, 1990 #48
1736/37	Dougal Ged	Edinburgh	Two handled cup, compressed bun knop on handles, stepped and domed lid, with acorn finial, bell shaped bowl with slightly everted lip, 10 ½" ht, 59.5oz	Source uncertain

204

YEAR	MAKER	LOCATION	DESCRIPTION	SOURCE
1750/51	Ker & Dempster	Edinburgh	Two handled cup, bell shaped bowl chased on both sides with the badge of the Blue and Orange Society, identical armorials, festoons of fruit, flowers and leaves, leaf capped double scroll handles, on spreading foot, inscribed "Ex Dono Saml. Dukinfield Esqr. To Col. Jas. Thorne, 4th King's Own Regt. Of Foot", 5 ½" ht, 18.8oz	Sotheby's November 3, 1966 #42
1751 ca	Ker & Dempster	Edinburgh	Two handled cup with cover, gold, King's Prize for the 1751 Leith races won by a horse called Traveller, engraved Royal Arms with the version used in England, whereas correct Scottish version was used on teapots (details per George Dalgleish of the National Museums of Scotland)	J. T. D'Arcy Hutton Collection Christie's Oct 4, 1959 #150 National Museums of Scotland H.1993.55 1-2
1752/53	William Gilchrist	Edinburgh	Two handled cup with cover, gold, wooden handle, gold capped with acanthus, the Kings Prize for 1753 won by the mare Lady's Thigh (details per George Dalgleish of the National Museums of Scotland)	Finlay pl. 85 Jules S. Bache Collection 1949 Metropolitan Museum of Art, NYC
1754/55	Ker & Dempster	Edinburgh	Two handled cup, upper body chased with rococo cartouches, panels of rococo flowers and scrolls, on circular molded foot, double scroll handles, 7" ht, 37.1oz	Christie's January 29, 1964 #170
1755/56	Lothian & Robertson	Edinburgh	Two handled cup, no details	Lyle Silver Review 1982 p 47
1755 ca	Ker & Dempster	Edinburgh	Two handled cup, Castle Grant	Cripps p 151
1755/56	Ker & Dempster	Edinburgh	Two handled cup, covered, lower part and center of cover repoussed with oblique fluted border, 8 ½" di, 36.4oz	Breadalbane Collection Sale 1935 #360
1760 ca	Milne & Campbell	Glasgow	Two handled cup, plain, baluster shape, scroll handles, 5" ht, 15.4oz	Nicholas Shaw Catalog Winter 2001 p73
1764/65	Alexander Gardner	Edinburgh	Two handled cup, with spout for feeding	National Museums of Scotland MEQ 1144 1975.299
1764/65	*Alexander Gardner*	*Edinburgh*	*Two handled feed cup, baluster body, curved spout, S scroll handles, 3 ½" ht, 4oz*	*Nobel Collection Sotheby's Gleneagles August 28, 1975 #50 Finlay 1991 #92*
1765/66	Patrick Robertson	Edinburgh	Two handled cup, bell shaped body, applied reeded mid-rib, above which is engraved a unicorn passant on a coronet, leaf capped scroll handles, 7 ¾" ht, 46.6oz	Sotheby's Gleneagles August 25, 1997 #153
1765/66	Alexander Gardner	Edinburgh	Two handled spout cup, shaped outline, covered spout, ebonized wood finial to raised cover (unmarked), crest and motto, 5 ¾" ht, 8.6oz	Dundee Museums and Art Galleries 1986-140

YEAR	MAKER	LOCATION	DESCRIPTION	SOURCE
1768/69	William Dempster or William Davie	Edinburgh	Two handled cup, chased and repoussed with swags of flowers, lower part chased with banding of foliated strap work, 22.5oz	Breadalbane Collection Sale 1935 #162
1771/72	"Tait" (Benjamin Tait)	Edinburgh	Two handled cup, plain, no details	National Museums of Scotland MEQ 1333 1980.62
1771/72	Lothian & Robertson	Edinburgh	Two handled cup, covered, no details	Finlay 1991 #99 National Museums of Scotland 1963.37 a
1772/73	Patrick Robertson	Edinburgh	Two handled cup, vase shaped body chased with lobes below, scroll band and swags, lobed pedestal foot and cover, berried leafy borders, 8" ht	Sotheby's Easton Neston May 19, 2005 #908
1772/73	William Davie or William Dempster	Edinburgh	Two handled invalid cup, baluster body, reeded everted lip, 2 strap handles, curved spout, everted skirt base, crested above initials, 3 ¾" ht, 4.7oz	Sotheby's Scone Palace April 14, 1980 #108
1784/85	W & P Cunningham I	Edinburgh	Two handled cup, covered, reeded handles, crest of Graham, 9 ½" ht, 26.7oz	Nicholas Shaw Catalog Autumn 1999 p59
1788/89	William Davie Or William Dempster	Edinburgh	Two handled cup, covered, 23 ¾" ht, 126oz 10d	Sotheby's Picture Book June 13-14 1977 #594
1790 ca	William Byres	Banff	Two handled cup, covered, engraved in cartouche "MD"	Bell of Aberdeen Grantully Castle Antiques National Museums of Scotland MEQ 957
1790/91	William Dempster	Edinburgh	Two handled cup, (Note: William Davie was deceased by this date), no details	Philips Glasgow Auction Summer 1991
1791/92	William Robertson (continued)	Edinburgh	Two handled cup, bell shaped body, trumpet foot, with borders of bright cut foliage and pendants, reeded loop handles, later engraved with shields enclosing names and date 26th July 1862, foot also engraved with names, 11" ht, 30.6oz	Sotheby's Gleneagles August 30, 1973 #36
1793/94	Dick & McPherson	Edinburgh	Two handled cup, vase shaped body, engraved on one side with arms of the city of Edinburgh, on the other an inscription and date 1809, 9 ½" ht, 25.7oz	Sotheby's Gleneagles August 28, 1975 #53
1799/1800	W & P Cunningham I	Edinburgh	Two handled cup, covered, vase shaped with the Royal Arms of Scotland and Arms of Arthur Forbes, 7th of Culloden, 17" ht, 71.5oz	Sotheby's Gleneagles August 25, 1997 #130 National Museums of Scotland K.1998.419

YEAR	MAKER	LOCATION	DESCRIPTION	SOURCE
1800/01	Alexander Gardner & Co	Edinburgh	Two handled cup, vase shaped, engraved with a band of foliate scroll motifs at the rim, pedestal foot, each side with engraved date, base engraved "Silver wedding Feb 17th 1912 from Mr. and Mrs. Arthur Sassoon", 10 1/8" ht	Christie's London UK 2002 #250
1801/02	McHattie & Fenwick	Edinburgh	Two handled covered cup, urn form urn finial, waisted cover, minor dents, 12 ½" ht, 30 oz	Skinner, Inch, Bolton, MA USA 1991 #224
1801/02	WM	Edinburgh	Two handled cups, pair, no details	The Maple Swan Collection
1802/03	McHattie & Fenwick	Edinburgh	Two handled cup, presented to D. Hay 1804	National Museums of Scotland MEQ 807
1804/05	W & P Cunningham I	Edinburgh	Two handled cup and cover, Queen Ann form, lower half of body applied with alternate lobes and straps below the midriff, leaf capped scroll handles, 11 ½" ht 53oz	Private Collection Sotheby's February 28, 1991
1804/05	W & P Cunningham I	Edinburgh	Two handled cup, urn shaped body, splayed foot, bright cut work around the base, 9" ht, 8 3/8" over handles	Cincinnati Art Museum 1936.406
1805 ca	Dick & Robertson	Edinburgh	Two handled cup, engraved in cartouche	National Museums of Scotland MEQ 1306
1805/06	James Douglas	Edinburgh	Two handled cup, tapering circular section cup with angular handles attached to body with leaf motifs, raised pedestal foot, supported on later ebonized plinth with a silver collar, 11" ht, 35.5oz	Christie's London UK 2001 #113
1806/07	McHattie & Fenwick	Edinburgh	Two handled cup, engraved "Dalkeith Farmers Club"	National Museums of Scotland MEQ 1529
1807/08	Cunningham & Sons	Edinburgh	Two handled presentation cup, given to Captain William Dalgleish, Scotscraig, 9" ht, 24.9oz	Nicholas Shaw Catalog 2004 p104
1808/09	James McKay	Edinburgh	Two handled cup, 10" ht	Antiques Magazine vol 31 p93
1810 ca	James Erskine	Aberdeen	Two handled cup, of Campana shape, bright cut festoons of flowers and vacant cartouche, 10 1/8" ht, 19.1oz	Nicholas Shaw Catalog Winter 2001 p74
1812/13	Alexander Henderson	Edinburgh	Two handled cup, no details	Lorentz Antiques Toronto 1991
1813–18	MM obscured	Edinburgh	Two handled cup, semi-fluted body, presentation inscription "From Robert Mac Farlane, Esq, AlloA to Mrs. Alexander MacFarlane on the occasion of her marriage 20 September 1814", 9 ¾" ht, 26oz	Christie's London UK 2004 #118
1814/15	N & G mark	Edinburgh	Two handled cup, racing trophy	Christie's NY October 1988 #241

YEAR	MAKER	LOCATION	DESCRIPTION	SOURCE
1815/16	George McHattie	Edinburgh	Two handled cup, applied reeded rim above a reeded band, engraved inscription to both sides, one later, partly fluted lower body, 3 ½" ht, 3.5oz	Bonhams London UK 2005 #329
1816/17	Robert Gray & Sons	Glasgow Edinburgh assay	Two handled cup, covered, of Campana shape, engraved with crest and motto "DOMINUS FIDUCIA MEA," 9 1/8" ht, 32oz	Nicholas Shaw Catalog Winter 2000 p79
1817/18	James Howden	Edinburgh	Two handled presentation cup, given by Major Sir John Hope for a Troop Race 10th July 1818, 9" ht, 22.2 oz	Nicholas Shaw Catalog 2005 p100
1820/21	Charles Bendy (also Hay Leith)	Edinburgh / Leith	Two handled presentation cup, no details	National Museums of Scotland MEQ 1332
1821/22	Robert Gray & Son	Glasgow	Two handled cup, inscribed, 16 ¼"ht, 145oz 10d	Sotheby's Gleneagles August 28, 1976 #56
1821/22	Robert Gray & Son	Glasgow	Two handled cup, covered, different from the above, 139oz 16d	Sotheby's November 27, 1985 #125
1825/26	Morton retailer	Edinburgh	Two handled silver-gilt cup, embossed and chased with hunting scene, spreading circular foot, square base, domed cover, royal crown finial, 16 3/8" ht, 101 oz 2d	Sotheby's London UK 2007 #147
1836/37	Leonard Urquhart	Edinburgh	Two handled presentation cup, no details	National Museums of Scotland MEQ 810 1962.1881
1879/80	James Nasmyth & Co	Edinburgh	Two handled presentation cup, no details	National Museums of Scotland MEQ 723
1886/87	William Marshall	Edinburgh	Two handled cup, chased with vacant cartouche	National Museums of Scotland MEQ 855
1891/92	George Edward & Sons	Glasgow	Cup and cover, ovoid body on spreading foot chased with spiral fluted foliage, body chased on one side with Viking boats and on the other with yachts, detachable cover with triton finial, 27" ht, 144oz	Christie's London UK 2006 #57
1903/04	Hamilton & Inches	Edinburgh	Two handled cup, trophy, one side engraved with inscription, the other with various names, inscriptions recognizes those involved with the Bardhill Swimming Club, 17 ½" long over handles	Christie's London UK 2006 #493
1929/30	Hamilton & Inches	Edinburgh	Two handled cup, silver challenge, part fluted with thistle and Celtic motifs, handles mounted with knights on horseback, engraved inscription, 5 ¼" ht	Christie's London UK 2004 #141

Dinnerware

Plate 20. One of two covered Entrée Dishes 1829/30 by Marshall & Son, Edinburgh. Courtesy of a private collector. Photograph by Janice M Dietert.

Dish Crosses and Dish Rings

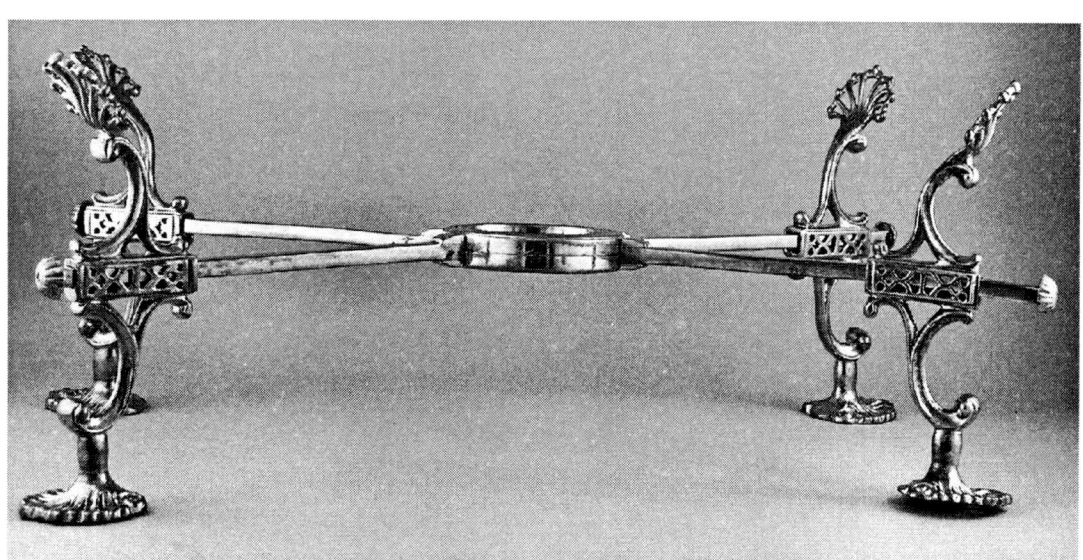

Plate 21. Dish Crosses and Dish Rings. Top – A Dish Ring 1693/94 by James Cockburn, Edinburgh. Photograph courtesy of A C Cooper Ltd, London and The Maple Swan Collection. Bottom – A Dish Cross 1767/68 by WD, probably William Dempster, Edinburgh. Courtesy of The Phoenix Collection. Photograph by Janice M Dietert.

YEAR	MAKER	LOCATION	DESCRIPTION	SOURCE
	DISH CROSSES AND DISH RINGS		***DINNERWARE***	
1693/94	James Cockburn	Edinburgh	Dish ring, Coat of Arms, Arms of David Carnegie, 4th Earl of Northesk, possible a second owner	The Maple Swan Collection
1736/37	Hugh Penman	Edinburgh	Dish ring, plain baluster ring, on spreading circular base (strengthened), with scroll handle, 2 ¾"ht, 3oz	Christie's Glasgow November 12, 1991 #271
1750 ca	Hugh Ross	Tain	Dish ring, on 3 paw feet, no details	National Museums of Scotland MEQ 1578 1984
1751/52	Dougal Ged	Edinburgh	Dish cross, exceptional example with clear marks, 13.7oz	How of Edinburgh 1937 #106
1751/52	Not available	Edinburgh	Dish cross, shaped double height cross arms with S-scroll terminals and shell feet, 11" wide, 14oz 3d	Sotheby's London UK July 5, 2006 #226
1756/57	Robert Gordon	Edinburgh	Dish cross, on 4 shell feet, leaf dish rests, simple arms, 12" long, 3 ¼" ht, 18oz	Minneapolis Institute of Art 74.63.29.4
1758/59	WD Probably William Dempster	Edinburgh	Dish cross, sliding scroll supports, shell pattern feet, marked on the bars, crest below a coronet, 21.4oz	Sotheby's January 26, 1967 #23 N Bloom Antiques
1761/62	Lothian & Robertson	Edinburgh	Dish cross, no burner, adjustable shell and scroll supports, 13" wide, 18oz	Christie's Glasgow November 18-19, 1992 #696
1765 ca	Milne & Campbell	Glasgow	Dish cross, shell decorated arms with banner, 16"di, 21.8oz	Nicholas Shaw Catalog 2005 p96
1765/66	Ker & Dempster	Edinburgh	Dish ring, no details	National Museums of Scotland MEQ 1972.274
1765/66	*Ker & Dempster*	*Edinburgh*	*Dish ring on 3 shell feet, the ring applied with 3 suspended swags of scroll work and shell design, 18.3oz*	*Scottish Art Review Vol XIII #3 back cover 1972* *How of Edinburgh advertisement*
1766/67	James Gilliland and Daniel Ker	Edinburgh	Dish cross, large, on 4 adjustable shell and scroll feet, circular lamp frame, lamp missing, engraved with crest and motto, 12oz 2d	Christie's March 24, 1975 #183 Christie's July 18, 1978 #64
1767/68	William Dempster	Edinburgh	Dish cross, typical form, lacking central burner, sliding feet-cum-dish supports, pierced as shell motifs, 12 ¾" across, 22oz 4d	Sotheby's Gleneagles August 28, 1985 #148 JH Bourdon-Smith London The Phoenix Collection

YEAR	MAKER	LOCATION	DESCRIPTION	SOURCE
1770/71	James Gilliland	Edinburgh	Dish cross, without a burner	National Museums of Scotland MEQ 1966.990
1771/72	Patrick Robertson	Edinburgh	Dish cross, sliding supports with scroll brackets and pierced shell rests, marked on each arm, 11", 13oz	Sotheby's Gleneagles August 29, 1977 #186
1776/77	W & P Cunningham I	Edinburgh	Dish cross, with sliding central ring, with baluster finials to the ends of the bars, on 4 pierced shell feet, central ring pierced with 6 pedal flower head with scalloped surround, 14 ¾", 17.7oz	Bonhams the Scottish Sale August 24, 2005 #34
1780/81	Patrick Robertson	Edinburgh	Dish cross, no details	The Maple Swan Collection
1780 ca	AG mullet above, possibly Alexander Gardner	Edinburgh	Dish cross, scissor form with sliding brackets, pierced shell feet and dish supports, beaded central aperture, crest on one arm, 13" wide, 13oz 18 d	Sotheby's NY USA 1999 #498
1782/83	Patrick Robertson	Edinburgh	Dish ring, no details	National Museums of Scotland MEQ 1571
1783/84	William Davie or William Dempster	Edinburgh	Dish cross, typical X form, flower head terminals to arms, 4 sliding brackets below arrow-shaped dish supports, 12 ½", 14.5oz	Bonhams The Scottish Sale, August 21, 2003 #42
1784/85	William Davie or William Dempster	Edinburgh	Dish cross without burner, 12 ¾" long, 14.8oz	Nicholas Shaw Catalog Winter 2001, p76
1794/95	Francis Howden	Edinburgh	Dish cross form with adjustable lamp holder (no lamp), one support engraved script "WD", 13 ½", 17oz	Lyon & Turnbull, The Murray Collection August 20, 2003 # 193
1794/95	Francis Howden	Edinburgh	Dish cross with pierced adjustors, 13" wide, 13oz	Gorringes LLP Lewes July 26, 2007 #1181A
1894/95	Hamilton & Inches	Edinburgh	Dish ring with foliage and a dog, 8 ¼" di, 12.3oz	Nicholas Shaw Catalog 2005 p105

ENTRÉE DISHES

YEAR	MAKER	LOCATION	DESCRIPTION	SOURCE
1809/10	James McKay	Edinburgh	Entrée dishes, set of 3, covered	The Maple Swan Collection
1820/21	George McHattie	Edinburgh	Entrée serving dish, with cover, lamp and stand, also marked "Hay" of Leith	National Museums of Scotland 1969.406 & a-d
1829/30	Marshall & Son	Edinburgh	Entrée dishes, pair, with covers and handles, borders with flowers and ivy leaves, handles similarly cast, 11 ½", 118oz	Private Collection

YEAR	MAKER	LOCATION	DESCRIPTION	SOURCE
	EPERGNES			
1781/82	WD William Davie or William Dempster	Edinburgh	Epergne, on four foliate feet and a domed open work base pierced and chased with flowers and leaves, eight supporting branches each with circular or oval baskets, all but two with crests, 20" ht, 150oz	Christie's NY USA 1997 #320
1794/95	W & P Cunningham I	Edinburgh	Epergne, no details	Antiques Magazine vol 122, p 718
1795/96	William Robertson	Edinburgh	Epergne, with central oval basket, 6 side baskets, on 4 legs, 22 ¾" ht, 29 ¼" wide	Indianapolis Museum of Art 78.96 a-I TR #2426
1806/07	Patrick Cunningham & Sons	Edinburgh	Epergne, oval central bowl, 4 small circular bowls	National Museums of Scotland MEQ 1610
	JUGS			
1701/02	Thomas Ker	Edinburgh	Jug, no details	How's Notes II, 1972, p7 Private Collection UK
1713/14	Colin McKenzie	Edinburgh	Covered jug, chased with strap work panel, engraved "1869", 65.2oz	Sotheby's Olympia April 5, 2005, #228
1716/17	Mungo Yorstoun	Edinburgh	Jug, plain, pear shaped body, on a circular molded foot, with molded party covered spout, shallow domed lid with acorn finial, fluted scroll thumb piece, chased later with bands of scrolling foliage on a matted ground, crest and coronet, 8 ½" ht, 37.3 oz	Christie's October 16, 1963
1718/19	Edward Penman Maker and assayer	Edinburgh	Ale? jug, plain pear shaped body, silver harp shaped handle, short molded spout, low domed lid with acorn finial, body later engraved with the Arms Lynam impaling Moreton, 6" ht, 13.9oz	Sotheby's June 22, 1960 How of Edinburgh Sotheby's February 1987 #66
1795 ca	William Robertson	Edinburgh	Water jug, silver-mounted Chinese blue and white, mount of an escalloped bordered rim, hinged dome lid with ball finial, secured with silver rivets to the jug, Chinese export ware porcelain with short spout, painted with lake fishing scene, 9 ½' ht	Christie's Lanarkshire UK 1997 #121
1800/01	W & P Cunningham I	Edinburgh	Hot water jug, called a coffee jug, oval, fluted and decorated with a collar of bright cut foliage and flowers, crest and motto in an oval cartouche, 8 ¼" ht, 21.5oz	Sotheby's Gleneagles, August 27, 1979 3192
1804/05	W S Cockburn	Edinburgh assay	Jug, engraved, "David Murray from R Leith Volunteer"	National Museums of Scotland MEQ 1077

YEAR	MAKER	LOCATION	DESCRIPTION	SOURCE
1807/08	Patrick Cunningham & Sons	Edinburgh	Water jug, baluster form, beaked cast spout with Bacchus mask, handle cast as vine stocks, lower body with acanthus leaf band engraved and shoulder with bands of fruiting vines and foliage, 7 ½" ht, 18oz	Christie's Lanarkshire UK 1997 #189
1809/10	Not available	Edinburgh	Jug/pitcher, swelling sides tapering to high neck and everted lip, molded handle with bearded masks, repousse decoration on exterior with grape vines, leaves and clusters, 6 5/8" di	Carnegie Institute Museum of Art 78.36.21
1810/11	Patrick Cunningham & Sons	Edinburgh	Claret jug, baluster form on a spreading foot, chased with band of fruiting vines between stylized foliage borders, short Bacchic mask decorated spout, entwined vine tendril handle, gilt interior, 6 ½" ht, 15oz	Christie's Lanarkshire UK 1998 #479
1819/20	W & P Cunningham II	Edinburgh	Lidded jug, no details	National Museums of Scotland MEQ 694
1820/21	Francis Howden	Edinburgh	Wooden jug, with silver mounts	National Museums of Scotland MEQ 930 1968.492
1822/23	George Fenwick	Edinburgh	Lidded jug, chased with thistles around the middle	National Museums of Scotland MEQ 695
1825/26	Robert Gray & Son	Glasgow	Hot water jug, with silver handle, chased with vine and grape decoration, engraved on the base "TMF", 9 7/8" ht	Nicholas Shaw Catalog Winter 2000 p78
1825/26	James McKay	Edinburgh	Jug, baluster robustly decorated with leaf, flower and scroll motifs on a granulated ground, ivory insulated handle, hinged lid, 8 ½" ht, 20oz gross	Christie's London UK 2002 #160 2003 #152
1831/32	George Paton	Edinburgh	Claret jug, no details	National Museums of Scotland MEQ 1105
1834/35	Andrew Wilkie	Edinburgh	Lidded jug, no details	National Museums of Scotland MEQ 1297 1978
1837/38	Lawrence Aitchison	Glasgow	Jug, plain body with hinged lid, 4 ¾" ht	Christie's Melbourne, AU 2004 #537
1840/41	James & William Marshall	Edinburgh	Jug, high shouldered baluster shape, angular handle with scrolled thumb piece, side hinged lid with foliate finial, short spout with mask motif, cartouche with "FEAR GOD IN LIFE", and crest of Somervale, Scotland, 10" ht, 30 oz	Richie's Toronto CA 1996 #2043
1841/42	Andrew Wilkie	Edinburgh	Wine jug, presented to Mr. Adam Brydon 1841, 8 ½" ht, 32.4oz	Nicholas Shaw Catalog Winter 2002/3 p88

YEAR	MAKER	LOCATION	DESCRIPTION	SOURCE
1845/46	Marshall & Sons	Edinburgh	Presentation claret jug, ovoid part-fluted body chased in relief with a frieze of birds and flowers, cartouche with arms of Earl of Eldon, late inscribed for a shooting prize award to "John, 3rd Earl of Eldon", 15 ½" ht, 42 oz	Christie's London UK 2007 #150
1846/47	WM	Edinburgh	Claret jug, quatrefoil form, embossed throughout with panels of flowers and scrolls, 11 ½" ht, 18 oz	Gorringes LLP, East Sussex UK 2006 #1413
1852/53	JM	Glasgow	Lidded jug, baluster form, chased in high relief with flowers and scrolls, vacant central cartouche, scroll handle, pedestal support, 15 ¼" ht, 41 oz 9d	Christie's London UK 2000 #18
1860/61	Charles Robb & Son	Edinburgh	Claret jug, no details	National Museums of Scotland H.1995.200
1865/66	J Muirhead	Glasgow	Claret jug, ovoid form, engine turned decanter, cartouche either side, one with a presentation inscription, ivory insulated handle, hinged lid, 12 ¼" ht, 26oz gross	Christie's London UK 2001 #11
1866/67	John Pears Hutton	Edinburgh	Jug, for water, chased classical scenes, 14 1/8" ht, 4"di base	Huntley House Museum Edinburgh HH2104/62
1867/68	James McKay	Edinburgh	Jug, for water, Presented to" Rev. Henry R...., Kelso 1868", 14 5/8" ht, 4 3/8" di, 4" di base	Huntley House Museum Edinburgh HH2104/61
1867/70	Crichton	Edinburgh	Covered jug, chased with strap work, panel engraved with "1869", 65.2oz	Sotheby's Olympia April 5, 2005, #228
1868/69	William Marshall	Edinburgh	Lidded jug, no details	National Museums of Scotland MEQ 1317
1869/70	William Marshall	Edinburgh	Claret jug, baluster shape, decorated with zodiac panels, 13 ½" ht, 24.7oz	Nicholas Shaw Catalog Winter 2000, p81
1871/72	Hamilton & Inches	Edinburgh	Claret jug of ovoid shape, engraved with floral and foliate swags and a blank cartouche, arched leaf capped handle, 13 ¼" ht, 21oz	Bonhams Trinity 2007 #96
1877/78	Not available	Edinburgh	Jug, for wine, no details, mm unclear	Aberdeen Museums and Galleries ABDAG001052
1879/80	Hamilton & Inches	Edinburgh	Lidded jug, no details	National Museums of Scotland MEQ 930 1968.492
1880/81	John Reid	Glasgow	Hot water jug, ovoid, embossed with four alternate roundels depicting various Chinese figures and panels of exotic birds in scrolls surround, domed cover with fluted knopped finial, floral chased handle, 9 2/3" ht, 23 oz	Bonhams London UK 2004 #370

YEAR	MAKER	LOCATION	DESCRIPTION	SOURCE
1886/87	JR	Glasgow	Claret jug, baluster form on pedestal foot, profusely decorated with birds, animals, masks and caryatid figures, female caryatid scroll handle, helmet shaped spout with hinged lid, 12 ½" ht, 28 oz	Bonhams Solihull 2003 #403
1907/08	Hamilton & Inches	Edinburgh	Silver mounted claret jug, baluster shaped body etched with stars and with star-cut base, the mount mushroom shaped, embossed with thistles and strapwork, 9 ¼" ht	Christie's London UK 2000 #18
1913/14	R & W Sorley	Glasgow	Water jug, baluster form with Silenus mask spout, shallow domed cover, fluted thumbpiece, inset Queen Anne coin, presentation inscription underneath, 6 7/8" ht, 22 oz	Bonhams London UK 2004 #114

Plates

Plate 22. One of a pair of Ashets (meat platters) 1821/22 by George McHattie, Edinburgh. Courtesy of a private collector. Photograph by Janice M Dietert.

YEAR	MAKER	LOCATION	DESCRIPTION	SOURCE
	PLATES – DINNER/TABLE			
1671-73	Alexander Scott Deacon Edward Cleghorne I	Edinburgh	Dinner plates, set of 36, each engraved with "K" below a coronet, for the Earl of Kinghorne, 12 described in a family inventory with maker A. S. deacon E. C., sold after the death of the Lord of Strathmore and Kinghorne, 492 oz all	Silver Society Journal
1722/23	Henry Bethune	Edinburgh	Dinner plates, set of 18, circular with gadrooned edge, coat of Arms of Meaux or Meux quartering 3 others, set was originally larger, see below, 9 ¾" di, 20oz each	Wark, Huntington Library Book p114, #272
1722/23	Henry Bethune	Edinburgh	Dinner plates, set of 6 from the same set as in the Huntingdon Library Collection, original set was at least 2 dozen plates	Antiques Magazine vol 107 Potentially on the Market in Scotland in 1968
1761/62	Daniel Ker	Edinburgh	Dinner plate, second course dinner plate, shaped circular, with molded border, engraved with armorials, Arms of Drummond, 12 ¼" di, 30.7oz	Sotheby's October 25, 2004 or 1984 #225
1770 ca	Patrick Robertson	Edinburgh	Dinner plates, set of 6, no details	Antiques Magazine Bell of Aberdeen advertisement
1772/73	WD William Dempster or William Davie	Edinburgh	Meat plate/dish, ashet, oval with shaped edges and gadrooned border	Dundee Museums and Art Galleries 1968-15
1772/73	Patrick Robertson	Edinburgh	Dinner plates, set of 12, circular with gadrooned border, one side engraved with a crest, 9 ½" di, 204oz	Christie's NY USA 2000 #249
1772/73	Patrick Robertson	Edinburgh	Dinner plates, set of 24, circular with a gadrooned border, engraved with a coat-of-arms with an earl's coronet above arms of Scotland quartering Steward and Moray impaling Gray for Francis, 9th Earl of Moray and his wife, Jean Gray, 9 ¾" di, 411oz	Christie's London UK 2004 #69
1821/22	George McHattie	Edinburgh	Ashets, oval, pair, Scottish type, gadrooned borders, engraved with a crest of a prancing horse, an arrow pointing at its shoulders, above the motto "Onward", assayed February 15, 1822, 15 ¼" X 11 ¾", 82oz	Private Collection
1840/41	James McKay	Edinburgh	Soup plates, set of 12, no details	The Maple Swan Collection

YEAR	MAKER	LOCATION	DESCRIPTION	SOURCE
	SERVING AND OTHER DISHES			
1644-46	John Mylne Deacon Adam Lamb	Edinburgh	Sweetmeat dish, no details	Crichton Bros Jackson Marks p542
1646-48	Thomas Cleghorne	Edinburgh	Sweetmeat dish, circular body, chased with stylized flowers in center, 6 radiating ribbed leaves, flat handles shaped like the plumes of 5 feathers, initials "M/VG" and "AC", 3 ¾" di, 2.2oz	Shaw Collection Christie's Glasgow March 29, 1983 #14 National Museums of Scotland H.MEQ 1567
1650 ca	Thomas Moncur	Aberdeen	Sweetmeat dish, no details	Messrs. Jamieson and Carry, Aberdeen
1688/89	George Scott	Edinburgh	Saucepan, no details	Jackson Marks p543 Possibly Christie's as a source
1746/47	James Weems	Edinburgh	Saucepan, baluster form, V-shaped spout, part silver/part wooden handle, crest of an animal, 9" long, 10oz	Noble Collection Nicholas Shaw Catalog 2004 p98
1756/54	Ker & Dempster	Edinburgh	Chafing dish, circular form, ebony turned handle, stepped domed cover, ebony finial, lid engraved with a crest and garter below an earl's coronet, interior with another crest, 9" di, 15" overall, 35oz	Lyon & Turnbull The Murray Collection August 20, 2003 #197
1810 ca	William Jamieson	Aberdeen	Saucepan, no details	Hughes p78
1823/24	George McHattie	Edinburgh	Chafing dish, lamp and stand	National Museums of Scotland MEQ 819
1825/26	Alexander Edmonstoun	Edinburgh	Lipped saucepan, no details	National Museums of Scotland MEQ 704
1896/97	James Ferrier	Glasgow	Dessert dishes, part foliated, pierced shaped oval, spreading bases, 10 1/8" wide	Sotheby's London UK 2003 #153
	TUREENS			
1756/57	James Welsh	Edinburgh	Soup tureen and cover, oval bombe form on four scroll supports with ruffled shell and scroll headers, embossed cartouches engraved on one side with later arms, domed cover crested below rose finial, arms of Wood, of Mount House Co. Durham, 18 ¾" wide, 118oz 10d	Sotheby's NY USA 2006 #210
1763/64	Alexander Gardner	Edinburgh	Soup tureen, oval bombe form, chased with scrolls, on 4 ball and claw feet, cover with pumpkin finial, 14 1/8" wide, 124oz	Clayton Christie's Book p 206 #10 Apollo August 1966 vol 84 p80

YEAR	MAKER (continued)	LOCATION	DESCRIPTION	SOURCE
1778/79	Patrick Robertson	Edinburgh	Tureen, circular bombe form, gadrooned rim, on 4 foliate supports terminating in voluted feet, 2 reeded handles, domed lid with gadrooned band and screw on rosette of leaves from which issues an artichoke finial, Arms of Dundas of Fingast on body, lid with crest and motto of Dundas on the lid, 11 9/16"ht, 17" long, 145oz	National Museums of Scotland MEQ 842a-b 19683989a-b
1782/83	WD script William Davie or William Dempster	Edinburgh	Soup tureen, with cover, engraved with "HOC MENRIT INTEMERA FIDES", also arms of the city of Edinburgh, 12 3/8" ht, 19 3/4" long over the handle	Antiques Magazine vol 97 #906 Clayton Dictionary p366 #541 Thomas Campbell Museum, Camden NJ USA 1966-27
1784/85	PG (or possibly RG)	Edinburgh	Soup tureen, no details	Art Institute of Chicago 1984.62a-b
1791/92	William Robertson	Edinburgh	Tureen, no details	Edward & Sons, Glasgow Exhibition 1911, vol I, p107 #8
1797/98	Francis Howden	Edinburgh	Covered Tureen, no details	Christie's NY USA October 30, 1990 #296
1800/01	GG	Edinburgh	Tureen, no details	National Museums of Scotland MEQ 952 1969.688
1802/03	McHattie & Fenwick	Edinburgh	Soup tureen, no details	Antiques Magazine vol 95 #288 Bell of Aberdeen advertisement
1808/09	James McKay	Edinburgh	Covered soup tureen, bombe form, on 4 lion paw feet, engraved presentation to Crawford Tait, Esq. of Harvieston, 8 ½" ht, 124.4oz	The Maple Swan Collection
1810/11	George McHattie	Edinburgh	Covered tureen, with crest, no details	Nicholas Shaw Catalog Autumn 1999 p 59
1816/17	James McKay	Edinburgh	Soup tureen, no details	National Museums of Scotland MEQ 822a
1816/17	W & P Cunningham II	Edinburgh	Soup tureen and cover, oval on four lion's paw and acanthus foliage feet, reeded scroll bracket handles, domed cover with leaf-capped ring handle, body and cover with crest and motto, 16 ¾"wide, 104 oz	The Maple Swan Collection
1816/17	MM rubbed	Edinburgh	Regimental presentation soup tureen, no cover, partly gadrooned bombe oval, pedestal foot raised on four paw feet, gadrooned borders and hoop handles, engraved on one side with a Regimental badge and on the other with an 1817 presentation inscription, badge of Connaught Rangers, 15 3/8" wide, 76oz	Christie's London UK 1997 #68
				Sotheby's London UK 2005 #230

YEAR	MAKER	LOCATION	DESCRIPTION	SOURCE
1819/20	George Fenwick	Edinburgh	Soup tureen, bombe form, on 4 lion's paw feet, presentation to Mr. Alexander Henderson, cover surmounted by his crest, 15 3/8" long, 74.9oz	Nicholas Shaw Catalog Winter 2000 p77
1823/24	W & P Cunningham II	Edinburgh	Soup tureen and cover, oval bombe form, four cast acanthus headed paw supports, scrolled reeded handles either end, stepped domed cover, base and cover engraved with crest and motto "TRUE TO THE END", 10" ht, 16" wide, provenance S. J. Shrubsole	Butterfields Auctioneers Corp, San Francisco, CA USA 1991 #3116
1823/24	W & P Cunningham II	Edinburgh	Soup tureen with cover, liner by James Charles Edington, London, 1834, bulbous, foliate capped claw supports, crest and motto "TRUE TO THE END" for Hume, 17" di, 130oz 11d	*Sotheby's NY USA 1999 #430*
1823/24	George Fenwick	Edinburgh	Soup tureen with cover, bulbous, armorial engraved within a foliate cartouche and matted surround, leaf capped paw supports, the cover chased below the branch form handle with rococo ornament, 15 ½" wide, 74oz 14d	Sotheby's NY USA 1998 #545
1823/24	George Fenwick	Edinburgh	Sauce tureens, pair, with covers, oval on paw feet, 8 ¾" long, 64.5oz both	Nicholas Shaw Catalog Winter 2000 p78
1825/26	James McKay	Edinburgh	Soup tureen and cover, squat oval form on four ornate foliate scroll feet, domed cover with large handle decorated in relief with acorns and oak foliage, body with coat of arms on each side, cover with crest and motto "KIND HEART BE TRUE AND YOU SHALL NEVER RUE", 17" wide, 134oz	Woolley & Wallis, Salisbury UK 2007 #849
1830/31	James Howden & Co	Edinburgh	Soup tureen and cover, oval bombe form, applied rococo cartouches between scroll legs with cartouche and foliate headers, hoop handles, cover chased with rococo ornament, rose spring finial, also marked with AE in a shield, 17 ½" wide, 145oz 10d	Sotheby's NY USA 2005 #222
1833/34	George McHattie	Edinburgh	Soup tureen, bombe oval form, on 4 shell and scroll feet, Arms of Turnbull, 16" long, 96.1oz	Nicholas Shaw Catalog Autumn 1999 p59
1839/40	AW	Edinburgh	Soup tureens, pair, with covers, fluted bulbous, paw supports, engraved with armorials, 8 ½" wide, 52oz 5d	Sotheby's London UK 2004 #210
1876/77	J Crichton	Edinburgh	Soup tureen and cover, oval form on four beaded scroll supports, entwined tendril handles, domed cover, poppy finial, body chased with scrolling foliage enclosing a cartouche, engraved on one side with a coat of arms and on the other side with a crest, 18" wide, 102 oz	Christie's Lanarkshire UK 1998 #98
1910/11	Hamilton & Inches	Edinburgh	Soup tureens, pair, with covers, matching stands and ladles, oval form, domed covers, vase shaped finials, oval pedestal foot, with a presentation inscription, 9 2/3" wide, 59oz	Bonhams Solihull 2004 #221

Flatware

Plate 23. A Scots Fiddle Pattern Tea Straining Spoon 1730 ca by William Aytoun, Edinburgh. Courtesy of a private collector. Photograph by Janice M Dietert.

Fish Slices

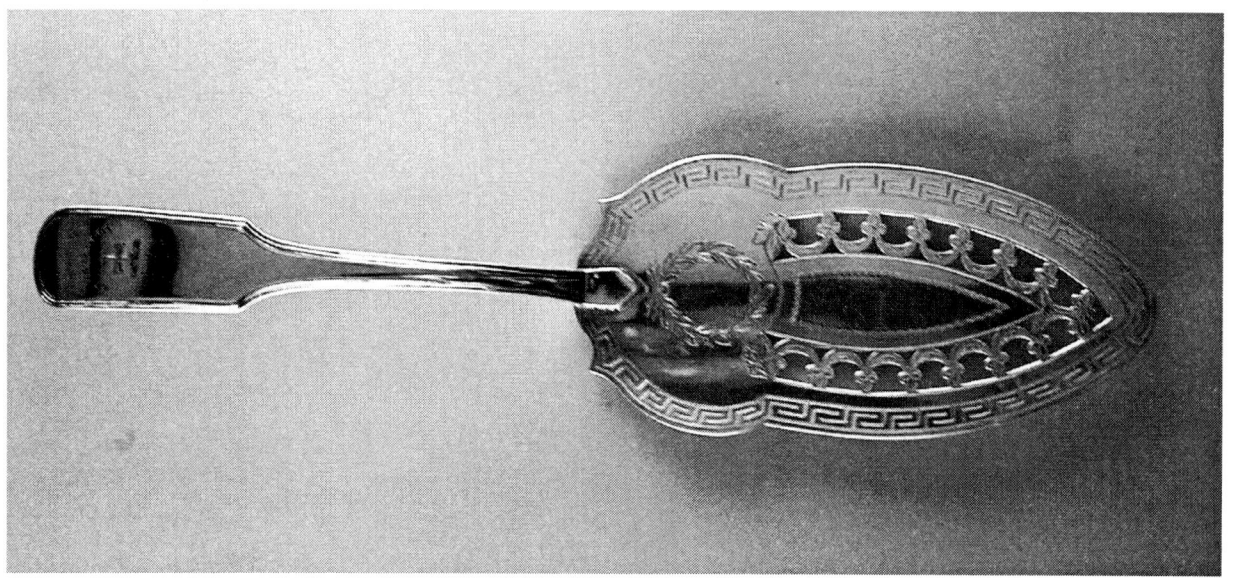

Plate 24. A Fish Slice 1807/08 by James Douglas, Edinburgh.
Courtesy of The Phoenix Collection. Photograph by Janice M Dietert.

YEAR	MAKER	LOCATION	DESCRIPTION	SOURCE
			FLATWARE	
	FISH SLICES			
1778/79	Peter Mathie	Edinburgh	Old English fish trowel, feather edged and crested, handle 11 3/8", 11 5/8"	Rabinovitch III #53, p76
1780/81	William Davie or William Dempster	Edinburgh	Fish slice, no details	Sotheby's Gleneagles August 1987 Lot 239
1784/85	Patrick Robertson	Edinburgh	Serving trowel, no details	Christie's Edinburgh November 21, 1990 #30
1790 ca	Charles Jamieson	Inverness	Long oval server in the shape of a fish	Rabinovitch IV #41, p140-141
1790 ca	James Erskine	Aberdeen	Cake slice/server, no details	Aberdeen Museums and Galleries ABDAG001306
1798/1800	Alexander Henderson	Edinburgh	Trowel with piercing and bright cut decoration, mm only	Private Collection
1799/1800	Francis Howden	Edinburgh	Fish slice, small with turned fruitwood handle	Private Collection
1799/1800	Alexander Spence	Edinburgh	Fish slice with green-stained ivory handle	Private Collection
1800 ca	Charles Fowler	Elgin	Fish slice, no details	National Museums of Scotland MEQ 132
1802/03	Robert Gray	Glasgow Edinburgh assay	Fish slice, no details	National Museums of Scotland MEQ 1195 1976.42
1802/03	Robert Keay I	Perth Edinburgh assay	Fish slice with filled round handle, unmarked, 11 ½"	Rabinovitch V #16, p160
1805/06	James Douglas	Edinburgh	Fish slice, 3 pierced circles, initial "C" on top, initial "R" underneath	Huntley House Museum Edinburgh HH3462/69
1806/07	Patrick Cunningham & Sons	Edinburgh	Fish slice, 11 ½", 5.9oz	Nicholas Shaw Catalog 2004 p106
1806/07	Robert Gray & Son	Glasgow Edinburgh assay	Fish slice, sharply curved blade, sometimes termed a "kidney server", fiddle handle, blade pierced with foliate pattern with engraved foliage as well	The Finial, v. 17/05 May/June 2007 p 5 (fig. 28)

YEAR	MAKER	LOCATION	DESCRIPTION	SOURCE
1807/8	James Douglas	Edinburgh	Fish slice, bright cut with Grecian key border, pierced swags, a vacant wreath, reeded fiddle handle, crest and motto "EX INDUSTRIA", 12" long	Joya Antiques, Washington, DC 1994 The Phoenix Collection
1810 ca	Robert Gray & Son	Glasgow Edinburgh assay	Acorn fish slice, pierced by vertical rear dolphin, monogrammed, 11" long	Rabinovitch VI #15 pp 234-235
1810/11	Robert Gray & Son	Glasgow Edinburgh assay	Fish slice, no details	Dundee Museums and Art Galleries 1962-701-1
1811/12	Ziegler	Edinburgh	Fish slice, 12 ¼" long, 4.1oz	Nicholas Shaw Catalog 2004 p106
1814/15	Francis Howden	Edinburgh	Kidney-shaped fish slice, script "R" on handle, 11 3/8" long	Rabinovitch VI #17 pp236-237
1815 ca	Jameson & Naughton	Inverness	Fish slice, 11 5/8" long, 4.1oz	Nicholas Shaw Catalog 2004 p106
1815/16	John McDonald	Edinburgh	Fish slice, fiddle pattern, sold with other items	Christie's London UK 2007 #417
1816/17	Mitchell & Russell	Glasgow	Fish slice, Kings pattern, reeded foliate pierced blade, monogrammed, handle with crest and motto "FORTES FORTUNA JUVAT", provenance Dr. J. H. Huffman, Toronto, 12 1/8" long, 5.4oz	Ritchie's Toronto CA June 5, 2007 #1104
1820-23	George McHattie	Edinburgh	Fish slice, no details	Aberdeen Museums and Galleries ABDAG001128
1821/22	Forrest (Retailer)	Edinburgh	Fish server, engraved script "B"	National Museums of Scotland MEQ 783
1824/25	GW	Glasgow	Fish slice, shaped blade with pierced and engraved decoration, initialed, 11 2/3" long, 5.5 oz	Lyon & Turnbull Edinburgh UK 2003 #335
1825 ca	James Pirie	Aberdeen	Fish slice, fiddle pattern, blade pierced and engraved with a fish and sprays of foliage within pricked dot borders, contemporary initials "Mc", 11 ¾" long 4oz	Christie's Lanarkshire UK 1998 #2
1825 ca	William Jamieson	Aberdeen	Fish slice with vertical fish, bright cut lines, 12"long	Rabinovitch V #54 pp 178-179
1825 ca	William Jamieson	Aberdeen	Fish slice, no details	Aberdeen Museums and Galleries ABDAG001128
1825 ca	William Jamieson	Aberdeen	Fish slice, plain fiddle pattern with shaped pierced blade, monogram, 11" long	Christie's London UK 1999 #10

YEAR	MAKER	LOCATION	DESCRIPTION	SOURCE
1825/26	CB	Edinburgh	Fish slice, fiddle pattern, pierced shaped center of blade with panels	Christie's London UK 2005 #525
1828/29	James McKay	Edinburgh	Fish slice, narrow, pierced blade in leafy design, handle terminates in shell design, 12" long, 2 ¾" wide	Birmingham Museum of Art 73.25
1830 ca	William Whitecross	Aberdeen	Fish slice, no details	Aberdeen Museums and Galleries ABDAG001305
1829/30	James Howden & Co	Edinburgh	Fish slice, Kings pattern, blade pierced with anthemions, monogrammed	Christie's Lanarkshire UK 1997 #815
1830/31	James McKay	Edinburgh	Fish slice, shaped with pierced scrolled panel, handle crested, 17 ¾" long 6oz	Bonhams London UK 2004 #307
1830/31	Robert Gray & Sons	Glasgow	Fish slice with plain unreeded blade, pierced squares, 12 3/8" long	Rabinovitch V #69 pp 182-183
1831/32	James Howden & Co	Edinburgh	Fish slice, no details	Antiques Magazine vol 95 p622
1833/34	Peter Arthur	Glasgow	Fish slice, solid handle, double reeding, script initials on back, 11 5/8"long	Rabinovitch V #72 pp182-183
1833/34	George White	Glasgow	Fish slice, fiddle pattern, with an initial, blade pierced and engraved with a fish motif surrounded by stars, 11 ¾" long, 5oz	Christie's London UK 2002 #237
1834/35	AW	Edinburgh	Fish slice with double reeded blade, arched lunettes, circles and stars pierced, 12 ¼" long	Rabinovitch V #73 pp182-183
1834/35	James Howden	Edinburgh	Fish slice, no details	National Museums of Scotland MEQ 935 1968.497
1834/35	Elder & Co	Edinburgh	Fish slice, no details	National Museums of Scotland MEQ 935
1835/36	AW	Edinburgh	Fish slice, single struck, Kings pattern, crest and motto "AMORE"	Christie's London UK 2007 #405
1836 ca	George Turvey	Glasgow	Fish slice, no details	Shrubsole NY 1992
1836/37	Elder & Co	Edinburgh	Fish slice, fiddle pattern, pierced with anthemion motifs	Christie's London UK 1998 #7
1839/40	William Cunningham	Edinburgh	Fish slice, single struck, Kings pattern, blade with pierced panel with cut out word "FISH" in elaborately scrolling letters, 5 oz	Christie's London UK 2004 #339
1840 ca	James Berry	Aberdeen	Fish slice, no details	Aberdeen Museums and Galleries ABDAG001378

YEAR	MAKER	LOCATION	DESCRIPTION	SOURCE
1840 ca	M Rettie & Son	Aberdeen	Fish slice, silver and ivory	Aberdeen Museums and Galleries ABDAG001294
1841/42	AW in shield	Edinburgh	Fish slice, no details	Antiques Mall, San Antonio TX, USA 1990
1841/42	Alexander Cameron	Dundee Edinburgh assay	Fish slice, fiddle pattern, shaped blade pierced and engraved with a fish within an outer border of water leaves and seaweed, engraved with initial "K", 11 ½" long, 4oz	Christie's Lanarkshire UK 1997 #34
1842/43	James McKay	Edinburgh	Fish slice, no details	Aberdeen Museums and Galleries ABDAG001029
1843/44	AW	Edinburgh	Fish slice, fiddle pattern, blade with a pierced panel of scrolls, crested, 5 oz	Woolley & Wallis Salisbury UK 2007 #141
1849/50	Robert Gray	Edinburgh	Fish slice, single struck, Kinds pattern	Christie's London UK 2005 #683

Forks

Plate 25. A pair of trefid Tableforks 1698/99 by Alexander Kincaid, Edinburgh. Courtesy of The Phoenix Collection. Photograph by Janice M Dietert.

YEAR	MAKER	LOCATION	DESCRIPTION	SOURCE
FORKS				
1698/99	Alexander Kincaid	Edinburgh	Forks, pair of trefids, with 4 prongs, part of a larger set, with a later Belgium import mark, block initials "M" over "TE"	Brand Inglis London The Phoenix Collection
1698/99	Thomas Cleghorne	Edinburgh	Fork, no details	National Museums of Scotland L1946.50
1698/99	Robert Bruce	Edinburgh	Fork, dog nose, 3 prongs	National Museums of Scotland MEQ 22
1698/99	Robert Bruce	Edinburgh	Forks, set of 10 dog nose, crest and motto of Haldane	Christie's July 1, 1982 # 70
1699/1700	Not available	Edinburgh	Forks, set of 6 dog nose, unclear, over struck	Private Collection UK
1700/01	John Seatoun	Edinburgh	Forks, set of 6, 3- pronged dog nose	Sotheby's October 13, 1960 # 125
1700/01	John Seatoun	Edinburgh	Forks, set of 6, 3- pronged dog nose, initials "A" and a thistle crest, 23.5oz total	Sotheby's October 13, 1960 # 113
1702/03	Colin McKenzie	Edinburgh	Table forks, set of 12, Hanoverian pattern, with tablespoons, each engraved with the crest of a stag's head issuing from a Viscount's coronet, with motto "HINC HONOR ET SALUS"	Private Collection UK
1704/05	Alexander Kincaid Over struck by __ B	Edinburgh	Forks, pair of dog nose, 3 pronged forks, later engraved "C" over "RB", 7" long	Private Collection UK
1704/05	Colin McKenzie	Edinburgh	Forks, set of 3 dog nose, 3 pronged forks with a crest	Sotheby's April 28, 1960 # 55 Shrubsole
1706/07	James Penman	Edinburgh	Forks, set of 4 dog nose, 3 pronged forks, intertwined and mirrored monogram "CWM"	Christie's June 22, 1960 # 99 How of Edinburgh Private Collection
1709/10	Colin McKenzie	Edinburgh	Fork, no details	National Museums of Scotland MEQ 937
1710/11	John Seatoun	Edinburgh	Forks, set of 5, dog nosed, 3 pronged, 6 7/8" long	Private Collection UK
1710/11	William Ged	Edinburgh	Forks, set of 12, probably Hanoverian, 3 pronged, crest and motto, 23oz	Sotheby's December 3, 1969
1712/13	James Yorstoun	Edinburgh	Forks, set of 3 dog nosed, with initials	Christie's January 22, 1960 # 99 How of Edinburgh

YEAR	MAKER	LOCATION	DESCRIPTION	SOURCE
1715 ca	William Ged	Edinburgh	Forks, pair of 3- pronged, crest of Robertson	National Museums of Scotland MEQ L1946.3-4
1715/16	Colin Campbell	Edinburgh	Forks, dog nosed, 3- pronged	Sotheby's April 28, 1960 # 55
1718/19	William Ged	Edinburgh	Forks, set of 3, Hanoverian 3- pronged, part of a larger set, initial "K"	Sotheby's January 31, 1979 # 137
1719/20	Henry Bethune	Edinburgh	Forks, set of 6, 3- pronged, trefid handles	Breadalbane Collection Sale 1935, Log 368
1719/20	James Tait	Edinburgh	Fork, Hanoverian, with 2- prongs	National Museums of Scotland
1719/20	James Tait	Edinburgh	Forks, pair, Hanoverian, with 2 prong, 7 ¼" long	Private Collection UK
1719/20	Mungo Yorstoun	Edinburgh	Dessert forks, set of 8, 3 -pronged Hanoverian, engraved crest and motto	Sotheby's July 4, 1968 # 156 Hancocks & Co, London UK
1719/20	Henry Bethune	Edinburgh	Forks, set of 6, 3 pronged dognose, contemporary script initial "F", 11 oz, possibly same as before	Sotheby's NY USA Oct 24, 2000 #195
1720 ca	Robert Cruickshank	Old Aberdeen	Forks, pair, 3 pronged, 7 1/7" long	Private Collection UK
1720 ca	Robert Cruickshank	Old Aberdeen	Fork, 3 pronged, different initials from previous lot	Sotheby's December 21, 1967 #222 Spinks London
1720/21	Henry Bethune	Edinburgh	Forks, set of 6, 3 -pronged, with a crest	Phillip Edinburgh March 29, 1964 # 141
1720/21	Henry Bethune	Edinburgh	Forks, set of 3, 3- pronged Hanoverian. 7 3/8" long, 6.9oz	Phillip Edinburgh October 21, 1983 # 85-88 Phillip Edinburgh October 19, 1990 # 99-101
1721/22	William Ged	Edinburgh	Forks, set of 12, 3 -pronged Hanoverian, with crest of Demi-lion	Sotheby's NY April 23, 1993 #300
1724/25	Alexander Edmonstoun I	Edinburgh	Forks, set of 6 Hanoverian, crest and motto of Campbell of Woodhall	Noble Collection Nicholas Shaw Catalog 2005 p89
1725 ca	Henry Bethune	Edinburgh	Fork, 3- pronged, fully marked, date not stated, 7 ¼", 1.8oz	Woolley & Wallis April 29, 2003 # 291
1725/26	Patrick Graham	Edinburgh	Forks, set of 11, 3- pronged, crest of intertwined rose and thistle with a motto, 7 ¼" long	Private Collection UK

YEAR	MAKER	LOCATION	DESCRIPTION	SOURCE
1727/28	William Aytoun	Edinburgh	Forks, set of 12, Hanoverian, 3- pronged, crest and motto	Christie's November 30, 1960 Christie's March 15, 1972
1727/28	James Ker	Edinburgh	Forks, set of 12, Hanoverian, 3- pronged, 24.6oz all	Sotheby's November 6, 1980, #126
1728/29	Henry Bethune	Edinburgh	Forks, set of 10, Hanoverian, 19.5oz all	Breadalbane Collection Sale 1935 # 354
1728/29	Henry Bethune	Edinburgh	Forks, pair, no details	National Museums of Scotland 1955.193 & a
1728/29	Henry Bethune	Edinburgh	Dessert forks, set of 6, no details	National Museums of Scotland 1983.30
1729/30	William Aytoun	Edinburgh	Forks, set of 12, 3- pronged, with coronet and crest of Fox, 23.1 oz	Christie's April 28, 1965 # 30 How of Edinburgh
1732/33	John Rollo	Edinburgh	Forks, set of 12, Hanoverian 3- pronged, crest and motto and coronet, 23oz	Christie's November 10, 1971 #107
1733/34	William Aytoun	Edinburgh	Dessert forks, set of 12, 3 -pronged, engraved with a coronet and initials "HA" 22oz	Christie's July 27, 1966 #130 Walter Willson Christie's March 15, 1972
1734/35	James Ker	Edinburgh	Forks, set of 12, 3- pronged, with 12 knives	How of Edinburgh 1937 #96
1738/39 & 1741/42	James Mitchelson	Edinburgh	Table forks, 3, no details	Sotheby's NY October 1991, #233
1740 ca	Michael Forrest	Canongate	Fork, 3- pronged, Hanoverian, crest of a fist holding 3 arrows, motto "Unite", (Note: apparently another single and a set of 4 exist with the same crest and motto), 8 3/8" long	Christie's May 15, 1981 #63 Phillips Edinburgh May 21, 1982 #118 Phillips Edinburgh Oct 22, 1982 #107
1740/41	Edward Lothian	Edinburgh	Forks, set of 12, Hanoverian, 3-pronged with knives, 22.3oz	How of Edinburgh 1937 #95
1741/42	James Ker	Edinburgh	Forks, set of 6, 3-pronged, 10oz	Christie's October 12, 1987 #184
1743/44	James Weems	Edinburgh	Forks, 3-pronged, with later initial "M", 6.4oz	Sotheby's February 24, 1966 # 97 Sotheby's April 11, 1968 # 7 JH Bourdon-Smith London

YEAR	MAKER	LOCATION	DESCRIPTION	SOURCE
1747/48	Robert Gordon	Edinburgh	Fork, 3- pronged, with initial "K"	Sotheby's January 31, 1979 #137
1749/50	Edward Lothian Over striking another	Edinburgh	Forks, set of 6, 3-pronged, crest and motto of Talbot	Private Collection
1749/50	Ebenezer Oliphant	Edinburgh	Fork, 3-pronged, engraved with initial "M", 24oz	Christie's April 25, 1979 #58
1750/51	Lothian & Robertson	Edinburgh	Forks, 3-pronged Hanoverian, with crest and motto, 23.8oz	Sotheby's April 23, 1981
1751-53	Ker & Dempster	Edinburgh	Table forks, composite set of five, Hanoverian pattern, with crest, motto and coronet, 10oz	Christie's Lanarkshire UK 1998 #5
1758/59	William Taylor	Edinburgh	Forks, set of 7, 3-pronged, 13.2oz	Christie's December 11, 1968
1760-65	Bayne & Napier & others	Glasgow and elsewhere	Table forks, composite of twelve, crest of Reid of Edinburgh	Metropolitan Museum of NY USA
1765/66	James Gilliland over striking another	Edinburgh	Forks, two small, Hanoverian pattern, three pronged, one engraved with initial "H", 5" long	Christie's Lanarkshire UK 1997 #124
1765/66	James Gilliland	Edinburgh	Fork, no details	National Museums of Scotland K.1998.450
1769/70	William Davie or William Dempster	Edinburgh	Serving fork, no details	The Maple Swan Collection
1770/71	William Ker	Edinburgh	Toasting fork, for toast or bannock, 4 tines, twisted horn handle with silver finial, swiveling hinge, 28" long	Sotheby's Scone Palace, April 23, 1979 # 70
1771/72	Patrick Robertson	Edinburgh	Dessert forks, set of 12, Hanoverian, three pronged, terminal, engraved with a script initial "H" below an earl and coronet, 15 oz	Sotheby's NY USA 1995 #289
1781/82	David Downie	Edinburgh	Toasting fork, no details	Jackson Marks p550
1781/82	W & P Cunningham I	Edinburgh	Forks, pair of 2- pronged, crest of a bird, 7 5/8" long, 1.3oz each	Wark, Huntington Library Collection p143, #334
1786/87	Patrick Robertson	Edinburgh	Serving fork, 6- pronged, crest and motto, 11 3/8" long	Huntley House Museum Edinburgh HH1299/51
1790 ca	John Leslie	Aberdeen	Forks, 3, no details	National Museums of Scotland MEQ 537-539

YEAR	MAKER	LOCATION	DESCRIPTION	SOURCE
1796/97	Alexander Henderson	Edinburgh	Table forks, set of 7, no details	Sotheby's Gleneagles August 1988 # 333
1800 ca	Francis Howden	Edinburgh	Oyster forks, pair, no details	National Museums of Scotland MEQ 1007-1008 1970.558-559
1800 ca	James Erskine	Aberdeen	Forks, set of 6, no details	National Museums of Scotland MEQ 531
1800 ca	*James Erskine*	*Aberdeen*	*Forks, set of 6,, crest and motto*	*Sotheby's Gleneagles August 1993 # 12*
1801/02	Alexander Henderson	Edinburgh	Table forks, set of five, fiddle pattern	Gorringes LLP East Sussex UK 2005 #1760
1806/07	John Ziegler	Edinburgh	Venison forks, 4, 2 pronged, crest and motto, 7 7/8" long	Huntley House Museum Edinburgh HH 1498/54
1807/08	Alexander Spence	Edinburgh	Table fork, bright cut, 8 1/8" long	Huntley House Museum Edinburgh HH 3463/69
1808-11	James McKay	Edinburgh	Table forks, mixed year fiddle pattern, set of six	Toovey's West Sussex UK 2007 #426
1813/14	MC John McDonald or Matthew Craw	Edinburgh	Table fork, upturned handle, English fiddle pattern, 8 1/8" long	Huntley House Museum Edinburgh HH3235/68
1816/17	James McKay	Edinburgh	Table forks, set of 4, small, with heraldry	S Wyler, NY 1993
1816/17	Mitchell & Russell	Glasgow	Table forks, set of eleven, double struck Queen's pattern, the reverses of prongs stuck with shells and reeding, engraved with a crest, motto and monogram	Christie's Amsterdam NE 2005 #45
1816/17	James & William Howden	Edinburgh	Table forks, set of six fiddle pattern, sold with others	Christie's Lanarkshire UK 1997 #309
1819/20	James McKay	Edinburgh	Table forks, set of six, fiddle pattern, engraved on reverse with a monogram, 14oz	Christie's Lanarkshire UK 1997 #68
1819/20	W & P Cunningham II	Edinburgh	Table fork, no details	Sotheby's Gleneagles August 1993 # 15

YEAR	MAKER	LOCATION	DESCRIPTION	SOURCE
1820 ca	Alexander Stewart	Tain	Table fork, fiddle pattern, three pronged engraved with a hand and dagger crest, 7 ¾" long, 2 oz	Christie's Lanarkshire UK 1997 #68
1820/21	Marshall & Sons	Edinburgh	Table fork, fiddle pattern 7 7/8" long, 2.1oz	The Silver Spoon Club Postal Auction July 12, 2007 #19
1821/22	PG	Glasgow	Table forks, set of six, fiddle and shell pattern, 15oz	Christie's Lanarkshire UK 1997 #391
1824/25	J & W Marshall	Edinburgh	Table fork, no details	Antique Center, San Antonio TX, USA 1998
1824/25	Marshall & Sons	Edinburgh	Table fork, set of seven, fiddle and shell pattern, with initials "R & MJ", 15oz	Gorringes LLP Lewes 2007 #2054
1830 ca	Andrew Davidson	Arbroath	Forks, 6, no details	National Museums of Scotland MEQ 303-308
1830 ca	Ronald Donaldson	Dundee	Child's fork, three pronged, fiddle pattern, terminal reverse with crest and motto, 4" long, 1oz	Sotheby's NY USA 1999 #507
1830 ca	George Elder	Banff	Table Forks, set of six, compressed fiddle pattern with shouldered stems, four prongs, engraved with initials "JBA", 12oz	Christie's Lanarkshire UK 1999 #26
1830 ca	Alexander Cameron	Dundee	Table forks, eleven, fiddle pattern, part of a larger canteen	Gorringes LLP East Sussex, UK 2006 #1746
1835 ca	Richard Maxwell	Tain	Forks, set of 6, fiddle pattern, crest and motto "In Defense", 7 ¾" long, 13.8oz	Noble Collection Nicholas Shaw Catalog 2005 p102
1840 ca	John Sellars	Wick	Forks, set of 6, Old English pattern, crest and motto of Sutherland, 8 ½", 15oz	Noble Collection Nicholas Shaw Catalog 2005 p102
1842/43	WC	Edinburgh	Table forks, set of six, fiddle pattern with shell cast finials, 12oz	Mullucks Wells Essex UK 2007 #142
1842/43	AW	Edinburgh	Dessert forks, set of ten, 10oz	Tring Auctions, Hertfordshire UK 2007 #271
1843/44	Donald McDonald	Glasgow	Table forks, set of twelve, fiddle pattern, engraved with an initial, 29.5oz	Christie's London UK 2005 #108

YEAR	MAKER	LOCATION	DESCRIPTION	SOURCE
1846/47	A M & Co	Edinburgh	Table forks, set of six, single struck, Kings pattern, sold with others	Christie's Lanarkshire UK 1997 #311
1851/52	J Mitchell Jr	Glasgow	Dessert forks, set of six, single struck Albert pattern	Christie's London UK 1999 #85
1876/77	MacKay & Chisholm	Edinburgh	Starter forks, set of six, fiddle pattern	O'Reilly Auctions, Dublin IR 2007 #333
1902/03	Charles Rennie MacKintosh (made by David Hyslop)	Glasgow	Pudding forks, pair, no details	Aberdeen Museums and Galleries ABDAG11014

Knives

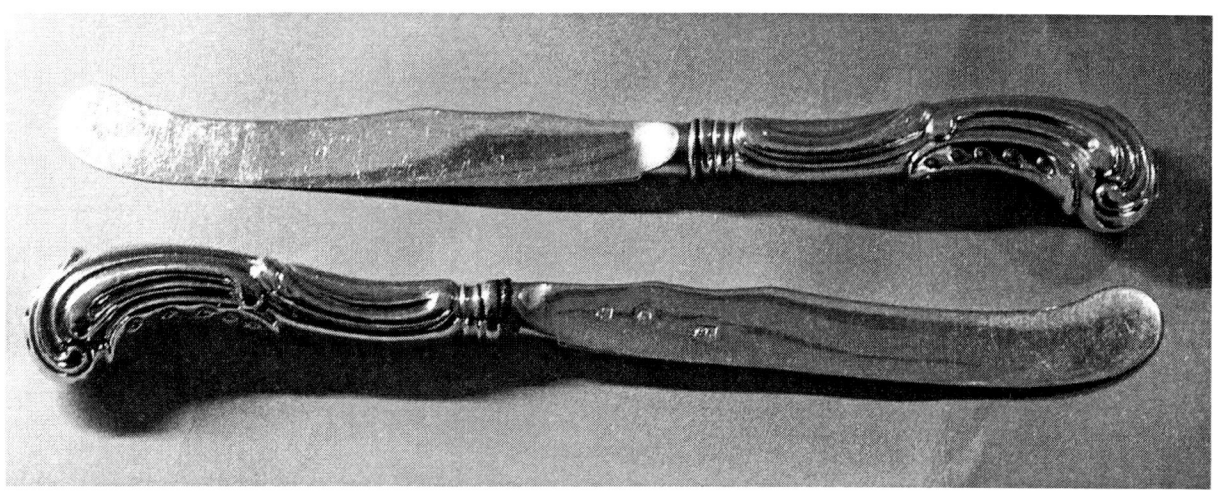

Plate 26. Two from a set of 12 1786-90 Dessert Knives by Patrick Robertson, Edinburgh. Courtesy of a private collector. Photograph by Janice M Dietert.

YEAR	MAKER KNIVES	LOCATION	DESCRIPTION	SOURCE
1690 ca	John Seatoun	Edinburgh	Knives, tapering cylindrical handles, stepped domed ends, mm only	Christie's July 26, 1972 # 339 How of Edinburgh
1709/10	Robert Bruce	Edinburgh	Knives, cannon handled, set of 8, part of a larger flatware and cutlery set, engraved "Mary Hay Lady Randerstone elder 1710",	Private Collection UK
1710 ca	Colin McKenzie	Edinburgh	Table knives, 2, no details	National Museums of Scotland MEQ 1102
1710/11	Colin McKenzie	Edinburgh	Table knives, set of 9, pistol handled, steel blades engraved with a monogram, with 5 similar unmarked cheese knives	Christie's July 26, 1972 # 332 How of Edinburgh
1720 ca	Not available	Edinburgh	Knives, set of 12, plain pistol handled, initials "KH"	Private Collection
1730 ca	Not available	Edinburgh	Dessert knives, set of 12, voluted pistol handles, original steel blades with cutler's mark "Wight"	Christie's Fingask Castle April 27, 1993 Private Collection
1730 ca	Not available	Edinburgh	Knives, set of 6, rat tail, voluted, pistol handled, en suit with knives above, later blades marked "DUN" slender and maybe reconverted forks	Christie's Fingask Castle April 27, 1993 Private Collection
1730 ca	Robert Luke II	Glasgow	Knives, 3, with silver grips	National Museums of Scotland MEQ 1099-1101 1974.407-409
1734/35	James Ker	Edinburgh	Table knives, set of 12, pistol grip, with forks, leaf capped volutes on handles	How of Edinburgh 1937 #96
1740/41	Edward Lothian	Edinburgh	Knives, set of 12, pistol grip, plain volute handles, with forks	How of Edinburgh 1937 #95
1745 ca	Lawrence Oliphant	Edinburgh	Table knives, set of 12 ,pistol handled, with steel blades	How of Edinburgh Private Collection
1760 ca	Patrick Robertson	Edinburgh	Table knives, set of 6, plain, tapering ovoid section handles with almost flat truncated terminals, each engraved with crest and motto of Craig of Riccarton, original steel blades with cutler's mark "BOOG," 10 ½" long	Lyon & Turnbull The Murray Collection August 20, 2003 # 195
1780 ca	Patrick Robertson	Edinburgh	Knives, set of 4, no details	National Museums of Scotland MEQ 845
1790 ca	Patrick Robertson	Edinburgh	Tea knives, set of 12, with slender blades and filled silver handles, blades marked 1789/90 or 1790/91 by Patrick Robertson, handles unmarked, crest	Bell of Aberdeen 1968 Private Collection

YEAR	MAKER (continued)	LOCATION	DESCRIPTION	SOURCE
			and motto "CORDA SERRATA PANDO" and viscount's coronet	
1800 ca	Charles Jamieson	Inverness	Dessert knife, narrow blade, handle with parallel incised lines to give it a reeded effect	Dundee Museums and Art Galleries 1978-697
1830 ca	William Ferguson	Elgin	Butter knives, pair, fiddle pattern, no details	Sotheby's Gleneagles August 1993 #6
1830 ca	Charles Jamieson	Inverness	Butter knife, fiddle pattern, sold with a teaspoon and dessert spoon by the same maker	Gorringes LLP East Sussex UK 2006 #1732
1836/37	RAF	Edinburgh	Butter knife, fiddle pattern, reeded blade, engraved initial, 1.3oz	Gildings Leicestershire UK 2007 #365
1839/40	Marshall & Sons	Edinburgh	Cheese knives, set of six, plain blade, partly reeded tapering handle, three handles with London marks	Christie's London UK 1998 #19
1873/74	Hamilton & Inches	Edinburgh	Butter knife, 6 ¾" long	The Phoenix Collection
1875/76	McKay & Chisolm	Edinburgh	Butter knives, pair, no details	The Maple Swan Collection
1878/79	William Marshall	Edinburgh	Butter knife, fiddle pattern, 7 ½" long	Gorringes LLP East Sussex UK 2006 #1666

Ladles

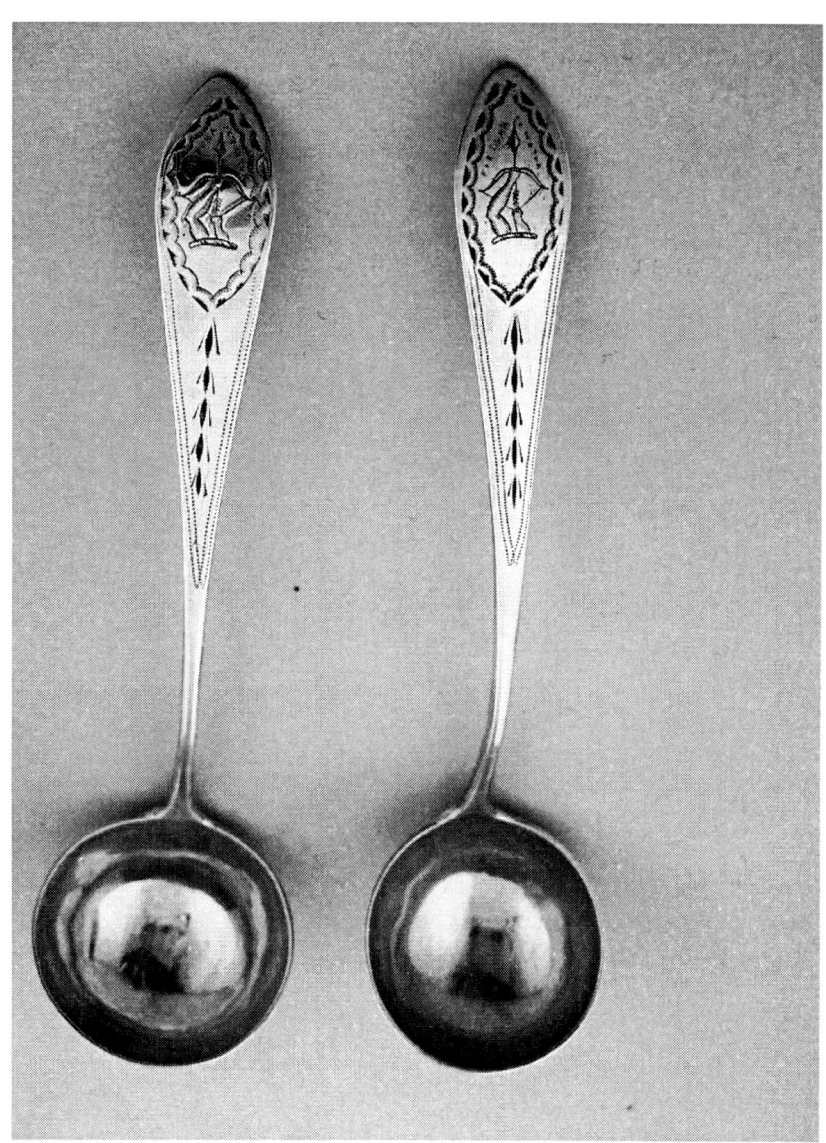

Plate 27. A pair of Sauce Ladles 1790 ca by James Douglas, Dundee. Courtesy of The Phoenix Collection. Photograph by Janice M Dietert.

YEAR	MAKER LADLES	LOCATION	DESCRIPTION	SOURCE
1704/05	Thomas Cumming	Glasgow	Ladle, exact form questionable	Glasgow Exhibition of 1911 Jackson Marks p519
1728/29	Patrick Graham	Edinburgh	Soup ladle, no details	Glasgow Exhibition 1911, vol I, p 111 #28
1733/34	William Aytoun	Edinburgh	Punch ladle, oval bowl, 17 ½" long	Nicholas Shaw Catalog 2004 p106
1735 ca	CD Possibly Charles Dickson I	Dundee	Punch ladle, plain circular bowl and socket, turned wood baluster handle, three marks CD in script, pot of lilies, script E, note: is most likely for Charles Dickson I but could also be for Charles Dickson II	Christie's Lanarkshire UK 1998 #100
1740/41	Edward Lothian Assayer – Dougal Ged	Edinburgh	Soup ladle, Old English pattern, sold with other items	Sotheby's NY USA 1997 #290
1745 ca	Alexander Johnston	Dundee	Punch ladle, no details	Christie's Edinburgh November 21, 1990 #25
1750 ca	Robert Wildgoose	Old Aberdeen	Soup ladle, no details	Grantully Castle Antiques Private Collection UK
1750 ca	John Steven	Dundee	Soup ladle, no details	National Museums of Scotland H.1996.33
1755 ca	Ker & Dempster	Edinburgh	Sugar sifter ladle, Hanoverian, engraved cipher below a coronet, 2oz	Woolley & Wallis January 26, 2005 # 742
1755/56	Ker & Dempster	Edinburgh	Sugar sifter ladle, Hanoverian with double drop, shallow bowl, engraved cipher below a coronet, mm only 4x, 2oz	Woolley & Wallis Auction, January 26, 2005 #742
1760 ca	JL	Glasgow	Soup ladle, plain Old English, circular bowl, script marriage initials 'JH/JB'	Christie's London UK 1999 #66
1763/34	Alexander Gardner	Edinburgh	Soup ladles, pair, no details	National Museums of Scotland MEQ 929-929 1968.989 a-b
1765 ca	Adam Graham	Glasgow	Punch ladle, 17 ¼" long	Nicholas Shaw Catalog Winter 2001 p80
1765 ca	Adam Graham	Glasgow	Soup ladle, Old English script, interlocking initials "H/EM", 14" long, bowl 4" di	Hunt Antiques, San Antonio, TX The Phoenix Collection

YEAR	MAKER	LOCATION	DESCRIPTION	SOURCE
1765 ca	Adam Graham	Glasgow	Soup ladle, Old English, no details	JH Bourdon-Smith London 1994
1765 ca	James Gordon	Aberdeen	Soup ladle, no details	Sotheby's Gleneagles August 1988 #432
1765 ca	William Craw	Canongate	Soup ladle, no details	Dundee Museums and Art Galleries 1978-696
1766/67	Alexander Gardner	Edinburgh	Sauce ladles, pair, scalloped bowl, twisted handle, crest and motto, 7 3/8" long	Huntley House Museum Edinburgh HH 3468/69
1766/67	Alexander Gardner	Edinburgh	Soup ladle, Old English pattern, with a crest of Menzies, 15" long, 7oz	Christie's London UK 2006 #118
1770 ca	James Gordon	Aberdeen	Soup ladle, Old English pattern, 13 1/8", 6.1oz	Nicholas Shaw Catalog Winter 2000 p89
1770 ca	William Davie or William Dempster	Edinburgh	Ladle, shell bowl, no details	National Museums of Scotland MEQ 1218
1770 ca	Milne & Campbell	Glasgow	Soup ladle, Hanoverian pattern, with shell attachment to bowl, script initial "B" also stamp of "Breadalbane" on handle, 14 ¾" long	The Phoenix Collection
1770 ca	Adam Graham	Glasgow	Soup ladle, plain Old English, 15" long	Christie's Lanarkshire UK 1997 #134
1770 ca	Milne & Campbell	Glasgow	Soup ladle, Hanoverian pattern with shell bowl, engraved with initial "R", 15" long	Christie's London UK 1999 #188
1770 ca	James Gordon	Aberdeen	Soup ladle, Old English pattern, 13" long	Gorringes LLP East Sussex UK 2006 #1582
1770/71	William Dempster or William Davie	Edinburgh	Soup ladle, Hanoverian, with shell bowl	JH Bourdon-Smith London Private Collection
1770/71	Gilliland & Ker	Edinburgh	Soup ladle, circular bowl, crest and motto, 14" long, 12oz	Campbell Museum, Camden, NJ USA 1966-27b
1771/72	James Reid (over striking another)	Edinburgh	Soup ladle, Hanoverian pattern, 7.2oz	JH Bourdon-Smith London Private Collection
1772 ca	James Cornfute	Perth	Soup ladle, round bowl, Hanoverian pattern, part of a large set	Brooklyn Museum 66.32.99
1772/73	William Davie or William Dempster	Edinburgh	Soup ladle, no details	Jackson Marks p549

YEAR	MAKER	LOCATION	DESCRIPTION	SOURCE
1774/75	WD (block) William Dempster or William Davie	Edinburgh	Ladle, no details	National Museums of Scotland H.1996.29
1775 ca	James Cornfute	Perth	Soup ladle, Old English, initials "JP", 13 13/4" long, 6.5oz	Nicholas Shaw Catalog Winter 2000 p89
1775 ca	James Cornfute	Perth	Soup ladle, no details	National Museums of Scotland MEQ 425
1775/76	William Davie or William Dempster	Edinburgh	Punch ladle, no details	The Maple Swan Collection
1776 ca	WD script William Davie or William Dempster	Edinburgh	Punch ladle, shell shaped, wooden handle, monogrammed "R" in script, 12 7/8" long overall	Huntley House Museum Edinburgh HH 2538/64
1777/78	Peter Mathie	Edinburgh	Soup ladle, no details	Sotheby's Gleneagles August 1987 #238
1779/80	James Hewitt	Edinburgh	Soup ladle, Old English, engraved "McM", 8.5oz	Sotheby's Gleneagles August 29, 1978 # 403
1779/80	James Hewitt	Edinburgh	Sauce ladle, no details	Jackson Marks p549
1779/80	Patrick Robertson	Edinburgh	Soup ladle, no details	Sotheby's Gleneagles 1990 # 9
1779/80	James Hewitt	Edinburgh	Soup ladle, no details	Jackson Marks p549
1780 ca	James Smith	Aberdeen	Soup ladle, no details	Sotheby's Hopetoun House, May 1990 #10
1780 ca	W M	Edinburgh	Soup ladle, no details	Sotheby's Gleneagles August 1988 #34
1780 ca	Thomas Borthwick	Inverness	Soup ladle, Old English, initials "GBM", 13 ¾" long	Sotheby's Gleneagles August 1993 #16
1780 ca	William Scott	Dundee	Soup ladle, feather edge, crest and motto "PRAETIO PRODESTION PRAESTAR", 14" long, 6.6oz	Nicholas Shaw Catalog Winter 2000 p89
1780 ca	John Leslie	Aberdeen	Punch ladle, no details	Aberdeen Museums and Galleries ABDAG000903

YEAR	MAKER	LOCATION	DESCRIPTION	SOURCE
1780 ca	William Law	Dundee	Soup ladle, no details	Dundee Museums and Art Galleries 1986-122
1780 ca	William Scott	Dundee	Soup ladle, Old English pattern, shallow circular bowl, with contemporary initials "A.K.C.", 14" long, 6oz	Christie's Lanarkshire UK 1998 #49
1780/81	James Welsh	Edinburgh	Soup ladle, Old English, no details	Private Collection
1780/81	Alexander Aitchison	Edinburgh	Soup ladle, no details	The Maple Swan Collection
1782/83	WD William Davie or William Dempster	Edinburgh	Soup ladle, bright cut, 15" long	Huntley House Museum Edinburgh HH3489/70
1782/83	James Gilliland	Edinburgh	Soup ladle, Old English	Christie's Melbourne AU 2001 #556
1783/84	James Gilliland	Edinburgh	Soup ladle, Old English, engraved initial	Christie's London October 1988 #14
1783/84	Francis Howden	Edinburgh	Soup ladle, Old English, with initials	Sotheby's Scone Palace April 10, 1978 #78
1783/84	IE Probably John Edmonstoun	Edinburgh	Punch ladle, with bone handle, bowl with scalloped edge, 17" long	Lyman Allyn Art Museum, New London, CT USA 1971.46
1784/85	J Clark (over struck)	Edinburgh	Soup ladle, no details	S Wyler, NY 1992
1784/85	Alexander Gardner	Edinburgh	Sauce ladles, pair, no details	Christie's London 1988 #14
1785/86	William Davie or William Dempster	Edinburgh	Sauce ladles, set of 5, 2 with crest and motto, 3 with erasures	William Walters Antiques, London, 1995
1785/86	Thomas Bryden	Glasgow Edinburgh assay	Soup ladles, pointed Old English pattern, crest and motto of Mackintosh, 11 ½" long, 3oz	JH Bourdon-Smith Catalog Autumn 1991 #41 p44
1785/86	James Hewitt	Edinburgh	Soup ladle, Old English, with bright cut stem, silver-gilt fluted bowl, initials	Sotheby's Scone Palace April 14, 1980 # 93
1785/86	Patrick Robertson	Edinburgh	Ladle, 14" long	Antiques Magazine vol 52, p313
1786/87	William Dempster or	Edinburgh	Soup ladle, Old English pattern, with shell bowl, monogrammed, 5.8oz	Bonhams Sale 15120 Aug 22

YEAR	MAKER	LOCATION	DESCRIPTION	SOURCE
	William Davie			2007 #70
1788/89	James Douglas	Edinburgh	Sauce ladles, pair, pointed Old English pattern, initials "F" or "T"	Private Collection
1788/89	Patrick Robertson	Edinburgh	Soup ladle, Old English, engraved "R C/2"	Sotheby's Gleneagles August 29, 1978 # 373
1789/90	James Douglas	Edinburgh	Toddy ladle, no details	Jackson Marks p 550
1789/90	Patrick Robertson	Edinburgh	Sauce ladles, 4, not pictured	Christie's London October 1988 #14
1789/90	David Marshall	Edinburgh	Soup ladle, pointed Old English	Christie's Melbourne AU 2001 #556
1790 ca	John Leslie	Aberdeen	Toddy ladles, pair, no details	National Museums of Scotland MEQ 548
1790 ca	James Cornfute	Perth	Soup ladle, no details	Sotheby's Gleneagles, August 1987 #238
1790 ca	Joseph Pearson	Dumfries	Soup ladle, Old English, initials "RS 13"	Sotheby's Gleneagles, August 1993 #313
1790 ca	MK (conjoined in an oval)	Edinburgh	Sauce ladle, pointed Old English pattern, script initial "G", 6 ¼" long, .5oz	EBAY 7378438884 January 14, 2006
1790 ca	William Clark	Greenock	Soup ladle, Old English, no details	JH Bourdon-Smith London 1994
1790 ca	John Leslie	Aberdeen	Toddy ladles, pair, no details	National Museums of Scotland MEQ 548
1790/91	Alexander Gardner	Edinburgh	Soup ladle, Old English pattern, initialed, sold with other items	Lyon & Turnbull Edinburgh UK 2005 #264
1790/91	Robert Gray	Glasgow Edinburgh assay	Soup ladle, shell bowl, with a crest and motto, 14" long	Bonhams London UK 2006 #189
1790/91	William Robertson	Edinburgh	Soup ladle, pointed Old English, handle with script initial "H", 15" long, 7.5 oz	Christie's East NY USA 1997 #63
1790/91	Patrick Robertson	Edinburgh	Sauce ladles, pair, not pictured	Christie's London October 1988 #15

YEAR	MAKER	LOCATION	DESCRIPTION	SOURCE
1790/91	Alexander Ziegler	Edinburgh	Soup ladle, pointed Old English pattern, with crest and motto, 6oz	Sotheby's Scone Palace April 10, 1978 # 119
1790/91	William Robertson	Edinburgh	Sauce ladles, pair, not pictured	Christie's London October 1988 #15
1790/91	John Leslie	Aberdeen	Sauce ladle, no details	Hyman Collection - Colonial Williamsburg
1790/91	George Christie	Edinburgh	Soup ladle, pointed Old English pattern, sailing ship crest and "RR" initials, 6oz	Woolley & Wallis January 26, 2005 # 212
1793/94	Alexander Ziegler	Edinburgh	Soup ladle, no details	Glasgow Exhibition 1911, vol I, p 111 #33
1794/95	Francis Howden	Edinburgh	Soup ladle, Old English, engraved "JB", 6.7oz	Sotheby's Gleneagles August 29, 1878 #421
1794/95	L_ mark		Soup ladle, Old English, no details	Wyler, NY USA1993
1794/95	William Robertson	Edinburgh	Soup ladle, Old English, engraved with an initial, 6.8oz	Christie's London UK 2001 #100
1795 ca	James Douglas	Dundee	Sauce ladles, pair, pointed Old English pattern, bright cut, engraved, crest and motto in oval medallion, probably of Hunter 5 ½" long	M Rafael, NY 1995 The Phoenix Collection
1795 ca	James Douglas	Dundee	Toddy ladle, pointed Old English pattern, 6 1/8" long	Nicholas Shaw Catalog Winter 2000 p82
1795/96	William Cunningham	Edinburgh	Sauce ladles, pair, no details	The Maple Swan Collection
1795/96	Robert Gray	Glasgow Edinburgh assay	Sauce ladle, Old English pattern, round bowl, slender stem	The Finial, vol 17/05 May/June 2007 p4 (fig. 7)
1796/97	Francis Howden	Edinburgh	Soup ladle, Old English pattern, with an initial, 14" long, 6oz	Christie's London UK 2003 #442
1796/97	Alexander Gardner	Edinburgh	Sauce ladle, pointed Old English pattern, initials "LHC", 15" long	Hyde Park Center, NY 1993 The Phoenix Collection
1796/97	Francis Howden	Edinburgh	Soup ladle, pointed Old English pattern, initials "SAR"	Private Collection
1797/98	Robert Wilson	Edinburgh	Soup ladle, with a crest, 5.4oz	Sotheby's Gleneagles Sept 1, 1981 #391

YEAR	MAKER	LOCATION	DESCRIPTION	SOURCE
1797/98	Francis Howden	Edinburgh	Ladle, for use with tureen of same date	National Museums of Scotland MEQ 953 1969.689
1798/99	Francis Howden	Edinburgh	Soup ladle, Old English, initials, 6.5oz	Sotheby's Hopetoun House November 15, 1977 # 111
1798/99	RW mark	Edinburgh	Soup ladle, Old English, crest	Jonathan Trace Antiques, NY USA 1992
1799/1800	Alexander Henderson	Edinburgh	Soup ladle, pointed Old English pattern, initials script "AGC", 15"long	Jonathan Trace Antiques, NY USA 1992 The Phoenix Collection
1799/1800	IG (over striking another)	Edinburgh assay	Soup ladle, Old English, 14"long	Hyde Park Center, NY USA 1993
1800 ca	James Erskine	Aberdeen	Soup ladle, Old English, with initials, 5oz	Christie's London UK 2001 #130
1800 ca	Robert Wilson	Edinburgh	Toddy ladles, with crest of Murray Threipland of Fingast	Bonhams The Scottish Sale August 21, 2003 #47
1800 ca	W & P Cunningham I	Edinburgh	Ladles, pair, silver hand twist punch	Silver Plus 1993
1800 ca	A Henderson	Edinburgh	Toddy ladles, 6, pointed Old English pattern	Sotheby's Gleneagles August 1993 #6
1800 ca	James Cornfute	Perth	Soup ladle, Old English	JH Bourdon-Smith London 1992
1800 ca	James Hewitt	Dumfries	Punch ladle, wood handle	JH Bourdon-Smith London 1992
1800 ca	JP mark & thistle		Punch ladle, no details	JH Bourdon-Smith London 1992
1800 ca	R D mark	Perth	Soup ladle, not pictured	Sotheby's London November 1987 #15
1800 ca	W H	Perth, Glasgow, or Paisley	Ladle, mark with an anchor, no details	Sotheby's London November 1987 #15
1800 ca	Thomas Davie	Greenock	Toddy ladle, no details	Sotheby's Gleneagles August 1987 #245
1800 ca	John Keith	Banff	Soup ladle, no details	Sotheby's Hopetoun House, April 1988 #13

YEAR	MAKER	LOCATION	DESCRIPTION	SOURCE
1800 ca	James Erskine	Aberdeen	Soup ladle, Old English	JH Bourdon-Smith London 1994
1800 ca	Charles Jamieson	Inverness	Soup ladle, Old English	JH Bourdon-Smith London 1994
1800 ca	David Gray	Dumfries	Sauce ladle, Old English, initials "PMcN"	Nicholas Shaw Catalog Autumn 1999 p 51
1800 ca	James Erskine	Aberdeen	Toddy ladle, no details	National Museums of Scotland MEQ 108
1800 ca	James Erskine	Aberdeen	Toddy ladle, pair, no details	National Museums of Scotland MEQ 546
1800 ca	Nathaniel Gillet	Aberdeen	Toddy ladle, no details	National Museums of Scotland MEQ 550
1800 ca	James Erskine	Aberdeen	Toddy ladles, pair, no details	National Museums of Scotland MEQ 571
1800 ca	John Sellar	Wick	Toddy ladles, 3 different ones, no details	National Museums of Scotland MEQ 255 MEQ93 MEQ891
1800 ca	Peter Lambert	Montrose	Soup ladle, no details	Dundee Museums and Art Galleries 1987-160
1800 ca	George Booth	Aberdeen	Toddy ladles, set of three, fiddle pattern, initialed, 3oz	Christie's London UK 1998 #257
1800/01	G & Mc	Edinburgh	Soup ladle, Old English pattern, 14 ½" long, 7oz	Christie's London UK 2005 #216
1801-03	Robert Keay	Perth Edinburgh assay	Sauce ladles, pair, Old English pattern, 7" long	Litchfield Auction Gallery, Litchfield, CT 1992 #372
1801/02	WM	Edinburgh	Soup ladle, Old English pattern, with cursive monogram, 5oz 14d	Butterfields Auctioneers San Francisco USA 1991 #1128
1802/03	Robert Gray	Glasgow Edinburgh assay	Soup ladle, Old English pattern, engraved with an initial, 6oz	Christie's London UK 2004 #606
1802/03	John Zeigler	Edinburgh	Soup ladle, Old English, crest and motto of Stirling, 6.5oz	Louis Wine, Toronto Canada 1991

YEAR	MAKER	LOCATION	DESCRIPTION	SOURCE
1804/05	Alexander Henderson	Edinburgh	Sauce ladle, no details	The Maple Swan Collection
1804/05	John Ziegler	Edinburgh	Toddy ladles, set of 6, no details	National Museums of Scotland MEQ 1087-1092 1973.244-249
1804/05	WM	Edinburgh	Soup ladle, Old English pattern, initialed, 15 1/8" long, 6oz	Lyon & Turnbull Edinburgh UK 2002 #365
1805/06	Robert Gray & Son	Glasgow Edinburgh assay	Soup ladle, fiddle pattern, crest, 13 ¾" long	Lorentz Antiques, Toronto Canada 1991 The Phoenix Collection
1805/06	W & P Cunningham I	Edinburgh	Sauce ladle, oar pattern, applied crest of stag on disk, 6 ¾" long	The Phoenix Collection
1805/06	IG (over striking)	Edinburgh assay	Soup ladle, no details	Sotheby's Hopetoun House April 1988 #15
1805/06	William Auld	Edinburgh	Soup ladle, Old English, monogrammed, *sold with another*	Christie's London UK 2006 #1508
1806/07	Alexander Edmonstoun II or III	Edinburgh	Toddy ladles, 3, no details	National Museums of Scotland MEQ 1587-1589
1806/07	*James Erskine*	Aberdeen	Sauce ladle, fiddle pattern, with script "AL", 6 ½"long	Nicholas Shaw Catalog Autumn 1999 p51
1806/07	W & P Cunningham I	Edinburgh	Toddy ladle, no details	National Museums of Scotland K.1998.1140
1806/07	TT	Edinburgh assay	Soup ladle, no details	Christie's London UK 1999 #92
1806/07	W & P Cunningham I	Edinburgh	Toddy ladle, Old English pattern, script initial "B", 6 1/8" long, .84 oz	The Silver Spoon Club Postal Auction July 12, 2007 #84
1807/08	TT	Edinburgh assay	Toddy ladle, Old English pattern, script initials	The Silver Spoon Club Postal Auction Feb 22, 2007 #95
1807/08	P Cunningham & Sons	Edinburgh	Soup ladle, (called a punch ladle), 13" long, 7oz	Eldred Co, Inc East Dennis, MA USA 2007 #290
1807/08	Alexander Spence	Edinburgh	Sauce ladles, pair, with twisted handles, 6" long	Christie's London UK 2000 #20

YEAR	MAKER	LOCATION	DESCRIPTION	SOURCE
1807/08	R Gray & Son	Edinburgh	Toddy ladles, pair, not pictured	Sotheby's Hopetoun House, April 1988 #12
1808/09	Robert Gray & Son	Edinburgh	Soup ladle, no details	Antiques Magazine vol 130 p536
1809/10	Alexander Henderson	Edinburgh	Sauce ladle, fiddle pattern, angled stem, crest and motto of Horseburgh	Shrubsole, NY 1995
1809/10	AR mark	Edinburgh assay	Soup ladle, no details	Lorentz Antiques Toronto Canada 1991
1809/10	Matthew Craw	Edinburgh	Sauce ladles, pair, no details	Bonhams London UK 2001 #323
1810 ca	Peter Ross	Aberdeen	Toddy ladle, fiddle pattern, 6 ½" long	Gorringes LLP East Sussex UK 2006 #1437
1810 ca	David Manson	Dundee	Punch ladle, lipped oval bowl with coin insert, sides engraved with two whaling ships and contemporary script monogram "ES", with flattened lower stem, spiral whalebone upper stem, plain silver terminal, 14 ½" long	Christie's London UK 1999 #86
1810 ca	Francis Howden	Edinburgh	Toddy ladle, script initial "M", 8 ½"long	The Phoenix Collection
1810 ca	John McQueen	Banff	Toddy ladle, no details	National Museums of Scotland MEQ 109
1810 ca	William Jamieson	Aberdeen	Soup ladle, fiddle pattern, 13"long	Nicholas Shaw Catalog Autumn 1999 p51
1810 ca	Robert Keay I	Perth	Toddy ladles, set of 6, no details	Sotheby's Gleneagles August 1988 #436
1810 ca	John Ewan	Aberdeen	Soup ladle, fiddle pattern, no details	JH Bourdon-Smith London 1994
1810 ca	David Izat	Banff	Soup ladle, fiddle pattern, no details	JH Bourdon-Smith London 1994
1810/11	Ziegler	Edinburgh	Ladle with crest, no details	National Museums of Scotland MEQ 822b
1810/11	Ziegler	Edinburgh	Ladle, no details	National Museums of Scotland MEQ 823 1965.1894
1810/11	R & D	Edinburgh assay	Sauce ladle, script "D"	V Gordin, Toronto, 1994

YEAR	MAKER	LOCATION	DESCRIPTION	SOURCE
1810/11	Francis Howden	Edinburgh	Toddy ladle, for use with the Trades Punch Bowl	National Museums of Scotland MEQ L.1962.689
1810/11	George Fenwick	Edinburgh	Toddy ladles, set of four, plain patterned, initialed "D. E. G." 3.2oz	Woolley & Wallis Salisbury UK 2007 #182
1810/11	Z mark Ziegler family	Edinburgh	Soup ladle, 13 ¾" long	Gorringes LLP, East Sussex UK 2004 #470
1812/13	Alexander Henderson	Edinburgh	Toddy ladle, oar pattern, with crest, motto and script initial "B", 6 1/8" long	The Silver Spoon Club Postal Auction April 21, 2006 #130
1813/14	James McKay	Edinburgh	Soup ladle, Kings pattern, sold with others	Christie's London UK 2001 #193
1813/14	Alexander Henderson	Edinburgh	Cream ladle, fiddle pattern, 6 1/8" long	City Museum of St. Louis MO USA 181.48
1815 ca	John Orr	Greenock	Soup ladle, Old English, initials "M.J.L.", 15 ½" long, 7.2oz	Nicholas Shaw Catalog 2004 p16
1815 ca	George & Alexander Booth	Aberdeen	Sauce ladle, fiddle pattern, initials "JEM", 6"	Nicholas Shaw Catalog Autumn 1999 p51
1816/17	D McDonald	Edinburgh assay	Ladle, plain, no details	Sotheby's London November 1987 #15
1817/18	John McDonald	Edinburgh	Sauce Ladles, pair, fiddle and shell pattern, 5 ½" long, 1.9oz	Weschelor's Washington, DC USA 2002 #240
1817/18	A W mm	Edinburgh assay	Soup ladle, no details	Antiques Mall, San Antonio TX
1817/18	WM mm	Edinburgh	Soup ladle, no details	Sotheby's Gleneagles August 1991 #11
1819/20	Mitchell & Russell	Glasgow	Toddy ladle, round bowl, with baleen handle, 8 ½" long	The Silver Spoon Club Postal Auction July 12, 2007 #33
1820 ca	George Booth	Aberdeen	Soup ladle, fiddle pattern, 14" long	Gorringes LLP, East Sussex UK 2006 #1932
1820 ca	John Glenny	Montrose	Sifter ladle, oar pattern, initialed "S"	Thomas Roddick & Medcalf Edinburgh UK Oct 31, 2006 #120

YEAR	MAKER PT	LOCATION Peterhead	DESCRIPTION Sauce ladle, no details	SOURCE National Museums of Scotland 1952.44
1820 ca	William Jamieson	Aberdeen	Soup ladle, Old English pattern, engraved with initials, 5.5 oz	Christie's London UK 2001 #156
1820 ca	Mark Hinchsliffe	Dumfries	Sauce ladle, fiddle pattern, with extra mark K, 6 ¾" long	The Phoenix Collection
1820 ca	William Simpson	Banff	Ladles, pair, no details	National Museums of Scotland MEQ 728-729
1820 ca	Alexander Cameron	Dundee	Sauce ladle, fiddle shaped	Hobart House 1991
1820 ca	Nathaniel Rae	Aberdeen	Toddy ladles, pair, no details	National Museums of Scotland H.1994.1076
1820 ca	George Booth	Aberdeen	Soup ladle, fiddle pattern, initial "M", 13 ½" long, 7.9oz	Nicholas Shaw Catalog 2004 p106
1820 ca	William Jamieson	Aberdeen	Soup ladle, Old English	Goodwin's, Edinburgh 1993
1820 ca	William Jamieson	Aberdeen	Sauce ladle, long fiddle pattern	Lorentz Antiques, Toronto Canada 1994
1820 ca	William Jamieson	Aberdeen	Toddy ladles, set of 12, no details	Hyman Collection, Colonial Williamsburg
1820 ca	D Frazer	Inverness	Soup ladle, Old English	Goodwin's, Edinburgh 1993
1820 ca	George & Alexander Booth	Aberdeen	Sauce ladle, fiddle pattern, initial "G", 7" long	Nicholas Shaw Catalog Autumn 1999 p51
1820 ca	Alexander Cameron	Dundee	Sauce ladle, fiddle pattern, initial "M", 6" long	Nicholas Shaw Catalog Autumn 1999 p51
1820 ca	Mark Hinchsliffe	Dumfries	Sauce ladle, fiddle pattern, initial "C", 6 ¾" long	Nicholas Shaw Catalog Autumn 1999 p51
1820 ca	David Gray	Dumfries	Toddy ladle, fiddle pattern, initial "C", 7 ¾" long	Nicholas Shaw Catalog Autumn 1999 p51
1820 ca	William Whitecross	Aberdeen	Soup ladle, fiddle pattern, engraved "ABD" 13" long	Nicholas Shaw Catalog Autumn 1999 p52

YEAR	MAKER	LOCATION	DESCRIPTION	SOURCE
1820 ca	Thomas Davie	Greenock	Soup ladle, Old English	Goodwin's, Edinburgh 1992
1820 ca	James McKay	Edinburgh	Toddy ladles, set of 5, no details	Sotheby's Gleneagles August 1987 #245
1820 ca	Charles Murray	Perth	Punch ladle, no details	Hyman Collection, Colonial Williamsburg
1820 ca	Alexander Cameron	Dundee	Soup ladle, fiddle pattern, crest of a stag and motto "Watch Well", 14 ½"long	Nicholas Shaw Catalog Autumn 1999 p52
1820 ca	William Clark	Greenock	Soup ladle, fiddle pattern, initial "M", 13"long	Nicholas Shaw Catalog Autumn 199 p52
1820 ca	Charles Murray	Perth	Punch ladle, 15 ¼"long	Nicholas Shaw Catalog Autumn 1999 p61
1820 ca	Robert Keay I	Perth	Fiddle pattern, soup ladle, initial "H", 13 ½" long	Nicholas Shaw Catalog Autumn 1999 p52
1820 ca	David Gray	Dumfries	Toddy ladles, pair, fiddle pattern, circular bowls, initials "K" on the reverse	Christie's Lanarkshire UK 1998 #30
1820 ca	David Gray	Dumfries	Toddy ladle, fiddle pattern with shouldered stem and circular bowl, initials "W. N."	Christie's Lanarkshire UK 1998 #35
1820 ca	Charles Murray	Perth	Toddy ladle, fiddle pattern, initialed	Lyon & Turnbull Edinburgh UK 2003 #288
1820 ca	Alexander Cameron	Dundee	Punch ladle, plain circular bowl, partly spiral whalebone stem	Christie's Lanarkshire UK 1998 #32
1821/22	Dick & McPherson	Edinburgh	Sauce ladle, Kings pattern, with monogram "A", sold with others	Christie's Lanarkshire UK 1997 #813
1821/22	William Allen	Edinburgh assay	Sauce ladle, no details	Antiques Magazine vol 130 p536
1821/22	G I	Edinburgh assay	Syrup ladles, pair, fiddle pattern #5 & 6	Lorentz Antiques, Toronto Canada 1994
1822/23	Alexander Cameron	Dundee Edinburgh assay	Sauce ladle, no details	The Maple Swan Collection

YEAR	MAKER	LOCATION	DESCRIPTION	SOURCE
1822/23	W & P Cunningham II	Edinburgh	Soup ladle, shell shaped, fiddle pattern, shell, 13 5/8" long, 8.5oz	Nicholas Shaw Catalog Winter 2000 p89
1822/23	James McKay	Edinburgh	Punch ladle, no details	Luddington p64
1823/24	B McCallum	Glasgow	Soup ladle, no details	Silver Plus 1993
1823/24	WE	Edinburgh	Toddy ladle, fiddle pattern, initials, 6" long, .71oz	The Silver Spoon Club Postal Auction July 2, 2007 #29
1824/25	Alexander Edmonstoun	Edinburgh	Ladles, set of 6, king's pattern, initial "M", 6" long, 6.3oz	Nicholas Shaw Catalog Autumn 1999, p51
1824/25	George McHattie	Edinburgh	Punch ladle, no details	National Museums of Scotland MEQ 1134
1825 ca	Peter Ross	Aberdeen	Sauce ladle, fiddle pattern, initials "JRSG", 6 ½" long	Nicholas Shaw Catalog Autumn 1999 p51
1825 ca	Robert Keay	Perth	Sauce ladle, fiddle pattern, 6" long	Nicholas Shaw Catalog Autumn 1999 p51
1825 ca	Alexander King	Petershead	Soup ladle, fiddle pattern	Nicholas Shaw Catalog 2005 p94
1825 ca	R & R Keay	Perth	Toddy ladle, fiddle pattern, initial "D", 6 ¾" long	Nicholas Shaw Catalog Autumn 1999 p51
1825 ca	William Ferguson	Elgin	Toddy ladle, fiddle pattern, with a monogram removed, marks "WF and PHD"	Thomas Roddick & Medcalf, Edinburgh UK Oct 31, 2006 #138
1825/26	IM	Edinburgh	Punch ladles, pair, no details	National Museums of Scotland 1961.10-11a
1825/26	William Marshall & Son	Edinburgh	Soup ladle, King's pattern, no details	Whirligig Antiques, Austin, TX USA 1993
1825/26	William Marshall & Son	Edinburgh	Soup ladle, fiddle pattern	M Getz Antiques, Washington, DC USA 1993
1825/26	James McKay	Edinburgh	Sauce ladle, no details	Joya's Antiques, Washington, DC USA 1994
1826/27	WP	Edinburgh	Toddy ladle, single struck, Kings pattern, 6" long	The Silver Spoon Club Postal Auction, April 21, 2006 #9

YEAR	MAKER	LOCATION	DESCRIPTION	SOURCE
1826/27	James McKay	Edinburgh	Toddy ladles, no details	National Museums of Scotland 1959.587
1826/27	Angus McDonald	Glasgow	Punch ladle, no details	Argentum, San Francisco, CA USA 1993
1826/27	M & S	Glasgow	Soup ladle, no details	Asprey, NY, 1993
1827/28	Peter Sutherland	Edinburgh	Soup ladle, Kings pattern, engraved with initial "C"	Christie's Lanarkshire UK 1997 #83
1828/29	AW	Edinburgh	Soup ladle, fiddle pattern, initialed, sold with another	Christie's London UK 2006 #1508
1828/29	N L	Glasgow	Sauce ladles, pair, no details	Silver Plus 1993
1829/30	JH mm	Edinburgh	Ladle, Old English, no details	Keene Antiques Center, NH USA1993
1829/30	A Mitchell, William Mitchell	Glasgow	Sauce ladle, fiddle pattern	Elizabeth Austin Antiques, 1993
1830 ca	Andrew Davidson	Arbroath	Toddy ladle, no details	National Museums of Scotland MEQ 51
1830 ca	John McQueen	Banff	Punch ladle, no details	Aberdeen Museums and Galleries ABDAG001045
1830 ca	John McQueen	Banff	Toddy ladles, pair, oar end pattern, plain circular bowls, initials "J H W"	Christie's Lanarkshire UK 1998 #29
1830 ca	Robert Naughton	Inverness	Toddy ladle, fiddle pattern, oval bowl	Christie's Lanarkshire UK 1998 #33
1830 ca	Joseph Pozzi	Elgin	Toddy ladle, matched pair, fiddle pattern with chamfered and shouldered stem and oval bowl, one engraved with initials "F J T"	Christie's Lanarkshire UK 1998 #45
1830 ca	John McRay	Inverness	Toddy ladles, pair, plain fiddle pattern with shouldered stems and oval bowls	Christie's London UK 2000 #415
1830 ca	John McRay	Inverness	Toddy ladles, fiddle pattern, initialed "D/M Mc J", 1oz	Woolley & Wallis Salisbury UK 2007 #201
1830/31	David McDonald	Glasgow	Soup ladle, fiddle pattern, engraved with an initial	Christie's London UK 2005 #611

YEAR	MAKER	LOCATION	DESCRIPTION	SOURCE
1832/33	Robert Gray & Son	Glasgow	Soup ladle	The Finial v 17/05 May/June 2007 p6 (fig 30)
1832/33	Alexander Cameron	Dundee Edinburgh assay	Shifter ladle, no details	The Maple Swan Collection
1833/34	W C	Edinburgh	Sauce ladle, with initials, no details	Milne & Arne Antiques, Washington DC USA 1994
1833/34	Robert Gray	Glasgow	Punch ladle, wooden handle, 19" long	JH Bourdon-Smith Catalog Autumn 2001 #43, p57
1833/34	James Cruikshanks	Glasgow	Soup ladle, fiddle pattern, with other items	Christie's London UK 2005 #606
1834/35	D C Raitt	Glasgow	Punch ladle, no details	Sotheby's Gleneagles August 1987 #250
1835 ca	John Seller	Elgin	Toddy ladle, fiddle pattern 1 oz	Sotheby's NY USA 1996 #515
1835/36	Alexander Mitchell	Glasgow	Soup ladle, fiddle, thread and shell pattern, part of a larger service	Christie's London UK 2007 #1531
1836/37	Elder & Co	Edinburgh	Punch ladle, 14 ½" long	Nicholas Shaw Catalog Autumn 1999 p61
1840 ca	Robert Robertson	Cupar	Punch ladle, circular bowl with a tapering silver handle, heightened by two double scroll motifs, twisted whale bone handle, 16 ½" long (listed as a toddy ladle)	Christie's London UK 2000 #415
1840 ca	Alexander Davidson	Perth	Toddy ladle, fiddle pattern, initialed "H", 1 oz	Woolley & Wallis Salisbury UK 2007 #146
1840/41	Adam Burgess	Dumfries Edinburgh assay	Toddy ladle, fiddle pattern with shouldered stem and circular bowl	Christie's Lanarkshire 1998 #37
1840/41	John Strurrok	Montrose	Sauce ladle, fiddle pattern, 6" long	Nicholas Shaw Catalog Autumn 1999 p51
1843/44	Finlay & Field	Glasgow	Toddy ladle, King variant pattern, 7" long	The Silver Spoon Club Postal Auction April 21, 2006 #11

YEAR	MAKER	LOCATION	DESCRIPTION	SOURCE
1846/47	D. C Rait	Glasgow	Toddy ladles, set of 4, with twisted stems, 6" long	JH Bourdon-Smith Catalog Autumn 2001 #43 p57
1853/54	Muirhead & Arthur	Glasgow	Toddy ladle, single struck, Queens pattern, 6 2/3" long	The Silver Spoon Club Postal Auction April 21, 2006 #10

Marrow Spoons & Scoops

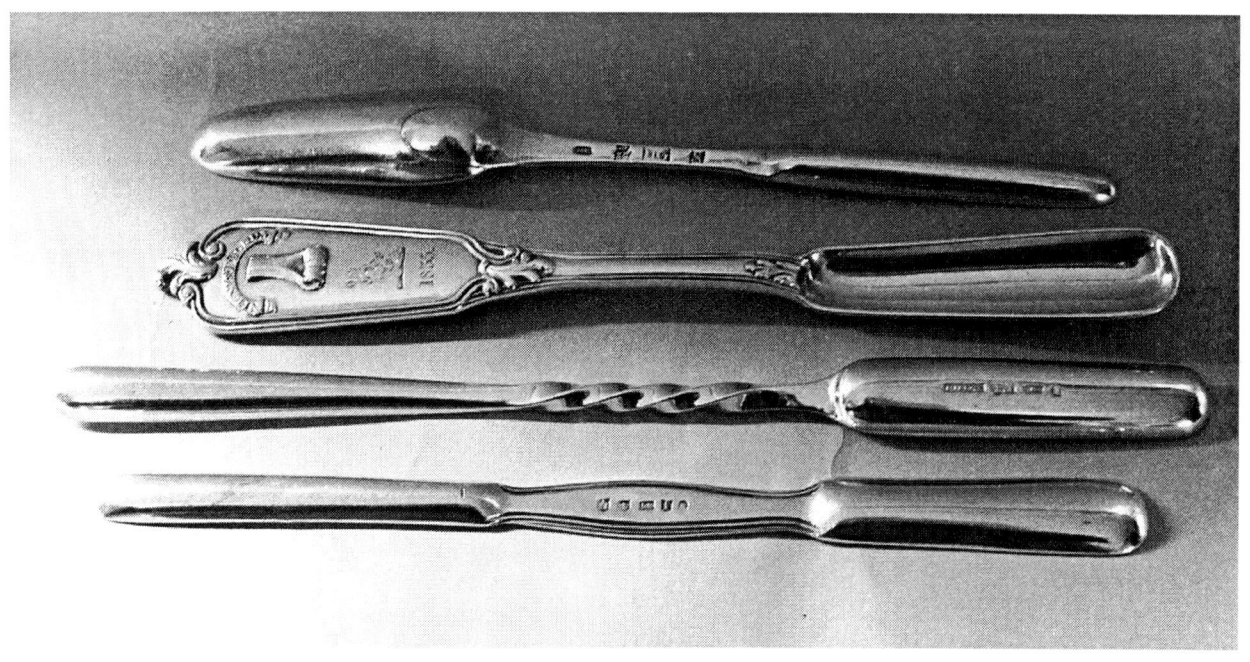

Plate 28. Four Marrow Scoops.
Top – 1747/48 by Dougal Ged, Edinburgh; 2nd from Top – 1840/41 Bone Marrow Club by WC, Edinburgh.
2nd from Bottom – 1815/16 twisted stem example by George McHattie, Edinburgh
Bottom – 1811/12 bulbous connection example by John Ziegler, Edinburgh.
Courtesy of a private collector. Photograph by Janice M Dietert.

YEAR	MAKER MARROW SPOONS & SCOOPS	LOCATION	DESCRIPTION	SOURCE
1700/01	Alexander Kincaid	Edinburgh	Marrow spoon, 3oz	Christie's Edinburgh March 29, 1983 #58 National Museums of Scotland MEQ 1558
1734/35	James Ker	Edinburgh	Marrow spoon, with cipher of the Earl of Hopetoun	Phillips Edinburgh August 24, 2001 #555
1735 ca	George Cooper	Aberdeen	Marrow scoop, no details	Dundee Museums and Art Galleries 1966-238-1
1735 ca	George Cooper	Aberdeen	Marrow scoop/spoon, no details	Dundee Museums and Art Galleries 1966-238-2
1745/46	Dougal Ged	Edinburgh	Marrow spoon, conventional form with crest	Phillips Edinburgh August 24, 2001 #556
1747/48	Dougal Ged	Edinburgh	Marrow scoop, the larger end with a slightly ridged and tongued drop, 8 ½" long	Private Collection
1748/49	William Aytoun	Edinburgh	Marrow scoop, the larger end unusually broad with an extended drop, 8 7/8" long, 1.5oz	Bonhams The Scottish Sale, July 18, 2002 #251
1750 ca	Robert Gordon	Edinburgh	Marrow spoon, crest and motto of Porterfield	National Museums of Scotland A1922.393
1750 ca	Alexander Shirras	Banff	Marrow scoop, marks – BANF, AS, S - each in an engrailed punch, the N is backward in the town letter	Grantully Castle Antiques Private Collection
1760 ca	Alexander Johnston	Dundee	Marrow scoop, no details	Dundee Museums and Art Galleries 1979-390
1760 ca	Colin Allan	Aberdeen	Marrow scoop, 9", 1.4oz	Nicholas Shaw Catalog Winter 2001 p80
1761/62	Not available	Edinburgh	Marrow scoop, no details	Freeman & Co, Philadelphia PA USA 1998 #139
1767/68	Patrick Robertson	Edinburgh	Marrow spoon, 8 ¾" long, 2.1oz	Nicholas Shaw Catalog Winter 2001 p80

YEAR	MAKER	LOCATION	DESCRIPTION	SOURCE
1767/68	Patrick Robertson	Edinburgh	Marrow scoop, no details, sold with other items	Sotheby's NY USA April 5, 2007 #412
1767/68	James Gilliland	Edinburgh	Marrow scoop, narrow end slightly waisted, short stem, 8 ½" long, 1.2oz	Nicholas Shaw Catalog 2005 p57 #10
1770 ca	James Gordon	Aberdeen	Marrow scoop, no details	Aberdeen Museums and Galleries ABDAG001009
1770 ca	James Wildgoose	Aberdeen	Marrow scoop, 8 ½" long	Gorringes LLP, East Sussex UK 2006 #1634
1775 ca	James Gordon	Aberdeen	Marrow scoop, 8 ½" long, 1.4oz	Nicholas Shaw Catalog Autumn 1999 p57
1775 ca	William Scott	Dundee	Marrow scoop, 8 ¾", 1.9oz	Nicholas Shaw Catalog Winter 2001 p80
1775/76	Patrick Robertson	Edinburgh	Marrow scoop	Sotheby's Gleneagles August 1988 #33 or #333
1775/76	Patrick Robertson	Edinburgh	Marrow scoop, crest of Sharp	Hyman Collection – Colonial Williamsburg
1778 ca	John Argo	Banff	Marrow scoop, no details	Private Collection UK
1778/79	Peter Mathie	Edinburgh	Marrow scoop, 8 5/8" long	The Phoenix Collection
1778/79	James Gilliland	Edinburgh	Marrow scoop, plain, the larger scoop with a slight drop, 8 ½" long	Private Collection
1780 ca	James Smith	Aberdeen	Marrow scoop, plain, conventional form, marked "IS" and "ABD", 8 ¾" long	Morris Collection Christie's Scotland July 3, 1984 #83 Christie's Lanarkshire UK 1998 #52
1780 ca	Robert Gray	Glasgow	Marrow scoop, plain conventional form	Christie's Lanarkshire UK 1997 #133
1780/81	WD script William Davie or William Dempster	Edinburgh	Marrow scoop, conventional form, 8 7/8" long	Bonhams the Scottish Sale, August 24, 2005 #52

YEAR	MAKER	LOCATION	DESCRIPTION	SOURCE
1781/82	William Davie or William Dempster	Edinburgh	Marrow scoop, but called a spoon in the catalog, 1.7oz	Sotheby's Gleneagles, August 29, 1978 #351
1782/83	William Davie or William Dempster	Edinburgh	Marrow scoop, details	Sotheby's, Scone Palace April 10, 1978 #133
1783/84	Patrick Robertson	Edinburgh	Marrow spoon, crested with a bull, 8 ¾" long, 1.8oz	Nicholas Shaw Catalog Autumn 1999 p57
1783/84	Patrick Robertson	Edinburgh	Marrow scoop or spoon, unclear, 9 ½" long, 1.3oz	Woolley & Wallis, June 28, 2000 #103
1783/84	Patrick Robertson	Edinburgh	Marrow spoon, the stem with a narrow scoop in the terminal, the bowl oval, 8 ¾" long, 1.8oz	Nicholas Shaw Catalog 2001 p83
1790 ca	Alexander Gardner	Edinburgh	Marrow scoop, with initial "C"	JH Bourdon-Smith London 1993
1790 ca	AG Probably Alexander Gardner	Edinburgh	Marrow scoop, sold with others	Christie's London UK 2006 #1723
1790 ca	AG Probably Alexander Gardner	Edinburgh	Marrow scoop, engraved with initials, 8 7/8" long, 1.5oz	Christie's London 2002 #214
1792/93	William Robertson	Edinburgh	Marrow scoop, narrow stem, narrower smaller end that merges in outline, 9 ½" long, 1.4oz	Nicholas Shaw Catalog 2005 p57 #7
1797/98	John Leslie	Aberdeen	Marrow scoop, no details	Hobart House, CT USA 1991
1799/1800	Not available	Edinburgh assay	Marrow scoop, no details	Dundee Museums and Art Galleries 1978-764
1800 ca	George Christie	Edinburgh	Marrow scoop/spoon, somewhat confusing description	Dundee Museums and Art Galleries 16962-709-1
1804/05	Simon Cunningham	Edinburgh	Marrow spoon, no details	Jackson Marks p550
1810/11	John McDonald	Edinburgh	Marrow scoop, crest and motto, 8 7/8" long	Huntley House Museum Edinburgh HH3230/68
1810/11	Patrick Cunningham & Sons	Edinburgh	Marrow scoop, no details	National Museums of Scotland MEQ 1057

YEAR	MAKER	LOCATION	DESCRIPTION	SOURCE
1811/12	John Ziegler	Edinburgh	Marrow scoop, with a bulbous connection	Private Collection
1811/12	George McHattie	Edinburgh	Marrow scoop, 8 ½" long	Gorringes LLP, East Sussex UK 2006 #1252
1813/14	Robert Gray & Son	Glasgow Edinburgh assay	Marrow scoop, 8 ½" long	Gorringes LLP, East Sussex UK 2006 #1635
1815/16	MM not distinct	Edinburgh	Marrow scoop, 10" long	Gorringes LLP, East Sussex UK 2006 #1251
1815/16	George McHattie	Edinburgh	Marrow scoop, with a twisted stem, Heron retailer	Private Collection
1815/16	James & William Marshall	Edinburgh	Marrow scoop, 10 ½" long, 1.9oz	Nicholas Shaw Catalog Winter 2001 p80
1816/17	James McKay	Edinburgh	Marrow scoop, no details	Eldred Co, Inc, East Dennis, MA USA 2000 #82
1817/18	Robert Gray & Son	Glasgow Edinburgh assay	Marrow spoon, no details	Hyman Collection – Colonial Williamsburg
1820 ca	William Jamieson & Co	Aberdeen	Marrow scoop, no details	National Museums of Scotland MEQ 540
1820 ca	William Jamieson	Aberdeen	Marrow scoop, 8 ½" long, 1.3oz	Nicholas Shaw Catalog Winter 2001 p80
1820 ca	Peter Ross	Aberdeen	Marrow scoop, with an engraved initial	Bonhams Sale 15120 Aug 22, 2007 #174
1824/25	Robert Gray & Sons	Glasgow	Marrow scoop, sold with other items	Christie's London UK 2002 #211
1825/26	William Marshall	Edinburgh	Marrow scoop, 9 ½" long, 1.5oz	Nicholas Shaw Catalog 2004 p108
1837/38	A. M.	Glasgow	Marrow scoop, no details	Nicholas Shaw Catalog 2005 p92
1837/38	AGW	Edinburgh	Marrow scoop, engraved with initial "B" on back of scoop, sold with others	Weschler's Washington DC USA 2004 #1181

YEAR	MAKER	LOCATION	DESCRIPTION	SOURCE
1840/41	WC	Edinburgh	Marrow scoop, Bone Marrow Club of Edinburgh, dated 1835, made for Andrew Rutherford, Club member	Private Collection
1842/53	J M	Glasgow	Marrow scoop, 8 4/5" long	Musee de Beaux Arts, Montreal Canada
1872/73	D. D.	Edinburgh	Marrow scoop, fiddle pattern, 7 ¾" long, 1.8oz	Nicholas Shaw Catalog 2005 p92
1873/74	G & M Crichton	Edinburgh	Bone marrow club scoop, for J. Turnbull	Hyman Collection – Colonial Williamsburg

Skewers

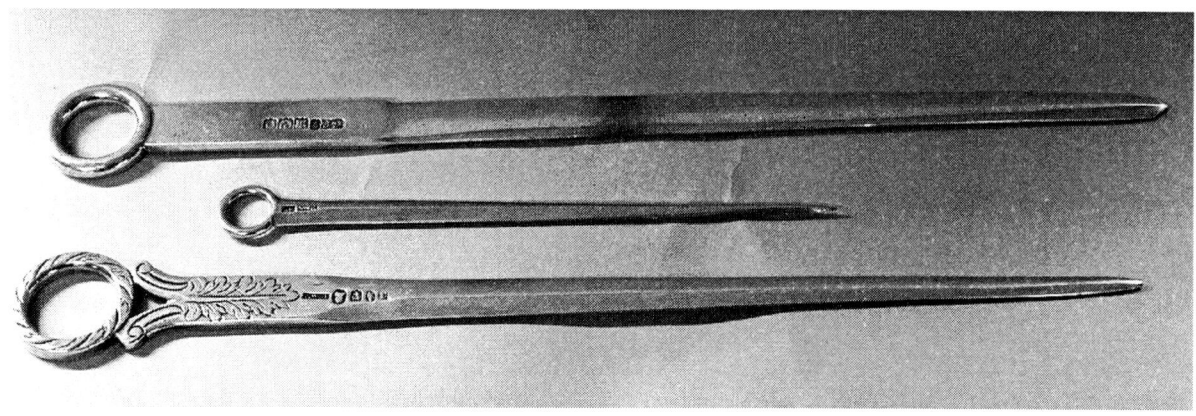

Plate 29. Top – one long skewer from a set of 4, 1820/21 by George Fenwick, Edinburgh.
Center – tiny Skewer 1800 ca by Robert Naughton, Inverness.
Bottom – leaf-decorated Skewer by Heron, Greenock, 1828/29 Glasgow assay
Courtesy of a private collector. Photograph by Janice M Dietert.

YEAR	MAKER SKEWERS	LOCATION	DESCRIPTION	SOURCE
1770 ca	John Steven	Dundee	Skewer, plain, tapered	Dundee Museums and Art Galleries 1967-60
1795/96	Robert Gray	Glasgow Edinburgh assay	Meat skewer with a large oval ring terminal, 11 2/3" long, 3.3oz	Woolley & Wallis Salisbury UK 2007 #204
1796/97	Robert Gray	Glasgow Edinburgh assay	Meat skewer, ring handle, plain tapering form, 7 ¼" long 3 oz	The Silver Spoon Club Postal Auction July 12, 2007 #31
1799/1800	McHattie & Fenwick	Edinburgh	Skewer, no details	Glasgow Exhibition 1911, vol I, p120 #176
1800 ca	Robert Naughton	Inverness	Skewer, small, no details	Private Collection
1800/01	Robert Gray	Glasgow Edinburgh assay	Meat skewer, plain tapering form with ring handle, engraved with initial "B", 12" long	Christie's Lanarkshire UK 1997 #100
1807/09	T. T	Edinburgh assay	Meat skewer	Janet Sisler Antiques, St. Louis, 1991
1808/09	Dick & McPherson	Edinburgh	Meat skewer, plain tapering form, ring handle, engraved with a crest and motto of Duncan, possibly of Park Hill, Arbroath, or Sunnyside, Montrose, 12" long	Christie's Lanarkshire, UK 1997 #86
1811/12	W. H.	Edinburgh assay	Meat skewer, crest and motto	Hobart House CT, USA 1991
1814/15	George Fenwick	Edinburgh	Meat skewers, pair, ring handles, shell join, with crest and motto, sold with other items	Christies, East NY USA 1999 #332
1820/21	George Fenwick	Edinburgh	Long skewers, with a ring end, set of 4	Private Collection
1823/24	Marshall & Sons	Edinburgh	Meat skewer, monogrammed "E. M. A."	National Museums of Scotland 1964.542
1828/29	Heron	Greenock Glasgow assay	Skewer, with leaf decoration	Private Collection

YEAR	MAKER	LOCATION	DESCRIPTION	SOURCE
1830 ca	William Ferguson	Elgin	Meat skewer, no details	National Museums of Scotland A.1960.442
1831/32	Robert Gray & Sons	Glasgow	Meat skewer, stylized Kings pattern, one side with a shell, the other with an anthemion, plain ring end, 13" long, 3.5oz	Christie's Lanarkshire UK 1998 #462

Spoons

Plate 30. Spoons – Hash and Serving Spoons.
Top – 1745 ca Hanoverian Hash Spoon by James Glen, Glasgow.
2nd from Top – 1703/04 Trefid-Hanoverian pattern Hash Spoon by Colin McKenzie, Edinburgh.
2nd from Bottom – 1776/77 Onslow pattern Hash Spoon by WD, Edinburgh.
Bottom – 1865 ca Fiddle pattern Serving Spoon by John MacKay of Elgin.
Courtesy of The Phoenix Collection. Photograph by Janice M Dietert.

YEAR	MAKER SPOONS	LOCATION	DESCRIPTION	SOURCE
1572-74	William Cok	Edinburgh	The Cunningham spoon, seal top, with a damaged bowl	How Spoon Book, vol II, p324-325 National Museums of Scotland H.MEQ 139
1576 ca	Robert Gairdyne I	Dundee	Spoon, seal top, marks – lily, pot, RG	Private Collection UK
1577-79	James Cok III Deacon William Cok	Edinburgh	The Jackson Spoon, seal top	How Spoons Book, Vol II p328-339 Jackson Collection National Museum of Wales
1579-81	George Heriot II Deacon Edwart Hairt	Edinburgh	The Cunningham Spoons, disk ends, 7 spoon set (shaved)	How Spoons Book, vol II p332-333 National Museums of Scotland H.MEQ 9
1583-85	Adam Craig Deacon Thomas Annand	Edinburgh	The Sanders Spoon, disc end, engraved with initials "IS/EW", maker and Deacon could be reversed	How Spoon Book, vol II, p336-337 Christie's Glasgow March 1983 #63 Asprey, London
1589 ca	George Cunningham I	Canongate	The Canongate Spoon, disk end, initials block "DM/MD"	Jackson Marks p953 National Museums of Scotland MEQ 26
1591/92	James Crawford	Edinburgh	Spoon, seal top	Jackson Marks p512
1600 ca	AB mark	Aberdeen	Spoon, no details	National Museums of Scotland MEQ 1577
1600 ca	Johnathan Kirkwood	Glasgow	Spoon, disc end, marks – K, K, K, being (IK in monogram)– initials "NG" on back of bowl, engraved CD/1600, there is another and possibly a 3rd of these spoons	Sotheby's November 6, 1969 #168 Sotheby's August 28-29, 1978 #370 Phillip Edinburgh October 19, 1984 #70 Spink London How Spoons vol II p340-341 Private Collection UK

YEAR	MAKER	LOCATION	DESCRIPTION	SOURCE
1600 ca	Johnathan Kirkwood	Glasgow	Spoon, disc end, from same set as above, initials "NG" on the back of the bowl, CD/1600	Sotheby's Gleneagles August 29, 1978 #370
1600 ca	Johnathan Kirkwood	Glasgow	Spoon, disc end, apparently from the same set as the others above, initials "NG" on the back of the bowl	Unclear where this is but it does exist
1608-10	John Lindsay	Edinburgh	The Falkland Palace Spoon	How Spoons Book vol II, p342-343 Private Collection UK
1609/10	Gilbert Kirkwood	Edinburgh	Spoon, slip top	How Spoons Book vol II, p350-351 Private Collection UK
1611 ca	Gilbert Kirkwood	Edinburgh	Spoon, disc end	National Museums of Scotland MEQ 140 1943.342
1611-13	George Crawford	Edinburgh	Spoon, disc end	How Spoons Book vol II, p 346-347 Private Collection UK
1612 ca	Gilbert Kirkwood	Edinburgh	Spoon, disc end	How Spoons Book vol II, p344-345 Private Collection UK
1615 ca	Alexander Reid I & George Crawford marks	Edinburgh	Spoons, pair, disk end, initials "IH" over "EE"	Glasgow Art Gallery, 1952 acquisition
1625 ca	Robert Ker	Canongate	Spoon, The Oliphant spoon, disc end, pinwheel decoration on disc	Finlay 1991 #36 Private Ownership
1626 ca	George Robertson I	Edinburgh	Spoon, no details	National Museums of Scotland MEQ 47
1630 ca	Robert Gairdyne	Dundee	Spoon, disc end, with letter "L/EL", possibly for Lady Elizabeth Lyon, 5 7/8" long	Private Collection UK
1637-39	George Robertson Deacon John Scott	Edinburgh	Spoon, disc end, initial "W", 7 1/8" long	How Spoons Book vol II, p 346-347 Private Collection UK
1637-39	George Crawford Deacon John Scott	Edinburgh	Spoon, disc end, engraved initials "AC" on the back of the bowl, initials "M" later, crest, 7 ¼" long, 1.5oz	Nicholas Shaw Catalog 2004 p96

YEAR	MAKER	LOCATION	DESCRIPTION	SOURCE
1640 ca	John Scott Deacon Adam Lamb	Edinburgh	Spoon, disc end, disk initialed "AL", back of bowl "MD"	Sotheby's Gleneagles August 25, 1977 #25
1640 dated	Thomas Lindsay II	Dundee	Spoon, Puritan, initials "WI/SW" on the bowl, leaf engraving on the upper stem	How of Edinburgh Private Collection National Museums of Scotland MEQ 1176
1640-42	Thomas Cleghorne I As Deacon also	Edinburgh	Spoon, no details	Jackson Marks p 542 Glasgow Exhibition
1642-44	Adam Lamb	Edinburgh	Spoon, disc end, front stem engraved with foliate designs at the joint, disk initialed "AG", back of bowl "EG", 7 3/8"	Phillips London April 24, 1997 #22
1644-46	Maker unmarked Deacon Adam Lamb	Edinburgh	Spoon, disc end, engraved with stylized foliage and date "1646", initialed "EE" on the reverse	Sotheby's London January 30, 1972 #190
1646-48	John Scott Maker and Deacon	Edinburgh	Spoon, disc end	How Spoons Book vol II p 346-347
1648-50 or 1665-67	Peter Neilson Deacon George Cleghorne	Edinburgh	Two spoons, no details	Jackson Marks p313 Stirling-Maxwell Collection
1649 ca	Alexander Scott	Edinburgh	Puritan spoon	Royal Academy Exhibition 1911 Glasgow vol I, p 109 #1
1650 ca	Thomas Moncur	Aberdeen	Spoon, disc end	National Museums of Scotland MEQ 1577
1651 ca	James Symontoun	Edinburgh	Spoon, no details	National Museums of Scotland 1958.43
1651-53	Adam Burrell Deacon James Fairbairn	Edinburgh	Spoon, disc end, with shaped terminal, some pitting	Sotheby's Lennoxlove June 24, 1980 #268
1651-53 Or 1657-59	George Cleghorne	Edinburgh	Puritan Spoon	How Spoons Book vol II p 354-355 Private Collection UK
1653 ca	George Cleghorne	Edinburgh	"The Barncleuch Spoon", puritan spoon, with owner's initials on back, "OH/MD", 7 ½" long, 2oz	Sotheby's Gleneagles, August 30, 1982 #483

YEAR	MAKER	LOCATION	DESCRIPTION	SOURCE
1653/54 Or 1659-61	Alexander Scott	Edinburgh	Puritan spoon	How Spoons Book vol II, p356-357
1660 ca	Patrick Borthwick	Edinburgh	"The Christchurch Puritan spoon", mm only	Christchurch College, Cambridge, UK
1660 ca	Thomas Moncur	Aberdeen	Spoons, set of 3, disc end, engrave "LWE", 6 7/8" long	Christie's Glasgow July 3, 1984 #91 Clayton p81 #16
1665-67	Alexander Reid	Edinburgh	Spoon, with oval bowl, flat spreading trefid, initials	Christie's June 22, 1960 #95 How of Edinburgh
1665-67	David Boig Deacon James Symontoun	Edinburgh	Puritan spoon, engraved "RM" on back of bowl	Finlay 1991 # 33 How Spoons Book, vol II, p 358-359 National Museums of Scotland MEQ 40
1667-69	Alexander Reid	Edinburgh	Puritan spoon	National Museums of Scotland MEQ 616
1670 ca	AC or AG		Spoon, trefid engraved with stylized leaf decoration, back of terminal "RP" initials, back of bow "MB", 8 1/8" long	Phillips November 1998 #205
1672-78	AG	Aberdeen	Spoon, trefid pattern	National Museums of Scotland MEQ 52
1675 ca	WM	Perth	Spoon, trefid, initials "B/HI", also with Breadalbane stamp	National Museums of Scotland MEQ 141
1675-81	Edward Cleghorne Deacon Alexander Reid	Edinburgh	"The Price-Woods Spoons", set of 4 trefids, letter "H" under a semicircle, one of the earliest known sets, 7 3/8" long, 5.8oz	Noble Collection Sotheby's Gleneagles August 1994 Finlay 1991 #53 Nicholas Shaw Catalog 2004 p96
1675 ca	*Edward Cleghorne*	*Edinburgh*	*Not available*	*Christie's April 23, 1965 #169*
1675 ca	George Rolland	Edinburgh	Spoons, set of 6, rat tailed, flat notched top trefids, handle with engraving, formal foliage	Christie's December 19, 1910 #120
1675-77	George Rolland	Edinburgh	Large spoon, no details	Jackson Marks p 543

YEAR	MAKER	LOCATION	DESCRIPTION	SOURCE
1675-77	Alexander Reid III	Edinburgh	Large spoon, no details, may be related to prior one	Jackson Marks p 543
1680 ca	WM	Perth	Trefid spoon, with Breadalbane stamp, initials "B/H"	National Museums of Scotland MEQ 726.7
1680 ca	Robert Gardiner (Gairdyne)	Perth	Spoon, trefid, initials and date 1726, probably different from the pair below	Phillips or Christie's February 11, 1961
1680 ca	Robert Gardiner (Gairdyne)	Perth	Spoons, pair, trefid, initials "KC"	Christie's June 13, 1907 #268 National Museums of Scotland MEQ 142-143
1681 ca	Alexander Reid	Edinburgh	Spoon, trefid, repaired over the date letter, initials "AH/ES", probably dated 1681/82 based on similar dated spoons with the same initials	Christie's South Kensington December 14, 1999 #138
1681/82	Edward Cleghorne	Edinburgh	Spoons, trefid, decorated with foliage over the top of the stem and back of bowl	Christie's July 11, 1960 #138
1681/82	Alexander Reid	Edinburgh	Spoons, set of 5, trefid, silver-gilt, 7.2oz	Christie's October 12, 1966 #106
1681/82	Alexander Reid	Edinburgh	Spoon, trefid, initials "AH/ES", different from the repaired spoon, possibly part of the set of 5 that sold in 1966, 1.5oz	Christie's South Kensington December 14, 1999 #138
1681/82	Alexander Reid Assayer Borthwick	Edinburgh	Spoons, set of 5, trefid, engraved initials "AH/ES", gilt, 7oz 15d	Christie's March 24, 1948 #98 Christie's October 12, 1966 #106
1681/82	Edward or Marion Cleghorne	Edinburgh	Trefid spoon, back of bowl and stem decorated with foliage, probably part of a larger set	Christie's November 6, 1960 #138
1681/82	Edward Cleghorne	Edinburgh	Spoons, rat tailed, bowl and stem decorated with foliage, possibly part of the pair listed below	Christie's July 11, 1960 #138 Christie's November 30, 1960 #95 How of Edinburgh Collection
1681/82	Alexander Reid	Edinburgh	Spoon, trefid, 8" long	Christie's Glasgow November 18-19 1992, #567
1682ca	Marion (Mitchell) Cleghorne	Edinburgh	Spoons, pair, decorated trefid, foliage on handles and back of bowls, block initials "GH/EF", Heriot family spoons, initials possibly for George Heriot and Elizabeth Ferguson, 7 7/8" long	Tessiers London 1994-95 The Phoenix Collection Private Collection England
1682/83	James Cockburn	Edinburgh	Spoons, set of 6, trefids, no details	Jackson Marks p 543

YEAR	MAKER	LOCATION	DESCRIPTION	SOURCE
1685 ca	William Law	Edinburgh	Spoon, trefid, decorated bowl, initials "AG/SB"	Sotheby's Hopetoun House April 29, 1987 #52
1685 ca	James Cockburn	Edinburgh	Spoons, set of 10, trefids, initials "M/AB" over "KR", also listed as a single spoon	Shaw Collection Christie's Glasgow March 29, 1983 #60 Christie's Edinburgh May 26, 1998 #10
1685 ca	Not available	Not available	Spoons, pair, trefid pattern	Sotheby's Hopetoun House April 1987 #51
1685 ca	Not available	Montrose	Spoons, set of 3, shaped tops, possibly Montrose initials	Christie's February 19, 1947 #37 How of Edinburgh Collection
1685/86	Robert Brock	Glasgow	Spoons, pair, trefid, initials "AG/IR", 7 5/8" and 7 ¾" long	Crichton Brothers Private Collection UK
1685/86	Robert Bruce	Edinburgh	Spoons, pair, trefids	Christie's December 17, 1930 #63
1685/86	Matthew Cochquin	Ayr	Spoon, trefid pattern	Finlay 1991 #45 How Spoons book vol II
1685/86	James Stirling	Glasgow	Dessert spoon, trefid, initials "AP", 5 1/3" long	How Spoons Book vol II, ch V, sect V, pl3 Christie's Glasgow March 29, 1983 #44 Phillips London April 24, 1977 #24 National Museums of Scotland MEQ 1555
1685 ca	James Stirling	Glasgow	*Spoon, small rat tail, initial, one third of this lot*	*Christie's June 19, 1957 #62* *How of Edinburgh Collection*
1685 ca	Robert Brock	Glasgow	Spoons, set of 6, rat tailed, trefid handles, oval bowls, regilt, 7 ¾" long	Scottish Art Academy Exhibit 1939 #420
1688 ca	Robert Elphinstone	Inverness	Tablespoons, set of 6, trefids, terminals initials "M/ID/AD", 8" long	Private Collection UK How Spoons Book, vol II Ch V, sect V

YEAR	MAKER	LOCATION	DESCRIPTION	SOURCE
1686/87 ca	James Stirling	Glasgow	Dessert spoon, trefid, initials script "L"	Shaw Collection Christie's March 29, 1983 #45
1688/89	James Law	Edinburgh	Spoons, set of 6, trefids, initials "WI" over "MC", 10oz 19d	Sotheby's Scone Palace April 1979 #78
1689/90	James Stirling	Glasgow	Spoon, set of 5, trefids, date letter "I", initials "WG/HB", 7 ¾" long	Private Collection UK
1690 ca	William Scott Elder	Banff	Spoons, pair, trefids with initials	Christie's December 5, 1950 #103 Thomas Lumley Ltd
1690 ca	George Walker	Aberdeen	Spoons, set of 6, rat tailed, shield top, 9oz 15 d	Christie's February 18, 1942 #49
1690 ca	George Yorstoun	Edinburgh	Spoon, child's, trefid, 4 1/8"	Noble Collection Nicholas Shaw Catalog 2005 p89
1690 ca	Not available		Spoon, trefid	National Museums of Scotland MEQ 134 1936.256
1690 ca	William Scott	Aberdeen	Spoon, trefid	Art Treasures Exhibition 1932 #492 How of Edinburgh Collection
1690 ca	William Scott	Banff	Spoon, rat tailed, one third of a lot	Christie's June 19, 1957 #62 How of Edinburgh Collection
1690 ca	Robert Bruce	Edinburgh	Spoon, trefid, initials "AC" over "MC", 2oz	Christie's Glasgow March 29, 1983 #62
1690 ca	Thomas Cleghorne	Edinburgh	Spoons, trefid, no details	National Museums of Scotland MEQ 134
1690 ca	Robert Brock	Glasgow	Large spoon, trefid, initials, one of 3 items in the lot	Christie's June 19, 1957 #62
1690/91	Robert Brock	Glasgow	Spoon, trefid, no details	National Museums of Scotland MEQ 1160 1976.7
1690/91	Robert Brock	Glasgow	Spoon, trefid, broad terminal, initials "RMED" in monogram, distinctive style, 7 7/8" long	Private Collection
1690/91	Robert Brock	Glasgow	Spoon, trefid, back of bowl with a ribbed rat tail, rounded terminal	How of Edinburgh
1691/92	Robert Inglis	Edinburgh	Spoon, set of 10, trefids, crest of a unicorn for Stewart of Appin, 19oz	Shaw Collection Christie's Glasgow March 29,

YEAR	MAKER (continued)	LOCATION	DESCRIPTION	SOURCE
1691/92	*Robert Inglis*	*Edinburgh*	*Spoon, no details*	1983 #59 Christie's Scotland November 14, 1985 #270
1693 ca	Not available	Edinburgh	Spoons, pair of trefids	Sotheby's Hopetoun House April 1987 #52
1693 ca	Alexander Forbes	Edinburgh	Spoon, trefid, found in a well in 1834. (Note: this Sotheby's citation was also found for a pair of unspecified maker spoons listed earlier)	Sotheby's Hopetoun House April 29, 1987 #51 Christie's Scotland November 25-27, 1997 #309
1693/94	George Yorstoun	Edinburgh	Spoon, trefid	Christie's June 8, 1909 #130
1694/95	Robert Bruce	Edinburgh	Spoons, set of 4, no details	National Museums of Scotland L.396.12-12c
1694/95	Robert Brock	Glasgow	Spoon, trefid	Christie's November 14, 1945 #131 How of Edinburgh Collection
1694/95	Robert Brock	Glasgow	Spoons, pair, trefids, engraved initials	Christie's March 13, 1963 #17
1695 ca	Andrew Gilmour	Edinburgh	Spoon, trefid, decorated, described as an elaborate 17th century spoon	Dundee Museums and Art Galleries 1967-23
1695 ca	Thomas Cleghorne	Edinburgh	Spoons, set of 4, trefid, repairs and wear, initials "M/HT/BB", maker a little uncertain	Phillips London July 24, 1997 How of Edinburgh
1695 ca	George Robertson	Aberdeen	Spoon, dog nose, later initialed	Sotheby's July 30, 1970 #226
1695/96	Marion (Mitchell) Cleghorne	Edinburgh	Spoons, pair, rat tailed, "MM" script initial, stamped foliage, initials of Revd. Hugh Thomson and Barbara Barr, He was ordained in 1691	Christie's July 26, 1960 #146 Thomas Lumley Ltd National Museums of Scotland
1695 ca	William Lindsay	Aberdeen	Spoon, trefid, decorated, stem engraved "Achnagat"	Noble Collection Nicholas Shaw Catalog p 96
1695 ca	Not available	Glasgow	Spoons, set of 5, trefids	Christie's December 17, 1912 #117

YEAR	MAKER	LOCATION	DESCRIPTION	SOURCE
1695 ca	George Yorstoun	Edinburgh	Teaspoon, dog nose, block initials "I/TM", maker most likely, 4 ½" long	The Phoenix Collection
1695/96	Thomas Ker	Edinburgh	Dessert spoon, trefid, 7 ½" long	Huntley House Museum Edinburgh HH3456/69
1695/96	Thomas Cleghorne	Edinburgh	Spoons, pair, trefid	National Museums of Scotland L1983.33
1696/97	Thomas Ker	Edinburgh	Spoon, dog nose, initials "MAGIL"	Sotheby's November 7, 1968 N. Bloom Antiques
1696/97	Thomas Ker	Edinburgh	Spoons, set of 3, dog nose	Private Collection
1697/98	William Law	Edinburgh	Spoons, no details	Jackson Marks p 544
1697/98	James Penman	Edinburgh	Spoons, set of 5, trefids, initials "M/T/KY", 8oz	Christie's Glasgow March 29, 1983 #61
1698/99	James Penman	Edinburgh	Spoon, dog nose, no details	National Museums of Scotland MEQ 1299
1698/99	Colin McKenzie	Edinburgh	Spoons, set of 3, trefids, with initials	Christie's November 6, 1946, #79
1698/99	Not available	Edinburgh	Spoon, dog nose	National Museums of Scotland MEQ 1299 1978.86
1699/1700	Alexander Kincaid	Edinburgh	Spoons, no details	Jackson Marks p544
1700 ca	Colin McKenzie	Edinburgh	Straining spoon	National Museums of Scotland MEQ 119
1700/01	Thomas Ker	Edinburgh	Tablespoons, set of 6, dog nose, 7 ½" long	Private Collection UK
1700 ca	George Walker	Aberdeen	Tablespoons, set of 6, trefids, marked – GW, AB, D – in an engrailed punch, the terminals have initials "M/IA/IS", 7 5/8" long	Private Collection UK
1700 ca	Stephen Agate	Old Aberdeen	Tablespoons, no details	Private Ownership
1700 ca	William Scott	Aberdeen	Tablespoons, set of 6, wavy end, terminals engraved, 7 ½" long	Private Collection UK
1700/01	John Luke II	Glasgow	Spoon, trefid, no details	Christie's May 12, 1926 #41
1701/02	William Burton	Edinburgh	Spoon, dog nose, engraved with the initials "IP"	National Museums of Scotland MEQ 28

YEAR	MAKER	LOCATION	DESCRIPTION	SOURCE
1701/02	John Luke II	Glasgow	Spoon, dog nose, initials "M/RM/ES", 2oz 2d	Sotheby's Gleneagles August 1990 vol 27 #26
1702/03	David Dunlop	Canongate	Spoons, set of 6, dog nose, engraved with the initials "R.G.H.G", 7 ¾" long, 11.1oz	Noble Collection Nicholas Shaw Catalog 2001 p99
1702/03	Mungo Yorstoun	Edinburgh	Spoon, no details	Jackson Marks p544
1702/03	John Luke, II	Glasgow	Spoon, dog nose, no details	Sotheby's Gleneagles 1990
1702/03	Colin McKenzie	Edinburgh	Tablespoons (with forks), set of 11, Hanoverian, each engraved with the crest of a stag's head issuing from a Viscount' coronet, with motto "HINC HONOR ET SALUS"	Private Collection UK
1702/03	Thomas Ker	Edinburgh	Tablespoons, set of 6, wavy ended or dog nosed, crest and motto, 13.6oz	Christie's July 6, 1972 #14
1703/04	Colin McKenzie	Edinburgh	Hash spoon, transition Hanoverian, trefid, rat tailed, block initials "M" over "MN" over "LD", on reverse later script initials "D", 18" long, 12 oz	Lorentz Antiques Toronto Canada 1993 The Phoenix Collection
1703/04	Thomas Ker	Edinburgh	Tablespoons, set of 6 dog nose, rat tailed, marks worn, crest and motto worn, 13oz 13d	Christie's June 8, 1961 #156 Christie's July 5, 1972 #14
1703/04	John Seatoun	Edinburgh	Spoons, set of 3, no details	National Museums of Scotland 1943.314-316
1703/04	Thomas Cleghorne	Edinburgh	Spoon, no details	Jackson Marks p544
1704/05	John Seatoun	Edinburgh	Spoon, no details	National Museums of Scotland MEQ 19
1704/05	*John Seatoun*	*Edinburgh*	*Spoons, rat tailed spoon, no details*	*Jackson Marks p 544*
1704/05	John Penman II	Edinburgh	Tablespoon, rat tailed, with coat of arms	Christie's June 24, 1986 #159 Phillips May 20, 1988 #81
1704/05	John Seatoun	Edinburgh	Spoon, wavy ended or dog nosed, 7 ½" long	Christie's Glasgow November 19, 1992 #654
1705 ca	Thomas Ker	Edinburgh	Tablespoon, pair, dog nose tablespoons	National Museums of Scotland MEQ 1307-08 1978.94-95
1705 ca	David Dunlop	Canongate	Tablespoons, set of 6, wavy end, different from the set of 6 in the Nicholas Shaw 2004 catalog	Private Collection UK 1972 ca

YEAR	MAKER	LOCATION	DESCRIPTION	SOURCE
1705 ca	John Luke II	Glasgow	Spoon, trefid, town mark with bell on the left, and the G (not reversed) on the right, initials "SM", stamped Breadalbane, 8 1/8" long	Private Collection UK
1705 ca	Simon Le Revier	Aberdeen	Hash spoon, also a pair of gravy spoons, but with different marks, Jackson calls it a large rat-tailed basting spoon	Jackson Marks p526 Dover ed p485
1705/06	John Luke II	Glasgow	Tablespoons, set of 12, dog nosed, rat tailed, terminals with initials "IB/MW", presumably different from the other set of 12 if the initials were recorded correctly	Sotheby's Gleneagles August 30, 1982 #478
1705/06	Patrick Murray I	Edinburgh	Spoon, rat tailed spoon, no details	Jackson Marks p 545
1705/06	James Luke, II	Glasgow	Spoons, set of 12, dog nose, initials "IB MB", 25oz	Christie's April 26, 1972 #116
1705/06	John Luke II	Glasgow	Basting spoon, tubular handles, fluted bands, rat tailed, called a ladle in the Grimdex, 10oz 5d	Christie's May 12, 1926 #46
1706/07	John Seatoun	Edinburgh	Tablespoon, dog nose, 7 7/8" long, 2oz	M Klein Auction, Chicago September 12, 2004 #103
1706/07	Colin McKenzie	Edinburgh	Tablespoon, dog nose pattern, with rat tail bowl, engraved with contemporary initial "K"	Thomas Roddick & Medcalf, Edinburgh UK Mar 28, 2006 #124
1707/08	John Luke II	Glasgow	Tablespoon, dog nose or wavy end, large, one from the original set, script initials "HA", coronet above, 2.3oz	Sotheby's London UK Oct 31, 1974 #92 Bran Inglis Bonhams London UK 2005 #198
1707/08	John Luke II	Glasgow	Spoons, set of 6, dog nosed, coronet above script initials "HA" (or "JA"), 14oz 4d	Christie's July 5, 1972 #11
1707/08	Robert Inglis over striking John Seatoun Assayer James Penman	Edinburgh	Tablespoons, set of 6, early make, dog nosed, initials "MWF, ML", rat tailed, tops of spoons molded with drops, reverse of stem with engraved initials, 30oz	Christie's July 5, 1972 #10
1707/08	Mungo Yorstoun	Edinburgh	Hash spoon, rat tail, dog nosed, 6oz 15d	Christie's June 25, 1947 #133 How of Edinburgh Collection
1707/08	James Tait	Edinburgh	Hash spoon, Breadalbane	Sotheby's NY April 1990 #427
1707/08	James Tait	Edinburgh	Hash spoon, rat tail, shield top, 9oz	Hyman Collection – Williamsburg VA USA

YEAR	MAKER	LOCATION	DESCRIPTION	SOURCE
1708 ca	John Luke II	Glasgow	Tablespoons, set of four, Hanoverian pattern with rat tail bowls, engraved with contemporary initials "AM/EH",	Lyon & Turnbull February 20, 2004 #259; also 2004 #454
1708/09	Thomas Ker	Edinburgh	Tablespoons, dog nose, terminal initialed "JB/JB", 8" long, 2oz	How of Edinburgh Woolley & Wallis June 28, 2000 #105
1709/10	John Seatoun	Edinburgh	Tablespoons, set of 4, dog nose, with crest of a winged spur and motto	Private Collection UK
1709/10	Patrick Murray	Edinburgh	Dessert spoons, set of 6, rat tailed, dog nosed, 11oz 12d	Christie's May 29, 1968 #75
1709/10	James Seatoun	Edinburgh	Tablespoons, set of 6, with forks, dog nosed, crest	Scottish Exhibition Glasgow 1911 Christie's December 13, 1933 #55 Girdwood Collection
1710 ca	John Luke II	Glasgow	Hash spoons, pair, marks – IL in heart, D town mark, "h" date mark, 16" long	Private Collection UK
1710 ca	James Falconer	Glasgow	Spoon, rat tailed, no details	Glasgow Exhibition 1901 Jackson Marks p568
1710 ca	George Robertson	Aberdeen	Chocolate spoon, no details	Aberdeen Museums and Galleries ABDAG011150
1710 ca	George Robertson	Aberdeen	Tablespoons, set of 3, wavy end, terminals engraved with "A/I" beside "S", en suite with similar ones by Simon le Revier Old Aberdeen, 7 ¾" long	Private Collection UK
1710 ca	Simon Le Revier	Aberdeen	Tablespoons, set of 3, wavy end, terminals engraved "A/I" beside "S", en suite with similar ones by George Robertson in the same collection	Private Collection UK
1710 ca	William McLean	Inverness	Hash spoon, applied rat tail, tubular tapering handle, spiral fluted knop, unscrewing and containing a wooden spirtle, initials "IMT"	Shaw Collection Christie's Glasgow March 29, 1983 #38 How of Edinburgh Private Collection UK
1710/11	John Seatoun	Edinburgh	Tablespoon, dog nose, terminal engraved "JHM", 8 1/5" long	Private Collection UK
1711/12	James Tait	Edinburgh	Spoons, set of 6, no details	National Museums of Scotland L.396.32-21e
1711/12	James Tait	Edinburgh	Tablespoons, set of, 6 Hanoverian rat tailed, with initials "WM or WI" or "IW"	Bonhams The Scottish Sale, August 21, 2003 #56

YEAR	MAKER	LOCATION	DESCRIPTION	SOURCE
1712/13	John Seatoun	Edinburgh	Tablespoons, dog nose, initials removed, later crest of an ostrich head and 2 feathers, 2 oz	Bonhams July 18, 2002 #250
1712/13	Robert Ker	Edinburgh	Large spoon, no details	Jackson Marks p 545
1712/13	James Mitchelson	Edinburgh	Hash spoon, Hanoverian pattern with a rat tail, 15 ¾" long, 8.8oz	Bonhams Sale 15120 Aug 22, 2007 #61
1713/14	Alexander Kincaid	Edinburgh	Spoons, set of 6 rat tailed, 13.5oz	Breadalbane Collection Sale 1935 #358
1713/14	Patrick Murray I	Edinburgh	Tablespoons, set of 6, dog nosed, crest of a boar's head, 8" long	Private Collection UK
1713/14	Charles Duncan	Edinburgh	Spoons, set of 6, Hanoverian rat tailed, initials "IS ID"	Not available
1713/14	Colin McKenzie	Edinburgh	Spoons, pair, no details	National Museums of Scotland MEQ 149
1713/14	Colin McKenzie	Edinburgh	Spoons, pair, no details	National Museums of Scotland 1955.192-a
1714/15	James Mitchelson	Edinburgh	Tablespoon, set of 6, wavy end or dog nosed, crested, 12.3oz	Sotheby's August 3, 1967 #246 Grantully Castle Antiques
1715 ca	George Robertson	Aberdeen	Teaspoon, Hanoverian, rat tailed, script initials "ME", 4 5/8" long	The Phoenix Collection
1715 ca	Mungo Yorstoun	Edinburgh	Teaspoons, pair, rat tailed, Hanoverian	National Museums of Scotland MEQ 2021
1715/16	Alexander Kincaid	Edinburgh	Tablespoons, Hanover, rat tailed, script initials "JD, CB" on the reverse, later below "RC", 8" long	M Rafael, NYC 1995 The Phoenix Collection
1715/16	Thomas Ker	Edinburgh	Spoons, rat tailed, no details	Jackson Marks p 545
1716/17	John Seatoun	Edinburgh	Spoons, rat tailed, no details	Jackson Marks p545
1716/17	Kenneth McKenzie	Edinburgh	Hash spoon, rat tailed, 9.3oz	Breadalbane Collection Sale 1935, #357
1716/17	Robert Inglis	Edinburgh	Tablespoons, set of 4, engraved initials "MF F MF", part of a lot, 30 oz	Christie's July 5, 1972 #10
1716/17	Henry Bethune	Edinburgh	Spoons, rat tailed, no details	Jackson Marks p 545

YEAR	MAKER	LOCATION	DESCRIPTION	SOURCE
1716/17	John Seatoun	Edinburgh	Tablespoons, set of 6, rat tailed, tops engraved with a crest, 15oz 6d	Christie's June 17, 1937 #276 Sotheby's Scone Palace April 14, 1980 #59
1717/18	William Ure	Edinburgh	Spoon, rat tailed, no details	Jackson Marks p 545
1717/18	John Seatoun	Edinburgh	Tablespoons, set of 11, rat tailed, 24oz 6d	Christie's February 14, 1934 #29
1718 ca	John Walker	Aberdeen	Teaspoon, rat tailed	National Museums of Scotland MEQ 123
1718/19	Patrick Turnbull	Edinburgh	Hash spoon, rat tailed, 15 1/3" long	Sotheby's NY November 1, 1947 #378
1718/19	James Mitchelson	Edinburgh	Hash spoon, rat tailed, no details	Jackson Marks p 545
1719/20	William Aytoun	Edinburgh	Tablespoons, 5 Hanoverian, rat tailed, crest and motto	JH Bourdon-Smith Catalog 1993
1719/20	Mungo Yorstoun	Edinburgh	Spoon, rat tailed, set, no details	Jackson Marks p 546
1719/20	Alexander Simpson	Edinburgh	Spoon, rat tailed, set, no details	Jackson Marks p 546
1719/20	James Inglis	Edinburgh	Spoon, rat tailed, no details	Jackson Marks p 546
1719/20	James Mitchelson	Edinburgh	Tablespoon, Hanoverian, initials and crest	Sotheby's September 13, 1979 #32
1719/20	William Aytoun	Edinburgh	Tablespoons, one (1719/20) and five (1723/24), Hanoverian pattern, with a crest and motto	Lyon & Turnbull Edinburgh UK 2004 #242
1719/20	William Scott	Banff	Tablespoon, rat tailed, Hanoverian pattern, terminal with initials "WD/EP", 7 ¾" long	Private Collection UK
1720 ca	Simon McKenzie	Inverness	Tablespoons, Hanoverian, rat tailed	National Museums of Scotland MEQ 726.7
1720 ca	Charles Dickson I	Dundee	Tablespoons, set of 6	National Museums of Scotland MEQ 211-216 1956.713-718
1720 ca	Robert Innes	Edinburgh	Hash spoon, rat tailed, 15 ½" long	Sotheby's April 23, 1993 #341
1720 ca	William Aytoun	Edinburgh	Spoon, date letter indistinct, marriage initial and later crest and motto above, 17 ½" long, 9oz	Christie's November 19, 1993 #226

YEAR	MAKER	LOCATION	DESCRIPTION	SOURCE
1720 ca	Robert Innes	Inverness	Tablespoon, Hanoverian pattern, rat tail bow, marriage initials "M/WA", 7" long	Christie's London UK 1998 #8
1720 ca	John Walker	Aberdeen	Tablespoon, Hanoverian pattern with rat tail bowl, engraved initials "WL CF TL"	Thomas Roddick & Medcalf, Edinburgh UK Oct 31, 2006 #9
1720/21	David Mitchell	Edinburgh	Spoon, no details	Jackson Marks p 546
1721/22	William Aytoun	Edinburgh	Hash spoon, rat tailed, crest and motto of Pitcairn of that Ilk, 14 ¾" long, 8oz	Sotheby's November 11, 1993 #201
1721/22	David Mitchell	Edinburgh	Tablespoon, Hanoverian rat tailed, crest and motto, "VERTUTIS GLORIA MERCES", 8"long	The Phoenix Collection
1721/22	James Clarke	Edinburgh	Spoon, no details	Jackson Marks p 546
1722 ca	Charles Dickson I	Dundee	Tablespoon, Hanoverian, rat tailed, script initials "JT" over "MP", 8 1/8" long	Connecticut Shop 1992 The Phoenix Collection
1722/23	Kenneth McKenzie	Edinburgh	Dessert spoons, set of 7 rat tailed, 8.5oz	Sotheby's Gleneagles August 27, 1979 #215
1722/23	Henry Bethune	Edinburgh	Tablespoons, pair, rat tailed, Hanoverian, 8 1/8" long	The Phoenix Collection
1722/23	Colin Campbell	Drysdale	Spoon, no pictures	Cripps p 150
1723 ca	Simon McKenzie	Inverness	Hash spoon, rat tailed, 16 ½" long	Jonathan Trace Inc., NY 1994
1723 ca	Simon McKenzie	Inverness	Hash spoon, tubular, 19 1/6" long, 10oz wt	Christie's Glasgow March 1983 #38
1723/24	Charles Blair	Edinburgh	Tablespoon, no details	Jackson Marks p 546
1724/25	Alexander Edmonstoun	Edinburgh	Tablespoons, no details	Jackson Marks p 546
1725 ca	James Tait	Edinburgh	Tablespoons, pair, Hanoverian pattern, with initial "K", with other items	Christie's London UK 2003 #463
1725 ca	George Robertson	Aberdeen	Tablespoon, Hanoverian pattern, contemporary initials "IL/EG"	Thomas Roddick & Medcalf, Edinburgh UK Oct 31, 2006 #10
1725 ca	James Brown	Perth	Tablespoon, Hanoverian pattern, rat tail bow, initials "MO"	Thomas Roddick & Medcalf, Edinburgh UK Oct 31, 2006 #130

YEAR	MAKER	LOCATION	DESCRIPTION	SOURCE
1725 ca	Robert Gilchrist (or McGilchrist)	Glasgow	Hash spoon, Hanoverian, rat tailed, terminal with initials "DP", 14 3/8" long, 7.5oz	Sotheby's Scone Palace April 23, 1979 #73 How of Edinburgh Bonhams the Scottish Sale August 21, 2003 #74
1725/26	Archibald Ure	Edinburgh	Tablespoon, no details	Jackson Marks p 546
1725/26	Maker not listed in Grimdex	Edinburgh	Hash spoon, rat tailed, 9oz 3d	Christie's May 6, 1903 #71
1726/27	Dougal Ged	Edinburgh	Hash spoon, Hanoverian, rat tailed, engraved with initial "B", 15 ½"long, 9oz	Christie's London November 22, 2000 #76
1726/27	David Mitchell	Edinburgh	Tablespoon, no details	National Museums of Scotland MEQ 72
1726/27	James Tait	Edinburgh	Tablespoon, no details	Jackson Marks p 546
1726/27	James Ker	Edinburgh	Hash spoon, maker incorrectly listed as J Kincaid, not pictured	Sotheby's Hopetoun House April 1988 #5
1726/27	David Mitchell	Edinburgh	Hash spoon, rat tailed, ribbed stern, initials, 9oz 8d	Christie's July 19, 1939 #64
1727/28	Henry Bethune	Edinburgh	Hash spoon, rat tailed, Hanoverian, 15 11/16" long	The JB Speed Art Museum Louisville KY USA
1727/28	Charles Duncan or Charles Dickson I	Edinburgh	Hash Spoon, rat tailed Hanoverian, 9oz	Breadalbane Collection Sale 1935 #135
1727/28	David Mitchell	Edinburgh	Tablespoons, set of 6, Hanoverian, terminal with initials	Sotheby's Gleneagles August 29, 1974 #92
1727/28	James Tait	Edinburgh	Hash spoon, Hanoverian, rat tailed, 7.8oz	Sotheby's Gleneagles August 29, 1974 #013
1727/28	Patrick Graham	Edinburgh	Tablespoon, Hanoverian no details	National Museums of Scotland MEQ 1023 1970.574
1727/28	*Patrick Graham*	*Edinburgh*	*Tablespoon, no details*	*Cripps p 150* *Breadalbane Collection*
1728/29	Alexander Kincaid	Edinburgh	Tablespoons, pair, dog nose, block initials	National Museums of Scotland MEQ 1045-1046 1971.267-268

YEAR	MAKER	LOCATION	DESCRIPTION	SOURCE
1728/29	Patrick Graham	Edinburgh	Tablespoon, no details	Jackson Marks p 564
1728/29	William Aytoun	Edinburgh	Tablespoons, set of 12, with forks, rat tailed, crest and motto	Christie's November 30, 1960 #177
1728/29	James Ker	Edinburgh	Tablespoons, set of 6, rat tailed with forks	Christie's February 3, 1954 #98
1728/29	James Tait	Edinburgh	Tablespoons, pair, Hanoverian rat tail pattern, with others	Bonhams London UK 2003 #359
1729/30	Archibald Ure	Edinburgh	Tablespoon, no details	National Museums of Scotland MEQ 125 1933.337
1729/30	William Aytoun	Edinburgh	Tablespoon, no details	Jackson Marks p 546
1730 ca	William Aytoun	Edinburgh	Tea strainer spoon, Scots fiddle pattern	Private Collection
1730 ca	Robert Luke II	Glasgow	Tablespoons, pair, no details	National Museums of Scotland MEQ 182-183
1730 ca	George Cooper	Aberdeen	Tablespoons, 2, no details	National Museums of Scotland MEQ 512
1730 ca	Johan Gott-helf-Bilsings	Glasgow	Tablespoons, pair, Hanoverian, script initial "JC" over "TJ", 8 ½" long	D Robinson, NJ 1994 The Phoenix Collection
1730 ca	James Mitchelson	Edinburgh	Tablespoons, pair, Hanoverian, in a fitted case	Christie's December 1977 #141 Christie's January 30, 1978 #19
1730 ca	Colin Mitchell	Canongate	Tablespoon, Hanoverian, no details	National Museums of Scotland MEQ 346 1956-848
1730/31	Charles Duncan or Charles Dickson I	Edinburgh	Tablespoons, pair, no details	W B Smith Glasgow Exhibition 1911 vol I, p 103, #14
1730/31	James Mitchelson	Edinburgh	Tablespoons, set of 12, Hanoverian pattern, backs of bowls with double strap drop, each with "S" below an earl's coronet	Private Collection UK
1731/32	Charles Dickson I Or Charles Duncan	Edinburgh	Tablespoons, set of 6, Hanoverian, initials "AD/ED", 14.8oz	Sotheby's Gleneagles August 27, 1979 #217
1731/32	James Mitchelson	Edinburgh	Tablespoons, set of 5, with a crest	Christie's February 17, 1960

YEAR	MAKER	LOCATION	DESCRIPTION	SOURCE
1732/33	IM (or WI) in an oval	Edinburgh	Teaspoon, probably by William Jamieson or possibly John Main	National Museums of Scotland MEQ 1516
1732/33	George Forbes	Edinburgh	Tablespoons, no details	Jackson Marks p 547
1733/34	Hugh Gordon	Edinburgh	Hash spoon, Hanoverian, engraved with a cipher, 16 18" long, 7oz 10d	Christie's Glasgow March 29, 1983 #57
1733/34	Edward Lothian	Edinburgh	Tablespoons, Hanoverian, engraved with an initial below a coronet	Sotheby's Gleneagles August 29, 1983 #387
1734/35	William Marshall I Assayer – Archibald Ure	Edinburgh	Spoon, No details	Davis, English Silver at Williamsburg
1734/35	James Mitchelson	Edinburgh	Tablespoons, set of 3, no details	Sotheby's December 16, 1976 #80
1734/35	James Mitchelson	Edinburgh	Tablespoons, set of 6, Hanoverian, 5 with identical initials, 6th with different initials, 13.1oz	Sotheby's August 24, 1974 #93
1734/35	William Aytoun	Edinburgh	Tablespoon, set of three, Hanoverian pattern, engraved with monogram "S.H"	Christie's Lanarkshire UK 1997 #126
1735 ca	Robert Luke	Glasgow	Tablespoon, Hanoverian pattern, initial "C", with rare divided town mark	Thomas Roddick & Medcalf, Edinburgh UK Mar 28, 2006 #149
1735 ca	John Rollo	Edinburgh	Teaspoons, pair, Scots fiddle, initials "MC"	Private Collection
1735/36	James Mitchelson	Edinburgh	Tablespoons, set of 6 Hanoverian, terminals with initials	Sotheby's Gleneagles August 29, 1983 #93
1735/36	James Ker	Edinburgh	Dessert spoons, set of 7 Hanoverian, plus one shortened spoon, chased, decorated on both sides with scrolls, flowers, and leaves, empty scroll medallion on the reverse, 8" long	M Rafael, NY 1993 The Phoenix Collection
1735/36	John Rollo	Edinburgh	Spoon, no details	Jackson Marks p 547
1735/36	James Ker	Edinburgh	Tablespoons, set of 6, Hanoverian, not pictured	Sotheby's Gleneagles August 1987 #231
1736/37	Hugh Penman	Edinburgh	Spoon, no details	Jackson Marks p547
1736/37	Kenneth McKenzie	Edinburgh	Tablespoons, pair, Hanoverian, 8 3/8" long	The Phoenix Collection

YEAR	MAKER	LOCATION	DESCRIPTION	SOURCE
1737/38	Dougal Ged	Edinburgh	Tablespoons, set of 5, no details	National Museums of Scotland H.1996.13.1-5
1737/38	James Ker	Edinburgh	Tablespoons, 3 Hanoverian, initials "GH" over "SH", 8" long	Goodwin's Edinburgh, 1993 The Phoenix Collection Auction, source unclear
1737/38	Edward Lothian	Edinburgh	Spoons, 3, no details	
1738/39	James Ker	Edinburgh	Tablespoons, set of 11, Hanoverian, terminals lightly engraved with a crest, 25oz	Sotheby's Scone Palace April 14, 1980 #17
1738/39	Lawrence Oliphant	Edinburgh	Tablespoons, set of 8, Hanoverian, crest of a rock and motto "Firm", 2 were later initialed "N", 24.9oz	Sotheby's Gleneagles August 25, 1997 #28
1738/39	James Weems	Edinburgh	Teaspoons, pair, no details	W B Smith Glasgow Exhibition 1911, vol I, p116, #100
1738/39	William Aytoun	Edinburgh	Tablespoons, 4, no details	National Museums of Scotland H.1996.11-12
1738/39	James Mitchell	Edinburgh	Tablespoon, pair, Hanoverian pattern, with other items	Christie's London UK 2000 #275
1738/39	Lawrence Oliphant	Edinburgh	Tablespoon, Hanoverian pattern, with others	Bonhams Solihull 2003 #308
1739/40	James Hally	Edinburgh	Tablespoons, pair, Hanoverian pattern, with engraved betrothal initials, 5.2oz	Bonhams Sale 15120 Aug 22, 2007 #72
1739/40	James Ker	Edinburgh	Spoon, no details	Jackson Marks p 547
1739/40	James Tait	Edinburgh	Tablespoons, set of 6, Hanoverian, terminal with the initials "MF", 13.2oz	Sotheby's Scone Palace, April 14, 1980, #121
1739/40	James Mitchell Assayer – Dougal Ged	Edinburgh	Tablespoons, no details	Sotheby's Gleneagles August 1991 #14
1740 ca	George Cooper	Aberdeen	Tablespoons, set of 5, no details	National Museums of Scotland MEQ 515
1740 ca	Patrick Murray III	Edinburgh	Teaspoons, set of 3 Scots fiddle, with unusually broad stems	Private Collection
1740 ca	Alexander Johnston	Dundee	Tablespoons, pair, Hanoverian pattern, triple drop heel, crest and motto of Hunton, 4oz	Christie's Lanarkshire UK 1997 #39

YEAR	MAKER	LOCATION	DESCRIPTION	SOURCE
1740 ca	George Cooper	Aberdeen	Tablespoon, Hanoverian pattern, with rat tail bowl, marriage initials "M/AC/BB"	Christie's Lanarkshire UK 1997 #24
1740 ca	Hugh Ross	Tain	Tablespoon, Hanoverian pattern, triple drop heel, oval bowl, contemporary inscription "Mrs. J. G."	Christie's Lanarkshire 1998 #9
1740 ca	Dougal Ged	Edinburgh	Teaspoons, 3 Scots fiddle pattern, wavy stem, mm only, middle marked, script initials "WMl", 4 7/8" long	Gebelein's East Arlington, VT 1991 The Phoenix Collection
1740 ca	Alexander Johnson	Dundee	Tablespoons, set of 6 Hanoverian, crest of Hunter, marks include script "K"	Mary Cooke London, 1995
1740 ca	AT probably Adam Tait	Edinburgh	Teaspoon, Hanoverian, mm only, middle marked	Pickford Spoons Book p87 #93
1740/41	James Ker	Edinburgh	Tablespoons, set of ten, Hanoverian pattern, with an initial, with other spoons	Christie's London UK 2004 #125
1740/41	James Hally Assayer – Dougal Ged	Edinburgh	Hash spoon, Hanoverian, with initials "IM IR", 6.4oz	Sotheby's Hopetoun House March 27, 1984 #21
1740/41	Charles Dickson II	Edinburgh	Tablespoon, no details	National Museums of Scotland MEQ 217 1956.719
1740/41	Charles Dickson II	Edinburgh	Tablespoons, 2, no details	National Museums of Scotland H.1996.7
1740/41	James Ker Assayer – Dougal Ged	Edinburgh	Tablespoons, set of 8, Hanoverian, initials "TJC", mm over striking self	Schredds Antiques London 2005
1740/41	James Mitchelson	Edinburgh	Tablespoons, set of 4, Hanoverian, crest and motto, "NON DEGENER" for Wedderburn	Sanda Lipton London 1995 The Phoenix Collection
1740/41	James Ker	Edinburgh	Spoon, no details	Jackson Marks p 547
1740/41	Ebenezer Oliphant	Edinburgh	Spoon, no details	Jackson Marks p 547 Breadalbane Collection
1741/42	James Mitchelson	Edinburgh	Tablespoons, set of 3, Hanoverian, sold with one earlier spoon by James Tait, terminals with initials	Bonhams December 20, 1979 #275

YEAR	MAKER	LOCATION	DESCRIPTION	SOURCE
1741/42	Ebenezer Oliphant	Edinburgh	Tablespoons, set of 6, chased, Hanoverian pattern	National Museums of Scotland H.1996.17
1741/42	James Ker Assayer – Dougal Ged	Edinburgh	Hash spoon, with hook support at back, top chased with scrolls and shells, crest, 6oz 9d	Christie's February 14, 1934 #53
1741/42	James Ker	Edinburgh	Tablespoons, set of 12, plain, ribbed handles, 27oz 10d wt	Christie's January 2, 1946 #10
1741/42	Lawrence Oliphant	Edinburgh	Hash spoon, no details	Jackson Marks p 547
1741/42	William Aytoun	Edinburgh	Spoon, no details	Jackson Marks p 547
1741/42	Charles Blair	Edinburgh	Tablespoons, set of three, Hanoverian pattern, with others	Bonhams London UK 2003 #484
1742/43	James Ker	Edinburgh	Tablespoon, Hanoverian pattern	Christie's Lanarkshire UK 1998 #540
1743/44	Robert Low	Edinburgh	Tablespoon, Hanoverian pattern, with another	Lyon & Turnbull, Edinburgh UK 2007 #258
1743/44	William Aytoun	Edinburgh	Hash spoon, Hanoverian pattern, with a crest and motto, 13 ¼" long	Lyon & Turnbull, Edinburgh UK 2004 #238
1743/44	William Aytoun	Edinburgh	Hanoverian hash spoon, 13" long, 5.9oz	Nicholas Shaw Catalog 2005 p92
1743/44	Lawrence Oliphant	Edinburgh	Tablespoons, pair, Hanoverian, with script initials "GT/ED", 8 3/8" long	The Phoenix Collection
1743/44	Alexander Aitchison I Over striking Robert Low	Edinburgh	Tablespoon, Hanoverian, with initials "MJ", 8 ½" long	The Phoenix Collection
1743/44	Alexander Campbell	Edinburgh	Tablespoon, Hanoverian, with script initial "E", 8 1/8" long	The Phoenix Collection
1744/45	William Aytoun	Edinburgh	Tablespoon, pair, probably Hanoverian, 3.3oz	Breadalbane Collection Sale 1935 #354
1744/45	Edward Lothian	Edinburgh	Tablespoons, set of 3 Hanoverian	Sotheby's Scone Palace April 13, 1976 #29
1745 ca	John Steven	Dundee	Hash spoon, engraved with the crest of Scrymsoure of Tealing	Private Collection
1745 ca	James Brown & Francis Brown	Perth	Tablespoon, Hanoverian pattern with faceted long drop heel, initial "A"	Thomas Roddick & Medcalf Edinburgh UK Oct 31, 2006 #131

YEAR	MAKER	LOCATION	DESCRIPTION	SOURCE
1745 ca	John Steven	Dundee	Hash spoon, Hanoverian, terminal with initials "JMF", 7.3oz	Sotheby's Scone Palace April 19, 1977 #65
1745 ca	John Steven	Dundee	Hash spoon, plain, Hanoverian, probably different from the initialed one as acquired in 1964	Dundee Museums and Art Galleries 1694-60
1745 ca	Dougal Ged	Edinburgh	Teaspoon, Scots fiddle, with initials "MC"	Private Collection
1745 ca	James Glen	Glasgow	Tablespoons, pair, Hanoverian, script initials "JC" over "MM", 8 ¼" long	Hobart House, CT 1993 The Phoenix Collection
1745 ca	James Glen	Glasgow	Tablespoon, no details	National Museums of Scotland MEQ 188
1745 ca	Ebenezer Oliphant	Edinburgh	Teaspoon, Scots fiddle, with script initial "A", 5 ¼" long	The Phoenix Collection
1745 ca	James Glen	Glasgow	Tablespoons, set of 20 Hanoverian, not pictured	Sotheby's Hopetoun House, April 1988 #7
1745 ca	James Glen	Glasgow	Hash spoon, Hanoverian	Metropolitan Museum NYC AC #33.120.92
1745 ca	Edward Lothian	Edinburgh	Hash spoon, no details	Sotheby's NY October 27, 1982 #356
1745 ca	James Glen	Glasgow	Hanoverian hash spoon, with script initials "DK", 14" long	The Phoenix Collection
1745/46	Edward Lothian	Edinburgh	Tablespoons, set of 9	National Museums of Scotland MEQ L.1983.328-i
1745/46	William Taylor	Edinburgh	Tablespoons, pair, Hanoverian pattern	Christie's London UK 2003 #403
1746/47	James Mitchelson	Edinburgh	Tablespoons, set of 12, Hanoverian pattern, crest and motto "TANDEM" for Cunningham, with other items – note maker listed as John Main in catalog	Christie's London UK 2002 #207
1746/47	Hugh Penman	Edinburgh	Tablespoons, pair, Hanoverian, with the initials "HJ/L"	Bonhams The Scottish Sale August 21, 2003 #48
1746/47	William Davie or William Dempster	Edinburgh	Hash spoon, Hanoverian, arms, scratch weight, 15" long	Rothstein Antiques NY 1993 Koopman London 1993
1746/47	Dougal Ged	Edinburgh	Hash spoon, no details	National Museums of Scotland MEQ 34 1923.365

YEAR	MAKER	LOCATION	DESCRIPTION	SOURCE
1746/47	John Welsh	Edinburgh	Tablespoon, Hanoverian, no details	Shredd's Antiques London 1996
1747 ca	Samuel Telfer	Glasgow	Tablespoon, no details	Jackson Marks p569
1747/48	CL maker's mark	Edinburgh	Spoon, no details	Jackson Marks p 547
1747/48	Hugh Penman	Edinburgh	Tablespoons, pair, Hanoverian pattern, 8 ¼" long, 4.5oz	Christie's London UK 2002 #21
1748/49 and 1757/58	Robert Low	Edinburgh	Tablespoons, set of five, Hanoverian pattern, with a foliate initial, 11.7oz	Bonhams Edinburgh UK 2005 #48
1748/49	Ker & Dempster	Edinburgh	Tablespoon, Hanoverian pattern, script "O" initial, 8 1/8" long, 2.2oz	The Silver Spoon Club Postal Auction July 12, 2007 #174
1748/49	Robert Gordon	Edinburgh	Tablespoons, set of 12, Hanoverian, crest and motto, 30oz 2d	Sotheby's November 6, 1980 #127
1748/49	William Gilchrist	Edinburgh	Spoon, no details	Jackson Marks p 547
1748/49	Robert Gordon	Edinburgh	Tablespoon, Hanoverian, with script initials "R & MF", 8 3/8" long	The Phoenix Collection
1748/49	James Weems	Edinburgh	Teaspoons, pair, no details	W B Smith Glasgow Exhibition 1911, vol I, p 116, #101
1749/50	Ker & Dempster	Edinburgh	Tablespoons, set of 6, 13.5oz	Breadalbane Collection Sale 1935 #374
1749/50	William Aytoun	Edinburgh	Tablespoons, set of six, Hanoverian pattern, crested, Provenance Thomas Graham of Airth, Airth Castle, Stirlingshire, and to Mrs. George Booth by descent	Christie's London UK 2002 #152
1749/50	Charles Dickson II	Edinburgh	Tablespoons, set of 12, 27.5oz	Christie's Glasgow July 3, 1984 #65 Morris Collection
1749/50	Robert Low	Edinburgh	Hash spoon, engraved with initials	Sotheby's Gleneagles August 29, 1974 #96 JH Bourdon-Smith London
1749/50	James Mitchell	Edinburgh	Apostle spoons, pair, (conversions)	National Museums of Scotland MEQ 784
1749/50	IM in a rectangle James McKenzie I	Edinburgh	Tablespoon, Hanoverian, with script initials "AO", 8 ½" long	The Phoenix Collection

YEAR	MAKER or James Mitchelson	LOCATION	DESCRIPTION	SOURCE
1749/50	James Mitchell	Edinburgh	Tablespoons, set of 3	National Museums of Scotland H.1996.10
1749/50	Hugh Gordon	Edinburgh	Tablespoons, set of 6 Hanoverian	Shredd's Antiques London 1996
1750 ca	Colin Allan	Aberdeen	Mote spoon, no details	Aberdeen Museums and Galleries ABDAG000906
1750 ca	HR conjoined Possibly Hugh Ross of Tain	Tain	Mote spoon, long narrow handle, with pierced surface and rays	Lyman Allyn Art Museum, New London, CT USA 1948.11
1750 ca	Colin Allan	Aberdeen	Hash spoon, no details	National Museums of Scotland MEQ 507
1750 ca	Hugh Ross	Tain	Teaspoon, Scots fiddle, with initials "IP", 4 5/8" long	Nicholas Shaw Catalog 2002/03 p91
1750 ca	James Glen	Glasgow	Serving spoon, no details	Sotheby's Gleneagles August 1987 #233
1750 ca	*James Glen*	*Glasgow*	*Serving spoon, crest and initials*	*Hyman Collection – Williamsburg VA* *How of Edinburgh Collection*
1750 ca	Hugh Ross	Tain	Tablespoons, set of 6, Hanoverian	Lyle Annual Review 1983 Sotheby's
1750 ca	Alexander Shirras	Banff	Hash spoon, 15 ½" long, 7oz 5d	Christie's Glasgow March 1983 #23
1750 ca	William Taylor	Edinburgh	Teaspoon, Scots fiddle , block initials "M/RM", 4 ¾"	The Phoenix Collection
1750 ca	John Steven	Dundee	Tablespoon, Hanoverian, with initial "A"	Thomas Roddick & Medcalf Sale Edinburgh November 10, 2003 #397
1750 ca	John Steven	Dundee	Tablespoon, Old English pattern, initialed, with other	Bonhams Solihull 2003 #308
1750 ca	Hugh Penman	Edinburgh	Teaspoons, pair, Scots fiddle pattern, initial "M"	Thomas Roddick & Medcalf, Edinburgh UK Oct 31, 2006 #55

YEAR	MAKER	LOCATION	DESCRIPTION	SOURCE
1750 ca	James Hill	Edinburgh	Teaspoons, pair, Scots fiddle pattern, script initials	The Silver Spoon Club Postal Auction Feb 22, 2007 #30
1750/51	Edward Lothian	Edinburgh	Tablespoon, no details	The Maple Swan Collection
1750/51	James Hewitt	Edinburgh	Tablespoon, no details	National Museums of Scotland MEQ 128 1933.338
1750/51	Ker & Dempster	Edinburgh	Tablespoons, set of 12, Hanoverian, initial "A"	Sotheby's Gleneagles August 1993 #18
1751/52	Lothian & Robertson	Edinburgh	Tablespoons, set of 6, 14.5oz	Breadalbane Collection Sale 1935 #361
1752/53	IM in a rectangle James McKenzie I or James Mitchelson	Edinburgh	Tablespoon, no details	Jackson Marks p 548
1752/53	Dougal Ged	Edinburgh	Spoons, not pictured	Cripps p 150
1752/53	Ker & Dempster	Edinburgh	Hash spoon, engraved with a monogram	Sotheby's Gleneagles August 29, 1974 #95 JH Bourdon-Smith Catalog London
1752/53	Lothian & Robertson	Edinburgh	Hash spoon, terminal engraved with "Ex Domo JR", 18 ½" long, 8oz	Mary Cooke London Private Collection
1752/53	Ebenezer Oliphant	Edinburgh	Tablespoons, set of 6, initials in script "IMD", 8 3/8" long	Royal Ontario Museum Toronto Canada 977.227.6 a-f
1753/54	Ker & Dempster	Edinburgh	Tablespoons, set of 11, Hanoverian, with crest and motto	Sotheby's Gleneagles August 29, 1974 #100
1753/54	Ker & Dempster	Edinburgh	Tablespoons, set of 12 Hanoverian, crested with motto "AT SPES INFRACT" with coronet for the 2nd Earl of Hopetoun	Sotheby's Gleneagles August 25, 1997 #27
1753/54	James Weems	Edinburgh	Hash spoons, no details	Jackson Marks p 548
1754/55	Robert Low	Edinburgh	Hash spoon, Hanoverian	Breadalbane Collection Sale 1935 #362

YEAR	MAKER	LOCATION	DESCRIPTION	SOURCE
1754/55	Lothian & Robertson	Edinburgh	Tablespoon, misdated as 1740 in catalog	Bonhams the Scottish Sale August 21, 2003 #50
1755 ca	Alexander Shirras	Banff	Tablespoon, Hanoverian pattern, 2.5oz	Lyon & Turnbull, Edinburgh UK 2004 #467
1755 ca	Thomas Johnston	Montrose	Tablespoon, Hanoverian pattern, initial "B"	Thomas Roddick & Medcalf, Edinburgh UK Oct 31, 2006 #118
1755 ca	Lothian & Robertson	Edinburgh	Teaspoon, Scots fiddle, with initials "CS" #5, with lion crest and motto	Private Collection
1755 ca	AIT Alexander Aitchison	Edinburgh	Teaspoon, Scots fiddle, with script initials "JL"	The Phoenix Collection
1755 ca	I (dot) W maker's mark		Teaspoon, Scots fiddle, 4 5/8" long	The Phoenix Collection
1755 ca	James Hewitt	Edinburgh	Teaspoons, set of 4, Scots fiddle, block initials "IMT", 4 5/8" long	The Phoenix Collection
1755 ca	Thomas Johnston	Montrose	Hash spoon, 14 ½" long, 8oz	Christie's Glasgow March 1983 #25
1755 ca	Peter Spaulding	Edinburgh	Teaspoons, set of 3, Scots fiddle pattern, initial "M"	Thomas Roddick & Medcalf, Edinburgh UK Oct 31, 2006 #63
1755 ca	Alexander Shirras	Banff	Tablespoon, Hanoverian pattern, initial "G" above "MG", one from a larger set	Thomas Roddick & Medcalf, Edinburgh UK Mar 28, 2006, #55
1755/56	Ker & Dempster	Edinburgh	Spoon, no details	Jackson Marks p 548
1755/56	Peter Cuthberton	Canongate	Tablespoons, pair, Hanoverian	National Museums of Scotland H.1993.32-33
1756/57	Patrick Robertson	Edinburgh	Tablespoons, set of 12 Hanoverian, with crest and motto of Dunbar, 28oz	Sotheby's Hopetoun House November 15, 1977 #103
1756/57	Lothian & Robertson	Edinburgh	Hanoverian tablespoon, crest and script initials "H" below crest, 8 3/8"	Gebelein's, East Arlington, VA USA The Phoenix Collection
1756/57	Lothian & Robertson	Edinburgh	Hanoverian hash spoon, not picture 7oz wt	Sotheby's London June 18, 1987 #183
1756/57	Robert Gordon	Edinburgh	Spoon, no details	Jackson Marks p548

YEAR	MAKER	LOCATION	DESCRIPTION	SOURCE
1757/58	James Gilliland	Edinburgh	Tablespoons, pair, Hanoverian, 8 ¼" long	Donahoue Antiques, Ottawa, Canada, 1994 The Phoenix Collection
1757/58	James Clark	Edinburgh	Spoon, no details	Jackson Marks p 548
1757/58	Robert Gordon	Edinburgh	Tablespoons, set of 12, Hanoverian, crest and motto, 29oz 16d wt	Sotheby's November 6, 1980 #128
1757/58	John Clark	Edinburgh	Tablespoon, Hanoverian pattern, engraved "JH" over "BE"	Woolley & Wallis April 20, 2005 #282
1758/59	Lothian & Robertson	Edinburgh	Hash spoon, 7oz	Breadalbane Collection Sale 1935 #153
1758/59	James Gilliland	Edinburgh	Tablespoon, Hanoverian, date wrong in the catalog	Bonhams the Scottish Sale August 21, 2003 #50
1758/59	Robert Gordon	Edinburgh	Spoons, with crossed leaves, crest and motto, 5oz	Woolley & Wallis, April 29, 2003 #286
1758/59	Dougal Ged Assayer – Hugh Gordon	Edinburgh	Hash spoon, maker over struck later	Sotheby's Gleneagles August 23, 1976 #110
1758/59	Lothian & Robertson	Edinburgh	Hash spoon, no details	The Maple Swan Collection
1758/59	Archibald Ure over struck by Gordon	Edinburgh	Spoon, date letter over struck by 1758, initial "G", 15 ¼" long, 7oz 11d	Not available
1759/60	Dougal Ged	Edinburgh	Tablespoons, pair, Hanoverian, initials script "RC"	Sanda Lipton, London 1995
1759/60	William Taylor	Edinburgh	Tablespoons, set of 3, Hanoverian, initials script "W/AC"	Mary Cooke, London 1995
1759/60	James Gilliland	Edinburgh	Spoon, no details	Jackson Marks p 548
1759/60	John Clark Assayer – Hugh Gordon	Edinburgh	Tablespoon, set of 3, Hanoverian pattern, with others	Bonhams London UK 2003 #484
1759/60	Lothian & Robertson	Edinburgh	Tablespoon, set of 10, Hanoverian pattern, with a crest and motto	Lyon & Turnbull, Edinburgh UK 2004 #240

YEAR	MAKER	LOCATION	DESCRIPTION	SOURCE
1760 ca	Milne & Campbell	Glasgow	Basting spoon, Hanoverian pattern, with a crest, 16 ½" long, 8oz	Sotheby's NY USA 1995 #13
1760 ca	Milne & Campbell	Glasgow	Basting spoon, Hanoverian pattern, faceted single drop, initialed "AC" and "MC", 16 ½" long, 8oz	Christie's London UK 1998 #33
1760 ca	Milne & Campbell	Glasgow	Basting spoon, Hanoverian pattern, with initial "M", 15" long, 8oz	Christie's London UK 1998 #252
1760 ca	Milne & Campbell	Glasgow	Tablespoons, pair, Hanoverian pattern, with script "H", sold with others	Bonhams London UK 2003 #359
1760 ca	Milne & Campbell	Glasgow	Tablespoon, Hanoverian pattern, with others	Christie's London UK 2007 #804
1760 ca	Milne & Campbell	Glasgow	Tablespoons, set of 6, Hanoverian pattern	Lyon & Turnbull, Edinburgh UK 2004 #438
1760 ca	Colin Allan	Aberdeen	Tablespoon, Hanoverian pattern 2.3oz	Lyon & Turnbull, Edinburgh UK 2004 #466
1760 ca	"Reid" mark	Edinburgh	Teaspoon, Scots fiddle, script initials "JL", 4 ¾" long	The Phoenix Collection
1760 ca	J Steven	Dundee	Tablespoons, Hanoverian, with initials	JH Bourdon-Smith 1994
1760 ca	Colin Allan	Aberdeen	Tablespoons, 4 Hanoverian	Sotheby's NY April 1992, #425
1760 ca	Milne & Campbell	Glasgow	Tablespoons, 10 Hanoverian	Goodwin's Antiques, Edinburgh 1992
1760 ca	Milne & Campbell	Glasgow	Tablespoons, 8 Hanoverian, crest and motto of Buchannan	JH Bourdon-Smith 1993
1760 ca	MM mark		Teaspoon, Scots fiddle	National Museums of Scotland MEQ 1516
1760 ca	John Baillie	Inverness	Masking spoon, initials "IS", 7" long	Nicholas Shaw Catalog 2002/03 p91
1760 ca	William Napier	Glasgow	Teaspoon, Scots fiddle, block initial "I", 5" long	The Phoenix Collection
1760 ca	Colin Allan	Aberdeen	Tablespoon, Old English, script initial "J", 8 ¾" long	The Phoenix Collection
1760 ca	James Clark	Edinburgh	Teaspoon, Scots fiddle, with script initial "L", 4 5/8" long	The Phoenix Collection
1760 ca	James Welsh	Edinburgh	Teaspoon, Scots fiddle, with script initials "W/EK", 4 5/8" long	The Phoenix Collection
1760 ca	IMC (conjoined)	Edinburgh	Teaspoon, Scots fiddle with remnant script initials, 4 5/8" long	The Phoenix Collection

YEAR	MAKER	LOCATION	DESCRIPTION	SOURCE
1760 ca	J (dot) W	Glasgow	Tablespoon, Hanoverian, with script initials "TP", 8 ¾" long	The Phoenix Collection
1760 ca	John Clark	Edinburgh	Teaspoons, set of 6, of slender form, with the initials "DE" over "E", mm only, 5 3/16" long	Private Collection
1760 ca	David Warnock	Glasgow	Hash spoon, no details	National Museums of Scotland MEQ 192
1760 ca	Benjamin Lumsden	Montrose	Tablespoon, Hanoverian pattern, with initials 'W. R. B. F'	Christie's Lanarkshire, UK 1997 #44
1760 ca	William Napier	Glasgow	Teaspoons, Scots fiddle pattern, set of 3	Thomas Roddick & Medcalf, Edinburgh UK Oct 31, 2006 #89
1760 ca	James Weems	Edinburgh	Tablespoons, set of 3, Hanoverian pattern, with others	Bonhams Solihull 2003 #308
1760/61	Alexander Gardner	Edinburgh	Basting spoon, Hanoverian pattern, with 2 set of initials, sold with other items, 15" long	Thomas Roddick & Medcalf, Edinburgh UK Oct 31, 2006 #89
1760/61	James Weems	Edinburgh	Tablespoons, set of 3, Hanoverian pattern, with initial "M", 7.2oz	Bonhams Sale 15120 Aug 22, 2007 #73
1760/61	Lothian & Robertson	Edinburgh	Hash spoon, Hanoverian, 16 1/8" long, 7.5oz	Nicholas Shaw Catalog 2005 p92 #4
1760/61	James Somervail	Edinburgh	Tablespoons, no details	Jackson Marks p 548
1760/61	Lothian & Robertson	Edinburgh	Hash spoon, Hanoverian, 16 1/8" long, 7.5oz	Nicholas Shaw Catalog 2005 p02
1760/61	Alexander Gardner	Edinburgh	Hash spoon, Hanoverian, engraved with the initials "DL/CR", 15 ¼" long, 7.6oz	Nicholas Shaw Catalog 1999 p57
1761/62	Dougal Ged	Edinburgh	Tablespoon, Hanoverian pattern, with initial "S"	Christie's Lanarkshire UK 1997 #102
1761/62	Lothian & Robertson	Edinburgh	Dessert spoons, pair, Hanoverian, chased	Bonhams July 18, 2002 #252
1761/62	William Dempster or William Davie	Edinburgh	Tablespoon, no details	Jackson Marks p 548
1761/62	William Dempster or William Davie	Edinburgh	Tablespoons, set of 6 Hanoverian, with initials, 12.8oz	Sotheby's Gleneagles August 30, 1982 #461

YEAR	MAKER	LOCATION	DESCRIPTION	SOURCE
1762/63	Robert Gordon	Edinburgh	Tablespoons, set of 12, with initial "G", 29.7oz	Sotheby's Hopetoun House March 27, 1984 #25c
1762/63	Ker & Dempster	Edinburgh	Tablespoons, Old English pattern	Bonhams the Scottish Sale August 21, 2003 #52
1762/63	Gilliland & Ker	Edinburgh	Tablespoon, misdated in Jackson as 1767/68	Jackson Marks p 549
1762/63	William Taylor	Edinburgh	Tablespoons, pair, no details	WB Smith Glasgow Exhibition 1911 vol I, p110, #7
1763/64	Lothian & Robertson	Edinburgh	Dessert spoons, set of 6, Hanoverian pattern, initial "M"	Lyon & Turnbull, Edinburgh UK 2004 #444
1763/64	Not available	Edinburgh	Hash spoon, mm mark indistinct, 15 ¼" long, 6.9oz	Sotheby's Gleneagles August 25, 1008 #31
1763/64	Gilliland & Ker	Edinburgh	Dessert spoon, set of 6 Hanoverian, with winged hourglass crest and motto	Sotheby's Gleneagles August 29, 1968 #179 Private Collection
1763/64	Robert Gordon	Edinburgh	Tablespoons, set of 6 Hanoverian, crest of a flaming heart over a starfish, motto "SUPER TOTUM"	Bonhams the Scottish Sale August 21, 2003 #55
1763/64	Ker & Dempster	Edinburgh	Hash spoon, engraved with a monogram	Sotheby's Gleneagles August 29, 1974 #95 JH Bourdon-Smith London
1763/64	John Clark	Edinburgh	Tablespoons, set of 5, one 1759, initials	Sanda Lipton, London 1995
1763/64	John Taylor	Edinburgh	Hash spoon, no details	Jackson Marks p 549
1763/64	William Davie or William Dempster	Edinburgh	Hash spoon, with a crest, 16" long, 8.5oz	JH Bourdon-Smith Catalog 1996, p15 #38
1763/64	Robert Gordon	Edinburgh	Tablespoons, set of 6 Hanoverian, with crest and motto "SUPER SIDERA VOTUM", 8 ½" long, 14.4oz	Nicholas Shaw Catalog 2000 p89
1763/64	Lothian & Robertson	Edinburgh	Tablespoon, pointed Old English, erased initials, 8 ½" long	The Finial Postal Auction March/April 2004 #132 Leopard Antiques #S1161
1763/64	John Clark	Edinburgh	Tablespoons, pair of Hanoverian, with script initials "JM/AT", 8 ½" long	The Phoenix Collection

YEAR	MAKER	LOCATION	DESCRIPTION	SOURCE
1764/65	Edward Lothian	Edinburgh	Apostle spoons, pair, no details	National Museums of Scotland 1943.308-309
1764/65	Francis Howden	Edinburgh	Apostle's spoon, no details	National Museums of Scotland 1943.307
1764/65 & 1767/68	Francis Howden	Edinburgh	Apostle's spoons, set of 4, 2 from each year	National Museums of Scotland 1943.310-313
1764/65	Milne & Campbell	Glasgow	Hash spoons, no details	Jackson Marks p 549
1764/65	James Gilliland	Edinburgh	Tablespoons, 6 Old English	Silver Plus 1993
1765 ca	Adam Graham	Glasgow	Tablespoons, set of 11, Hanoverian pattern, with another	Christie's London UK 2007 #474
1765 ca	Adam Graham	Glasgow	Tablespoons, set of 10, Hanoverian pattern, engraved initials	Lyon & Turnbull, Edinburgh UK 2004 #436
1765 ca	Adam Graham	Glasgow	Tablespoons, set of 7, Hanoverian pattern	Lyon & Turnbull, Edinburgh UK 2004 #440
1765 ca	Milne & Campbell	Glasgow	Tablespoon, Hanoverian pattern, script initials, 8 ½" long, 2.2oz	The Silver Spoon Club Postal Auction July 12, 2007 #46
1765 ca	Adam Graham	Glasgow	Tablespoons, set of 6, no details	National Museums of Scotland MEQ 189
1765 ca	William Scott	Perth	Hash spoon, with Breadalbane stamp	National Museums of Scotland MEQ 295
1765 ca	William Craw	Canongate	Tablespoons, set of 6, initials "JM", on reverse, 8 5/8" long	Huntley House Museum Edinburgh HH1800/58
1765 ca	MK conjoined	Edinburgh	Teaspoons, Scots fiddle	National Museums of Scotland MEQ 1274
1765 ca	James Welsh	Edinburgh	Salt shovel, Scots fiddle	National Museums of Scotland MEQ 992 1970.543
1765 ca	William Davie or William Dempster	Edinburgh	Mustard spoon, Hanoverian, chased with foliage	Bonhams July 18, 2002 #262
1765 ca	James Dempster	Edinburgh	Masking spoon, Scots fiddle, with initials "JC"	Private Collection

YEAR	MAKER	LOCATION	DESCRIPTION	SOURCE
1765 ca	Patrick Robertson	Edinburgh	Hash spoon, Hanoverian, engraved with monogram, 6.5oz	Sotheby's Scone Palace April 10, 1979 #48
1765/66	James Gilliland	Edinburgh	Tablespoons, Hanoverian, with initials, 12.7oz	Sotheby's Gleneagles August 30, 1982 3462
1765/66	Ker & Dempster	Edinburgh	Gravy spoons, Onslow pattern, engraved with a crest and motto	Sotheby's Gleneagles September 1, 1981 #419
1765/66	W (star) D probably William Dempster	Edinburgh	Tablespoons, Hanoverian, with crest, 8 ½" long	The Phoenix Collection
1765/66	Ker & Dempster	Edinburgh	Serving spoon, no details	National Museums of Scotland 1954.265
1765/66	WD (said to be) William Drummond	Edinburgh	Tablespoons, (Note: this mark was probably used by Dempster or Davie), no details	Jackson Marks p 549
1766 ca	James Gordon	Aberdeen	Tablespoons, set of 6, no details	National Museums of Scotland MEQ 519
1766/67	MK conjoined	Edinburgh	Tablespoon Hanoverian, script monogram, possibly James McKenzie, 8 1/8" long	The Phoenix Collection
1766/67	John Steven	Dundee	Tablespoon, no details	Jackson Marks p 549
1767/68	WD script William Dempster or William Davie	Edinburgh	Serving spoon, Onslow pattern	eBay November 5, 2005 #6576445868 NYS
1767/68	James Gilliland	Edinburgh	Tablespoons, set of 5 Hanoverian, initial "H", 8 1/8" long, 12.2oz	Nicholas Shaw Catalog 2000 p89
1767/68	Benjamin Tait	Edinburgh	Tablespoon, no details	Jackson Marks p 549
1766/67	Patrick Robertson	Edinburgh	Dessert spoons, 2	Glasgow Exhibition 1911, vol I, p118 #144
1767/68	William Taylor	Edinburgh	Hash spoon, Hanoverian, with later initials, 16 3/8" long, 7.7oz	Bonhams the Scottish Sale August 21, 2003 #72
1768/69	James Gilliland	Edinburgh	Tablespoons, set of 6 Hanoverian, with initial "W" with another spoon, 13.4oz	Sotheby's Gleneagles September 1, 1981 #405

YEAR	MAKER	LOCATION	DESCRIPTION	SOURCE
1768/69	Patrick Robertson	Edinburgh	Tablespoons, set of 11 Hanoverian, with crests, 21.8oz	Sotheby's Hopetoun House November 15, 1977 #46
1768/69	Alexander Ziegler	Edinburgh	Tablespoon, no details	Bonhams July 18, 2002 #253
1768/69	Lothian & Robertson	Edinburgh	Tablespoons, pair, Hanoverian, 2 crests and mottos	Sanda Lipton, London 1995
1768/69	Patrick Robertson	Edinburgh	Tablespoon, no details	Jackson Marks p 549
1769/70	Daniel Ker	Edinburgh	Salt spoon, no details	Jackson Marks p 659
1770/71	J B mark	Edinburgh	Sugar spoon, no details	Jackson Marks p 549
1770 ca	Patrick Robertson-Gordon	Edinburgh	Spoon, no details	Cripps p151
1770 ca	JL	Glasgow	Tablespoons, pair of Old English, initial script "C", actually a set of 8	Schredds Antiques, London 1995
1770 ca	JL	Glasgow	Dessert spoon, set, Old English, matching tablespoons above, 7" long	Schredds Antiques, London 1996 The Phoenix Collection
1770 ca	John Argo	Banff	Tablespoon, marks – BA, IA – Old English pattern	National Museums of Scotland MEQ 349-351 1956.851-853
1770 ca	Peter Spaulding	Canongate	Teaspoons, set of 3, Scots fiddle pattern	Glasgow Exhibition 1901 Jackson Marks p591
1770 ca	Michael Forrest	Canongate	Hash spoon, no details	National Museums of Scotland MEQ 363 1956.865
1770 ca	Bayne & Napier	Glasgow	Serving spoon, Hanoverian, not pictured	Sotheby's Gleneagles August 1987 #235
1770 ca	Adam Graham	Glasgow	Serving spoon, not pictured	Sotheby's Gleneagles August 1987 #237
1770 ca	Milne & Campbell	Glasgow	Tablespoons, set of 3	National Museums of Scotland H.1996.14 (1-3)
1770 ca	Milne & Campbell	Glasgow	Tablespoons, set of 4, with initials	Lyon & Turnbull, Edinburgh UK 2004 #461
1770 ca	Adam Graham	Glasgow	Tablespoons, pair, Hanoverian pattern, with script initials, with other items	Bonhams London UK 2003 #359

YEAR	MAKER	LOCATION	DESCRIPTION	SOURCE
1770 ca	James Gordon	Aberdeen	Basting spoons, pair, Old English pattern, with script initial "M", 12 " long, 5.5oz	Christie's London UK 2007 #805
1770 ca	Milne & Campbell	Glasgow	Tablespoon, Hanoverian pattern, initials removed, 8 3/8" long, 2.2oz	The Silver Spoon Club Postal Auction July 12, 2007 #102
1770 ca	James Gordon	Aberdeen	Tablespoon, Hanoverian pattern, three script initials	The Silver Spoon Club Postal Auction Feb 22, 2007 #97
1770 ca	Alexander Thompson	Aberdeen	Hash spoon, Hanoverian, with initial "M" on the back, 16" long, 6.9oz	Nicholas Shaw Catalog 2001 p69
1771/72	James Gilliland	Edinburgh	Hash spoon, Hanoverian, 15" long, 7.7oz	Bonhams the Scottish Sale August 24, 2005 358
1771/72	Patrick Robertson	Edinburgh	Tablespoon, Hanoverian, single drop, inscribed with "Richmond" on the back, 8 ½" long	Woolley & Wallis, June 28, 2000 #44
1772/73	Patrick Robertson	Edinburgh	Tablespoons, set of 11, Hanoverian pattern, with initials "H" and an earl's coronet, 25oz	Christie's Lanarkshire, UK 1998 #6
1772/73	Ker Probably for William Ker	Edinburgh	Tablespoons, set of 3, Hanoverian pattern, decorated with fruit, C-scrolls and foliage, crested and initialed, 7oz	Lyon & Turnbull, Edinburgh UK May 25, 2006 #303
1772/73	William Davie or William Dempster	Edinburgh	Tablespoon, no details	Lorentz Antiques, Toronto Canada 1991
1772/73	James Welsh	Edinburgh	Tablespoon, pair-of Hanoverian	Sotheby's NY April 14, 1982 #220
1773 ca	James Taylor	Glasgow	Hash spoon, sold with another, 10.2oz	Breadalbane Collection Sale 1935 #367
1773/74	George Auld	Edinburgh	Dessert/fruit spoons, 4	National Museums of Scotland 1996.15
1773/74	James Gilliland	Edinburgh	Hash spoon, feathered border	Hyman Collection - Colonial Williamsburg
1774/75	Alexander Aitchison & Son	Edinburgh	Tablespoon, feather edged, Old English, crest and mottos "LUCIO NON URO" and "VIRTUTE ET VALORE", 8 ½" long	The Phoenix Collection
1775 ca	Alexander Thompson	Aberdeen	Tablespoon, Hanoverian pattern, with initials " C G"	Christie's Lanarkshire UK 1997 #23

YEAR	MAKER	LOCATION	DESCRIPTION	SOURCE
1775 ca	John Argo	Banff	Teaspoon, Hanoverian pattern, 4 ¾" long, .35oz	The Silver Spoon Club Postal Auction July 12, 2007 #149
1775 ca	Alexander Thompson	Aberdeen	Spoon, no details	Luddington p 145
1775 ca	Alexander Thompson	Aberdeen	Tablespoon, worn bowl end	Medford Antiques, New Jersey USA 1994
1775 ca	John Taylor	Greenock	Tablespoon, worn end	D Robinson, New Jersey USA 1994
1775 ca	William Scott	Dundee	Hash spoon, Old English, with Breadalbane stamp, 15" long, 5.9oz	Nicholas Shaw Catalog 1999 p57
1775 ca	David Downie	Edinburgh	Teaspoon, Scots fiddle	Private Collection
1775/76	William Davie or William Dempster	Edinburgh	Dessert spoons, set of 6 Hanoverian, 6.5oz	Private Collection
1775/76	William Davie or William Dempster	Edinburgh	Dessert spoons, set of 6 Hanoverian, with crest and motto	Breadalbane Collection Sale 1935 #143
1775/76	WD script William Davie or Dempster	Edinburgh	Serving spoon, pierced Old English	National Museums of Scotland MEQ 933
1776/77	WD script William Davie or Dempster	Edinburgh	Serving spoon, Onslow pattern, crest of a double singed spur, 12" long	The Phoenix Collection
1776/77	William Davie or William Dempster	Edinburgh	Sugar spoon, no details	Jackson Marks p549
1776/77	Patrick Robertson	Edinburgh	Tablespoon, no details	DW Hyslop Glasgow Exhibition 1911 vol I, p110 #18
1777 ca	Taylor & Hamilton	Glasgow	Serving spoon, Hanoverian, 11" long, 3.4oz	Nicholas Shaw Catalog 2001 p79
1777/78	W S mark	Edinburgh	Tablespoons, 6 Old English	L Wine, Toronto Canada, 1994 The Phoenix Collection
1777/78	James Dempster	Edinburgh	Tablespoon, no details	Jackson Marks p 549
1778/79	Patrick Robertson	Edinburgh	Serving spoon, Old English, 2 arms holding an orb, 12"	Lorentz Antiques, Toronto, Canada, 1994 The Phoenix Collection

YEAR	MAKER	LOCATION	DESCRIPTION	SOURCE
1778/79	Alexander Aitchison	Edinburgh	Tablespoons, 5 Old English	Louis Wine Antiques, Toronto CA, 1991
1778/79	James Hewitt	Edinburgh	Gravy spoons, pair, with the crest and motto of Coutts	Private Collection
1778/79	James Hewitt	Edinburgh	Dessert spoons, set of 12	Private Collection
1778/79	Alexander Ziegler	Edinburgh	Teaspoon, Scots fiddle	Private Collection
1780 ca	Robert Gray	Glasgow	Tablespoon, Old English pattern, with another	Lyon & Turnbull, Edin UK 2007 #258
1780 ca	William Scott	Dundee	Hash spoon, no details	Sotheby's Gleneagles August 1987 #242
1780 ca	Milne & Campbell	Glasgow	Tablespoons, 6, not pictured	Sotheby's Hopetoun House, April 1988 #11
1780 ca	Hugh Ross	Tain	Masking spoon, no details	National Museums of Scotland K.2003.1048
1780 ca	William Scott	Dundee	Tablespoons, set of 12 feather edged, crest and motto "PRAETIO PRUDENTIA", 8 ¾" long, 25.5oz	Nicholas Shaw Catalog 2000 p89
1780 ca	WM mark		Teaspoons, set of 5 Scots fiddle, 4 7/8" long	The Phoenix Collection
1780 ca	JL	Glasgow	Tablespoon, Old English pattern, initials "IP", with other spoons	Christie's London UK 2007 #474
1780/81	William Davie or William Dempster	Edinburgh	Dessert spoons, set of 4, feather edged, Old English, with a crest and motto	Sotheby's Gleneagles August 29, 1978 #376
1780/81	W & P Cunningham I	Edinburgh	Tablespoon, no details	Jackson Marks p 550
1780/81	William Davie or William Dempster	Edinburgh	Dessert spoons, set of 4, feather edged, Old English, with a crest and motto	Sotheby's Gleneagles August 29, 1978 #376
1780/81	Patrick Robertson	Edinburgh	Tablespoons, set of 3	National Museums of Scotland H.1996.8
1780/81	Patrick Robertson	Edinburgh	Serving spoon, no details	National Museums of Scotland MEQ 526
1780/81	W & P Cunningham I	Edinburgh	Spoons, set of 8, no details	National Museums of Scotland L.396.33-33g

YEAR	MAKER	LOCATION	DESCRIPTION	SOURCE
1781/82	Archibald Ochiltree	Edinburgh	Tablespoons, pair of dog nose, rat tailed	Sotheby's Scone Palace April 10, 1978 #106
1781/82	Taylor & Howden	Edinburgh	Tablespoons, with later chased handles, 8oz	Bonhams the Scottish Sale August 24, 2005 #49
1782/83	Francis Howden	Edinburgh	Spoon, no details	Jackson Marks p 550
1782/83	William Dempster or William Davie	Edinburgh	Gravy spoons, set of 4, pointed Old English pattern, with a stag's head crest and motto	Private Collection
1782/83	Patrick Robertson	Edinburgh	Tablespoons, Old English, with crest and motto, 27.5oz	Sotheby's Gleneagles August 29, 1983 #385
1782/83	James Wright	Glasgow	Tablespoons, set of 6, 12.7oz	Breadalbane Collection Sale 1935 #146
1783 ca	James Smith	Aberdeen	Tablespoons, set of 3	National Museums of Scotland MEQ 526
1783/84	Alexander Gardner	Edinburgh	Serving spoons, pair, Onslow pattern	National Museums of Scotland MEQ 920-921 1921.482-483
1783/84	Robert Bowman	Edinburgh	Spoon, no details	Jackson Marks p 550
1783/84	James Welsh	Edinburgh	Tablespoon, pointed Old English pattern, with script initials "JB", 7 5/8" long	The Phoenix Collection
1783/84	Taylor & Howden	Edinburgh	Tablespoon, Old English, with script initial "J", 8 5/8" long	The Phoenix Collection
1783/84	Neil Paton	Edinburgh	Tablespoon, sailing ship crest and motto	Thomas Roddick & Medcalf, Edinburgh UK Oct 31, 2006 #54
1784/85	David Marshall	Edinburgh	Tablespoon, Hanoverian pattern, with incuse mark, with other spoons	Christie's London UK 2004 #125
1784/85	Alexander Edmonstoun	Edinburgh	Teaspoon, Scots fiddle, with incuse duty mark, with the initials "NF"	Private Collection
1784/85	David Marshall	Edinburgh	Teaspoons, set of 6 feather edge, Old English, 2.3oz	Breadalbane Collection Sale 1935 #144
1784/85	James Gilliland	Edinburgh	Teaspoon, pointed Old English pattern, feather edge, with initials "GT"	The Phoenix Collection
1784/85	Alexander Spence	Edinburgh	Teaspoons, pair, fully marked Scots fiddle pattern	National Museums of Scotland MEQ 917-918 1968.479-480

YEAR	MAKER	LOCATION	DESCRIPTION	SOURCE
1784/85	W & P Cunningham I	Edinburgh	Serving Spoon, no details	National Museums of Scotland A.1963.441
1784/85	Peter Mathie	Edinburgh	Hash spoon, no details	National Museums of Scotland MEQ 775
1784/85	James Hewitt	Edinburgh	Tablespoons, 11 Old English, initial "W"	JH Bourdon-Smith London, 1993
1784/85	Alexander Gardner	Edinburgh	Hash spoon, Old English pattern, engraved initials	Christie's October 19, 1988 #14
1785 ca	James McEwan	Glasgow	Tablespoon, Hanoverian, with script initial "F", 8 5/8" long	The Phoenix Collection
1785 ca	David Edmund	Edinburgh	Large Teaspoons, set of 6, Scots fiddle pattern	Thomas Roddick & Medcalf, Edinburgh UK Oct 31, 2006 #54
1785/86	James Hewitt	Edinburgh	Tablespoons, set of 3, pointed Old English pattern, with others	Gorringes LLP, East Sussex UK 2006 #1545
1785/86	Thomas Duffus	Edinburgh	Dessert spoons, set of 6, pointed Old English pattern, with a crest and motto, with another spoon	Bonhams London UK 2007 #202
1785/86	Alexander Gardner	Edinburgh	Serving spoon, Old English, 12 5/8" long, 3.5oz	M Klein Auction, Chicago USA September 12, 2004 #116
1785/86	James Dempster or James Douglas	Edinburgh	Teaspoons, set of 12, no details	The Maple Swan Collection
1785/86	David Marshall	Edinburgh	Tablespoon, no details	Jackson Marks p 550
1786/87	Alexander Gardner	Edinburgh	Hash spoon, not pictured	Sotheby's Gleneagles August 1990 #9
1786/87	Alexander Ziegler	Edinburgh	Dessert spoons, 2, Old English pattern	Sotheby's Gleneagles August 1993 #14
1788/89	William Davie or William Dempster	Edinburgh	Gravy spoons, pair, no details	The Maple Swan Collection
1788/89	James Gilliland	Edinburgh	Tablespoons, set of 6 Old English, with the initial "B: and numbered 1-6, 11.3oz	Sotheby's Scone Palace April 19, 1977 #70
1788/89	Neil Paton	Edinburgh	Gravy spoons, pair of pointed Old English pattern, with the initial "A"	Private Collection
1789/90	William Davie or	Edinburgh	Gravy spoons, pair of Old English, with a crest and motto, 5.9oz	Sotheby's Gleneagles August 29,

YEAR	MAKER	LOCATION	DESCRIPTION	SOURCE
	William Dempster			
1789/90	James Hewitt	Edinburgh	Dessert spoon, pointed Old English pattern, engraved with "E", 6.7oz	Sotheby's Gleneagles August 39, 1978 #383
1789/90	Francis Howden	Edinburgh	Tablespoon, 3 Pointed Old English pattern, with initials, 6.2oz	Sotheby's Scone Palace April 23, 1982 #477
1789/90	Patrick Robertson	Edinburgh	Gravy spoons, set of 4 pointed Old English pattern, with the crest of a flaming rock and a motto	Sotheby's Scone Palace April 23, 1979 #48
1789/90	Patrick Robertson	Edinburgh	Serving spoons, pair, pointed Old English pattern, crest and motto of Campbell "Follow me", initials "CC" in a badge/cartouche, 12 ½" long	Private Collection
1789/90	Patrick Robertson	Edinburgh	Hash spoons, set of 4, engraved with initials, 12oz	M Rafael, NYC USA 1993 The Phoenix Collection
1789/90	Alexander Gardner	Edinburgh	Hash spoon, no details	Christie's October 19, 1988 #16
1789/90	Alexander Ziegler	Edinburgh	Stuffing spoons, pair of Old English	Jackson Marks p 550
1789/90	Patrick Robertson	Edinburgh	Tablespoons, set of 12, pointed Old English pattern, with a crest and motto, 26oz	Firestone & Parsons, Boston MA, USA 1993
1790 ca	John Argo	Banff	Hash spoon, no details	Christie's Lanarkshire UK 1998 #7
1790 ca	John Leslie	Aberdeen	Gravy spoon, Old English, with initial "M", 11 ½" long, 2.7oz	National Museums of Scotland MEQ 471
1790 ca	James Cornfute	Perth	Spoons, pair, pointed Old English, no details	Nicholas Shaw Catalog 2005 p92
1790 ca	James Cornfute	Perth	Tablespoons, 12 pointed Old English, no details	Sotheby's Gleneagles August 1987 #241
1790 ca	Richard Dickson	Perth	Spoons, 5, no details	Sotheby's Gleneagles August 1987 #244
1790 ca	James Cornfute	Perth	Spoons, pair, pointed Old English, no details	Sotheby's Gleneagles August 1991 #14
1790 ca	Francis Howden	Edinburgh	Teaspoon, pointed Old English pattern, bright cut engraved with script initials "NH", 5 ½" long, .45oz	Sotheby's Gleneagles August 1987 #241
				The Silver Spoon Club Postal Auction July 12, 2007 #146

YEAR	MAKER	LOCATION	DESCRIPTION	SOURCE
1790 ca	Alexander Gardner	Edinburgh	Teaspoon, pointed Old English pattern, bright cut engraved initials script "MW", 5" long	The Silver Spoon Club Postal Auction April 21, 2006 #38
1790 ca	John Leslie	Aberdeen	Tablespoon, feather edge pattern, script initials "AMH", 8 3/8" long, 2.3 oz	The Silver Spoon Club Postal Auction July 12, 2007 #125
1790 ca	Patrick Robertson	Edinburgh	Spice sifter spoon, pointed Old English pattern, 4 ¼" long, .32oz	The Silver Spoon Club Postal Auction July 12, 2007 #63
1790/91	WA Possibly William Auld	Edinburgh	Tablespoons, set of 6, pointed Old English pattern, engraved with a monogram, 11oz	Christie's Lanarkshire UK 1997 #600
1790/91	Alexander Spence	Edinburgh	Dessert spoons, set of 10, pointed Old English pattern, with contemporary initials	Christie's Lanarkshire UK 1999 #776
1790/91	Patrick Robertson	Edinburgh	Serving spoons, pair, engraved with initials	Christie's October 19, 1988 #15
1790/91	William Robertson	Edinburgh	Serving spoons, pair, engraved with initials	Christie's October 19, 1988 #15
1790/91	Alexander Henderson	Edinburgh	Dessert spoons, 6-8 pointed Old English	Asprey London 1991
1790/91	Francis Howden	Edinburgh	Tablespoons, 6, pointed Old English pattern, initials "HS"	Sotheby's Gleneagles August 1993 #11
1790/93	W & P Cunningham I	Edinburgh	Spoons, 6, pointed Old English	Shrubsole, London UK 1991
1790/91	Francis Howden	Edinburgh	Gravy spoons, pair of pointed Old English pattern, with the initial "S"	London Silver Vaults Private Collection
1791/92	Alexander Gardner	Edinburgh	Tablespoons, set of 12 Old English, with crest and motto, 26oz	Sotheby's Gleneagles August 31, 1992 #16
1791/95	Alexander Ziegler	Edinburgh	Tablespoons, pointed Old English pattern, with the initial "K", 11.8oz	Sotheby's Blair Castle September 12, 1980 #141
1791/92	Francis Howden	Edinburgh	Serving spoons, pair, no details	Sotheby's Hopetoun House April 1989 #7
1792/93	William Robertson	Edinburgh	Tablespoon, no details	DW Hyslop Glasgow Exhibition 1911, vol I, p111, #20
1793/94	Robert Gray	Glasgow Edinburgh assay	Serving spoon, Old English, with the initial "F"	M Getz Antiques, Washington DC, USA, 1993

YEAR	MAKER	LOCATION	DESCRIPTION	SOURCE
1793/94	Alexander Gardner	Edinburgh	Dessert spoon, pointed Old English	Levine, Inc. Alexandria VA USA, 1994
1794/95	William Robertson	Edinburgh	Tablespoon, no details	Jackson Marks p 550
1794/95	George Christie	Edinburgh	Tablespoons, 3 Hanoverian, initial script "E", 8 ½" long	Goodwin's Edinburgh UK 1993 The Phoenix Collection
1794/95	William Robertson	Edinburgh	Serving spoons, pair, no details	The Maple Swan Collection
1795 ca	James Douglas	Dundee	Teaspoons, set of pointed Old English pattern, with script initials "BN"	National Museums of Scotland MEQ 895
1795 ca	William Byres	Banff	Teaspoons, 4, no details	M Raphael, NYC USA 1993
1795 ca	James Douglas	Dundee	Teaspoon, pointed Old English pattern, script initial, 5 ¼" long, .35oz	The Silver Spoon Club Postal Auction July 12, 2007 #148
1795 ca	Alexander Ziegler	Edinburgh	Teaspoon, pointed Old English pattern, bright cut engraved with script initials, 5 9/16" long, .35oz	The Silver Spoon Club Postal Auction July 12, 2007 #140
1796/97	Alexander Spence	Edinburgh	Tablespoon, no details	Jackson Marks p 550
1796/97	Robert Gray	Glasgow Edinburgh assay	Hash spoon, no details	Hyman Collection – Colonial Williamsburg
1796/97	James McKay	Edinburgh	Gravy spoons, pair of fiddle and thread pattern, crest of Drummond, 7.5oz	Sotheby's Gleneagles August 27, 1979 #228
1796/97	William Robertson	Edinburgh	Tablespoons, set of 6 pointed Old English pattern, with initials, 13.4oz	Sotheby's Blair Castle September 12, 1980 #JE
1796/97	William Robertson	Edinburgh	Dessert spoons, set of 12, with the initial "H"	Private Collection
1796/97	Alexander Spence	Edinburgh	Spoons, set of 6 Old English & thread pattern, with the initials "WD"	Private Collection
1797/98	Alexander Spence	Edinburgh	Gravy spoons, pair, no details	Glasgow Exhibition 1911, vol I, p112, #39
1797/98	HW	Edinburgh assay	Dessert spoons, set of 11 Old English, with 2 sets of initials, 10.5oz	Sotheby's Gleneagles August 29, 1983 #382

YEAR	MAKER	LOCATION	DESCRIPTION	SOURCE
1797/98	Alexander Gardner & Co	Edinburgh	Tablespoons, Old English, engraved with initials "JD"	Bonhams the Scottish Sale August 24, 2005 #53
1797/98	Robert Gray	Glasgow Edinburgh assay	Serving spoon, pointed Old English pattern, crest and motto "CERTUM PETE FINUM", 12" long	The Phoenix Collection
1798/99	Thomas Duffus	Edinburgh	Spoon, no details	Jackson Marks p 550
1798/99	W & P Cunningham I	Edinburgh	Gravy spoon, pointed Old English pattern	Christie's Lanarkshire UK 1998 #550
1798/99 and 1799/1800	Alexander Ziegler	Edinburgh	Tablespoons, set of 12, pointed Old English pattern, with a later initial, 22.5oz	Christie's London UK 2005 #107
1799/1800	Patrick Robertson	Edinburgh	Serving spoon, date letter double struck and likely wrong, too late for that maker, 12 ½" long	Sotheby's Gleneagles August #13
1799/1800	Alexander Gardner & Co	Edinburgh	Spoon, no details	Jackson Marks p 550
1799/1800	Robert Keay I Assayed – Edinburgh	Perth	Hash spoon, crest and motto	Hyman Collection – Colonial Williamsburg
1799/1800	Matthew Craw	Edinburgh	Tablespoons, set of 4, Hanoverian pattern, initialed, 7.5oz	Humberts Fine Art, Hawkhurst 2007 #313
1800 ca	Edward Livingstone	Dundee	Teaspoon, set of 6, pointed Old English, 5 with script initials "RI/IJ/K" and one with script "K", with other spoons	Bonhams London UK 2005 #36
1800 ca	William Ritchie	Perth	Teaspoons, pairs, pointed Old English, initialed	Woolley & Wallis, 2007 #144
1800 ca	William Clark	Greenock	Tablespoon, pointed Old English, with Breadalbane stamp	National Museums of Scotland MEQ 48
1800 ca	James Sinclaire	Wick	Spoon, fiddle pattern	Luddington p145 Gubbins Collection
1800 ca	Alexander Ross	Dingwall	Spoon, no details	Luddington p145 Gubbins Collection
1800 ca	Charles Fowler	Elgin	Spoon, fiddle pattern	Luddington p145 Gubbins Collection

YEAR	MAKER	LOCATION	DESCRIPTION	SOURCE
1800 ca	William Ritchie	Perth	Dessert spoons, 6, no details	Sotheby's Gleneagles August 1991 #14
1800 ca	John Keith	Banff	Teaspoon, Old English	Sotheby's Gleneagles August 2003 #6
1800 ca	James Douglas	Dundee	Dessert spoons, set of 7 Old English	Sotheby's Gleneagles August 1993 #10
1800 ca	Nathaniel Gillet	Aberdeen	Dessert spoons, set of 6 Old English, with the initial "H"	Sotheby's Gleneagles August 1993 #12
1800 ca	Nathaniel Gillet	Aberdeen	Teaspoons, set of 6	Sotheby's Gleneagles August 1993 #12
1800 ca	John Leslie	Aberdeen	Teaspoons, 2 Old English	Sotheby's Gleneagles August 1993 #12
1800 ca	J McQueen	Banff	Teaspoons, 3 Old English	Sotheby's Gleneagles August 1993 #12
1800 ca	Peter Lambert	Banff	Teaspoons, 2 Old English	Sotheby's Gleneagles August 1993 #12
1800 ca	AC	Greenock	Teaspoon, Old English	Sotheby's Gleneagles August 1993 #12
1800 ca	AC	Greenock	Teaspoon, Scots fiddle pattern, also with "S" mark	Sotheby's Gleneagles August 1993 #12
1800 ca	James Erskine	Aberdeen	Serving spoon, no details	National Museums of Scotland MEQ 895
1800 ca	John Keith	Banff	Dessert spoons, set of 4	National Museums of Scotland MEQ 484-487
1800 ca	James Erskine	Aberdeen	Gravy straining spoon	National Museums of Scotland MEQ 510
1800 ca	WM	Edinburgh	Salt spoons, pair of fiddle pattern, script initial "W", 3 ¾" long	The Phoenix Collection
1800 ca	AC	Greenock	Teaspoon, pointed Old English pattern, with script initials "MT", 5 ½" long	The Phoenix Collection
1800 ca	James Erskine	Aberdeen	Teaspoons, set of 5, pointed Old English pattern, engraved "A & IS", sold with a masking spoon by another	Christie's London UK 2006 #537

YEAR	MAKER	LOCATION	DESCRIPTION	SOURCE
1800 ca	James Pearson	Dumfries	Teaspoon, Oar pattern, script initials, 5 1/3" long, .42oz	The Silver Spoon Club Postal Auction July 12, 2007 #151
1800 ca	John Argo	Banff	Sugar spoon, oar pattern, script initials, 5 9/16" long, .32	The Silver Spoon Club Postal Auction July 12, 2007 #147
1800 ca	John Heron	Greenock	Tablespoons, set of 6, pointed Old English, initial "B"	The Silver Spoon Club Postal Auction June 23, 2006 #70
1800/01	IM	Edinburgh	Serving spoon, pointed Old English pattern, initial "B", 12" long	Gorringes LLP, Lewes 2007 #1481
1800/01	John Ziegler	Edinburgh	Hash spoon, no details	Jackson Marks p 550
1800/01	Alexander Ziegler	Edinburgh	Dessert spoons, set of 9 Old English	Sotheby's Gleneagles August 1993 #14
1800/01	Lothian & Robertson	Edinburgh	Tablespoons, set of 6, date too late for these makers, 11.6oz	Sotheby's Hopetoun House, November 13, 1978 397
1801/02	Francis Howden	Edinburgh	Tablespoon, no details	Jackson Marks p550
1801/02	Francis Howden	Edinburgh	Stuffing spoon, 2oz 10d	Warman PG 27th ed, 1993 p585
1801/02	Alexander Henderson	Edinburgh	Serving spoon, Old English, crest and motto "CAVE ADSUM", 12" long, 3.4oz	Nicholas Shaw Catalog 2001 p79
1801/02	IM	Edinburgh	Serving spoon, no details	National Museums of Scotland MEQ 894
1802/03	Alexander Ziegler	Edinburgh	Serving spoon, pointed Old English pattern, with coat of arms, 12 ¾" long, 3.5oz	Nicholas Shaw Catalog 2001 p79
1802/03	Matthew Craw	Edinburgh	Serving spoons, pair, pointed Old English pattern, with crest and motto, another pair also	Sanda Lipton, London 1995
1802/03	Matthew Craw	Edinburgh	Tablespoon, no details	Jackson Marks p 550
1802/03	Alexander Henderson	Edinburgh	Serving spoons, pair, no details	S Wyler, NY, 1992
1802/03	WM	Edinburgh	Hash spoon, Old English, with script initial "A"	Floyd & Ritas, Toronto Canada, 1994
1802/03	WM	Edinburgh	Tablespoons, pair of Old English	Whirligig Antiques, Austin TX USA, 1993

YEAR	MAKER	LOCATION	DESCRIPTION	SOURCE
1802/05	Robert Gray	Glasgow Edinburgh assay	Dessert spoon, 6 Old English, with initial "J"	Sotheby's Gleneagles August 1993 #10
1802/03	Alexander Henderson	Edinburgh	Basting spoon, pointed Old English pattern, with others	Christie's Lanarkshire UK 1997 #98
1804/05	John Ziegler	Edinburgh	Dessert spoon, pointed Old English pattern, script initials "RMW", with other spoons	Bonhams London UK 2003 #221
1804/05	Alexander Edmonston	Edinburgh	Serving spoon, pointed Old English pattern, with crest and motto	Mary Cooke London 1995
1804/05	Robert Gray & Son	Glasgow Edinburgh assay	Serving spoon, Old English, 12 ¾" long	M Getz Antiques, Washington DC USA, 1993
1804/05	Alexander Spence	Edinburgh	Spoons, pair, inscribed with initials "JB" or "IB", no details	High Museum of Art, Atlanta GA USA 68.1000.21 A & B
1805/06	John Ziegler	Edinburgh	Tablespoon, Old English pattern, script initials "WE/E", 5" long, 2.3oz	The Silver Spoon Club Postal Auction July 12, 2007 #114
1805/06	Mitchell & Russel	Glasgow Edinburgh assay	Spoon, no details	Jackson Marks p 550
1805/06	Alexander Henderson	Edinburgh	Serving spoon, no details	National Museums of Scotland H.1996.38
1806/07	Alexander Henderson	Edinburgh	Teaspoon, pointed Old English pattern	Silver Queen, VA USA 1992
1806/07	WC	Edinburgh	Tablespoon, fiddle pattern	E Austin, Charleston SC USA 1983
1806/07	Robert Gray & Son	Glasgow Edinburgh assay	Teaspoon, set of 12 Old English, initials "JW", 5 3/8" long, 5.2oz	Sanda Lipton London #3076
1807/08	James McKay	Edinburgh	Salt spoon, no details	The Maple Swan Collection

YEAR	MAKER	LOCATION	DESCRIPTION	SOURCE
1807/08	John Ziegler	Edinburgh	Hash spoon, Old English, strainer grooved, with script initial "A"	Floyd & Ritas Toronto Canada 1994
1807/08	Francis Howden	Edinburgh	Dessert spoon, 6 Old English, with initials "HS"	Sotheby's Gleneagles August 1993 #11
1807/08	William Hanney	Paisley Edinburgh assay	Teaspoon, Paisley fiddle pattern	E Austin, Charleston SC USA 1983
1807/08	Robert Gray & Son	Glasgow Edinburgh assay	Teaspoon, Old English, with script initials "MH"	The Phoenix Collection
1808/09	WM	Edinburgh	Hash spoon, fiddle pattern, with script initials "RN"	Lorentz Antiques Toronto Canada 1991
1808/09	Alexander Henderson	Edinburgh	Serving spoon, pair, with crest	D Voth NYC USA 1993
1808/09	Alexander Edmonston	Edinburgh	Tablespoon, no details	The Maple Swan Collection
1808/09	James Nasmyth	Edinburgh	Tablespoon, later decorated as a berry spoon	The Maple Swan Collection
1809/10	N & D	Edinburgh	Tablespoon, later decorated as a berry spoon	The Maple Swan Collection
1809/10	ID or LG	Edinburgh	Teaspoons, pair of fiddle pattern, 5 ¼" long	The Collection, Trumansburg NY USA 1995 The Phoenix Collection
1809/10	Z for Ziegler	Edinburgh	Tablespoons, pair of fiddle pattern, with crest of sun, script initial "P"	Floyd & Ritas Toronto Canada 1994
1809/10	James McKay	Edinburgh	Dessert spoons, 6 Old English	Scarlet Fox, VA USA 994
1809/10	Alexander Henderson	Edinburgh	Dessert spoons, 6 fiddle pattern	Louis Wine, Toronto Canada 1991
1810 ca	William Constable	Dundee	Serving spoons, pair of pointed Old English, script initial "F", 12 ½" long	National Museums of Scotland MEQ 239-240 1956.741-742
1810 ca	WA	Forres	Spoon, fiddle pattern, no details	Luddington p145 Gubbins Collection

YEAR	MAKER	LOCATION	DESCRIPTION	SOURCE
1810 ca	William Jamieson	Aberdeen	Tablespoons, 6 Old English, with initial "D"	Sotheby's Gleneagles August 1993 #8
1810 ca	WC	Greenock	Teaspoon, pointed Old English pattern, script initial "M?", 5 ½" long, .45oz	The Silver Spoon Club Postal Auction July 12, 2007 #21
1810 ca	William Jamieson	Aberdeen	Dessert spoon, fiddle pattern, script initial "M", 6 ½" long, .9oz	The Silver Spoon Club Postal Auction July 12, 2007 #23
1810 ca	David Gray	Dumfries	Teaspoon, oar pattern, interlocked script initials "AK", 5 ¾" long, .58oz	The Silver Spoon Club Postal Auction July 12, 2007 #24
1810 ca	AM	Perth	Egg spoons, set of 4, Old English pattern, monogrammed, sold with other items	Bonhams London UK 2006, #187
1810/11	John McDonald	Edinburgh	Tablespoon, Old English pattern, retailed by Hay, script initials, crest?, 8 ½" long	The Silver Spoon Club Postal Auction April 21, 2006, #21
1810/11	AR	Edinburgh assay	Tablespoon, fiddle pattern, with script initials "HR"	Lorentz Antiques Toronto Canada 1994
1810/11	A R	Edinburgh assay	Teaspoons, set of 5, no details	The Maple Swan Collection
1812/13	William Cunningham	Edinburgh	Salt spoons, 2, no details	The Maple Swan Collection
1813/14 and 1820/21	Francis Howden	Edinburgh	Dessert spoons, pointed Old English pattern, script initials "RMW", with another	Bonhams London UK 2003 #221
1813/14	Francis Howden	Edinburgh	Salt spoons, pair, no details	Sotheby's Gleneagles August 1988 #124
1814/15	James McKay	Edinburgh	Tablespoon, fiddle pattern	F Milwee, Washington DC USA, 1994
1815 ca	WS	Peterhead	Spoon, fiddle pattern, no details	Luddington, p145 Gubbins Collection
1815 ca	Robert Keay I	Perth	Tablespoons, pair of fiddle pattern, with script initial "T", 8 7/8" long	Hyde Park Center NY USA 1993 The Phoenix Collection
1815 ca	Jameson & Naughton	Inverness	Dessert spoon, fiddle pattern, 6 7/8" long	The Silver Spoon Club Postal Auction July 12, 2007 #83

YEAR	MAKER	LOCATION	DESCRIPTION	SOURCE
1815/16	Not available	Edinburgh	Tablespoons, King's pattern, with script initials "AH"	Antique Emporium, Raleigh NC USA, 1995
1815/16	Robert Keay I	Perth Edinburgh assay	Hash spoon, oar pattern, with a crest	Hyman Collection – Colonial Williamsburg
1816/17	Robert Keay I	Perth Edinburgh assay	Hash spoon, fiddle pattern	Hyman Collection – Colonial Williamsburg
1816/17	Charles Dalgleish	Edinburgh	Salt spoons, 3, fiddle pattern, retailed by Watson	M Getz Antiques, Washington DC USA 1993
1817/18	Mitchell & Russell	Glasgow	Hash spoon, no details	Perdue & Podner 1991
1818/19	Charles Dalgleish	Edinburgh	Salt spoon, no details	The Maple Swan Collection
1819/20	John Heron	Paisley	Hash spoon, shell, fiddle pattern, with initials	Hyman Collection – Colonial Williamsburg
1820 ca	John McQueen	Banff	Spoons, fiddle pattern	Luddington p145 Gubbins Collection
1820 ca	Adam Burgess	Dumfries	Spoon, Old English pattern	Luddington p145 Gubbins Collection
1820 ca	Alexander Stewart	Inverness	Tablespoons, 6, no details	Sotheby's Gleneagles August 1991 #10
1820 ca	William Jamieson	Aberdeen	Serving spoon, no details	Sotheby's Hopetoun House April 1989 #8
1820 ca	David Gray	Dumfries	Hash spoon, fiddle pattern	Shrubsole, NY 1993
1820 ca	Mark Hinchsliffe	Dumfries	Teaspoons, set of 6, oar pattern, with other spoons	Christie's London UK 2007 #804
1820 ca	William Jamieson	Aberdeen	Teaspoon, fiddle pattern, script initials, .42oz	The Silver Spoon Club Postal Auction July 12, 2007 #184
1820 ca	John McQueen	Banff	Spoon, oar pattern, script initials "W", table or tea?	The Silver Spoon Club Postal Auction April 21, 2006 #23

YEAR	MAKER	LOCATION	DESCRIPTION	SOURCE
1820 ca	David Gray	Dumfries	Salt spoon, fiddle pattern, script initial "P", 3 ¾" long, .32oz	The Silver Spoon Club Postal Auction July 12, 2007 #47
1820 ca	Alexander Cameron	Dundee	Teaspoon, fiddle pattern, script initials "HG", 5 2/3" long, .45oz	The Silver Spoon Club Postal Auction July 12, 2007 #25
1820 ca	James Davie	Greenock	Teaspoon, fiddle pattern, script initials, 5 2/3" long, .48oz	The Silver Spoon Club Postal Auction July 12, 2007 #22
1820/21	Charles Dalgleish	Edinburgh	Mustard spoon, no details	The Maple Swan Collection
1820/21	Francis Howden	Edinburgh	Hash spoon, no details	Gebelein Antiques VT USA 1993
1820/21	Charles Dalgleish	Edinburgh	Teaspoons, set of 6, no details	The Maple Swan Collection
1821/22	George Fenwick	Edinburgh	Mustard spoons, 2, no details	The Maple Swan Collection
1823/24	Mitchell & Son	Glasgow	Serving spoon, fiddle pattern	M Getz Antiques, Washington DC USA, 1993
1823/24	William Hannay	Paisley Glasgow assay	Teaspoon, 2, no details	E Austin Charleston, SC USA 1993
1823/24	Marshall & Son	Edinburgh	Teaspoon, fiddle pattern, with plow crest, 5 3/8" long	The Phoenix Collection
1824/25	AW	Edinburgh	Mustard spoon, no details	The Maple Swan Collection
1824/25	Not available		Hash spoon, no details	Gebelein, VT USA 1993
1824/25	M & S	Glasgow	Spoon, no details	Sotheby's Hopetoun House April 1988 #11
1824/25	PG	Edinburgh	Serving spoon, fiddle pattern	Hyde Park Center, NY USA 1993
1825/26	W & P Cunningham II	Edinburgh	Teaspoons, 6, no details	Sotheby's Hopetoun House April 1988 #20
1826/27	Robert Gray & Son	Edinburgh	Teaspoons, 6 fiddle pattern	Scarlet Fox, VA USA 1993
1826/27	AW	Edinburgh	Serving spoons, pair, fiddle pattern	S Wyler, NY USA 1992
1827/28	AW	Edinburgh	Salt spoon, no details	The Maple Swan Collection

YEAR	MAKER	LOCATION	DESCRIPTION	SOURCE
1827/28	W R	Glasgow	Salt spoon, King's pattern	M Getz Antiques, Washington DC USA 1992
1827/28	Peter Aiken	Glasgow	Basting spoon, Hanoverian pattern, 11 ½" long, 3oz	Bonhams London UK 2004 #376
1828/29	Peter Aiken	Glasgow	Teaspoon, no details	Silver Queen, VA USA 1992
1828/29	WM over AM	Edinburgh	Mustard spoon, King's pattern, crest and motto	V Gordin Toronto Canada 1994
1829 ca	William Whitcross	Aberdeen	Teaspoon, fiddle pattern, script initials, 5 5/8" long, .64oz	The Silver Spoon Club Postal Auction July 12, 2007 #185
1830 ca	William Jamieson	Aberdeen	Dessert spoon, fiddle pattern, with initial "D"	Sotheby's Gleneagles August 1993 #8
1830 ca	David Gray	Dumfries	Teaspoons, 6 fiddle pattern	Silver Plus, VA USA 1993
1830 ca	George Booth	Aberdeen	Sugar spoon, fiddle pattern, script initial "B", foliated, 5 ½" long	The Silver Spoon Club Postal Auction April 26, 2006 #164
1830/31	Adam Elder or Alexander Edmonston	Edinburgh	Teaspoons, 5 fiddle pattern, 5 3/8" long	Ithaca, NY Show 1992
1830/31	DE	Edinburgh	Teaspoon, fiddle pattern, 5 3/8" long	Ithaca, NY Show 1994
1830/31	James Nasmyth	Edinburgh	Tea caddy spoon	Hobart House, CT USA 1994
1830/31	James McKay	Edinburgh	Tablespoons, pair, no details	The Maple Swan Collection
1831/32	John Law II	Edinburgh	Tablespoons, pair, fiddle pattern, 8 ¾" long, 4.5oz	The Silver Spoon Club Postal Auction July 12, 2007 #85
1834/35	John Mildridge	Glasgow	Teaspoon, 6, no details	Silver Plus, VA USA 1993
1835 ca	Alexander Mollison	Aberdeen	Masking spoon, pointed Old English pattern, engraved "A & IS", sold with matching five teaspoons by another	Christie's London UK 2006 #537
1835/36	James McKay	Edinburgh	Salt spoon, King's pattern	M Getz Antiques, Washington, DC USA 1993
1835/36	WR	Glasgow	Mustard spoon, no details	Antique Mall San Antonio, TX USA 1998

YEAR	MAKER	LOCATION	DESCRIPTION	SOURCE
1836/37	George Whyle	Glasgow	Sifter spoon, Old English pattern, 6 7/8" long, 1.2oz	The Silver Spoon Club Postal Auction July 12, 2007 #30
1837/38	J & W Marshall	Edinburgh	Mustard spoon, fiddle pattern, gilded bowl, with a crest, 4 1/8" long, .5oz	The Silver Spoon Club Postal Auction July 12, 2007 #86
1837/38	Peter Aiken	Glasgow	Sugar sifter, no details	Sotheby's Gleneagles August 1993 #6
1840 ca	Robert Keay II	Perth	Teaspoon, oar pattern, script initials "EB", 5 ½" long, .42oz	The Silver Spoon Club Postal Auction July 12, 2007 #26
1846/47	Samuel Weir	Edinburgh	Salt spoon, fiddle pattern	The Silver Spoon Club Postal Auction Feb 22, 2007 #35
1850/51	Charles Robb	Edinburgh	Dessert spoons, set of 3	National Museums of Scotland MEQ 1016
1854/55	Robert Keay II	Perth Glasgow assay	Teaspoon, single struck Queens pattern, 5 ½" long, .68oz	The Silver Spoon Club Postal Auction July 12, 2007 #28
1856/57	JL	Glasgow	Dessert spoons, 6 shell pattern	Salt City Antique Show, Syracuse NY USA 1993
1858/59	Charles Robb & Son	Edinburgh	Teaspoons, set of 12, 5 ½"	The Phoenix Collection
1865 ca	MacKay	Elgin	Serving spoon, fiddle pattern, monogram probably "HR"	The Phoenix Collection
1866/67	JW	Edinburgh	Teaspoons, 6, King's pattern	Silver Plus Virginia USA 1993
1888/89	R Tennant	Glasgow	Teaspoon, set of 6, fiddle pattern, numbered 5,7,9,10,11, 12, with block letters "N.S.", 4 2/3" long, 2.3oz	The Silver Spoon Club Postal Auction July 12, 2007 #126
1903/04	R & W Sorley	Glasgow	Teaspoons, set of 6, oar pattern, 5 ½" long, 2.7oz	The Silver Spoon Club Postal Auction July 12, 2007 #127

Sugar Tongs

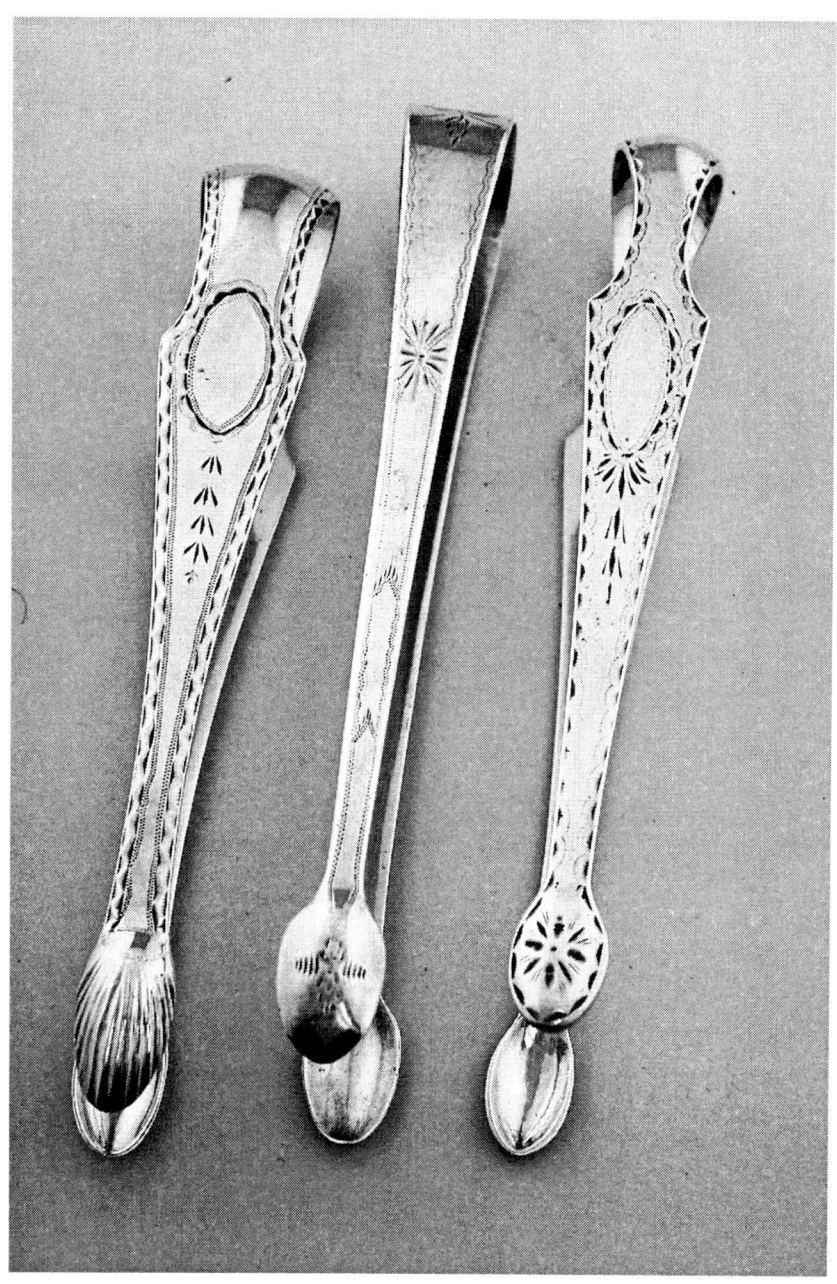

Plate 31. Three Sugar Tongs
Left – 1790 ca by Peter Mathie, Edinburgh
Center – 1800 ca by James Erskine, Aberdeen
Right – 1790 ca by PH, Paisley
Courtesy of a private collector. Photograph by Janice M Dietert.

YEAR	MAKER SUGAR TONGS	LOCATION	DESCRIPTION	SOURCE
1745 ca	James Ker	Edinburgh	Sugar tongs, no details	National Museums of Scotland L1980.6
1760/61	Alexander Aitchison	Edinburgh	Sugar tongs, no details	Jackson Marks p 548
1780 ca	Not available		Sugar tongs, spoon grips	E Austin, Charleston, SC USA 1991
1783/84	James Dempster	Edinburgh	Sugar tongs, engraved, shell grips	E Austin, Charleston, SC USA 1993
1785 ca	James Cornfute	Perth	Sugar tongs, bright cut	E Austin, Charleston, SC USA 1992
1785 ca	NG Possibly Nathaniel Gillet	Possibly Aberdeen	Sugar tongs, with feather edge, shell bowls, with other items	Christie's London 2004 #133
1790 ca	Alexander Ziegler	Edinburgh	Sugar tongs, plain pattern, with others	Sotheby's NY USA 1999 #486
1790 ca	Alexander Ziegler	Edinburgh	Sugar tongs, fiddle pattern, anthemion terminals, initial "S", with others	Sotheby's NY USA 1999 #485
1790 ca	Peter Mathie	Edinburgh	Sugar tongs, bright cut, wiggle work edging on the swelled arms, slender bowl engraved with cattails, the bow with initials "MB", 5 ½" long, 1.1oz	New Orleans Auction Galleries, 2002 #464
1790 ca	IM	Edinburgh	Sugar tongs, plain pattern, with others	Sotheby's NY USA 1999 #485
1790 ca	RW	Edinburgh	Sugar tongs, thread border, initials "SH", with others	Sotheby's NY USA 1999 #485
1790 ca	William Robertson	Edinburgh	Sugar tongs, plain, possibly with a thread border and plain bowls, 5 7/8" long, 1.5oz	Johnboy's Antiques Emporium eBay #190140029600 Aug 2007
1790 ca	Patrick Robertson	Edinburgh	Sugar tongs, no details	Shrubsole, NY 1991
1790 ca	Peter Mathie	Edinburgh	Sugar tongs, bright cut	Toby's, Connecticut USA 1993
1790 ca	Alexander Ziegler	Edinburgh	Sugar tongs, bright cut	Antique Emporium Raleigh, NC USA 1995
1790 ca	PH	Paisley	Sugar tongs, bright cut decoration, 5 ¾" long	The Phoenix Collection
1790 ca	Peter Mathie	Edinburgh	Sugar tongs, bright cut, with vacant cartouche on each side, shell nips	The Phoenix Collection

YEAR	MAKER	LOCATION	DESCRIPTION	SOURCE
1790 ca	Alexander Ziegler	Edinburgh	Sugar tongs, bulge pattern, bright cut, with the initials "WJE"	Private Collection
1795 ca	Edward Livingstone	Dundee	Sugar tongs, shaped fluted bowl, 5 5/8" long, 1.6oz	Nicholas Shaw Catalog Winter 2000 p90
1800 ca	IM	Edinburgh	Sugar tongs, plain, 5 ½" long	The Phoenix Collection
1800 ca	William Hannay	Paisley	Sugar tongs, plain with reeding and shell nips, script initial "J", 6" long	The Phoenix Collection
1800 ca	William Hannay	Paisley	Sugar tongs, no details	Bernfelds CT USA 1991
1800 ca	PH	Paisley	Sugar tongs, no details	Gebelein, VT USA 1991
1800 ca	IM	Edinburgh	Sugar tongs, no details	Delmar, NY USA 1992
1800 ca	A * G	Edinburgh	Sugar tongs, no details	National Museums of Scotland MEQ 722 1964.1882
1800 ca	James Erskine	Aberdeen	Sugar tongs, bright cut decoration, with script initial "D" in an oval cartouche	The Phoenix Collection
1800 ca	John Ziegler	Edinburgh	Sugar tongs, fiddle pattern, initials "JW"	Sotheby's NY USA 1999 #494
1800 ca	Francis Howden	Edinburgh	Sugar tongs, with others	Bonhams London UK 2003 #224
1800 ca	Peter Mathie	Edinburgh	Sugar tongs, with wiggle work borders and initials, with others	Sotheby's NY USA 1999 #483
1800 ca	Alexander Ziegler	Edinburgh	Sugar tongs, with wigglework borders and initials "EJS", with others	Sotheby's NY USA 1999 #483
1800 ca	William Auld	Edinburgh	Sugar tongs, with wigglework borders and the initial "B", with others	Sotheby's NY USA 1999 #483
1804/05	JO script	Edinburgh	Sugar tongs, plain with shell nips, 6" long	Toby's CT USA 1993 The Phoenix Collection
1805 ca	Robert Keay I	Perth	Sugar tongs, fiddle pattern, with fluted bowl, 5" long, 1.4oz	Nicholas Shaw Catalog Winter 2001 p82
1805 ca	James Erskine	Aberdeen	Sugar tongs, plain, engraved with initial "D", 5 ¾" long, 1.6oz	Nicholas Shaw Catalog Winter 2001 p 82
1808/09	Cunningham & Simpson	Edinburgh	Sugar tongs, no details	National Museums of Scotland 1945.40
1808/09	Alexander Henderson	Edinburgh	Sugar tongs, plain pattern, initials "WF", with others	Sotheby's NY USA 1999 #485

YEAR	MAKER	LOCATION	DESCRIPTION	SOURCE
1809/10	William Constable	Dundee Edinburgh assay	Sugar tongs, Old English pattern, with others	Woolley & Wallis Salisbury UK 2007 #211
1810 ca	William Hannay	Paisley	Sugar tongs, reeded border, with fluted bowl, engraved initials "WJA", 5 ¾" long, 1.3oz	Nicholas Shaw Catalog Winter 2001 p82
1810 ca	James McKay	Edinburgh	Sugar tongs, plain with shell grips	E Austin, Charleston, SC USA 1993
1810 ca	William Haney	Paisley	Sugar tongs, with shell grips and thread pattern stems, initialled, sold with other items	Christie's London UK 1998 #93
1810 ca	David Manson	Dundee	Sugar tongs, no details	Christie's London UK 1999 #96
1810 ca	Robert Gray & Son	Glasgow Edinburgh assay	Sugar tongs, fiddle pattern, initial "S", with others	Sotheby's NY USA 1999 #471
1810/11	Alexander Reid	Glasgow Edinburgh assay	Sugar tongs, fiddle pattern, initial "AB", with others	Sotheby's NY USA 1999 #471
1810/11	Austen	Dundee Edinburgh assay	Sugar tongs, plain with fluted bowls, with other	Woolley & Wallis, Salisbury UK 2007 #211
1810/11	Alexander Henderson	Edinburgh	Sugar tongs, fiddle pattern, initials "SJJ", with others	Sotheby's NY USA 1999 #486
1812/13	Alexander Edmonstoun	Edinburgh	Sugar tongs, fiddle pattern, with others	Sotheby's NY USA 1999 #486
1814/15	James Nasmyth	Edinburgh	Sugar tongs, fiddle pattern, anthemion terminals, initials "JA", with others	Sotheby's NY USA 1999 #485
1815 ca	J & G Heron	Paisley	Sugar tongs, fiddle pattern with initials and numbered "17"	Christie's London UK 1999 #96
1815/16	Alexander Henderson	Edinburgh	Sugar tongs, fiddle pattern, shell terminals, initials "JG", with others	Sotheby's NY USA 1999 #481
1815/16	Matthew Craw	Edinburgh	Sugar tongs, fiddle pattern, shell terminals, initial "M", with others	Sotheby's NY USA 1999 #481
1817/18	Charles Dalgleish	Edinburgh	Sugar tongs, no details	National Museums of Scotland MEQ 646
1818/19	SZ	Edinburgh	Sugar tongs, fiddle pattern, anthemion terminals, with others	Sotheby's NY USA 1999 #485

YEAR	MAKER	LOCATION	DESCRIPTION	SOURCE
1818/19	Alexander Henderson	Edinburgh	Sugar tongs with rounded shell nips, in a banner "Elness", boar's head crest and motto "PER ACTUM INTENTIO", for Urquhart, 6" long	The Phoenix Collection
1820 ca	David Gray	Dumfries	Sugar tongs, fiddle pattern, engraved with the initial "D", 5 ½" long, 1.6oz	Nicholas Shaw Catalog Winter 2001 p82
1820 ca	Charles Murray	Perth	Sugar tongs, fluted bowl, engraved initials "MA to MS", 6 ¼" long, 2.5oz	Nicholas Shaw Catalog Winter 2001 p82
1820 ca	Alexander Cameron	Dundee	Sugar tongs, fiddle pattern, plain, engraved with the initial "D", 6 ¼" long, 1.8oz	Nicholas Shaw Catalog Winter 2001 p82
1820 ca	George Booth	Aberdeen	Sugar tongs, fiddle pattern, plain, 6" long, 1.3oz	Nicholas Shaw Catalog Winter 2000 p90
1820 ca	Alexander Cameron	Dundee	Sugar tongs, fiddle pattern, with shell bowls	Lyon & Turnbull Edinburgh UK 2003 #286
1820 ca	Alexander Cameron	Dundee	Sugar tongs, a short fiddle pair, with others	Woolley & Wallis, Salisbury UK 2007 #211
1820 ca	William Constable	Dundee	Sugar tongs, fiddle pattern, single drop bowls, with others	Woolley & Wallis, Salisbury 2007 #211
1822/23	Mitchell & Son	Glasgow	Sugar tongs, Kings pattern, with others	Sotheby's NY USA 1999 #483
1822/23	David McDonald	Glasgow	Sugar tongs, fiddle pattern, anthemion bowls, initial "J", with others	Sotheby's NY USA 1999 #486
1823/24	JM	Glasgow	Sugar tongs, wavy shells	Shrubsole NY USA 1993
1824/25	Philip Grierson	Glasgow	Sugar tongs, fiddle pattern, anthemion bowls, initials "MY", with others	Sotheby's NY USA 1999 #486
1825 ca	John Sellar	Wick	Sugar tongs, fiddle pattern, plain, 6 ¼" long, 1.9oz	Nicholas Shaw Catalog Winter 2001 p82
1825 ca	William Whitecross	Aberdeen	Sugar tongs, fiddle pattern, plain, engraved with the initials "JW", 5 7/8" long, 1.5oz	Nicholas Shaw Catalog Winter 2000 p90
1825 ca	David Gray	Perth	Sugar tongs, plain fiddle pattern, engraved with initials "AS"	Christie's Lanarkshire UK 1998 #720
1828/29	Robert Tennet	Glasgow	Sugar tongs, fiddle pattern, initials "PMC", with others	Sotheby's NY USA 1999 #471
1827/28	AR	Glasgow	Sugar tongs, fiddle pattern, initials "JC McC", with others	Sotheby's NY USA 1999 #471

YEAR	MAKER	LOCATION	DESCRIPTION	SOURCE
1829/30	W Semple Jr	Glasgow	Sugar tongs, Queens pattern, 5 ¾" long, 1.6oz	Richie's Toronto CA 1996 #2069
1830 ca	Peter Gill & Son	Aberdeen	Sugar tongs, fiddle pattern, Initials "M" or "W"	Sotheby's NY USA 1998 #509
1830 ca	William Whitecross	Aberdeen	Sugar tongs, no details	Sotheby's NY USA 1998 #516
1830 ca	Robert Naughton	Inverness	Sugar tongs, fiddle pattern with fluted bowls, with others	Woolley & Wallis, Salisbury UK 2007 #211
1831/32	TK	Glasgow	Sugar tongs, fiddle pattern, with shell nips, script monogram "GB", 5 ¾" long, 1.5oz	Spencer Marks Antiques, MA USA 2006 Item #277
1832/33	TK	Glasgow	Sugar tongs, fiddle pattern, anthemion terminals, initials "WGC", with others	Sotheby's NY USA 1999 #481
1832/33	James & William Marshall	Edinburgh	Sugar tongs, fiddle pattern, anthemion bowls, with others	Sotheby's NY USA 1999 #485
1833/34	Peter Aitken	Glasgow	Sugar tongs, fiddle pattern, anthemion bowls, 5 ¾" long	Antiques Antiques, North Wales eBay #160147292611 2 Aug 2007
1833/34	James Douglas	Edinburgh	Sugar tongs, no details	National Museums of Scotland MEQ 646
1834/35	George Drummond	Glasgow	Sugar tongs, fiddle pattern, shell grips, script initials, 6 ½" long, 1.7oz	The Silver Spoon Club Postal Auction July 12, 2007 #45
1835/36	Samuel Weir	Edinburgh	Sugar tongs, fiddle pattern, shell terminals, with others	Sotheby's NY USA 1999 #481
1836/37	J Fettes	Glasgow	Sugar tongs, Kings pattern, with others	Sotheby's NY USA 1999 #483
1838/39	Emslie & Mollison	Aberdeen	Sugar tongs, fiddle pattern, plain, engraved with the initial "H", 5 7/8" long, 1.3oz	Nicholas Shaw Catalog Winter 2000 p90
1840/41	Robert Gray & Son	Glasgow	Sugar tongs, fiddle pattern, initials "RJ", with others	Sotheby's NY USA 1999 #471
1842/43	WH	Glasgow	Sugar tongs, fiddle pattern, anthemion bowls, with others	Sotheby's NY USA 1999 #486
1845/46	J & W Mitchell	Glasgow	Sugar tongs, Queens pattern, initials "MWM", sold with others	Sotheby's NY USA 1999 #454
1846/47	JMK & Son	Edinburgh	Sugar tongs, no details	National Museums of Scotland MEQ 713 1964.1851
1848/49	RG	Edinburgh	Sugar tongs, no details	National Museums of Scotland MEQ 749 1969.1820

YEAR	MAKER	LOCATION	DESCRIPTION	SOURCE
1848/49	Marshall & Son	Edinburgh	Sugar tongs, Kings pattern, with shell terminals, 6 ½" long, 1.7oz	New Orleans Auction Galleries, 2002 #468
1848/49	Marshall & Son	Edinburgh	Sugar tongs, Kings pattern, with others	Sotheby's NY USA 1999 #483
1851/52	MacKay & Chisholm	Edinburgh	Sugar tongs, Kings pattern with groove shell bowls, initials	S. T. Freeman & Co, Philadelphia PA USA 2002 #362
1854/55	DD	Glasgow	Sugar tongs, Queens pattern, initials "AMB", 6 ½" long, 11.7oz	Britannia Collectables eBay #14014720266 Aug 2007
1854/55	George Jamieson	Aberdeen	Sugar tongs, no details	National Museums of Scotland MEQ 837
1855/56	DG	Glasgow	Sugar tongs, fiddle pattern, anthemion bowls, with others	Sotheby's NY USA 1999 #481
1856/57	Robert Scott	Glasgow	Sugar tongs, Queens pattern, initials "EB", with others	Sotheby's NY USA 1999 #457
1856/57	David Dow	Glasgow	Sugar tongs, Queens pattern, initials "JC", with others	Sotheby's NU USA 1999 #457
1859/60	MH	Glasgow	Sugar tongs, fiddle pattern, with shell terminals, initials "I ? SH", 6 ½" long	New Orleans Auction Galleries 2003 #918
1861/62	MH	Glasgow	Sugar tongs, fiddle pattern, anthemion terminals, initials "JSH", with others	Sotheby's NY USA 1999 #471
1861/62	Crichton Brothers	Edinburgh	Sugar tongs, Kings pattern, with others	Sotheby's NY USA 1999 #483
1862/63	WM	Edinburgh	Sugar tongs, fiddle pattern, initials "RF", with others	Sotheby's NY USA 1999 #486
1865/66	W Alexander & Son	Glasgow	Sugar tongs, Old English pattern, bright cut borders, with a lion's head crest, with others	Sotheby's NY USA 1999 #454
1866/67	PW	Edinburgh	Sugar tongs, fiddle pattern, anthemion bowls, initials "IW", with others	Sotheby's NY USA 1999 #485
1867/68	JW	Edinburgh	Sugar tongs, King's pattern	E Austin, Charleston, SC USA 1993
1870/71	Robert Gray & Son	Glasgow	Sugar tongs, Kings pattern, initials "EH", with others	Sotheby's NY USA 1999 #483
1872/73	Hamilton & Inches	Edinburgh	Sugar tongs, fiddle pattern, shell bowls, crest and motto, "OPTIMA EST VERITAS", with others	Sotheby's NY USA 1999 #481
1874/75	Robert Tennet	Glasgow	Sugar tongs, Old English pattern, engraved with leaves, initial "L", with others	Sotheby's NY USA 1999 #457

YEAR	MAKER	LOCATION	DESCRIPTION	SOURCE
1879/80	William Coghill	Glasgow	Sugar tongs, Queens pattern, anthemion terminals, initials "CE", sold with others	Sotheby's NY USA 1999 #454

Ink Pots & Inkstands

Plate 32. Ink Pots and Inkstands. 1742/43 Inkstand with 3 members by Robert Gordon, Edinburgh.
Photograph courtesy of George Dalgleish and the National Museums of Scotland.

INK POTS AND STANDS

YEAR	MAKER	LOCATION	DESCRIPTION	SOURCE
1742/43	Robert Gordon	Edinburgh	Inkstand, oblong, pie crust and shell border, rococo decoration, with 3 members – quill stand, ink bottle, and blotter powder bottle – trough, engraved with a full coat of arms	National Museums of Scotland MEQ 621 1962.1029
1785/86	William Davie or William Dempster	Edinburgh	Ink pot and sander, cylindrical body with flat top, small sander nozzle, each section with crest of a cat and the motto "Touch Not The Cat Bot A Glove" for McPherson and others	Finlay 1991 # 100
1785/86	*WD script* *William Davie or William Dempster*	*Edinburgh*	*Ink holder and stand*	*National Museums of Scotland* *MEQ 1037*
1807/08	George Fenwick	Edinburgh	Ink holder, no details	National Museums of Scotland MEQ 1969.5
1813/14	George Fenwick	Edinburgh	Inkstand, no details	National Museums of Scotland MEQ 1067
1820/21	James McKay	Edinburgh	Inkstand, shell like, with silver mounted glass inkpot (silver lid, handle, mounted foot), inverted funnel, foot below shell bowl, single silver handle on the shell, fully hallmarked, 4 ½" ht, 5 ½" X 3 ½"	Silver Plus Antiques, Central Village, CT USA 1992
1837/38	Robb & Whittet	Edinburgh	Inkstand, in the shape of a curling stone, hinged lid with silver handle opens to reveal ink and blotter powder bottles, cover heavily chased with scrolls and flower heads, handle with two initials on terminal end, cartouche on lid with presentation inscription, full marks on lid and bottom	National Museums of Scotland MEQ 717
1842/43	Marshall & Son	Edinburgh	Inkstand, rectangular, two facetted glass bottles with engraved octagonal flat tops, pierced conical taperstick with a snuffer, shaped gallery scroll pierced scroll and shell feet, 10 ½" long, 23.8 oz (silver)	Neals Nottingham England UK 2007 #374
1843/44	William Marshall	Edinburgh	Inkstand, no details	National Museums of Scotland MEQ 1141
1851/52	William Marshall	Edinburgh	Inkstand, no details	National Museums of Scotland MEQ 1570
1856/57	JM	Glasgow	Inkstand, oblong with engraved leaf, flower and rocaille motifs below a scroll motif rim, on four scroll feet, each side with a pen rest, supports for the two mounted glass bottles, with a silver taperstick, 8 ¾" long, 19oz (silver)	Christie's London UK 2003 #81

YEAR	MAKER M & C	LOCATION	DESCRIPTION	SOURCE
1881/82		Edinburgh	Inkstand, shaped rectangular base on four pad feet, central oval pen rest engraved with a presentation inscription, central clock mounted with an urn-form vessel, flanked by two elaborately decorated urn, four vessels, 10 5/8" long	Christie's London UK 2001 #86
1882/83	H Crichton & Co	Edinburgh	Inkstand, presented to Sir Archibald C. Campbell, Bart.	National Museums of Scotland MEQ 1059
1898/99	Hamilton & Inches	Edinburgh	Enameled inkstand	National Museums of Scotland MEQ 1965.1879
1902/03	Hamilton & Inches	Edinburgh	Inkstand, rectangular on four canted feet, gadrooned egg and dart borders, with a pen trough, two inkwell covers concealing glass inkwells, central hinged compartment, 11 ½" long, 63oz	Christie's NY USA 2005 #139
1903/04	MacKay & Chisholm	Edinburgh	Enameled inkstand, architectural design with columns, three enameled panels, center panel with coat of arms, right panel motto "PRUDENTIA ET ANIMIS", left panel name on a banner "William Strang Steel"	National Museums of Scotland MEQ 808
1906/07	Hamilton & Inches	Edinburgh	Inkstand, circular, gadrooned edge, center silver mounted cut glass bottle, Arms of the Royal Scots Greys, 11 5/8" di, 29oz	Nicholas Shaw Catalog 2005 p106
1973/74	Michael Rowe	Edinburgh assay	Inkwell, double, no details	Aberdeen Museums and Galleries ABDAG011209 acquired in 2005

Miscellaneous

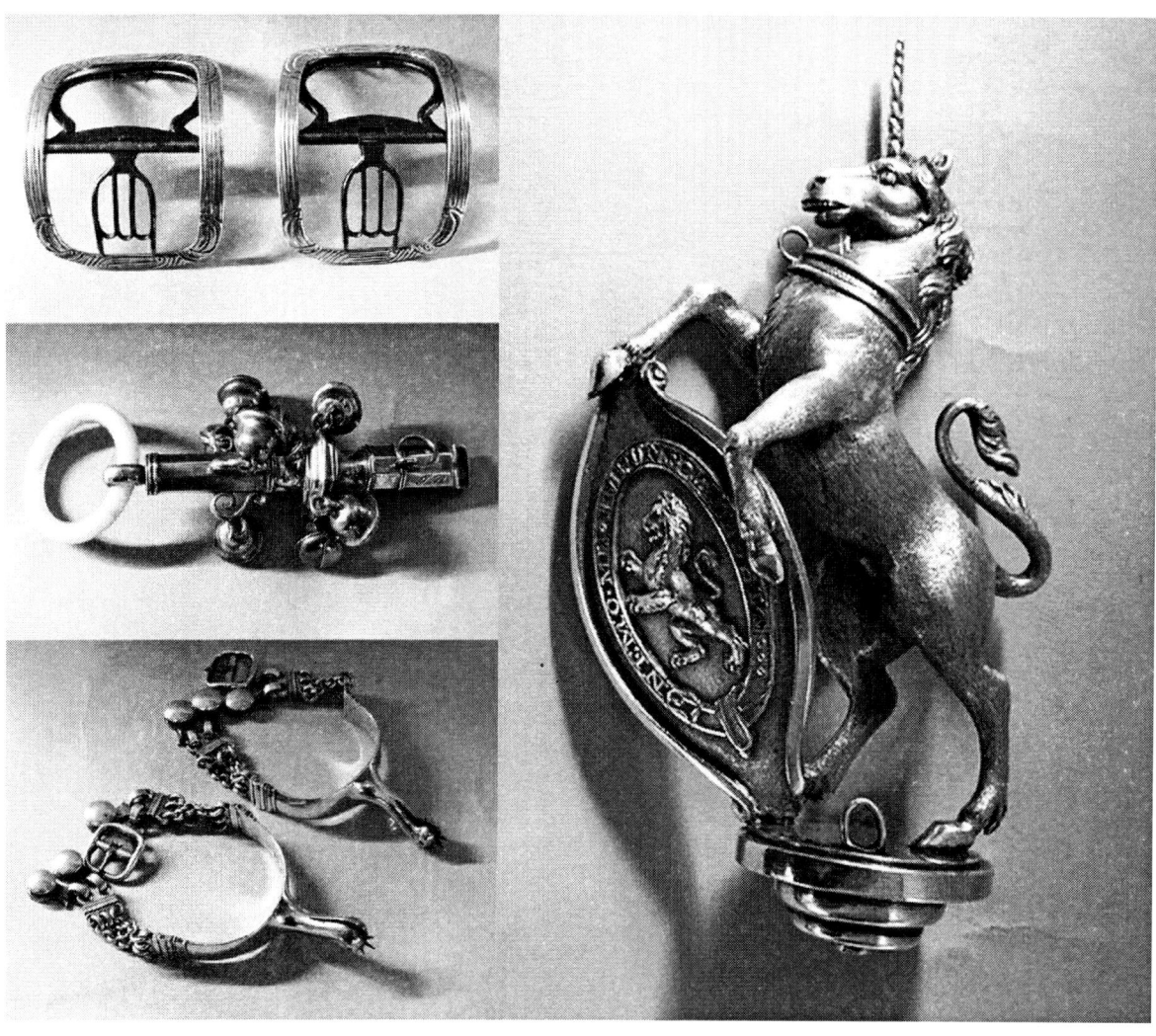

Plate 33. Top Left – Pair of Buckles 1780 ca by William Scott, Dundee;
Center Left – Child's Rattle 1745 ca by James Glen, Glasgow
Lower Left – Pair of Spurs 1807/08 by James McKay, Edinburgh
Right – Cast top (London made) of the Green Rod. This top was made specifically for
The Scottish coronation of George IV in 1821.
All courtesy of a private collector. Photographs by Janice M Dietert.

YEAR	MAKER	LOCATION	DESCRIPTION	SOURCE
			MISCELLANEOUS AND SPECIAL COLLECTIONS	
1530-50 ca	Vh possibly for John Vaitch	Edinburgh	The Methune Cup, silver gilt rock crystal, 7" ht	Finlay 1991 #17 Clayton Dictionary p251 #49 Hearst Collection Los Angeles County Museum of Art CA USA
1565 ca	Not available		The McLeod Cup, apparently a secular cup similar in outline to the Forgue Communion Cup	Finlay 1991 p22
1565-75	James Cok I Deacon George Heriot II	Edinburgh	The Erskine Ewer	Erskine, Lord Swaythling How of Edinburgh Private Collection On loan to National Museums of Scotland Finlay 1991 #22
1608-10	Hugh Lindsay	Edinburgh	The Lanark Racing Bell	Lanark Town Council Finlay 1991 #34
1608-10	Adam Wilson	Edinburgh	Midside Maggie's Girdle	National Museums of Scotland NA 338
1611-13	Robert Dennistoun Deacon David Palmer	Edinburgh	The Heriot Cup, Nautilus Cup	Heriot's Hospital Trust Glasgow Exhibition 1911 vol I, p123 #21 On loan to National Museums of Scotland Finlay 1991 #32
1612 ca	Thomas Ramsay	Perth	The Rattray Arrow, with four unmarked medals appended to the arrow, all in a fitted case	Finlay 1991 #37 Perth City Art Gallery and Museums
1612 ca	Thomas Ramsay	Perth	The Rattray Ball, with a number of unmarked medals appended to the ball	Perth City Art Gallery and Museum
1617 (one year)	George Robertson I Deacon George Crawford	Edinburgh	The Edinburgh City Mace	Corporation of the City of Edinburgh Finlay 1991 #29

YEAR	MAKER	LOCATION	DESCRIPTION	SOURCE
1648 dated	Andrew Dennistoun Deacon George Cleghorne	Edinburgh	Seal of the Barony of Portsburgh 1648	National Museums of Scotland 145
1650 ca	Walter Melville	Aberdeen	Mace, of King's College, Aberdeen	King's College, Aberdeen
1669 ca	Thomas Moncur	Glasgow	Trumpet	Private Collection UK
1674 (one year)	Thomas Cleghorne	Edinburgh	Traveling writing set, presented to Nicol Sommerveil Clerk of the Incorporation of Goldsmiths in 1674	Finlay 1991 #54 Nicol Sommerveil Messrs. Cunningham The Incorporation of Goldsmiths, Edinburgh National Museums of Scotland MEQ 1238
1675 ca	Robert Brock	Glasgow	Trumpet	Private Collection UK
1686/87	Zacharias Mellinus	Edinburgh	Holyrood Sanctus Bell	Finlay 1991 #33 Scottish Catholic Hierarchy on loan to National Museums of Scotland KJ1970.14
1695 ca	George Scott	Edinburgh	Powder horn, silver mounted	National Museums of Scotland LK89 1961.2232
1695 ca	Walter Scott	Aberdeen	Bowl, described as a sugar bowl, but too early for that purpose, decorated, circular molded foot, 2 bands of flutes, shield, 5 ¾" di	Jackson 2 vols p980 # 1329
1698/99	William Clerk	Glasgow	Silver sword hilt	Finlay 1991 #35
1700 ca	Patrick Gairdyne	St Andrews	Table bell, plain, molded edge to bow, tall baluster handle, engraved with crest, 5 oz 5d	Christie's January 26, 1972 #126
1701 ca	James Penman	Edinburgh	Silver-mounted mirror, plain molded borders, the cantle of cresting pierced and chased cherubs, fruit and scrolling foliage, a vacant cartouche and a baron's coronet, 29" ht, 41oz	Christie's December 14, 1988 #238
1702-04	Thomas Ker	Edinburgh	Barber's shaving basin and ewer, arms of Hamilton quartering Melrose, ewer 7 5/8" ht, 21.3oz, basin 13 9/16" X 9 5/8", 25.4oz	Sotheby's London October 16, 1961 #156 Garrard Ltd, London Finlay 1991 #64 Alcorn Museum of Fine Arts

YEAR	MAKER (continued)	LOCATION	DESCRIPTION	SOURCE
1703 ca	RI (Probably Robert Inglis)	Edinburgh	Child's rattle, the center formed as a ribbed sphere, 2 crescent shaped branches, one being the mouthpiece for a whistle, the other holding a coral teether (broken), inscribed "RB 1703"	Boston MA USA p328-329 #251 Christie's October 19, 1988 #288
1703/04	Colin McKenzie	Edinburgh	The Keir Toilet Service	Hon. Marion Steward, daughter of the 5th Lord Blantyre Stirling of Keir Glasgow Exhibition 1911 vol I, p124 #29 Christie's March 24, 1982 Clayton Christie's p86, #1 Finlay 1991 #62 National Museums of Scotland K.2004314
1706/07	Thomas Ker	Edinburgh	The Hopetoun Ewer and Basin and Box (set)	Finlay 1991 #64 National Museums of Scotland 1512-13 MEQ 1556
1710 ca	Robert Bruce	Edinburgh	Pin cushion, oblong on 4 pad feet, with applied reeded bands, chased wriggle work, reverse engraved with later initials "EA" and a ducal coronet, 6 ½" wide	Shaw Collection Christie's Glasgow March 29, 1983 #102 National Museums of Scotland MEQ 1565
1713/14	Colin Campbell	Edinburgh	Bell, of plain design, engraved with a crest, baluster handle capped with a bead, tongue missing, 4 ½" ht, 5oz	Sotheby's April 28, 1960 #56 S J Phillips Ltd London UK, London UK
1715 ca	William Scott	Elgin	The Huntley Sporran	Clayton's Dictionary p383 #565 Private Collection UK
1715 ca	Henry Bethune	Edinburgh	Sword with silver hilt, Jacobite inscription on the blade	Finlay 1991 #89 National Museums of Scotland LA124
1716/17	Alexander Kincaid	Edinburgh	Whiskey flask, with crest and motto	National Museums of Scotland MEQ 1038 1970.589
1718/19	Henry Bethune	Edinburgh	Snuffer tray, no details	National Museums of Scotland MEQ 562

YEAR	MAKER	LOCATION	DESCRIPTION	SOURCE
1719/20	Henry Bethune	Edinburgh	Snuffer tray, crest and motto	Christie's NY USA October 20, 1990 #319
1720 ca	Johan Got-helf-Bilsings	Glasgow	Bible hasp clips, faceted edges in Scandinavian style, plain ball fasteners, 4 heart shaped bracket mounts, 7"	Christie's Glasgow October 24, 1995 #478 National Museums of Scotland H.1996.263
1721/22	William Aytoun	Edinburgh	Oblong snuffer tray, 4 feet, shaped border, scroll handle, 7 ½" long, 9oz 15d	Scottish Art Academy Exhibit #427 Stirling-Maxwell Collection Christie's February 4, 1958 #141
1730 ca	Robert Luke	Glasgow	Dog collar, plain band, inscribed between molded borders "John Crawford of Mitoun Esq: Owner 1732", sliding retainer, 4 slots and 2 applied rings, 5 ½" di, 5oz 1d	Sotheby's July 24, 1980 #29
1735 ca	I D	Edinburgh	Flask, mm only, probably Edinburgh, compressed pear shaped body, fitted with detachable base, engraved at borders with bands of stiff leafage simulating a girdle, chained, screw on stopper, similar to Alexander Kincaid flask 1716ca, 6 ¼" ht, 10.4oz	Sotheby's February 20, 1975 #93 Sotheby's April 19, 1977 #101
1735 ca	Patrick Gordon	Banff	Ewer, no details	Crichton Brothers Jackson Marks p591
1735/36	Dougal Ged	Edinburgh	Hanging lamp, for a kettle	National Museums of Scotland MEQ 1983.29c
1739/40	William Aytoun Assayer David Mitchell	Edinburgh	Library lamp, lamp with reflector and snuffers, circular molded base, on 4 scroll feet, plain stem with open work bracket, for 2 missing candle branches, shaped pan for a pair of plain snuffers, plain oblong adjustable reflector curved in at both ends, ring handle at top, snuffers with mm only, 20 ½" ht, 53oz	Christie's October 14, 1970 #114 National Museums of Scotland MEQ 1063
1740 ca	Colin Allan	Aberdeen	Table bell, plain, molded bow, plain rib above and baluster handle, marks AD in 2 lobes and a fish head, 4 ½" ht, 4oz 14d	Christie's November 27, 1963 #120
1740 ca	Colin Mitchell	Canongate	Lochiel's broadsword, no details	Private Ownership
1740/41	Dougal Ged	Edinburgh	Snuffer stand, plain molded border, on 4 hoof feet, shaped handle with fleur-de-lis, baron's crest and motto	Shrubsole NY USA 1981 E2081 Antiques Magazine 1974 vol 106, p943
1740/41	Ebenezer Oliphant	Edinburgh	The Traveling Canteen of Prince Charles Edward Stuart	Christie's London March 1962 Clayton Christie's p194, #41

YEAR	MAKER (continued)	LOCATION	DESCRIPTION	SOURCE
	James Glen	Glasgow	Child's rattle, rattle with whistle, octagonal mouthpiece with initials "JB", hung with 8 bells, mm only, 6" overall, 3oz 2d	Clayton Dictionary p323, #684 Finlay 1991 #72 National Museums of Scotland MEQ 1584 (or 1384)
1745 ca	James Weems Assayer Hugh Gordon	Edinburgh	Brandy warmer, plain baluster body, turned wood handle at right angles to lip rising from a shell motif, engraved with a crest, 9" long, 10 oz all	Sotheby's August 28-29, 1978 How of Edinburgh Private Collection
1746/47	Not available	Edinburgh	Trophy, Harrow on the Hill Trophy, silver arrow, shaft inscribed "Thos Saunders won ye Arrow at Harrow ye Hill 3 Avgst 1749", not marked, 24" long, 10oz 19d	Noble Collection Nicholas Shaw Catalog 2004 p98
1749 ca				Sotheby's November 13, 1975 #125
1750 ca	Samuel Telford	Glasgow	Beefsteak tongs, one round and one oval finger grips, long strap arms and corrugated inside, 10 7/8" long	Museum of Fine Art, Boston MA USA 33.131
1750 ca	Hugh Gordon	Edinburgh	Snuffer tray, not pictured	Park-Berne 46 p7 Rudkin Collection
1750 ca	AP	Provincial	Pap boat, plain, typical form, engraved on underside with contemporary initials, mm only, AP 3X's, 4" wide, 1oz 15d	Sotheby's February 13, 1975 #132
1750 ca	John Steven	Dundee	Table bell, no details	Dundee Museums and Art Galleries 1986-123
1750 ca	WD probably William Dempster	Edinburgh	Gold child's rattle, no details	National Museums of Scotland 1957.118
1750 ca	Probably Ebenezer Oliphant	Edinburgh	Spirit flask, flattened oval, detachable cup, screw cap, mm only, 5 ¾" ht, 10oz 5d	Sotheby's NY USA Oct 6, 2006 #339
1751/52	Lothian & Robertson	Edinburgh	Flask, tapering oval body, one side with later monogram and 2 crests above the name "Capesthorne", one the detachable oval beaker forming the base, screw on cap with detachable cork-shaped top, 8" ht, 12.8oz	Sotheby's May 8, 1969 Christie's February 9, 1972 #149
1753/54	Lothian & Robertson	Edinburgh	Crumb hook or cream scoop, no details	Finlay 1991 National Museums of Scotland 1956.1498

YEAR	MAKER	LOCATION	DESCRIPTION	SOURCE
1755 ca	Colin Allan	Aberdeen	Child's rattle, coral on one end and a whistle on the other	JH Bourdon-Smith Catalog 1977 p16 #33
1756/57	John Clark	Edinburgh	Microscope, no details	Files of the National Museums of Scotland
1758/59	John Clark	Edinburgh	The White Rod of Scotland	Finlay 1991 #92
1760/61	William Dempster	Edinburgh	Snuffer tray, no details	Private Collection
1763/64	James Hill	Edinburgh	Snuffer Tray, no details	Jackson Marks p 549
1767/68	Ker & Dempster	Edinburgh	Blackjack, silver mounted leather, cylindrical form, slightly flared toward the base, silver lined, with scalloped edges to the rim and foot mount, the S-shaped handle with mounted heart-shape kick, applied rococo cartouche to front of body, with a C-scroll engraved border, crest and motto, "ESSE QUAM VIDERI" above an inscription, 7 1/3" ht	Lyon & Turnbull, Edinburgh UK May 25, 2006 #337
1767/68	John Clark	Edinburgh	Presentation Malacca walking stick, silver handle of curved tapering form, trefoil termination, inscribed "Jon Rob, Dunblain 1768", 38 5/8" long	Christie's Scotland April 4, 1987 #142
1767/68	Patrick Robertson	Edinburgh	Blackjack, leather tankard, silver lining, cylindrical, leather work by Wilson of Edinburgh, 7 3/8" ht, (Note: this may be the same as the one dated the following year)	Huntley House Museum Edinburgh HH2820/65
1768/69	*Patrick Robertson*	*Edinburgh*	*Blackjack, with plain engrailed foot and lip mounts to the cylindrical body, silver lining, scroll handle, plain mount to the lower junction of the handle initialed "CHW", 7 ½" ht*	*Shaw Collection Christie's Glasgow March 29, 1983 #72*
1770 ca	James Gordon	Aberdeen	Ewer, small, no details	Aberdeen Museums and Galleries ABDAG001041 acquired in 1981
1770 ca	Milne & Campbell	Glasgow	Tea infuser, silver and fruitwood, 4 ½" ht, 5 ½" di	Dallas Museum of Art TX USA 1990.99
1770 ca	"Ker"	Edinburgh	Child's rattle, no details	National Museums of Scotland MEQ 1175 1976.22
1770ca	*William Ker*	*Edinburgh*	*Child's rattle, knopped octagonal body, hung with a pendant ring and 8 bells, mm only, 5 ½" long*	*Sotheby's May 27, 1976*
1770 ca	HR (dot between)	Possibly Tain	Bottle holder, with a tapered collar ring much as used with wine, trefid end and attachment, heavy possibly originally gilt	Lyon & Turnbull, Edinburgh UK late 2007 or early 2008 auction

YEAR	MAKER	LOCATION	DESCRIPTION	SOURCE
1771/72	Patrick Robertson	Edinburgh	Crumb hook/scoop, typical curved blade with turned wooden handle, 10 ¼" long	Sotheby's Gleneagles August 23, 1976 #102 Sotheby's Scone Palace April 10, 1978 #48
1776/77	Patrick Robertson	Edinburgh	Argyll, plain oval body with loop handle, straight spout, wriggle decoration to top and detachable cover, 4 ½" ht, 15.8oz	Sotheby's Scone Palace April 23, 1979 #42 National Museums of Scotland MEQ 1325
1780 ca	William Scott	Dundee	Buckles, pair	Private Collection
1780 ca	Alexander Gardner	Edinburgh	Spurs, pair, no details	National Museums of Scotland MEQ 1523/1524 1982
1780 ca	Peter Mathie	Edinburgh	Ewer, possibly for cream	Aberdeen Museums and Galleries ABDAG000918
1781/82	William Davie or William Dempster	Edinburgh	Asparagus tongs, no details	National Museums of Scotland MEQ 70
1782/83	Patrick Robertson	Edinburgh	Shape of a Pilgrim's flask, pull off silver cap on a chain, crest of a unicorn's head, initials "WK", 6 ¼" ht, 8.8oz	Sanda Lipton, London #2943
1784/85	Not available	Edinburgh assay	Nutmeg grater, no mm, .7oz	Bonhams The Scottish Sale August 21, 2003 #33
1785 ca	William Davie or William Dempster	Edinburgh	Boot powderer, crest and motto of Campbell of Balcaldine, 4 ½" long, 4oz	Nicholas Shaw Catalog Winter 2002/03 p86
1785/86	Alexander Ziegler	Edinburgh	Buckle, no details	The Maple Swan Collection
1785/86	WD Script William Davie or William Dempster	Edinburgh	Whiskey flask, no details	National Museums of Scotland MEQ 1035
1787 ca	Francis Howden	Edinburgh	Oblong silver shoe buckles, original steel fastenings, decorated with flowers at the corners, between intertwined ribbons, each engraved with "JH 1787", marked "FH" thistle, King's head, 2 7/8" X 2 7/16"	Private Collection Christie's Fingask Castle, April 27, 1993
1790 ca	W & P Cunningham I	Edinburgh	Wax jack, straps supporting the spindle and sconce springing from a saucer, shaped base, chain secured extinguisher, 4 ½" ht, 4oz	Sotheby's Gleneagles August 25, 1997 #141
1791/92	Patrick Robertson or	Edinburgh	Crumb scoop, no details	National Museums of Scotland

YEAR	MAKER	LOCATION	DESCRIPTION	SOURCE
	ER mark			MEQ 859
1791/92	Patrick Robertson or ER mark	Edinburgh	Crumb scoop or cream skimmer, no details, unclear if related to prior entry	The Maple Swan Collection
1791/92	WD script William Dempster	Edinburgh	Double cups/scoops on a turned wooden handle connected to a long silver sleeve, bowl like cups on either side of the end, by this date William Davie was deceased, maker is most likely Dempster	The Maple Swan Collection
1792/96 and 94/95	Robert Gray	Glasgow Edinburgh assay	Fox head stirrup cup	National Museums of Scotland MEQ 1315
1795 ca	William Robertson	Edinburgh	Buttons, set of 4, circular engraved with fox hunting scenes, 1"di	Sotheby's Gleneagles August 30, 1977 #163
1795/96	William Robertson	Edinburgh	Hound's head stirrup cup, inscribed around the collar "Won by Capt. A. Gordon's Dog Dubskelper at Barnbauckle Hill 12th Nov. 1793 beating seven others", 11.3oz	Sotheby's Gleneagles August 29, 1977 #186
1795/96	William Robertson	Edinburgh	Hip flask, plain oval body with bands of prick dot engraving, 6 1/8", 10.2oz	Nicholas Shaw Internet Catalog 2006
1797/98	W & P Cuningham I	Edinburgh	Centerpiece on four tapering legs, each with cast fox head suspending fruiting vine garlands, supporting oval pierced basket, reeded upward scrolling handles, crested, 17 ¾" ht, 13 ¾" long, 56oz	Bonhams Sale 15120 Aug 22, 2007 #26
1800 ca	Robert Gray	Glasgow Edinburgh assay	Shoe buckles, pair, oval with flowers and foliate scrolls	Private Collection
1800 ca	Dick & McPherson	Edinburgh	Papboat, completely plain, 4 ½" long, 1.6oz	Nicholas Shaw Catalog 2001 p75
1800 ca	Edward Livingston	Dundee	Shoe buckles, pair	Dundee Museums and Art Galleries 1962-691-1=2
1800 ca	John McDonald	Edinburgh	Wax jack, oval form with spindle and snuffer, on circular base with thumb piece handle, 6" ht, 4.3oz	Nicholas Shaw Catalog 2005 p98
1800 ca	John Argo	Banff	Gold ring, no details	National Museums of Scotland NJ 127
1800 ca	JH	Edinburgh	Asparagus tongs, few details, but possibly earlier	The Maple Swan Collection

YEAR	MAKER	LOCATION	DESCRIPTION	SOURCE
1800 ca	William Scott	Dundee	Shoe buckles, pair, oblong form, hinged steel pins	Sotheby's NY USA 1999 #484
1800/01	M & F	Edinburgh	Spirit flask, shaped oval, detachable cup, sides set with four loops, engraved initials on one side and a crest on the other, 6" ht, 8oz	Christie's London UK 2004 #193
1804/05	James Douglas	Edinburgh	Oval flask, with molded threaded cap, removable oval cup from lower body, crest and motto of Maxwell of Springkell, marked on neck and cup, 9" ht, 22oz	Christie's NY USA, October 17, 1996 #315
1805/06	JO	Edinburgh	Brandy flask, no details	National Museums of Scotland 1962.775B
1805/06	Dick & McPherson	Edinburgh	Wax jack, no details	National Museums of Scotland MEQ 1132
1806 ca	I A (dot between)	Provincial	Captain's calipers by the maker I dot a, probably not by John Argo but rather another maker, engraved with floral detail, 6 2/3" long	Lyon & Turnbull, Edinburgh UK May 25, 2006 #333
1807/08	James McKay	Edinburgh	Spurs, pair	Private Collection
1808/09	James Douglas	Edinburgh	Silver mounted gavels, pair, no details	National Museums of Scotland MEQ 1983.7-8
1809/10	Dick & McPherson	Edinburgh	Taper stand, no details	National Museums of Scotland MEQ 860
1810 c a	McHattie & Fenwick	Edinburgh	Buttons, 2, engraved "Lanark Renfrewshire Hunt"	National Museums of Scotland MEQ 1974
1813/14	James McKay	Edinburgh	Spurs, pair, with chains and buckles, cased	Asprey Small Collectables Catalog 1990 p20 #82
1814/15	MM rubbed	Edinburgh	Spirit flask, typical form, engraved leaf motifs, crest with motto above	Christie's London UK 2002 #148
1815/16	James McKay	Edinburgh	Deep bowl on circular spreading foot with a short stem, later engraved with "The Harbottle Coursing Meeting of 1874", 6 ¼" ht, 9oz	Christie's Lanarkshire 1998 #256
1817/18	George McHattie	Edinburgh	Vase or cup, no details	National Museums of Scotland MEQ 711
1817/18	James & William Howden	Edinburgh	Snuffer stand, no details	The Maple Swan Collection
1817/18	George Fenwick	Edinburgh	Lid of entrée dish, plain, numbered "15" in the handle well, handle lacking, additional "G.F.TOBAGO" mark, 10 3/16" X 7 3/16", 25oz	Private Collection

YEAR	MAKER	LOCATION	DESCRIPTION	SOURCE
1818/19	W & P Cunningham II	Edinburgh	Wine cooler	Clayton Christie's p264 #2
1819/20	Robert Gray & Son	Glasgow	Snuffer trays, two, plain oblong form with gadrooned sides, ends with applied shell and acanthus foliage, 9 ¾" wide, 16oz	Christie's Lanarkshire UK 1998 #565
1820 ca	William Jamieson	Aberdeen	Spirit lamp, circular stand on 4 scroll feet,	Christie's February 3, 1965 #124
1820 ca	AD mm	Aberdeen	Table bell, no details	Dundee Museums and Art Galleries 1978-637
1820 ca	Francis Howden	Edinburgh	Chain of Office, Provost of Leith, gold badge and chain, upright oval, cast figure of justice, engraved "1834 First Provost Adam White", on reverse side 2 masted ship in front of a pier, rowing boat in the foreground 1 7/8" X 2 3/8"	Huntley House Museum Edinburgh museum number not available
1820 ca	George Booth	Aberdeen	Sugar sifter, no details	Dundee Museums and Art Galleries 1970-314
1820 ca	Edward Livingstone	Dundee	Shoe buckles, pair, no details	National Museums of Scotland TBX 135 a,b 1985
1820 ca	W & P Cunningham II	Edinburgh	Extinguisher, no details	National Museums of Scotland MEQ 786
1820/21	George Fenwick	Edinburgh	Candle snuffers, pair, no details	National Museums of Scotland H.1996.30
1820/21	Richard Haxton	Edinburgh	Oval nutmeg grater, lid set with red carnelian agate, interior fitted with original iron grater, ring at the other end, mm only	Private Collection
1820/21	George McHattie	Edinburgh	Wine coolers, pair, bucket-shaped, applied horizontal hoops, upright loop handles, later chased, complete with collars and liners, 9" ht, 135oz	Christie's London UK 1999 #78
1822/23	George McHattie	Edinburgh	Snuffer scissor, 6 ¾" long, 5.1oz	Nicholas Shaw Catalog 2005 p100
1823/24	W & P Cunningham II	Edinburgh	Crumb scoop, coronet and crest of Gordon, Earl of Aberdeen	Nicholas Shaw Catalog 2005 p100
1823/24	Robert Gray & Son	Glasgow	Coursing trophy, no details	National Museums of Scotland K.2002.368
1824/25	George Fenwick	Edinburgh	Snuffers, scissor form, box engraved with crest and motto	Christie's East NY USA 1999 #240

YEAR	MAKER	LOCATION	DESCRIPTION	SOURCE
1825 ca	Not available	Edinburgh	Dog whistle shaped like a dog's head	Shrubsole NY USA 2006 #04-24
1825/26	George McHattie	Edinburgh	Brandy pan and cover, hinged spout flap, 4 ½" di, 11oz 10d	Private Collection
1828/29	Marshall & Sons	Edinburgh	Centerpiece, no details	National Museums of Scotland MEQ 1237
1828/29	D C Rait	Glasgow	Whiskey flask, rectangular, with crest and motto, engraved to Robert Dick, Esq	National Museums of Scotland MEQ 1128
1828/29	James Howden & Co	Edinburgh	Fox head stirrup cup, 5" long, 4 5/8" across, 6oz	JH Bourdon-Smith Catalog 1999 p54 #41
1828/29	James McKay	Edinburgh	Brandy pan, traditional squat baluster form, turned wood handle, with crest, motto and initials for Balfour of Fernie Castle, 6 7/8" ht, 5.5oz gross	Lyon & Turnbull, Edinburgh UK 2004 #356
1830/31	William Marshall	Edinburgh	Edinburgh Academy in full relief, whole set in silver gilt rim and mount, fully marked, 2" di	Private Collection
1831/32	James Howden	Edinburgh	Goose egg decapitator, monogrammed, Elder & Co retailers	Nicholas Shaw Catalog 2005 p100
1834/35	Andrew Wilkie	Edinburgh	Meat bone holder, no details	National Museums of Scotland 4.1995.685
1834/35	TJR	Edinburgh	Nutmeg grater, no details	National Museums of Scotland MEQ 1217
1835/36	Andrew Wilkie	Edinburgh	Meat bone holder, presumably this is different from the National Museums of Scotland grip made the year earlier	Sotheby's Gleneagles August 1987 #308
1836/37	James McKay	Edinburgh	Combination fork and knife, no details	National Museums of Scotland MEQ 1319
1836/37	William Marshall	Edinburgh	Presentation cup, no details	National Museums of Scotland MEQ
1838/39	James Nasmyth	Edinburgh	Presentation lancet or scalpel box	National Museums of Scotland VJ15
1838/39	Mitchell & Russell	Glasgow	Early Victorian pap boat, reeded edge, unengraved, marked in base of bowl	Private Collection
1839/40	Robb & Whittet	Edinburgh	Nutmeg grater, no details	National Museums of Scotland MEQ 919

YEAR	MAKER	LOCATION	DESCRIPTION	SOURCE
1840/41	William Marshall	Edinburgh	Butter dish, no details	National Museums of Scotland MEQ 1127
1843/44	James McKay	Edinburgh	The Weill Cup, presented to Patrick Weill by Practical Gardeners	National Museums of Scotland A.1878.50
1849/50	EM	Edinburgh	Presentation Trowel, no details	National Museums of Scotland MEQ 1286
1855/56	J Mc	Edinburgh	Ewer, no details	National Museums of Scotland H.1995.638
1856/57	Michael Crichton	Edinburgh	Baton, no details	Private Collection 2005
1856/57	J & W Marshall	Edinburgh	2 handled piggin	Private Collection
1858/59	CMB	Edinburgh	Stirrup cup, cast in the form of a ram's head, gilt interior, 4 ¾" wide, 4oz 9d	Sotheby's London UK 2006 #252
1858/59	Walker Crichton	Edinburgh	Centerpiece, statuette of Sir Walter Scott, Presentation 1861	National Museums of Scotland MEQ 1606
1825/29	JR	Edinburgh	Ram's head snuff mull, horns terminating in thistle mount, set with faceted quartz, hinged lid thistle embossed, crested shield, sold with various tools, 7½" ht	Bonhams Sale 15120 Aug 22, 2007 #3
1859/60	J & W Marshall	Edinburgh	Crumb scoop or cream skimmer	The Maple Swan Collection
1869/70	Charles Robb & Son	Edinburgh	2 handled piggin	Private Collection
1871/72	G & MC	Edinburgh	2 handled piggin	Private Collection
1874/75	Hamilton & Inches	Edinburgh	Christening set, no details	National Museums of Scotland 1978.102
1878/79	James Nasmyth & Co	Edinburgh	Egg timer, no details	National Museums of Scotland H.1991.1
1879/80	McKay & Chisholm	Edinburgh	Piggin with lug type handles, engraved "to James Marshall Findlay.....", 2 ½" ht, 10.5oz	JH Bourdon-Smith Catalog 1991 p47 #34
1880 ca	William Robb	Ballater	Shoe buckles, pair	Aberdeen Museums and Galleries ABDAG008693

349

YEAR	MAKER	LOCATION	DESCRIPTION	SOURCE
1880/81	McKay, Cunningham & Co	Edinburgh	Centerpiece, no details	National Museums of Scotland H.1995.107
1881/82	J & W Marshall	Edinburgh	Piggin, engraved "John Alexander, 20 Feb 1857", 2 ½" ht, 6.5oz	JH Bourdon-Smith Catalog 1991 p47 #34
1884/85	Marshall & Son	Edinburgh	Spades, 2 pairs, one pair 8" long, the other pair 6" long, 10oz all	JH Bourdon-Smith Catalog 1999 p60 #41
1889/90	George M Millard	Edinburgh	Rare Victorian hunting horn	Private Collection
1890/91	Marshall & Sons	Edinburgh	Argyle, engraved with the arms of Tristram, 5 ¾" ht, 17.1oz	JH Bourdon-Smith Catalog #47 Spring 2007 p 57
1897/98	J M T	Edinburgh	Buckles, pair, with Celtic knotwork decoration, 1 2/3" long X 1 ½" wide	eBay #160140507525 July 2007
1902/03	Brook & Son	Edinburgh	Piggin, with bold banding, 2 7/8" ht, 6" across, 13oz	JH Bourdon-Smith Catalog 1999 p57 #41
1903/04	Hamilton & Inches	Edinburgh	Heraldic menu holders, modeled as the crest of Blair of Dunrod, sold with other items	Bonhams London UK 2004 #371
1907/08	Young & Tatton	Edinburgh	Dirk and Skene Dhu, no details	National Museums of Scotland LC90 1969
1909/10	Hamilton & Inches	Edinburgh	Crumb hook, standard form, rat tailed curved blade, turned dark wood handle	Private Collection
1910/11	Hamilton & Inches	Edinburgh	Crumb scoop, curved blade, ebony turned handle, 11 2/3" long, 7.4oz gross	eBay #320138527789 July 2007
1920/21	Henry Roy Tatton	Edinburgh	Napkin ring, no details	The Maple Swan Collection
1972/73	RA	Edinburgh assay	Skene Dhu, no details	The Maple Swan Collection
1978	Grant McDonald	Edinburgh	Rosebowl, for the 500th Anniversary of the Edinburgh Assay Office	National Museums of Scotland MEQ 1981.48
1982/83	T E	Edinburgh	Highland dirk, no details	The Maple Swan Collection
1989	Maureen Edgar	Edinburgh	Silver mounted vase, no details	National Museums of Scotland MEQ 1616
1990/91	T E	Edinburgh	Dress sporran, no details	The Maple Swan Collection

YEAR	MAKER	LOCATION	DESCRIPTION	SOURCE
2003	William Kirk	Edinburgh	Two containers on a slate base	National Museums of Scotland K2004.22 1-3
	SPECIAL COLLECTIONS			
1999-2000	Malcolm Appleby	Edinburgh	Table center, Millennium Collection	Scottish Goldsmith's Trust on permanent loan to Bute House, Edinburgh UK
1999-2000	Adrian Hope	Edinburgh	Culler set, Millennium Collection	Scottish Goldsmith's Trust on permanent loan to Bute House, Edinburgh UK
1999-2000	Gordon Burnett	Edinburgh	Clock, Millennium Collection	Scottish Goldsmith's Trust on permanent loan to Bute House, Edinburgh UK
1999-2000	Sara Cave	Edinburgh	Condiment set, Millennium Collection	Scottish Goldsmith's Trust on permanent loan to Bute House, Edinburgh UK
1999-2000	John Creed	Edinburgh	Floor-standing candle holders, Millennium Collection	Scottish Goldsmith's Trust on permanent loan to Bute House, Edinburgh UK
1999-2000	Maureen Edgar	Edinburgh	Condiment set, Millennium Collection	Scottish Goldsmith's Trust on permanent loan to Bute House, Edinburgh UK
1999-2000	Marion Kane	Edinburgh	Vases, pair, Millennium Collection	Scottish Goldsmith's Trust on permanent loan to Bute House, Edinburgh UK
1999-2000	William Kirk	Edinburgh	Rose/fruit bowl, Millennium Collection	Scottish Goldsmith's Trust on permanent loan to Bute House, Edinburgh UK
1999-2000	Michael Lloyd	Edinburgh	Water jugs, pair, Millennium Collection	Scottish Goldsmith's Trust on permanent loan to Bute House, Edinburgh UK
1999-2000	Helen Marriott	Edinburgh	Candlesticks, two pairs, Millennium Collection	Scottish Goldsmith's Trust on permanent loan to Bute House, Edinburgh UK

YEAR	MAKER (continued)	LOCATION	DESCRIPTION	SOURCE Edinburgh UK
1999-2000	Grant McCaig	Edinburgh	Fruit bowl, Millennium Collection	Scottish Goldsmith's Trust on permanent loan to Bute House, Edinburgh UK
1999-2000	Roger Millar	Edinburgh	Wine cooler/ice bucket, Millennium Collection	Scottish Goldsmith's Trust on permanent loan to Bute House, Edinburgh UK
1999-2000	Linda Robertson	Edinburgh	Condiment set, Millennium Collection	Scottish Goldsmith's Trust on permanent loan to Bute House, Edinburgh UK
1999-2000	Graham Stewart	Edinburgh	Claret jugs, pair, Millennium Collection	Scottish Goldsmith's Trust on permanent loan to Bute House, Edinburgh UK
1999-2000	Nicola Williams	Edinburgh	Feature bowl and candlesticks, Millennium Collection	Scottish Goldsmith's Trust on permanent loan to Bute House, Edinburgh UK
2005	Sarah Cave	Edinburgh	Claret jug and beakers, designed for Sir Cameron Mackintosh, Jug 10 2/3" ht, 23.7oz	Silver of the Stars, International Tour 2007/08 National Museums of Scotland 2008 Exhibition
2005	John Creed	Edinburgh	Irn Bru jug, goblets and tray, designed for Ian Rankin, OBE, jug 10 2/3" ht, 20.6oz	Silver of the Stars, International Tour 2007/08 National Museums of Scotland 2008 Exhibition
2005	Colin O'Dubhghaill	Edinburgh	Tricycle teapot, sugar bowl and banjo spoon, designed for Billy Connolly, CBE, teapot 8 2/3" ht, 60.3oz	Silver of the Stars, International Tour 2007/08 National Museums of Scotland 2008 Exhibition
2005	Sarah Hutchinson	Edinburgh	Teapot and cups, designed for Sharleen Spiteri, teapot 9 ½" ht, 54.4oz	Silver of the Stars, International Tour 2007/08 National Museums of Scotland 2008 Exhibition

YEAR	MAKER	LOCATION	DESCRIPTION	SOURCE
2005	Michael Lloyd	Edinburgh	Quaich, designed for Sir Sean Connery, 5 7/8" di, 13.2oz	Silver of the Stars, International Tour 2007/08 National Museums of Scotland 2008 Exhibition
2005	Grant McCaig	Edinburgh	Whiskey set, designed for Robbie Coltrane, OBE, jug 6 ¼" ht, 17.8oz	Silver of the Stars, International Tour 2007/08 National Museums of Scotland 2008 Exhibition
2006	Marion Kane	Edinburgh	Coffeepot, mug and cream jug, designed for Ewan McGregor, 999 silver, coffeepot 13 ¾" ht, 67.7oz	Silver of the Stars, International Tour 2007/08 National Museums of Scotland 2008 Exhibition
2006	Roger Millar	Edinburgh	Hot chocolate pot and mugs, designed for Nicola Benedetti, pot 10 2/3" ht, 34.8oz	Silver of the Stars, International Tour 2007/08 National Museums of Scotland 2008 Exhibition
2006	Linda Robertson	Edinburgh	Teapot, designed for Lulu, OBE, 4 ¾" ht, 51oz	Silver of the Stars, International Tour 2007/08 National Museums of Scotland 2008 Exhibition
2006	Graham Stewart	Edinburgh	Absinthe goblet and spoon, designed for Alexander McQueen, goblet 8 ¼" ht, 78oz,	Silver of the Stars, International Tour 2007/08 National Museums of Scotland 2008 Exhibition

Mugs

Plate 34. A Mug 1739/40 by Patrick Murray III, Edinburgh.
Courtesy of The Phoenix Collection. Photograph by Janice M Dietert.

General Mugs

Plate 35. A Mug 1734/35 by Dougal Ged, Edinburgh.
Courtesy of The Phoenix Collection. Photograph by Janice M Dietert.

MUGS

YEAR	MAKER	LOCATION	DESCRIPTION	SOURCE
	GENERAL			
1684/85	IS (pillar in between)	Edinburgh	Mugs, pair, (apparently), bell shaped body, engraved opposite handles above the molded girdle with armorials, scroll handles applied beaded rat tails, on rim feet, Arms of Wyohe, of Davenham, County Chester, 3 ¾" ht, 13.4oz	Park Lane Loan Exhibition, pl XVII, #29 Sotheby's March 16, 1961 #72
1684/85	IS (pillar in between)	Edinburgh	Mug, similar to the pair above, 4"ht, 7oz	Sotheby's June 2, 1949 #101 Christie's October 16, 1963 #171 S J Phillips Ltd London UK
1709 ca	William Clerk	Glasgow	Mug, plain tapering cylindrical, on reeded rim foot, molded lip, scroll handle with rat tail extension, mm 2X's, 3 3/8" ht, 6oz 5d	Christie's March 29, 1983 #52 Shaw Collection National Museums of Scotland MEQ 1556 1983
1710 ca	Robert Innes	Inverness	Mug, small bell shaped, applied with girdle and lobe straps above slight ring foot, reeded strap handle, engrave with contemporary initials "M/S MK/ K MK", 1 ¾" ht, 1oz 9d	Sotheby's June 30, 1981 #172
1710 ca	Simon McKenzie	Inverness	Mug, for a child, may be a thistle mug	Metropolitan Museum AC #63.53.7
1710 ca	Not available	Edinburgh	Mug, 4 ¾" ht, 16.5oz	Sotheby's April 29, 1986
1710/11	Henry Bethune	Edinburgh	Mugs, pair, no details	The Maple Swan Collection
1711/12	James Mitchelson	Edinburgh	Mug, no details	The Maple Swan Collection
1711/12	David Mitchell	Edinburgh	Mug, small, circular, plain, with scroll handle, central band on slightly spreading rim base, 3 ½" ht, 5oz	Phillips May 15, #91 Sotheby's March 20, 1975 #183
1711/12	Colin McKenzie	Edinburgh	Mug, straight sided, plain strap handle, engraved underneath "RY/EC", 3 1/8" ht, 6.3oz	J H Bourdon-Smith Catalog #47 Spring 2007 p15
1711/12	Colin Campbell	Edinburgh	Mug, with date letter variant, no details	Jackson Marks p 546
1712/13	John Seatoun	Edinburgh	Mug, tapering, cylindrical, molded lip and base, scroll handle with later initials, with crest and motto, 3 ½" ht, 7.4oz	Sotheby's December 1, 1976 #107
1712/13	Colin McKenzie	Edinburgh	Mug, cylindrical, simple handle, 3 ¼" ht	Wark, Huntington Library Book #60
1712/13	Thomas Ker	Edinburgh	Mug, plain cylindrical, reeded feet and rim, 3 ½" ht, 5oz	Christie's February 5, 1947 #89

YEAR	MAKER	LOCATION	DESCRIPTION	SOURCE
1713/14	Edward Penman	Edinburgh	Mugs, pair, cylindrical, molded thumbstops, Napier crest and motto, 3 1/6" ht, 10oz 12d both (5oz 6d ea)	Christie's February 17, 1960 #131
1713/14	James Mitchelson	Edinburgh	Mug, later gilt, tapering cylindrical body, inscribed above a reeded girdle, scroll handle, molded lip and base, 3" ht, 4.8oz	Sotheby's December 4, 1958
1713/14	John Seatoun	Edinburgh	Mug, cylindrical, bulbous sides, reeded base, scroll handle, 3 ¼" ht, 5oz 8d	Christie's May 18, 1938 #70
1714/15	Alexander Kincaid	Edinburgh	Mugs, pair, straight sided, with molded borders, scroll handles, 3 1/8" ht, 9oz both (4oz 10d ea)	Sotheby's May 17-19, 1988 #993 (unsold) Christie's March 8, 1989 #197
1715 ca	William Ged	Edinburgh	Mug with slight tapering body, Arms of Maxwell, 3 ½" ht	Christie's London March 4, 1992 #191 Hyman Collection, Colonial Williamsburg
1715 ca	*William Ged*	*Edinburgh*	*Mug with slightly tapering body, full Arms of Maxwell and gift inscription, 3 ¾" ht, 8.2oz*	*Sotheby's Gleneagles 1990 #136*
1715/16	John Seaton	Edinburgh	Mugs, pair, plain, cylindrical crest and motto, initials "M/JB", 3 ¼", 11.8oz both	JH Bourdon-Smith Catalog Autumn 1999, p20, #41
1715/16	Colin Campbell	Edinburgh	Mug, plain, reeded foot, slightly convex sides, scroll handle, 3 ¼" ht, 4oz 18d	Christie's March 19, 1934 #142 Gardner Collection
1716/17	Henry Bethune	Edinburgh	Mugs, pair, each on a molded foot, shaped bodies with scroll handle, 3" ht, 8.6oz both	Christie's July 12-13, 1983 #78
1717/18	Mungo Yorstoun	Edinburgh	Mugs, pair, initial "C" 2x's, crest and motto of Crichton, 2 7/8" ht, 11oz 14d	Christie's December 20, 1974 #15 Clayton Christie's Book p 116 Sotheby's August 29, 1978 #440
1717/18	Charles Blair	Edinburgh	Mug, cylindrical, scroll handles, inscription, 3 1/5" ht, 6oz 1d	Christie's October 28, 1953 #47 Jackson Marks p 545
1717/18	William Ged	Edinburgh	Mug, cylindrical, molded foot and rim, 3" ht, 6oz 5d	Christie's July 31, 1950 #128
1717/18	Archibald Ure	Edinburgh	Mugs, pair, cylindrical engraved, initials, 3 1/6" ht, 12oz 12d both, (6oz 6d ea)	Christie's June 22, 1960 #100 Shrubsole

YEAR	MAKER	LOCATION	DESCRIPTION	SOURCE
1717/18	Mungo Yorstoun	Edinburgh	Mugs, pair, small, no details	National Museums of Scotland MEQ 1292-1293 1978.79-80
1718/19	Patrick Turnbull	Edinburgh	Mug, no details	The Maple Swan Collection
1718/19	Alexander Simpson	Edinburgh	Mug, no details	The Maple Swan Collection
1718/19	Patrick Turnbull	Edinburgh	Mug, cylindrical, slightly everted rim, reeded base, with the initial "C", flaring lip, 2 7/8" ht, 4oz 3d	Christie's April 26, 1966 #115 C. Vander Collection Sotheby's NY USA April 1990 #445
1718/19	Edward Penman	Edinburgh	Mug, baluster body with high loop handle, 4 7/8" ht, 9oz	California-European Art Exchange Inventory #2618
1718/19	Alexander Kincaid	Edinburgh	Mugs, pair, straight sides, initials "PC MB", 3" ht, 9oz 13d	Sotheby's November 26, 1968 #233 How of Edinburgh Scottish Arts Review, vol XII #3 back cover Antiques Magazine vol 121, p 1311 S. Wyler Advertisement
1718/19	Charles Dickson I or Charles Duncan	Edinburgh	Mug, plain, baluster form, scroll handle, 4 ½" ht, 7oz	Christie's London March 1992 #192
1718/19	Not available		Mug, plain, no details	Connoisseur Magazine May 1939, vol 103 p35 How of Edinburgh advertisement
1719/20	Robert Inglis	Edinburgh	Mug, half pint, initials "A/RI" under base, 3 ½" ht, 5.8oz	JH Bourdon-Smith Catalog 2004 Nicholas Shaw Antiques 2004
1719/20	Archibald Ure	Edinburgh	Mugs, pair, cylindrical initials, slightly tapering, 3 ¼" ht, 11oz 12d both (5oz 16d ea)	Christie's November 2, 1960 #166
1719/20	Not available		Mug, plain, no details	Connoisseur Magazine May 1939 vol 103 p35 How of Edinburgh advertisement
1719/20	Kenneth McKenzie	Edinburgh	Mug, slightly tapering body, on rim foot, with a strap handle, 3 ½" ht, 4.3oz	Sotheby's Hopetoun House, June 20, 1988 #151

YEAR	MAKER	LOCATION	DESCRIPTION	SOURCE
1719/20	Charles Dickson I or Charles Duncan	Edinburgh	Mug, half pint, slightly shaped body, tucked into a molded rim foot, everted lip, plain capped scroll handle, crest and motto of Lockhart	Lyon & Turnbull February 20, 2004 #253
1719/20	Alexander Kincaid	Edinburgh	Mug, plain, tapering cylindrical shape, single scroll handle with marriage initials, 3" ht, 5oz	Christie's Edinburgh April 29, 1982 #50
1719/20	Archibald Ure	Edinburgh	Mugs, pair, on molded feet, scroll handles, one has the initials "AM HM", 3 3/8" ht, 11oz 12d the other has the initials "AM JL",	Christie's November 10, 1971 #135
1719/20	Robert Inglis	Edinburgh	Mug on spreading foot, engraved "R.A.I." on base, 3 ½" 5.9oz	Nicholas Shaw Catalog 2004 p101
1720 ca	N R		Dram cup, 1 ½"ht, 1oz	Nicholas Shaw Catalog 2002/03 p84
1720 ca	James Tait	Edinburgh	Mug, straight sided, on flaring foot	Country Life June 1987 p114 JH Bourdon-Smith advertisement
1720 ca	George Robertson	Aberdeen	Mugs, pair of plain tapering cylindrical, each on molded rim foot, everted lip, faceted scroll handle, engraved on lower terminal with initials "ICW", 3 ½" ht, 11oz	Shaw Collection Christie's March 29, 1983 #34
1720 ca	James Mitchelson probably	Edinburgh	Mug on spreading rim foot, molded girdle, leaf capped loop handle, later body chasing, (said to be William Jamieson based on Jackson), 2 1/8" ht	Christie's Glasgow July 12, 1983, #195
1720/21	James Mitchelson	Edinburgh	Mug, slight barrel shape, flat foot, engraved initials "AG", 3" ht 5.3oz	Christie's December 15, 1971 #293 Christie's London UK 2002 #17 Nicholas Shaw Catalog 2002/03 p84
1721/22	James Tait	Edinburgh	Mug, with added lip above initials, scroll handle on spreading stepped rim, 3 ½" ht, 6.4oz	Sotheby's February 14, 1980 #55
1723/24	James Mitchelson	Edinburgh	Mug, shaped outline, on molded foot, with a crest and motto, 5.4oz	Christie's April 13, 1977 #98
1723/24	Kenneth McKenzie	Edinburgh	Mug or cup	Jackson Marks p546 notes (Christie's source)
1724/25	Alexander Kincaid	Edinburgh	Mug, 3 ½" ht	Scottish Art Academy Exhibition 1939 #458 J. Cathcart White Collection

YEAR	MAKER	LOCATION	DESCRIPTION	SOURCE
1724/25	Alexander Kincaid	Edinburgh	Mug, no details	National Museums of Scotland 1943.248
1725/26	Edward Penman	Edinburgh	Mug, no details	The Maple Swan Collection
1725/26	James Ker	Edinburgh	Mug, cylindrical, on molded foot, lip and rim, 3 ¾" ht, 5oz 17d	Christie's July 17, 1963 #122
1725/26	James Mitchelson	Edinburgh	Mug, 3.1" ht	Wark, Huntington Book #64
1725 ca	Robert Luke	Glasgow	Mug, plain, 6oz 4d	Christie's March 5, 1946 #122
1726/27	Alexander Kincaid	Edinburgh	Mug, circular shaped body, molded base, *leaf capped handle*, initials "JS JT", 3" ht, 5oz 16d	Christie's May 18, 1966 #77
1726/27	Charles Blair	Edinburgh	Mug, partly fluted, shaped outline, molded foot, 2 ¾" ht, 5oz 5d	Christie's March 13, 1968 #64
1727/28	James Ker	Edinburgh	Mugs, pair, slightly tapering cylindrical with tuck in or plain spreading base and slightly everted lip, engraved opposite handles, variation of Arms of Hamilton of Pencartland, 4 ½" ht, 15.3oz	Scottish Art Review vol XII, #2 back cover 1969 How of Edinburgh advertisement JH Bourdon-Smith Catalog 2004, p24, #45
1727/28	Not available	Edinburgh	Mug, slightly tapering cylindrical, slightly flaring at rim, plain capped scroll handle, tucked in base on spreading foot, 3 ¼" ht, 6.8oz	Sotheby's Gleneagles August 25, 1977 #159
1727/28	James Ker	Edinburgh	Mug, plain, nearly straight sided, tucked on a spreading stepped base, plain capped single scroll handle, 3 3/8" ht	Lyon & Turnbull February 20, 2004 #245
1728/29	James Ker	Edinburgh	Mug, tapering cylindrical form on spreading foot, scroll handle, 3" ht, 5.2oz	Sotheby's November 26, 1969 #194 Christie's April 22, 1970
1728/29	*James Ker*	*Edinburgh*	*Mug, tapering cylindrical form on spreading foot, scroll handle, 3" ht, 5.7oz*	*Sotheby's London December 19, 1993 #193*
1730 ca	Johan Got-helf-Bilsings	Glasgow	Mug, straight-sided with a molded girdle crest and motto, faceted double scroll handled, scratch weight on base "7=10", repaired at handle, 3 ¾" ht, 7oz 5d	Sotheby's NY USA Oct 18, 2001 #297
1730 ca	Alexander Kincaid	Edinburgh	Mug, mm only, baluster form with flaring rim, molded foot, S-scroll handle with leaf grip, engraved script initials "JS/GW", thought to have been presented to George Washington at his Christening in 1732, Provenance: Dr. S. Weir Mitchell, antiquarian, 3 1/8" ht, 5oz 5d	Christie's NY USA 1990 #88

YEAR	MAKER	LOCATION	DESCRIPTION	SOURCE
1730 ca	Robert Luke	Glasgow	Mug, almost cylindrical body, tucked in base and spreading foot, scroll handle, 3 ½" ht,	Sotheby's April 13, 1976 #50
1730 ca	Robert Luke	Glasgow	Mug, plain, tapering cylindrical form, on spreading foot, plain scroll handle, retaining traces of engraved initials, 3 ¼" ht, 6oz	Christie's Glasgow November 16, 1994 #680
1730 ca	George Cooper	Aberdeen	Mugs, pair, slightly tapering cylindrical bodies, each engraved with crest and motto, on spreading feet, scroll handle, 3 ½" ht, 12oz 1d both	Sotheby's London June 18, 1987 #234
1731/32	James Ker	Edinburgh	Mug, engraved with animal head and crest, motto probably for Fairlie, part of a suite with bowl and stand	JH Bourdon-Smith Spring 1983 viewing
1732/36	Hugh Penman	Edinburgh	Mug, on spreading foot, with scroll handle, 4.5oz (possibly Henry Bethune or misdated)	Christie's July 12, 1983, #199 (unsold)
1733/34	Hugh Penman	Edinburgh	Mug, plain baluster body, with plain capped scroll handle, body tucked on a spreading foot, 3 ¼" ht, 4.8oz	Sotheby's Gleneagles, August 25, 1997 #161
1734/35	Colin Campbell	Edinburgh	Mugs, pair, one patched, initials "EQ ID", 3 ¾" ht, 10oz 10d	Christie's Glasgow March 1983 Christie's Edinburgh November 21, 1990 #38
1734/35	*Colin Campbell*	*Edinburgh*	*Mugs, pair, no details*	*The Maple Swan Collection*
1734/35	Dougal Ged	Edinburgh	Mug, baluster, with crest and motto '"VERTUTIS FORTUNA COMES"', 3" ht	Goodwin's Edinburgh 1992 The Phoenix Collection
1735ca	Robert Luke II	Glasgow	Mug, baluster form, on spreading foot, crest and motto of Folis	Nicholas Shaw Catalog 2005 p91
1735/36	Dougal Ged	Edinburgh	Mug, small baluster form, on spreading circular foot, everted lip and scroll handle, 3 ¼" ht, 5oz	Christie's Scotland November 25-28, 1997 #107
1735/36	Dougal Ged	Edinburgh	Mugs, pair, plain, shaped outline, each on spreading foot, plain capped double scroll handle, 4 1/3" ht, 21oz both (10oz 10d ea)	Christie's July 6, 1977 #162
1735/36	William Aytoun	Edinburgh	Mugs, pair, pear shaped initials and crest, 3 1/3" ht 12oz 5d both (6oz 3d ea)	Christie's May 11, 1960 #122 Scottish Arts Review vol XV, #3 back cover How of Edinburgh advertisement
1735 ca	George Cooper	Aberdeen	Mugs, pair, no details	Finlay 1991 pl 108
1735 ca	*George Cooper*	*Aberdeen*	*Mugs, pair, no details*	*Sotheby's London June 1987 #234*

YEAR	MAKER	LOCATION	DESCRIPTION	SOURCE
1735 ca	Robert Luke	Glasgow	Mug, tucked in cut base on flat foot, crest and motto "THURE ET TURE", 3 ½" ht, 6.1oz	Nicholas Shaw Internet Catalog October 1999
1736/37	Hugh Penman	Edinburgh	Mug, baluster body on spreading foot, reeded rim, double scroll handle, 3" ht, 3.6oz	Sotheby's April 30, 1985 #127
1736/37	James Campbell	Edinburgh	Mug, plain on rim foot, with slightly everted lip, scroll handle, 3 1/8" ht, 5.3oz	Christie's May 15, 1963 #69
1737/38	James Ker	Edinburgh	Mugs, pair, curved sides, scroll handle, 3" ht, 11oz 13d both (5oz 17d ea)	Christie's May 8, 1939 #44 Christie's May 11, 1960 #121
1737/38	James Ker	Edinburgh	*Mugs, pair, plain, curved sides, 3" ht*	*Louis Wine, Ltd, Toronto Canada 1996*
1737/38	Alexander Farquharson	Edinburgh	Mug, small, no details	Jackson Marks p 547
1738/39	Edward Lothian	Edinburgh	Mug, plain baluster, on spreading circular foot, engraved opposite handle with coat of arms of MacFarlane, capped scroll handle, 3 1/3" ht, 4.5oz	Christie's Glasgow July 4, 1989 #103
1738/39	James Ker	Edinburgh	Mug, baluster body, engraved with initials, double scroll handle, on spreading foot, 3 1/8" ht, 5.9oz	Sotheby's Gleneagles August 29, 1983 #489
1738/39	William Dempster (either wrong maker or wrong year)	Edinburgh	Mug, engraved and later chased with monogram, scrolls and floral sprays on a matted ground, leaf capped double scroll handle, on molded rim foot, 3 ¼" ht, 6.7oz	Sotheby's April 28, 1960 #136 Simon Kaye Antiques
1739/40	James Ker	Edinburgh	Mug, no details	Jackson Marks p 547
1739/40	Patrick Murray III Assayer Archibald Ure	Edinburgh	Mug, baluster form, script initials "DL" over "EC", 3 5/8" ht	JH Bourdon-Smith Catalog 1993 The Phoenix Collection
1739/40	James Ker	Edinburgh	Mug with extensive repousse decoration	National Museums of Scotland 1900.275
1739/40	Not available Assayer Archibald Ure	Edinburgh	Mug, plain shaped outline, on spreading foot, with scroll handle,	Christie's July 11, 1960 #115 Christie's February 1, 1961 #112 Simon Kaye Antiques
1740 ca	John Baille	Banff	Mugs, pair, shaped, plain, fluted, scroll handles, 15oz both (7oz 10d ea)	Christie's March 14, 1944 #107 How of Edinburgh Collection
1740 ca	Robert Luke	Glasgow	Mug, double scroll handle, 3" ht, 5oz 14d	Sotheby's June 26, 1975 #160

YEAR	MAKER	LOCATION	DESCRIPTION	SOURCE
1740 ca	Alexander Johnston	Dundee	Mug, half pint, plain, slightly waisted cylindrical form, molded circular base, plain scroll handle with old repair, base engraved with contemporary initials "E & MK", 4 marks, A I (struck twice), pot of lilies, script L, 3 ¾" ht, 6oz	Christie's Glasgow November 16, 1994 #692
1740 ca	Robert Luke	Glasgow	Mug, plain, on circular molded foot, body of shaped outline, scroll handle, engraved with initials, 3 1/8", 5oz 12d	Christie's December 20, 1974 #125
1740 ca	Robert Luke	Glasgow	*Mug, plain, tapered cylindrical body, on tucked in base, everted lip, doubled scroll handle, 3" ht, 5oz 14d*	*Sotheby's June 26, 1975 #160*
1740 ca	John Baillie	Inverness	Mugs, pair, plain, each of shaped outline, on rim foot, faceted double scroll handle, patched, marks IB, IM, 3 ½" ht, 11oz	Shaw Collection Christie's March 29, 1983 #42
1740 ca	John Baillie	Inverness	*Mugs, pair, plain, each on rim foot, slightly everted lip, scroll handle, 3 3/8" ht, 11oz*	*Christie's July 3, 1984 #160*
1740/41 & 42/43	Edward Lothian	Edinburgh	Mugs, pair, plain, each on circular molded foot, bodies of shaped outline, double scroll handles, engraved with crest and motto, 3 3/8" ht, 12.4oz both	Christie's November 10, 1971 #76
1740/41	William Aytoun	Edinburgh	Mug, baluster body, double scroll handle, shaped plinth, 3 3/8" ht	Thomas Roddick and Metcalf, Dumfries March 13, 2000
1740/41	Edward Lothian	Edinburgh	Mug, baluster form	S J Phillips Ltd London UK London 2006 #19812
1740/41	Dougal Ged	Edinburgh	Mug, baluster form, engraved with crest and motto of Balfour, "VIRTUS AD ACTHERA TENDIT", 3 ½" ht, 6.4oz	Nicholas Shaw Catalog 2001 p71
1742/43	Edward Lothian	Edinburgh	Mug, baluster form, 3 ¼" ht, 5.9oz	JH Bourdon-Smith Catalog Autumn 2002 p23
1742/43	Thomas Mitchell	Edinburgh	Mug, baluster, with initials "EPS", 3 ¾" ht, 6.5oz	JH Bourdon-Smith Catalog Autumn 1997, p17 #39
1742/43	*Thomas Mitchell*	*Edinburgh*	*Mug, baluster form, scroll handle, raised circular foot, initials, 3 3/8" ht, 6oz*	*Bonhams October 24, 2000*
1742/43	Edward Lothian	Edinburgh	Mug, dumpy baluster shape, 3 ½" ht, 5.8oz	J H Bourdon-Smith Catalog #47 Spring 2007 p15
1742/43	*Edward Lothian Assayer Edward Lothian*	*Edinburgh*	*Mug, 3 1/3" ht, 2 ¾" di*	*JH Bourdon-Smith Catalog 1993*
1742/43	Edward Lothian	Edinburgh	Mug, baluster, plain, 3 ½" ht	W T Wilkenson, London 1995

YEAR	MAKER	LOCATION	DESCRIPTION	SOURCE The Phoenix Collection
	Assayer Edward Lothian			
1743/44	William Aytoun	Edinburgh	Mug, baluster body, on spreading foot, chased around armorials, with scrolls and rococo, leaf capped handle, 6 ¾" ht, 22.7oz	Sotheby's Gleneagles September 1, 1998 #559
1743/44	Ebenezer Oliphant	Edinburgh	Mugs, pair, baluster form, later initials, double scroll handles, on spreading bases, 3 ½" ht, 11oz both	Sotheby's Gleneagles August 29, 1983 #504
1744/45	William Aytoun	Edinburgh	Mug, no details	Jackson Marks p547
1744/45	Lawrence Oliphant	Edinburgh	Mug, silver gilt, heavily chased, acanthus capped scroll handle	Finlay 1991 p80 National Museums of Scotland MEQ 1177
1744/45	Alexander Campbell	Edinburgh	Mug, squat baluster form, applied scroll handle, spread circular foot, 3 ¼" ht, 5oz	Bonhams London UK 2007 #163
1745 ca	William Davie or William Dempster Assayer Hugh Gordon	Edinburgh	Pint mugs, pair, baluster shape, chased with contemporary band of scroll, shell and floral motifs, on spreading base, 5" ht, 26oz	Sotheby's June 13, 1974
1747/48	Edward Lothian	Edinburgh	Mugs, baluster, on a domed foot, scroll handle, engraved with initials, 3 ½" ht, 6oz	Christie's London UK 2002 #228
1747/48	Edward Lothian	Edinburgh	Mugs, pair, baluster form, both engraved with a script initial "D", 3 ¼" ht, 12.1oz	Nicholas Shaw Catalog 2004, p99
1747/48	*Edward Lothian*	*Edinburgh*	*Mugs, pair of plain baluster shape, each on a spreading circular foot, with scroll handle and molded rim, engraved with script initial "D", 3 ¼" ht, 11oz 19d both*	*Christie's May 18, 1988 #364*
1747/48	Ker & Dempster	Edinburgh	Mugs, pair, no details	Burlington Magazine 1939, vol 74, p71
1747/48	Ker & Dempster Assayer Hugh Gordon	Edinburgh	Mug, plain, shaped outline, on rim foot, double scroll handle, engraved with an initial, 3 ½" ht, 5oz 12d	Christie's July 26, 1960 #139
1749/50	Edward Lothian	Edinburgh	Mug, with later inscription, "Property of M & S goods collection", 2 ¾" ht, 6oz	Sotheby's NY October 12, 1990 #161
1750/51	Edward Lothian	Edinburgh	Mug, baluster form, on stepped foot, double scroll handle, crest and motto of	Bonhams Sale 15120 Aug 22,

YEAR	MAKER	LOCATION	DESCRIPTION	SOURCE
			McCulloch, 3 ½" ht, 6.2oz	2007 #17
1752/53	James Gilliland	Edinburgh	Mug, baluster outline, on slightly shaped stepped spreading foot, molded lip, plain capped double scroll handle, 3 ½" ht, 7oz 10d	Christie's Glasgow March 29, 1983 #382
1758/59	Edward Lothian Assayer – Hugh Gordon	Edinburgh	Mug, squat baluster form, front engraved with foliated script initials "SL", 3 ½" ht, 6oz	Christie's London UK 2006 #719 Christie's London UK 2007 #1352
1760 ca	James Law	Aberdeen	Mug, split sides, 5 ¼" ht	JH Bourdon-Smith London 1996
1761/62	William Davie or William Dempster	Edinburgh	Mug, baluster, on low foot, crest and motto, 3" ht, 6.3oz	Nicholas Shaw Internet Catalog, October 1999
1761/62	Robert Gordon	Edinburgh	Mug, baluster form, plain capped double scroll handle, on spreading foot, crest and motto of Ross of Priesthill, 3 1/3" ht, 6.2oz	Sotheby's Scone Palace April 10, 1978 #66
1764/65	Ker & Dempster	Edinburgh	Mug with restrained swags of flowers and foliage, engraved "1766/Ex Dono/Margt. Carruther", en suite with a salver	Scottish Art Review vol VI, 1956 p 41 #1 Bell of Aberdeen advertisement
1765 ca	Adam Graham	Glasgow	Mug, baluster, half pint, engraved with script initials "HD", 3 ½" ht, 7.6oz	Nicholas Shaw Catalog Winter 2002/03 p84
1765 ca	Adam Graham	Glasgow	Mug, baluster form, leaf capped double scroll handle, molded rim foot, 4 ½" ht, 12oz	Sotheby's February 3, 1972 #157
1765 ca	Adam Graham	Glasgow	Mug, baluster form, on a conforming foot, leaf capped handle, side with initials, engraved "1726" underneath, 3 ¾" ht, 7oz	Christie's London UK 2002 #229
1765 ca	Adam Graham	Glasgow	Mug, cylindrical with tucked in base, on molded spreading circular base, engraved initials, enclosing a small set of initials, leaf capped multi-scroll handle, 4" ht, 10oz	Christie's East NY, USA 1997 #201
1765/66	Robert Clark	Edinburgh	Mug, small, no details	Jackson Marks p549
1769 ca	Milne & Campbell	Glasgow	Mug, no details	Sotheby's Gleneagles August 1987 #293
1770 ca	Milne & Campbell	Glasgow	Mug, baluster half pint, engraved with initials "G.C.W.", 3 3/8" ht, 5.6oz	Nicholas Shaw Catalog Winter 2001 p73
1770 ca	James Gordon	Aberdeen	Mug, no details	Aberdeen Museums and Galleries ABDAG011099

YEAR	MAKER	LOCATION	DESCRIPTION	SOURCE
				National Museums of Scotland
1776/77	Patrick Robertson	Edinburgh	Mug, large with straight sides, for beer, engraved with swags	
1777/78	Patrick Robertson	Edinburgh	Mugs, pair, engraved band, crest of Davidson of Cantroy, 4" ht, 14oz	Sotheby's October 4, 1976 #186
1781/82	William Davie or William Dempster	Edinburgh	Mug, pear shaped, plain, loop handle, monogram on one, 2 ½" ht, 6oz both, (3oz 5d ea)	Christie's March 24, 1965 #143
1782/83	Alexander Gardner	Edinburgh	Mug, cylindrical, initials monogram, 27oz 1d	Sotheby's June 2, 1977
1782/83	William Davie or William Dempster	Edinburgh	Mug, engraved, no details	National Museums of Scotland MEQ 820
1788/89	H & S	Edinburgh	Mug, large, engraved "AF", monogram, small dents, 21oz	Sotheby's NY USA 2003 #48
1791/92	William Robertson	Edinburgh	Mug, cylindrical, crest and motto of M'Adam of Ayrshire, mid rib height of 4 3/8", 9.6oz	Nicholas Shaw Internet Catalog 2004
1800 ca	John Keith	Banff	Mug, for beer, no details	Dundee Museums and Art Galleries 1964-141-1
1800 ca	James Confute	Perth	Mug, of slight tapering form with scroll handle, 3 ¾" ht, 4.3oz	Bonhams Sale 15120 Aug 22, 2007 #247
1810 ca	Robert Keay I	Perth	Christening mug, cylindrical, engraved with a stag's head crest, 2 7/8" ht, 4.1oz	Nicholas Shaw Catalog Winter 2001 p84
1810 ca	William Jamieson	Aberdeen	Christening mug, monogrammed "HL"	Aberdeen Museums and Galleries ABDAG008654 acquired 1988
1813/14	W & P Cunningham I	Edinburgh	Mug, baluster form, on spreading foot, chased throughout, crest and motto of Robertson	Nicholas Shaw Catalog 2005 p105
1815 ca	George Booth	Aberdeen	Mugs, pair of tot mugs	Aberdeen Museums and Galleries ABDAG008796 acquired in 1992
1816/17	James McKay	Edinburgh	Mug, for a child,	Shrubsole NY USA 1991
1825 ca	William Stephen Ferguson	Peterhead	Mug, plain slightly tapering cylindrical form, band of applied molding to base and rim, reverse scroll handle, contemporary initials "AM", 3 ½" ht, 5oz	Christie's London UK 1998 #70
1830 ca	William Jamieson	Aberdeen	Mug, plain baluster, engraved "From ITM to B. E. Crawford", 3 3/8" ht, 3.9oz	Nicholas Shaw Catalog Winter 2000 p80

YEAR	MAKER	LOCATION	DESCRIPTION	SOURCE
1838/39	James Nasmyth & Co	Glasgow	Christening mug, campana form, embossed with "C" cartouche flanked by flowers and leaves on a frosted ground, leaf capped scroll handle, presentation engraving	Bonhams London UK 2003 #297
1842/43	Marshall & Sons	Edinburgh	Mug, Gothic style	National Museums of Scotland H.1993.570
1845/46	Marshall & Sons	Edinburgh	Mug, octagonal, 4 cast figures on alternate panel, crest and motto "I HOPE", 3 ¾" ht, 7.5oz	Nicholas Shaw Catalog Autumn 1996 p25, #38
1861/62	J M	Glasgow	Mug with engraved panels, in its original case, 3 ½" ht, 4.9oz	JH Bourdon-Smith Catalog Autumn 1997 p17, #39
1865/66	J McKay & Sons	Glasgow	Christening mug, engraved with entwined decoration on a linear ground and two shaped reserves, one monogrammed, scroll handle, spread circular foot	Bonhams London UK 2007 #280
1865/66	EM	Edinburgh	Christening mug, of urn form, decorated with geometric scrollwork, crest and initials in a buckle and belt surround, handle with goats and terminal	Christie's Lanarkshire UK 1997 #80 Bonhams London UK 2006 #294
1881/82	J Reid	Glasgow	Christening mug, decorated with 6 different animals, retailed by D C Rait & Sons, 3 7/8" ht, 6.6oz	Nicholas Shaw Catalog Winter 2001 p77
1898/99	KC or KG	Edinburgh	Christening mug, engraved "Robert Kern Dewar"	National Museums of Scotland MEQ 1820

Thistle Mugs

Plate 36. A Thistle Mug 1710 ca by George Robertson, Aberdeen.
Courtesy of The Maple Swan Collection.

YEAR	MAKER THISTLE	LOCATION	DESCRIPTION	SOURCE
1688 ca	Robert Elphinstone	Inverness	Thistle mug, miniature	Private Collection UK
1690 ca	William Scott	Banff	Thistle mug, miniature, engraved with initials "AC/MC" above a calyx of applied beaded lobes, double scroll handle,	Dreweatt Neate, Donnington April 12, 2000 #492
1690 ca	MR conjoined	Inverness	Thistle mug, engraved with 2 contemporary sets of initials above reeded girdle, everted lip, lower part of body with applied lobes terminating in inverted hoops at rim foot, double scroll handle, 3 ¼" ht, 5oz 13d	Sotheby's March 6, 1958 #148
1690 ca	William Clerk	Glasgow	Thistle mug, inverted bell form, on circular rim foot, body applied with straps below a molded rib, beaded scroll handled, marked under base, 3 ½" ht, 5oz	Christie's London March 2, 1994 #114
1690 ca	George Walker	Aberdeen	Thistle mugs, pair, each on a rim foot, applied lobing to lower body, molded girdle with band of pricked dots, scroll handle with curved oval thumbpiece, applied with band of corded decoration with pricked dot and wriggle work bands, inscribed with initials "IS/MM", 3 marks under base – GW, ABD, gothic D – 4" ht, 10oz	Christie's Glasgow November 16, 1994 #684
1693/94	James Cockburn	Edinburgh	Thistle mugs, pair, engraving, applied leaves, mid-rib, initials below mid girdle, 3 ¼" ht, 13.2oz	Sotheby's April 24, 1969 #264
1693/94	John Seatoun	Edinburgh	Thistle mug, half pint, girdle with arrow topped lobes, applied vertical leaves, reeded mid-rib, flat scroll handle, initials below the lip "AD/MR", 3" ht, 7.1oz	Christie's November 7, 1945 #77 Christie's March 19, 1934 #150 Gardner Collection Munro Collection Wark, Huntington Library #52 Hughes p 129 #178
1693/94	James Cockburn	Edinburgh	Thistle mug, initials above applied girdle, 3" ht, 6oz	Christie's Edinburgh August 27-28, 1987 #105
1693/94	William Clerk	Glasgow	Thistle mugs, pair, no details	Connoisseur Magazine p206 vol 90
1694 ca	Robert Brock	Glasgow	Thistle mug, applied lobing to lower body, on rim foot, applied molded girdle, scroll handle, engraved with contemporary initials, 3 ¼" ht, 6oz	Sotheby's Gleneagles October 24, 1995 #479
1694 ca	Walter Graham	Canongate	Thistle mug, may be the miniature listed next and not full size, no details	Finlay 1991 text p120 Private Collection UK
1694 ca	Walter Graham	Canongate	Thistle mug, miniature, may be same as above, unclear if full size and miniature both exist, no details	Private Collection

YEAR	MAKER	LOCATION	DESCRIPTION	SOURCE
1694/95	Andrew Law	Edinburgh	Thistle mug with double girdle, vertical leaf appliqué, beaded strap handle, initials "B/B", 3 1/6" ht, 6.2oz	Sotheby's November 30, 1973 #137 Antiques Magazine April 1ol 73 Bell of Aberdeen advertisement Christie's October 16, 1963, #170
1694/95	Robert Brock	Glasgow	Thistle mug, inverted bell shape, slightly flaring rim, reeded collet foot, gadrooned border, molded mid-rib, scroll capped scroll handle, base engraved with initial "H", 3 ½" ht, 6.3oz	Christie's London UK 2001 #83
1694/95	James Cockburn	Edinburgh	Thistle mug, dot above leaves, 3" ht, 5oz 12d	Sotheby's Gleneagles August 27, 1979 #248 Luddington p49 courtesy of Sotheby's
1694/95	John Seatoun	Edinburgh	Thistle mug with vertical leaves, beaded handle, 6oz 18d	Christie's June 8, 1921 #22 Christie's February 9, 1926 #75 Tessiers London
1694/95	John Seatoun	Edinburgh	*Thistle mug, 2 reeded mid-ribs, vertical leaves, rat tail handle, 3 ¼" ht, 6oz 18d*	*Christie's May 30, 1904 #97* *Scottish Art Review 1968 vol XI #4 back cover* *How of Edinburgh advertisement* *Holland p215*
1694/95	James Seatoun	Edinburgh	*Thistle mug, with applied leaves, 2 bands of reeding, block initials "WF/BF", 3 14/"" ht*	*JH Bourdon-Smith Catalog 2005 p8 #46* *Christie's London UK 2005 #44*
1694/95	George Yorstoun	Edinburgh	Thistle mug, double girdle, long thing applied lobes, triple scroll handle	Jackson Marks p544 Jackson Collection National Museum of Wales
1694/95	Andrew Law	Edinburgh	Thistle mug, with applied curved leaves, reeded mid rib band, reeded handled, engraved "Fordoun", 3 3/8" ht, 7.3oz	Nicholas Shaw Catalog 2000 p65
1694/95	Andrew Law	Edinburgh	Thistle mug, tapering circular section, applied lobes, reeded handle, initials "B/IB", 7oz	Christie's London UK 2000 #378
1695/96	William Scott Elder	Banff	Thistle mug, Huntley Trophy, strap handle with horizontal notches (thumb grip), applied lobes,	Country Life August 1964 vol 136 p331 Holland p215

YEAR	MAKER	LOCATION	DESCRIPTION	SOURCE
1695/96	Andrew Law	Edinburgh	Thistle mugs, pair, reeded mid band, vertical leaves, 10oz 7d both (5oz 3d ea)	Christie's June 23, 1920 #47
1695 ca	John Seatoun	Edinburgh	Thistle mug, lobed leaf, engraved initials, girdle, 3 ½" ht, 5oz 15d	Burlington Magazine November 1970 vol 112 p82
1695 ca	John Seatoun	Edinburgh	Miniature thistle mug, strap handle, applied leaf lobes, 1 ½" ht, 1 ¾" across top	Goodwin's Edinburgh 1995 The Phoenix Collection
1695 ca	Colin McKenzie	Edinburgh	Miniature thistle mug, with girdle and lobe, 1 ½" ht, 1.1oz	Hyman Collection – Colonial Williamsburg
1695 ca	William Scott	Banff	Miniature thistle mug, loop handle center entwined, initials "RR IE", 1 5/8" ht	Scottish Art Review 1943, p58 #13 How of Edinburgh advertisement How Exhibition 1992 pl 169
1695 ca	William Scott	Banff	Miniature thistle mug, strap handle, handle different from the one above, applied lobes, girdle, 1 ¾" ht, 1oz	Sotheby's NY October 28, 1992 #348 How of Edinburgh 1973
1695 ca	*William Scott*	*Banff*	*Miniature thistle mug*	*National Museums of Scotland H.1996.275*
1695 ca	William Scott younger	Aberdeen	Thistle mug, probably, *few details given*, dram size	Aberdeen Museums and Galleries ABDAG001386
1696/97	Andrew Law	Edinburgh	Thistle mug, vertical leaves mid rib, beaded scroll handle, 3" ht, 5oz 17d	Christie's March 19, 1934 #147 Connoisseur Magazine 1934 vol 93 p348 How of Edinburgh 1936 #52 Private Collection UK
1696/97	Alexander Forbes	Edinburgh	Thistle mug, vertical leaves, foot and lip with chain pattern, handle with thumb ridges, 3 ¼" ht, 5oz 13d	Christie's July 23, 1930 Scottish Art Academy Exhibit 1939 #914 J Cathcart-White Collection Finlay 1991 #48 Antiques Magazine October 1949 vol 56 National Museums of Scotland 1943.249

YEAR	MAKER	LOCATION	DESCRIPTION	SOURCE
1696/97	Robert Bruce	Edinburgh	Miniature thistle mug, engraved "MR" under coronet on bottom	National Museums of Scotland MEQ 1556 1983
1696/97	James Cockburn	Edinburgh	Pair of thistle mugs, 2 handled, 3 ¼" ht	Christie's March 18, 1959 #122 Christie's Scottish Picture Files
1696/97	Andrew Law	Edinburgh	Pair of thistle mugs, originally misdated as 1682/83, slight chance they are confused with the Andrew Law pair of 1695/96	Glasgow Exhibition 1911, vol I, p123, #20 Herriot's Hospital Trustees, on loan to National Museums of Scotland Jackson Marks p544
1697/98	John Seatoun	Edinburgh	Thistle mug with pointed vertical leaves, reeded mid rib, beaded strap handle, script initials "IB MC", 3" ht, 4oz 15d	How Exhibition 1992 #27 pl 16
1697/98	Robert Bruce	Edinburgh	Thistle mug with vertical leaves, reeded mid rib, beaded scroll handle, 3 ¼" ht, 5oz 6d	Christie's May 16, 1916 #17
1698/99	William Clerk	Glasgow	Thistle mugs, pair, vertical leaves, beaded scroll handle	Art Treasure Exhibition 1932 #502 How of Edinburgh Collection
1698/99	Robert Bruce	Edinburgh	Thistle mug with vertical leaves, beaded scroll handle, 3" ht, 5oz 6d	Christie's March 19, 1934 #145 Gardner Collection Connoisseur Magazine 1934 vol 93 p348
1698/99	*Robert Bruce*	*Edinburgh*	*Thistle mug with applied leaves, a reeded mid rib, with crest of Montgomery of Newton, 3 ¼" ht, 5.2oz*	*Nicholas Shaw Catalog 2004 p95*
1698/99	William Clerk	Glasgow	Thistle mugs, pair, strap handles with beading, broad girdle, applied lobes almost vertically, straight body, 8.7oz both	Apollo 1933 vol 25 p18 How of Edinburgh advertisement Connoisseur Magazine 1939 vol 103 p35 How of Edinburgh advertisement Christie's London How of Edinburgh 1936 #54
1698/99	William Clerk	Glasgow	Thistle mug, marked – WC, Tree etc., S, 5.3oz	How of Edinburgh 1936 #55 Private Collection
1699/1700	Robert Bruce	Edinburgh	Thistle mug with vertical leaves, reeded mid ribs, 4 oz 14d	Christie's July 31, 1918 #130

YEAR	MAKER	LOCATION	DESCRIPTION	SOURCE
1700 ca	Alexander Forbes	Edinburgh	Miniature thistle mug, reeded girdle, contemporary and later initials, 1 ½" ht	Sotheby's June 15, 1978 #25
1700 ca	George Walker	Aberdeen	Miniature thistle mug, typical thistle shape, applied vertical strap work and beeding below the girdle, engraved with initials above, scroll handle, on rim foot, 1 ¾" ht	Sotheby's July 20, 1982 #151
1700 ca	William Scott II	Banff	Thistle mug, miniature, reeded strap handle	Grantully Castle Antiques Scottish Art Review vol XIV 1973 back cover How of Edinburgh advertisement
1700 ca	William Scott II	Banff	Miniature thistle mug, vertical strap work applied below molded girdle, molded strap handle, rim foot, mm only 1 ¾" ht, 1oz, unclear if different from above	Sotheby's NY USA October 28, 1992 #348
1700 ca	John Seaton	Edinburgh	Thistle mug, thistle form, beaded cut car straps above reeded spreading support, later script initials "EJC" above wigglework girdle, beaded scroll handle, 4" ht, 5oz 7d	Sotheby's NU USA 2000 #213
1700/01	James Penman	Edinburgh	Thistle mug with applied girdle, beaded strap handles, applied lobes, initials underneath "IR;S", 3 3/16" ht, 5oz	Alcorn, Museum of Fine Art #32.407 p327 #249 Gift of Lady Edith Playfair 1932
1700 ca	Alexander Kincaid	Edinburgh	Miniature thistle mug, cipher	Sotheby's June 15, 1978 #25 How Exhibition 1992
1700 ca	mm only		Miniature thistle mug, possibly attributable to Alexander Forbes of Edinburgh or Alexander Kincaid of Edinburgh, 1 ¾" ht	Christie's April 15, 1964 #103
1700 ca	Colin McKenzie	Edinburgh	Miniature thistle mug, engraved initial on front, girdle no leaf, 1 3/8" ht	Sotheby's November 28, 1968 #40 How of Edinburgh
1700 ca	Colin McKenzie	Edinburgh	Thistle mug, girdle, base engraved with the initial "G", mm only, 2 ½" ht	Christie's October 11, 1972 #240
1700 ca	James Penman	Edinburgh	Miniature thistle mug, mm only, leaf lobing, molded girdle, scroll handle, beaded thumb piece, initials "KJ", 1 2/3"	Christie's Edinburgh November 21, 1990 #35
1700/01	John Seaton	Edinburgh	Thistle mug, no details	The Maple Swan Collection
1700/01	Alexander Forbes	Edinburgh	Thistle mug with vertical leaves, corded scroll handle, 7.4oz	Christie's June 19, 1935 #94 How of Edinburgh 1936 #56 Christie's Glasgow November 16, 1994 #685

376

YEAR	MAKER (continued)	LOCATION	DESCRIPTION	SOURCE
1701/02	Edward Penman Assayer – James Penman	Edinburgh	Thistle mug, spiraled leaves at the base, mid rib band, beaded handle, 3 ½" ht, 3 ¼" across the top	Connoisseur Magazine 1939 vol 103 p35 How of Edinburgh advertisement
1701/02	Colin McKenzie	Edinburgh	Thistle mugs, pair, girdle, no leaf, initials "IL" underneath, 3 ¼" ht, 11oz 4d	Shrubsole London 1991 The Phoenix Collection
1701/02	Colin McKenzie	Edinburgh	Thistle mug, no leaf, possibly one of the above, 3 ¼" ht, 6oz	Sotheby's Gleneagles August 28, 1975
1701/02	John Seatoun	Edinburgh	Thistle mug, 5.9oz	Christie's NY October 18, 1989 #134
1701/02	Robert Inglis	Edinburgh	Thistle mugs, pair, vertical leaves	Connoisseur Magazine 1932, vol 90 p206 How of Edinburgh 1937 #57
1702/03	Robert Bruce	Edinburgh	Thistle mug, double girdle, no applied leaves, plain scroll handle, 3 ¼" ht, 5oz	Christie's July 1, 1931 #84 Seaford House Exhibition 1929 #535 trust Duke of Hamilton
1703/04	George Scott Jr	Edinburgh	Thistle mugs, pair, strap handle, beaded decoration, girdle, leaf decoration, initials underneath "IH IL", 3 14/" ht, 10oz	Christie's March 1993 #112 Hyman Collection – Colonial Williamsburg
1703 ca	George Walker	Aberdeen	Thistle mug, vertical leaves, reeded mid band, 5oz 5d	Sotheby's April 26, 1979 #138 Sotheby's October 11, 1979 Sotheby's Hopetoun House November 13, 1978 #96
1703/04	Thomas Cleghorne III	Edinburgh	Thistle mug, pair, lobed leaves below a mid girdle, initials opposite the beaded strap scroll handle, 3" ht, 10.6oz	Christie's March 24, 1940 #86 Scottish Art Academy Exhibition 1931 #109 Ashburton Collection Glasgow Empire Exhibition 1939 #190 Scottish Art Academy Exhibit 1939 #942 Noble Collection
				Sotheby's Gleneagles September 1, 1981 #458

YEAR	MAKER	LOCATION	DESCRIPTION	SOURCE
1703/04	Robert Bruce	Edinburgh	Thistle mug, large, lobed leaves below a reeded girdle, with leaf capped scroll handle, engraved later "Presented to Duncan by his mother Ellen Carline McPherson McDonald of Glencoe, 25th December 1995", 3 7/8" ht	Christie's Glasgow September 8, 1987 #101
1703/04	Richard Rae	Edinburgh	Thistle mug, with applied leaves below a reeded girdle, beaded rat tail to the strap scroll handle, later crest (shorted and lighter than average), 2 ¾" ht, 4.1oz	Sotheby's Hopetoun House November 13, 1978 #63
1704/05	John Luke II	Glasgow	Thistle mug, thistle form on rim foot, applied lobes, reeded girdle, partly beaded strap handle, 3 3/8" ht, 4.5oz	Christie's Lanarkshire UK 1997 #122
1704/05	Patrick Murray I	Edinburgh	Thistle mug, presumed to be, no details	Jackson Marks p 544
1704/05	John Luke II	Glasgow	Thistle mug, no details	Jackson Marks p568
1704/05	John Penman II	Edinburgh	Thistle mug, no leaf, reeded rib, reeded scroll handle, 3 ½" ht, 5oz 7d	Christie's March 19, 1934 #146 Bell of Aberdeen advertisement Gardner Collection
1704/05	John Luke II	Glasgow	Thistle mugs, pair, girdle, pointed leaf, later crest and motto under lip, 3" ht, 10oz 4d	Sotheby's February 28, 1974 #118
1704/05	John Luke II	Glasgow	*Thistle mug, one of above pair, crest of Murdoch and MacMurdoch, 3 " ht, 5oz*	*Christie's London UK 2005 #42*
1705 ca	John Munro	Inverness	Miniature thistle mug, applied reeded girdle below flared rim, double scroll handle, ridged foot, 2" ht, 1oz 9d	Sotheby's March 27, 1984 #93
1705 ca	RI Robert Inglis	Edinburgh	Miniature thistle mug, small case script initial "h" mid rib, leaf straps	Christie's August 13, 1941 #69 How of Edinburgh Collection
1705 ca	George Robertson	Aberdeen	Thistle mug, pair, girdle, no leaf, initials "MWL/MG", 3" ht	Christie's February 28, 1973
1705 ca	George Walker	Aberdeen	Thistle mug, on molded foot, applied lobes, with small cut card tongues between them, girdle, strap loop handle with reeded bands, base with a monogram, unclear if same as previous by this maker, 3 ½" ht, 6oz	Shaw Collection Christie's Glasgow March 29, 1983 #36
1705 ca	Not available		Thistle mug, plain	Waldron Book #591
1705 ca	William McLean	Inverness	Thistle mug, thistle form on rim foot, applied molded girdle, scroll handle, plain thumbpiece, engraved initials "K" and "MB" conjoined, engraved scratch weight under base 1oz 13d, 2" ht, 1.5oz	Christie's London UK 1999 #274

YEAR	MAKER	LOCATION	DESCRIPTION	SOURCE
1705/06	Robert Inglis	Edinburgh	Thistle mug, reeded band, spreading lip, initials "M/AM/CR", scroll handles, no lobes, 5oz 11d	Christie's November 14, 1945 #116 Crichton Brothers Gees, Clark Art Institute p62 #14
1705/06	George Scott	Edinburgh	Thistle mugs, pair, no leaf, mid rib scroll handle, girdle, 3" ht, 2.6oz	Park Lane Exhibition 1929 #701 Mr. Goldie-Tanbaman Christie's February 28, 1973 #170 Christie's Negative #739756 Garrard Ltd, London UK
1705/06	John Luke II	Glasgow	Thistle mug, beaded handle, vertical leaf girdle, initials "IL EG", 3" ht, 5oz 13d	Christie's June 28, 1965 #149 Clayton Christie's Book p 106
1705/06	Colin McKenzie	Edinburgh	Thistle mug, pair, plain, no applied leaves, initials "IB/HG", old repairs, 3.1" ht, 10oz 10d	Christie's April 8, 1937 #180 Ivory Collection Connoisseur Magazine 1939 vol 103 p29 Guille advertisement Christie's NY April 1989 #574 Sotheby's London June 5, 2001 #391
1705/06	John Luke II	Glasgow	Thistle mug, no details	National Museums of Scotland 1936.279
1705/06	*John Luke II*	*Glasgow*	*Thistle mug, no details*	*Jackson Marks p568*
1706/07	Alexander Kincaid	Edinburgh	Thistle mug, applied girdle, no leaf, low foot, strap handle, 3" ht, 4oz 5d	Sotheby's June 21, 1973 #149
1706/07	Alexander Kincaid	Edinburgh	Thistle mug, with engraved leaves, script initials "JM" or "IM"	National Museums of Scotland MEQ 791 1965.1882
1707 ca	John Luke II	Glasgow	Thistle mugs, pair, each with everted lip, calyx of appliqué lobes, double scroll beaded handles, each engraved with later date crest and initials "RS/AS" dated 1688, 10oz both	Phillips Edinburgh December 4, 1997 #333 Lyon & Turnbull February 20, 2004 #264
1707/08	John Seaton	Edinburgh	Thistle mug, no applied leaves, bell shaped body, flared rim, applied girdle above, initials "W*N" below a later crest, scroll handle, unusually tucked in on spreading foot, 3 3/8" ht, 4.5oz	Sotheby's Gleneagles September 2, 1981 #452
1707/08	Thomas Ker	Edinburgh	Thistle mug, vertical leaves, beaded mid rib, 4oz 6d	Christie's February 12, 1918 #37 Christie's May 21, 1952 #151

YEAR	MAKER	LOCATION	DESCRIPTION	SOURCE
1708/09	John Luke II	Glasgow	Thistle mug, partly fluted, on rim foot, lower part of body applied with flutes, reeded band above, everted lip, reeded scroll handle, engraved with crest and motto, 3" ht, 5oz 4d	Christie's January 31, 1979 #195 Country Life, July 5, 1979 p11 #166 How of Edinburgh
1708/09	Patrick Turnbull	Edinburgh	Thistle mug, no leaf, mid rib plain, scroll handle, 3oz 8d	Christie's March 26, 1908 #28
1708/09	John Luke II	Glasgow	Thistle mug, bell shaped, 12 applied lobes, applied girdle, engraved opposite handle initials "F/RG"	Royal Ontario Museum, Toronto Canada 980.99.1e
1709/10	Robert Inglis	Edinburgh	Thistle mug, with later handle and foot, engraved at the lip with initials, shallow fluting below a decorative tooled band, 3 ½" ht, 5.1oz	Sotheby's December 16, 1971 #164
1709/10	*Robert Inglis*	*Edinburgh*	*Thistle mug with fluting on body and foot*	*eBay UK 2007*
1709/10	Alexander Forbes	Edinburgh	Thistle mugs, pair, plain no leaves, engraved inscription	Connoisseur Magazine April 1939 vol 103 p187
1709/10	Charles Blair	Edinburgh	Thistle mug, plain, bell shaped, everted lip, rat tail handle 3" ht, 4oz 5d	Christie's July 5, 1939 #125 Sotheby's December 17, 1964 #285
1709/10	John Luke II	Glasgow	Thistle mug, beaded mid rib, vertical leaves, beaded scroll handle, 3 ¼" ht, 6oz 3d	Christie's March 19, 1934 #145 How of Edinburgh Scottish Art Academy Exhibit 1939 #944 National Museums of Scotland Gardner Collection Connoisseur Magazine 1934 vol 93 p348
1709/10	John Luke II	Glasgow	Thistle mug, vertical leaves, molded mid rib, apparent weight difference from the one above, 3 ¼" ht, 5oz 5d	Christie's February 5, 1947 #90 Hyman Collection – Colonial Williamsburg
1710 ca	Henry Bethune	Edinburgh	Thistle mugs, pair, no applied leaves, initials opposite handle "IT/RB", applied molded girdles, simple loop handles	Sotheby's March 6, 1990
1710 ca	George Robertson	Aberdeen	Thistle mug, Queen Anne, on molded rim foot, lower part of body with applied fluting, reeded rib above, scroll handle, engraved with initials "M/IG/LD", mm only, 3 ½" ht, 5oz 5d	Christie's July 3, 1984 #126 Phillips Edinburgh October 24, 1986 #181 Shaw Collection Christie's Glasgow March 29,

YEAR	MAKER (continued)	LOCATION	DESCRIPTION	SOURCE 1983 #35
1710 ca	*George Robertson*	*Aberdeen*	*Thistle mug, with mid rib band, lobed, applied leaves, scroll handle*	*The Maple Swan Collection*
1710 ca	Thomas Ker	Edinburgh	Miniature thistle mug, bell shaped body on a rim foot, molded girdle, scroll handle, initials and later date of 1724, 1 5/8"ht, 1oz	Christie's December 10, 1980 #128
1710 ca	*Thomas Ker*	*Edinburgh*	*Miniature thistle mug, 1 ½" ht*	*How Exhibition 1992*
1710 ca	Simon McKenzie	Inverness	Miniature thistle mug, vertical leaves, mid rib scroll handle, engraved "Suddie", 1oz 12d	Christie's December 13, 1933 #68 Jackson Marks p771 #1000 Girdwood Collection How of Edinburgh Collection J. R. Medrum Finlay text 1991 p120 Possibly Metropolitan Museum
1710 ca	Not available		Thistle mugs, pair, applies ribs, Trustees of Duke of Hamilton	Park Lane Exhibition 1929 #699
1710/11	John Seaton	Edinburgh	Thistle mug, no applied leaves, molded applied girdle, scroll handle, with later monogram and date "1883", 3 ¼" ht, 5.6oz	Christie's November 8, 1972 #80
1710/11	Colin McKenzie	Edinburgh	Vertical leaves, reeded mid rib, scroll handle, 5oz 15d	Christie's June 9, 1943 #46
1711/12	John Seaton	Edinburgh	Thistle mugs, pair, bell shaped, everted lips, applied molded girdle, part faceted molded scroll handle, on reeded foot, undersides engraved "RE", 3 ¼" ht, 13.7oz	Sotheby's October 5-10, 1987 #54
1711/12	Colin Campbell	Edinburgh	Thistle mug, mid girdle, no leaf, initials "RDS" underneath, widening to lip, 5oz 10d	Christie's June 24, 1981 #41 Christie's December 17, 1930 #49
1711/12	James Mitchelson	Edinburgh	Thistle mug, mid rib, scroll handle, unclear if same as below, 7oz 5d	Christie's March 23, 1945 #141
1711/12	James Mitchelson	Edinburgh	Thistle mug, on a circular tall foot, no leaf, girdle, 3 ½" ht, 7oz 15d	Christie's June 24, 1981 #48
1715 ca	Simon McKenzie	Inverness	Thistle mug, miniature	Private Collection UK
1716/17	Henry Bethune	Edinburgh	Thistle mug, applied girdle, later crest and motto	Sotheby's November 28, 1968 #260
1720 ca	Hugh Ross	Tain	Thistle mug, miniature, mm only, heavy gauge traditional thistle shape, lobed body below molded central band, strap handle, engraved with betrothal initials	Lyon & Turnbull, February 20, 2004 #318

381

YEAR	MAKER (continued)	LOCATION	DESCRIPTION	SOURCE
	William Scott the Younger	Aberdeen	"AS/MF", 1 7/8" ht Thistle mug, miniature, on molded rim foot, strap handle, 2 marks – WS conjoined, ABD, 1 ½" ht, 1 ¾" di,	Christie's Scotland November 14, 1985 #292
1720 ca	M Possibly Simon McKenzie	Inver	Thistle mug, miniature	National Museums of Scotland MEQ 1679 1984
1720 ca	RI Probably Robert Innes	Inverness	Thistle mug, miniature, strap handle, girdle, applied lobes, initials "WR/IM", 1 1/2" ht, 1 2/3" di at the mouth, different from 1705ca mug	How of Edinburgh Royal Ontario Museum Toronto Canada 988.33.138
1730 ca	Alexander Forbes	Aberdeen	Thistle mug, miniature, inverted bell shape on round foot rim, applied lobes, reeded girdle, S-handle, 1 2/3" ht, 1 ¾" di at the rim	Shrubsole NY USA Royal Ontario Museum Toronto Canada 988.33.139
1730 ca	Hugh Ross	Tain	Miniature thistle mug, applied girdle, squat body on spreading foot, engraved with initials "D M/H", mm on base, HR conjoined, 1 ½" ht, 2" di,	Phillips Edinburgh November 21, 2000 #276
1730 ca	Alexander Forbes	Aberdeen	Miniature thistle mug, slightly molded foot, lower part of body with applied calyx of petals, molded rib above, reeded scroll handle, engraved with a cipher, possibly the same as the one in the Royal Ontario Museum, 1 ¾" ht,	Christie's April 15, 1969 #103
1747ca	Samuel Telford	Glasgow	Thistle mug, vertical leaves, mid rib, 3" ht	Scottish Art Academy Exhibit 1939 #916 Stirling-Maxwell Bt
1760 ca	Hugh Ross	Tain	Thistle mug, pear shaped, 5 4/8" ht, 3 3/8" di	San Diego Museum of Art CA USA 64:25
1769 ca	Milne & Campbell	Glasgow	Thistle mug, no details	Sotheby's Gleneagles August 1987 #293
1775 ca	Milne & Campbell	Glasgow	Thistle mugs, pair, boar's head crest, motto "Fit via vi", 3 ¼" ht, 11oz 11d	Christie's June 24, 1981 #47
1777/78	Patrick Robertson	Edinburgh	Thistle mugs, pair, engraved band, crest of Davidson of Cantroy, 4" ht, 14oz	Sotheby's October 14, 1976 #186
1781/82	William Davie or William Dempster	Edinburgh	Thistle mug, pear shaped, plain, loop handle, monogram on one, 2 ½" ht, 6oz both (3oz 5d ea)	Christie's March 24, 1965 #143
1816/17	James McKay	Edinburgh	Miniature thistle mug, no details	Shrubsole NY 1991
1818/19	George McHattie	Edinburgh	Thistle mug, circular and on spreading circular foot, short stem with compressed beaded knop, thistle shaped body embossed with double rib at	Christie's Lanarkshire UK 1997 #116

YEAR	MAKER (continued)	LOCATION	DESCRIPTION	SOURCE
			the waist, reeded lip, 5 3/8" ht, 6.5oz	
1820/21	W & P Cunningham II	Edinburgh	Thistle mug, circular, on spreading circular foot, short stem with compressed beaded knop, thistle-shaped body embossed about the waist with double rib, reeded borders to foot and lip, 8" ht, 15.1oz	Christie's Lanarkshire 1997 #115
1829/30	D C Raitt	Glasgow	Thistle mug, serpentine handle, flaring foot, base chased and embossed with foliate lobes, foliate cartouche with monogram, 4" ht, 5oz	Skinner, Inc Boston MA USA 2004 #493
1830 ca	David Mason	Dundee	Thistle cup/mug, no details, uncertain if similar to earlier thistle mugs in form	Dundee Museums and Art Galleries 1986-126

Mustard Pots

Plate 37. Mustard Pots. A 1841/42 Mustard Pot by James McKay, Edinburgh. Photograph courtesy of I. Franks Antique Silver, London Silver Vaults, London.

MUSTARD POTS

YEAR	MAKER	LOCATION	DESCRIPTION	SOURCE
1729/30	William Aytoun	Edinburgh	Dry mustard pot, baluster bun type, no finial, on molded spreading foot, with a reeded band applied to the body, the unpierced dome pull off cover engraved with simulated scroll and foliate piercing, lower body with crest and motto of Cunningham, 4 ¼" ht, 3.6oz	Noble Collection Christie's March 29, 1983 #79 Nicholas Shaw Catalog 2005 p89
1745 ca	James Glen	Glasgow	Mustard vase, inverted pear shape, initials below molded shoulder, spreading base, detachable cover with swirl lobes and fluted, engraved with flowers, diaper and other motifs, baluster finial, 6 1/8" ht, 7oz	Sotheby's December 1, 1982
1769/70	Patrick Robertson	Edinburgh	Mustard pot, drum form, pierced with scrollwork (some repairs), the slightly domed lid engraved with a crest (worn), with other items	Christie's London UK 2003 #459
1780 ca	Patrick Robertson	Edinburgh	Mustard pot, no date given, no details	Dundee Museums and Art Galleries 1971-981
1786/87	David Downie	Edinburgh	Mustard pot, urn shaped, with domed lid, 5 1/8" ht, 4.4oz	Nicholas Shaw Catalog 2005 p95
1786/87	ID	Edinburgh	Mustard pot, plain oval form with bead borders, scroll handle and pierced shell thumbpiece, fitted with a clear glass liner, said to be James Dempster but possibly by James Douglas	Christie's London UK 2000 #89
1788/89	Thomas Duffus	Edinburgh	Mustard Pot, no details	Jackson Marks p550
1790 ca	James Douglas	Edinburgh	Mustard pot, plain, oval, reeded handle, urn shaped thumb piece, oval domed lid, original blue glass liner, marked on base and lid, engraved initials "WES", 2 ¼" ht, 2oz 10d	Private Collection
1793/94	Francis Howden	Edinburgh	Mustard pot, oval with straight sides, pierced and engraved with an oval cartouche and narrow borders, crested, with a blue glass interior, 3' ht, 3.3oz	Waddington, McLean & Co Ltd, Toronto CA 1995 #125
1795/96	Alexander Henderson	Edinburgh	Mustard pot, no details	Jackson Marks p550
1795/96	George Fenwick	Edinburgh	Mustard pot, oval with bright cut leaves, shell thumb piece, script initials "G.E.C.", 3 3/8" ht, 9.2oz	Nicholas Shaw Catalog 2004 p102
1798/99	W & E	Edinburgh	Mustard pot, oval body, angular scroll handle, domed lid with ball finial, initialed, 3 ½" ht, with other items	Sotheby's Billinghurst 1998 #17212
1809/10	J. F.	Edinburgh assay	Mustard pot, no details	National Museums of Scotland MEQ 815

YEAR	MAKER	LOCATION	DESCRIPTION	SOURCE
1810/11	RK over striking Possibly Robert Keay I	Edinburgh assay	Mustard pot, mm over struck with "RK" mark, no details	Sotheby's Gleneagles August 1987 #299
1811/12	Francis Howden	Edinburgh	Mustard pot, no details	The Maple Swan Collection
1812/13	W & P Cunningham II	Edinburgh	Mustard pot, plain bellied form with stylized gadrooned border, 3 lion mask and paw feet, lid with ball finial, engraved with script "H", thread edge handle, gilt interior, 3 ¾" ht, 7.3oz	Bonhams London UK 2005 #142
1815/16	WP also retailer mark J & W Howden Co	Edinburgh	Mustard pot, squat circular on lion mask and paw feet, shell, acorn and oak leaf rim, ribbed shell-capped handle and domed with ball finial, gilt interior and traces of exterior gilt, with other items	Christie's London UK 2007 #73
1819/20	Not available	Edinburgh	Mustard pot, lid with shell finial and flared rim, lion mask terminating in paw feet, with other items	Lyon & Turnbull Edinburgh UK 2001 #273
1823/24	George McHattie	Edinburgh	Mustard pot, circular, drum-shaped pot	JH Bourdon-Smith London 1993
1824/25	James McKay	Edinburgh	Mustard pot, circular section form with later foliate scroll and floral motifs, the hinged lid with a shell form thumbpiece, with a conforming cobalt glass interior	Christie's London 2001 #111
1825/26	George McHattie	Edinburgh	Mustard pot, drum shaped, original blue glass liner, 2 ½" di, 4oz 8d	Private Collection
1825/26	George McHattie	Edinburgh	Mustard pot, glass with silver mounts, 10 sided, 4 ½" ht, 2 1/8" di	Huntley House Museum Edinburgh HH3225/68
1827/28	George Paton	Edinburgh	Mustard pot, circular shaped, crest, 2 ½" ht, 4.7oz	Nicholas Shaw Catalog Autumn 1999 p62
1841/42	James McKay	Edinburgh	Mustard pot, drum-shaped, slightly domed lid, pierced thumbpiece, crested, reeded borders, 3" ht, 4" wide	L Frank Antique Silver, London UK 2007 #d0624
1842/43	Leonard Urquhart	Edinburgh	Mustard pot, no details	National Museums of Scotland MEQ 853 1966.1000
1849/50	Not available	Edinburgh	Mustard pot, plain drum-shaped mustard pot	S J Phillips Ltd London UK London 2006 #19581
1860/61	J & W Marshall	Edinburgh	Mustard pot, tall, cylindrical, gadrooned border	Private Collection
1897/98	John Crichton	Edinburgh	Mustard pots, pair, cut glass with silver mounts and hinged lids, 1 ¾" di	Huntley House Museum Edinburgh HH3568/71

Porringers & Bleeding Bowls

Plate 38. A Bleeding Bowl 1749/50 by Dougal Ged, Edinburgh.
Courtesy of The Phoenix Collection. Photograph by Janice M Dietert.

PORRINGERS AND BLEEDING BOWLS

YEAR	MAKER	LOCATION	DESCRIPTION	SOURCE
1675-77	William Law	Edinburgh	Porringer, 2 handled, scroll handles, initials under the lip "TS/SM", bulbous body, possibly originally with a lid	Finlay 1991 # 55 National Museums of Scotland MEQ 1460
1689/90	James Penman	Edinburgh	Porringer/bleeding bowl, single handled, circular bowl, initials "BM", trefoil handle pierced with clovers, 5 ½" di, 7.5oz	Noble Collection Crichton Brothers Sotheby's November 6, 1997 #190 Exhibited in Old Scottish Silver Loan Collection Empire Exhibition, Glasgow 1938 #60
1710 ca	AD	Aberdeen	Bleeding bowl, initials in block "WS" on handle, 4.9oz	Philadelphia Museum of Art 1925-21-3 Bulletin February Vol XXII 1928 p22 #118
1722/23	Henry Bethune	Edinburgh	*Porringer/bleeding bowl, single handled, with pierced triangular handle, engraved initials on handle "EW to EP", the underside of handle bears an impression of another mark, possibly ID above, 5.5oz*	Shaw Collection Christie's March 29, 1983 #101 Finlay 1991 pl 71
1745 ca	James Glen	Glasgow	Porringers, pair, lower part of bodies chased with floral sprays and scrolls around vacant cartouches, scrolling monster handles, on rim bases, also stamped "M", 3" ht, 15oz 1d both	Sotheby's December 9, 1976
1748/49	Ker & Dempster Assayer Hugh Gordon	Edinburgh	Porringer, circular body, engraved on one side with contemporary crest and motto above chased decoration of flowers, scrolls and foliage, sides applied with snake entwining scroll handles, 6 ¼", 6oz 15d	Sotheby's August 28, 1969 #163
1749/50	Dougal Ged	Edinburgh	Porringer/bleeding bowl, single handled, with rococo pierced handle, script monogram "AP" or "AS" on front, 4 ¼" di, 5 ¾ over handle	The Phoenix Collection
1749/50	Patrick Robertson Assayer Hugh Gordon	Edinburgh	Porringer/bleeding bowl, compressed circular bowl, everted lip, cast handle formed as a leaf, engraved with a later crest, 4 ¾" di, 7oz 18d	Sotheby's December 3, 1959 #132
1749/50	*Patrick Robertson Over striking another possibly Edward Lothian*	*Edinburgh*	*Porringer/bleeding bowl, single handled, plain, circular with everted lip, handled shaped as a stylized acanthus leaf, with a crest, motto and coronet, 8.7oz*	*Shaw Collection Christie's Glasgow March 29, 1983 #100*
1755/56	Ker & Dempster	Edinburgh	Porringer, 2 handled, in 17th century style, lower body chased, handles with dolphin masks and foliage, 3" ht, 6.4oz	Christie's July 29, 1964 #138

YEAR	MAKER	LOCATION	DESCRIPTION	SOURCE
1755/56	Dougal Ged	Edinburgh	Porringer/bleeding bowl, single handled, circular with triangular stylized acanthus leaf handle, inscribed "Betty Dunbar gifted by her Grandmama, Lady Hempriggs", 6oz	Scottish Arts Review, vol 14,#3 back cover How of Edinburgh
1755/56	Ker & Dempster	Edinburgh	Porringer, no details	National Museums of Scotland MEQ 705 1964.1843
1755/56	*Ker & Dempster*	*Edinburgh*	*Porringer, with cover, no details*	*Antiques Magazine vol 63, p305 Shrubsole advertisement*
1761/62	James Gilliland	Edinburgh	Porringer, no details	Antiques Magazine vol 127, p828 Gebelein advertisement
1764/65	Benjamin Tait	Edinburgh	Porringer, 2 handled, of flared cylindrical form, with scroll handles, initials on the underside, on a rim foot, 2 ½" ht, 5.3oz	Sotheby's Hopetoun House, November 10, 1980 #74
1765/66	Ker probably for William Ker	Edinburgh	Porringer, circular section with part fluting and a rococo cartouche, with 2 applied reeded handles, 2 ¾" ht, 3oz	Christie's London UK 2004 #616
1811/12	Robert Gray & Son	Glasgow Edinburgh assay	Bleeding bowl, leaves on handle, script initials on the front	National Museums of Scotland MEQ 1296 1978.83

Quaichs

Plate 39. A Quaich 1808/09 by Matthew Craw, Edinburgh.
Courtesy of The Phoenix Collection. Photograph by Janice M Dietert.

QUAICHS

YEAR	MAKER	LOCATION	DESCRIPTION	SOURCE
1632 ca	Not available		Quaich, wooden with gold band around the rim, 4 lugs, gifted by James Roughead to John Pringle Lister Burgess of Edinburgh Anno 1632, not marked, 3 5/8" di	Huntley House Museum Edinburgh HH3527/70
1640 ca	Robert Gairdine I (or II)	Dundee	Quaich, no details	Dundee Museums and Art Galleries 2004-112
1663-81	Edward Cleghorne I	Edinburgh	Quaich, used as a communion cup by the Kirk of Alvah, (also indicated under Communion cups)	Burns p 401
1665-67	Alexander Reid II Deacon James Symontoun	Edinburgh	Quaich, large, with 2 lugs	Jackson Marks p542 Private Collection UK
1669-71	William Law Deacon Alexander Reid	Edinburgh	Quaich, exterior with line staves, interrupted by a triple band decorated with groups of hatched lines at intervals, center of the bowl engraved with a mirror monogram of "R" beneath a Baron's coronet, other Arms and initials as well, 10 5/8" over lugs, 3" ht, 7 1/16" di, 14.2oz	Firestone & Parsons 1962 Boston Museum of Fine Art 1962.168
1670 ca	Thomas Moncur	Glasgow	Quaich on a rim foot, lug with ends down turned, decorated with panels of leaves, engraved near foot, 3 narrow bands engraved around the body, panels of roses and tulips near the lip, block initials "M/RS/CL" inside with stave lines	Jackson vol 2, part III, p743, Fig 971 & 972
1670 ca	Not available		Quaich, no details	Antiques Magazine 1948 vol 53 p147
1675 ca	Not available		Quaich, silver mounted wood, Arms of Bruce on one lug, Arms of Sinclair on the other lug, unmarked, 10" over lugs	Nicholas Shaw Catalog Winter 2002/03 p81
1675-80 ca	Thomas Moncur	Glasgow	Quaich, no details	Private Collection UK
1680 ca	Not available		Quaich, alternating panels of thistle, rose and leaves, initials, mark indistinct but struck 3X, 8" long, 6.5oz	Sotheby's Hopetoun House May 1990 #108
1680 ca	Not available		Quaich, not marked, no details	Lyle Annual Review 1983 p598
1680 ca	Robert Brock	Glasgow	Quaich, on rim foot, arms of Campbell of Arkinglass, initials "IC" on one handle, 9" over handles	Shaw Collection Sotheby's Picture File Christie's March 29, 1983 #56 Art Institute of Chicago 1984.66 N.E7940

YEAR	MAKER	LOCATION	DESCRIPTION	SOURCE
1680 ca	*Robert Brock*	*Glasgow*	*Quaich, 2 lugs, on circular rim foot, body with simulated staves, outside with alternating panels of flowers, lugs engraved with rope borders, initials "IC" on one lug, and "IS" on the other, arms of Campbell of Ardkinglas*	*Information from a Private Collector*
1680 ca	Thomas Lindsay II	Dundee	Quaich, no details	Private Collection UK
1680-85	James Penman	Edinburgh	Quaich, with 2 lugs, mm only	Private Collection UK
1681/82	William Law Assayer John Borthwick	Edinburgh	Quaich, on rim foot, lugs with down turned ends, bottom panels of leaves 3 narrow hatched bands and upper panels of alternating flower heads, Arms of Earl of Abercorn (Hamilton), 10 5/8" long, 2 5/8" ht, 7" bowl di	Museum Silver Shop, NY USA advertisement
1681/82	William Law	Edinburgh	Quaich, with 16 staves, marked, initials on lugs "MG and "MPV", 7 5/8" di, 10" over lugs	Huntley House Museum Edinburgh HH3527/70
1682/83	William Law Assayer – John Borthwick	Edinburgh	Quaich, hemispherical and engraved with staves between side handles, initialed "BA/K" and "IL/K", further initialed "GMD" below the lip, 6" di, 7oz 5d	Sotheby's NY USA 1999 #504
1683/84	Robert Brock	Glasgow	Quaich, marks - RB, town mark, RB	Private Collection UK
1685/86	James Penman	Edinburgh	Quaich, engraved flower, staves, no initials on lugs, 9 1/3" over lugs, 6" di bowl, 8oz	Connoisseur Magazine 1938 vol 101, p71 Sotheby's March 10, 1938 #68
1685/86	James Penman	Edinburgh	Quaich, similar to the one above, with script initials	Burlington Magazine 1939 Finlay 1991 #47 National Museums of Scotland 1943.263
1685/86	William Law	Edinburgh	Quaich, no details	Antiques Magazine 1962 vol 81, p20
1687/88	John Luke I	Glasgow	Quaich, no details, note: rare piece carrying the mark of John Luke I	Private Collection UK
1690 ca	MC Possibly Matthew Coquhoun	Possibly Ayr	Quaich, circular on circular collet foot, two shaped handles, engraved below rim with floral panels, reeding and "V" motifs, handles engraved with foliated borders and monograms "M*F" and "I*C", 9" long, 8oz	Sotheby's London UK Feb 28, 1974 #117 Christie's London UK 2005 #45
1690 ca	Robert Elphinstone	Inverness	Quaich, small 2 lugged	Private Collection UK
1694/95	Robert Brock	Glasgow	Quaich, no details	Jackson Marks p568

YEAR	MAKER	LOCATION	DESCRIPTION	SOURCE
1695 ca	John Seaton	Edinburgh	Quaich, miniature, 1oz	How of Edinburgh 1936 #59 Metropolitan Museum AC#63.53.9
1698/99	William Clerk	Glasgow	Quaich, decorated with staves and flower heads, lugs with initials "SG" on one and "IG" on the other, 7 ¼" di, 14oz 10d	Clayton Dictionary #423 Christie's April 15, 1959 #112 Christie's May 19, 1898 Hyman Collection – Colonial Williamsburg
1700 ca	Not available		Quaich, no details	Antiques Magazine 1948 vol 53 p147
1700 ca	Colin McKenzie	Edinburgh	Quaich, no details	Antiques Magazine 1948 vol 53 p147
1700 ca	*Colin McKenzie*	*Edinburgh*	*Quaich, staff engraved, mm only, 6" over lugs, 3oz 14d*	*Sotheby's November 1, 1990 #233* *How of Edinburgh 1937 #87*
1700 ca	William Law	Edinburgh	Quaich, stave lines inside and out, 4 7/8" across lugs,	Hyman Collection - Colonial Williamsburg Antiques Magazine August 1998 p194
1700/01	Colin McKenzie	Edinburgh	Quaich, 3.6oz (Note: not entirely clear this is different from some others listed 1700ca)	How of Edinburgh 1936 #60
1700/01	Thomas Ker	Edinburgh	Quaich, simulated stave lines inside and outside, initials "IS"	Antiques Magazine 1961 vol 79 p97
1700/01	Robert Ker	Edinburgh	Quaich, not pictured, 5 5/8" over lugs	Clayton Christie's Book p228 Christie's Glasgow July 3, 1984 #66
1704 ca	William McLean	Inverness	Quaich, silver mounted, mm indistinct	Private Collection UK
1704/05	John Luke II	Glasgow	Quaich, lower body faint leaves in panels, 3 bands above, panels of flowers alternating near lip, 7 ½" long, 14oz 5d	Country Life April 28, 1960 vol 127 p914 Auction sale Christie's March 23, 1960 #158
1705 ca	Thomas Cumming	Glasgow	Quaich, mm only	Grantully Castle Antiques 1968ca

YEAR	MAKER	LOCATION	DESCRIPTION	SOURCE
1705/06	Robert Inglis Assayer James Penman	Edinburgh	Quaich, no details	Hayden p296
1707 ca	James Falconer	Glasgow	Quaich, initials on lugs, one "MC", the other "II"	National Museums of Scotland MEQ 800
1707/08	James Falconer	Glasgow	Quaich, decorated with flowers in alternating panels near lip, 10" over lugs	Country Life June 17, 1965 vol 137 p 1535 Sotheby's March 4, 1965 #162
1707/08	William Clerk	Glasgow	Quaich, initials on lugs "AC" and "WC", alternating panels of flower heads near rim, outside simulated stave lines, 12 1/8" across lugs, 7 ¾" bowl di, 16oz	How Exhibition 1992 #32, pl 18
1709/10	John Seatoun	Edinburgh	Quaich, staff engraved initials "CM & AK", 11 1/3" overall	Christie's June 24, 1981 #75
1709/10	William Clerk	Glasgow	Quaich, similar to the 1707 example	Breadalbane Collection Sale 1935 #205 Connoisseur Magazine 1939, vol 103, p73
1709/10	*William Clerk*	*Glasgow*	*Quaich, no details*	*Burlington Magazine 1937 vol 71, pp 278-283*
1709/10	*William Clerk*	*Glasgow*	*Quaich, 10 7/8" wide, 14.1oz*	*Metropolitan Museum AC#68.141.7*
1710 ca	Charles Blair	Edinburgh	Quaich, miniature, 1.5oz	How of Edinburgh 1936 #61
1710 ca	Robert Ker	Edinburgh	Quaich, engraved hoops and staves, initials on lugs "AD ER", mm only, 8 ½" over lugs, 5 ½" di bowl, 6oz 14d	Christie's February 25, 1970 #101 Sotheby's February 28, 1974 #10 Blair September 1980 #35 Christie's 1984 #66 The Morris Sale Christie's Edinburgh May 26, 1998 #57 Bonhams The Scottish Sale August 21, 2003 #14
1710 ca	William Scott	Aberdeen	Quaich, stave lines inside and outside, but worn on the outside, initials on lugs "ED" and "TS"	Aberdeen Museums and Galleries ABDAG001361
1711/12	Edward Penman	Edinburgh	Quaich, no details	Dundee Museums and Art Galleries 1966-26

YEAR	MAKER	LOCATION	DESCRIPTION	SOURCE
1712/13	William Hodgert	Glasgow	Quaich, 7 7/8" across lugs, 6.5oz	Hayden, p223 How of Edinburgh 1937 #63
1713/14	James Tait	Edinburgh	Quaich, very plain, down turned ends of lugs, 5" di	Connoisseur Magazine February 1939 p2 Crichton Brothers advertisement
1713/14	Robert Inglis	Edinburgh	Quaich, large, 2 lugs, exterior with Tudor roses and tulips in alternating panels, handles engraved "IMC" and "AC", 6 5/8" di, 10.3oz	Breadalbane Collection Sale 1935 #200 Jackson Marks p 545 Apollo July 1938 p10-12 Connoisseur Magazine 1935 vol 96 p55
1715 ca	William Ged	Edinburgh	Quaich, initials "GS" and MK" on lugs, 7 ½" over the lugs, 6oz	Sotheby's Gleneagles August 29, 1994 #139
1715 ca	MP	Edinburgh	Quaich, lugs with initials "EY" and "IP", also initials underneath, 5" over lugs, 3oz	Sotheby's NY April 12, 1994 #289
1715/16	Alexander Kincaid	Edinburgh	Quaich, no details	Fine Arts Museum of San Francisco CA USA (loan item)
1716/17	Colin McKenzie	Edinburgh	Quaich, 2 lugs, large size	Private Collection UK
1716/17	Alexander Kincaid	Edinburgh	Quaich, exterior of the bowl surrounded by two bands intersected with vertical bands, top of the lug handles engraved with initials "IW" or "MN" within zig-zag borders, 7" over handles, 5oz	James Robinson Inc, NY USA Northeast Auctions, Manchester NH USA 2006 #1424
1716/17	*Alexander Kincaid*	*Edinburgh*	*Quaich, 5.4oz*	*Connoisseur Magazine 1936 vol 98 p241*
1719/20	Robert Inglis	Edinburgh	Quaich, plain bowl, engraved with stave lines inside and outside, 2 lugs edged with a band of simple diagonal hatched decoration, engraved "ER" and "WW", 7 ½" over lugs	JH Bourdon-Smith Catalog 2004 p11 #45
1719/20	*Robert Inglis*	*Edinburgh*	*Quaich, marked below lip, 7 ½" over lugs, 5oz*	*Scottish Art Review vol X, #1* back cover *How of Edinburgh advertisement*
1719/20	James Tait	Edinburgh	Quaich, 6.3oz	Connoisseur Magazine 1943 vol 112, p68

YEAR	MAKER	LOCATION	DESCRIPTION	SOURCE
1719/20	James Tait	Edinburgh	Quaich, initials "M/GS/MK" at the lip, 7 ½" over the lugs, 6oz	Sotheby's Gleneagles August 29, 1994 #138
1720 ca	Charles Blair	Edinburgh	Quaich, 2 ¾" di	Phillips April 21, 1978 #129
1720 ca	Not available Assayer – Edward Penman	Edinburgh	Quaich, no details	Lyle Silver Review 1982 p 87
1720 ca	William Ged	Edinburgh	Quaich, initials "AML" on each lug, 5 ¼" over lugs, 2oz	JH Bourdon-Smith Catalog Autumn 2005, p20 #40
1720 ca	William Scott, younger	Banff	Quaich, engraved with staves, initials "L.F.C." and "CP" on either lug, 3.6oz	Nicholas Shaw Catalog Winter 2001 p68 Bonhams Edinburgh UK 2005 #116
1720 ca	Simon McKenzie	Inverness	Quaich, 4 ¾" across the lugs, 2oz	How of Edinburgh Notes on Antique Silver vol I 1941 p20
1721/22	Robert Luke	Glasgow	Quaich, no details	Antiques Magazine 1969 vol 96 p405
1721/22	Not available Assayer – Edward Penman	Edinburgh	Quaich, initials "WJ" and date "1714", no mm overall, 2X town mark, 12" long, 20oz	Apollo June 1974 vol 99 p486 Christie's February 2, 1974 Christie's March 27, 1956 #89 Christie's London July 5, 2005 #46
1722/23	Charles Dickson I or Charles Duncan	Edinburgh	Quaichs, set of 4	Holland p213
1725 ca	Johan Got-helf-Bilsings	Glasgow	Quaich, 2.5oz	How of Edinburgh 1936 #62 How of Edinburgh 1937 #89 Shaw Collection Christie's Glasgow March 29, 1983 #53
1725 ca	Robert Cruickshank	Aberdeen	Quaich, miniature, 2 lugs, on rim foot, engraved with simulated staves inside and out, shaped lugs with a band of hatching, initials "MF" and "GSM" respectively, 4" over lugs, 1oz	Shaw Collection Christie's Glasgow March 20, 1983 #37 Aberdeen Museums and Galleries ABDAG001241

YEAR	MAKER	LOCATION	DESCRIPTION	SOURCE
1725 ca	Charles Blair	Edinburgh	Quaich, miniature, mm only, 4 ½" wide, 1oz 10d	Sotheby's November 13, 1975 #124
1725 ca	Hugh Ross	Tain	Quaich, engraved 4 1/5" long	Sotheby's Gleneagles August 1993 #169
1725 ca	George Robertson	Aberdeen	Quaich, 3 lugged	National Museums of Scotland L.1972.5
1725/26	Johan Got-helf-Bilsings	Glasgow	Quaich, no details	Antiques Magazine 1970 vol 98 p872 Spink Ltd London
1729/30	James Anderson	Edinburgh	Quaich, plain, on collar foot with flange, maybe with a later crest, profile of lugs slight raised	Brand Inglis 1980 p137 #153
1730 ca	Johan Got-helf-Bilsings	Glasgow	Quaich, initials "CLL", 4 ¼" over lugs, 1oz 17d	Sotheby's April 29, 1986 #96
1730 ca	Johan Got-helf-Bilsings	Glasgow	Quaich, larger example than the previous listing, 4 ¾" bowl di, 6.2oz	Christie's March 29, 1968
1730 ca	James Baillie	Banff	Quaich, border on lugs, no clear initials	Bell of Aberdeen advertisement
1730 ca	Robert Innes	Inverness	Quaich, simulated stave lines inside, border on lugs, no initials, 4" over lugs	Sotheby's Hopetoun House April 1988 #48
1730/31	Alexander Kincaid	Edinburgh	Quaich, bowl incised with 16 stave lines, chevron borders on lugs, no initials, 7 ½" over lugs, 5.5oz	Apollo May 1973, vol 97 p3 JH Bourdon-Smith London 1996 Christie's November 23, 1977 #168 Sotheby's Gleneagles August 29, 1977
1735 ca	Edward Lothian	Edinburgh	Quaich, with 3 lugs, crest and motto "A HUNDRED TO ONE", leaves on lugs	Finlay 1991 # 65 National Museums of Scotland L.1969.679
1735 ca	Alexander Kincaid	Edinburgh	Quaich, no details	Lyle Silver Review 1982 p87
1736/37	Charles Blair	Edinburgh	Quaich, large size, flowers in alternating panels	National Museums of Scotland L.1938.536 Antiques Magazine 1949 vol 56, p272

YEAR	MAKER (continued)	LOCATION	DESCRIPTION	SOURCE Holland p213
1736/37	*Charles Blair*	*Edinburgh*	*Quaich, initials "IH K"*	*Sotheby's April 7, 1938 #114*
1737/38	David Mitchell Assayer Archibald Ure	Edinburgh	Quaich with 2 lugs	National Museums of Scotland MEQ 135
1740 ca	Not available		Quaich, engraved on lugs "EY" and "IP", 5" over lugs, 3.4oz	Nicholas Shaw Catalog Autumn 2005 p20 #46
1740 ca	Robert Innes	Inverness	Quaich, engraved staves, initials "SM" and "AM" on either lug, 4 7/8" over lugs, 1.5oz	Nicholas Shaw Catalog 2004 p94
1740 ca	John Baillie	Inverness	Quaich, on rim foot	How's Notes on Antique Silver vol I 1941 p20 The Maple Swan Collection
1740 ca	IB (probably Bilsings or Baillie)	Inverness or Glasgow	Quaich, on details	National Museums of Scotland H.1994.1098
1740 ca	John Baillie	Inverness	Quaich, 1 ½" X 5 1/8" X 1 ¼"	Musee de Beaux Arts, Montreal Canada 1981.Ds.21
1740 ca	Alexander Johnston	Dundee	Quaich, plain, circular, shaped hollow lug handles	Dundee Museums and Art Galleries 1994-310
1743 ca	James Glen	Glasgow	Quaich, no details (Note: cannot tell if this is the same as other Glen quaichs listed)	Breadalbane Collection How's Notes on Antique Silver p569
1745 ca	James Glen	Glasgow	Quaich, engraved thistles on either lug, 4 5/8" over lugs, 2.4oz	Nicholas Shaw Catalog 2004 p94
1748/49	Colin Allan	Aberdeen	Quaich, no details	National Museums of Scotland SJA 35
1750 ca	John Baillie	Inverness	Quaich, lugs with initials "A/MK", and "M/MK", 3" di	Antique Collector April 1973 p73
1750 ca	John Steven	Dundee	Quaich, no details	Sotheby's Hopetoun House April 1988 #41
1750/51	Robert Low	Edinburgh	Quaich, no details	Jackson Marks p548

YEAR	MAKER	LOCATION	DESCRIPTION	SOURCE
1751/52	Lothian & Robertson	Edinburgh	Quaich, initials on lugs, 6 1/8" over lugs, 3oz 12d	Clayton Christie's Book p182 Christie's February 27, 1974 #149
1751/52	*Lothian & Robertson*	*Edinburgh*	*Quaich, later engraved with initials, 6 1/16" di, 3oz*	*Bonhams London UK 2005 #47*
1751/52	Lothian & Robertson	Edinburgh	Quaich, staff lines in bowl, 3 script Gothic initials on each lug, 3 ½" di, 3.6oz	JH Bourdon-Smith Catalog Autumn 2005 p20 #46
1760 ca	IH		Quaich, 2 lugs, sides engraved "D. McK" and "E. McD", the upper surface of one leg engraved "1733"	Bonhams August 21-23, 2003 #157
1761/62	William Dempster or William Davie	Edinburgh	Quaich, simulated stave lines on the upper half outside, Arms on lugs	Los Angeles Museum Exhibition March 21-April 29, 1962 #227
1765 ca	Adam Graham	Glasgow	Quaich, shaped handles slightly engraved, 3 ½" di, 2oz	Breadalbane Collection Sale 1935 #204
1765/66	Ker & Dempster	Edinburgh	Quaich, silver, double lugged, shaped, 3" di, 3oz	Breadalbane Collection Sale 1935 #197
1770 ca	Alexander Stewart	Inverness	Quaich, lugs engraved "MML" and "IF", 3" di	Antique Collector April 1973 p74
1770 ca	Alexander Stewart	Inverness	Quaich, no details	Clayton Christie's Book p 182 #6
1770/71	James Gilliland	Edinburgh	Quaich, no details	Breadalbane Collection Jackson Marks p 549
1773/74	Alexander Gardner	Edinburgh	Quaich, no details	Jackson Marks p549
1775 ca	James Taylor	Glasgow	Quaich, initials "KMD AMD", also additional script initial, 3 ½" id, 3oz 10d	Sotheby's February 26, 1976 #163
1775/76	J M mark	Glasgow	Quaich, no details	Antiques Magazine vol 96 p405
1780 ca	Not available	Inverness	Quaich, border on lugs, no initials, mm indistinct, 5 ½", 3oz	Sotheby's Hopetoun House April 1988 #65
1780 ca	Thomas Borthwick	Inverness	Quaich, dated "1783", 2 ¾" di, 4.6oz	Christie's 1984 The Morris Sale #151
1780 ca	Thomas Borthwick	Inverness	Quaich, engraved initials, 2 ¾" di bowl, 3.5oz	Christie's July 3, 1984 The Morris Sale #152

YEAR	MAKER	LOCATION	DESCRIPTION	SOURCE
1780 ca	Milne & Campbell	Glasgow	Quaich, 5 1/8" long	Museum of Art, Rhode Island School of Design, Providence RI USA 75.117.10
1780 ca	Thomas Borthwick	Inverness	Quaich, lugs initials "RC" and "AMcK", 3" di	Antique Collector April 1973 p74
1780 ca	Thomas Borthwick	Inverness	Quaich, lugs initials "MR" and "DMK", 3.6oz	Philadelphia Museum of Art 1925-21-2 Bulletin February vol XXII 1928 p22 #118
1780 ca	Thomas Borthwick	Inverness	Quaich, lugs initials "EM" and possibly "IMK", 2 7/8" di	Antique Collector April 1973 p74
1780 ca	AG	Edinburgh or Glasgow	Quaich, mm only, shallow circular, engraved decoration, initialed and plain lug handles, sold with others	Sotheby's Devon UK 1996 #509
1790 ca	Charles Jamieson	Inverness	Quaich, no details	Connoisseur Magazine 1932 vol 90 p205
1793/94	Alexander Gardner	Edinburgh	Quaich, one lug, with engraved date "1793", possibly mm only, piece possible not all correct	Sotheby's August 23, 1976 #12, withdrawn
1793/94	R G	Glasgow Edinburgh assay	Quaich, wooden with 2 half bands, one with thistle and the other hallmarked RG mm, 3 3/8" di	Huntley House Museum Edinburgh HH3338/68
1800 ca	Charles Jamieson	Inverness	Quaich, circular bowl, ring foot, crest on one lug of a crowing gamecock, 5 ¼" wide	Royal Ontario Museum, Toronto Canada 928.13.2
1800 ca	Charles Jamieson	Inverness	Quaich, no details	National Museums of Scotland MEQ 1
1800 ca	Charles Jamieson	Inverness	Quaich, lugs initialed "Dundee Museum and Art Galleries" and "HM", 3" di	Antique Collector April 1973 p75
1808/09	Matthew Craw	Edinburgh	Quaich, one lug with script initials "JMcL", 4 5/9" over lugs	Goodwin's Edinburgh 1991 The Phoenix Collection
1809/10	W & A Ziegler	Edinburgh	Quaich, thistle lugs, won by "The Auld Man", 3" di	JH Bourdon-Smith Catalog Autumn 2002 p23 #44
1810 ca	Charles Jamieson	Inverness	Quaich, no details	Connoisseur Magazine 1934 vol 93, p347
1810 ca	Donald Fraser	Inverness	Quaich, no details	National Museums of Scotland 1961.99

YEAR	MAKER	LOCATION	DESCRIPTION	SOURCE
1810 ca	Charles Jamieson	Inverness	Quaich, lugs initialed "DMK" and "FM"	Antique Collector 1973 p75
1814/15	Not available	Edinburgh	Quaich-shaped bowl, quatrefoil bowl, 3 lobed fluted thin handles, plain slight flared rim, foot, no mm, 4" di, 6 ½" over lugs, 4oz 7d	Private Collection
1814/15	N & G	Edinburgh	Quaich, not pictured	National Museums of Scotland MEQ 1225
1815 ca	Jameson & Naughton	Inverness	Quaich, plain form with hollow handles, on a plain collet foot, the undersides of the handles each engraved with initials, 4" over handles, 21oz 2d	Christie's London UK 2002 #7
1816 dated	Edward Livingstone	Dundee	Quaich, with rays inside and out, engraving inside the rim	National Museums of Scotland 1298 1978-85
1816/17	A?	Edinburgh assay	Quaich, silver mounted wood, inside rim inscribed "Queen Mary's Yew Tree cut at Cruikston May 1816"	Sotheby's London UK 2005 #259
1818/19	Francis Howden	Edinburgh	Quaich, no details	Clayton Christie's Book, p182
1820 ca	Robert Naughton	Inverness	Quaich with inscription, 2 ¾" di bowl, 2.7oz	Breadalbane Collection Christie's July 3, 1984 #50 The Morris Sale Aberdeen Museums and Galleries ABDAG001363
1821/22	JH script	Edinburgh	Quaich, inscribed "Presented to Peter Black", 3" di, 2oz 4d	Sotheby's February 26, 1976 #161
1828/29	Peter Aiken	Glasgow	Quaich, no details	Hyman Collection - Colonial Williamsburg
1829/30	Alexander Edmonstoun	Edinburgh	Quaich, small, embossed fox head handles, gilt lined, retailer J & W Marshall, 4 3/8" X 2 5/8" di X 1 1/8" ht	Huntley House Museum Edinburgh HH2047-60
1830 ca	Peter Arthur or Peter Aiken	Glasgow	Quaich, engraved crest and motto, "Clarior Hinc Honos", of Buchanan, 4" di, 1.5oz	Nicholas Shaw Catalog Winter 2001 p75
1830/31	D C Rait	Glasgow	Quaich, no details	Hobart House, CT USA advertisement
1830/31	W F & Co	Edinburgh	Quaich, 4" over lugs, 1oz 15d	Clayton Christie's Book p 182 Christie's February 27, 1974 #145

YEAR	MAKER	LOCATION	DESCRIPTION	SOURCE
1830/31	Robert Gray & Son	Glasgow	Quaich, no details	National Museums of Scotland L.1980.2
1831/32	AW Possibly Andrew Wilkie	Edinburgh	Quaich, wooden, bound with cane, 2 half bands of silver, one with a thistle, one hallmarked, 2 3/8" di	Huntley House Museum Edinburgh HH2229/68
1831/32	G P	Edinburgh	Quaich, no details	Sotheby's Gleneagles August 1987 #307
1832/33	D C Rait	Glasgow	Quaich, no details	Dundee Museums and Art Galleries 1986-141
1833/34	Elder & Co	Edinburgh	Quaich, the circular section bowl decorated with birds in a landscape and a vacant shield on either side, with other items	Christie's London UK 2003 #416
1833/34	Robert Keay & Son	Perth Edinburgh assay	Quaich, chased heavily, engraved "Won by W. Proctor 1879", 4 1/8" di, 2.4oz	Nicholas Shaw Catalog Winter 2001 p77
1835/36	Elder & Co	Edinburgh	Quaich, small size, no details	Francis E Fowler Foundation
1835/36	James McKay	Edinburgh	Quaich, small size, no details	Francis E Fowler Foundation
1837/38	Not available	Edinburgh	Quaich, silver mounted treen, presented to George Martin, Esq., 3 1/6" di	Nicholas Shaw Catalog Winter 200 p91
1839/40	D C Rait	Glasgow	Quaich, small size, no details	Francis E Fowler Foundation
1840/41	Peter Aiken	Glasgow	Quaich, no details	Dundee Museums and Art Galleries 1978-659
1841/42	J & W Marshall	Edinburgh	Quaich, no details	Clayton Christie's Book p 182
1842/43	J & W Marshall	Edinburgh	Quaich, crest of a dog, with motto "Jamais Arrierre", 1" ht, 2.1oz	Nicholas Shaw Catalog Winter 2000 p91
1849/50	J & W Marshall	Edinburgh	Quaich, engraved "Achleeks Curling Club", 2 ½" di	JH Bourdon-Smith Catalog Autumn 2002 p23 #44
1875/76	John Hay	Edinburgh	Quaich, fox's head on each lug, body chased with flowers, 4 ½" di, 2.5oz	Nicholas Shaw Catalog Winter 2001 p77
1875/76	P Mathie	Edinburgh	Quaich, fox head thumbpiece, chased throughout, 3 ½" over lugs, 1.7oz	Nicholas Shaw Catalog 2005 p104

YEAR	MAKER	LOCATION	DESCRIPTION	SOURCE
1878/79	Hamilton & Inches	Edinburgh	Quaich, leaf handled	National Museums of Scotland MEQ 1301
1879/80	Hamilton & Inches	Edinburgh	Quaich, engraved "Highland Borders 90"	Asley Antiques MA USA 1993
1880 ca	Ferguson & McBean	Inverness	Quaichs, pair, silver mounted, carved wood decorated with mythical Celtic beasts, interwoven snake lugs, silver rim foot and central boss, engraved "SQUAB AS I", one in cherry, one in Laburnum	Lyon & Turnbull, Edinburgh UK 2004 #468
1891/92	John Crichton	Edinburgh	Quaich, with 2 lugs	National Museums of Scotland MEQ 1337
1896/97	MacKay & Chisholm	Edinburgh	Quaich, circular shape on stepped rim, foot engraved with crest of a lion rampant, 8" di, 7.1oz	Nicholas Shaw Catalog Winter 2000 p91
1896/97	Ferguson & McBean	Inverness Edinburgh assay	Quaich, silver mounted wood, wood carved in relief with two panther-like animals, the handles carved with intertwined serpents, interior set with raised silver and engraved bosses	Christie's London UK 2002 #6
1897/98	Edwards & Sons	Glasgow	Quaich, each lug pierced with date of Queen Victoria's Jubilee, 1 5/8" ht, 2.2oz	Nicholas Shaw Catalog Winter 2001 p84
1898/99	JWK	Edinburgh	Quaich, small plain on circular spreading rim foot, shaped lug handles, engraved "SCUAB AS I", 2 ¼" di	Christie's Lanarkshire UK 1998 #280
1900/01	R & HB Kirkwood	Edinburgh	Quaich shaped bowl	National Museums of Scotland MEQ 846
1901/02	MacKay & Chisholm	Edinburgh	Quaich, no details, sold with others	Christie's London UK 2007 #513
1901/02	Hamilton & Inches	Edinburgh	Quaich, plain form with shaped handles, 13 ¾" over handles, 29oz	Bonhams Solihull 2006 #436
1907/08	Brook & Son	Edinburgh	Quaichs, pair, with lugs, "….Presented to the Edinburgh Society of Musicians…."	National Museums of Scotland MEQ 1109
1907/08	M N B	Edinburgh	Quaich	National Museums of Scotland MEQ 1300
1907/08	Brook & Son	Edinburgh	Pair of lugged quaichs, presented to the Edinburgh Society of Musicians	National Museums of Scotland MEQ1511
1907/08	Hamilton & Inches	Edinburgh	Quaich, plain, inscribed below bowl as from Mrs. McDonald Stuart of Dalross, with the date 1909, 7 5/7" di	Huntley House Museum Edinburgh HH3340/68

YEAR	MAKER	LOCATION	DESCRIPTION	SOURCE
1907/08	Hamilton & Inches	Edinburgh	Quaich, of Scottish Regimental interest	Lyon & Turnbull, Edinburgh UK 2002 #284A
1915/16	Brook & Son	Edinburgh	"The Ranger Quaich"	National Museums of Scotland L.1938.12
1918/19	William Robb	Ballater Edinburgh assay	Plain, 4" long	Nicholas Shaw Catalog 2005 p104
1957/58	Mackay & Chisolm	Edinburgh	Quaich, circular bowl, 3 5/8" across lugs	Royal Ontario Museum, Toronto Canada 974.150.19

Salts

Plate 40. Two from a set of 4 human mask (possibly Jacobite) Salts 1743/44 by Ebenezer Oliphant, Edinburgh.
Courtesy of a private collector. Photograph by Janice M Dietert.

YEAR	MAKER	LOCATION	DESCRIPTION	SOURCE
			SALTS	
1670 ca	Patrick Gairdyne	St Andrews	Master salt, St Mary, single, standing form	St Mary's College, St Andrews Finlay 1991 #40
1694 ca	Robert Brock	Glasgow	Trencher salt cellar, circular, reeded borders, engraved with initials "IL/MM", 3" di, 1oz 2d	Sotheby's London August 31, 1992 #169
1694/95	Robert Brock	Glasgow	Salt trencher, circular, with crest, 3 1/8" di, 1.2oz	Noble Collection Nicholas Shaw Catalog 2005 p87
1710/11	William Ged	Edinburgh	Trencher salts, set of 4 oval shaped, with concave sides, each with initials "HA" below a viscount's coronet	Clayton Dictionary p314 #448
1710/11	*William Ged*	*Edinburgh*	*Trencher salts, set of 4*	*National Museums of Scotland MEQ 1464.1-4*
1712/13	Henry Bethune	Edinburgh	Salts, pair, octagonal, Napier crest, 3oz 8d both (1oz 14d ea)	Christie's February 17, 1960 #132
1713/14	Not available	Edinburgh	Trencher salt, oblong with cut corners, accompanying 1729/30 Patrick Graham salts	Sotheby's November 14, 1983 #90 How of Edinburgh
1715/16	Henry Bethune	Edinburgh	Trencher salts, pair, probably oblong with cut corners, sometimes called octagonal, with identical crests and mottos, 2 ¾", 4oz both	Sotheby's April 28, 1960 #54
1716/17	Henry Bethune	Edinburgh	Salt, one of a set of 3, the other two are 1719/20, with oblong cut corners, incurved sides, and oval bowl, on stepped base and reeded border, base stamped "Breadalbane", 2 ¾" long, 9oz total	Breadalbane Collection Sale 1935 #150 Christie's June 13, 2000 #247 withdrawn JH Bourdon-Smith Catalog Autumn 2000
1718/19	Patrick Turnbull	Edinburgh	Salts, pair, octagonal shaped, 3" wide	Scottish Art Academy Exhibition 1939 #419 Noble Collection
1719/20	Henry Bethune	Edinburgh	Two salts of a set of 3 (3rd is 1716/17), as described for the pair, base stamped "Breadalbane", 2 ¾" long, 9oz	Breadalbane Collection Sale 1935 #150 Connoisseur Magazine 1935 vol 96 p55 JH Bourdon-Smith Catalog Autumn 2000

YEAR	MAKER (continued)	LOCATION	DESCRIPTION	SOURCE
1719/20	Alexander Simpson	Edinburgh	Trencher salts, pair octagonal, with engraved initials "AT" over "SH", 2 7/8" long, 4oz 10d	Christie's London UK 2000 #247 lot withdrawn Walter P Chrysler Park-Bernet NY USA Oct 18, 1956 #26 Christie's NY USA 2004 #603 S J Phillips Ltd London UK London 2006 #25565
1722/23	Not available	Edinburgh	Trencher salt, oblong with cut corners, sold with 1729/30 Patrick Graham pair	Sotheby's November 14, 1963 #90 How of Edinburgh
1723/24	Patrick Graham	Edinburgh	Salts, pair, small, octagonal, 2oz 5d both (1oz 12d ea)	Christie's May 1, 1940 #91
1728/29	James Ker	Edinburgh	Trencher salts, pair, oblong with cut corners, with incurved sides above a molded border, 6.6oz	Christie's July 10-11, 1987 #346
1728/29	James Ker	Edinburgh	Trencher salt, no details	National Museums of Scotland 1952.45
1729/30	Patrick Graham	Edinburgh	Trencher salts, pair, sold with 2 other Edinburgh salts, oblong with cut corners, engraved with initials, 3" wide, 10.1oz for 4 salts	Sotheby's November 14, 1963 #90 How of Edinburgh
1729/30	James Mitchelson Assayer Archibald Ure	Edinburgh	Salts, pair, oblong, with cut corner, incurved sides, molded borders, 2 ½" long, 5.6oz	Sotheby's Gleneagles August 1987 #287 Delieb Book p54
1730 ca	George Cooper	Aberdeen	Salts, pair, 3 footed	National Museums of Scotland MEQ 945
1732/33	James Mitchelson	Edinburgh	Trencher salts, pair, oblong with cut corners and incurved sides, initials "ICM", late inscribed underneath "Eigg" and "George IInd 1732", 3" long, 3.5oz	Sotheby's Gleneagles August 19, 1996 #138 Christie's Edinburgh May 26, 1998 #67
1734/35	Archibald Ure	Edinburgh	Salts, set of 4, oblong with cut corners	Antiques Magazine vol 104
1734/35	*Archibald Ure Assayed Archibald Ure*	*Edinburgh*	*Salts, 4, oblong with cut corners*	*Christie's NY USA 1984 p92*

YEAR	MAKER	LOCATION	DESCRIPTION	SOURCE
1734/35	*Archibald Ure*	*Edinburgh*	*Trencher salts, set of 4, concave sides, engraved with crest and motto, 6.5oz*	*Christie's January 24, 1973 #186*
1734/35	William Aytoun	Edinburgh	Salts, pair of oblong, with cut corners, crest of an animal, with motto	Clayton Christie's Book p182 #1 Christie's London June 24, 1981
1734/35	James Ker	Edinburgh	Salts, pair, oblong with cut corners, 1 1/3" ht	Scottish Art Academy Exhibition 1939 #431 Sir R G Gilmour, Private Collection UK
1735 ca	James Mitchelson	Edinburgh	Salts, set of 3 circular shape, each on 3 hoof feet, with chased foliage about the shoulder, sold with one salt by William Dempster, 10.5oz for 4,	Christie's Glasgow April 12, 1983 #66
1735 ca	Colin Mitchell	Canongate	Salts, pair, no details	National Museums of Scotland 1858.119 a+ b
1735/36	James Tait	Edinburgh	Salts, set of 4, compressed circular, corded rims, hoof feet, with later blue glass liners, 2 ½" di, 10.2oz	Sotheby's December 1, 1982 #
1736/37	James Ker	Edinburgh	Salts, circular pair, each on 3 high scroll feet, band of applied molded drops to shallow bowls, 9.7oz	Christie's January 29, 1969 Simon Kaye Antiques
1737/38	Edward Lothian	Edinburgh	Salts, set of 4, circular, rope work rims, hoof feet, 9oz	Phillips Bayswater June 18, 2001 #392
1737/38	*Edward Lothian*	*Edinburgh*	*Salts, set of 4, circular, rope work rims, hoof feet, 9.2oz*	*Bonhams Sale 15120 Aug 22, 2007 #15*
1740 ca	Alexander Forbes	Aberdeen	Salts, pair circular, on 3 hoof feet, 2" di, 3.7oz	Nicholas Shaw Catalog Winter 2001 p69
1740 ca	Johann Got-helf-Bilsings	Glasgow	Salt cellars, pair, compressed circular, engraved with crest and motto below reeded rims, 2 ½" di, 5oz 15 d	Sotheby's Gleneagles August 27-28, 1975 #233
1740 ca	John Baillie	Inverness	Salts, pair, circular shaped, footed	National Museums of Scotland 1517-1518 1982
1741/42	James Ker Assayer Dougal Ged	Edinburgh	Trencher salt, oblong with cut corners, single to match 3 London salts to make a set of 4, London Salts by David Williaume 1722/23	Christie's July 5, 1972 #22
1741/42	James Ker	Edinburgh	Salts, pair, compressed circular shape, corded borders, on 3 hoof feet, initials, 2 ½" di, 5.7oz	Sotheby's June 18, 1964 #132

YEAR	MAKER	LOCATION	DESCRIPTION	SOURCE
1742/43	Edward Lothian	Edinburgh	Salts, set of 4, plain circular shape, molded rim, on 3 hoof feet, with crest, 10oz all	Christie's June 22, 1966 #135
1743/44	Ebenezer Oliphant	Edinburgh	Salts, set of 4, circular, each on 3 unusual human period male face feet attachments, beaded rim, engraved with the crest of a stag's head, crest is stated to be that of Hunter, but possibly is Dick, very unusual feet, the faces may be a Jacobite tribute to Prince Charles, 2 ¾" di, 16oz	Christie's Edinburgh April 29, 1992 Private Collection
1743/44	Edward Lothian	Edinburgh	Salts, set of 4 circular, each with a crest and motto, 2 ½" di, 10.9oz	Sotheby's Gleneagles September 1, 1981 #444 Sotheby's Gleneagles August 1988 #458
1743 ca	James Glen	Glasgow	Salt cellars, pair, gilt interiors, reeded rims, plain, on hoof feet, 2 ½" di, 4oz 16d	Sotheby's March 25, 1965 #85
1744/45	William Aytoun	Edinburgh	Salts, pair, circular on 3 hoof feet, rope edge border, 1 ½" ht, 5.54oz	Nicholas Shaw Catalog 2004 p101
1744/45	James Mitchelson Assayer Hugh Gordon	Edinburgh	Salt cellars, pair, compressed circular shape, each engraved with crest and motto, below a molded rim, on 3 hoof feet, with 2 later blue glass liners, 2 ½" di, 5oz	Sotheby's Gleneagles August 29, 1983 #503
1744/45	James Mitchelson	Edinburgh	Salt cellars, pair, no details	The Maple Swan Collection
1744/45	William Aytoun	Edinburgh	Salts, pair, circular, on 3 hoof feet, with rope edge border, 2 ¼" di 5.5oz	Nicholas Shaw Catalog 2004 p101
1744/45	Not available	Edinburgh	Salt, single, compressed circular shape, on 3 hoof feet, mm rubbed, 2 ¾" di, 2.5oz	Sotheby's Chester December 13-16, 1983 #1162 Sotheby's Chester February 15-17, 1984 #1210
1746/47	Robert Gordon	Edinburgh	Salts, set of 4, shell shaped, on 3 pad feet, 3 ¼" wide, about 11oz both (2oz 5d ea)	Christie's January 7, 1939 #244 Hearst Collection
1746-58	JL	Glasgow	Salt cellars, 2, chased with floral festoons, each on 3 hoof feet, mark rubbed, engraved, 2 ½" di	Sotheby's May 24, 1970 #65
1747/48	Ebenezer Oliphant Assayer Hugh Gordon	Edinburgh	Salt cellars, pair, cauldron shaped, on pad feet, gilt lined, chased with foliage	Christie's March 21, 1977 #262
1747/48	James Mitchell	Edinburgh	Salt cellars, set of 4, each on 3 hoof feet, engraved with a crest and motto,	Christie's March 28, 1984 #193

YEAR	MAKER Assayer Hugh Gordon	LOCATION	DESCRIPTION mm IM figure between, glass liners, 10oz 4d	SOURCE
1747/48	Ebenezer Oliphant	Edinburgh	Salt cellar, compressed circular shape, gilt interior possibly later, 2 ¾" di	Sotheby's Hopetoun House November 12, 1979 #59
1748/49 And 1733/34	James Mitchell	Edinburgh	Salts, two, caldron form, gadrooned rim, later bright cut engraved bow tied swags between stepped hoof feet, later one with Mitchell's mark Overstriking another and probably done later, 2 ½" di, 4oz	Bonhams London UK 2006 #465
1750/51	William Taylor	Edinburgh	Salts, pair, circular, on feet	JH Bourdon-Smith London 1993
1751/52	Ker & Dempster	Edinburgh	Salts, set of 6, compressed circular shape, repoussé and chased with flowers and foliage, gadrooned rims, on 3 hoof feet, 2 ¾" di, 19.3oz	Sotheby's June 2, 1965 #31
1751/52	William Davie or William Dempster	Edinburgh	Salts, pair, circular, chased	Harbor View Antique Center, Toronto Canada, 1994
1752/53	Ker & Dempster	Edinburgh	Cauldron salts, set of 4, crimped border, 2 ½" di	JH Bourdon-Smith Catalog Autumn 2001 p 37, #43
1753/54	Robert Gordon	Edinburgh	Salts, pair of compressed circular shape, with molded rims, gilt interiors, on 3 hoof feet, 2 ¾" di, 5.6oz	Sotheby's Scone Palace April 13, 1976 #107
1753/54	Lothian & Robertson	Edinburgh	Salts, 3, oval, each on 4 mask and paw feet, with gadrooned edges	Private Collection UK
1755/56	James Gilliland	Edinburgh	Salts, set of 4, circular, mask feet, chased flowers, 2 ¾" di	Scottish Art Academy Exhibit 1939 #423 HM Queen Mary Collection
1755/56	Not available	Edinburgh	Salt, single, plain circular shape, molded rim, on 3 hoof feet, sold with 2 similar Edinburgh 1817/18 salts, mm rubbed 6.9oz for 3	Christie's December 20, 1967 #168 Sotheby's May 2, 1968 #6
1755/56	Robert Low	Edinburgh	Salt, chased below the corded rim with ragged hair motif, gilt interior, on 3 lion paw feet, sold with 3 matching salts dated 1836/37 by T A Finlayson, 2 ¾" di, 16.6oz for 4	Sotheby's May 14, 1981 #257
1757/58	Dougal Ged	Edinburgh	Salts, pair of compressed circular shape, with crimped everted rims, each on 3 feet, en suite with a pair of 1772 salts by Patrick Robertson	Scottish Art Review vol IV #3 Bell of Aberdeen advertisement
1757/58	Robert Gordon	Edinburgh	Pair of cauldron salts, on 3 hoof feet, with gadrooned rims and later blue glass liners, 2 1/8", 4.6oz	Bonhams the Scottish Sale August 24, 2005 #5

YEAR	MAKER	LOCATION	DESCRIPTION	SOURCE
1758/89	Benjamin Coutts	Edinburgh	Salts, pair, circular, with beaded rim, on 3 hoof feet, 2 3/8" di	JH Bourdon-Smith 1993 The Phoenix Collection
1758/59	John Edmonstoun	Edinburgh	Salts, pair, circular gadrooned borders, on 3 hoof feet, 4.5oz	Philips Edinburgh August 24, 2001 #554
1758/59	Lothian & Robertson	Edinburgh	Salt, single, squat circular form, crimped everted rim, on 3 shell feet, with crest	Christie's Glasgow August 14, 1984 #166
1758/59	Lothian & Robertson	Edinburgh	Salts, pair, gadrooned rims and gilt interiors, on 3 shell feet, crest, sold with 1854 salt spoons with the same crest, 2 ½" di, 7.1oz with spoons	Sotheby's June 25, 1968
1759/60	James Weems	Edinburgh	Salts, pair of compressed circular shape, with everted crimped rims, on hoof supports, with later blue glass liners, 2 ½" di, 5.6oz	Sotheby's Gleneagles August 29, 1978 #356
1759/60	Dougal Ged	Edinburgh	Salts, pair of compressed circular shape, with everted scalloped edges, on 3 cabriole legs, with reeded toe capped feet, 1 ½" ht, 2 5/8" di, 4.3oz	Sotheby's Gleneagles August 29, 1978 #356
1759/60 and 60/61	WD William Dempster or William Davie	Edinburgh	Salts, set of 4, circular with scalloped rims, gilt interiors, each on 3 hoof feet, 13.1oz all	Christie's July 20, 1966 Christie's April 26, 1967 #22 Simon Kaye Antiques
1759/60	Ker & Dempster	Edinburgh	Salt, plain circular shape, scalloped projecting rim, on 3 shell feet, sold with 3 others, 2 from 1760/70 MK conjoined and one 1785-86 James Hewitt, 2 ½" di, 10.4oz all	Sotheby's October 29, 1959 #60
1759/60	William Dempster or William Davie	Edinburgh	Salts, pair, cauldron form, on 3 hoof feet, scalloped rims, gilt interior, 4.3oz	Bonhams Sale 15120 Aug 22, 2007 #8
1760 ca	William Craw	Canongate	Salts, pair, compressed circular shape, with fluted rims, on 3 hoof feet, 2 ½" di, 3.8oz	Sotheby's Gleneagles August 30, 1982 #501
1761/62	William Taylor	Edinburgh	Salt, circular shape, on 3 hoof feet, initials, paired with a London salt	Christie's January 18, 1982 #223 Christie's March 15, 1982 #58
1761/62	Ker & Dempster and William Dempster	Edinburgh	Salts, 3, circular on hoof feet, initials, paired with a London salt	Christie's July 12-13, 1983 #54
1762/63	Patrick Robertson	Edinburgh	Salt, claw and ball feet, beaded rim, pierced oval, sold with 4 electroplated salts	Christie's Edinburgh November 17, 1993 #713 Christie's Glasgow February 10, 1994 #1328

YEAR	MAKER	LOCATION	DESCRIPTION	SOURCE
1762/63	Not available	Edinburgh	Salts, set of 4, squat circular form, on 3 shell and hoof feet	Christie's Glasgow UK Nov 15, 1984 #164
1762/63	Marks rubbed	Edinburgh	Salts, pair, caldron form, initials underneath "BWM", non-matching blue glass liners, 3" di	Gorringes LLP, East Sussex UK 2006 #1273
1763/64	James Hewitt	Edinburgh	Salts, set of 4, compressed circular shape, scalloped rims, shell and pad feet, with crests, 9oz all	Christie's South Kensington October 30, 1990 #370
1765 ca	Adam Graham	Glasgow	Salts, pair, circular, on 3 hoof feet, with thumb print pie crust scalloping around the edge, molded rim, 2 ½" di	Blum Antiques St Petersburg, FL 1993 The Phoenix Collection
1765 ca	Adam Graham	Glasgow	Salt, no detail	National Museums of Scotland MEQ 54
1765 ca	Adam Graham	Glasgow	Salts, pair of circular shape on 3 hoof feet, engraved initial "B", 2 1/8" di, 3.1oz	Nicholas Shaw Catalog 2004 p101
1765 ca	Adam Graham	Glasgow	Salt, single, compressed circular shape, with flame border, on shell ended legs and feet	National Museums of Scotland MEQ 618 1982.1026
1765/66	Not available	Edinburgh	Salts, pair, compressed circular shape, on 3 hoof feet, mm rubbed, 2 ½" di, 4oz	Sotheby's June 1, 1967 #169
1765/66	Gilliland & Ker	Edinburgh	Salts, pair, compressed circular shape, plain, with reeded and gadrooned rims, on 3 hoof feet, 2 ½" di, 4.9oz	Sotheby's October 10, 1968 Koopman London
1767/68	Patrick Robertson	Edinburgh	Salts, pair, circular salts, with flame gadroon rims, on 3 pad feet	San Antonio Antiques, TX USA 1988 The Phoenix Collection
1767/68	William Dempster or William Davie	Edinburgh	Salts, pair, circular with blue liners, like the following 1769 pair	Mary Cooke Antiques London 1995
1768/69	Alexander Gardner	Edinburgh	Salts, pair, no details	Dundee Museums and Art Galleries 1963-739-2-3
1769/70	MK conjoined	Edinburgh	Salts, pair, plain circular shape, everted scalloped rim, on 3 shell feet, sold with 2 other 1759/60 and 1785/86 Edinburgh, possibly by James McKenzie, 2 ½" di	Sotheby's October 29, 1959 #60
1769/70	William Dempster or	Edinburgh	Salts, pair, circular, blue liners, on hoof feet	Mary Cooke Antiques London

YEAR	MAKER	LOCATION	DESCRIPTION	SOURCE
	William Davie			1995
1770 ca	Robert Clark	Edinburgh	Salts, pair, 3oz	Warman Price G, 27th ed 1993 p584
1770 ca	Not available	Possibly Banff	Salt, plain circular on 3 hoof feet, with a gadrooned rim, marks B, A, B, 2" di	Christie's London UK 1999 #41
1770 ca	Milne & Campbell	Glasgow	Salts, pair, circular with blue glass liners	Private Collection
1771/72	Patrick Robertson	Edinburgh	Salts, set of 7, two with mm only, oval on claw and ball feet, open work sides with applied trailing vine leaves between corded borders, clear glass liners, 3 ¼" wide, 16.5oz	Christie's Lanarkshire UK 1998 #59
1771/72	Patrick Robertson	Edinburgh	Salts, set of 4, oval, waved, gadrooned rim, bequest, pierced foliage and birds, 3 ¼" long	Victoria & Albert Museum 1981 Seabright
1771/72	*Patrick Robertson*	*Edinburgh*	*Oval salt*	*Hughes p 93* *Victoria & Albert Museum*
1772/73	Patrick Robertson	Edinburgh	Salts, pair of compressed circular shape, with crimped everted rims, each on 3 feet, en suite 1757 Dougal Ged pair	Scottish Art Review 1953 vol IV, #3 Bell of Aberdeen advertisement
1776/77	Probably Alexander Gardner	Edinburgh	Salts, pair, navette shaped, bead rims with ring handles, sides chased with flower head roundels and husk swags over pierced fluted slats, part fluted lower body on a fluted oval foot, gilt interiors, both fitted with unmarked silver liners, 5" over handles, 5.5oz	Bonhams London UK 2003 #443 Bonhams London UK 2204 #366
1777	Possibly Patrick Robertson mm double struck	Edinburgh	Salts, set of 4, oval with open work sides, on 4 ball and claw feet, sold with other items	Christie's London UK 2001 #142
1780 ca	Benjamin Lumsden	Aberdeen	Salts, pair, circular, on 3 hoof feet, petal shaped borders, gilded interior, 4.1oz	Shaw Collection Christie's Glasgow March 29, 1983 #30
1780 ca	William Scott	Dundee	Salts, pair, no details	Dundee Museums and Art Galleries 1969-168
1780 ca	James Gordon or James Douglas	Aberdeen	Salts, pair, with blue glass liners	Aberdeen Museums and Galleries ABDAG011131
1785/86	James Hewitt	Edinburgh	Salt, plain circular shape, everted scalloped rim, on 3 shell feet, sold with others earlier Edinburgh, 2 ½" di	Sotheby's October 29, 1950 #60

YEAR	MAKER	LOCATION	DESCRIPTION	SOURCE
1786/87	James Dempster or James Douglas	Edinburgh	Salt cellar, no details, note: James Douglas was also making silver that year	Jackson Marks p 550
1790 ca	Not available		Salts, pair, boat shaped	JH Bourdon-Smith Catalog 1993
1790 ca	Robert Keay I	Perth	Salts, pair, oval shape	National Museums of Scotland MEQ 1079-80 1972
1790 ca	M & F	Edinburgh	Salts, pair, boat shaped, 4" across, with another matched London pair	Gorringes LLP, East Sussex UK 2006 #1788
1790 ca	W & P Cunningham I	Edinburgh	Salts, set of 4, boat shaped with reeded rim and two reeded flat handles, on a conforming foot, gilt interiors, 5" long, 10.5oz	Christie's London UK 2002 #144
1790 ca	Francis Howden	Edinburgh	Salts, set of 4, oval on spreading foot, with gadrooned borders, 4 ½" wide, 14oz	Christie's Lanarkshire UK 1998 #53
1790/91	James Dempster or James Douglas	Edinburgh	Salt, most likely James Douglas as maker since James Dempster was deceased by this time, no details	Antiques Magazine 1953 vol 63 p160 Shreve advertisement
1790/91	Peter Mathie	Edinburgh	Salts, pair of circular shape, on 3 hoof feet, with rope edge border, engraved "R", 2 ½" di, 5.3oz	Nicholas Shaw Catalog Winter 2001 p75
1795 ca	James Erskine	Aberdeen	Salt cellars, pair of oval shape, 2 bands of bright cut engraving, laurel leaf cartouche, 3 3/8" long, 2.6oz	Nicholas Shaw Catalog 2004 p107
1795 ca	George Christie	Edinburgh	Salts, pair, paneled cellars, reeded rim and base, on bracket feet, crest of dexter arm clasping a spur and a script "C", 3 ¾" X 2 3/8" X 2 3/8" ht, 2oz each	Minneapolis Institute of Art 77.22.48 1,2
1795/96	William Robertson	Edinburgh	Salts, set of 4, oval, bright cut with blue liners, 2 rubber crests	J M Simmons Antiques, London 1995
1795/96	W & P Cunningham I	Edinburgh	Salts, pair, boat shaped	The Gordons, Plattsburgh NY USA 1995
1800 ca	McHattie & Fenwick	Edinburgh	Salts, set of 4, boat shaped	JH Bourdon-Smith Catalog London 1993
1800 ca	GB George Bain or George Booth	Edinburgh	Salts, pair, boat shaped, no date letter, possibly just assayed in Edinburgh, 3 7/8" X 2 1/8"	Huntley House Museum Edinburgh HH2533-64

YEAR	MAKER	LOCATION	DESCRIPTION	SOURCE
1800 ca	W & P Cunningham I	Edinburgh	Salts, set of 6, boot shaped supported on a conforming foot, gilt interiors, later engraved with an initial, 3 ¾" long, 15oz	Christie's London UK 2004 #597
1800 ca	George Booth	Aberdeen	Salts, pair, square shaped on a conforming pedestal foot, rims with foliate scroll and flower motifs, engraved with a crest, gilt interiors, with blue glass liners, 3 ¼" long, 5oz	Christie's London 2002 #217
1805 ca	Robert Gray & Son	Glasgow Edinburgh assay	Salts, pair, no details	Sotheby's Gleneagles August 1991 #124
1806/07	John McDonald	Probably Edinburgh	Salts, set of 4, boat form, gilt lined, on a rim foot with gadrooned rims, 4" long, sold with other items, indicated as Glasgow	Christie's NY USA 1997 #86
1810 ca	Possibly John Heron	Greenock	Salt, cylindrical form on a swept, circular foot, 4" ht	Gorringes LLP, East Sussex UK 2006 #570
1810 ca	William Jamieson	Aberdeen	Salts, set of 4, oval boat shape with gilt interiors, oval pedestal foot, bright cut engraved cartouche on either side, 8 oz	Christie's London UK 2007 #843
1810/11	George Fenwick	Edinburgh	Salt dish, no details	National Museums of Scotland H.1994.1128
1815 ca	Jameson & Naughton	Inverness	Salts, pair of boat shaped	Noble Collection Nicholas Shaw Catalog 2005 p103
1815 ca	*Jameson & Naughton*	*Inverness*	*Salts, pair, boat shaped on spreading oval base and rim foot, 4 " long, 3oz*	*Christie's London UK 1999 #7*
1820 ca	William Jamieson	Aberdeen	Salts, set of 4, no details	Dundee Museums and Art Galleries 1971-978-1 - 4
1821/22	J Neville	Glasgow	Salts, pair, no details	Goodwin's, Edinburgh 1993
1823/24	CB	Edinburgh	Salts, set of 4, top and foot decorated with ornamental band, crest of Gibson-Carmichael, with 2 others by Paul Storr	Royal Ontario Museum, Toronto Canada 961.123.8 c-f
1823/24	James McKay	Edinburgh	Salts, set of 3, caldron type each on 3 lion's mask and claw feet	Christie's London UK 2005 #614
1824/25	James McKay	Edinburgh	Salts, pair, circular on 4 shell feet, engraved with crest of Balfour, gadrooned rims, 2 ¼" ht, 3" di, 11.9oz	Bonhams Edinburgh UK 2005 #27

YEAR	MAKER	LOCATION	DESCRIPTION	SOURCE
1826/27 and 1828/29	James McKay	Edinburgh	Salts, pair, circular with gadrooned borders, on 3 lion's mask and paw feet, 3 ½" di, sold with others	Eubank Guidford 2007 #570
1828/29	F & S	Edinburgh	Salts, pair, oval form, gadrooned borders, spiral fluted sides, on pad feet, sold with others	Christie's London UK 2000 #74
1828/29	James McKay	Edinburgh	Cauldron salts, pair, on 4 legs, with mermaid crest, 12oz	JH Bourdon-Smith Catalog Autumn 2005 p26 #46
1832/33	George Paton	Edinburgh	Cauldron salts, pair, on 3 lion mask feet, scrolled leaves on rim, 3" di, 7.2oz	Nicholas Shaw Catalog Autumn 1999 p62
1839/40	J & W Marshall	Edinburgh	Salts, pair, no details	National Museums of Scotland MEQ 113-14
1847/48	R & S	Aberdeen Edinburgh assay	Salts, pair, caldron form, gadrooned borders, on 3 stepped hoof feet, blue glass liners, sold with other items	Bonhams London UK 2006 #305
1859/60	JH	Edinburgh	Salts, 3 of a set of 4, with other items	Christie's Lanarkshire UK 1997 #594
1862/63	James McKay	Edinburgh	Salt cellars, pair, no details	The Maple Swan Collection
1866/67	James McKay	Edinburgh	Salt, one of a set of 4, with other items	Christie's Lanarkshire UK 1997 #594
1872/73	George & Michael Crichton	Edinburgh	Salts, 4, no details	National Museums of Scotland MEQ 880
1883/84	R & CD	Glasgow	Salts, set of 4, circular on four ball feet, with chased base, the side formed of four cast and chased elephants in Indian ceremonial dress, each with a cranberry glass liner, 2" ht	Christie's London UK 2006 #144
1888/89	Hamilton & Inches	Edinburgh	Salts, pair, no details	National Museums of Scotland MEQ 1180-81 1976.27-28
1893/94	Hamilton & Inches	Edinburgh	Salts, pair on stands, each on oval stand with everted border and reeded rim alternated by four fluted foliated ornaments, raised square center, the oval salt cellars on rectangular base, partly gadrooned body with reeded rim and two angular handles, 8 ¾" wide stand, 18.8oz	Christie's Amsterdam NE 2004 #201
1897/98	J Reid	Glasgow	Salts, four novelty, cast as swans, glass liners spoons and case, 3" long, 7oz 5d	Sotheby's London UK Oct 22, 1998 #293

YEAR	MAKER	LOCATION	DESCRIPTION	SOURCE
1926/27	Brook & Son	Edinburgh	Salts, pair, triangular shaped, Traprain design	National Museums of Scotland MEQ 1612
1929/30	Brooks & Sons	Edinburgh	Traprain salts, pair, 4 ½" di , 10oz	Nicholas Shaw Catalog Winter 2002/03 p89
1930/31	Brook & Son	Edinburgh	Traprain salts, pair, 2" ht, 9.6oz	Bonhams Edinburgh UK 2005 #17

Salvers

Plate 41. A Salver 1740 ca by Robert Luke, Glasgow.
Courtesy of The Phoenix Collection. Photograph by Janice M Dietert.

SALVERS, STANDS AND WAITERS

YEAR	MAKER	LOCATION	DESCRIPTION	SOURCE
1717/18	Henry Bethune	Edinburgh	Shallow dish or tray, no details	National Museums of Scotland MEQ 1347
1718/19	Charles Duncan	Edinburgh	Teapot stand, engraved in center with a cipher "EL" under an earl's coronet, shallow circular dish on plain flaring rim, attributed to Charles Dickson I but most likely by Charles Duncan, 1 3/16" ht, 7 5/16" di, 11.9oz	Alcorn, Museum of Fine Art, p331 #253
1719/20	James Mitchelson	Edinburgh	Teapot stand, underside engraved with initials "AH", circular, scalloped rim, center engraved with the crest of Burnside, 6 1/3" di, 7oz	Bonham Sale 10914, #9
1719/20	James Mitchelson	Edinburgh	Waiter, circular, simple molded rim, 3 panel supports, crest and motto "THINK ON" for MacLellan of Barclay, 7" di, 8oz 12d	Sotheby's London Sept 1, 1998 #551
1719/20	Henry Bethune	Edinburgh	Teapot stand, perfectly plain, circular with upturned edge on narrow rim foot, with its teapot, 6 ¾" di	Sotheby's Gleneagles, August 27-28, 1970 #114
1719/20	James Mitchelson	Edinburgh	Salver, plain circular, simple molded raised rim, on 3 panel feet, center with armorials of McLean of Barclay, 7" di, 8.6oz	Sotheby's Gleneagles September 1, 1998 #551
1720 ca	William Ged	Edinburgh	Salver, no details	National Museums of Scotland MEQ L.1983.21
1720/21	Thomas Hay	Edinburgh	Teapot stand, circular engraved with a crest and a ship inscribed "The Happy Union," on narrow rim foot, 6 ½" di 7.2oz	Sotheby's Gleneagles, August 27-28, 1971 #137
1721/22	Henry Bethune	Edinburgh	Teapot stand on rim foot, sides later chased with flowers, scrolls, foliage, with crest and motto, 6 ½" di, 6.6oz	Christie's July 25, 1973 #189
1724 ca	Alexander Forbes	Aberdeen	Salver, Chippendale border, engraved initials "M/JA/JS", 8 ½"di, 15oz	Nicholas Shaw Catalog 1999 p62
1725 ca	James Mitchelson	Edinburgh	Salver, small hexagonal shape	National Museums of Scotland MEQ 934
1725 ca	Robert Luke	Glasgow	Salver, on foot, possibly a tazza, later engraved with armorials of Drummond quartering Home, chased with scrolls, flowers and foliage, 5 ¼" di, 6oz	Sotheby's January 14, 1960 #56
1725 ca	Robert Luke	Glasgow	Teapot stand as shallow dish on low rim foot	How of Edinburgh advertisement p107 illustration
1725/26	Henry Bethune	Edinburgh	Teapot stand, no details	National Museums of Scotland MEQ 1980.4

YEAR	MAKER	LOCATION	DESCRIPTION	SOURCE
1725/26	James Ker	Edinburgh	Salvers, pair, wavy borders, circular, molded beaded edge	National Museums of Scotland MEQ 1235-1236 1977.34-35
1725/26	William Aytoun	Edinburgh	The Annandale Stand, crest of Johnston, Marquess of Annandale	How of Edinburgh 1937 #92 Private Collection UK
1726/27	Henry Bethune	Edinburgh	Teapot stand, on rim foot, dish form, plain border, initials "IAS", 7" di, 8oz 5d	Shaw Collection Christie's Glasgow March 29, 1983 #84
1727/28	James Ker	Edinburgh	The Johnson Tea Service Tray (also called Ford Set Tray), engraved with armorials for Johnson	How's Notes on Antique Silver I, p23, 1941
1728/29	James Ker	Edinburgh	Waiters, pair, square, crest, motto under a coronet	Sotheby's June 25, 1953 #114
1728/29	James Ker	Edinburgh	Circular waiter (stand), hoof feet, scalloped molded rim, 7 ½" di 7oz 16d	Christie's November 8, 1950 #159
1729/30	James Mitchelson	Edinburgh	Circular salver with shaped wavy border, on rim foot, engraved initials below an earl's coronet, wavy border teapot stand, description described as by William Jamieson, see note in italics below, 8" di, 10.9oz	Sotheby's August 29, 1978 #423 National Museums of Scotland MEQ 1295 1978.82
1729/30	*James Mitchelson Assayer Archibald Ure*	*Edinburgh*	*Salver, no details. (Note: this mark is attributed to William Jamieson but more likely for James Mitchelson but read upside down)*	*Jackson Marks p546*
1729/30	James Ker Assayer Archibald Ure	Edinburgh	Stand with wavy border, molded edge, 2 crests, on rim foot, 12 points, 8 ½" di, 12oz 19d	Sotheby's Book p819 Sotheby's November 18, 1970 #225 N Bloom & Sons
1729/30	James Ker Assayer Archibald Ure	Edinburgh	Square waiter, crest, motto in worn cartouche, on bracket feet, 6 7/8" wide, 10oz 19d	Clayton Christie's Book p182 Christie's July 5, 1972 #25 How of Edinburgh
1729/30	James Mitchelson	Edinburgh	Square waiter, crest and motto of Haig, 4 ¾", 6oz 15d	Christie's October 29, 1959 #65 Sotheby's December 12, 1963 366 Christie's Glasgow March 1983 #74
1729/30	James Mitchelson	Edinburgh	Teapot stand, no details	National Museums of Scotland MEQ 1983.24

YEAR	MAKER	LOCATION	DESCRIPTION	SOURCE
1729/30	Not available	Edinburgh	Salver, shaped, square, marked on each foot, mm not clear, panel feet, crest and motto, 10 ½" wide, 22oz	Christie's NY USA April 12, 1994 #290
1729/30	Not available	Edinburgh	Salver, shaped, square/octagonal, with alternate straight and convex sides, between indentations, center with a crest and motto, mm unclear, 10 ½" wide, 22oz, one mark on each, on 4 shaped panel supports	Sotheby's NY USA April 12, 1994 #290
1729/30	Henry Bethune	Edinburgh	Teapot, stand, wavy border, on rim foot, molded edge, 12 points, with 1727 Ker tea service	Apollo 1934, vol XXV p20 Wilson & Sharp advertisement
1729/30	*Henry Bethune*	*Edinburgh*	*Salver/tray, on cylindrical foot, scalloped wavy rim, molded edge, crest and motto "Will God I Shall", part of the early Tea Service, the rest by Ker*	Brooklyn Museum 63.95.1
1730 ca	George Cooper	Aberdeen	Salver, Chippendale border, engraved in center with vacant oval in scrolling foliage cartouche, on 3 hoof feet, 6 ¾" di, 6oz 8d	Sotheby's June 26, 1968 Spink
1730 ca	George Cooper	Aberdeen	Salver, on central trumpet shaped foot, slight raised molded border, possibly a tazza, 9 7/8" di, 17oz 6d	Christie's July 26, 1972 #359
1730 ca	Robert Luke	Glasgow	Salver, on foot, circular, later engraved with brickwork roundel enclosing arms of Orr of Barrowfield, Scotland, below foliate mantling, helm, crest and motto "BONIS OMNIA BONA", molded rim, on trumpet shaped foot, 9 ½" di, 18oz 8d	Christie's Nov 21, 1957 Sotheby's Gleneagles August 31 – Sept 1, 1987 #281 Provenance: J Stuart Stevenson Esq.
1730 ca	Robert Luke	Glasgow	Waiter, square form, re-entrant corners, shell and acanthus engraved inner border, on four hoof feet, 6 1/3" wide, 9oz	Lyon & Turnbull Edinburgh UK 2004 #475
1730 ca	George Cooper	Aberdeen	Salver, later engraved in center with armorials, foliate mantling and mottos, flat chased with diaper and fruits, Chippendale rim, 3 scroll feet, 6" di, 5oz	Sotheby's April 30, 1985 #78
1730 ca	George Cooper	Aberdeen	Salver, square, shaped corners, chased out border, 8" across	Queen's Silver p 66 pl 10
1730 ca	George Cooper	Aberdeen	Salver, no details	National Museums of Scotland MEQ 46
1730 ca	Robert Luke II	Glasgow	Salver, with wavy border, with molded edge, 14 points, 7 7/8", 10.8oz	Nicholas Shaw Catalog 2005 p91
1730 ca	George Cooper	Aberdeen	Salver, Chippendale border, engraved in center with vacant oval in scrolling foliage cartouche, on 3 hoof feet, 6 ¾" di, 6oz 8d	Sotheby's June 26, 1968 Spink Ltd London
1730 ca	Robert Luke II	Glasgow	Shaped square salver, on 4 hoof feet, flat chased border of shells and scrolls, 6 1/8", 8.8oz	Nicholas Shaw Catalog 2005 p91

YEAR	MAKER	LOCATION	DESCRIPTION	SOURCE
1730ca	Robert Luke	Glasgow	Salver, engraved with motto, shaped molded border, 7 ½" di, 7oz 9d	Sotheby's September 23, 1973 #4
1730 ca	George Cooper	Aberdeen	Waiter, Chippendale border, flat chased with band of fruit and flowers, center with later crest and initial, 6" di, 6oz 4d	Sotheby's August 29-30, 1977 #184
1730 ca	George Cooper	Aberdeen	Waiter, plain shaped square, on 4 bun feet, slightly raised border, incurved angles, engraved on reverse side with initials "PAS", 4 ¾" di, 4oz 9d	Christie's July 3, 1984 #121
1730 ca	George Cooper	Aberdeen	Waiter, plain square, on scroll feet, flat molded border with shaped angels, reverse engraved with initials, 5 ¾" square, 6oz 9d	Christie's June 2, 1976 #163
1730 ca	George Cooper	Aberdeen	Salver or teapot stand, no details	Hyman Collection - Colonial Williamsburg G1996-221
1730 ca	Robert Luke	Glasgow	Teapot stand, no details	National Museums of Scotland 1958.129
1730 ca	George Cooper	Aberdeen	Waiter, square, no details, may be same as before	Aberdeen Museums and Galleries ABDAG001359
1730 ca	George Cooper	Aberdeen	Teapot stand, shaped circular form, 3 scroll and hoof feet, 6" di	Morris Collection Clayton Dictionary p171 #10 Christie's July 3, 1984 #119 Christie's London UK 1999 #18
1730 ca	George Cooper	Aberdeen	Tea tray, large circular, on 4 feet, scalloped border, chased with a band of scrolls, flowers and foliage, 20 ½" di, 114oz	Scottish Art Review vol VI 1956 p41 #1 Bell of Aberdeen advertisement Aberdeen Museums and Galleries
1730 ca	George Cooper	Aberdeen	Salver, the Duff Family Salver, with coat of arms, crest and motto	Aberdeen Museums and Galleries ABDAG001002 acquired in 1975
1731/32	James Mitchelson	Edinburgh	Teapot stand, no details, originally attributed to John Main	Wilson & Sharp Ltd Finlay #77 National Museums of Scotland MEQ 1983.23
1731/32	William Aytoun	Edinburgh	Salver, octagonal, on 4 bracket feet, crest and motto of Hathorn or Stewart, 13 ¾", 48oz	Apollo October 1988 vol 88 p95 De Haviland Antiques advertisement

YEAR	MAKER (continued)	LOCATION	DESCRIPTION	SOURCE
				Sotheby's July 4, 1968 #160
1731/32	Henry Bethune	Edinburgh	Waiter, shaped square, molded border incurved at angles, crest and motto in center on 4 hoof supports, 6 ¼", 10.6oz, note: also indicated as 1730/31	Sotheby's Gleneagles, August 28, 1975 #46 Christie's Scotland November 25-27, 1997 #113
1731/32	James Tait	Edinburgh	Circular with a bath border, initials on underside, on 3 hoof feet, 7 ½" di, 9.6oz	Sotheby's February 10, 1966 Vander Collection
1731/32	James Ker	Edinburgh	Salver, circular teapot stand, wavy border and molded beaded edge, with sugar bowl, 9 points, 7 ¾" di	JH Bourdon-Smith Catalog 1983 p14 The Maple Swan Collection
1731/32	William Aytoun	Edinburgh	Tray, octagonal, engraved, on bracket feet, 11", 50oz	National Museums of Scotland MEQ 1585-86 1985
1732/33	James Mitchelson	Edinburgh	Salver, plain square, molded border, 5 ½" square, 9oz 15d	Christie's April 10, 1923 #7
1732/33	William Aytoun	Edinburgh	Waiter, square, on 4 bracket feet, molded border with incurved corners, crest and motto, 6 1/7", 15.1oz	Christie's July 6, 1972 How of Edinburgh
1733/34	William Aytoun	Edinburgh	Salvers, pair, square, cut corners, center with crest and motto in a rib and above, 20.5oz	How of Edinburgh 1937 #107
1733/34	William Aytoun	Edinburgh	Stand, wavy border, molded edge with bowl, Arms of Menzies impaling Campbell, 12 points	How of Edinburgh advertisement Clayton Dictionary p33 #43
1733/34	William Aytoun	Edinburgh	Stand on rim, wavy border, molded edge, 8" di, 11oz 14d	Christie's February 27, 1980 #137
1733/34	William Aytoun	Edinburgh	Salver, shaped circular, molded rim, on rim foot, 8" di, 11oz	*Christie's December 14, 1988 #185*
1733/34	William Aytoun	Edinburgh	Salver, with wavy border, molded rim, stand	*Lyle Silver Review 1982 p91*
1733/34	William Aytoun	Edinburgh	Tea pot stand, wavy border on rim, part of Girdwood Tea Service	Christie's December 13, 1933 #36 December 13, 1967 #22 Treasures From Scotland Houses Edinburgh 1967 #149-152 Collections of Girdwood and Noble

YEAR	MAKER	LOCATION	DESCRIPTION	SOURCE
1733/34	James Ker	Edinburgh	Salvers, pair, on 4 feet, one with detachable tazza base (central foot), 14" di	Scottish Art Academy Exhibit #899 Stirling-Maxwell Collection National Museums of Scotland MEQ 1585-56 1985
1733/34	Archibald Ure	Edinburgh	Teapot stand, with wavy border, with molded edge, initials "AH", probably 12 points, 7" di, 8.5oz	Christie's London July 10-11, 1984 #375 Picture file Negative #25239
1733/34	William Aytoun	Edinburgh	Salvers, pair, square, incurved corners, each on 4 bracket feet with molded borders, center with full armorials for Wauchope quartering, Wauchope of Edmondstone, each with scratch weights "25.8", "26:4", 10 ¾" wide, 49oz	Christie's June 13, 2000 #231
1733/34	James Tait	Edinburgh	Teapot stand, shaped circular molded border, on rim foot, 12 points, originally sold/appeared with a teapot in 1965, 8 ½" di, 9oz	Christie's Glasgow April 12, 1983 #171
1733/34	Ebenezer Oliphant (said to be)	Edinburgh	Salver, shaped circular with plain ground and molded border on 4 hoof feet, 10 ½" di, 22oz, note: either the date or maker is incorrect, Oliphant did not become a freeman until 1737	Christie's London UK 2004 #140
1734/35 & 1738/39	James Mitchelson	Edinburgh	Salvers, matched pair, both borders with 6 points, 21.4oz both	How of Edinburgh 1937 #105
1734/35	William Aytoun	Edinburgh	Salver, on 3 pad feet, flat chasing, 7 ¾" di	Schredds of Portobello, London 2005
1734/35	James Ker	Edinburgh	Salver, shaped, chased, crest and motto, coronet of Hope, part of the Hopetoun Service, 9 3/8" wide	Clayton Dictionary #651 Christie's June 15, 1977 #121 National Museums of Scotland 1211 1977.10
1734/35	Edward Lothian	Edinburgh	Waiter, square, rounded corners, molded border, 6 ½" square, 10oz 10d	Christie's June 25, 1946 #96
1734/35	*Edward Lothian*	*Edinburgh*	*Salver, no details*	*Jackson Marks p547*
1734/35	James Ker	Edinburgh	Salver, square, shaped molded border, center with coat of arms, 4 hoof feet	Sotheby's April 24, 1978 #128
1734/35	James Ker	Edinburgh	Salvers, pair square on 4 hoof feet, chased with scrolling foliage and shells on a matted ground, engraved with later crest, motto and coronet, 5 ¾" wide, 16.2oz	Christie's November 24, 1976 #50
1734/35	James Tait	Edinburgh	Waiter, shaped circular form with pie-crust molded border, on 3 hoof feet, 7 ½" di, 9.5oz	Lyon & Turnbull, Edinburgh UK 2006 #118

YEAR	MAKER	LOCATION	DESCRIPTION	SOURCE
1734/35	James Tait	Edinburgh	Waiter, shaped circular form on 3 scrolled hoof feet, with ogee cusped and molded border, the reverse with traces of betrothal initials, 7" di, 9oz	Christie's Lanarkshire UK 1997 #16
1735 ca	Alexander Farquharson	Edinburgh	Waiter, square with in turned corners, on 4 hoof feet, chased with shells and foliate scrolls, 5 ¾" wide, 8oz	Christie's Scotland May 23, 1996 #446
1735 ca	Robert Luke II	Glasgow	Salver, Chippendale border, 3 hoof feet, flat chased flowers, fruits and shell, 8", 11.8oz	Nicholas Shaw Catalog 2005 p93
1735 ca	George Cooper	Aberdeen	Salver, plain, on central foot	Private Collection
1735 ca	Robert Luke II	Glasgow	Teapot stand, wavy border, on plain rim feet, 7 ¾" di, 10oz	Shaw Collection Christie's Glasgow March 1983 JH Bourdon-Smith London
1735 ca	George Cooper	Aberdeen	Waiter, marks include a gothic A or E	Aberdeen Museums and Galleries ABDAG001003
1735 ca	George Cooper	Aberdeen	Teapot stand, circular, monogram "JG"	Aberdeen Museums and Galleries ABDAG008579
1735/36	Dougal Ged	Edinburgh	Waiter, shaped circular form on 3 hoof feet, engraved with a crest, 7" di, with another item	Christie's London UK 2002 #156
1735/36	James Mitchelson	Edinburgh	Salver, plain shaped, circular, on 4 hoof feet, with molded waved border, 10 1/8" di, 20oz	Christie's April 26, 1966 #
1735/36	Dougal Ged	Edinburgh	Salver, circular, no details	Christie's Edinburgh November 21, 1990 #103
1735/36	James Ker	Edinburgh	Salver, acquired 2004-05 by Edinburgh City Museum, no details	Huntley House Museum 2004-05
1735/36	James Ker	Edinburgh	Tray, a modified oblong, scrolled borders in between, 14 ½" X 11 ½", 37oz	Pictured in Furniture & Silver article
1735/36	Edward Lothian	Edinburgh	Salver, circular, raised scalloped rim, 12.5oz	Yale University Art Gallery 1959.17.8
1735/36	William Aytoun Assayer Archibald Ure	Edinburgh	Salver, no details	Sotheby's London August 1989 #212
1735/36	James Mitchelson	Edinburgh	Salver, shaped circular, on 4 hoof feet, molded wavy border, 10 ½" di, 20oz	Christie's April 26, 1966 #144

YEAR	MAKER	LOCATION	DESCRIPTION	SOURCE
1735/36	James Mitchelson	Edinburgh	Salver, shaped border, on 3 feet, engraved arms, 9" di, 17oz 14d	Scottish Art Academy Exhibit #962 Christie's April 12, 1954 #158
1735/36	John Rollo	Edinburgh	Salver, plain, circular, on 4 scroll and shell feet, molded border, 14" di, 49oz 13d	Christie's April 24, 1950 #130
1735/36	William Aytoun	Edinburgh	Salver, modified square, reeded shaped border, central shield with coat of arms inside, on 4 shell feet	Dewar Collection Sotheby's London 1987
1735/36	James Ker	Edinburgh	Urn stand, quatrefoil shape, plain center, bounded by an engraved shell, scroll and hatched border, on 4 stump supports, 14 ½" long, 36.5oz	Phillips, Edinburgh July 22, 1983 #245 How of Edinburgh Scottish Art Review vol XVI 1984 #1 National Museums of Scotland MEQ 1574 1984
1735/36	James Mitchelson	Edinburgh	Salver, shaped circular on molded foot, with center shaped molded rim, crest and motto, 7oz	Christie's December 9, 1970 #57
1736/37	Edward Lothian	Edinburgh	Salver, plain, shaped circular, on 4 scroll feet, 8 ¾" di, 13.9oz	Nicholas Shaw Catalog Winter 2001 p71
1736/37	James Mitchelson	Edinburgh	Salver, small circular, bath border, 7 ½" di, 11oz 10d	Private Collection Sotheby's Gleneagles August 27, 1990
1736/37	William Aytoun	Edinburgh	Salver, circular, reeded bath type border with scrolls, 6 points, 2 central script initials "LW" or "SW", 7 3/8" di, 11oz	JH Bourdon-Smith London 1994
1736/37	James Ker	Edinburgh	Salvers, set, Castle Grant	Cripps p150
1736/37	Lawrence Oliphant	Edinburgh	Snuffer tray, shaped hour glass form, on 4 feet, molded border, rising scroll handle, with crest and motto, 5.4oz	Christie's March 24, 1982 #70
1736/37	Dougal Ged	Edinburgh	Salver, octagonal, molded border, flowers and fruits, engraved baskets, 15 ½" di, 65oz	Christie's June 25, 1946
1737/38	Dougal Ged Assayer Archibald Ure	Edinburgh	Waiters, pair, with shaped borders	James Robinson NY USA 1993

YEAR	MAKER	LOCATION	DESCRIPTION	SOURCE
1737/38	Edward Lothian	Edinburgh	Waiter, Chippendale border, later chased with shells, diaper work, flowers, and foliage, on 3 hoof feet, 6" di, 7.2oz	Sotheby's January 14, 1970 #162
1737/38	William Aytoun	Edinburgh	Salver, ascribed to "WA", 9" di, no details	Wilson & Sharp Glasgow Exhibition 1911 vol I, p120 #46
1737/38	Dougal Ged	Edinburgh	Salver, shaped circular on 3 hoof feet, chased with a band of shells, foliage and scrolls on a matter ground, center with later coat of arms and coronet, 9" di, 12.9oz	Christie's October 8, 1980 #182
1738/39	James Ker	Edinburgh	Salver, circular on 3 hoof feet, shaped molded rim, center chased with border of shells, flowers and foliage, 8 ¼" di, 10.2oz	Christie's February 19, 1964 #161 Sotheby's ? June 4, 1987 #111
1738/39	James Ker	Edinburgh	Waiter, on 3 hoof feet, plain, slightly raised shaped border, 6" di, 6.5oz	Christie's Glasgow March 27, 1984 #262
1738/39	*James Ker*	*Edinburgh*	*Waiter, circular, quite plain, Chippendale border, on hoof feet, marked on base and rim, 6" di, 6.9oz*	*Sotheby's January 13, 1966 #? Koopman London*
1738/39	Edward Lothian	Edinburgh	Salver, shaped circular, molded border with later wiggle work decoration, 8" di, 23.5oz	Sotheby's Olympia April 12, 2005 #265
1738/39	William Aytoun	Edinburgh	Salver, large, on 4 shell and scroll feet, with molded border, center flat chased band of scrolling foliage and cartouches, with flowers, dipper work between with a coat of arms, 15 1/8", 50oz	Christie's May 4, 1977 #164
1738/39	James Tait	Edinburgh	Salver, shaped circular, crested with a Chippendale border, on 3 hoof feet, 7 ½" di, 8.6oz	Sotheby's Scone Palace, April 23, 1979 #94
1738/39	James Ker	Edinburgh	Salver or waiter, no details	Jackson Marks p 547
1738/39	Edward Lothian	Edinburgh	Salver, shaped circular section, bright cut engraved zig-zag motif, on 3 pod feet, 8" di, 10oz, note: weight different from other of the same year	Christie's London UK 2001 #104
1738/39	Edward Lothian	Edinburgh	Teapot stand, shaped circular on 3 hoof feet, molded rim, border flat chased of shells, flowers, scrolls and lappets, 8" wide, sold with a London teapot	Christie's, East NY USA 1999 #225
1739/40	James Ker	Edinburgh	Salver, 8" di, no further details	Glasgow Exhibition 1911, vol I, p121, #48
1739/40	James Ker Assayer Archibald Ure	Edinburgh	Salver, shaped square with notched canted corners, on 4 knurled and shell supports, oblong cartouche with crest, flat chased with shaped panels of birds on matted ground, rococo decoration, molded border, applied rim, 9 ¼" wide,	Christie's NY USA October 16-17, 1995 #445

YEAR	MAKER (continued)	LOCATION	DESCRIPTION	SOURCE
1739/40	Lawrence Oliphant Assayer Archibald Ure	Edinburgh	Salver, shaped circular, on 3 hoof feet, with molded scalloped border, center chased with band of baskets of fruit, flowers and trellis work, engraved with crest and motto, 8 7/8" di, 12.9oz	Christie's November 10, 1971 #44 Christie's June 14, 1972 #116
1739/40	*Lawrence Oliphant*	*Edinburgh*	*Salver, shaped circular, on 3 hoof feet, with molded scalloped border, center chased with band of baskets of fruit, flowers and trellis work, engraved with crest and motto, 8 ¾" di, 10.5oz*	*Sotheby's April 19, 1973 #102*
1739/40	James Ker Assayer Archibald Ure	Edinburgh	Salver, shaped circular on 3 hoof feet, chased with band of shells, foliage and scrolls, possibly the same as the one in the Glasgow Exhibition, 8" di, 12.5oz	Christie's October 31, 1973 #
1739/40	James Mitchell Assayer David Mitchell	Edinburgh	Salver, circular, on 3 hoof feet, with scalloped molded rim, center chased with broad band of flowers and shells and rococo panels, engraved with crest, 7 ¾" di, 9.7oz	Christie's January 2, 1964 #173
1739/40	James Mitchell	Edinburgh	Salver, circular, flat chased with flowers, fruit, and diaper panels below shaped molded edge, raised on 4 hoof feet, 10" di, 18oz	Phillips November 6, 1991 #199
1739/40	James Ker Assayer David Mitchell	Edinburgh	Salver, center engraved with crest and motto, probably of Dick of Prestonfield, flat chased band of flowers, foliage and baskets of fruit, Chippendale border of 4 volute and shell supports, 13 ¾" di, scratch weight 42:19, 42.1oz	Sotheby's Gleneagles August 28, 1995 #168
1740 ca	George Cooper	Aberdeen	Salver, no details	National Museums of Scotland MEQ 511
1740 ca	Colin Allan	Aberdeen	Salver, circular, Chippendale border, center plain except for narrow band of later chased scrolls and flowers, on 4 hoof like supports, 18oz 17d	Sotheby's December 5, 1968 #
1740 ca	John Baillie	Inverness	Salvers, square shaped, incurved corners, on bracket feet, 3 marks IB, INS, X dotted, 5 ½" wide, 9.94oz	Phillips May 20, 1988 # 111
1740 ca	George Cooper	Aberdeen	Waiter, shaped circular, on 3 feet, 6 7/8" di, 6oz 7d	Christie's July 3, 1984 # 118
1740 ca	George Cooper	Aberdeen	Waiter, no details	Aberdeen Museums and Galleries ABDAG001355
1740 ca	George Cooper	Aberdeen	Teapot stand, circular on three hoof feet, molded rim, border flat chased, block initials on reverse "I * L", 6 7/8" di, with a teapot	Christie's NY USA 1999 #312
1740 ca	Alexander Johnston	Dundee	Waiter, no details	Private Family Descent UK

YEAR	MAKER	LOCATION	DESCRIPTION	SOURCE
1740 ca	George Cooper	Aberdeen	Waiter, no engraved, scalloped border with 18 indents and 9 points alternating with 9 crescents, on 3 feet	Clayton Dictionary p171 #11 Christie's Glasgow July 3, 1984
1740 ca	Robert Luke II	Glasgow	Salver, chipped border, on 3 pad feet, chased border, crest of an arrow through a pelican, city mark partitioned into segments, 8" di	JH Bourdon-Smith London 1995 The Phoenix Collection
1740/41	William Aytoun	Edinburgh	Waiter, shaped hexagonal, on 3 paw feet, fluted molded border, center engraved with initials "JWO", scratch weight 7:14, 6 ¾" wide, 7oz	Christie's Scotland November 25 – 27, 1997 #109
1740/41	William Aytoun	Edinburgh	Waiter, circular on paw feet, chased with flower heads, foliage and scrolls on matted ground, raised shaped molded border, 8 2/3" di, 9oz	Christie's Glasgow August 16, 1983 #
1740/41	James Ker	Edinburgh	Salver, circular, with Chippendale border, engraved with crest and motto, chased with band of fruit clusters and flower heads in scroll cartouches, on 3 hoof feet, 8" di, 8.6oz	Sotheby's November 22, 1973 #171 Sotheby's April 27, 1978 #136
1740/41	Dougal Ged	Edinburgh	Snuffer tray, hourglass form, molded border, shaped ends, on 4 hoof feet, flat pear shaped handle, decorated with fleur-de-lis, baron's coronet above the crest of a stag's head, motto below, 6 3/8" long, 5.9oz	Christie's March 26, 1969 #84 Spink London probably Shrubsole NY USA
1740/41	William Gilchrist	Edinburgh	Salver, circular, on 3 hoof feet, scalloped molded rim, center chased with border of flowers and shells in rococo panels, 8 3/8" di, 12.2oz	Christie's January 29, 1964 #
1740/41	Edward Lothian	Edinburgh	Teapot stand, circular on 3 scroll feet	Scottish Art Review 1967 vol XI, p32 #2 Muirhead Moffat advertisement
1740/41	William Aytoun Assayer Dougal Ged	Edinburgh	Salver, circular with Chippendale border, on 4 paw feet, chased with border of shells, scrolls, leaves and flowers, possibly the same as the Christie's 1983 auction, 8 7/8" di, 10oz	JH Bourdon-Smith London 1992 Sotheby's March 12, 1984 #618 The Phoenix Collection
1741/42	Edward Lothian	Edinburgh	Salver, shaped circular form, on 3 volute feet, flat chased band of foliage, shaped molded border, crest of a stag's head, listed as being by Dougal Ged with Lothian as assay master, but records state Ged was assay master at the time, 8 ½" di 14oz	Christie's Edinburgh April 29, 1992 #49
1741/42	James Mitchell	Edinburgh	Salver, shaped circular form, molded scalloped border, on 3 hoof feet, chased band of flowers, shells and scrolls, center with an initial, 8 ½" di, 11.9oz	Christie's January 30, 1963
1741/42	James Mitchell	Edinburgh	Salver, on 3 hoof feet, molded border, chased with shell work and scrolls, engraved with a crest, 8 ½" di, 10.4oz	Christie's May 7, 1969 Christie's December 17, 1969 #194

YEAR	MAKER	LOCATION	DESCRIPTION	SOURCE
1741/42	James Ker	Edinburgh	Waiters, pair, Chippendale border, on 3 pad feet, crest of a lion passant holding a branch with leaves	Sotheby's July 4, 1968 #52
1741/42	Edward Lothian Assayer Dougal Ged	Edinburgh	Salver, 8 ¾" di, 11oz	Christie's NY USA April 14, 1990 #296
1741/42	William Dempster Assayer Dougal Ged	Edinburgh	Salver, chased, circular, on 4 hoof feet, Finlay may have cited the assayer instead of the maker as it carried William Dempster's mark as well	Finlay 1991 pl 78 Nobel Collection Christie's June 24, 1981 Christie's Negative #967766
1741/42	Ebenezer Oliphant Assayer Dougal Ged	Edinburgh	Salver, circular, on 4 shell feet, molded scalloped rim, chased with a band of fruit and flowers, 13" di, 35oz	Christie's November 20, 1950 #143
1742/43	James Mitchelson	Edinburgh	Salver, shaped circular form on 3 hoof feet, flat chased with a band of flowerheads, foliage and scrolls on a matted ground, engraved crest and motto, underside engraved with initials "MS", 8" di, 10oz	Christie's Lanarkshire UK 1998 #478
1742/43	Edward Lothian	Edinburgh	Salver, circular, on 3 feet, chased border, marked with a castle, no assayer mark, date letter and mm on underside of applied border	N & I Franklin, London 1995
1742/43	William Aytoun	Edinburgh	Salver, Chippendale border, on 3 paw supports, flat chased with band of ornament, 6 ½" di, 7.3oz	Sotheby's March 14, 1974 #152
1742/43	James Ker	Edinburgh	Waiters, pair, shaped circular form, Chippendale border, on 3 hoof feet, crest of a lion holding a branch in its dexter front camb, 5 ¾" di, 14.7oz	Sotheby's July 14, 1968 #52 Spink Ltd London
1742/43	Ebenezer Oliphant	Edinburgh	Salver, circular, molded border, on 3 hoof feet, chased with a band of fruit, flowers, and scrolls , with a crest and motto, 9 7/8" di, 17oz	Christie's January 24, 1973 #185
1743 ca	Robert Luke II	Glasgow	Salver, shaped border, flat chased band of fruit, flowers and rococo ornamentation, 7 ¾" di, 11.5oz	Breadalbane Collection Sale 1935 #355
1743 ca	James Glen	Glasgow	Salver, circular, flat chased broad band of rococo ornamentation, molded raised border, on 3 paw feet, 7 ¾" di, 10.6oz	Sotheby's Gleneagles August 25, 1997 #150
1743/44	Robert Low	Edinburgh	Salver, Chippendale border, on 3 hoof feet, center with initials 5 ¾" di, 6.2oz	Sotheby's September 26, 1974 #105 Christie's Australia July 20, 1993 #714
1743/44	William Aytoun	Edinburgh	Salver, shaped circular form, molded border, on 4 paw feet, chased with flowers and foliage, 8 ¾" di, 10.5oz	Christie's June 23, 1976 #71

YEAR	MAKER	LOCATION	DESCRIPTION	SOURCE
1743/44	William Dempster or William Davie	Edinburgh	Salver, shaped circular form, chased with scrolls and foliage, on 3 paw feet, crest and motto of Stewart of Appin or of Ardsheal, or one of the Appin families, accompanying a 3 legged coffeepot 1740/41 by James Ker, 9" di, 17.3oz	Apollo Magazine 1933 vol 17 How of Edinburgh advertisement
1743/44	Charles Dickson II	Edinburgh	Waiter, circular form, shell and scalloped border, on 3 scroll feet, crest and motto of Bruce of Mowance, Shetland, 6 1/8" di	Lyon & Turnbull February 20, 2004 #254
1743/44	Dougal Ged	Edinburgh	Salver, shaped square, molded border, band of flat chased scrolling foliage, flowers and shell motifs, on 4 hoof feet, crest and motto, 10 ¾" across, 19.4oz	Sotheby's December 1, 1982 #132
1743/44	James Mitchell	Edinburgh	Waiter, square, chased, chipped border, 3 pad feet, 6" square, 5oz 18d	Sotheby's April 24, 1986 #189
1743/44	Robert Luke II	Glasgow	Salver, shaped circular, on 3 hoof feet, flat chased with a band of flower heads, foliage, and scrolls, engraved with script initial "R" within shaped border, 7 ½", 9.92oz	Nicholas Shaw Catalog Winter 2000, p67
1743/44	Robert Gordon	Edinburgh	Square waiter, raised border, 8 ¼" across, 14oz 10d	Christie's June 25, 1946 #92 Sotheby's October 31, 1963 #157
1743/44	Dougal Ged and Ebenezer Oliphant	Edinburgh	Waiters, pair, crest and motto, 6 ½" di,	JH Bourdon-Smith London 1994
1743/44	Ebenezer Oliphant	Edinburgh	Waiters, pair, plain, octagonal, molded borders, 6 ½" di, 14oz 5d both (7oz 13d ea)	Christie's February 3, 1943 #131 How of Edinburgh Collection
1743/44	James Weems	Edinburgh	Salvers, pair, rococo, crest and motto of the Earl of Weems, 10"	Shrubsole 1993 Sotheby's April 23, 1993 #293 JH Bourdon-Smith Catalog 2005
1743/44	James Ker	Edinburgh	Salvers, 2 of different sizes, volute and shell feet, shell border, flat chased decoration, 17 ¾" di and 12 ¾" di, 114.5oz all	Sotheby's May 3, 1984 #81
1743/44	Hugh Penman	Edinburgh	Salver, plain center bordered near the waved rim with chased flowers, shell motifs and scrolls, 9 ½" di, 9.7oz	Sotheby's July 20, 1967 #60
1743/44	James Weems	Edinburgh	Salver, shaped square, raised and applied border, on 4 hoof feet, later applied with a monogrammed roundel, flat chased with blooms and foliate scrolls on a matted ground, 10 ½" wide, 20.7oz	Sotheby's Gleneagles August 31, 1981 #455
1743/44	Ebenezer Oliphant	Edinburgh	Waiter, shaped circular on 3 hoof feet, with double scroll border, 6 2/3" di, 6.5oz	Bonhams Sale 15120 Aug 22, 2007 #13
1744/45	James Ker	Edinburgh	Salver & pair of waiters – set, shell and scroll border, chased inside band,	Christie's March 7, 1979 #11

YEAR	MAKER	LOCATION	DESCRIPTION	SOURCE
	Assayer Hugh Gordon		8 1/3" di and 6 1/3" di, 30oz	Christie's Negative #918599
1745 ca	James Ker	Edinburgh	Spoon tray, plain oval, shaped border chased with flowers, foliage and scale work, 6 5/8" di, 2oz 5d	Christie's July 25, 1973
1745 ca	Robert Luke II	Glasgow	Waiter, hexafoil. On 3 curved hoof feet, chased with a band of scrolls, foliage and rococo ornament, molded shaped border, engraved with initial "R", 7 ½" di, 9oz 18d	Christie's May 20, 1987 Nicholas Shaw Catalog Winter 2000 p67
1745 ca	James Glen	Glasgow	Waiter, plain shaped circular, on 3 scroll feet, molded border, center engraved with initials, 7 ¾" di, 12oz 18d	Christie's December 18, 1970
1745 ca	James Glen	Glasgow	Stand, for a chocolate pot, no details	Aberdeen Museums and Galleries ABDAG001310
1745 ca	William Aytoun	Edinburgh	Waiter, crested, Chippendale rim, on 3 paw feet, 5 ¾" di, 6oz 17d	Sotheby's July 12, 1962 Sotheby's December 19, 1963
1745 ca	Robert Luke II	Glasgow	Waiter, shaped circular flat chased, border of scrolls, diaper and foliage, molded rim, on 3 hoof feet, 7 ¾" di, 9oz 2d	Sotheby's April 29, 1986 Jackson Marks p 520
1745 ca	William Davie or William Dempster	Edinburgh	Waiter, crested, Chippendale rim, initials on base, on 3 hoof feet, 6" di, 8oz	Sotheby's June 25, 1964
1745 ca	James Glen	Glasgow	Salver, large circular, base engraved with initials "HA", based has been mounted, 4 marks – IG, tree, IG, S - 9.77oz	Christie's Glasgow May 20, 1983 #240
1745 ca	James Ker Assayer Hugh Gordon	Edinburgh	Salver, shaped circular, on 4 hoof feet, chased with band of fruit, flowers, scrolls, with molded shell and scroll border, engraved with initials, 8 ½"di, 12oz 4d	Christie's February 23, 1970
1745 ca	James Glen	Glasgow	Salver, plain with mark "M"	Tessier's, London UK 1994
1745ca	*James Glen*	*Glasgow*	*Salver, no details*	*Sotheby's Gleneagles August 1994*
1745 ca	James Glen	Glasgow	*Salver, small circular*, plain, escalloped border, base engraved with initial "I/MF", on 3 hoof feet, 6 1/8" di, 6.9oz	Christie's Glasgow May 20, 1983 #600
1745 ca	James Glen	Glasgow	Salver, engraved shell and foliage, molded escalloped border, 8" di, 11oz 17d	Christie's June 19, 1913 #69
1745 ca	James Glen	Glasgow	Salver on 3 paw feet, shell, foliate and scroll border, crest and motto 23oz 5d	Christie's July 31, 1963 #173

YEAR	MAKER	LOCATION	DESCRIPTION	SOURCE
1745 ca	James Glen	Glasgow	Waiter, circular form on 3 short legs with hoof feet, 6" di, 7oz	Lyon & Turnbull, Edinburgh UK 2006 #336
1745 ca	James Glen	Glasgow	Waiter, shaped circular form, molded borders, stylized shell decoration on 3 hoof feet, crested, with mark "N" in a rectangle, 6" di, 7oz	Lyon & Turnbull Edinburgh UK 2003 #231
1745 ca	James Glen	Glasgow	Waiter, shaped circular form, on 3 pad feet, chased with rococo foliated and shell motifs, 7 7/8" di, 10oz	Christie's London UK 2003 #413
1745/46	James Ker	Edinburgh	Salver, on 4 scroll and shell feet, shell border, flat chased with arms of Nisbet, 15 1/6" di, 50 or 59oz	Christie's Glasgow March 29, 1983 #68 Shaw Collection Christie's May 26, 1998 #63
1745/46	James Ker	Edinburgh	Salver, same description as above, matching a smaller version of the preceding salver, 13 ¾" di, 37oz	Christie's Glasgow March 29, 1983 #69 Shaw Collection Christie's May 26, 1998 #64
1745/46	James Glen	Glasgow	Waiter or teapot stand, shaped, small circular	Private Collection
1745/46	James Ker	Edinburgh	Spoon tray, oblong, everted, chased rim	Christie's London July 25, 1973 #176 Christie's Negative # 744575
1746 ca	Not Available		Waiter, circular on 3 hoof feet, shaped molded shell rim, 6 ¾" di	Christie's February 3, 1965 #124
1746/47	Not available		Salver, scroll border, 10" di, 10oz	Christie's July 3, 1894 #130
1746/47	Dougal Ged	Edinburgh	Salver, on 4 feet, crest and motto "FIDES SUFFICUT" of Sir Peter Halket	Portland Art Museum, Portland OR USA 60.13
1747/48	Ebenezer Oliphant Assayer Hugh Gordon	Edinburgh	Salver, circular, engraved in center with crest and motto within a border of flat chased shells, fruit and flowers, rim applied with scroll and rococo motifs, on 3 rococo volute feet, 13" di, 42oz	Sotheby's May 20, 1982 #74
1747/48	James Gilliland Assayer Hugh Gordon	Edinburgh	Salver, shaped circular, flat chased within a shell and scroll border, typical foliage and flowers, initials on underside, on 3 hoof feet, 7 ¼" di, 8oz	Sotheby's January 16, 1975 #122
1747/48	Ebenezer Oliphant Assayer Hugh Gordon	Edinburgh	Salver, shaped circular, on 3 feet, border pierced and cast with vines and scrolls, engraved with later crest, 8" di, 13oz 8d	Christie's July 30, 1975 #195 Christie's December 10, 1975 #87 Sotheby's July 20, 1978 #132

YEAR	MAKER	LOCATION	DESCRIPTION	SOURCE
1747/48	Ker & Dempster Assayer Hugh Gordon	Edinburgh	Salver, shoulder engraved with cartouche and crest of Buchanan of Touch, inscribed "AUDACES JUVO" (I will help the brave ones), border chased with flower heads, scrolls, and scallop motifs, raised rim with cast shell motifs, on 4 scroll and leaf capped feet, 13 ¾" di, 49oz	Phillips Glasgow April 19, 1984 #101
1747/48	Block "WD" Probably William Dempster	Edinburgh	Waiter, chased with shells, scrolls, flowers and fruit, on 3 cabriole legs, pad feet, 6 ½" di	JH Bourdon-Smith Catalog 1993 The Phoenix Collection
1747/48	James Ker	Edinburgh	Waiters, pair, on 3 hoof feet, shell and scroll border, initials below earl's coronet, 7" di, 18oz 15d	Sotheby's October 27, 1987
1747/48	Ebenezer Oliphant	Edinburgh	Salver, on 3 rococo volute feet, crest and motto, shell and scroll border, chased interior, catalog listed maker as Hugh Gordon, 12 ¾" di, 42oz	Christie's April 24, 1975 #162 Sotheby's May 20, 1982
1747/48	Ebenezer Oliphant	Edinburgh	Salver, circular, on 3 hoof feet, chased with a border of scrolls, shells and flower heads, with raised shaped scroll and shell rim, 8 2/3" di, 13oz	Bonhams The Scottish Sale, August 24, 2005 #15
1747/48	William Davie or William Dempster Assayer Hugh Gordon	Edinburgh	Waiter, shaped circular, on 3 short scroll feet, surface flat chased with band of fruit and foliage, raised border with molded rim, 6 ½" di, 6.5oz	Christie's November 21, 1989 #53
1747/48	James Ker Assayer Hugh Gordon	Edinburgh	Waiters, pair, shaped circular, each lightly engraved with initials below an earl's coronet within a trellis work and foliate scroll cartouche, molded rim with shells at intervals, on 3 hoof feet, 7" di, 18oz 15d	Sotheby's December 22-27, 1987 #261
1748 ca	James Mitchelson Assayer Hugh Gordon	Edinburgh	Salver, shaped circular, later initials, chased with a broad band of matted fruit and scrolls, applied scroll border with shell motifs at intervals, hoof supports, mm wrongly ascribed to John Main, 9 1/8" di, 13oz	Sotheby's Sussex February 20, 1996 #738 Sotheby's Sussex July 4-12, 1995
1748/49	James Weems Assayer Hugh Gordon	Edinburgh	Waiter, engraved with crest, Chippendale border, on hoof feet, 6" di, 7oz 15 d	Sotheby's March 9, 1961 #31
1748/49 *1740	James Mitchelson Assayer Dougal Ged	Edinburgh	Waiter, shaped circular, on 3 hoof feet, flat chased with band of diaper, shells and foliage, wrongly ascribed to John Main, probably assigned to wrong year, should be 1740/41, 8 ½" di, 10oz	Christie's Edinburgh November 17-18, 1993 #738
1748/49	Lawrence Oliphant	Edinburgh	Salver, shaped circular, center engraved with crest, flat chased band of diaper work and flowers, shell motifs, and cartouches, molded border, on 3 hoof feet, 10 ½" di, 16oz	Sotheby's Gleneagles August 26-27, 1991 #178

YEAR	MAKER	LOCATION	DESCRIPTION	SOURCE
1748/49	William Aytoun Assayer Hugh Gordon	Edinburgh	Salver, shaped circular, plain, with applied scroll and shell border, on 3 hoof feet, 9 ¼" di, 12oz 4d	Sotheby's Gleneagles September 1, 1987 #284
1748/49	Ker & Dempster Assayer Hugh Gordon	Edinburgh	Salver, shaped circular, on 3 volute feet, flat chased with band of foliage and scrolls, fluted shell, foliage, and scroll border, engraved with coat of arms of MacDowall and Garthland, Galloway, 11" di, 26oz	Christie's May 26, 1998 #83
1748/49 *1740ca	James Ker Assayer Dougal Ged	Edinburgh	Salver, shaped circular, on 3 hoof feet, surface flat chased with band of fruit and foliage, raised border with molded rim, engraved with 2 crests, date letter slightly rubbed, probably really 1740/41, 7 5/8"di, 8oz	Christie's November 21, 1990 #41
1748/49	Ker & Dempster Assayer Hugh Gordon	Edinburgh	Salver, shaped circular, on 3 hoof feet, flat chased with band of fruit and foliage, retaining traces of an engraved coat of arms within shell and scroll border, 9 ½" di, 14.5oz	Christie's Edinburgh November 18, 1993 #722
1748/49	Robert Low Assayer Hugh Gordon	Edinburgh	Salver, shaped circular, on 3 hoof feet, chased with a band of fruit, flowers and scrolls, molded foliage and scroll border, engraved with a monogram 9 ¼" di, 15oz 4d	Christie's May 20, 1987 #365
1748/49	Charles Dickson II	Edinburgh	Salver, Chippendale border on 3 paw feet, 11" di, 18.1oz	Sotheby's Gleneagles August 28, 1968 #139
1748/49	James Ker	Edinburgh	Salver, shaped circular	Christie's Edinburgh November 21, 1990 #41
1748/49	William Aytoun	Edinburgh	Salver, no details	Sotheby's Gleneagles August 1987 #283
1748/49	William Aytoun Assayer Dougal Ged	Edinburgh	Waiter, chased, on 3 cast feet, 7 ½" di, 8oz	Phillips May 29, 1981 #54
1748/49	Lawrence Oliphant	Edinburgh	Salver, circular, crest, chased border, 10 ¼" di, 16oz	Sotheby's Gleneagles August 1991 #178
1749/50	Ebenezer Oliphant	Edinburgh	Salvers, 3, no details	National Museums of Scotland MEQ 707
1749/50	Ebenezer Oliphant Assayer Hugh Gordon	Edinburgh	Waiter, engraved in center with later crest within a narrow band of chased scrolls and fruit, shell and scroll rim, on 3 hoof feet, 7" di, 7oz 18d	Sotheby's Dec15, 1966 #31 Sotheby's June 15, 1972 #42 Sotheby's May 10, 1973 #146 JH Bourdon-Smith, London UK
1749/50	James Gilliland	Edinburgh	Salver, circular, engrave in center with later foliate monogram, shell and scroll	Sotheby's August 20, 1973 #70b

YEAR	MAKER	LOCATION	DESCRIPTION	SOURCE
			border, on 3 hoof feet, 7 ½" di, 8oz 16d	
1749/50	IS Assayer Hugh Gordon	Edinburgh	Salver, later engraved with scrolling foliate designs, Chippendale border, resting on 4 volute feet capped with foliage, mm said to be "IS", 16 ¼" di, 60oz 13d	Sotheby's January 14, 1960 #84 Antiques Magazine February 1987 Shrubsole advertisement Christie's NY USA 1984 #304
1749/50	Edward Lothian Assayer Hugh Gordon	Edinburgh	Salver, shaped circular, center with engraved crest, flat chased with foliage and rococo motifs below similarly decorated border, on 4 claw and ball feet, 12 ½" di, 29oz 2d	Sotheby's June 16, 1977 #252 Sotheby's September 22, 1977 #121 Sotheby's January 19, 1978 #213
1749/50	Ker & Dempster Assayer Hugh Gordon	Edinburgh	Salver, shaped circular, on 3 claw feet, chased with band of flowers and scrolls, molded shell and scroll border, engraved with later coat of arms and motto, 9" di, 14oz 5d	Christie's May 29, 1985 #172
1749/50	James Weems	Edinburgh	Salver, shaped circular, on 3 hoof feet, applied shell and scroll rim, ground later chased with flowers and scrolling foliage, with presentation inscription, 9 ½" di, 14.5oz	Christie's August 16, 1982 #206 Christie's May 29, 1985 #172
1749/50	Ker & Dempster Assayer Hugh Gordon	Edinburgh	Salver, circular, molded below the leaf decorated scroll border, on 3 hoof feet, 8 ½" di,	Sotheby's December 8, 1977 #120
1750 ca	Colin Allan	Aberdeen	Salver, Chippendale border, on 3 hoof feet, crest and motto "IN GOD IS ALL" for Fraser, 6 1/8", 5.4oz	Nicholas Shaw Catalog Winter 2000 p68
1750 ca	Colin Allan	Aberdeen	Salver, molded C-scroll border with inset circlets, engraved with fish scales and a single bee, 7 ½" di, 10oz	Nicholas Shaw Catalog 2004 p99
1750 ca	Colin Allan	Aberdeen	Waiter, square, on 4 scroll feet, monogram in circular medallion, 5 ¾" square, 5oz 12d	Christie's July 21, 1954 #36
1750 ca	Colin Allan	Aberdeen	Salver, on 3 scroll feet, scrolls and shells	Christie's Glasgow March 1983
1750 ca	Colin Allan	Aberdeen	Salver, circular, decorated with scrolls and floral elements, marks "ABD and CA", border with indentations, semicircular, with initials "WHC", on 3 pad feet, 8 ½" di, 12oz	Mary Cooke Antiques London 1996
1750 ca	WS		Salver, with crest and motto, on 3 hoof feet, mm struck twice, 9 ½" di, 16oz	Christie's Glasgow March 1983 #18

YEAR	MAKER	LOCATION	DESCRIPTION	SOURCE
1750 ca	Colin Allan	Aberdeen	Salver, no details	National Museums of Scotland MEQ 1110
1750 ca	Colin Allan	Aberdeen	Salver, The Gordon Family Salver	Aberdeen Museums and Galleries ABDAG001039
1750 ca	James Glen	Glasgow	Tray, presentation with inscription and Arms of the City of Glasgow, given to Richard Oswald, applied and chased border, 22" di, 145oz	Scottish Art Review vol VI 1958 p41 Bell of Aberdeen advertisement
1750 ca	James Taylor	Glasgow	Salver, shaped border, inside band of alternating diaper work, flowers and fruit	National Museums of Scotland MEQ 1108
1750 ca	Colin Allan	Aberdeen	Salver, no details	Dundee Museums and Art Galleries 1961-242
1750 ca	James Glen	Glasgow	Waiter, shaped circular on 3 hoof feet, with fluted shell and scroll border, with a griffon crest within a strapwork foliate cartouche (center with a tiny pinhole), 6 1/3" di, 9oz	Christie's London UK 2000 #159
1750 ca	Colin Allan	Aberdeen	Salver, shaped circular form on 4 hoof feet with indented and fluted border, with a crest and motto, reverse with initials "JE, JA, G" and original scratch weight 16=9, 9 ½" di, 16oz	Christie's Lanarkshire UK 1998 #65
1750 ca	James Glen	Glasgow	Waiter, shaped circular form, pie-crust rim, on 3 hoof feet, center later engraved with flowers and foliage, 6" di, 8oz	Bonhams London UK 2004 #280 Bonhams London UK 2005 #520
1750 ca	Alexander Shirras	Banff	Salver, no details	National Museums of Scotland MEQ 622
1750/51	Not available	Edinburgh	Salver, shell and scroll rim, on 3 hoof feet, chased with scrolls, flowers, leafage and shell ornamentation, 9 ½" di, 15.1oz	Sotheby's March 12, 1959 #51
1750/51	William Gilchrist	Edinburgh	Waiter, shaped circular form, applied Chippendale border, pad feet, engraved with later crest and motto, script initials underneath, 5 7/8" di, 6.7oz	Sotheby's June 11-14, 1985 #964
1750/51	Robert Gordon	Edinburgh	Salver, circular, leaf and floral scroll border, on 3 scrolled and pad feet, engraved and chased with flowers, fruit and shell decoration, 9 2/3" di, 16.4oz	Christie's Australia July 20, 1993 #725
1750/51	Ker & Dempster	Edinburgh	Salvers, pair, shell, scroll and foliate rims, claw and ball feet, border chased with flower sprays, scrolls and shell motif, identical crests and mottos in the centers, 11" di, 54oz all	Sotheby's October 21, 1965

YEAR	MAKER	LOCATION	DESCRIPTION	SOURCE
1750/51	Ker & Dempster	Edinburgh	Salver, shaped circular, shells around rim, crest and motto of Campbell, Earls of Breadalbane, 9 7/8" di, 20.1oz	Christie's London UK 2000 #1 Nicholas Shaw Catalog Winter 2000 p72
1750/51	Robert Low	Edinburgh	Salver, hexagonal, chased floral border, on 3 legs, initials "R" "RF" and "1763", 8 5/8" over points	Huntley House Museum Edinburgh HH3188/68
1751/52	James Mitchelson or James McKenzie I	Edinburgh	Salver, shaped circular on 3 feet, chased border, 8 ¾" di, 12oz 4d	Butterfields Auctioneers Corp, San Francisco, CA USA 1997 #7304
1751/52	Ker & Dempster	Edinburgh	Salver, circular, chased shell and scroll border, on 3 claw and ball feet, chased flowers, fruit and scrolls, later engraved inscription and names, 12 7/8" di, 23.3oz	Phillips Edinburgh December 16, 1983 #197 Phillips Edinburgh January 20, 1984 #50
1751/52	Lothian & Robertson	Edinburgh	Salver, shaped circular form, 13 1/8" di	Private Collection UK
1751/52	Robert Low	Edinburgh	Salver, shaped circular form, scroll and foliage border, on 3 hoof feet, the ground chased with a band of decoration, 8 ¾" di, 16.3oz	Christie's October 14, 1987 #195
1751/52	James Mitchell	Edinburgh	Waiters, pair, circular, shaped molded shell and foliage rims, on 3 hoof feet, chased border of flowers and scrolls, 6" di, 11.4oz	Christie's July 31, 1963 #153
1751/52	Edward Lothian	Edinburgh	Salver, no details	National Museums of Scotland MEQ 795
1751/52	Lothian & Robertson	Edinburgh	Salver, initials "N/CE", scratch weight 16:9	National Museums of Scotland A.1943.270
1751/52	John Clark	Edinburgh	Waiter, with shell and scroll border, flat chased, 7" di, 9.5oz	JH Bourdon-Smith Catalog Autumn 1993 p30 #41
1751/52	John Clark	Edinburgh	*Waiter, shell and scroll rim, pad feet, crested, 7" di, 8.8oz*	*Christie's London 1999 #171*
1751/52	Robert Low	Edinburgh	Salver, shaped circular, on 3 hoof feet, edge finely chased with fruit, flowers and scale work, underside inscribed "Isobel Tweedie's Gift to Isobel Crawfurd, 1753", 8 ¾" di, 15oz 7d	Private Collection
1751/52	*Robert Low*	*Edinburgh*	*Salver, no details*	*Jackson Marks p 548*
1751/52	Lothian & Robertson	Edinburgh	Salver, circular, shell and scroll border, on 3 hoof feet, 7 ¼", 8.8oz	Sotheby's Scone Palace April 23, 1979 #70

YEAR	MAKER	LOCATION	DESCRIPTION	SOURCE
1752/53	Ker & Dempster	Edinburgh	Salver, shaped circular form, applied shell and leaf border, on 3 short scroll feet, center with a crest and motto "THIS I'LL DEFEND", 9 ¼" di, 14oz	Bonhams London UK 2006 #474
1752/53	James Gilliland	Edinburgh	Salver, shaped circular form, shell and scroll border, on 3 hoof feet, chased with a band of fruit, foliage and scrolls, 10 ¾" di, 18.9oz	Christie's January 28, 1970 #181
1752/53	James Gilliland	Edinburgh	Salver, shaped circular form, applied border, on 3 hoof feet, the ground chased with a narrow frieze of arabesques, crest and motto, 11" di, 18.5oz	Christie's March 5, 1991 #251
1752/53	Robert Gordon	Edinburgh	Waiters, pair, plain, molded shell and scroll border, on 3 hoof feet, center with crest and motto of Spottiswoode of Dunipace, 6 1/8" di, 14.5oz	Christie's November 10, 1960 #40 Asprey London
1753/54	James Gilliland	Edinburgh	Salver, shell and scroll border, on 3 feet, chased, underside with initials, 7 ¼" di, 7.2oz	Sotheby's March 17, 1966
1753/54	Robert Gordon	Edinburgh	Salvers, pair, shaped circular form, centers with a crest, an eagle, and motto "CONSILIO NON IMPETU" of Agnew, 7" di, 15.1oz	Sotheby's Gleneagles August 19, 1996 #133
1753/54	Ker & Dempster	Edinburgh	Salver, circular, shell and scroll border, later Arms of Sefton, 10 ½" di, 18oz	Christie's October 27, 1987 #426
1753/54	Robert Gordon	Edinburgh	Waiters, pair, crest and motto, 6 ½" di, 16oz	Antiques Magazine Bell of Aberdeen advertisement Sotheby's Gleneagles August 1996 #133
1753/54	*Robert Gordon*	*Edinburgh*	*Waiter, no details*	Antiques Magazine 1970 vol 94 p948
1753/54	John Edmonston	Edinburgh	Small tray, no details	Jackson Marks p 548
1753/54	Lothian & Robertson	Edinburgh	Waiter, no details	Christie's Edinburgh November 21, 1990 #47
1754/55	IM in a rectangle James McKenzie I or James Mitchelson	Edinburgh	Waiter, shaped circular form, scroll and shell border, band of foliate decoration, center with a crest and motto of McDonald and McDowell, 7 2/3" di, 8oz	Sotheby's January 16, 1975 #123
1755/56	Robert Gordon	Edinburgh	Salver, shaped circular, flat chased with foliage, flowers and shells within a matching border, on 3 hoof feet, center with later armorials and supporters below a crest and motto, 9 ¼" di, 12.7oz	Sotheby's January 16, 1975 #123
1755/56	Ker & Dempster	Edinburgh	Salver, scroll and shell border, center crest and motto within rococo chasing, on 3 hoof feet, 7" di, 6.5oz	Sotheby's Gleneagles August 29, 1977 #180

YEAR	MAKER	LOCATION	DESCRIPTION	SOURCE
1756/57	Hugh Gordon	Edinburgh	Salver, shaped circular, center crest, scroll and shell rim, on 3 hoof feet, 8" di, 9.9oz	Sotheby's Gleneagles August 27, 1979 #193
1756/57	Not available	Edinburgh	Waiters, pair, gadrooned and shell, 7" di, 18oz 12d both (9oz 6d ea)	Christie's July 3, 1984 #129
1756/57	Robert Gordon	Edinburgh	Salver, circular, on 3 hoof feet, molded gadrooned border, shell and foliate border, crest and motto, 7 ¼" di, 10.1oz	Christie's May 21, 1986 #196
1756/57	Lothian & Robertson	Edinburgh	Salver, shaped circular form, scroll and shell rim, on 3 hoof feet, crest in the center, 8" di, 10oz	Sotheby's Gleneagles August 27-28, 1979 #191
1757/58	Robert Low	Edinburgh	Salver, shaped circular, chased with a narrow band of flowers and foliage, on 3 hoof feet, 11" di, 20.3oz	Scottish Art Review vol III, #2 Bell of Aberdeen advertisement
1757/58	William Taylor	Edinburgh	Small salver, no details	Jackson Marks p 548
1758/59	William Ker	Edinburgh	Salver, shaped circular, on 3 hoof feet, gadrooned rim, border of bright cut trailing vines and wiggle work, center with armorials, since William Ker was not yet a freeman at this time, either the maker is wrong or the date should be later, 11 ¼" di, 25.9oz	Sotheby's September 14, 1978 #118
1758/59	John Clark	Edinburgh	Waiters, pair, 7 ¼" di, 17oz both	Sotheby's NY USA October 1990 #307 Shrubsole, NY USA
1759/60	Robert Gordon	Edinburgh	Salvers, pair, plain, circular with crest and motto of Dundas, with gadrooned borders, on hoof feet, 7 ½", 27oz	Sotheby's Gleneagles, August 29, 1983 #500 The Maple Swan Collection
1759/60	Lothian & Robertson	Edinburgh	Salver, 8 ¾" di	Antiques Magazine 1957 vol 71, p10 Gebelin advertisement (Boston USA)
1759/60	Lothian & Robertson	Edinburgh	Salver, oblong, open border, rococo strap work, 10 ½" X 7 ¾"	Scottish Art Academy Exhibit 1939 #891
1759/60	MW	Edinburgh	Salver, small, maker not identified, no details	Jackson Marks p 548
1759/60	Ebenezer Oliphant	Edinburgh	Waiter, with shell and scroll border, flat chased, engraved "W", 6 ¼" di, 6.5oz	Nicholas Shaw Catalog Autumn 1999 p55
1759/60	Ebenezer Oliphant	Edinburgh	Waiter, shaped circular, shell and scroll border, initialed, 6 2/3" di, 7oz	Christie's London UK 1997 #3

YEAR	MAKER	LOCATION	DESCRIPTION	SOURCE
1759/60	Lothian & Robertson	Edinburgh	Waiter, shaped circular with a shell and scroll border and pad feet, repaired in the center, 7 ½" di, 8oz	Christie's London UK 1998 #106
1760 ca	Milne & Campbell	Glasgow	Salver, shaped circular form on 3 hoof feet, chased with a border of scrolling foliage, with a shell and scroll border, 8 ¾" di, 10.9oz	Bonhams Sale 15120 Aug 22, 2007 #113
1760 ca	Not available	Edinburgh	Waiter, with chased border of flowers, shell, armorials in center, 7 1/8" di, 8.9oz	Bonhams the Scottish Sale, August 21, 2003 #52
1760 ca	James Gilliland	Edinburgh	Salver, no details	Dundee Museums and Art Galleries 1961-679
1760/61	Lothian & Robertson	Edinburgh	Salver, scroll and shell decoration, molded rim, on 3 hoof feet, border of flowers and exotic birds, center with a crest, 9 ½" di, 13.8oz	Sotheby's March 11, 1971 #72 Sotheby's Dec 22, 1971 #192
1760/61	Lothian & Robertson	Edinburgh	Salver, circular, scroll and shell border, on 3 pad feet, leaping hound and wheat sheaf crest, 7 ½" di, 9.1oz	Sotheby's April 11-13, 2000 #148
1760/61	William Dempster or William Davie	Edinburgh	Salver, shaped circular form, shell and scroll border, on 3 hoof feet, chased band of flowers and foliage, later initialed, 8 ¼" di, 12.1oz	Sotheby's April 12-13, 1988 #28
1761/62	John Robertson	Edinburgh	Salver, shaped, circular, on 3 hoof feet, made out of an earlier footed tazza, 8 ½" di, 10oz 10d	Private Collection
1761/62	John Robertson	Edinburgh	Salver, no details	Jackson Marks p 548
1761/62	William Dempster or William Davie	Edinburgh	Waiter, chased, has repairs	Moreland House Antiques, VA USA
1761/62	William Dempster or William Davie	Edinburgh	Salver, shaped circular, on 3 hoof feet, 7" di	Private Collection
1761/62	John Clark	Edinburgh	Salver, circular, with chased border of flowers, foliate shells and scale ornament, scroll and shell pattern rim, on 3 hoof feet, underside with later initials, 7 ½" di, 8.7oz	Sotheby's January 16, 1970 #163
1761/62	John Clark	Edinburgh	Salver, miniature, made to match larger salver by Clark, initials possibly for marriage of John Wilson, Provost of Dunfermline and Katherine Stevenson in 1743, 3" di, 2 ¼" ht	Sotheby's October 19, 1970 #200
1761/62	WD William Dempster or William Davie	Edinburgh	Waiters, pair, circular, shaped acanthus leaf molded rim and chased floral design, on 3 pad feet, engraved crest and motto "I WILL DEFEND", possibly the same as a previous pair, 7 ¼" di, 14oz	Dreweatt Neate Turnbridge Wells 2007 #31

YEAR	MAKER	LOCATION	DESCRIPTION	SOURCE
1761/62	Lothian & Robertson	Edinburgh	Salvers, pair, circular on 3 hoof feet, shell and scroll rim, the border flat chased with grapevine, center with a crest and motto, 10"di, 37oz 10d	John Bell of Aberdeen Christie's NY USA 1999 #380
1761/62	IO Possibly James Oliphant	Edinburgh	Salver, on 3 hoof feet, shell decorated rim, chased scroll and floral border, *crest and motto*, 8 ½" di, 10.5oz	Sotheby's November 16-17, 1981 #423
1761/62	James Oliphant	Edinburgh	*Salver, circular, lightly chased floral and fruit decoration, chased shell and scroll border, on 3 hoof feet, crest and motto, 8 ½" di, 11oz*	*Phillips Edinburgh March 22, 1985 #93*
1761/62	William Dempster or William Davie	Edinburgh	Salvers, pair, circular, band of flat chased flowers and leaves, raised and applied scroll and shell border, *pad feet*, 7 ½" di, 14.8oz both	Sotheby's July 24-27, 1984 #1566
1762/63	Robert Gordon	Edinburgh	Waiter, shaped circular form, scroll and foliate borders, band of fruit decoration, center with crest and motto of Robertson of Lanarkshire	Bonhams July 5, 2001 #556
1762/63	William Dempster or William Davie	Edinburgh	Teapot stand, oval, applied shell and scroll border, on 4 hoof feet, sold as a matching tea service	Sotheby's London June 8, 1995 #136
1762/63	William Dempster or William Davie	Edinburgh	Salver, circular, border with shells, chased out border, scroll and leaves, on 3 scroll feet, 12 ½" di	Antiques Magazine 1965 vol 88 p730 Shreve advertisement
1763/64	Not available	Edinburgh	Salver, circular, on 3 hoof feet, molded shell and scroll border, with band of *flowers and foliage*, 7 ¼" di, 8.5oz	Christie's November 27, 1963 #61
1763/64	James Gilliland	Edinburgh	Salver, shaped circular, with crest and motto of Stirling, 9" di, 12.5oz	Nicholas Shaw Catalog Winter 2000 p92
1763/64	MK conjoined Possibly James McKenzie I	Edinburgh	Salver, or kettle stand, slight dished, 8 ¾" di, 15oz 10d	Private Collection
1763/64	Lothian & Robertson	Edinburgh	Salver, circular form, molded border, shaped gadrooned mount, center engraved with a crest and motto, 14' di, 43oz	Christie's London UK 2004 #137
1764/65	Ker & Dempster	Edinburgh	Salver, chased band of flowers and foliage, engraved in center "1766"/Ex *Dono/Margt. Carruthers"*, with a mug	Scottish Art Review vol VI, p41 #4 Bell of Aberdeen advertisement
1764/65	Gilliland & Ker	Edinburgh	Teapot stand, shell and scroll border, inscribed "A present from A.G. & S. G. to their niece MG in James Court 12th June 1765", 7" di, 9.2oz	Nicholas Shaw Catalog 2004 p102
1764/65	Marks worn	Edinburgh	Waiter, circular with shell and scroll border, with plain ground and 3 pad feet, repairs to border, erased ground and thin, 6" di, 5oz	Christie's London UK 2007 #114

YEAR	MAKER	LOCATION	DESCRIPTION	SOURCE
1764/65 possibly	Alexander Gardner	Edinburgh	Waiter, shaped circular form, with shell and scroll cast edge and piecrust molded border, chased border of scrolls and foliage, crested with a motto "ASSIDUITATE NON DESIDIA", on 3 hoof feet, crest of Loch family, 7 ¼" di, 7oz	Lyon & Turnbull Edinburgh UK 2006 #277
1765 ca	Adam Graham	Glasgow	Salver, hexagonal, gadrooned border, engraved "MM", 12 ¾", 33.9oz	Nicholas Shaw Catalog Autumn 1999 p53
1765 ca	Adam Graham	Glasgow	Salver, shaped circular form, border of shells, center with engraved crest of clansman, 8" di, 10oz 8d	Sloans & Kenyon Chevy Chase, MD USA 2006 #701
1765 ca	Alexander Johnston	Dundee	Slaver, circular, on 3 hoof feet, gadrooned border, crest, 7 ¼" di, 9oz	Christie's October 26, 1977 #171
1765 ca	Adam Graham	Glasgow	Salver, circular, on 3 hoof feet, molded foliate and scroll border, chased with a band of flowers, scrolls and foliage on a matted ground, with later names, 7 1/8" di, 8.8oz	Christie's December 8, 1971 #158
1765 ca	Adam Graham	Glasgow	Salver, circular, with shell and scroll border, flat chased with trailing foliage, on 3 hoof feet, 8" di, 9.5oz	Sotheby's Scone Palace April 14-16, 1980 #124
1765/66	Gilliland & Ker	Edinburgh	Teapot stand, with teapot, chased with flowers and scrolls, on 3 hoof feet, shell and scroll border, inscriptions on base, 29.8oz both	Christie's February 27, 1957
1765/66	James Gilliland	Edinburgh	Salver, small with band of flowers and foliage, shaped shell and scroll rim, on 3 hoof feet, 7 ¼" di, 7.6oz	Sotheby's Gleneagles August 28, 1975 #67
1765/66	Patrick Robertson	Edinburgh	Teapot stand, on rim foot, engraved with a spray of leaves, crest and motto, and later inscriptions, 6" di, 5.7oz	Christie's April 13, 1977 #125
1766/67	Not available	Edinburgh	Salver, circular, flat chased with band of floral scrolls within a raised and applied scroll and shell border, on 3 hoof feet, 7" di, 6oz 16d	Sotheby's Gleneagles, #211
1766/67	James Gilliland	Edinburgh	Waiter, circular, shell and scroll border, center engraved with coat of arms of Ramsay, kin of the Earls of Dalhousie, whole on 3 hoof feet, 7 ¼" di, 7oz	Bonhams March 6, 2001 #163
1766/67	Ker & Dempster	Edinburgh	Plate stand, circular, on 3 leaf capped scroll supports with shell feet, pierced aprons between cast with open work shell, foliage and scrolls, 7 7/8" di, 19oz	Christie's March 27, 1984 #264 Christie's November 15, 1984 #193
1766/67	William Ker	Edinburgh	Salver, engraved in center with later initials, flat chased below scroll and shell border, band incorporating flowers, leaves and similar motifs, on 3 hoof feet, 8 ½" di, 10oz 12d	Sotheby's October 12, 1972 #188 Sotheby's January 11, 1978 #74

YEAR	MAKER	LOCATION	DESCRIPTION	SOURCE
1766/67	Alexander Gardner	Edinburgh	Salver, shaped circular, engraved crest and motto within applied scroll and shell border, on pad supports, 7 ½" di, 9oz 14d	Sotheby's January 26-28, 1988 #1768
1766/67	Alexander Gardner	Edinburgh	Salver, shaped circular, engraved in center with coat of arms with greyhound supporters and headed by a crest, scroll and shell border, arms of Seton of Colbeg, County Sterling, on 3 hoof feet, 10" di, 22oz 3d	Sotheby's May 1, 1969 #
1766/67	James Gilliland	Edinburgh	Salver, shaped circular, with shell and scroll border, on hoof feet, center chased with foliate scrolls, 7 ¼" di, 7.25oz	Phillips London September 23, 1994 #195
1766/67	Ker & Dempster	Edinburgh	Salver, shaped circular outline, C-scroll molded border, on 4 paw feet, chased border, engraved quartered arms of Ford of Abbeyfield, 15" di, 54oz	Lyon & Turnbull Edinburgh UK 2006 #399
1767/68	Daniel Ker	Edinburgh	Salver, circular, border with shells, chased out border, 7 ¼" di	Styles Antiques 2004
1767/68	W * D William Dempster	Edinburgh	Salver, 7" di, no further details	Glasgow Exhibition 1911, vol I, p120 #47
1768/69	Alexander Ziegler	Edinburgh	Waiter, shaped circular, on 3 bracket feet, scroll and shell border, flat chasing, 7 3/8" di, 7.5oz	Shaw Collection Christie's Glasgow March 29, 1983 #76
1768/69	Patrick Robertson	Edinburgh	Salver, circular, with shaped gadrooned rim, linen fold border, engraved with pairs of flowers alternating with scroll work, 9 ¼" di, 19oz	Sotheby's NY USA October 2-5, 1979 #342
1768/69	WD Probably William Dempster	Edinburgh	Waiter, shaped circular form on 3 hoof feet, chased band of flower heads and foliage within a shell and scroll border, 7 ¼" di, 7oz	Christie's Lanarkshire UK 1998 #562
1769/70	Patrick Robertson	Edinburgh	Salver, circular form, gadrooned rim, later engraved foliate scroll motifs, on 4 paw feet, later withdrawn from sale, 13 5/8" di, 38oz	Christie's London UK 2002 #221
1769/70	William Dempster or William Davie	Edinburgh	Salvers, circular, Arms of Keith-Falconer, Earl of Kintore, circular, shells on trim, chased border, 11 ¾" di, 49.2oz	Sotheby's NY USA April 8-9, 1981 #912
1770 ca	James Taylor	Glasgow	Waiter, with bath border, with crest, 8 1/8" di, 9.3oz	Nicholas Shaw Catalog 2005 p91
1770 ca	Alexander Thompson	Aberdeen	Salver, shaped circular, shell border, 8 1/8" di, 7.7oz	Nicholas Shaw Catalog Winter 2000 p72
1770 ca	Adam Graham	Glasgow	Salver, circular, on pad feet, beaded border, engraved with a crest and the initial "R", 7 ½" di	eBay #7392845190 NY USA February –March 2006

449

YEAR	MAKER	LOCATION	DESCRIPTION	SOURCE
1770/71	James Hewitt	Edinburgh	Salver, shaped circular, gadrooned edged, narrow chased outer band, 7" di, 7.7oz	Lyon & Turnbull Edinburgh UK 2004 #493 Nicholas Shaw Catalog 2005 p95
1770/71	W * D Probably William Dempster	Edinburgh	Stand, oval, chased with shells and scrolls, on 3 pad feet, engraved vacant oval cartouche, 8 5/8" long, 6 ¼" wide	Asprey London 1992 The Phoenix Collection
1772/73	Patrick Robertson	Edinburgh	Teapot stand, no details	The Maple Swan Collection
1772/73	William Davie or William Dempster	Edinburgh	Teapot stand, oval, gadrooned rim, on 4 pad feet, eagle crest and motto, 7 ¾" long X 5 ¼" wide	Virginia Museum of Fine Arts, Richmond VA USA 70.9.335
1773/74	William Davie or William Dempster	Edinburgh	Salver, on 3 pad feet, gadrooned edge, engraving in center, crest or script initials 7" di	Fogg Art Museum Harvard University Boston MA USA 1948.50
1773/74	Patrick Robertson	Edinburgh	Platter, no details	The Maple Swan Collection
1773/74	Patrick Robertson	Edinburgh	Waiters, pair, oval, gadrooned border, crest and motto	Sotheby's London June 1987 #301
1773/74	Alexander Gardner	Edinburgh	Salver, shaped circular, initials within scrolling foliage, raised and applied gadrooned border, 7 1/8", 9.4oz	Sotheby's Gleneagles September 1, 1981, #441
1774/75	Alexander Gardner	Edinburgh	Stand, no details	Firestone & Parsons, Boston USA 1992
1774/75	WD William Davie or William Dempster	Edinburgh	Teapot stand, oval on 4 scroll feet, plain elevated rim, engraved foliage border, 7 7/8" long, 7oz	Christie's London UK 2002 #122
1775 ca	Milne & Campbell	Edinburgh	Stand, oval, with teapot, chased bands, gadrooned edge	Sotheby's October 31, 1974 #38
1775/76	WD William Davie or William Dempster	Edinburgh	Waiter, circular shape, gadrooned rim, 3 scroll and stepped hoof feet, later Victorian inscription, 7 7/8" di, 12oz	Bonhams London UK 2005 #313
1775/76	James Gilliland	Edinburgh	Salver, oval, engraved with foliate sprigs, beneath an applied gadrooned border, on 4 hoof feet, 8 ½" long, 8.3oz	Sotheby's Gleneagles August 27, 1979 #212
1776/77	James Gilliland	Edinburgh	Stand, part of a tea service, 2 crests with a stag and star	Connoisseur Magazine March 1947

YEAR	MAKER	LOCATION	DESCRIPTION	SOURCE
1776/77	William Davie or William Dempster	Edinburgh	Salver, on 4 ball and claw feet, shaped beaded edge, embossed swag near the border, arms and motto "VIRESCIT VULNERE VIRTUS", 13 ¾" di	Firestone and Parsons, Boston USA Antiques Magazine vol 17 p1226
1777/78	Alexander Gardner	Edinburgh	Waiter, teapot stand, oval, beaded border, scroll feet, center engraving, 6 2/3" X 5", 8.2oz	eBay #7392153455 Scotland February – March 2006
1777/78	Patrick Robertson	Edinburgh	Salver, gadrooned border, crest, motto and baron's coronet, on 3 hoof feet	Sotheby's NY USA April 16-17, 1980 #709
1777/78	James Hewitt	Edinburgh	Teapot stand, oval on 4 hoof feet, center with a monogram, sold with another	Christie's Lanarkshire UK 1997 #148
1778/79	Gilliland & Ker	Edinburgh	Teapot stand, oblong form, on bun feet, the lattice work grid base formed of interlaced silver wire, 7 ½" long, 4.5oz	Christie's Lanarkshire UK 1997 #132
1778/79	William Davie or William Dempster	Edinburgh	Salver, 13" di, no details	Glasgow Exhibition 1911, vol I, p122 #66
1778/79	Patrick Robertson	Edinburgh	Salver, no details	Glasgow Exhibition 1911, vol I, p 121, #60
1779/80	William Dempster or William Davie	Edinburgh	Teapot stand, oval, rooster crest and motto	JH Bourdon-Smith 1992
1780 ca	William Dempster or William Davie	Edinburgh	Teapot stand, no details	National Museums of Scotland MEQ 1344
1780 ca	Milne & Campbell	Glasgow	Salver, shell and scroll border, heavy chasing	Sotheby's April 5, 1982 #204
1780 ca	Patrick Robertson	Edinburgh	Teapot stand, with teapot, no details	Dundee Museums and Art Galleries 1986-73
1780 ca	Robert Gray	Glasgow	Teapot stand, unengraved oval shaped	Private Collection
1780 ca	James Gordon	Aberdeen	Teapot stand, no details	Aberdeen Museums and Galleries ABDAG001337
1780 ca	James Law	Aberdeen	Teapot stand, oval, motto "My Trust in God"	Aberdeen Museums and Galleries ABDAG008882
1780/81	Patrick Robertson	Edinburgh	Waiters, pair, plain, circular, beaded rim, on 3 shaped feet, crest and motto of Hay, 7" di, 15oz 1d both (7oz 10d ea)	Christie's April 26, 1966 #98

YEAR	MAKER	LOCATION	DESCRIPTION	SOURCE
1780/81	William Dempster or William Davie	Edinburgh	Waiter or teapot stand, small circular, decorated with band of rounded foliage, gadrooned edge, on 3 hoof feet, 6 1/8" di, 6oz 14d	Private Collection
1783/84	William Dempster or William Davie	Edinburgh	Teapot stand, with teapot, no details	The Maple Swan Collection
1783/84	William Dempster or William Davie	Edinburgh	Teapot stand – part of 4 piece service	Country Life May or June 1968, vol 143
1784/85	Patrick Robertson	Edinburgh	Salvers, pair, beaded borders, pre duty mark, 8" di, 25oz	Private Collection
1784/85	William Dempster or William Davie	Edinburgh	Waiters, pair, circular, 7" di	Country Life May or June 1968, vol 143
1784-86	William Dempster or William Davie	Edinburgh	Salver, circular, 13" di	Country Life May or June 1968, vol 143
1784/85	William Dempster or William Davie	*Edinburgh*	Teapot stand, on 4 leaf capped cabriole legs, with claw feet, with teapot	Clayton Dictionary p307 #645
1784/85	Alexander Gardner	Edinburgh	Teapot stand, oval, on 4 feet, with crest and motto, sold with its teapot	Chrichton Bros, London UK Christie's NY USA 1999 #281
1785/86	Not available	Edinburgh	Salver, circular, beaded outer and inner border, cast shell and scroll feet, later engraved flat, 12" di, 26oz, *no mm*, with incuse duty mark	Lyon & Turnbull Edinburgh UK 2004 #492
1785/86	William Dempster or William Davie	Edinburgh	Salver, with center crest and motto, flat chased band of fruit, flower, etc, on 3 hoof feet, 9" di, 13oz	Sotheby's Gleneagles August 29, 1978 #378
1786/87	William Dempster or William Davie	Edinburgh	Salver, 13 1/8" di, 30oz 10d	Private Collection
1788/89	Patrick Robertson	Edinburgh	Salver, circular, flat chased scrolls, scale work and foliage, on 3 feet, 8 ½", 12.7oz	Sotheby's Scone Palace, April 23, 1979 #44
1788/89	James Dempster or James Douglas	Edinburgh	Teapot stand, no details	National Museums of Scotland MEQ 1118
1788/89	Patrick Robertson	Edinburgh	Tray, oval, on 6 bracket feet, bright cut band and armorials in center, 27 ½" X 19 ½", 137oz	Christie's London UK 2005 #797 eBay #7389358628 February 2006 UK
1789/90	David Marshall	Edinburgh	Salver/teapot stand, 1" X 3 1/8" X 5 7/8"	Musee De Beaux Arts Montreal Canada 1947.Ds.2

YEAR	MAKER	LOCATION	DESCRIPTION	SOURCE
1789/90	Francis Howden	Edinburgh	Salver, circular, no details	The Maple Swan Collection
1789/90	Patrick Robertson	Edinburgh	Teapot stand, octagonal, on 4 fluted straight feet	Finlay 1991 # 98
1789/90	W & P Cunningham I	Edinburgh	Stand, part of a service	Christie's May 1-2, 1991 #236
1789/90	Francis Howden	Edinburgh	Salver, circular, reeded border, on 4 panel feet, Arms of Drummond quartering Forbes and Williams, 12 ¼", 25.8oz	Sotheby's Gleneagles August 27, 1979 #222
1790/91	W & P Cunningham I	Edinburgh	Teapot stand, oval, bright cut with a band of formal quatrefoils below the raised applied border, on panel feet, 7 ¾" wide, 6.6oz	Sotheby's Gleneagles August 29, 1983 #495
1790/91	Francis Howden	Edinburgh	Teapot stand, oval, bright cut decoration, 6 7/8" long, 4oz	Nicholas Shaw Catalog 2005 p99, #1
1790/91	Francis Howden	Edinburgh	Teapot stand, oval, bright cut, engraved, 6 7/8" long, 4oz	Nicholas Shaw Catalog 2005 p99
1790/91	W & P Cunningham I	Edinburgh	Waiter, circular, 3 footed, engraved large armorials with crest and motto, within an elaborate foliate scroll surround, 6" di, with other items	Christie's, East NY USA 1999 #240
1790/91	W & P Cunningham I	Edinburgh	Teapot stand, shaped oval on 4 tab feet, with other items	Christie's NY USA 2003 #102
1791/92	William Robertson	Edinburgh	Teapot stand, 4 piece service	Country Life February 13, 1964, vol 135 p31 Bracher & Sydenham advertisement Finlay 1991 pl 98
1791/92	William Robertson	Edinburgh	*Teapot stand, on 4 plain panel supports, part of a 4 piece service, 8 3/8" X 6 1/8"*	*Sotheby's Gleneagles August 31, 1992, #147* Private Collection
1791/92	George Christie	Edinburgh	Waiter, no details	Jackson Marks p550
1791/92	William Robertson	Edinburgh	Salver, no details	Dundee Museums and Art Galleries 963-346
1791/92	William Dempster	Edinburgh	Tray, oval, molded rim with threaded edge, threaded end handles with foliated mountings, 20 ¼" X 14 ¾" excluding handles, 68oz	Rockville, MD US Collection
1792/93	William Robertson	Edinburgh	Salver, roundel in the center, enclosing a later inscription, bright cut border, with a later fitted case, 12", 30oz	Sotheby's Blair Castle, Sept' 12, 1980 #107

YEAR	MAKER	LOCATION	DESCRIPTION	SOURCE
1792/93 and 1798/99	W & P Cunningham I	Edinburgh	Salvers, matched pair, pointed oval form, 4 bracket feet, boar's head crest and motto "FOLLOW ME", 8 ¾" long, 16oz both	Lyon & Turnbull Edinburgh UK 2007 #244
1793/94	W & P Cunningham I	Edinburgh	Tray, large oval, center with 2 armorials, Arms are those of the City of Edinburgh and of Stirling Bt, 30" long, 189oz	Christie's January 22, 1947 #59 Sotheby's March 20, 1970 Sotheby's Scone Palace April 19, 1977 #100
1793/94	Thomas Sempill	Edinburgh	Teapot stand, shaped oval with bright cut engraved decoration and initials "P.Y.E.W", sold with its teapot, 12" wide	Christie's Lanarkshire UK 1997 #52
1794/95	W & P Cunningham I	Edinburgh	Salver, circular with beaded borders, on 3 bracket feet with shell tips, with a dog crest, 12" di, 28oz	Christie's, East NY USA 2000 #206
1794/95	Alexander Gardner	Edinburgh	Teapot stand, oval, possibly with engraved foliate band on paneled feet, with reeded rim, sold with its teapot	Christie's London UK 2005 #429
1794/95	Alexander Spence	Edinburgh	Teapot stand, part of a 4 piece service	Sotheby's Gleneagles, September 1, 1998 #542
1794/95	Dick & McPherson	Edinburgh	Waiters, pair, 7 ½" di, 20oz 8d	Sotheby's April 24, 1975 #75
1794/95	Francis Howden	Edinburgh	Salver, oval, 7 ½" di	Antiques Magazine vol 51, p343 Shreve advertisement
1794/95	Alexander Spence	Edinburgh	Salvers, pair, oval, gadrooned rim, bright cut leaf border, Arms	Christie's October 14, 1959 #99
1794/95	W & P Cunningham I	Edinburgh	Teapot stand, 4 piece set, 6 ¾" di	Christie's March 2, 1966 #179
1794/95	Peter Mathie	Edinburgh	Meat dishes, 2, presentation dishes of different sizes, gadrooned borders, 24 ¼" long and 17" long	Sotheby's London 1987 #436 Monroe Collection
1795 ca	W & P Cunningham I	Edinburgh	Salvers, pair, no details	Antiques Magazine vol 72 p590 Shreve advertisement
1795 ca	W & P Cunningham I	Edinburgh	Salver, circular, 20" di, 104oz 7d	Sotheby's November 28, 1974 #230
1795 ca	Edward Livingstone	Dundee	Teapot stand, octagonal	Finlay 1991 # 111
1795/96	Francis Howden	Edinburgh	Tray, miniature, 3' long X 1 ½" wide, .9oz	Wark, Huntington Library book p162 #370

454

YEAR	MAKER	LOCATION	DESCRIPTION	SOURCE
1795/96	Graham & McLean	Edinburgh	Teapot stand, engraved "JB", part of a 4 piece service, pot by same makers	N & I Franklin Private Collection
1796 ca	James Erskine	Aberdeen	Teapot stand, oblong	Finlay 1991 #109
1797 ca	Cunningham & Simpson	Edinburgh	Salver, circular, on 3 claw and ball feet, 12" di, 27oz 1d	Sotheby's November 28, 1968 #250
1797/98	A? Cunningham	Edinburgh	Teapot stand	Sotheby's July 1, 1959 #147
1797/98	W & P Cunningham I	Edinburgh	Salver, circular on 3 hoof feet, raised border, center engraved with crest of Fettes, 13 7/8" di, 17.3oz	Bonhams Sale 10914, #24
1798/99	M & C	Edinburgh	Salver, circular, with reeded border, on 3 panel feet, 10" di, 20.2oz	Sotheby's Hopetoun House, November 15, 1977 #94
1799/1800	W & P Cunningham I	Edinburgh	Teapot Stand, on 4 panel feet, with teapot	Woolley & Wallis, April 24, 2000 #314
1800 ca	RG	Provincial	Waiter, oval form with gadrooned rim on 4 panel feet, marks "RG" and "thistle", 6 ½" di, 4oz	Christie's London UK 2001 #102
1800 ca	Edward Livingstone	Dundee	Teapot stand, octagonal shape with a crest and initial, molded border, panel supports, sold with its teapot	Sotheby's NY USA 1999 #435
1800/01	W & P Cunningham I	Edinburgh	Teapot stand, on 4 bracket feet, monogrammed "MW", 6 ½" long, with a teapot	Christie's London UK 2000 #176
1800/01	James McDonald	Edinburgh	Salver, with crest and motto, 13 7/8" di, 34oz	Sotheby's NY USA October 22, 1993 #325
1800/01	McHattie & Fenwick	Edinburgh	Salver, no details	Antiques Magazine vol 91 #810 Bell of Aberdeen advertisement
1800/01	McHattie & Fenwick	Edinburgh	Tray, date 21 July 1800, 17 ½" long, 61oz	Sotheby's December 1, 1966, #170 Christie's May 20, 1987
1800/01	*McHattie & Fenwick*	*Edinburgh*	*King's Prize Tray, to the Royal Company of Archers, with 2 crests and arms*	*National Museums of Scotland*
1800/01	W & P Cunningham I	Edinburgh	Teapot stand, oval, bright cut engraved foliate decoration, sold with its teapot	Gorringes LLP, East Sussex UK 2006 #1531

YEAR	MAKER	LOCATION	DESCRIPTION	SOURCE
1801/02	Francis Howden	Edinburgh	Salvers, 12oz	Lorentz Antiques Toronto Canada 1991
1801/02	McHattie & Fenwick	Edinburgh	Salver, initial "R", 10" di, 38oz 19d	Sotheby's April 28, 1977 #83
1801/02	M & S	Edinburgh assay	Salver, crest and motto, oval, swags of flowers, drapes and scrolls, 10 ¾" di, 20oz	Sotheby's NY USA April 13, 1988 #173
1801/02	McHattie & Fenwick	Edinburgh	Salver, circular, panel supports, formal cartouche, arms of Buchanan of Leny, Stirlingshire, 10" di, 20oz	Sotheby's NY USA 1999 #439
1802/03	W & P Cunningham I	Edinburgh	Salver, plain circular outline, gadrooned border, 4 shell and bracket feet, inscribed on reverse as gift in 1805 from R R Cunningham to David Boyle, 12 1/3" di, 36.5oz	Christie's London UK 1999 #33
1802/03	W & P Cunningham I	Edinburgh	Salver, plain circular form, on 4 reeded panel feet, center with shield-shaped coat of arms within ribbon tied foliage mantling, 15" di, 52oz	Christie's London UK 1999 #255
1802/03	W & P Cunningham I	Edinburgh	Trays, pair, no details	Sotheby's Hopetoun House April 1988 #79
1802/03	N I	Edinburgh	Teapot stand, oval, engraved, gift to the Royal Company, 4 piece set	Christie's November 19, 1919 #42
1804/05	McHattie & Fenwick	Edinburgh	Tray, rectangular, later engraved "Robert Jeffrey, Edinburgh 5 May '52"	National Museums of Scotland H.1992.1830
1804/05	M & S	Edinburgh assay	Salver, 9" di	James Robinson NY USA, 1991
1804/05	McHattie & Fenwick	Edinburgh	Tray, oblong form on 4 ball feet, border of crossed squares, central cartouche within a Greek key pattern border, 6" long, 5oz	Bonhams Sale 15120 Aug 22, 2007 #14
1805/06	Dick & McPherson	Edinburgh	Salver, a graduated pair, shaped circular form, on 3 shaped scroll supports, shell and gadrooned rim, center with a crest and motto, largest 11 7/8" di, 47oz both	Christie's London UK 2005 #335
1805/06	John McDonald	Edinburgh	Salver, circular, 20 ¼" di, 94oz	Sotheby's Gleneagles August 29, 1977 #171
1805/06	McHattie & Fenwick	Edinburgh	Teapot stand, oval on 4 bracket feet, with gadrooned border, sold with another	Christie's Lanarkshire UK 1997 #148

YEAR	MAKER	LOCATION	DESCRIPTION	SOURCE
1806/07	W & P Cunningham I	Edinburgh	Salvers, pair, gadrooned borders, central armorials of Kincraigie, 26.7oz	Sotheby's Hopetoun House April 1988 #76
1806/07	Francis Howden	Edinburgh	Teapot stand, rectangular with rounded corners, bright cut engraved with a floral band and the initial "W", sold with its teapot	Gorringes LLP, East Sussex UK 2006 #1479
1808/09	P Cunningham & Sons	Edinburgh	Salvers, pair, oblong, on 4 palmette and acanthus feet, gadrooned border, center with a monogram within a further engraved border of flowers and foliage, 10 ½" X 7 3/8", 38oz	Christie's Lanarkshire UK 1997 #162
1808/09	Cunningham & Simpson	Edinburgh	Tray, with 2 handles, gadrooned, 21 ½" long	Christie's October 11, 1972 #105
1808/09	Cunningham & Simpson	Edinburgh	Salver, oblong, gadrooned rim, border of flowers, Arms of Anderson of Lochtim, 16" wide, 55oz 16d	Christie's October 12, 1955 #96
1809/10	George Fenwick	Edinburgh	Tray, rectangular, rounded corners, raised molded lip, applied gadrooned rim, gadrooned handles with applied shell and acanthus leafage, 4 hairy paw and ball feet, coat of arms, crest and motto, 25 7/8" long, 111.2oz	Milwaukee Art Museum loan item #59 in catalog
1810 ca	William Jamieson	Aberdeen	Salver, no details	Aberdeen Museums and Galleries ABDAG001376
1810/11	George McHattie Also "Milby"	Edinburgh	Salver, no details	Sotheby's Hopetoun House April 1988 #71
1810/11	George McHattie	Edinburgh	Tray, with 2 handles, 21" long, 100oz	Christie's November 29, 1967 #120
1810/11	George Fenwick	Edinburgh	Tea tray, unclear if same as above	Sotheby's Gleneagles August 1988 #477
1810/11	George McHattie	Edinburgh	Salver, circular, on 4 ball and curved bracket feet, plain ground with 2 monograms, crest and motto "VIRTUTE ET FORTUNA", 16 7/8" di, 58oz	Christie's London UK 2004 #601
1810/11	George McHattie	Edinburgh	Salver, circular section on 4 ball and panel feet, crest and motto of Gardner, 17" di, 68oz, possibly the same as above	Christie's London UK 2003 #423
1810/11	James McKay	Edinburgh	Salver, circular form, robust leaf and shell motif rim, central engraved coat-of-arms surrounded by foliate, shell and scale motifs, on 3 leaf feet, 13" di, 40.5oz	Christie's London UK 2001 #108
1810/11	N & G	Edinburgh	Salver, circular form, on 3 bracket feet, with central engraved foliate initials, border of stippled foliage and flower heads, gadrooned rim, 10 2/3" di, 21.5 oz	Bonhams sale 15120 Aug 22, 2007 #19

YEAR	MAKER	LOCATION	DESCRIPTION	SOURCE
1811/12	James McKay	Edinburgh	Salver, gadrooned edged rim, engraved with vines and grapes, 13" di, 33oz	Nicholas Shaw Antiques 2004
1811/12	James Finlayson	Glasgow	Salver, circular, rope border, leaf and vine engraved border	JH Bourdon-Smith Catalog 1992
1811/12	James McKay	Edinburgh	Salver, circular, gadrooned edge with outer band of vines and grapes, engraved, 13" di, 33oz	Nicholas Shaw Catalog Winter 2002/03, p87
1812/13	George Fenwick	Edinburgh	Tray, oblong, no details	The Maple Swan Collection
1812/13	*George Fenwick*	*Edinburgh*	*Salver, oblong, no details*	*Antiques Magazine vol 88 p603*
1812/13	*George Fenwick*	*Edinburgh*	*Salver, oblong, reticulated, Arms in center, engraved elements each corner, 4 ball feet*	*Sotheby's London 1987 #136*
1812/13	James McKay	Edinburgh	Salver, reticulated, rope and shell border	Sotheby's NY USA 1991 #327
1812/13	James McKay	Edinburgh	Salvers, pair, crest and motto, 7 ¾" di, 23oz	Sotheby's November 28, 1968 #249
1812/13	George McHattie	Edinburgh	Salvers, pair, circular form, on 3 bracket feet with shell motif, applied gadrooned border, 9" di, 30oz both	Christie's East NY USA 2001 #448
1812/13	W & P Cunningham II	Edinburgh	Salver, circular on ball and claw feet, border of ovolo motifs interspersed with foliage, center with a coat-of-arms, 18 1/8" di, 85oz	Christie's London UK 2000 #76
1812/13	W & P Cunningham II	Edinburgh	Salver, circular form, on 3 claw and ball feet, gadrooned shell and scroll border, 12 ½" di, 33oz	Bonhams Sale 15120 Aug 22, 2007 #18
1813/14	George McHattie	Edinburgh	Waiter, circular, gadrooned borders, later embossed scroll, swag and cupid decoration, crested, on 3 bracket feet, 7 7/8" di, 10oz	Lyon & Turnbull Edinburgh UK 2002 #452
1813/14	W & P Cunningham II	Edinburgh	Salver, plain, heavy circular, gadrooned border, 2 scroll and scale work claw and ball feet, center engraved with impaled arms said to be of Collyer and Chancellor, 6 1/8" ht, 8oz 12d	Private Collection
1814/15	W & P Cunningham II	Edinburgh	Salver, circular, with cast rococo border, armorials in center	Finlay 1991 # 102
1814/15	W P	Edinburgh	Salvers, pair, William Parlen or William Peat possible makers	Burlington Magazine October 1970 vol 112, p39
1814/15	Robert Gray & Son	Glasgow Edinburgh assay	Waiter, circular form with a gadrooned border, on 3 lion's mask and paw feet, 5 7/8" di, 6oz	Bonhams Solihull 2004 #47

YEAR	MAKER	LOCATION	DESCRIPTION	SOURCE
1815 ca	William Jamieson	Aberdeen	Salver, oblong, vacant cartouche	Aberdeen Museums and Galleries ABDAG008824
1815/16	W & P Cunningham II	Edinburgh	Stand, no details	Sotheby's Gleneagles August 1988 #480
1815/16	Peter Aiken	Glasgow Edinburgh assay	Salver, no details	JH Bourdon-Smith London 1993
1815/16	WP	Edinburgh	Slaver, circular form, gadrooned edge, cast shell applications, on 3 paw feet, later engraved central initials within a garter, 10 ¾" di, 23oz 8d	Butterfields Auctioneers Corp, San Francisco, CA USA 1996 #5355
1816/17	Mitchell & Russell	Glasgow Edinburgh assay	Salver, circular, cast applied border, 11" di, 27.4oz	Nicholas Shaw Catalog Winter 2001 p77
1816/17	Alexander Henderson	Edinburgh	Salver, applied rim with gadrooned and shell motif, on 3 shell feet, monogrammed in script "CM" in center	Cincinnati Art Museum, Cincinnati OH USA 1936.403
1817/18	Elder & Co	Edinburgh	Tray, 26" long X 17" wide	Dayton Art Institute, Dayton OH USA 32.5.3
1817/18	James McKay	Edinburgh	Salvers, pair, circular, crest of Moncrieff, 10"di, 36oz	Antiques Magazine vol Bell of Aberdeen advertisement
1817/18	Mitchell & Russell	Glasgow Edinburgh assay	Salver, circular form with ovolo border, on 3 scroll feet, crested, 9" di, 16oz	Lyon & Turnbull Edinburgh UK 2005 #275
1818/19	George Fenwick	Edinburgh	Salvers, pair, rectangular on 4 winged and foliate clad feet, gadrooned border with flowers at intervals, central initials "EW", reverse inscribed "To Elizabeth Milner", 12" long, 46oz	Christie's NY USA, 2000 #190
1818/19	Peter Aiken	Glasgow Edinburgh assay	Salver, 20 ½" di, 21oz	Sotheby's NY USA April 27, 1990
1818/19	Mitchell & Russell	Glasgow Edinburgh assay	Salver, circular with an applied border of floral motifs, initialed, 11" di, 28oz	Christie's London UK 1997 #111

YEAR	MAKER	LOCATION	DESCRIPTION	SOURCE
1818/19	Robert Gray & Son	Glasgow Edinburgh assay	Salver, circular form, applied ovolo border, on 3 winged paw feet, chased band of foliage, flowers and diaper panels, 18" di, 88oz 18d	Butterfield's Auctioneers Corp, San Francisco, CA USA 1993 #4709
1819/20	James Howden Also AC	Edinburgh	Salver, no details	National Museums of Scotland MEQ 795 1965.1866
1819/20	James McKay	Edinburgh	Salver, no details	National Museums of Scotland MEQ 1096
1820 ca	Peter Ross	Aberdeen	Waiter, circular, with beaded rim	Aberdeen Museums and Galleries ABDAG011112
1820 ca	Peter Ross	Aberdeen	Waiter, plain circular, on 3 hoof feet, beaded rim, 6" di	Morris Collection Christie's Scotland July 3, 1984 #109 Christie's London UK 1998 #55
1820/21	James McKay	Edinburgh	Salver, chased, on scroll and lion paw feet, arms and crest of Bannerman, 7 ¼" di, 12.2oz	JH Bourdon-Smith Catalog Autumn 2005 p26 #46
1820/21	James McKay	Edinburgh	Salver, shaped circular form, paw feet, armorials, 7" di, 12oz	Christie's Lanarkshire UK 1998 #73
1820/21	CB	Edinburgh	Teapot stand, circular, 3 footed, part of a service	Christie's, East NY USA 1998 #52
1823/24	Mitchell & Son	Glasgow	Salver, circular with a husk and scroll border decorated with a wide flat chased frieze around a plain circular cartouche, initialed in the center, 12 1/3" di, 33oz	Christie's London UK 1999 #53
1825 ca	James Pirie	Aberdeen	Waiter, on 3 bracketed feet, rope border, 6 ¾" di, 8oz	Christie's Glasgow March 1983 #28
1825 ca	James Pirie	Aberdeen	Waiter, circular, no details, possibly the same as before	Aberdeen Museums and Galleries ABDAG001377
1825/26	Mitchell & Son	Glasgow	Salver, with inscribed dedication to a minister of the Borough of Glasgow, engraved by Gray & Son, 18 ½" di, 88oz	UK Antique Shop
1826/27	P. G.	Glasgow	Salver, gadrooned border, chased, 11 ½" di, 30oz	JH Bourdon-Smith Catalog Autumn 1991 p47 #34
1827/28	Robert Gray & Son	Glasgow	Salver, gadrooned border, chased, 8 ¾" di, 14.5oz	JH Bourdon-Smith Catalog Autumn 1991 p47 #34

YEAR	MAKER	LOCATION	DESCRIPTION	SOURCE
1828/29	Script IO Possibly James Orr	Greenock probably Edinburgh assay	Teapot stand, oval form, bright cut engraved with roundels and wigglework borders centered by a wreathe cartouche, on 4 bracket supports, sold with other items	Bonhams London UK 2004 #474
1830 ca	James McKay	Edinburgh	Tray, no details	National Museums of Scotland MEQ 145
1832/33	AA	Glasgow	Presentation salver, circular, on foliate feet, shell and foliate rim, date presentation on "Dec 3, 1832 to John Campbell, Esq. MD by the inhabitants of Largs", 11 ¾" di, 27.7oz	Ritchies, Toronto CA 2007 #1116
1833/34	Elder & Co	Edinburgh	Salver, shaped circular form, foliate scroll and shell cast edge, engraved border, crested and initialed in center, 3 shell and scroll cast bracket feet, 13" di, 34oz	Lyon & Turnbull Edinburgh UK 2005 #284
1835/36	Marshall & Sons	Edinburgh	Waiter, circular, rococo style, applied rim of reeded scrolls and leaves, chased band of foliate design, 3 scroll feet, armorial with motto in a banner, 6 ¼" di, with other items	Butterfields Auctioneers Corp, San Francisco, CA USA 1988 #1506
1836/37	Lawrence Urquhart	Edinburgh	Salver, circular, chased	JH Bourdon-Smith London 1993
1836/37	A G Wighton	Edinburgh	Salver, with shell decorations	JH Bourdon-Smith London 1993
1837/38	William Cunningham	Edinburgh	Salver, circular form, crested, 9 ½" di, 19oz	Hampstead Auctions, Ltd, Hampstead UK, 2007 #23
1839/40	RK Probably Robert Keay II	Perth Edinburgh assay	Salver, plain circular form with reeded border and three cast shell and foliate feet, 8" di, 12.5oz	Christie's London UK 2003 #418
1844/45	William Marshall	Edinburgh	Salver, no details	National Museums of Scotland MEQ 934
1860/61	Charles Robb & Son	Edinburgh	Salver, presentation, oval, 20" X 14"	Huntley House Museum Edinburgh HH2188/62
1904/05	Hamilton & Inches	Edinburgh	Teapot stand, octagonal, bright cut decoration, 6 ¼" long, 4.6oz	Nicholas Shaw Catalog 2005 p107
1905/06	Brook & Son	Edinburgh	Salver, no details	National Museums of Scotland MEQ 1109

YEAR	MAKER	LOCATION	DESCRIPTION	SOURCE
1930/31	R. W. Sorley	Glasgow	Tray, rectangular, with 2 handles, 23 ½" across handles, 85oz	Nicholas Shaw Catalog 2005 p107
1974/75	Hamilton & Inches	Edinburgh	Tray, circular, *last piece struck with the thistle mark*	National Museums of Scotland MEQ L.198.47

Sauceboats

Plate 42. A Sauceboat 1763/64 by Alexander Gardner, Edinburgh.
Courtesy of The Phoenix Collection. Photograph by Janice M Dietert.

YEAR	MAKER	LOCATION	DESCRIPTION	SOURCE
			SAUCEBOATS	
1730/31	James Mitchelson	Edinburgh	Sauceboats, pair, double lipped	Private Collection UK
1733/34 & 1734/35	James Ker	Edinburgh	Sauceboats, pair, marked in consecutive years, double lipped	Clayton Christie's p 176 #5 Christie's London November 27, 1976 #170
1735 ca	Robert Luke	Glasgow	Sauceboat, or cream boat, oval, everted shaped rim, chased with shells and scrolls above stepped pad supports, scroll handle, 6 ½" di, 5oz	Sotheby's Sussex January 17, 1990 #1980
1738/39	James Mitchelson	Edinburgh	Sauceboat, double lipped, on oval molded foot, molded drop beneath the spouts, double scroll handles, scalloped rim, engraved twice with crest and motto, hand holding dagger upright, "DUM SPIRO SPERO", 11.2oz	Finlay 1991 p69 Christie's July 3, 1968 #111 National Museums of Scotland MEQ 944
1740 ca	IG		Sauceboats, 2 oval, crested, flying scroll handles, decorated with overlapping tongue motifs, each on 3 pad supports, 7 ¾", 15oz 10d	Sotheby's June 29-30, 1981 #193
1745 ca	James Glen	Glasgow	Sauceboat, lip and shaped everted rim engraved with flowers, foliage and a shell, leaf capped double scroll handle, on 3 paw supports, underside has initials, 6 7/8", 8oz 5d	Sotheby's March 12, 1984 Sotheby's November 29, 1984
1745 ca	James Glen	Glasgow	*Sauceboat, on 3 trefoil and paw feet, scrolling everted rim chased with foliage and scrolls and double scroll handle, 6oz 5d*	*Christie's October 14, 1987*
1745 ca	Johnathan Buck or Johann Got-helf Bilsings	Limerick Glasgow	Sauceboat, on 3 shell and mask feet, body later repoussed and chased with fruit, foliage and trelliswork, scalloped rim, rising scroll handle formed as a sea serpent, 7oz 7d	Christie's March 13, 1968
1745 ca	James Glen	Glasgow	Sauceboat, plain, base engraved with initials, on paw feet, 5.9oz	Phillips January 24, 1986
1745 ca	Hugh Gordon	Edinburgh	Sauceboat, shallow, on knurled hoof feet, shaped rim chased with arabesques, double scroll handle, engraved with a crest, 7 ½", 6.75oz	Christie's March 21, 1988
1746/47	Not Available Assayer Hugh Gordon	Edinburgh	Sauceboat, small, on 3 scroll and hoof feet, double scroll handle and shaped border chased with shells, flowers and scrolls, 4oz 2d	Christie's December 7, 1966 #118 Christie's July 5, 1967 #111 De Havilland
1746/47	Dougal Ged Assayer Hugh Gordon	Edinburgh	Sauceboat, oval, initials below the shaped rim, flat chased with flowers and foliage, leaf capped scroll handle, shell headed volute feet, 7", 8oz 12d	Sotheby's October 2, 1980 #50

YEAR	MAKER	LOCATION	DESCRIPTION	SOURCE
1746/47	John Clark	Edinburgh	Sauceboat, oval, everted waved rim, leaf capped double scroll handle, on 3 hoof feet, 6oz 10d	Sotheby's Hopetoun House, April 26, 1988 #59
1747/48	CL mark	Edinburgh	Sauceboat, no details	Jackson Marks p 544
1747/48	Robert Gordon Assayer Hugh Gordon	Edinburgh	Sauceboat, oval, typical shallow design, projecting waved lip, somewhat pointed spout, with crest and motto on one side, on 3 claw feet headed by lobed motifs, 8 ½" 9oz 14d	Sotheby's July 4, 1968
1748/49	James Weems Assayer Hugh Gordon	Edinburgh	Sauceboat, engraved with a monogram below the everted rim, flat chased with flower, scroll and shell motifs, leaf capped double scroll handle, on 3 paw feet, 8", 6oz 11d	Sotheby's July 5, 1973 #172 Sotheby's Gleneagles August 27-28, 1979 #235 Sotheby's Hopetoun House November 10-11, 1980 #47
1751/52	Hugh Gordon	Edinburgh	Sauceboats, pair, no details	Antiques Magazine August 1992 vol 58 p 50
1751/52	Lothian & Robertson	Edinburgh	Sauceboat, no details	Sotheby's NY USA February 1985
1751/52	Dougal Ged	Edinburgh	Sauceboats, pair, on 3 shell and scroll feet, scroll handle, gadrooned rim, 30.7oz	How of Edinburgh 1937 #109
1753/54	Not available	Edinburgh	Sauceboat, *plain scalloped rim*, flying scroll handle, on 3 shell feet, with a crest, 9oz	Christie's June 3, 1959
1753/54	Lothian & Robertson	Edinburgh	Sauceboat, scalloped border, flying scroll handle, on 3 shell feet, 5.4oz	Christie's October 30, 1974 #192
1754/55	Lothian & Robertson	Edinburgh	Sauceboat, chased and on a spreading foot	Christie's Edinburgh November 21, 1990 #40
1755/56	Patrick Robertson	Edinburgh	Sauceboat, inverted pear shaped body, chased floral decoration, leaf capped high C-scroll handle, on stepped oval pedestal foot, 7 ¼" long, 9oz	Bell of Aberdeen 1969 Lyon & Turnbull The Murray Collection sale August 20, 2003, #190
1755/56	Ker & Dempster	Edinburgh	*Sauceboat, oval, chased and embossed floral foliate and scroll decoration, wavy border, on 3 shell feet, the base with a crest and motto*, 9.4oz	Phillips Edinburgh June 9, 1995 #291
1755/56	William Taylor	Edinburgh	Sauceboat, oval, shaped rim, flying scroll handle, 3 hoof feet, crest and motto, 7" long, 8.4oz	Sotheby's March 12, 1984 #610

YEAR	MAKER	LOCATION	DESCRIPTION	SOURCE
1755/56	William Gilchrist	Edinburgh	Sauceboat, on 3 paw supports, plain oval body with shaped flaring tip, flying scroll handle, 7 ½" long, 9oz	Sotheby's Edinburgh UK 1993 #125
1756/57	William Dempster or William Davie	Edinburgh	Sauceboat, oval, wavy rim, leaf capped flying scroll handle, 3 supporters headed by shell motifs, 7" long, 8oz	Sotheby's March 3, 1975 #86
1756/57	Ker & Dempster	Edinburgh	Sauceboat, chased with flowers, fruit and scrolls, leaf capped scroll handles, on 3 mask and shell feet, 7.4oz	Christie's April 14, 1982 #180
1756/57	Lothian & Robertson	Edinburgh	Sauceboat or creamboat, of inverted pear shape form, on spreading domed foot, with everted scalloped rim, acanthus capped flying scroll handle, monogram and initials 6 7/8", 7.6oz	Christie's January 26, 1979 #189 Bonhams The Scottish Sale August 24, 2005 #2
1757/58	William Dempster or William Davie	Edinburgh	Sauceboats, pair, oval with gadrooned foot, leaf capped scroll handles, crest and motto "AD ARDUA VIRTUS", 8" long, 18.6oz	Bonham the Scottish Sale August 21, 2003 #19 JH Bourdon-Smith Catalog Summer 2004 p15 #45
1758/59 and 61/62	Robert Gordon	Edinburgh	Sauceboats, 2, oval, each on spreading circular foot, gadrooned border, foliage capped scroll handle, 21oz both	Christie's October 14, 1970 #112 Simon Kaye Antiques
1760 ca	Patrick Robertson	Edinburgh	Sauceboat, oval body, supports headed with flowering foliage on a matted ground, later engraved with Royal Arms, inscribed from Queen Victoria to the royal company of Archers, mm rubbed, 7 ½" long, 12.7oz	Sotheby's May 8, 1975 #138
1760 ca	Milne & Campbell	Glasgow	Sauceboat, on 3 lion's mask and paw feet, with a serpent scroll handle, chased scroll rim, 7" long, 6.5oz	Woolley & Wallis 2004 #412
1760 ca	Milne & Campbell	Glasgow	Sauceboat, oval bellied form, wavy border, leaf-capped scroll handle, on a stepped oval foot, 8oz	Bonhams London UK 1995 #168
1760/61	Robert Gordon	Edinburgh	Sauceboat, inverted pear shaped body, gadrooned rim, leaf capped double scroll handle, on oval gadrooned spreading base, crest and motto in a riband, 7 ¾" long, 9.1oz	Sotheby's Scone Palace, April 19, 1977 #86 Private Collection
1761/62	William Dempster or William Davie	Edinburgh	Sauceboat, with cyma edge	Bonhams September 26, 1975 #561
1761/62	*William Dempster or William Davie*	*Edinburgh*	*Sauceboat, on 3 hoof feet, shaped rim, with flying scroll handle, 4.3oz*	*Bonhams Sale 15120 Aug 22, 2007 #6*
1761/62	Robert Gordon	Edinburgh	Sauceboat, gadrooned edge, leaf capped handle, on raised gadrooned foot, 9" over handle	JH Bourdon-Smith Catalog 2000 #42

YEAR	MAKER	LOCATION	DESCRIPTION	SOURCE
1762/63	Robert Gordon	Edinburgh	Sauceboats, pair, oval baluster form, gadrooned lips, leaf capped double scroll handles, decorated bases, 8 ½" long, 19.1oz both	Sotheby's March 31, 1966
1762/63 and 67/68	William Dempster or William Davie	Edinburgh	Sauceboats, 2, matching, gadrooned rims, pedestal bases, leaf capped double scroll handles, identical crests, 8 ½" long, 19.5oz both	Sotheby's July 6, 1967 #188
1762/63	*William Dempster or William Davie*	*Edinburgh*	*Sauceboats, pair, no details*	*Apollo July 1967 vol 86 p66*
1763/64	Alexander Gardner	Edinburgh	Sauceboat, oval, gadrooned flared rim, leaf capped double scroll handle on gadrooned foot, each side chased with a band of flowers and leaves, crest and motto "TOUJOUR PRET" under spout, 8 ¾" long over handle, 5 ½" ht	Christie's July 9, 1986 #248 Shrubsole London 1991 The Phoenix Collection
1763/64	Alexander Gardner	Edinburgh	Sauceboats, pair, oval inverted pear shaped body, chased with floral swags on upper part, bordered with semi lobing, shell lined bowl backs applied with leaf capped double scroll handle	Sotheby's Gleneagles August 28, 1969 #86 Bonhams the Scottish Sale August 24, 2005 #497
1765 ca	Adam Graham	Glasgow	Sauceboat, not marked, maker speculated, no details	Sotheby's NY USA October 1991 #366
1765 ca	Adam Graham	Glasgow	Sauceboat, slightly everted rim, wide leaf capped double scroll handle, inverted pear shaped body, 4" wide	Linden & Co Antiques, London 2006 #1642
1765 ca	Adam Graham	Glasgow	*Sauceboat, or cream boat, oval form, chased, leaf capped flying scroll handle, feet headed and terminated by shell motifs, 6 ¼" long, 5.3oz*	Sotheby's December 9, 1976 #34
1765/66	Ker & Dempster	Edinburgh	Sauceboats, pair, gadrooned border, scroll handle, segmented legs on 3 shell feet, 28oz both	Phillips Glasgow June 6, 1988 #340
1765/66	Ker & Dempster	Edinburgh	Sauceboat, or cream boat, oval form, chased, leaf capped flying scroll handle, feet headed and terminated by shell motifs, 6 ¼" long, 5.3oz	Sotheby's December 9, 1976 #34
1766/67	Daniel Ker	Edinburgh	Sauceboat, oval, wavy rim, flying scroll handle, pad supports, 6 ¾" long, 4oz 14d	Sotheby's Gleneagles August 31, 1999 #497
1766/67	*Daniel Ker*	*Edinburgh*	*Sauceboat, boat shaped on 3 hoof feet, scroll handle, scalloped rim, 4.7oz*	*Bonhams Edinburgh UK 2005 #4*
1766/67	Alexander Gardner	Edinburgh	Sauceboat, oval, repousse and chased with flower sprays, lobed and fluted rim and foot, double scroll leaf capped handle, 9 ½" wide, 11oz 6d	Sotheby's May 3, 1962 #154
1768/69	Alexander Ziegler	Edinburgh	Sauceboats, pair, no details	National Museums of Scotland 1961.544-555

YEAR	MAKER	LOCATION	DESCRIPTION	SOURCE
1768/69	Alexander Gardner	Edinburgh	Sauceboat, no details	The Maple Swan Collection
1769/70	Patrick Robertson	Edinburgh	Sauceboat, boat shaped body on a pedestal foot, leaf capped handle, 8 ½" long, 7.5oz	Christie's London UK 2003 #414
1770 ca	James Gordon	Aberdeen	Sauceboats, pair, plain oval, on 3 feet, with rising leaf capped scroll handle, engraved with crest, mm only, 15oz 5d both	Christie's July 3, 1984 #102
1770 ca	Adam Graham	Glasgow	Sauceboat, shell and floral chasing to inner rim, double scroll handle, oval tall plain base, 4" ht	JH Bourdon-Smith London
1770/71	William Ker	Edinburgh	Sauceboat, no details	Antiques Magazine October 1967 Bell of Aberdeen advertisement
1771/72	James Gilliland	Edinburgh	Sauceboat, oval inverted pear shaped body, chased with flowers and foliage below a waved rim, leaf capped scroll handle, on spreading foot, mate to next one, 8", 5.9oz	Sotheby's Scone Palace April 13, 1976 #122
1771/72	James Gilliland	Edinburgh	Sauceboat, mate to the one preceding, 8", 5.9oz	Sotheby's Gleneagles August 29, 1978 #418
1773/74	James Gilliland	Edinburgh	Sauceboat, oval, chased in rococo style, vacant cartouche, waved rim, leaf capped handle, oval molded foot, 7 ½", 5.9oz	Sotheby's Hopetoun House November 15, 1977 #39
1775 ca	Benjamin Lumsden	Aberdeen	Sauceboat, no details	Aberdeen Museums and Galleries ABDAG000099
1776ca	Milne & Campbell	Glasgow	Sauceboat, no details	Connoisseur Magazine 1934 vol 93 p 347
1776/77	Patrick Robertson	Edinburgh	Sauceboats, pair, gadrooned borders, bracket feet, double scroll handles, crest and motto of Bruce, 8" long, 22oz	JH Bourdon-Smith Catalog Autumn 1999 p38 #41
1781/82	James Gilliland	Edinburgh	Sauceboat, oval inverted pear shaped body, flat chased with fruit, swags, 2 vacant cartouches, leaf capped scroll handle, spreading base, 7 ½", 5.9oz	Sotheby's Blair Castle September 12, 1980 #41
1783/84	James McEwan	Glasgow Edinburgh assay	Sauceboats, pair, no details	Antiques Magazine vol 63 Shreve advertisement
1783/84	Davie Downie	Edinburgh	Sauceboat, crest of Stanhope, 4 ¾" ht, 6.7oz	National Museums of Scotland K.2004.206 Nicholas Shaw Catalog Autumn 1999 p54

YEAR	MAKER	LOCATION	DESCRIPTION	SOURCE
1784/85	James Gilliland	Edinburgh	Sauceboat, tall helmet shaped body, high hoop handles, 12.4oz	Sotheby's Gleneagles August 31, 1999 Private Collection
1784/85	Peter Mathie	Edinburgh	Sauceboat, no details	The Maple Swan Collection
1786/87	Patrick Robertson	Edinburgh	Sauceboat, gadrooned, crest and motto of MacKay, 8" long, 10oz	Sothebys' London UK 1993 #152 JH Bourdon-Smith Catalog Autumn 1997 p31 #39
1786/87	William Davie or William Dempster	Edinburgh	Sauce tureens, pair, with covers, classical vase shape, on conforming foot, beaded borders, urn finials, 5 ½" ht at handles, 25.9oz	Bonhams Sale 10914 #23
1788/89	Francis Howden	Edinburgh	Sauceboats, pair, oval, engraved either side with crest and helm within foliate mantling, beaded borders, capped loop handles, on oval pedestal base, 8 ½" long, 20.8oz both	Sotheby's Hopetoun House November 15, 1977 #124
1793/94	Peter Mathie	Edinburgh	Sauceboat, no details	Jackson Marks p 550
1898/99	Hamilton & Inches	Edinburgh	Sauceboats, pair, oval outline, with shaped everted rim, on 3 shell-capped hoof feet, leaf-capped flying scroll handle, 11' ht, 23.5oz	Lyon & Turnbull, Edinburgh UK 2006 #299
1904/05	Hamilton & Inches	Edinburgh	Sauceboats, pair, oval outline, double scroll handles, on shell shaped feet, 7" across, 16oz	Gorringes LLP, East Sussex UK 2006 #1438

Strainers & Squeezers

Plate 43. An oval Orange Strainer 1765 ca by Adam Graham, Glasgow.
Courtesy of The Maple Swan Collection.

STRAINERS AND SQUEEZERS

YEAR	MAKER	LOCATION	DESCRIPTION	SOURCE
Pre-1689	William Scott I	Aberdeen	Strainer, pierced in concentric circles, small bowl, small flat shaped handle, pierced with stylized Celtic cross	Hyman Collection - Colonial Williamsburg L1986-130
1730 ca	George Cooper	Aberdeen	Strainer, shallow bowl form, one shaped handle pierced with a trefoil, engraved with initials "AFS", mm 3X's, 4 ¼" di, 3oz 7d	Christie's July 3, 1984 #127 Provenance John Noble Esq., Sale, Christie's London June 24, 1981 #70
1730 ca	George Cooper	Aberdeen	*Strainer, circular with one handle and a clasp*	*Clayton Dictionary p156 #2 and 2a* *Christie's Glasgow July 3, 1984*
1730 ca	George Cooper	Aberdeen	*Tea strainer, lug handle, no details*	*Aberdeen Museums and Galleries ABDAG001358*
1740 ca	James Ker	Edinburgh	Orange strainer, crest under coronet on handles	National Museums of Scotland MEQ 1559 1983 Shaw Collection Christie's Glasgow March 29, 1983 #75
1740 ca	*James Ker*	*Edinburgh*	*Strainer, 2 pierced handles, mm only 3X's, 6 ¾" wide*	*Christie's February 16, 1981 #303*
1740 ca	Dougal Ged	Edinburgh	Lemon strainer, no details	Dundee Museums and Art Galleries 1978-658
1740 ca	Dougal Ged	Edinburgh	Strainer, typical form with 2 shaped tab handles, one handle engraved on reverse with a shell, mm only under one handle, sold with other items	Christie's NY USA 1999 #315
1740/41	Dougal Ged	Edinburgh	Lemon strainer, plain, circular with 2 shaped lug handles, asymmetrical piercing, 6 5/8" long, 3oz	Bell of Aberdeen 1951 Nicholas Shaw Catalog Winter 2000 p85
1750-80	Not available	Possibly Scotland	Strainer, small, Old English, pierced bowl, molded rim, slim shaped flat handles, crest of Drummond, positioning cleats under handles, 4 ¾" long	Hyman Collection - Colonial Williamsburg L1988-470
1760 ca	Alexander Gardner	Edinburgh	Tea strainer, circular simple pierced bowl below a molded rim, crest and motto, open scroll handled, marked on handle, 4 ½" di, 2.1oz	Sotheby's Hopetoun House March 27, 1984 #134
1760 ca	JS Probably John Steven	Dundee	Punch strainer, circular shallow bowl with scrolled clip, open reeded handle, hinged and folding, 11 ¾" long	Lyon & Turnbull Edinburgh UK 2004 #290

YEAR	MAKER	LOCATION	DESCRIPTION	SOURCE
1765 ca	Adam Graham	Glasgow	Orange strainer, oval shaped bowl, 2 handled, rococo feathering, star outline among punch circules in bowl, 4 marks, 11 5/8" wide	Christie's Glasgow July 2, 1983 #153 The Maple Swan Collection
1765 ca	Adam Graham	Glasgow	Orange strainer, circular, with open work foliate handles, molded rim, overlapping circles as punched pattern, (Note: different from oval shaped strainer by Graham), 7 7/8" or 8 5/8"	Christie's June 24, 1986 #163 Probably also Christie's Edinburgh April 26, 1989 #106
1765 ca	Adam Graham	Glasgow	Strainer, circular, pierced as a flower head between side handles, 4" di (bowl), 3oz, note: unclear if same as prior circular example	Sotheby's NY USA 1998 #239
1770 ca	WD Possibly William Davie	Edinburgh	Lemon strainer with pierced circular bowl and scroll handle, bright cut with a feather motif, 4" di, 2.4oz	Sotheby's Gleneagles August 29, 1978 #420
1770 ca	Not available	Possibly Scotland	Strainer, deep bowl, foliate small scale Old English piercing, everted gadrooned rim, flat neo-classical pierced handles, positioning studs	Hyman Collection - Colonial Williamsburg L1988-46
1770 ca	James Dempster	Edinburgh	Lemon strainer, no details	The Maple Swan Collection
1773/74	Patrick Robertson	Edinburgh	Orange strainer, no details	National Museums of Scotland MEQ 1205
1775 ca	Alexander Thompson	Aberdeen	Tea strainer, no details	Aberdeen Museums and Galleries ABDAG001312
1775 ca	Patrick Robertson	Edinburgh	Strainer, circular pierced bowl with threaded edge, with a C-scroll handle, 4" di	Lyon & Turnbull, Edinburgh UK The Murray Collection Sale August 20, 2003 #176
1775 ca	*Patrick Robertson*	*Edinburgh*	*Strainer, wirework heart-shaped handles terminating in C-scrolls, pierced 6 petaled flower motif, crested, 1.5oz*	Bonhams London UK 2004 #87
1782/83	William Davie or William Dempster	Edinburgh	Lemon strainer, 2 handles, 5 ½" di, 13 1/8" over handles	Huntley House Museum Edinburgh HH3144/67
1782/83	William Davie or William Dempster	Edinburgh	Strainer, foliate, Old English piercing, everted molded rim, short rococo handles, inset shell, crest on side of bowl	Hyman Collection - Colonial Williamsburg L1989-138 Jackson Marks p463
1784/85	Robert Gray	Glasgow Edinburgh assay	Lozenge bowl, wide flat rim, foliate Old English piercing, one short rococo handle over dip	Hyman Collection - Colonial Williamsburg L1989-362 Jackson Marks p 551

YEAR	MAKER	LOCATION	DESCRIPTION	SOURCE
1789/90	William Dempster or William Davie	Edinburgh	Punch strainer, pierced with a star within a border of circles, engraved on exterior with the crest of a man's head and motto "DURIS NON FRANGOR", flat shaped reeded handle, 6" long over handles, 3oz, note: most likely made by William Dempster given the later date	Northeast Auction, Manchester, NY USA 2007 #1401
1790 ca	JS	Dundee	Punch strainer, no details	Dundee Museums and Art Galleries 2004-134
1790 ca	RG probably Robert Gray	Glasgow Edinburgh assay	Lemon strainer, circular section bow with a reeded rim and applied double scroll handle, 5 ½" long	Christie's London UK 2001 #216
1790 ca	Robert Dickson	Perth	Strainer, lemon strainer, circular with single loop handle, fan pattern, punched holes	The Maple Swan Collection
1801/02	James Douglas possibly	Edinburgh	Strainer, mm JD in an oval	Shrubsole London 1991
1804/05	Script JO		Strainer, shell decorations	Toby's, CT USA 1993
1810 ca	Robert Keay I	Perth	Lemon strainer, circular form, simply pierced around a flowerhead, 4" di, 12oz	Bonhams Sale 15120 Aug 22, 2007, #277
1810/11	James Newlands & Philip Grierson	Glasgow Edinburgh assay	Lemon strainer, oval bowl, plain loop handles, engraved with small crest of a demi-leopard, motto "sans tache", Edinburgh marks for 1810/11	Private Collection
1811/12	Robert Gray & Son	Glasgow Edinburgh assay	Strainer, oval flattened bowl, gadrooned rim, heavy Old English piercing, spoon type handles cast with a foliate surround, stamped crest of Langlands	Hyman Collection - Colonial Williamsburg L 1988.146
1813/14	Robert Gray & Son	Glasgow Edinburgh assay	Lemon strainer, no details	National Museums of Scotland MEQ 1066
1815/16	Not available	Edinburgh	Strainer, oval with gadrooned border and scroll handles, initialed "ALM", 10 ½" long, 4oz 9d, mm indistinct	Sotheby's NY USA 1998 #553
1816/17	D M	Edinburgh assay	Lemon squeezer, no details, possibly by David Manson of Dundee	The Maple Swan Collection
1820 ca	George Jamieson	Aberdeen	Tea strainer, no details	Aberdeen Museums and Galleries ABDAG000063 acquired 1987

YEAR	MAKER	LOCATION	DESCRIPTION	SOURCE
1820 ca	Mitchell & Russell	Glasgow	Lemon strainer, shallow pierced circular bowl, with gadrooned edge, twin lyre handles with shell detail, 11 ¾" wide, 4oz, date letter indistinct	Lyon & Turnbull, Edinburgh UK 2007 #240
1821/22	Robert Gray & Son	Glasgow	Punch strainer, oval form, simply punched with two lyre-shaped side handles incorporating shell detail, gadrooned border, 11 ¾" long, 6.7oz	Bonhams Sale 15120 Aug 22, 2007 #117
1822/23	Mitchell & Russell	Glasgow	Punch strainer, with small brackets on each handle, engraved with the crest of Brodie, 13" long	JH Bourdon-Smith Catalog Autumn 2001 p57 #43
1822/23	Mitchell & Sons	Glasgow	Lemon strainer, no details	Sotheby's NY USA October 1990 #126
1823/24	JM	Glasgow	Strainer, wavy shells	Shrubsole 1993
1825/26	Robert Gray & Son	Glasgow	Strainer, oval flattened bowl, gadrooned rim, heavy Old English piercing, cast lyre form handles, shell terminals, positioning studs	Hyman Collection - Colonial Williamsburg L1988-138
1826/24	Robert Gray & Son	Glasgow	Lemon strainer, one handle and a clip, decorated rim	Private Collection
1827/28	D C Rait	Glasgow	Lemon strainer, harp shaped handles, flowered rim	National Museums of Scotland MEQ 56
1830/31	Robert Gray & Son	Glasgow	Strainer, oval with egg and dart border between lyre handles, 12" long, 7oz 1d	Sotheby's NY USA 1997 #245
1830/31	*Robert Gray & Son*	*Glasgow*	*Lemon strainer*	*National Museums of Scotland MEQ 744*
1832/33	D C Rait	Glasgow	Strainer, 2 handled, no details	ADC Heritage NYC US 1993
1857/58	JW	Edinburgh	Strainer, King's pattern, no details	Elizabeth Austin, Charleston SC USA 1993
1905/06	Hamilton & Inches	Edinburgh	Lemon squeezer, 7 1/8" di, 7.2oz	Nicholas Shaw Catalog Winter 2002/03 p89

Tankards

Plate 44. A Tankard 1695/96 by Alexander Forbes, Edinburgh.
Courtesy of S. J. Shrubsole, NY USA.

TANKARDS

YEAR	MAKER	LOCATION	DESCRIPTION	SOURCE
1663-81	Edward Cleghorne I	Edinburgh	Peg Tankard, Scandinavian type, 3 claw and ball feet, lower body heavily chased, foliate thumbpiece	Finlay 1991 # 49 Scottish Art Academy Exhibit 1939 #965 Stirling-Maxwell Collection
1685/86	James Cockburn	Edinburgh	Tankards, pair, lion thumb pieces, 7" ht, 65oz 10d	Antiques Magazine March 1960 vol 77 Sotheby's March 24, 1960 #37 Christie's June 9, 1943 #65 Thomas Lumley Collection One in Huntley House Museum Edinburgh HH3529/70 (stolen) One in National Museums of Scotland MEQ 1597
1690 ca	Robert Cruikshank	Aberdeen	Tankard, plain, on reeded base, scroll handle, engraved	Finlay 1991 #40
1695 ca	James Cockburn	Edinburgh	Tankard, eagle like thumbpieces, 31oz 3d	Connoisseur Magazine April 1955 Advertisement picture
1695/96	Alexander Forbes	Edinburgh	Tankard, gadrooned base and cover, ram's horn spiral thumbpiece, 8 ¼" ht, 42.5oz	BFAC 1901 B.43 (from Grimdex) J. P. Morgan Collection #123 Sotheby's NY USA 2002 #158 Shrubsole NY USA 2005 #03-06
1695/96	James Cockburn	Edinburgh	Tankard, fully marked, mm 4X's on handle, 8 ¾" ht, 43oz 10d	Jackson vol II, p 768 Sotheby's NY USA October 28, 1992 #339 Christie's July 19, 1907 #166 The Maple Swan Collection
1697/98	Mungo Yorstoun	Edinburgh	Tankard, gadrooned base and lid, cockscrew thumbpiece, Arms, crest and motto, fluted baluster finial, 8" ht, 35oz	Christie's June 23, 1976 #109
1697/98	Robert Bruce	Edinburgh	Tankard, decorated cut card work, gadrooning, 2 rat tails on handle, 8 ½"	Clayton Dictionary p 400 #606 Finlay 1991 #58 National Museums of Scotland MEQ 1159
1698/99	John Seatoun	Edinburgh	Tankard, large, no details	Finlay 1991 text p121 Private Collection UK

YEAR	MAKER	LOCATION	DESCRIPTION	SOURCE
1699/1700	Robert Bruce	Edinburgh	Tankard, cut card work, foliate top, acorn finial, Arms, 7 ¼" ht, 30oz	Sotheby's Oct 23, 1991 #113 Sotheby's NY USA Nov 21, 1997 Hyman Collection - Colonial Williamsburg Antiques Magazine Aug 1998 p195
1699/1700	Thomas Ker	Edinburgh	Tankard, gadrooned border, rat tail handle, vase shaped finial, 7 ¼" ht, 30oz 19d	Christie's May 20, 1904 #46 Christie's June 8, 1921 #35 Wilson and Sharpe
1699 ca	Thomas Cumming	Glasgow	Tankard, molded domed lid, double knopped finial, gadrooned border, scroll handled with applied beaded spine and scrolled thumbpiece, tapering cylindrical sides, reeded applied girdle on gadrooned foot, also engraved armorials and later inscription, marked on base and cover, 7 7/8" ht, 30oz 16d	Sotheby's January 28, 1971 #100
1700/01	Edward Penman	Edinburgh	Tankard, gadrooned lid and base, cut card work on girdle, elaborate thumbpiece	Finlay 1991 #49
1700/01	John Seatoun	Edinburgh	Tankard, 34.3oz	How's Notes on Antique Silver, 1942 vol II, p8 Queen Charlotte Loan Exhibition 1929
1701/02	Thomas Ker	Edinburgh	Tankard, no details	Finlay 1991 text p21 Private Collection UK
1701/02	George Scott Assayer – James Penman	Edinburgh	Tankard, no details	Jackson Marks p 544
1702/03	John Seatoun	Edinburgh	Tankard, plain tapering cylindrical body, girdle, cut card work on top, gadrooned base, initials	Holland p85 Sotheby's November 18, 1965 #180
1702/03	Robert Inglis Assayer – James Penman	Edinburgh	Tankard, possible earlier date letter (misread?), crest and motto of Gordon of Knockspock, no picture	Sotheby's London 1991 #70 Christie's May 22, 1991 Christie's Edinburgh November 13, 1991 #281 Christie's Edinburgh April 29 #72
1703/04	Robert Inglis	Edinburgh	Tankard, gadrooned feet and cover, baluster finial, rib scroll handle 7 ¼" ht	Seaford House Exhibition 1929 #526 Private Collection UK

YEAR	MAKER	LOCATION	DESCRIPTION	SOURCE
1703/04	Thomas Ker	Edinburgh	Tankard, plain, tapering cylindrical body, applied reeded girdle, flat lid, baluster finial, handle with beaded rat tail, plain reeded foot, 7 ½" ht, 31oz	Scottish Art Review 1953, vol IV #4 Bell of Aberdeen
1704/05	John Seatoun Assayer – Patrick Murray	Edinburgh	Tankard, initials in foliate on front, repairs to cover, 6 ½" ht, 31oz	Sotheby's NY Dec 15, 1988 p180
1704/05	John Seatoun	Edinburgh	Tankard, slightly domed cover, cut card work on top, handle and thumbpiece, decorated leaves, gadrooned border, 31oz 9d	Christie's February 3, 1910 #138 Connoisseur Magazine 1926 vol 76 #304 advertisement
1704/05	Edward Penman	Edinburgh	Tankard, gadrooned foliate foot, high foliate thumbpiece, with cut card work, 37oz	Scottish Art Review Vol III #4 Bell of Aberdeen National Museums of Scotland 1955.61
1705 ca	John Luke II	Glasgow	Tankard, 8 1/8" ht	Private Collection UK
1705 ca	Robert Inglis	Edinburgh	Tankard, later inscription underneath, 8" ht, 25oz 13d	Sotheby's February 28, 1991 #217
1705/06	Alexander Forbes	Edinburgh	Tankard, straight sided, tapering cylindrical, applied girdle, high domed lid, compressed ball finial, foliate thumbpiece, 10 ¼" ht, 50.6oz	Sotheby's February 20, 1964 #85 Finlay 1991 #67 National Museums of Scotland MEQ 1568
1706/07	Edward Penman	Edinburgh	Tankard, engraved with the Edinburgh coat of arms, gift to William Neilson, June 1710, 4 7/8" ht, 3 7/8" di top	Huntley House Museum Edinburgh HH1471/53
1707/08	John Luke II	Glasgow	Tankard, engraved "The gift of the – Woolen Manufactors of Glasgow to Thomas Manaden", 7 ½" ht, 29oz	Christie's Dec 11, 1923 #99
1707/08	Patrick Murray I	Edinburgh	Tankard, plain tapering cylindrical body, applied girdle, stepped dome finial, ball and button finial, corkscrew thumbpiece, scroll handle with beaded rat tail, 2 adorsed coat of arms in oval escutcheons, betrothal initials, scratch weight under base 40:7, Arms of Hope, 8" ht, 38oz	Christie's January 29, 1999 #20
1707/08	Patrick Murray I	Edinburgh	Tankard, later spout added, slightly tapering form, heavy molded base rim, midband, engraved coat-of-arms under spout, domed hinged lid, with baluster finial, scroll thumbpiece S-scroll handle with applied rat-tail, inscribed on bottom as presented by "the Coney Island Jockey Club" and date 1902, scratch weight 40:7, 8" ht, 39oz 10d, note: this could be the previous tankard restored or a mate to the prior tankard by this maker	Sotheby's NY USA 1998 #322

YEAR	MAKER	LOCATION	DESCRIPTION	SOURCE
1708/09	Henry Bethune	Edinburgh	Tankard, no details	Jackson Marks p545
1709/10	John Seatoun	Edinburgh	Tankard, Arms of Hepburn quartering Rutherford impaling Suttie, cylindrical domed cover, acorn finial, 8 ½" ht, 43oz	Christie's November 28, 1979 #42 Christie's February 28, 1934 #82
1709/10	James Tait	Edinburgh	Peg tankard, tapering cylindrical form, acorn finial, domed cover, 8 1/3" ht	Scottish Art Academy Exhibition 1939 #913
1709/10	Colin McKenzie	Edinburgh	Tankard, arms, crest and motto "Ense et…", bulbous body tucked in at base	Holland p 217 Sotheby's April 16, 1953 #162 Finlay 1991 #67
1709/10	Colin McKenzie	Edinburgh	Tankard, no details	National Museums of Scotland 1953.172
1709/10	Robert Bruce	Edinburgh	Tankard, large, no details	Private Collection UK
1710/11	Henry Bethune	Edinburgh	Tankard, tapering cylindrical body, on molded spreading foot, reeded applied girdle, stepped domed lid, acorn finial, scroll handle, applied rat tail, armorials, pouring lip added at a later date, 7 7/8" ht, 27oz	Christie's London March 18, 1986 #224
1710/11	Patrick Turnbull	Edinburgh	Tankard, tapering cylindrical body, applied molded reeded girdle, of spreading stepped domed and reeded foot, cockscrew thumbpiece, no finial, scroll handle with applied rat tail, 7 ½" ht, 33.6oz	Sotheby's Edinburgh April 28, 1992 #104 The Maple Swan Collection
1711/12	James Mitchelson	Edinburgh	Tankard, tapering cylindrical body, engrave with 2 sets of armorials, one with supported, the other between crossed foliate sprays, below the reeded girdle, double dome cover, acorn finial, scroll handle, 8 ½" ht, 31oz	Sotheby's Gleneagles August 29, 1983 #508
1711/12	Colin McKenzie	Edinburgh	Tankard, stepped cover, baluster finial, slightly shaped body, 8 ½" ht, 40oz 8d	Christie's June 24, 1981 #73 Christie's March 20, 1963 #94 Connoisseur Magazine May 1953 Noble Collection Provenance of Pamela Campbell
1715 ca	James Ker over striking another maker Assayer Edward Penman over struck by Hugh Gordon	Edinburgh	Tankard, circular cartouche enclosing monogram and earl's coronet, tapering cylindrical body, girdle, stepped domed lid, baluster bun finial, 8 ½" ht, 40.1oz	Sotheby's Scone Palace April 10, 1978 #98

YEAR	MAKER	LOCATION	DESCRIPTION	SOURCE
1715/16	John Seatoun	Edinburgh	Tankard, mid rib, acorn finial, domed cover, 8" ht, 25oz 5d	Chris April 24, 1929 #54 Park Lane Exhibition 1929 #250 Private Collection UK
1715/16	William Ged Assayer – Edward Penman	Edinburgh	Tankard, tapering cylindrical form, with girdle, initials "WC/MC", 7 ½" ht, 36.3oz	Apollo April vol 95 p346 Sotheby's February 3, 1972 #167 How of Edinburgh JH Bourdon-Smith Catalog 2004 vol 45 p19
1716/17	Colin McKenzie	Edinburgh	Tankard, plain, tapering, cylindrical, spreading circle foot, scroll handle, mid rib, corkscrew thumbpiece, stepped cover, acorn finial, 8 ½" ht, 37oz	Christie's London UK Oct 19, 1988 #204
1716/17	Colin McKenzie Assayer – Edward Penman	Edinburgh	Tankard, molded pedestal foot, tapering body, scroll handle, stepped lid, acorn finial, 8 ½" ht, 37.2oz	Bonhams Sale 10914, #33
1716/17	James Mitchelson	Edinburgh	Tankard, tapering cylindrical body, on molded foot, reeded girdle, stepped domed lid, acorn finial, foliate thumbpiece, scroll handle with rat tail, Arms, crest and motto "CURO DUM QUIESCO" of Maxwell, 8 ½" ht, 40oz	Christie's Glasgow March 29, 1983 #91 Shaw Collection
1716/17	Colin McKenzie	Edinburgh	Tankard, plain form, straight sided, scroll handle, flattened spreading foot, stepped lid, acorn finial, 8 ½" ht, 37.2oz	Christie's London UK 1999 #262 Nicholas Shaw Catalog Winter 2002/03 p82
1717/18	Henry Bethune	Edinburgh	Tankard, tapering, cylindrical, applied girdle, acorn finial, Arms of Rigg of Dounfield, 8 ½" ht, 36.8oz	Sotheby's May 3, 1962 Antiques Magazine vol 83 p68 Shrubsole advertisement
1717/18	Patrick Turnbull	Edinburgh	Tankard, tapering cylindrical body, on spreading reeded foot, applied girdle, engraved with Arms for the Earl of Hopetoun, stepped domed lid, acorn finial, handle with rat tail leaf capped thumbpiece, lid and base engraved with a flower, 8 ¾" ht, 48oz	Clayton Christie's Book p 132 Christie's June 15, 1977 #127
1717/18	*Patrick Turnbull*	*Edinburgh*	*Tankard, no picture*	*Antiques Magazine vol 116, p84* *Shrubsole advertisement*
1717/18	William Ged	Edinburgh	Tankard, cylindrical, mid rib, domed cover, acorn finial, leaf thumbpiece, rat tail on handle, 44oz	Christie's July 26, 1938 #266 Sotheby's April 24, 1958 #148 Jessop Antiques
1719/20	Robert Inglis	Edinburgh	Tankard, marked on body and lid, slightly tapering, cylindrical girdle, 2/3 way down the body, volute thumbpiece, domed lid, 7" ht, 25oz 2d	Sotheby's Gleneagles Aug 27, 1979 #260

YEAR	MAKER	LOCATION	DESCRIPTION	SOURCE
1720 ca	Robert Luke	Glasgow	Tankard, plain cylindrical body, applied molded girdle, on spreading base, domed lid, acorn finial, leaf shaped thumbpiece, double scroll handle, scratch weight "34 Ou 5 dr", 8 ½" ht, 34oz 12d	Sotheby's Hopetoun House April 26, 1988 #66 Sotheby's Nov 17, 1988 #101 Sotheby's Gleneagles Aug 31 – Sept 1, 1987 # 286
1720 ca	Robert Luke	Glasgow	Tankard, smaller size, tapered cylindrical body, reeded girdle, double scroll handle, hinged domed lid, acorn finial, molded base, 8 ½" ht, 34oz 15d	Scottish Art Review vol VII 1959 p37 #2 Bell of Aberdeen advertisement Sotheby's April 24, 1958 #149 Sotheby's June 19, 1955 #104
1720 ca	Johan Got-helf Bilsings	Glasgow	Tankard, miniature	Private Collection UK
1720/21	Henry Bethune	Edinburgh	Tankard, slightly bulbous form on molded circular, late arms of Ogilvy above reeded girdle, domed cover, acorn finial, open work corkscrew thumbpiece, reverse scroll handle, 8 ½" ht, 42oz	Christie's Edinburgh April 27, 1988 #61
1722/23	Charles Dickson I or Charles Duncan	Edinburgh	Tankard, straight sided, stepped lid, acorn finial, coronet, crest and motto of Hope, 8 ¾" – 9" ht, 41.9oz	Christie's June 15, 1977 #128 Bonhams The Scottish Sale August 21, 2003 #45 Nicholas Shaw Antiques 2004
1722/23	Alexander Kincaid	Edinburgh	Tankard, tapering cylindrical body, initials above applied molded reeded low girdle, on spreading domed foot, reeded acorn finial, leaf thumbpiece, scroll handle with applied rat tail	Sotheby's May 17, 1913 #44
1724/25	James Tait	Edinburgh	Tankard, shaped body, domed cover, acorn finial, shield with later monogram, foliate thumbpiece, scroll handle, 36oz	Christie's July 9, 1954 #146 Scottish Art Review 1955 vol V, p41 #3 Bell of Aberdeen advertisement Shaw Collection Christie's Glasgow March 29, 1983 #90 Christie's Edinburgh November 21, 1990 #43
1725 ca	William Aytoun Assayer Edward Penman	Edinburgh	Tankard, no details	William Walter Ltd, London 1991
1725 ca	Not available	Edinburgh	Tankard, plain, center finial	Waldron p633

YEAR	MAKER	LOCATION	DESCRIPTION	SOURCE
1725 ca	Robert Luke	Glasgow	Tankard, slightly bulbous body, tucked in on a broad low base, domed stepped lid with a bell finial on stem, scroll handle, full armorials, opposite handle with supporters, arms include three crowns, 35.2oz	Connoisseur Magazine 1950 vol 125 p60 How of Edinburgh advertisement
1725/26	James Tait	Edinburgh	Tankard, no details	The Maple Swan Collection
1726/27	Not available	Edinburgh	The "Small Hopes" Tankard, no details, no mm	Private Collection UK
1728/29	James Mitchelson	Edinburgh	Tankard, with arms	Sotheby's March 7, 1957 #149
1729/30	Charles Dickson I or Charles Duncan Assayer – Edward Penman	Edinburgh	Tankard, initial "M/JL/KR" on front, acorn finial, 8 ¼" ht, 32oz 17d	Burlington Magazine 1970 vol 112, p64 Sotheby's November 19, 1970 #228
1729/30	*Charles Dickson I or Charles Duncan*	*Edinburgh*	*Tankard, no picture*	*Christie's February 15, 1933 #169*
1729/30	*Charles Dickson I or Charles Duncan*	*Edinburgh*	*Tankard, no details*	*The Maple Swan Collection*
1730 ca	Robert Luke	Edinburgh	Tankard, large bulbous body, chased band of scrolls, corkscrew and leaf on top, 9" ht, 44oz	Christie's February 24, 1937 #72
1730 ca	Robert Luke	Glasgow	Tankard, exceptionally large	Private Collection UK
1730 ca	Robert Cruickshank	Aberdeen	Tankard, large straight sided, tapering cylindrical	King's College, Aberdeen
1730/31	James Mitchelson	Edinburgh	Tankard, baluster body, engraved with a monogram in a scrolling foliate cartouche, double scroll handle, domed lid, baluster finial, on spreading base, silver added where a later pouring spout was removed, patch marked with modern hallmarks, 8 ½" ht, 30.5oz	Sotheby's December 5, 1968 # Simon Kaye Antiques
1743 ca	James Glen	Glasgow	Tankard, quart capacity, baluster body, spiral handle, 15.2oz	Breadalbane Collection Sale 1935 #124
1750 ca	Not available	Aberdeen	Tankard, no details	National Museums of Scotland MEQ 640
1765 ca	William Craw	Canongate	The Trotter Tankard, engraved opposite the handle with the arms of Trotter of Mortonhall impaling Trotter Charterhall, the lid with the Trotter crest below the motto	Clayton Dictionary p 172, #4 and p183 #15 Huntley House Museum Edinburgh

YEAR	MAKER	LOCATION	DESCRIPTION	SOURCE
1776/77	Patrick Robertson	Edinburgh	Tankard, quart size, no details	National Museums of Scotland MEQ 1184
1785/86	Patrick Robertson	Edinburgh	Tankard, cylindrical, flat hinged lid with overhanging gadrooned edge, reeded bands on sides, 6 ¾" ht, 32oz	Sotheby's October 31, 1974 #34 Finlay 1991 #100
1785/86	*Patrick Robertson*	*Edinburgh*	*Tankard, lidded, no details*	*National Museums of Scotland MEQ 1336*
1800-20ca	AD, CSB	Arbroath	Tankard, fish head shaped, mid rib, domed cover, monogram, 9 ½" ht, 47oz	Christie's March 11, 1958 #51
1810ca	John Keith	Banff	Tankard for beer, no details	National Museums of Scotland K.2003.932
1810/11	Not available	Edinburgh	Tankard, slightly tapering cylindrical, with two horizontally reeded bands, hinged lid with a modified gadrooned motif border, C-handle, 4 ½" ht, 18.3oz, mm rubbed	Christie's London UK 2000 #365
1854/55	James McKay	Edinburgh	Tankard, loop handle, 5 7/8" ht	Bonhams London UK 2001 #415

Tazzas

Plate 45. A Tazza 1698/99 by John Yorstoun, Edinburgh.
Courtesy of The Phoenix Collection. Photograph by Janice M Dietert.

YEAR	MAKER	LOCATION	DESCRIPTION	SOURCE
			TAZZAS	
1665-70 ca	Alexander Scott	Edinburgh	The Strathmore Tazza. Originally a tazza or raised fruit dish, mentioned in Lord Strathmore's inventory of 1695	Finlay 1991 #52 Seaford House Exhibition 1929 #15 National Museums of Scotland MEQ 799
1669-71 Or 1674/75	William Law Deacon Alexander Reid	Edinburgh	Tazza on foot, raised reeded edge, semi-gadrooned rim, Arms of Dick impaling Nairne, simple non-gadrooned foot, 11 1/5" di, 17oz	Finlay 1991 #51 Sotheby's London June 1989 #207 Sotheby's July 18, 1987 #207 Sotheby's April 8, 1954 #86 National Museums of Scotland MEQ 1619 1990
1675-77	James Penman Deacon William Law	Edinburgh	Tazza on foot, center laurel wreath with initials "WH/ID", Arms of Hogg of Cammo, 13" di, 21.5oz	Apollo November 1966 vol 84 p124 How of Edinburgh Sotheby's auction November 17, 1966 Christie's March 7, 1894 #137 National Museums of Scotland MEQ 856
1683ca	Robert Brock	Glasgow	Tazza, circular on trumpet foot, cut out foot, gadrooned rim, 9 7/8" di	Scottish Art Academy Exhibition 1939 #950 Collection of Mrs. Stuart-Stevenson
1692/93	James Cockburn	Edinburgh	Tazzas, pair, on foot, gadrooned, 9 ¼" di, 24oz both	Brett p499 Sotheby's Gleneagles August 28, 1969 #176
1695/96	Robert Bruce	Edinburgh	Tazzas, pair, small, each with bold gadroon border, on trumpet foot, underside with initials, 5 ½" di, 8.1oz both	Sotheby's April 15, 1971 #179 Bank of Scotland Collection Edinburgh
1697/98	Robert Inglis	Edinburgh	Tazza, plain foot, gadrooned border, 10" di	Jackson 2 vols p268-269 fig 285
1698/99	John Yorstoun	Edinburgh	Tazza, on spreading pedestal foot, plain but with gadrooned border, underside engraved "B", 8 ¾" di, 12.5oz	Brian Beet Sotheby's August 30-31, 1993 #151 JH Bourdon-Smith London 1994

YEAR	MAKER (continued)	LOCATION	DESCRIPTION	SOURCE The Phoenix Collection
1698/99	John Yorstoun Assayer – James Penman	Edinburgh	Tazza, rope twist gadrooning, stepped domed foot with flanged base, monogrammed "B" on underside, 8 ¾" di, 12oz 4d, note: this is possibly a mate to the prior one based on the direct family sale, alternatively there is only one tazza that changed hands several times in 1993	Family Descent Butterfields Auctioneers Corp San Francisco, CA USA 1993 #4707
1699/1700	Robert Brock	Glasgow	Tazza, no details	National Museums of Scotland 1952.50
1700/01	John Seatoun Assayer – James Penman	Edinburgh	Tazza, circular, engraved with a coat-of-arms, and later with a differing crest, on a spreading foot, with gadrooned borders, engraved beneath with the initial "S", 11" di, 21oz, Arms of Wyndham impaling Leveson quartering Gower, for Catherine lady Wyndham (b. 1670)	Christie's London UK 2005 #454
1703/04	Patrick Murray I	Edinburgh	Tazzas, pair, gadrooned border, later armorials and flat chasing, later added 4 feet, 15 ¼" di, 120.5oz both	Sotheby's July 24, 1980 #135
1704/05	Thomas Ker Assayer Edward Penman	Edinburgh	Tazzas, pair, later engraved over erased coronet above interlocking script initials over garland "KD" or "DK", 11 ½" di, 57.9oz	Sotheby's Book p589 Sotheby's March 16, 1961 #113 How of Edinburgh
1705/06	Alexander Forbes	Edinburgh	Tazzas, pair, no details	Private Collection UK
1705/06	George Scott Jr	Edinburgh	Tazza, on central spreading foot, molded border, initials "MM/L/MG", en suite with a pair of cups, 9 ¾" di	Christie's Feb 28, 1973 #170 Christie's Negative #739757 Garrards London
1706/07	Colin McKenzie	Edinburgh	Tazza, on foot, engraved with coat of arms between knight and horse supporters, with molded border, 8 ½" di, 17.4oz	Christie's June 23, 1976 #77
1706/07	Thomas Cleghorne III Assayer James Penman	Edinburgh	Tazza, on trumpet foot, later crest and motto, molded plain border, crest of crescent moon, motto "ACTOR DUM PROCREDIOR", 10 ½" di, 24oz	Christie's March 23, 1978 #18 Christie's Negative #900736
1707/08	Walter Scott	Edinburgh	Tazza, plain, on trumpet foot, molded border, initials, 5 ¾" di, 6.3oz	Christie's April 23, 1970 #77 National Museums of Scotland MEQ 1073 1972.266
1708/09	John Seatoun	Edinburgh	Tazzas, pair, deep, or fruit dishes	Finlay 1991 #66
1708/09	Robert Bruce	Edinburgh	Tazza, plain, everted, trumpet shaped foot, 10" di, 16.3oz	Christie's April 10, 1934 #120

YEAR	MAKER	LOCATION	DESCRIPTION	SOURCE
1708/09	Patrick Turnbull	Edinburgh	Tazzas, pair, circular, depressed centers, crest and motto, on spreading foot, 11 ¼" di	Scottish Art Academy Exhibition 1939 #894 J Cathcart White Collection
1708/09	Patrick Turnbull	Edinburgh	Tazzas, pair, or stands, plain, no details, (Note: probably either the White Collection or the Breadalbane Collection pair)	National Museums of Scotland 1943, 251 + a
1708/09	Patrick Turnbull	Edinburgh	Tazza, stemmed, molded rim, on expanding stem and expanding foot, 9 ½" di, 21.2oz	Breadalbane Collection Sale 1935 #366
1709/10	Not available	Edinburgh	Tazzas, pair, on 3 later applied paw feet, molded border, center with Arms of Hope, 10 ¾" di, 66oz	Christie's June 15, 1977 #132
1709/10	Thomas Ker	Edinburgh	Tazzas, pair, central coat of arms	Linlithgow Collection Christie's London June 15, 1977 #132
1710 ca	George Robertson	Aberdeen	Tazza, marked BF, BF, 3 castles, Gothic a or e, I:J:R:I:J:F, engraved "AGNOSCAR ESENTU", over a Maltese cross crest in center	Aberdeen Museums and Galleries, ABDAG 001001
1710 ca	James Mitchelson	Edinburgh	Tazza, plain, on trumpet foot, molded rim, 9 ¾" di, 25oz 6d	Christie's March 19, 1934, #143 Gardner and How of Edinburgh Collection How of Edinburgh Collection
1710 ca	William Ged	Edinburgh	Tazza, on trumpet foot, plain molded border, underside with 2 sets of initials, 9 ¾" di, 18.8oz	Sotheby's April 15, 1971 Thomas Lumley Ltd
1710/11	John Seatoun	Edinburgh	Tazzas, pair, slightly raised arms. Arms of Johnston of Settam, 9 ¾" di, 37oz 5d both (18oz 12d ea)	Christie's December 17, 1930 #60
1710/11	Colin McKenzie	Edinburgh	Tazza, with arms, crest and motto	Finlay 1991 #69
1710/11	Colin McKenzie	Edinburgh	Tazza, arms crest and motto "ENSE ET ANIMO"	Sotheby's April 16, 1953 #161 National Museums of Scotland MEQ 1983.22
1710-16	Colin McKenzie	Edinburgh	Tazzas, pair, small, crest with motto below, no arms, same family but different tazzas from the above single, 5 ½" di, 12.7oz	Sotheby's April 16, 1953 #160
1710/11	I A (or IS)	Edinburgh	Tazzas, pair, 2 crescents above one below, arms and motto, repairs beneath engraving, mm could be John Seatoun, 10" di, 36oz 10d	Christie's NY USA February 11, 1982 #266

YEAR	MAKER	LOCATION	DESCRIPTION	SOURCE
1712/13	John Seatoun	Edinburgh	Tazzas, set of 3, 9 ¾" and 6 ¼"di, 33oz 5d for all	Christie's April 27, 1942 #101 How of Edinburgh Collection
1717/18	Alexander Kincaid	Edinburgh	Tazza, on central spreading foot, Arms of Lockhart, 8 ¼" di, 17oz	Christie's Glasgow March 29, 1983 #97 Scottish Art Review 1955 vol V, p41 #3 Bell of Aberdeen advertisement Christie's Edinburgh November 21, 1990 #44 Christie's Scotland November 14, 1985 #322
1717/18	Not available	Edinburgh	Tazza, or salver, carries variants of the assay master's mark, castle and date letter as noted in Jackson, apparently no mm	Jackson Marks p546 note
1717/18	Colin Campbell	Edinburgh	Tazza, on central spreading foot, plain molded rim, underside with initials "IW IT", 11 7/8" di, 24oz	Sotheby's November 10-11, 1984 #692
1719/20	Colin McKenzie	Edinburgh	Tazzas, pair, on capstan foot, undersides with contemporary initials and scratch weights, 5 ½" di, 12oz both	Park Lane Exhibition 1929 #464 Sotheby's NY USA April 1990 #444 The Maple Swan Collection
1725/26	Henry Bethune	Edinburgh	Tazza, plain, on central foot, waisted stem, underside with initials "G.D.W.", 11 ½" di, 27oz	Christie's May 16, 1916 #13 Christie's NY USA October 1984 #324
1726/27	James Mitchelson	Edinburgh	Tazza form dish with a crest, 8" di, 13.8oz	Christie's June 11, 1937 #118
1730 ca	Robert Luke	Glasgow	Tazza, plain, molded edge, center with circular matted ground, arms, crest and motto "BONIS OMNIA BONA", 9 ¼", 18.4oz	Sotheby's Gleneagles August 1987 #281
1730/31	James Ker	Edinburgh	Tazza, on central spreading foot, circular with slightly raised edge, initial "K" in center, possibly later, 9 ¼" di, 19.2oz	JH Bourdon-Smith Catalog 2004 p17 #45
1730/31	James Ker	Edinburgh	*Tazza, listed as a waiter, on spool central foot, molded rim, later engraved initials in the center, 20 oz*	Lyon & Turnbull, Edinburgh UK 2003 #366
1731/32	James Tait	Edinburgh	Tazza, on central foot, crest and motto of Haldane, 5 ¼" id, 6.5oz	Sotheby's October 29, 1959 #64 Shaw Collection Christie's Glasgow March 29, 1983 #98 Christie's Edinburgh May 26,

YEAR	MAKER (continued)	LOCATION	DESCRIPTION	SOURCE 1998 #66
1731/32	James Tait	Edinburgh	Tazza, Leith family tazza, few details, motto "Trustie to the End" above a cross	Aberdeen Museums and Galleries ABDAG 001116
1735 ca	George Cooper	Aberdeen	Tazza, plain, on central foot	Private Collection
1740 ca	Alexander Forbes	Aberdeen	Tazza, marks – AF, 3 castles, letter C	Private Collection UK
1955/56	Hamilton & Inches	Edinburgh	Tazza, no details	National Museums of Scotland H.1996.151

Tea

Plate 46. Some Components used in Serving Tea. Sugar Bowl 1731/32 by Archibald Ure, Edinburgh; Cream Boat 1740/41 by James Mitchell, Edinburgh. Salver 1739/40 by James Mitchelson, Edinburgh; Examples of Scots Fiddle Teaspoons by Ebenezer Oliphant, James Hewitt and WM, Edinburgh. Courtesy of The Phoenix Collection. Photograph by Janice M Dietert.

Tea Caddies

Plate 47. Tea Caddy 1792/93 by William Robertson, Edinburgh.
Courtesy of private collector. Photograph by Janice M Dietert

YEAR	MAKER	LOCATION	DESCRIPTION	SOURCE
	TEA CADDIES		***TEA***	
1685 ca	James Cockburn	Edinburgh	Tea caddy, hexagonal, with landscape scene, engraved around the panels	Finlay 1991 #23
1718/19	Henry Bethune	Edinburgh	Tea caddy, octagonal with stepped cover, crest 4 3/8"long, 4 ¾" ht	Fogg Art Museum, Harvard University, Hutchinson Collection 1949.114.3
1720 ca	Johan Got-helf-Bilsings	Glasgow	Tea caddy, oblong Queen Anne, applied reeded borders, cylindrical domed cover, engraved with coat of arms of Ferrier, probably impaling Galbraith with baroque cartouche, chased on shoulders with band of stylized foliage, cover engraved with a crest, fully marked on base and cover, mm 2X's, 4 ½" ht, 8oz	Christie's March 29, 1983 #51 Shaw Collection
1728/29	William Aytoun	Edinburgh	Tea caddies, pair, in later silver mounted shagreen box, oblong with molded borders, slightly raised covers conforming in outline with later crest below a scrolling motto, 31oz	Christie's March 22, 1978 #98 National Museums of Scotland 1255-57
1730 ca	George Cooper	Aberdeen	Tea caddies, octagonal pair, narrow molded bases, domed cap covers, baluster finials, each engraved with 2 baronial cartouches, one enclosing a later initial and sprays of flowers on the angles and tops, 15oz 13d	Christie's March 15, 1961
1730 ca	George Cooper	Aberdeen	Tea caddies, pair, rectangular upright body, canted corners, later engraved floral sprays and cartouches with script initial "M", pull off domed lids, turned finials, scratch initials on base script "GJB", 4 ¾" ht, 3 1/3" wide, 2 1/8" deep, 15oz	Lyon & Turnbull August 20, 2003 Bell of Aberdeen 1962 Sotheby's March 1, 1962
1730ca	George Cooper	Aberdeen	Tea caddies, pair (part of The Kirkhill Tea Service-five pieces), crest and motto of Gordon, based marked three towers, GC, Gothic A or E	Aberdeen Museums and Galleries ABDAG008505 and 008505 (acquired 1986)
1730 ca	*George Cooper*	*Aberdeen*	*Tea caddies, pair, part of a tea service*	*Connoisseur Magazine 1955 vol 135 p90*
1730 ca	George Cooper	Aberdeen	Tea caddy, octagonal, molded rim foot, similarly molded shoulder, circular stopper with baluster finial, engraved on side with script initial "B", engraved under base with initials "GR CF", 4 ½" ht, 9oz	Christie's March 29, 1983 #33 Provenance Shaw Collection Christie's July 3, 1984 #122
1730 ca	George Cooper	Aberdeen	Tea caddy, plain octagonal form, engraved on one side with crest and motto, detachable domed lid, marks are GC, 3 towers, gothic e, scratch weight 9:22, 4 ¾" ht, 9oz 17d	Sotheby's October 25, 1984 #269 Aberdeen Museums and Galleries ABDA G001004

YEAR	MAKER	LOCATION	DESCRIPTION	SOURCE
1735 ca	Robert Luke	Glasgow	Tea caddy, oval, with cover, chased floral and scroll bands, top and bottom of body	Finlay 1991 #107
1735 ca	George Cooper	Aberdeen	Tea caddies, pair, octagonal, in a wooden box	National Museums of Scotland L. 1980.S
1740 ca	George Cooper	Aberdeen	*Tea caddies, pair, octagonal, in a wooden box*	*National Museums of Scotland* MEQ 1590
1740 ca	Robert Luke	Glasgow	Tea caddie, no details	National Museums of Scotland MEQ 806
1745 ca	James Glen	Glasgow	Tea caddies, pair, rectangular, each on stepped molded foot, with band of flat chased flower heads and foliage to upper and lower body, stepped domed hinged lid with molded border and chased floral motif to center, side lock and key, 4 ½" ht, 20 oz both	Christie's April 12, 1983 #185 JH Bourdon-Smith Catalog Spring 1983
1750ca	James Glen	Glasgow	Tea caddies, pair, vase shaped, slightly elongated inverted pear form, shoulder decorated with deep chasing and repousse work, lids with similar band of chasing, large bud finials, Arms of the City of Glasgow, 27.1oz	How of Edinburgh, 1937, #102
1756/57	William Dempster or William Davie	Edinburgh	Tea caddies, pair, no details	Antiques Magazine vol 92 #268 Hammond advertisement
1761/62	William Dempster or William Davie	Edinburgh	Tea caddie, baluster ribbed, chased fruit and flower festoons, loose domed cover, molded foot, body with initial "M" 6 ½"ht, 8.7oz	Sotheby's October 17 1963 #29 How of Edinburgh
1762/63	William Dempster or William Davie	Edinburgh	Tea caddies, pair, inverted pear shape, engraved with the crest of Queen Elizabeth as Duchess, 5 ¼" ht	Queen's Silver p80, #24
1762/63	Alexander Gardner	Edinburgh	Tea caddies, set of 3, in original mahogany case, inverted pear bombe shaped bodies, low lids, all heavily chased, case on silver paw feet,	Apollo 1934 vol 20, p4 Bell of Aberdeen advertisement
1765/66	Not available	Edinburgh	Tea caddy, no details	Jackson Marks p969
1765/66	Patrick Robertson	Edinburgh	Tea caddies with case, no details	Jackson Marks p310
1765/66	Gilliland and Ker	Edinburgh	Tea caddie, oblong shape, raised flat-topped cover, ring finial, 3 7/8"ht, 6.1oz	Christie's March 19, 1975 #121
1770 ca	Milne & Campbell	Glasgow	Tea caddies with chased Chinese scene	Finlay 1991 #117 National Museums of Scotland MEQ 1068

YEAR	MAKER	LOCATION	DESCRIPTION	SOURCE
1770/71	Patrick Robertson	Edinburgh	Tea caddies, set of 3, oblong form with rounded corners, plain straight sides, reeded molded band at the foot and rim, covers with hinged fan-like tabs for finials, probably designed to fit in a case	Clayton Christie's p220 #7 Christie's November 24, 1976
1784/85	WD script William Davie or William Dempster	Edinburgh	Tea caddy, bright cut leaves and flowers	National Museums of Scotland MEQ 1191
1784/85	Alexander Spence	Edinburgh	Tea caddies, pair, oval, bright cut, with crest and motto of Halkett, hinged lids, 4 3/8" ht, 20.4oz	Nicholas Shaw Catalog Winter 2000
1789/90	Patrick Robertson	Edinburgh	Tea caddy, square, stepped lid, Arms of Wharton impaling McDuff quartering Duff, 4 ½" ht, 20.3 oz	Nicholas Shaw Catalog Autumn 1999 p54
1789/90	Alexander Spence	Edinburgh	Tea caddies, pair, each of oval form, body engraved with stylized bands and a crest within a navette-shaped panel, flat lockable flush hinged lid, oval urn finial, crest is a bird's head and neck, motto "SUFFICIT", 4 ¾", 19.5oz	Bonhams the Scottish Sale, August 21, 2003 #31
1792/93	William Robertson	Edinburgh	Tea caddy, oval dectagonal body, bands of bright cut decoration on top and bottom, vacant cartouche, domed hinged lid, ivory mushroom finial, 5 3/8" ht, 5" across, 11.3oz	eBay #6610400598 March 2006 London
1793/94	William Robertson	Edinburgh	Tea caddy, oval, flat hinged lid set with flower and leaf finial, led and body bright cut, front engraved with crest, an eagle flapping its wings, motto "ALTIORA PETO," original key, 5 ½" across, 4" ht	Private Collection
1795/96	W & P Cunningham I	Edinburgh	Tea caddy, with wood finial, vacant cartouche	National Museums of Scotland MEQ 1142
1795/96	*W & P Cunningham I*	*Edinburgh*	*Tea caddy, oval outline, swelling body with reeding top and bottom, sides chased in 3 bands of fluting and counter-fluting, vacant cartouche below the keyhole, dome lid with counter-fluting, block wooden finial*	*Finlay 1991 #101*
1801/02	W & P Cunningham I	Edinburgh	Tea caddy, double, beaded top edge	Apollo August 1969 vol 90 p2 Bell of Aberdeen advertisement
1801/02	W & P Cunningham I	Edinburgh	Tea caddy, double, lidded	National Museums of Scotland MEQ 1053-54
1802/03	James McKay	Edinburgh	Tea caddy, cube shaped, plain, reeded handle, crest 11oz	JH Bourdon-Smith London 1993
1802/03	John McDonald	Edinburgh	Tea caddy, rectangular with canted corners, body engraved with foliate and floral bands, cover with conforming decoration and wood pineapple finial, 4 ¾" ht, 9oz	Sotheby's London UK Mar 8, 2001 #532 Christie's NY USA 2004 #88

YEAR	MAKER	LOCATION	DESCRIPTION	SOURCE
1806/07	John McDonald	Edinburgh	Tea caddy, rectangular with canted corners, bright cut foliate and floral bands, wood pineapple finial, lock, 5" ht, 9oz 6d	Sotheby's London UK 2001 #532
1835/36	James McKay	Edinburgh	Tea caddy, of waisted casket form, engraved with strapwork on four cast feet, with lift-off cover, one cartouche with a presentation inscription, given to "Andrew Duncan by his brothers John and William", and dated 1st January 1846, the other cartouche with initials, 5 ¼" ht, 12oz	Christie's London UK 2002 #11
1835/36	TAF mark	Edinburgh assay	Tea caddy, no details	Sotheby's April 1989 #39
1844/45	William Cunningham	Edinburgh	Tea caddy, plain oblong body, griffin head crest, 12oz	JH Bourdon-Smith Catalog 1999 p50 #41
1895/96	Hamilton & Inches	Edinburgh	Tea caddy, no details	Bonhams London UK 2001 #427

Tea Kettles, Stands & Trays

Plate 48. The Kettle and Stand are 1758/59 by WD, probably William Dempster, Edinburgh. Courtesy of a private collector. Photograph by Janice M Dietert.

TEA KETTLES, KETTLE STANDS AND TRAYS

YEAR	MAKER	LOCATION	DESCRIPTION	SOURCE
1725/26	James Mitchelson	Edinburgh	Tea kettle with stand and lamp, insulated handle, curved spout, flattened spherical body, on 3 ball feet, stand like a strawberry dish, wood finial, crest and motto "AUGEOR DUM PROGREDIOR"	Apollo March 1973 vol 97, p2 Bell of Aberdeen advertisement National Museums of Scotland MEQ 1094
1727/28	Henry Bethune	Edinburgh	Tea kettle, stand and burner, compressed spherical body, flush lid with applied hinge, wooden knop, curved slightly flaring spout, 14 ½" ht, 89.9oz all, kettle 59.4oz, stand and burner 30.5oz	Private Collection UK
1729/30	Not available Assayer Archibald Ure	Edinburgh	Tea kettle and stand	Sotheby's June 8, 1959 #131
1731/32	James Mitchelson	Edinburgh	Tea kettle stand, circular with shaped rim, molded border, 10 points	Finlay 1991 #177 Wilson & Sharp Ltd
1731/32	James Mitchelson	Edinburgh	Tea kettle, flattened spherical body, simple curved spout, ball finial, silver handle, hanging lamp on chain, stand with rococo border on 3 cabriole legs that end in tall hoof feet, 54 oz	Christie's February 27, 1974 Clayton Christie's p152
1734/35	James Ker	Edinburgh	Tea kettle with stand, part of Hopetoun service, spherical body, chased lightly upper body and lid, wood ball finial, curved half fluted and half leaf capped spout, silver handle with fluting, insulated in center, arms below a coronet on body, lamp, stand with swag leaves, skirt connecting in center to the mouth of a human male face, on 3 leaf capped cabriole legs that end in hoof feet	Clayton Dictionary p419 National Museums of Scotland MEQ 1208-1211 MEQ 1207 a-c 1977, 6a-c
1734/35	William Aytoun	Edinburgh	Tea kettle and stand, compressed spherical tea kettle with stand and salver, stand on 3 shell and scroll feet, burner with domed hinged lid, the kettle later chased overall with scrolls, lattice-work, shells and foliage, with a part leather-covered swing handle and hinged flush lid, wooden ball finial, engraved twice with a coat of arms, stand unmarked, kettle patched, later Arms of Campbell of Succoth impaling Balbirnic for Archibald Campbell, 2nd Bt, 10 ¾" ht, 62oz	Christie's March 19, 1986 #234 Sotheby's Hopetoun House April 29, 1987 #59
1734/35	WI or IM in a plain oval William Jamieson or John Main	Edinburgh	Tea kettle, stand and burner, compressed body with later flame fluting top and bottom, flush lid with ivory mushroom finial, stand on 3 cabriole leaf topped legs ending in shell feet, festooned skirts, initials script "AA" below a coronet, 16 ½" ht	eBay #6612917586 March 2006
1735/36	William Aytoun	Edinburgh	Tea kettle, flattened spherical body, scrolled silver insulated handle, fluted curved spout, tall fall finial, stand with swag skirt of leaves, on "S" curved legs ending in shell feet, body rococo chased with decoration, 69oz	Antiques Magazine vol 41 p236 Bell of Aberdeen advertisement

YEAR	MAKER	LOCATION	DESCRIPTION	SOURCE
1736/37	James Mitchelson	Edinburgh	Tea kettle, slightly flattened spherical body, arms crest and motto, chased lightly with shells, leaves and diapering also on lid, wood finial, silver insulated handle, curved spout, lamp, stand with skirt of interlocking scrolls and circular plaque, on 3 "S" curved legs with shell insulated feet, tray with chased border and equipped with threaded central attachment for use as a silver table	National Museums of Scotland MEQ 638 & 639
1738/39	James Weems	Edinburgh	Tea kettle, no details	Antiques Magazine 1957 vol 71
1740ca	Robert Luke	Glasgow	Kettle and Stand, near spherical body, flat-chased with flowers, shells, and scrolls with two symmetrical cartouches, one with a crest and motto, slightly domed lid also chased, angular bud finial, foliated bird-neck spout, silver scroll swing handle with insulators, the stand on raised slender paw supports, with a pierced and cast apron featuring rococo masks, flowers and foliage pendant between, the detachable burner pendant on chains, marked on base, stand and burner, 15 ¾"ht, 93.8oz	Sotheby's Gleneagles August 30, 1982 #500
1748/49	James Weems	Edinburgh	Tea kettle, spherical, complete with stand and burner, 2 vacant asymmetrical cartouches within chased blossoms and scrolls, fluted spout, swing handle with shell and rococo mounts, flush hinged lid, wood finial, flat chased to match, stand with pendant looped ribbons between volute and hoof supports, burner suspended from chains, 12 ½" ht, 53oz all	Sotheby's Gleneagles August 27-28, 1979 #245
1749/50	William Aytoun Assayer Hugh Gordon	Edinburgh	Tea kettle, inverted pear shape, stand and burner, upper part of kettle chased with flowers, foliage, and scrolls on matted ground, fluted curved spout and domed cover, cone finial, scrolling swing handle, stand on 3 shell and scroll feet, pierced aprons between, 56oz	Christie's July 10-11, 1984 #331
1750ca	James Glen	Glasgow	Kettle on a Stand, inverted pear form, decorated round the shoulder with rococo flowers, foliage, etc., vacant cartouches, domed lid with bird finial, the stand with three leaf-capped scroll supports and shell feet, with a burner, 73oz	Scottish Art Review 1954 vol. V, # 1, p 40 Bell of Aberdeen advertisement
1750ca	James Glen	Glasgow	Kettle on Stand, inverted pear shaped body, shoulder chased with flowers and two rococo cartouches, one with a crest, with infant bacchanal finial, the stand on three hoof feet with floral apron	Shrubsole, NY 1981 E2081
1751/52	Ebenezer Oliphant	Edinburgh	Tea kettle and stand, inverted pear shaped body, chased around the shoulders with a cartouche, scrolls and foliage, cartouche with an inscription, domed lid with baluster finial, curved half-fluted leaf capped spout, stand with applied swags of scrolls and vines with rococo heads, on 3 leaf capped scroll legs ending in shell feet, possibly the one presented to James Stirling via the City of Glasgow for his report on the Clyde (Leadhills Reading Society)	Jackson Marks p549 Glasgow Exhibition 1911 vol I, p108 #21

YEAR	MAKER	LOCATION	DESCRIPTION	SOURCE
1752/53	Ebenezer Oliphant	Edinburgh	Kettle, stand and burner, inverted pear shape, upper body chased with a broad band of flowers and foliage on a matted ground, fluted leaf-capped curved spout, swing handle with caryatid emerging from the foliate scrolls, the domed lid decorated at the top and with foliate finial, the tripod topped with hound masks, complete with burner, marked on base of kettle and on stand, 15 ¾"ht, 74.8oz	Sotheby's June 29-30, 1981 #202
1752/53	Alexander Gardner	Edinburgh	Kettle, stand and lamp, inverted pear shaped body, shoulder chased with fruit, foliage and scrolls, bird's head spout, scroll swing handle, cone finial, the stand on three scroll and shell supports with pierced foliage and scroll aprons between, and with circular lamp, engraved with armorials, 58oz	Christie's March 31, 1971 #75
1753/54	Ker & Dempster Assayer Hugh Gordon	Edinburgh	Tea kettle and stand with lamp	Sotheby's NY USA 1981 #30
1753/54	Ker and Dempster	Edinburgh	Kettle and Stand, apparently London made with Ker and Dempster over striking the London maker's mark,	Probably existence
1753/54	William Gilchrist	Edinburgh	Tea kettle with stand, inverted pear shaped tapering body, domed lid, both heavily chased, artichoke finial, curved half fluted spout, silver handle with leaf capping, lamp, stand with heavy rococo leaf and flower skirt, 3 leaf capped "S" cabriole legs ending in shell feet, 73oz, probably awarded as a Leith race prize	Stirling Maxwell Collection Finlay 1991 #84 Lyon & Turnbull Edinburgh UK May 25, 2006 #338
1753/54	Robert Gordon	Edinburgh	Tea kettle, inverted pear body with dome lid, bird finial, multiscrolled insulated handle, chasing on upper body and lid, lamp, rococo skirt on stand, 3 "S" curved legs, leaf capped ending in shell feet	Apollo 1933 vol 17 pXIII How of Edinburgh advertisement
1755/56	William Dempster	Edinburgh	Tea kettle and stand, no details	National Museums of Scotland MEQ 1922.29a-b
1755/56	James Welsh Assayer Hugh Gordon	Edinburgh	Tea kettle, on stand with lamp, rococo chased pot with curved spout, cartouche, swing handle with reeded insulation on stand, on 3 feet, leaf capped knees to balls top 3 circular pad feet, skirt with flowers and leaves	Christie's NY USA April 2004 sale #1361 #107
1755/56	Ker and Dempster	Edinburgh	Kettle with tripod and burner, chased all over, presented from Archibald Stewart, Lord Provost, with crest and motto of Trotters of Dreghorn	Huntley House Museum, Edinburgh LR 60
1756/57	Robert Low	Edinburgh	Tea kettle, no details	Antiques Magazine 1959 vol 75
1756/57	James Welsh	Edinburgh	Tea kettle, 15" ht, 69oz	Christie's October 30, 1990 #223

YEAR	MAKER	LOCATION	DESCRIPTION	SOURCE
1758/59	William Dempster	Edinburgh	Tea kettle with stand and lamp, inverted pear body, domed lid, both chased, body with vacant cartouche, wood finial, curved spout with leaf end, insulated handle, 3 "S" curved leaf capped cabriole legs that end in shell feet	Private Collection
1786/87	Not available	Edinburgh	Tea kettle with swag decorations, no mm	National Museums of Scotland MEQ 872 1967.630
1789/90	Not available	Edinburgh	Tea kettle, oval, back and for the raffia-covered swag handle, no mm, 13 ½" long X 9" ht, 11 ½" ht with handle up, 52oz 12d	Private Collection How of Edinburgh
1835	James McKay	Edinburgh	Tea kettle and stand, elaborately decorated with cartouches, scrolls and flowers, on three shell feet, 11" ht, 82oz gross	Gorringes LLP, East Sussex UK 2006 #1476
1839-41	Robert Gray & Son	Glasgow	Tea kettle, lamp and stand, heavily reposed, engraved with name "Henrietta Cone Marsh", 11 ½" overall	Garth's Auctions Ohio USA, June 19, 2004 #817
1844/45	Leonard Urquhart	Edinburgh	Tea kettle, bombe form, body chased with scrolling foliage in panels, swing handle, part of a service	Christie's Amsterdam NE 1997 #92
1847/48	James McKay	Edinburgh	Tea kettle, no details	National Museums of Scotland MEQ 1163
1911/12	Edward & Sons	Glasgow	Tea kettle on stand, paneled oval body, scroll feet, wavy scroll borders, part of a service	Christie's London UK 1999 #58

Teapots

Plate 49. A Teapot 1735/36 by James Ker, Edinburgh.
Courtesy of Asprey Ltd., London.

TEAPOTS

YEAR	MAKER	LOCATION	DESCRIPTION	SOURCE
1714/15	Colin Campbell	Edinburgh	Teapot, plain bullet shaped, on circular molded spreading skirt foot, straight tapering spout, wooden capped loop handle, detachable cover with ball and button finial on a reeded mount, 17.4oz	Christie's June 25, 1969 #129 Sotheby's Nov 29, 1972 #76 Koopman Antiques London
1714/15	Colin McKenzie	Edinburgh	Teapot, no details	Finlay 1991 #133 Private Collection UK
1715 ca	Robert Cruickshank	Aberdeen	Teapot, flat lid applied hinge, wooden handle, straight spout, script initials "ABW", possession lineage engraved on side, 5 3/16" ht	Alcorn, Museum of Fine Art p330 #252 #1921.1971
1715/16	Colin McKenzie	Edinburgh	Teapot, apple shaped body, wood handle, pull off lid, wood knop finial, 4 ½" ht, 9" long, 17.1oz	Nicholas Shaw Antiques 2004 p95 National Museums of Scotland K2004.209
1716/17	Not available	Edinburgh	Teapot, apple shaped on low foot, initials "WF ID" for William Forbes and his wife, Janet Dyer, Bannfshire, silver handle, 18oz 13d	Christie's Scottish Picture File Sotheby's London UK July 25, 1935 #149 Crichton Collection
1716/17	Not available	Edinburgh	Teapot, apple shaped, flush hinged lid, straight tapering spout, leaf capped handle, 16oz	Christie's Glasgow Sept 20, 1983 #215
1716/17	Henry Bethune	Edinburgh	Teapot, apple shaped, plain capped double scroll silver handle, flattish lid with applied hinge, finial in the form of a heraldic wheat sheaf, with crest – an anchor, and motto 4 ¾" ht, 17.6oz	Sotheby's Gleneagles Aug 30, 1982 #493
1716/17	Henry Bethune	Edinburgh	Teapot, apple shaped, later chased and engraved with shells, strap-work, foliage and diaper work at the shoulder and on the slightly domed lid, straight tapering spout, double scroll handle, wood finial, 5 ¼" ht, 17oz	Sotheby's March 9, 1967
1716/17	Henry Bethune	Edinburgh	Teapot, apple shaped, straight tapering spout, almost flat hinged lid, silver mounted turned wood finial, plain capped silver scroll handle	Christie's NY USA Oct 20, 1998
1716/17	Henry Bethune	Edinburgh	Teapot, no details, earlier sale of prior Bethune pots	Connoisseur Magazine 1935 vol 96 p182
1718/19	Mungo Yorstoun	Edinburgh	Teapot, no details	Seaford House Exhibition 1929 #529 Abercrombie Collection
1718/19	Henry Bethune	Edinburgh	Teapot, apple shaped, with stand, plain tapering spout, wooden capped loop handle, flat lid with applied hinge, reeded acorn finial, 4 ¾" ht,	Sotheby's Gleneagles August 27-28 1970 #114

YEAR	MAKER (continued)	LOCATION	DESCRIPTION 25.3 oz including stand	SOURCE
1718/19	Charles Dickson I or Charles Duncan	Edinburgh	Teapot, apple shape, nearly flat lid with applied hinge, ball finial, straight tapering spout, capped and pointed loop wooden handle, body engraved with contemporary cipher "?B" under an Earl's coronet, base inscribed "EX DONO" and dated 1719, scratch weight 19:04, 4 ¾" ht, 19oz all	Christie's NY USA April 12, 1994 #288
1719/20	Colin McKenzie	Edinburgh	Teapot, apple shaped, wood handle, turned wood finial, Arms of Cunningham	Finlay 1991 #75
1719/20	Henry Bethune	Edinburgh	Teapot, ovoid or egg shaped, straight tapering spout, later crest, wood handle, reeded acorn finial, engraved "JL", 5 ¾" ht, 16.1oz	Finlay 1991 #75 Sotheby's Gleneagles August 1987 #280 National Museums of Scotland MEQ 1598
1719/20	Henry Bethune	Edinburgh	Teapot, apple shaped, on flat base, tapering straight spout, almost flat lid with applied hinge, acorn finial, capped wooden loop handle, 13.7oz	Sotheby's October 25, 1984 #268
1720 ca	George Robertson	Aberdeen	Teapot, bullet shaped, finely engraved on one side with contemporary armorials for John Urquhart, of Meldrum, Co Aberdeen, supporters and motto with initials on the other side, 2 later crests and mottos below, shoulders chased with flower clusters, foliage and scrolling strap work on matted ground, spherical finial on applied fluted motif and silver handle, straight tapering spout, on spreading rim foot, 6" ht, 29oz 7d	Sotheby's December 21, 1967 # 230
1720ca	George Robertson	Aberdeen	Teapot, The Urquhart Teapot, spherical, crest and 2 mottos, "PER MARE ET TERRAS" and "Meen Speak doe well", marked base - GR, GR, three towers, gothic A or E	Aberdeen Museums and Galleries ABDAG001000 (acquired 1969)
1720ca	George Robertson	Aberdeen	Teapot, silver, engraved, base marked - GR, ABD, GF, CF	Aberdeen Museums and Galleries ABDAG001006 (acquired 1973)
1720ca	George Robertson	Aberdeen	Teapot, spherical shape, no details	Dundee Museums and Art Galleries 1967-257
1720/21	Henry Bethune	Edinburgh	Teapot, octagonal, tall finial, wood handle, 15oz 5d	Christie's October 26, 1943 #42
1720/21	Henry Bethune	Edinburgh	Teapot, octagonal, no chasing evident, wood handle, on raised octagonal foot, straight spout, silver finial, cone with compressed ball in the middle	Antique Collector March 1949 SJ Phillips advertisement Christie's Picture File

YEAR	MAKER	LOCATION	DESCRIPTION	SOURCE
1720/21	Thomas Hay Assayer Edward Penman	Edinburgh	Teapot, apple shaped, silver handle, straight spout, acorn finial, conjoined "TH" mm, 5" ht, 19oz 16d	Sotheby's May 11, 1950 #141 Nicholas Shaw Catalog 2005 p88 Connoisseur Magazine 1950 vol 126 p224 Apollo 1950 vol 51 p32 Royal Scottish Museum Exhibition of 1948
1721/22	Colin McKenzie	Edinburgh	Teapot, apple shaped, hinge area repair on lid, ball finial, silver double scroll handle	Antiques Magazine 1959 vol 75 #238 James Robinson, NY advertisement Christie's East NY USA October 15, 1996 #353 Art Institute of Chicago
1722/23	James Mitchelson	Edinburgh	Teapot, barrel shaped, worn crest and motto for Seatoun family, flat lid, 18oz	Finlay 1991 #76 Christie's January 31, 1945 #59 Bell of Aberdeen Collection 1961 #7 National Museums of Scotland MEQ 1386
1722/23	Henry Bethune	Edinburgh	Teapot, egg shaped, crest and motto of Foulis, later chased decoration, 6" ht, 14oz 10d	Sotheby's Gleneagles August 1990 #173 Hyman Collection – Colonial Williamsburg Antiques Magazine June 1996 p845
1722/23	Charles Blair	Edinburgh	Teapot, circular apple shaped, silver handle, acorn finial, straight spout, 5 ¼" ht, 20.5oz	Christie's London July 1987 #219 Ivory Collection
1722/23	James Mitchelson	Edinburgh	Teapot, apple shaped, silver handle, acorn finial, straight spout, 4 ½" ht, 17oz 19d	Sotheby's NY USA April 23, 1993 #299 Thomas Lumley 1958 Exhibition of the Royal Ontario Museum Canada
1722/23	Colin Campbell	Edinburgh	Teapot, apple shaped body, wood handle, bud finial, 5 ½" ht, 15oz	Christie's NY USA October 20, 1999 #314 Nicholas Shaw Catalog 2000 p66 Nicholas Shaw Antiques 2004 Thomas Lumley 1951

YEAR	MAKER	LOCATION	DESCRIPTION	SOURCE
1722/23	James Tait	Edinburgh	Teapot, spherical, simple curved spout, wood handle possibly replaced, outside hinge on lid, 6" ht, 14oz	Apollo July 1940 vol 32 p28 #7 Mallet and Son
1722/23	William Aytoun	Edinburgh	Teapot, octagonal, wood handle, straight spout, 6"ht, 17.3oz	Nicholas Shaw Catalog 2005 p88
1723/24	William Aytoun	Edinburgh	Teapot, octagonal, ivory handle, later chasing, straight spout, 5 ½" ht, 16oz 14d	Christie's London Oct 25, 1989 Christie's May 26, 1905 #11
1723/24	Henry Bethune	Edinburgh	Teapot, plain, egg shaped, wood handle, exposed hinge on lid, straight spout, acorn finial, 5 ½" ht	Los Angeles County Museum Exhibition #171 Paul Rodman Maybury Collection
1723/24	James Ker	Edinburgh	Teapot, spherical, straight spout, 16oz 14d	Christie's April 6, 1910 #36 Christie's March 14, 1918 #43
1723/24	James Tait	Edinburgh	Teapot, spherical, lightly engraved around lid, cut card work around the spout, 18oz 3d	Christie's May 5, 1920, #104
1723/24	James Ker	Edinburgh	Teapot, no details	Jackson Marks p546 Crichton Brothers
1724/25	Henry Bethune	Edinburgh	Teapot, spherical, straight spout, ball finial, 6 ½" ht, about 23oz	Christie's Jan 7, 1939 #241 Hearst Collection
1725 ca	Not available		Teapot, no details	Jackson p952
1725 ca	Robert Luke	Glasgow	Teapot, curved spout, silver handle, ball finial	Antique Collection 1939
1725 ca	Robert Luke	Glasgow	Teapot, with stand	Connoisseur Magazine February 1939 p4 Bell of Aberdeen advertisement
1725 ca	Robert Luke	Glasgow	Teapot, later Victorian decoration added	Connoisseur Magazine May 1939 vol 103 p28
1725 ca	Robert Luke	Glasgow	Teapot, apple shaped, straight spout, wood handle, later arms, contemporary initials "C/JJ", 5 ½" ht, 17oz	Sotheby's London June 9, 1994 #309
1725 ca	Robert Luke	Glasgow	Teapot, spherical, on spreading circular foot, tapering straight spout, hinged domed lid, ball finial, leaf capped silver scroll handle, ivory insulators, marked on underside, lid is unmarked, 6 ½" ht, 19oz	Christie's London June 13, 2000 #230

YEAR	MAKER	LOCATION	DESCRIPTION	SOURCE
1725 ca	John Walker	Aberdeen	Teapot, apple shaped, curved spout, silver handle, part of a set	Sotheby's Gleneagles August 1987 #285
1725 ca	George Walker	Aberdeen	Teapot, spherical, silver handle, straight spout, light decoration, crest and coronet	Grimwade, The Queen's Silver #10
1725 ca	John Walker	Aberdeen	Teapot, plain circular tapering body, on reeded rim foot, double scroll handle with wood insulators, curved spout, initials on underside, 5 ¾" ht, 18oz 17d	Sotheby's London February 4, 1988 #23
1725ca	Robert Luke	Glasgow	Teapot, spherical, plain, slightly domed lid and hinge, straight spout, pedestal foot, silver handle, 6 ¾"ht	Bell of Aberdeen Collection, 1961, #13
1725 ca	George Robertson	Aberdeen	Teapot, wood handle	National Museums of Scotland MEQ 602
1725 ca	Robert Luke	Glasgow	Teapot, curved spout, silver handle, ball finial	Antique Collection 1939
1725/26	James Ker	Edinburgh	Teapot, elongated apple shape, flanged foot, with straight spout, lid with baluster finial, wood handle, applied hinge, crest and motto of Haig of Bemersyde, Rovburghshire, 5 ½" ht, 19oz	Finlay 1991 #34 Clayton Dictionary p306 #642 Christie's March 10, 1965 #53 Christie's Oct 14, 1959 #125 Christie's Oct 12, 1955 #63 Jackson #1272 Christie's Glasgow UK 1983 #83 Countess of Moray Collection
1725/26	William Aytoun	Edinburgh	Teapot, spherical, plain, straight spout	Park Lane Exhibition 1929 #419 Sassom Private Collection UK
1725/26	*William Aytoun*	*Edinburgh*	*Teapot, spherical, 6 ½" ht, 19.3oz*	*Christie's Oct 22, 19? #157* *Christie's Scottish Picture File*
1725/26	Henry Bethune	Edinburgh	Teapot, spherical, on plain spreading foot, domed lid, silver bud finial, silver handle	Clayton Christie's Silver Book p152 Christie's London Feb 27, 1974 Mallet & Son
1725/26	Henry Bethune	Edinburgh	Teapot, spherical	
1725/26	Henry Bethune	Edinburgh	Teapot, spherical, straight spout, later chased, silver handle, 6" ht, 22oz 10d	Sotheby's NY USA October 28, 1980 #526
1725/26	Edward Penman	Edinburgh	Teapot, lightly chased, curved spout, ivory handle, 6 ¼" ht, 19oz	Sotheby's May 29, 1969

YEAR	MAKER	LOCATION	DESCRIPTION	SOURCE
1725/26	*Edward Penman*	*Edinburgh*	*Teapot, no details*	*Holland p104*
1725/26	Edward Lothian	Edinburgh	Teapot, spherical, too early to be this maker, possibly Edward Penman	National Museums of Scotland 1952.185
1725/26	William Aytoun	Edinburgh	Teapot, spherical straight spout, baluster finial, silver handle, 6 ½" ht, 19oz 6d	Christie's October 22, 1951 #157 Hayden p130 National Museums of Scotland 1952.185
1725/26	William Aytoun	Edinburgh	Teapot, wood handle, ball finial, straight spout, external hinge, no decoration	Country Life 1959 p130-33a
1725/56	William Aytoun	Edinburgh	Teapot, not pictured	Connoisseur Magazine 1952 vol 130, p223
1725/26	James Ker	Edinburgh	Teapot, apple shaped, with crest and motto	National Museums of Scotland MEQ 1560 1983
1726ca	John Walker	Aberdeen	Teapot, no details, base marked IWR, IWR three crosses, engraved IGF?	Aberdeen Museums and Galleries ABDAG008631
1726/27	James Tait	Edinburgh	Teapot, spherical, with small decorated band	Christie's March 31, 1971 #80
1726/27	James Tait	Edinburgh	Teapot, plain, spherical, foot, curved spout, 6" ht, 13oz 19d	Christie's March 29, 1939 #61 Christie's London UK 2001 #139
1726/27	James Mitchelson	Edinburgh	Teapot, spherical, silver handle, ball finial, straight spout, no decoration, apparently different from the one below	Connoisseur Magazine December 1939 p2989
1726/27	James Mitchelson	Edinburgh	Teapot, spherical, Arms of Hairstans, Gladstans also, quart size, wiggle work decoration around lid, silver handle, straight spout, misattributed to John Main	Grimwade, The Queen's Silver #9
1726/27	Not available	Edinburgh	Teapot, spherical, straight spout, small band, period decoration around lip, silver handle, script initial in circular cartouche, with matching bowl one year later	Christie's March 31...#80, #81 Christie's Scottish Picture File How of Edinburgh
1727 ca	Johan Got-helf-Bilsings	Glasgow	Teapot, spherical, straight spout, silver handle, engraved band and crest, 6" ht, 18.1oz	Nicholas Shaw Catalog 2005 90
1727/28	Alexander Kincaid	Edinburgh	Teapot with stand, silver handle	Apollo March 1947 p68 How of Edinburgh 1937 #93
1727/28	James Ker	Edinburgh	Teapot, spherical, straight spout, silver handle, ball finial, crest, part of The Johnson Tea Service	Apollo 1934 vol 20 p25 Wilson and Sharp advertisement

YEAR	MAKER (continued)	LOCATION	DESCRIPTION	SOURCE
				How's Notes on Antiques Silver 1941, vol I, p23
1727/28	James Ker	Edinburgh	Teapot, spherical, part of a set	Finlay 1991 #34
1727/28	Thomas Mitchell	Edinburgh	Teapot, spherical, straight tapering spout, wood handle, plain dome lid, 6", 19oz	Gordon Small 1963 Sotheby's NY USA April 23, 1993 #298
1727/28	Patrick Murray I	Edinburgh	Teapot, spherical, straight spout, silver handle, ball finial, later chased, Arms of Carnegie and a quarter for Maule, motto "TACHE SANS TACHE", 6 ¾" ht, 22.3oz	Bonhams London UK 2004 #439 Nicholas Shaw Catalog 2005 p90
1727/28	Edward Penman	Edinburgh	Teapot, with sugar bowl, 2 crests and mottos, silver double scroll handle, 6 ½" ht, 30oz 15d total	Sotheby's December 14, 1972 #109 Koopman, London
1727/38	Alexander Kincaid	Edinburgh	Teapot, spherical, straight tapered spout, double scroll handle, ogee-molded circular base, stylized leaf band engraved near mouth, engraved "H" underneath, 6 1/8" X 9 1/8" X 4 3/8"	Musee Des Beaux Arts, Montreal Canada 1981.DS.31
1727/38	William Aytoun	Edinburgh	Teapot, spherical, double scroll silver handle, straight spout, ivory insulators, ball and button finial, scratch weight 21:4 underneath, 6 ½" ht, 10" long	Baruch Collection 1988 McKissick Museum, University of South Carolina, Columbia, SC USA 1.11
1727/28	Not available	Edinburgh	Teapot, spherical, on molded circular foot, straight spout, scroll handle, ball finial, chased at a later date with flowers, foliage, and scrolls on a matted ground, 2 coats of arms, 19.3oz	Christie's November 18, 1970 #94 Simon Kaye Antiques
1727/28	James Mitchelson	Edinburgh	Teapot, spherical, plain, on stepped spreading foot, capped curved spout, scrolling flutes, plain domed lid with applied hinge, ball finial, silver double scroll handle, 6 ¼" ht, 15.2oz	Sotheby's August 14, 1972 #44
1727/28	James Mitchelson	Edinburgh	Teapot, spherical, later decoration, silver handle, straight spout, original band decoration, is under later 1745ca decoration, 6 ¼" ht, 19oz 14d	Sotheby's February 26, 1942 #145 Christie's Scottish Picture File Connoisseur Magazine 1942 vol 109, p183 Christie's London May 1979 #145 Lyon & Turnbull February 20, 2004 #256

YEAR	MAKER	LOCATION	DESCRIPTION	SOURCE
1727/28	William Aytoun	Edinburgh	Teapot, spherical form, spreading circular foot, tapering spout, silver scroll handle with bone insulators, hinged lid with ball finial, 9 ¾" long, 19oz	Christie's NY USA 2000 #258
1728 ca	Johan Got-helf-Bilsings	Glasgow	Teapot, apple shaped, straight tapered spout, flush cover, banded baluster finial, silver C-scroll handle, capped by double leaf, one side engraved with crest and motto, engraved underneath with script initial "C", 5" ht, 16oz 15d	Christie's March 26, 1969 #85 Christie's Scottish Picture Files Sotheby's NY USA April 23, 1993 #297
1728/29	James Ker	Edinburgh	Teapot, spherical, applied hinge to lid, wooden loop handle, straight spout	Connoisseur Magazine v 103 February 1939 p2 Crichton Bros. advertisement
1728/29	James Ker	Edinburgh	Teapot, spherical, plain wooden loop handle, on circular stepped spreading foot, straight spout, domed lid with applied hinge, ball and button finial, 6" ht, 20.4oz	Sotheby's April 15, 1964 #101
1728/29	James Ker	Edinburgh	*Teapot, wood handle, straight spout, ball finial, 6" ht, 20oz 8d*	*Antiques Collector February 1964*
1728/29	James Ker	Edinburgh	*Teapot, wooden handle with a single curve, straight spout, 6 ¾" ht, 20oz 10d*	*Christie's April 8, 1937 #150 Ivory Collection*
1728/29	James Ker	Edinburgh	Teapot, misattributed to John Kincaid, decorated, wooden handle, narrow decoration near lid, straight spout, baluster finial, handle is double curved, engraved on bottom "Albany, NY October 10, 1878", 5 5/16" ht	Connoisseur Magazine January 1938 vol 101 p49 Peter Guille, NY advertisement Gess, Clark ART Institute p326-27 #226
1728/29	*James Ker*	Edinburgh	*Teapot, misattributed to John Kincaid*	*Antiques Magazine September 1962 vol 82*
1728/29	Henry Bethune Assayer Edward Penman	Edinburgh	Teapot, wood handle, straight spout, light decoration of stars around the lid	Sotheby's NY USA October 1990 #175
1728/29	Henry Bethune	Edinburgh	Teapot, spherical, engraved band around the lid, 18oz 7d	Christie's June 23, 1927 #35
1728/29	*Henry Bethune*	*Edinburgh*	*Teapot, spherical engraved band around the lid, 19oz*	*Christie's December 3, 1941 #3 How of Edinburgh Collection*
1728/29	Patrick Graham	Edinburgh	Teapot, spherical, chased on shoulders, 20oz 15d	Christie's June 28, 1916 #39
1728/29	*Patrick Graham*	*Edinburgh*	*Teapot, spherical, heavy later chasing, straight spout, silver handle*	*Antiques Magazine June 1996 Hyman Collection - Colonial Williamsburg G1995-068*

YEAR	MAKER	LOCATION	DESCRIPTION	SOURCE
1728/29	William Aytoun	Edinburgh	Teapot, spherical, engraved frieze around lid and rim, silver handle, 5 ½" ht, 17.8oz	Nicholas Shaw Catalog 1999 p53
1728/29	William Aytoun	Edinburgh	Teapot, spherical, later chased with hanging floral scrolls, crested cartouche, similarly decorated domed lid, urn finial, straight spout, leaf capped double scroll handle, on spreading base, 6" ht, 20.8oz	Sotheby's Dec 2, 1980 #228 Sotheby's April 7, 1981 #164 Christie's Monaco August 17, 1981 #216
1728/29	James Ker	Edinburgh	Teapot, spherical shape, straight spout, double scroll handle, ball finial on round lid with leaf and line border round mouth, arms, crest and motto "NUN QUAM NON PARATUS" for Johnson, part of the 4 piece Johnson Tea Service	Brooklyn Museum NY USA 63.95.1
1728/29	James Tait	Edinburgh	Teapot, spherical, straight spout, wiggle work around lid, patched from inside, possible fun finial, initials "SC" below the spout, double scroll silver hand, 6" ht, 22oz 16d	Sotheby's Gleneagles August 1994 #143 Sotheby's Gleneagles August 27-28, 1979 #182 Sotheby's Feb 21, 1980 #187
1729/30	*James Tait*	*Edinburgh*	*Teapot, spherical, slightly domed circular foot, ball finial, with diaper and chevron border where lid meets body, initial "EC" beneath the spout, 22.5oz*	*Lyon & Turnbull Edinburgh UK 2006 #119*
1729/30	James Mitchelson Assayer Archibald Ure	Edinburgh	Teapot, almost spherical body, curved spout, later chasing, silver double scroll handle, (Note: originally attributed to William Jamieson), 6" ht, 23oz 14d	Sotheby's Feb 1, 1973 N. Bloom Antiques
1729/30	William Aytoun	Edinburgh	Teapot, almost spherical form, on molded stepped spreading foot, straight tapering spout, double scroll silver handle, engraved narrow band round the mouth with zig-zag lines of ornament, lid similarly engraved near edge, 19.7oz	Christie's Dec 17, 1986 #225
1730 ca	George Cooper	Aberdeen	Teapot, no details	Mallet & Son 1930 p50
1730 ca	*George Cooper*	*Aberdeen*	*Teapot, with stand*	*Country Life April 1959 p130-33*
1730 ca	George Cooper	Aberdeen	Teapot, shell decoration	Hyman Collection - Colonial Williamsburg
1730 ca	George Cooper	Aberdeen	Teapot, ball shaped, light chased decoration around lid, silver handle, wood partitioned finial	Steppes Hill Farm, London 1995
1730 ca	George Cooper	Aberdeen	Teapot, apple shaped body, on spreading foot, straight tapering spout, silver scroll handle, ivory insulators, hinged lid with acanthus hinge, bud finial, repair to spout and base, 3 marks – 3 towers, Gothic e, A, GC – 9 5/8" long, 19oz	Christie's NY USA April 12, 1988

YEAR	MAKER	LOCATION	DESCRIPTION	SOURCE
1730 ca	George Cooper	Aberdeen	Teapot, spherical shape, on stepped spreading foot, shoulders chased with scrolls, flower heads, and foliage, hinged domed lid, wooden finial, partly fluted scroll spout, scroll handle, 6 2/3" ht, 21.8oz	Bonhams Aug 21-23, 2003 #119
1730 ca	George Cooper	Aberdeen	Teapot, spherical shaped, on molded circular foot, chased around the rim with bands of stylized foliage, straight tapering spout, leaf capped scroll handled, ivory baluster finial, 6" ht, 21oz	Christie's June 30, 1992 #206A
1730 ca	George Cooper	Aberdeen	Teapot, plain, inverted pear shape, on molded rim foot, straight spout, double scroll handle, hinged cover, baluster finial, mm 2X's, 19oz 10d	Christie's July 3, 1984 #124
1730 ca	George Cooper	Aberdeen	Teapot, shaped circular, on rim foot, wood insulation on handle, plain body, 3 marks – GC, 3 castles, gothic 3, 7 ¾", 8oz	Christie's March 18, 1986 #99
1730 ca	George Cooper	Aberdeen	Teapot, silver and wood, no details, based marked – GC,GC three towers, Gothic A	Aberdeen Museums and Galleries ABDAG001357
1730 ca	Robert Luke	Glasgow	Teapot, straight spout, silver handle, engraved monogram, 21oz	Christie's Nov 23, 1977 #169 Phillips July 14, 1978 #160 Christie's Scottish Picture File
1730 ca	Robert Luke	Glasgow	Teapot, straight spout, ball finial 17oz 5d	Christie's May 15, 1963 #52 Noble Collection
1730 ca	Robert Luke	Glasgow	Teapot, spherical, fluted spout, 5 ½" ht	Jackson Marks p952 #1276
1730 ca	Robert Luke	Glasgow	Teapot, spherical shape, plain, ball finial, tapered spout, double scroll handle, molded spreading foot, 6 " ht, 19oz 17d	Sotheby's Jan 26, 1967 #147
1730 ca	Robert Luke	Glasgow	Teapot, plain oviform body, on flat base, straight tapering spout, hinged flush lid, baluster finial, 5 ½" ht, 17oz 5d	Christie's May 15, 1963 #52
1730 ca	Robert Luke	Glasgow	*Teapot, plain, spherical, on circular molded foot, straight spout, baluster finial, hinged lid, 17oz 5d*	*Christie's September 19, 1979 #119*
1730 ca	Robert Luke	Glasgow	Teapot, spherical shape, straight spout, flat lid, later engraved with armorials of Lockart of Birkhill, Scotland, underside with contemporary initials "C/JJ", 5 ½" ht, 17oz	Sotheby's London June 9, 1994 #309
1730 ca	Robert Luke	Glasgow	Teapot, spherical, plain, circular molded foot, straight spout, double scroll handle, raised lid, ball finial, engraved with a monogram, 21oz	Christie's November 23, 1977 #169
1730 ca	Not available	Edinburgh	Teapot, 2 crests, straight spout, could be an Edward Penman pot	Waldron, p860

517

YEAR	MAKER	LOCATION	DESCRIPTION	SOURCE
1730 ca	Johan Got-helf-Bilsings	Glasgow	Teapot, 5 ¾"ht, 21oz	Lyle Annual Review 1982 p629
1730 ca	Johan Got-helf-Bilsings	Glasgow	Teapot, spherical shaped, engraved with scrolls, floral clusters, and 2 vacant cartouches, double scroll handle, on spreading base, slightly domed lid, baluster finial, 5 ¾" ht, 21oz 13d	Sotheby's Blair Castle September 12, 1980 #162
1730ca	Johan Got-helf Bilsings	Glasgow	Teapot, barrel shaped, straight spout, flat cover, silver acorn finial, leaf-capped handle	Hyman Collection-Colonial Williamsburg G1994-
1730ca	George Cooper	Aberdeen	Teapot, part of The Kirkhill Tea Service of five pieces, no details, based marked - three towers, GC, Gothic A or E	Aberdeen Museums and Galleries ABDAG008501 (acquired 1986)
1730ca	George Cooper	Aberdeen	Teapot, tapering spherical (apple?), silver scroll handle, dome lid, tubular spout, molded foot, 6"ht	Bell of Aberdeen Collection, 1961, #9
1730ca	George Cooper	Aberdeen	Teapot, spherical body, straight spout, silver handle, engraved near mouth	Hyman Collection-Colonial Williamsburg G1992-
1730/31	Not available	Edinburgh	Teapot, spherical, on spreading foot, with engraved shells, foliage and scrolls around the rim, straight tapering spout, silver plain capped double scroll handle, domed lid, flush hinge, orb finial, coat of Arms of Moubray of Cockairnie, Fife, 6 1/8", 22oz	Christie's Edinburgh Nov 21, 1990 #45
1730/31	Henry Bethune	Edinburgh	Teapot, spherical, later chased, straight spout, ball and button finial, applied hinge, silver double scroll handle, on molded domed foot, no leaf under finial knob, 10" long, 19oz	Christie's NY USA April 12, 1988 #40
1730/31	Henry Bethune	Edinburgh	Teapot, spherical, sold as part of a mixed tea service, finial has leaf under knob, silver handle, chasing probably slightly later, 6" ht, 21oz	Christie's Edinburgh June 10-11, 1984 #374 Christie's Scottish Picture File
1730/31	*Henry Bethune*	*Edinburgh*	*Teapot, spherical, straight spout, lightly engraved lid, 20oz 4d*	*Christie's Dec 3, 1925 #70*
1730/31	Not available	Edinburgh	Teapot, spherical, on spreading foot, with engraved shells, foliage and scrolls around the rim, straight tapering spout, silver plain capped double scroll handle, domed lid, flush hinge, orb finial, coat of Arms of Moubray of Cockairnie, Fife, 6 1/8", 22oz	Christie's Edinburgh Nov 21, 1990 #45
1730/31	Henry Bethune	Edinburgh	Teapot, spherical, straight spout, silver double scroll handle, ball and button finial, wooden insulators, 6 1/8"ht, 10"long	McKissick Museum, University of South Carolina, Columbia, SC USA 1.148 Baruch Collection

YEAR	MAKER	LOCATION	DESCRIPTION	SOURCE
1730/31	James Ker	Edinburgh	Teapot, spherical shape, no details	Dundee Museum and Art Galleries 1978-2060
1731/32	Archibald Ure	Edinburgh	Teapot, spherical, floral design and cartouche, with script initials "MG" and "DG", 6 3/8"ht, 9 3/8" long,	Huntley House Museum, Edinburgh HH 2128/61
1731/32	James Ker	Edinburgh	Teapot, curved spout, silver handle, arms of McLeod, 6" ht, 22oz	Christie's London May 1993 #114
1731/32	James Ker	Edinburgh	Teapot, spherical body, flat chased with flowers and scrolls near mouth, bun and button finial, curved spout, wood handle, 5 ½" ht, 20oz 4d	Sotheby's April 7, 1981 Sotheby's Scone Palace April 14, 1990 #119 Lyle Annual Review 1981 p627
1731/32	James Ker	Edinburgh	Teapot, spherical, chased with bands of scrolling foliage and flowers, cartouche enclosing a crest and motto on one side, 6 ½" ht, 24oz	Sotheby's Hopetoun House April 26, 1988 #58
1731/32	James Tait	Edinburgh	Teapot, later engraved initials below a coronet, straight tapering spout, scroll handle, hinged lid, spherical finial, 6" ht, 20oz	Sotheby's April 25, 1975 #149
1731/32	John Rollo	Edinburgh	Teapot, near spherical body, on stepped foot, plain capped silver double scroll handle, tapering straight spout, lid with applied hinge, silver bun and button finial, 6", 20.2oz	Christie's Nov 22, 1995 #126 Private Collection
1731/32	James Ker	Edinburgh	Teapot, spherical, flush hinged lid, silver handle, chased with fruits, flowers, later initials in cartouche, straight spout, 5 ½" ht, 20.8oz	Lyle Silver Review 1981 p116 Sotheby's Dec 16, 1976 #90
1731/32	James Ker	Edinburgh	Teapot, spherical, plain, straight spout, silver handle, ball finial	Christie's NY USA #1545, Sept 7, 2005 #315
1731/32	James Ker	Edinburgh	Teapot, plain spherical body	National Museums of Scotland 1983.27
1731/32	David Mitchell	Edinburgh	Teapot, spherical, ball finial, double scroll silver handle, band decoration on lid	Sotheby's Sale L05766 Nov 29, 2005 #157
1732/33	William Aytoun	Edinburgh	Teapot, spherical, straight spout, circular foot, engraved foliage, ball finial, 23oz 5d	Christie's Nov 12, 1952 #109
1732/33	William Aytoun	Edinburgh	Teapot, spherical, on stem and foot, silver scroll handle, straight spout, small engraved pattern surrounding lid, crest of Chartiers family, 6 ½" ht	Bell of Aberdeen Collection 1961, #14
1732/33	James Mitchelson	Edinburgh	Teapot, spherical, straight spout, 13oz 11d	Christie's July 13, 1932 #86

YEAR	MAKER	LOCATION	DESCRIPTION	SOURCE
1732/33	Archibald Ure	Edinburgh	Teapot, spherical, curved spout, engraving around lid	Scotland Art Academy Exhibition #948 Gilmour Collection
1732/33	*Archibald Ure*	*Edinburgh*	*Teapot, spherical, on spreading foot, chased at shoulders with band of foliage and hatching, straight spout, baluster finial, coat of arms, 12.3oz*	*Christie's July 30, 1945 #205*
1733/34	James Ker	Edinburgh	Teapot, spherical body, straight spout, silver handle, ball finial, delicate flat chasing, crest and motto "SANS PEUR" of Sutherland 24oz	Antiques Magazine 1961, vol 80, p498 Bell of Aberdeen advertisement Scottish Art Review vol VIII p35 #3 Bell of Aberdeen advertisement Christie's Glasgow March 29, 1983 #82 Shaw Collection Lyle Annual Review 1984 p753
1733/34	William Aytoun	Edinburgh	Teapot, spherical, part of The Girdwood Tea Service	Finlay 1991 #74 Ivory Collection
1733/34	William Aytoun	Edinburgh	Teapot, spherical, with contemporary armorials with supporters, shell and scrolling foliage on the shoulders and hinged lid, straight tapering spout, double scroll handle, spherical finial, on circular foot, 5 ¾" ht, 17.5oz	Sotheby's December 15, 1966 #113 Simon Kaye Antiques
1733/34	William Aytoun	Edinburgh	Teapot, spherical, flat chased shell and scroll work around mouth, engraved initials, straight spout, silver double scroll handle, on spreading stepped foot, with French duty marks, offered with swag border stand which had sold separately in 1983	Phillips Edinburgh June 9, 1995 #315
1733/34	James Mitchelson	Edinburgh	Teapot, spherical, on domed foot, straight tapering spout, reverse scroll handle with hardwood insulators, domed lid with applied hinge and ball finial, chased to shoulders and lid with band of shells and scrolls, contemporary betrothal initials "JL KM" underneath, (Note: originally attributed to William Jamieson), 6" ht, 21oz	Christie's Edinburgh May 26, 1988 #68
1733/34	Hugh Penman	Edinburgh	Teapot, spherical, on spreading circular molded foot, with straight tapering spout and shoulder and lid engraved with band of shells, scrolls and foliage, orb finial, 20oz	Christie's February 17, 1981 #148
1733/34	John Rollo	Edinburgh	Teapot, spherical, on spreading circular molded foot, straight tapering spout, silver double scroll handle with ivory insulators, hinged lid with bead finial and engraved foliage and shells on upper body and lid, side with script initial "W", 9 ¾" long, 19.5oz	Christie's NY USA April 17, 1996 #176

YEAR	MAKER	LOCATION	DESCRIPTION	SOURCE
1733/34	Kenneth McKenzie	Edinburgh	Teapot, straight spout, silver handle, light chasing near mouth, 6 ½", 24oz 3d	Untermeyer Collection #60 Metropolitan Museum of Art, NY USA Christie's February 11, 1960 #129
1733/34	James Tait	Edinburgh	Teapot, spherical, straight spout, engraved shell and straps, 18oz 13d	Christie's March 13, 1894 #45 Christie's November 7, 1945 #42
1733/34	*James Tait*	*Edinburgh*	*Teapot, spherical, straight spout, chased shells and foliage, baluster finial, double scroll handle, pedestal foot, 5 ½" ht, 18oz 13d*	*Christie's June 24, 1965 #19*
1733/34	James Mitchelson	Edinburgh	Teapot, spherical, straight spout, ball finial, chased with scrolls, 20oz 18d	Christie's October 24, 1937 #21
1733/34	*James Mitchelson*	*Edinburgh*	*Teapot, spherical, straight spout, silver handle, outside hinge, light period chasing*	*Apollo July 1940 vol 32, p20 #8* *Crichton Bros Shop*
1733/34	Edward Lothian	Edinburgh	Teapot, spherical, straight spout, engraved band of foliage, ball finial, 15oz	Christie's July 19, 1939 #98
1733/34	Edward Lothian	Edinburgh	Teapot, spherical, straight spout, light chasing, silver handle, ball finial, 19oz 10d	Apollo 1933 vol 17, p13 How of Edinburgh advertisement
1734 ca	Robert Luke	Glasgow	Teapot, bullet shaped, chased with shells, motifs, and scroll work, hinged lid, ball finial, scroll handle, fluted spout, on circular base, 5 7/8" ht, 22.5oz	Bonhams Knightsbridge February 22, 1994 #235A Bonhams London November 24, 1992 #167
1734 ca	Johan Got-helf-Bilsings	Glasgow	Teapot, plain, swan neck spout, wood handle, compressed spherical finial, molded circular foot, initials on under side, 6 ½" ht, 16oz 6d	Sotheby's March 16, 1961 #119
1734/35	Hugh Penman Assayer Archibald Ure	Edinburgh	Teapot, spherical, straight spout, ball finial, lightly chased, decorated around the mouth, silver handle, 17oz 13d	Shrubsole NY USA 1989 Christie's May 6, 1959 #149 Simon Kaye Antiques The Phoenix Collection
1734/35	William Aytoun	Edinburgh	Teapot, spherical, circular foot, engraved with scrolls, 18oz 16d	Christie's June 24, 1946 #86
1734/35	Alexander Kincaid	Edinburgh	Teapot, spherical, on high foot, shoulder chased with scrolls and flowers, 14oz 8d	Christie's November 23, 1932, #87 How of Edinburgh Collection Apollo 1933 vol 17, p13 How of Edinburgh advertisement
1734/35	Alexander Kincaid	Edinburgh	Teapot, spherical, chased at shoulder around the mouth with scrolls, masks and flower sprays, pear shaped finial, straight tapering spout, on spreading	Sotheby's January 27, 1966 Simon Kaye Antiques

YEAR	MAKER (continued)	LOCATION	DESCRIPTION pedestal base, 5 ½" ht, 15.2oz	SOURCE
1734/35	James Tait	Edinburgh	Teapot, spherical, straight spout, flat chased, ball finial, silver handle with wood insulators, initials "AH", 21oz	Christie's Glasgow March 29, 1983 Shaw Collection
173/35	James Ker	Edinburgh	Teapot, spherical form, slightly domed foot, upper body and lid flat chased with a band of shells and trailing foliage, leaf capped part fluted curved spout, 5 ¾" ht, 25.7oz	Bonhams Sale 15120 Aug 22, 2007 #12
1734/35	James Ker (continued)	Edinburgh	Teapot, spherical, straight spout, lightly chased, double scroll handle flush hinge, 6 ¼" ht, 22oz 8d	Sotheby's Gleneagles August 29, 1978 #435 Lyle Annual Review 1980 p638
1734/35	Edward Lothian	Edinburgh	Teapot, spherical, on circular molded foot, shoulder and border of lid engraved with bands of shells and foliage, baluster finial, 22oz	Christie's December 20, 1994 #194
1734/35	Edward Lothian	Edinburgh	Teapot, spherical, crest and motto of Hope, from The Hopetoun Service	Christie's June 15, 1977 #121
1734/35	James Ker	Edinburgh	Teapot, spherical, on circular molded foot, straight tapering spout, flush lid with baluster finial, shoulder with band of shells and scrolls, 19.4oz	Christie's June 18, 1969 #199 Simon Kaye Antiques
1734/35	Archibald Ure	Edinburgh	Teapot, on circular molded foot, almost spherical body, upper part chased with flowers and scrolls, straight spout, baluster finial, hinged lid, 21oz	Christie's April 12, 1967 #142
1735 ca	George Robertson	Aberdeen	Teapot, pear shape, flat chased on hinged lid and around rim on main body, straight spout, scroll wooden handle, 6 ¼" ht, 17.46oz	Nicholas Shaw Catalog Winter 2000 p66
1735 ca	George Cooper	Aberdeen	Teapot, plain, repair	Waldron #865
1735 ca	Not available		Teapot, spherical, straight spout, acorn finial, 4 ½" di	Scotland Art Academy Exhibition 1939 #89 Stuart-Stevenson Collection
1735 ca	Johan Got-helf-Bilsings	Glasgow	Teapot, spherical, tapering spout, engraved, 21oz 18d	Christie's July 17, 1946 #82
1735 ca	George Robertson	Aberdeen	Teapot, plain, straight spout, 19oz 4d	Christie's July 13, 1921 #86 Christie's June 11, 1937 How of Edinburgh Collection
1735 ca	George Cooper	Aberdeen	Teapot, tall apple shape, circular molded foot, straight spout, wooden handle, and finial, 17oz 4d	Christie's January 26, 1949 Nicholas Shaw Catalog 2000 p66
1735 ca	George Cooper	Aberdeen		

YEAR	MAKER	LOCATION	DESCRIPTION	SOURCE
1735 ca	George Cooper	Aberdeen	Teapot, with service	Scotland Art Academy Exhibition 1939 #959
1735 ca	Patrick Gordon	Banff	Teapot, spherical, straight spout, engraved, arabesque, 5" di	Scotland Art Academy Exhibition 1939 #970
1735 ca	George Cooper	Aberdeen	Teapot, spherical, silver and ivory, no details, base marked - GC, 3 castles, E	Aberdeen Museums and Galleries ABDAG008911 (acquired 1996)
1735 ca	Alexander Forbes	Aberdeen	Teapot, almost spherical, slightly flattened lid with applied hinge, baluster and bun finial, half fluted curved spout and capped silver scroll handle approximately 22oz	How's Notes on Antique Silver 1941 vol I, p.22.
1735 ca	Robert Luke	Glasgow	Teapot, with stand, no details	Private Collection UK
1735/36	James Mitchell	Edinburgh	Teapot, spherical, tapering spout, engraved around cover, mm described as IM with a rose above, most likely to be the IM figure between mark, 15oz 10d	Christie's October 22, 1952 #85
1735/36	James Ker	Edinburgh	Teapot, curved spout, wooden handle, lightly chased with shells, interior strainer punched with thistle design, scratch weight on bottom 24:2, 6 ¼"ht	Asprey London 1993 The Phoenix Collection
1735/36	William Aytoun	Edinburgh	Teapot, curved spout, light chasing, 7" ht	Sotheby's Picture Files
1735/36	Hugh Penman	Edinburgh	Teapot, straight spout, lightly chased, silver handle, ball finial, no heraldry, 6 ½" ht, 18oz 5d	Sotheby's December 13, 1973 #237
1735/36	Dougal Ged	Edinburgh	Teapot, spherical, flat chased shoulder decoration near mouth, straight tapering spout, wooden capped handle, lid with silver ball finial, on spreading foot, 16.3oz all	Sotheby's Gleneagles August 30, 1973 #70d Sotheby's June 13, 1974
1735/36	Dougal Ged	Edinburgh	Teapot, spherical, engraved later with 2 crests below lightly chased shoulders, straight tapering spout, double scroll handle, hinged lid with turned finial, on rim foot, 6" ht, 19.7oz	Sotheby's February 25, 1960 Simon Kaye Antiques
1736/67	William Aytoun	Edinburgh	Teapot, bullet on circular molded foot, single scroll handle with ebony insulator to the upper socket, lower end secured directly to the socket with a screw, partly fluted curved spout, engraved around mouth with shells, foliage and diaper work, lid with silver baluster finial, body with later coat of arms, crest and motto for A J Denneiston-Brown of Balloch Castle, Dumbartonshire, 22oz	Christie's December 17, 1986 #224
1736	James Ker	Edinburgh	Teapot, gold, wood handle, mm only, engraved depiction of Legacy with Jockeup and 1736 presentation date, 20oz 4d all in	Apollo December 1967 vol 86 p9 Clayton Dictionary p269 #541

YEAR	MAKER (continued)	LOCATION	DESCRIPTION	SOURCE
				Antiques Magazine October 1949 vol 56 Christie's July 5, 1972 #012 Christie's December 13, 1967 Christie's October 23, 1940 Rothechild & Noble Collections Firestone Parsons, Boston USA Ashton Bennet Collection Manchester City Art Gallery and Museum
1736/37	James Ker	Edinburgh	Teapot, spherical, fluted reverse spout, chased band of shells and flowers, 22oz 18d	Christie's December 19, 1956 #132
1736/37	James Ker	Edinburgh	Teapot, melon shaped, fluted and flat chased, James Ker over striking the mark of a London maker, Pere Pilleau	Connoisseur Magazine 1953 vol 132, p23 Garrard advertisement
1736/37	Dougal Ged	Edinburgh	Teapot, spherical body, diaper and scroll decoration at the shoulder, part fluted curved spout, crest and motto of Nairn, sold with 2 later pieces	Sotheby's December 19, 1995 #191 Sotheby's Gleneagles August 19, 1996 #137
1736/37	James Ker	Edinburgh	Teapot, spherical on circular molded foot, fluted spout formed as 2 reverse scrolls, ball finial on lid, chased around the shoulder and lid with bands of shells, scrolling foliage, with a crest, 22.7oz	Christie's December 19, 1956 # Sotheby's January 12, 1961 #147 Simon Kaye Antiques Christie's April 30, 1996 #79 Christie's Edinburgh May 26, 1998 #84
1736/37	David Mitchell	Edinburgh	Teapot, spherical, flat chased at the shoulder with formal scrolls, shells, and scale work, part fluted curved spout, simple scrolled capped handle, on spreading foot, crest a stag's head guardent and motto for Hunter-Blair, baronets of Blairquhan, Ayreshire, 24 oz	Sotheby's April 5-6, 1982 #203
1737 dated	James Ker	Edinburgh	Teapot, 18 carat gold, wood handle, single curve, straight spout, Royal arms and presentation date "1737", more heavily engraved than the 1736 example	Finlay 1991 #76 On loan to the National Museums of Scotland
1737/38	Charles Dickson II	Edinburgh	Teapot, bullet with flat chased decoration of flowers and foliate scrolls over the upper half of the body, possibly later, coat of arms with supporters and motto, possibly of Campbell and another, 19.8oz	Phillips Edinburgh May 17, 1991 #116

YEAR	MAKER	LOCATION	DESCRIPTION	SOURCE
1737/38	Hugh Gordon	Edinburgh	Teapot, spherical, on circular molded foot, partly fluted spout, scroll handle, upper body and lid engraved with shells, foliage and trellis work, lid with ball finial, 21oz	Christie's October 31, 1984 #152
1737/38	William Aytoun	Edinburgh	Teapot, spherical, on spreading molded foot, upper body and cover chased round the mouth with fruit, flowers and strap work, with C shaped handle, partly fluted curved spout, ball finial, some engraving removed, 20 oz	Christie's November 23, 1983 #146 Christie's May 9, 1984 #141 Christie's Scotland November 11, 1987 #? Sotheby's Gleneagles August 30, 1982 #503
	(continued)			
1737/38	James Ker	Edinburgh	Teapot, spherical, no foot, curved spout, chased, silver handle, ball finial, 19oz 18d	Apollo 1933 vol 17, p13 How of Edinburgh advertisement
1737/38	James Ker	Edinburgh	Teapot, spherical, curved spout, leaf capped silver loop handle, flat chasing, engrave script initials "JR", 4 ½" ht, 21.7oz	Nicholas Shaw Catalog 2002/03 p83 Woolley & Wallis April 20, 2005 #862c Bonhams The Scottish Sale August 24, 2005 #1
1737/38	George Forbes	Edinburgh	Teapot, spherical, curved spout, chased band of scrolls and flowers, ball finial, 25oz	Christie's July 26, 1939 #73 Jackson Marks p547
1737/38	Hugh Gordon	Edinburgh	Teapot, spherical, curved spout, partly fluted silver handle, ball finial, lightly chased with shells, 21oz	Christie's October 31, 1984 #152 Christie's Scottish Picture Files Negative #33889
1737/38	Edward Lothian	Edinburgh	Teapot, spherical, chased band of fruit, 23oz 10d	Christie's February 4, 1964 #60
1737/38	*Edward Lothian*	*Edinburgh*	*Teapot, no details*	*Antiques Magazine vol 67 p540*
1738/39	Dougal Ged	Edinburgh	Teapot, No details	Jackson Marks p547 Hamilton and Inches
1738/39	Archibald Ure	Edinburgh	Teapot, spherical, curved spout, light chasing, silver handle, 19oz 2d	Sotheby's Picture File
1738/39	*Archibald Ure*	*Edinburgh*	*Teapot, curved spout, lightly chased, 19oz 11d*	*Christie's December 13, 1961 #178* *Bell of Aberdeen Collection 1951 #15*

YEAR	MAKER	LOCATION	DESCRIPTION	SOURCE
1738/39	Archibald Ure	Edinburgh	Teapot, spherical, curved spout, lightly chased, silver handle 5 ½" ht, 19oz 12d	Apollo October 1948 vol 48 p18 Bracher & Snyder advertisement
1738/39	James Hally	Edinburgh	Teapot, spherical chased, mm I HY, 17oz 8d	Christie's March 7, 1962 #101
1738/39	James Weems	Edinburgh	Teapot, spherical, curved spout, original insulated silver handle, 6 ½" ht, 23oz 15d	Argentum Antiques, San Francisco CA USA 1996
1738/39	James Ker	Edinburgh	Teapot, contemporary flat chased decoration around mouth, lid with flush hinge and button and ball finial, curved semi-fluted spout, leaf capped silver loop handle, 9 ½" long, 21.5oz	JH Bourdon-Smith Catalog Spring 1983
1738/39	Charles Blair	Edinburgh	Teapot, on circular spreading foot, upper body flat chased with alternate cartouches of shells, and bunches of flowers within strap work, hinged lid with baluster finial, semi-fluted curved spout, silver plain capped loop handle, 6 7/8" ht, 22.8oz	Christie's Geneva? November 9, 1976 #53 Christie's Geneva? November 16, 1993 #13
1738/39	James Ker	Edinburgh	Teapot, on domed circular foot, upper part of body and cover flat chased, with band of flower heads, foliage and scrolls, orbed finial, straight tapering spout, leaf capped silver loop handle, 2 crests, one on each side, 19oz	Christie's Glasgow March 27, 1984 #270
1738/39	Not available	Edinburgh	Teapot, near spherical, flat chased with baskets of fruit, scrolls and diaper work at the shoulder, flat lid with bun finial, part fluted spout, leaf capped handle, 5 ½" ht, 19.6oz	Sotheby's Gleneagles August 29, 1983 #507
1739/40	James Mitchell	Edinburgh	Teapot, spherical, curved spout, original insulated silver handle, mm IM figure between, 6 ½" ht, 23oz 15d	Private Collection
1739/40	James Mitchell Assayer David Mitchell	Edinburgh	Teapot, no details, possibly the same as above	Christie's July 1987 #168
1739/40	Edward Lothian Assayer David Mitchell	Edinburgh	Teapot, spherical, on spreading foot, flat chased at shoulder with floral and fruit clusters within rococo matting, lid similarly decorated, spherical finial, molded curved spout, scroll handle, crest and motto of Buchan, 6" ht, 26oz	Sotheby's February 12, 1970 #195 Shrubsole NY USA Ticher Irish Silver, p28
1739/40	James Mitchell Assayer David Mitchell	Edinburgh	Teapot, spherical, on circular foot, partly fluted curved spout, shoulder and lid chased with flowers, wave ornament, and trellis work, orb finial, leaf capped silver loop handle, 21oz	Christie's March 25, 1981 #188 JH Bourdon-Smith Catalog Spring 1981
1739/40	James Ker Assayer David Mitchell	Edinburgh	Teapot, spherical, on spreading circular foot, partly fluted scroll spout, flush hinged lid, ball and button finial, engraved round mouth with band of shells, scrolls, and foliage, 23oz	Christie's March 19, 1986 #232

YEAR	MAKER	LOCATION	DESCRIPTION	SOURCE
1739/40	James Mitchell Assayer David Mitchell	Edinburgh	Teapot, spherical, on circular molded foot, partly fluted curved spout, upper part of body chased with flowers, fruit and foliage on matted ground, baluster finial, possibly one of the previous ones, 23oz	Christie's July 8, 1987 #167 Phillips Edinburgh March 20, 1987 #
1739/40	James Mitchell Assayer David Mitchell	Edinburgh	Teapot, compressed spherical, on circular molded foot, shoulder and lid chased with fruit, foliage and scrolls, partly fluted curved spout, baluster finial, 18.3oz	Christie's November 7, 1973 # Christie's March 20, 1974 #
1739/40	Dougal Ged Assayer David Mitchell	Edinburgh	Teapot, previously mis-ascribed to David Mitchell, near spherical with curved spout, chased at shoulder and on lid with scrolls, flowers, and foliage, curved half-fluted spout, silver plain capped scroll handle, with bun finial, crest below a motto placed between spout and mid-point of off side,	Holland Silver p 18 or 22
1739/40	David Mitchell	Edinburgh	Teapot, engraved under foot "IL, DK, KG, MC"	National Museums of Scotland MEQ 603
1739/40	James Hally Assayer David Mitchell	Edinburgh	Teapot, spherical, on molded circular foot, body chased round the shoulder and lid with flowers, fruit, shells, and strap work, curved spout chased with a shell, ball finial, 17.4oz	Christie's March 7, 1962 #101
1739/40	James Ker	Edinburgh	Teapot, spherical, short curved spout, silver handle, light chasing	Sotheby's November 3, 1949 #89
1739/40	James Ker Assayer Archibald Ure	Edinburgh	Teapot, no detail	Connoisseur Magazine 1950 vol 125 p68
1739/40	James Ker Assayer David Mitchell	Edinburgh	Teapot, compressed spherical, curved short spout, partly fluted silver handle, broadly decorated, end of spout with a slight notch	Christie's March 19, 1986 #232 Christie's Negative #66902
1739/70	James Mitchelson Assayer David Mitchell	Edinburgh	Teapot, chased, silver handle, curved spout, 21oz	Christie's March 25, 1981
1739/40	*James Mitchelson Assayer David Mitchell*	*Edinburgh*	*Teapot, silver circular handle, curved spout partly fluted, sold originally as a mixed set with a Lothian sugar bowl and a cream boat, 21oz*	*Christie's March 26, 1980 Pictured in Holland Silver p18*
1739/40	James Mitchelson Assayer David Mitchell	Edinburgh	Teapot, "S" shaped silver handle	Apollo January 1974 vol 99 p43 Asprey advertisement
1739/40	Not available Assayer David	Edinburgh	Teapot, spherical 20oz	Christie's December 7, 1955 #35

YEAR	MAKER Mitchell	LOCATION	DESCRIPTION	SOURCE
1739/40	Ebenezer Oliphant	Edinburgh	Teapot, curved spout, silver handle, chased body	JH Bourdon-Smith London, 1996
1739/40	Hugh Penman	Edinburgh	Teapot, flattened spherical body	National Museums of Scotland MEQ 1983.28
1740 ca	George Cooper	Aberdeen	Teapot and stand, spherical shaped, on spreading circular base, scroll spout with shell joint, leaf capped double scroll handle, wood insulators, shoulder and cover flat chased with border of scrolls and flowers, flat hinged cover surmounted by turned wood finial, handle engraved with block initials "I x L/R", shaped circular stand on 3 hoof feet, molded rim, border flat chased with similar decoration, engraved with block initials on reverse "I x L/R", each marked under base, 7" ht, 6 7/8" di, 30oz both	Christie's NY USA October 20, 1999 #312
1740 ca	George Cooper	Aberdeen	Teapot, spherical shape, chased at shoulders with diaper, scale ornament and foliage within outline of strap work, floral festoons and pendants below, fluted swan neck spout, wood handle and finial, son spreading rococo bordered foot, 5 ¾" ht, 15oz 18d	Sotheby's February 12, 1959 #150
1740ca	Alexander Johnston	Dundee	Teapot, spherical shape, no details	Dundee Museum and Art Galleries 1985-181
1740ca	Alexander Johnston	Dundee	Teapot, spherical shape, flat chased with flowers, shells, and scrolls round mouth, silver single scroll handle, spreading foot, domed lid with flush hinge, bun finial, with later initials, crest and motto, 23.9oz	Sotheby's Gleneagles September 1, 1981 #459
1740ca	Alexander Johnston	Dundee	Teapot, with stand, no details	Private Collection UK
1740ca	George Cooper	Aberdeen	Teapot, with stand and mashing spoon, spherical, on tall stem, silver scroll handle, fluted duck neck spout, decorated in rococo style, 7"ht	Bell of Aberdeen Collection, 1961, #10
1740ca	George Cooper	Aberdeen	Teapot, no details, marks - GC, d, three castles	Private collection, UK
1740ca	Johan Got-helf - Bilsings	Glasgow	Teapot, slightly compressed-spherical body, chased with scrolling foliage, floral and fruit clusters and shell ornament, a vacant cartouche on either side, molded curved spout, double scroll silver handle, applied hinged lid also chased as body, ball finial, 6 ¼'ht, 21.6oz (or 5 ¾"ht 21.6oz-Blair catalog)	Sotheby's Gleneagles August 30, 1973 #70c Sotheby's Blair Castle September 12, 1980 #162
1740 ca	George Cooper	Aberdeen	Teapot, spherical, on spreading circular foot, fluted curved spout, engraved around rim with diaper work and foliated scrolls, fluted baluster fruitwood finial, later wood handle, marked under base - GC, 3 castles, small gothic B, 6" ht, 16oz	Christie's Glasgow November 16, 1994 #681

YEAR	MAKER	LOCATION	DESCRIPTION	SOURCE
1740 ca	George Cooper	Aberdeen	Teapot, tapering spherical form, stepped spreading foot, shoulders flat chased with border of scrolls, trellis work, flower heads, foliage, hinged domed lid, straight tapering spout, wooden baluster finial, scroll handle, base engraved with initials "R*F", marked on base - GC, triple tower, gothic "e", 6 1/3" ht, 17oz	Phillips Edinburgh August 24, 2001 #629
1740 ca	George Cooper	Aberdeen	Teapot, spherical, curved spout, silver handle, light chasing, wooden finial, with stand, 7" ht	Nicholas Shaw Catalog 2005 p94
1740 ca	Robert Luke II	Glasgow	Teapot, spherical, flat chased at the shoulder with a band of scrolls, fruit and foliage, initial "R", 5 ¾" ht, 21oz 14d	Sotheby's Gleneagles 1998 #550
1740 ca	James Tait	Edinburgh	Teapot, shoulder and lid with chased decoration of flowers, foliage, scrolls and diaper work, short swan neck, spout reeded and fluted at the base, S-scroll handle capped with foliage, molded rim foot, 6" ht, 22.1oz	Sotheby's April 24, 1958 #96
1740 ca	Colin Allan	Aberdeen	Teapot, spherical, chased with flowers, shells and scrolls, 21oz 19d	Christie's April 15, 1931 #6 Christie's June 16, 1931 #19
1740 ca	IS mark	Banff	Teapot, 14oz	Lyle Silver Review 1983 p626 Sotheby's
1740 ca	Not available		Teapot, decorated, curved spout	Waldron #866
1740 ca	Johan Got-helf-Bilsings	Glasgow	Teapot, curved spout, wood handle, initials "IC" underneath, 5 ¾" ht, 15oz 8d	Sotheby's February 21, 1980 #168
1740 ca	Johan Got-helf-Bilsings	Glasgow	Teapot, curved spout, heavy later chasing, silver handle, 5 ¾" ht, 21oz 13d	Sotheby's Blair Castle September 1980 #162
1740 ca	*Johan Got-helf-Bilsings*	Glasgow	*Teapot, 5 ¾" ht, 16oz 6d*	*Lyle Annual Review 1981 p625* *Sotheby's*
1740 ca	Colin Allan	Aberdeen	Teapot, spherical, chased with flowers, shells and scrolls, 21oz 19d	Christie's April 15, 1931 #6 Christie's June 16, 1931 #19
1740/41	Charles Dickson II	Edinburgh	Teapot, oblong, 4 convex sides, pierced rectangular finial, silver handle	Antiques Magazine June 1996 p847 Wilson & Sharp Hyman Collection - Colonial Williamsburg G1999-201

YEAR	MAKER	LOCATION	DESCRIPTION	SOURCE
1740/41	Edward Lothian	Edinburgh	Teapot, no details	Antiques Magazine vol 88 410 Shrubsole advertisement
1740/41	James Mitchell	Edinburgh	Teapot, spherical, shoulder and collar chased with flowers and stylized floral motif, *sold with a later sugar bowl and cream boat*,	Christie's June 20, 1973 #
1740/41	James Mitchell	Edinburgh	Teapot, spherical, chased decoration, silver handle, different from those in post-1948 sales	National Museums of Scotland 1948.3
1740/41	James Mitchell	Edinburgh	Teapot, spherical, chased at shoulder with fruit, foliage, flowers and scrolls, leaf capped scroll handle, *domed lid, curved spout*, 6 ½" ht, 18.4oz	Sotheby's Scone Palace April 13, 1976 #54 Rix Antiques
1740/41	William Aytoun	Edinburgh	*Teapot, flattened spherical shape, curved spout, silver handle, crest and motto "FORGET NOT", 5 1/16" ht, 20.1oz*	Apollo 1933 vol 17 p13 How of Edinburgh advertisement Christie's Lanarkshire UK 1997 #54 Nicholas Shaw Catalog 2000 p70 Bonhams the Scottish Sale August 23, 2003 #11
1741/42	James Mitchelson	Edinburgh	Teapot, spherical, fluted spout, chased, 18oz 7d	Christie's April 24, 1964 #93
1741/42	*James Mitchelson*	*Edinburgh*	*Teapot, spherical form, partly fluted curved spout, upper body chased with band of flowers and scrollwork, lid with ball finial, on spreading foot, with two rococo cartouches with crest and initials, 18.8oz*	*Christie's April 24, 1968 #93 de Havilland Antiques*
1741/42	William Aytoun	Edinburgh	Teapot, spherical shape, upper body chased with a wide band of shell, scroll, floral and foliate motifs, two vacant cartouches, the lid similarly decorated, ball finial, curved spout, leaf-capped silver loop handle, spreading foot, 6"ht, 24.3oz	Sotheby's November 22, 1973 #188
1741/42	James Ker	Edinburgh	Teapot, small compressed spherical shape, chased round the mouth with flowers, fruit and foliage, partly fluted curved spout, conforming bullet shaped finial, fruit wood capped loop handle, patched, with a crest, 5"ht, 13.5oz	Christie's Scotland November 25-27, 1997 #108
1741/42	*James Ker*	*Edinburgh*	*Teapot, flattened spherical teapot, on raised foot, curved fluted spout, chasing on upper body, wooden handle, flattened ball finial*	Ian McCan Antiques 2004
1741/42	Robert Gordon	Edinburgh	Punch Pot, compressed spherical body, curved spout, flush-hinged lid at side, acorn finial, somewhat later coat of arms in rococo cartouche of Spearman impaling Young, inscription dated 1761, 6 ¼"ht, 30oz	Christie's October 14, 1992 #190; Christie's Edinburgh November 17-18, 1993 #725

YEAR	MAKER	LOCATION	DESCRIPTION	SOURCE
1742/43	James Mitchell	Edinburgh	Teapot, spherical, curved spout, mm IM figure between, 22oz 11d	Christie's December 7, 1955 #111
1742/43	*James Mitchell*	*Edinburgh*	*Teapot, silver handle with acanthus capped scroll thumbpiece, possibly same as above teapot, 23.2oz*	*How of Edinburgh 1937 #100*
1742/43	James Ker Assayer Edward Lothian	Edinburgh	Teapot, slightly compressed spherical body, flat chased around the flat hinged lid with scrolls and foliage, wood handle, curved spout, 5 ¾" ht, 18oz 13d	Sotheby's Gleneagles August 28, 1975 #64
1742/43	Robert Low	Edinburgh	Teapot, chased, curved spout, silver handle, 5 ¾" ht, 23oz 10d	Sotheby's October 24, 1985 #60
1742/43	James Campbell I	Edinburgh	Teapot, part of a 3 piece service, spherical, on spreading foot, partly fluted spout, shoulder and lid chased round the mouth with bunches of flowers and fruit in shells and scrollwork, catalog says by James Clark or Clarke	Sotheby's July 18, 1963 #297 Christie's July 5, 1967 #172 de Havilland Antiques
1742/43	Edward Lothian	Edinburgh	Teapot, offered with a sugar bowl 1744/45 probably by AG, shoulders and rim flat chased with foliage and flowers, ball finial, silver leaf capped single-scroll handle, ivory insulators, with a crest and motto, 6" ht	Sotheby's May 3, 1962 #12 Simon Kaye Antiques Sotheby's June 18, 1987 #251 Christie's (or Sotheby's) Scottish Picture files
1742/43	James Mitchelson	Edinburgh	Teapot, spherical shape, flat chased below the rim with shells, scroll and floral ornament, with two vacant cartouches, leaf-capped silver loop handle, partly lobed curved spout, on spreading base, flush hinged lid with a band of flat chased decoration, ball finial, 5 ¾" ht, 19oz	Sotheby's June 20-30 1981 #136 Sotheby's October 22, 1981 #186 Lyle Annual Review 1983 p626
1742/43	John Welsh	Edinburgh	Teapot, no details	National Museums of Scotland 1957.362
1743 ca	James Glen	Glasgow	Teapot and stand, inverted pear form, on circular molded foot, curved spout chased with shells and scrolls, terminating in a bird's head, with mask and shell scroll handle, shoulder chased with shells, flowers, scrolls, and 2 vacant rococo cartouches, hinged domed lid chased with a band of shells and scrolls, stylized bud finial, stand on 3 scroll feet, molded shell and scroll border chased with broad band of fruit, flowers, shells, and scrolls, 6 ½" ht, 32 oz all	Christie's February 9, 1972 #133 Sotheby's January 26, 1967 #94
1743ca	Robert Luke II	Glasgow	Teapot, almost spherical form, on circular molded foot, upper part of body and cover chased with flowers and scrolls, with partly fluted curved spout, ball finial, bearing town mark of tree, bell and fish, 21oz	Christie's July 13, 1966 #142
1743 ca	Not available	Glasgow	Teapot, bullet shaped, flat chased with collar of flowers, fruit and rococo decoration within scrolling foliage, semi fluted curved spout, leaf capped scroll	Sotheby's May 30, 1968 #193

YEAR	MAKER (continued)	LOCATION	DESCRIPTION	SOURCE
			handle, molded base, bun finial, flush hinged lid, mm rubbed, 5 ½" ht, 41oz 2d	
1743 ca	James Glen	Glasgow	Teapot, inverted pear shape, flat chased with scrolls and blooms, 2 vacant cartouches, domed cover, cone finial, loop handle, on spreading base, 6 ¼" ht, 23oz 10d	Sotheby's Scone April 14-15, 1983 #46
1743ca	James Glen	Glasgow	Teapot, artichoke finial, leaf end spout, no other details	National Museums of Scotland MEQ 180
1743ca	James Glen	Glasgow	Teapot, inverted pear body, heavily chased, bird's beak spout, artichoke finial,	Hyman Collection-Colonial Williamsburg G1997-11
1743 ca	James Glen	Glasgow	Teapot, no details	National Museums of Scotland MEQ 1186
1743/44	Edward Lothian	Edinburgh	Teapot, spherical shape, body with a frieze of arabesques, on rising circular foot, shell-fluted curved spout, leaf-capped scroll handle, artichoke finial, 5 ¾" ht, 20.5oz	Christie's January 4, 1988 #42
1743/44	Edward Lothian	Edinburgh	Teapot, spherical, chased around the shoulder with flowers, scrolls and fruit, curved spout, silver handle, 20oz 18d	Sotheby's London June 25, 2003 #316
1743/44	Edward Lothian	Edinburgh	Teapot, spherical, curved spout, silver handle, chased, 5 ½" ht, 20.1oz	Nicholas Shaw Catalog 2004 p100
1743/44	James Ker	Edinburgh	Teapot, from the Erskine Tea Service, initials "AE" on the bottom for the Erskine family, near spherical, chased, silver leaf capped loop handles, semi fluted curved spout	Christie's June 22, 1969 #101 Clayton Dictionary p 310 #651
1743/44	James Ker	Edinburgh	Teapot, spherical, straight spout, engraved, 22oz 10d	Christie's March 24, 1914 #59 E. A. Jones Book Ashburton Collection pl 58, #3 Farrer Collection
1743/44	William Aytoun Assayer Edward Lothian	Edinburgh	Teapot, spherical on a circular foot, partly fluted spout, 20oz 1d	Christie's May 5, 1950 #31
1743/44	William Aytoun	Edinburgh	Teapot, spherical, silver handle, curved partly fluted spout, cone finial, crest in a cartouche, initials "WFS", 20oz	Christie's May 18, 1988 #155 Christie's Negative #140465
1743ca	Johan Got-helf-Bilsings	Glasgow	Teapot, not pictured	Connoisseur Magazine 1954 vol 133 p6

YEAR	MAKER (continued)	LOCATION	DESCRIPTION	SOURCE
	Charles Dickson II	Edinburgh	Teapot, no details	Bell of Aberdeen advertisement Jackson Marks p547
1744/45	Hugh Penman	Edinburgh	Teapot, spherical, curved spout, Arms of Maxwell Baronet, 5 ¾" ht	Sotheby's March 23, 1993 #133 Scottish Art Review 1967 vol XI p32 #2 Moffat & Co advertisement
1744/45	Robert Low	Edinburgh	Teapot, spherical, flat chased at shoulder with floral and foliate swags, leaf capped silver loop handle, bud finial, part fluted curved spout, spreading foot, 6 ¼" ht, 18.6oz	Sotheby's Scone Palace April 13, 1976 #131
1745 ca	Robert Luke	Glasgow	Teapot, almost spherical form, on molded foot, curved spout, cast and chased with shells, scrolls and foliage, shoulder similarly chased, baluster finial to the slight raised cover, mm RL, 23oz	Christie's December 10, 1980
1745 ca	James Glen	Glasgow	Teapot, ogee shaped body, chased at shoulder with band of flowerheads, foliage, rococo and 2 vacant cartouches, on spreading foot, foliate and shell encased spout terminating in a serpent's head, leaf capped silver handle with wood fillets, and joined to body with a mouthless male mask, domed cover with acorn cone finial, 6 ½" ht, 25oz 14d	Sotheby's London June 18, 1987
1745 ca	James Glen	Glasgow	Teapot, globular body, resting on a spreading foot, engraved with "GB HL" on handle on the underside, part fluted curved spout, lid with ball finial, 6" ht, 19oz 14d	Sotheby's Hopetoun House April 29, 1987
1745 ca	James Ker	Edinburgh	Teapot, spherical body, hinged lid flat chased with fruit, flowers and scrolls, later engraved with a crest and motto, silver button and handle, 5 ½" ht, 20oz 16d	Sotheby's September 16, 1986
1745 ca	Johan Got-helf-Bilsings	Glasgow	Teapot, elongated spherical shape, curved spout, 5 ¼" di	Scotland Art Academy Exhibition 1939 #921 Provenance of Lord Glentanar
1745 ca	*Johan Got-helf-Bilsings*	*Glasgow*	*Teapot, bird's beak spout, 6 ½" ht*	*Sotheby's London June 1988 #248*
1745ca	George Cooper	Aberdeen	Teapot, silver and fruit wood, no details, Monogram "JG", based marked - GC, three towers, Gothic A	Aberdeen Museums and Galleries ABDAG008598
1745ca	Edward Lothian	Edinburgh	Teapot, spherical shape, no details	Dundee Museum and Art Galleries 1986-139

YEAR	MAKER	LOCATION	DESCRIPTION	SOURCE
1745 ca	Robert Luke	Glasgow	Teapot, curved spout, decorated	Christie's February 9, 1972 #132
1745 ca	James Glen	Glasgow	Teapot, spherical, on a spreading circular foot, with a leaf capped scroll handle with ivory insulators, partly fluted spout, lid with baluster finial, 5" ht, 21oz gross	Christie's London UK 1998 #84
1745/46	Edward Lothian	Edinburgh	Teapot, spherical, chased, wood handle, button finial, crest, curved leaf ending spout, 6 ½" ht, 23oz	Silver Vault IL USA 1994
1745/46	Edward Lothian	Edinburgh	Teapot, foliate finial, 6 ½" ht	Kovel's 1992 Price Guide p704
1745/46	Hugh Gordon	Edinburgh	Teapot, bullet shape, on spreading foot, chased around the rim and cover with shells, scrolls and foliage, partly fluted curved spout, leaf capped scroll handle, orb finial, old repair to base, 6" ht, 19oz	Christie's Scotland June 8-9, 1994
1745/46	Hugh Gordon	Edinburgh	Teapot, 7oz	Kovel's 1995 Price Guide p624
1746/47	James Ker	Edinburgh	Teapot, possibly misdated assayer listed as A. Ure, hemispherical on a spreading foot, hinged domed lid, ball finial, coat-of-arms of MacLeod of Cadboll, co. Ross, cypher, scratch weight 24:10 underneath, 6" ht, 23oz	Christie's London May 12, 1993 #114 Christie's London 2007 #86
1746/47	Robert Gordon	Edinburgh	Teapot, globular body and lid, part chased with shells, scrolls and foliage, part fluted spout, artichoke finial, 6 1/8" ht, 24oz gross	Christie's London 2004 #540
1746/47	James Ker	Edinburgh	Teapot, spherical, silver handle, curved spout, chased, repaired hinge, replaced finial, part of a 3 piece service	Sotheby's NY USA June 10, 1980 #433
1746/47	Edward Lothian Assayer Hugh Gordon	Edinburgh	Teapot, spherical, George II, flat chased at the shoulder and lid, scrolls enclosing clusters of fruit and shells, vacant cartouches on either side, semi-lobed spout, cone finial, loop handle, on spreading foot, 6" ht, 19oz 15d	Sotheby's June, 22, 1972 #190
1746/47	Robert Low Assayer Hugh Gordon	Edinburgh	Teapot, spherical, flush hinged lid, surround flat chased with a band of scroll enclosed blooms above and engraved crest and motto, fluted curved spout, leaf capped loop handle, spreading base, bud finial, 6" ht, 20oz	Sotheby's April 28-29, 1983 #1517
1746/47	Edward Lothian Assayer Hugh Gordon	Edinburgh	Teapot, spherical, George II, flat chased with a collar of foliage, rococo work and scrolls around the flush hinged lid, bud finial, part fluted leaf capped silver loop handle, on spreading dome foot, 5 ½" ht, 15oz 9d	Sotheby's November 12-13, 1979 #70 Lyle Annual Review 1981 p626
1746/47	Edward Lothian	Edinburgh	Teapot, spherical, silver loop handle, curved spout	Antiques Magazine 1948 vol 54 p387 James Graham & Sons, Inc. NY USA advertisement

YEAR	MAKER	LOCATION	DESCRIPTION	SOURCE
1746/47	Robert Low Assayer Hugh Gordon	Edinburgh	Teapot, spherical, on circular pedestal foot, circular body with partly chased C-scroll and foliate detail, circular lid, integral hinge, bud finial, leaf capped handle and spout, crest, repair to the foot, 21.5oz	Phillips Edinburgh December 4, 1997
1746/47	Robert Low	Edinburgh	Teapot, spherical, curved spout, flat chased, crest and motto "WITH HEART AND HAND", possibly same as above, 8 ¾" ht, 21.9oz	Noble Collection Nicholas Shaw Catalog 2004 p98
1746/47	Charles Dickson II	Edinburgh	Teapot, no details	Antiques Magazine 1958 vol 74
1746/47	Charles Dickson II	Edinburgh	Teapot, chased repaired foot, marked base, 6 ¾" ht, 21oz 16d	Sotheby's NY USA October 27, 1982 #376
1746/47	Edward Lothian Assayer Hugh Gordon	Edinburgh	Teapot, spherical, on circular molded foot, partly fluted curved spout, shoulder and cover chased with flowers and scrolls, cone finial, 19oz 10d	Christie's April 27, 1960
1747/48	Hugh Gordon	Edinburgh	Teapot, bullet shape, on domed circular foot, upper body and hinged lid chased with flower heads and foliate scrolls enclosing to each side a vacant rococo cartouche, partly fluted curved spout, scroll handle with acanthus leaf thumb piece, bud finial, 5 ½" ht, 21oz	Christie's Glasgow November 21, 1989 #51
1747/48	Ebenezer Oliphant Assayer Hugh Gordon	Edinburgh	Teapot, inverted pear shape, flat chased with band of flowers, shells and scrolls below the rim, leap capped loop handle, part lobed curved spout, on spreading base, dome lid with bud finial, 6 ½" ht, 21oz	Sotheby's February 18, 1982 #109
1747/48	Ebenezer Oliphant Assayer Hugh Gordon	Edinburgh	Teapot, inverted pear shape, on a rising circular foot, shell fluted rising curved spout, leaf capped scroll handle, dome hinged lid, artichoke finial, body and cover each chased with a frieze of arabesques, engraved with crest, 6 ¼", 21.8oz	Christie's London February 21, 1989 #348 Christie's July 11, 1989 #91
1747/48	Ebenezer Oliphant Assayer Hugh Gordon	Edinburgh	Teapot, inverted pear shaped, on rising circular foot, shell fluted rising curved spout, leaf capped scroll handle, domed hinged lid, artichoke finial, body and cover each chased with a frieze of arabesques, engraved with crest, 6 ¾" ht, 22oz	Lyle Silver Review 1982 p114
1747/48	Ebenezer Oliphant Assayer Hugh Gordon	Edinburgh	Teapot, pear shaped body, engraved with crest, flat chased around the cover with rococo and foliate motifs, bud finial, fluted curved spout, on spreading base, 6 ¾" ht, 22oz 1d	Sotheby's August 29-30, 1977 #189
1747/48	Ebenezer Oliphant	Edinburgh	Teapot, no crest, 6 ½" ht, 22oz 6d	Sotheby's December 18, 1982
1748/49 *1740 ca	William Gilchrist Assayer Dougal Ged	Edinburgh	Teapot, on spreading foot, compressed spherical body, hinged lid, flat chased with scrolls and other motifs, silver handle with ivory fillers, silver button,	Sotheby's Gleneagles, September 1, 1987 #291

YEAR	MAKER (continued)	LOCATION	DESCRIPTION	SOURCE
	James Mitchell	Edinburgh	wrong date, underside engraved with initials "AS", 20oz 12d	Phillips Edinburgh March, 20, 1987 #124
1748/49	James Mitchell	Edinburgh	Teapot, spherical, plain body, contemporary chased floral border, mm IM figure between, 20oz 13d	Christie's London UK 1999 #195
1748/49	Charles Dickson II	Edinburgh	Teapot, inverted pear shape on a circular spreading foot, upper body chased with shells, scrolls, flowers and foliage on a matted ground, 2 vacant oval cartouches, one later engraved with a crest and motto, hinged slightly domed lid with flat chased decoration, pine cone finial, partly fluted spout, leaf capped silver handle, with ivory insulators, 6" ht, 23oz gross	Christie's Scotland May 23, 1996 #529
1748/49 *1740	Ebenezer Oliphant Assayer Dougal Ged	Edinburgh	Teapot, spherical, on circular domed foot, plain lower body, chased with foliage to upper body and hinged lid, silver knop finial, partly fluted spout and loop handle, engraved with coat of arms supported by 2 male figures, arms are those of Duff for William Duff of Dipple and Braco, born in 1697, created Baron Braco of Kilbryde 1735 and Earl of Fife 1759, probably assigned to the wrong year, should be 1740/41, 7 ½" ht, 26oz	Spink London 1975 Christie's NY USA October 20, 1998
1748/49	James Mitchell Assayer Hugh Gordon	Edinburgh	Teapot, bullet shaped, on spreading stepped base, leaf capped scroll handle with insulators, shoulder flat chased with vacant cartouches on each side, scrolls, foliage and rococo, cover with pinecone finial, IM figure between mm, 6" ht, 23oz 10d	JH Bourdon-Smith Catalog Spring 1978
1748/49	Ebenezer Oliphant Assayer Hugh Gordon	Edinburgh	Teapot, chased decoration, 9 ½" from spout to handle, 21oz,	Sotheby's April 5-6, 1982 #208
1748/49	Ker & Dempster Assayer Hugh Gordon	Edinburgh	Teapot, inverted pear shape, chased on the shoulder and edge of domed cover with foliate scrolls and rococo on a matted ground, 2 vacant cartouches, spreading base, leaf capped loop handle, fluted curved spout, cone finial, 6 ½" ht, 23oz 10d	Christie's March 25, 1936 #40 Christie's July 28, 1936 #107
1748/49	James Mitchell	Edinburgh	Teapot, spherical, chased shoulder, mm IM figure between, either 22oz 14d or 20oz 2d	Christie's July 27, 1932 #50 How of Edinburgh Collection
1748/49	William Aytoun	Edinburgh	Teapot, high foot, chased, 19oz 4d	
1748/49	Edward Lothian	Edinburgh	Teapot, inverted pear shape, silver loop handle, chased, curved fluted spout, 20oz	Antiques Magazine December 1963 vol 84 p746 Bell of Aberdeen advertisement

YEAR	MAKER	LOCATION	DESCRIPTION	SOURCE
1748/49	IM in a rectangle James McKenzie I or James Mitchelson Assayer Hugh Gordon	Edinburgh	Teapot, inverted pear shape, curved fluted spout, leaf cap circular silver handle, acorn finial	Antiques Magazine vol 118 p 197 Robinson NY advertisement
1748/49	Ebenezer Oliphant	Edinburgh	Teapot, spherical, chased, 23oz 10d	Christie's May 25, 1938 #64
1749/50	Ker & Dempster Assayer Hugh Gordon	Edinburgh	Teapot, spherical, slightly squat, domed circular base, partly curved spout, hinged lid, pineapple finial, engraved on body with contemporary coat of arms of Nicholson, 6 5/8" ht, 10 5/8" long, 19.34oz	Nicholas Shaw Catalog Winter 2001 p71
1749/50	James Welsh	Edinburgh	Teapot, inverted pear shape, decorated with flat chasing around the body, hinged lid, pineapple finial, 2 3/8" ht, 20oz 18d	Nicholas Shaw Catalog 1999 p63 Nicholas Shaw Catalog, Winter 2000, p70
1749/50	William Dempster or William Davie Assayer Hugh Gordon	Edinburgh	Teapot, inverted pear shape, upper body flat chased with flowers, scrolls, and 2 vacant rococo cartouches, domed lid with foliage, part lobed curved spout, spreading base, bud finial, 6 ¼" ht, 17oz 16d	Sotheby's April 26, 1984 #111
1749/50	Ker & Dempster Assayer Hugh Gordon	Edinburgh	Teapot, inverted pear shaped body, chased with scrolls, shells, floral and fruit sprays, semi fluted curved spout, domed lid with cone finial, on molded rim foot, 7" ht, 4 ¾" di, 28oz 12d	Sotheby's April 28, 1960 #144
1749/50	IM in a rectangle James McKenzie I or James Mitchelson	Edinburgh	Teapot, upper part of inverted pear shape body, chased with floral sprays, scroll, scale work and shell ornaments, with a vacant cartouche on either side, hinged slightly domed lid, bud finial, leaf capped handle, molded circular foot, 6 ½" ht, 21oz 5d	Sotheby's March 22, 1973 #209 JH Bourdon-Smith Ltd, London UK Bonhams London UK 2005 #94
1749/50	John Rollo Assayer Hugh Gordon	Edinburgh	Teapot, spherical shape, with crest, chased with fruit swags, flowers and rococo decoration, swan neck spout, leaf capped handle, cone finial, on rim foot, (Note: should be a different maker since Rollo was no longer active at this point), 6" ht, 20oz 19d	Sotheby's July 12, 1962 #110
1749/50	William Aytoun	Edinburgh	Teapot, fluted spout, chased over the shoulder, 19oz 19d	Christie's June 28, 1906 #80
1749/50	Edward Lothian	Edinburgh	Teapot, vase shaped, chased on shoulder, 21oz 15d	Christie's November 24, 1943 #8 Noble Collection
1749/50	Edward Lothian	Edinburgh	Teapot, no details	Jackson Marks p548
1749/50	Not available	Edinburgh	Teapot, inverted pear form, circular base, body chased with flowers and two rococo cartouches, one engraved with a monogram, fluted scroll spout, leaf	Christie's NY USA 2004 #1059

YEAR	MAKER (continued)	LOCATION	DESCRIPTION	SOURCE
			clad handle with mask, ivory insulators, bud finial, mm lacking, 10 ½" long, 23oz gross	
1750 ca	Colin Allan	Aberdeen	Teapot, plain slightly compressed spherical shape, on stepped spreading circular foot, part shell clad curved spout, fruitwood handle, hinged lid, baluster finial, 6 ½" ht	Christie's Lanarkshire UK 1997 #119
1750 ca	James Glen	Glasgow	Teapot, no details	Sotheby's Hopetoun House April 1988 #68
1750 ca	Not available		Teapot, decorated, bird finial, said to be Scottish	Waldron p 867
1750 ca	Colin Allan	Aberdeen	Teapot, inverted pear shape, wood handle, service of 3 pieces, 5 ¼" ht	Christie's London July 1992 #100
1750 ca	Colin Allan	Aberdeen	Teapot, plain body, curved spout, replaced wood handle, multi level finial	Apollo 1934 vol 20 p4 Bell of Aberdeen advertisement
1750 ca	George Cooper	Aberdeen	Teapot, spherical, curved spout, wooden handle, deep chasing, engraved script initial "L", 6 ½" ht, 21.8oz	Nicholas Shaw Catalog 2001 p68
1750 ca	Alexander Johnson	Dundee	Teapot, compressed spherical shape, engraved with flowers and scrolls, 23oz 8d	Christie's July 28, 1930 #59
1750ca	James Glen	Glasgow	Teapot, no details	National Museums of Scotland MEQ 29
1750ca	Colin Allan	Aberdeen	Teapot, silver, no details, base marked - CA,CA,ABD, FF with a pelican crest	Aberdeen Museums and Galleries ABDAG001007
1750ca	Colin Allan	Aberdeen	Teapot, with stand, spherical on tall stem, silver scroll handle, fluted duck-neck spout, decorated in rococo style, 7"ht	Bell of Aberdeen Collection, 1961, #16
1750ca	Colin Allan	Aberdeen	Teapot, spherical body on stem, fluted duck-neck spout, silver scroll handle, decorated in rococo style, 6 ½"ht	Bell of Aberdeen Collection, 1961, #17
1750/51	Ker & Dempster	Edinburgh	Teapot, no details	Dundee Museum and Art Galleries 1964-26
1750/51	James Welsh	Edinburgh	Teapot, inverted pear shape, chased decoration	National Museums of Scotland MEQ 617 1962.1025
1751/52	Robert Gordon	Edinburgh	Teapot, no details	Antiques Magazine 1962 vol 82

YEAR	MAKER	LOCATION	DESCRIPTION	SOURCE
1751/52	James Welsh	Edinburgh	Teapot, inverted pear shape, on spreading circular foot, with fluted curved spout, leaf-capped scroll handle and domed hinged lid with artichoke finial, chased with a frieze of flowers and arabesques and engraved with two armorials within rococo cartouches, the underside with initials, 6"ht, 23.5oz	Christie's October 25, 1989 #193
1751/52	*James Welsh*	*Edinburgh*	*Teapot, chased floral leaf on silver handle, heavy*	*N & I Franklin, London 1994*
1752/53	William Dempster or William Davie	Edinburgh	Teapot, no details	Antiques Magazine vol 91 p22 James Robinson NY advertisement
1752/53	Ker & Dempster	Edinburgh	Teapot, compressed spherical on molded circular foot, flat lid and flush hinge, half-fluted curved spout, wooden loop handle with a thumb-piece, armorials within a brickwork and foliate strap-work cartouche, arms of Gordon impaling Brodie, 5"ht, 18.8oz	Sotheby's November 11 1993 #443 Sotheby's Gleneagles August 29, 1994 #137
1752/53	Dougal Ged	Edinburgh	Teapot, inverted pear shape, on molded foot, the upper part of the body chased with flowers, fruit and scrolls, with fluted curved spout, and cone finial, 7 ¼" ht, 22oz 10d	Christie's December 9 1959 #7 Sotheby's February 8, 1962 #177
1752/53	Lothian & Robertson	Edinburgh	Teapot, inverted pear shape, the shoulders reposed with flowers sprays and rococo scrolls enclosing plain cartouches on each side, leaf-capped silver handle, cone finial and ribbed swan-neck spout, 6 ½" ht, 23.7oz	Sotheby's February 26, 1976 #147
1752/53	James Gilliland	Edinburgh	Teapot, slightly compressed spherical, on domed foot, acanthus-capped loop silver handle, knop finial, 16.8oz	Bonhams Sale 15120 Aug 22, 2007 #1
1752-55ca	James Glen	Glasgow	Teapot, marks - GLN, town mark, GLS, S in an engrailed punch, may possibly be that of James Glen's widow	Jackson Marks p 569.
1753 ca	James Glen	Glasgow	Teapot, no details	National Museums of Scotland MEQ 29
1753/54	Lothian & Robertson	Edinburgh	Teapot, rectangular body, bird finial, curved spout, silver handle, comparatively small foot, 5 ¾" ht, 21oz 10d	Finlay 1991 #93 Sotheby's March 2, 1973 #18 Sotheby's October 31, 1974 #39 National Museums of Scotland MEQ 1112 1974.420
1754/55	Not available	Edinburgh	Teapot, squat hemispherical form, chased with fruit, scrolls, flowers and rococo cartouches, one initialed, the other vacant, part fluted spout, leaf-capped silver handle and knop finial, mm indistinct, 22oz	Christie's London UK 2007 #53

YEAR	MAKER	LOCATION	DESCRIPTION	SOURCE
1754/55	Ker and Dempster	Edinburgh	Teapot, inverted pear shaped body, domed flush hinged lid, chased with floral sprays and scrolls, the body also with armorial engraved cartouches headed by lions masks, bud finial, on spreading foot, with curved partly-fluted spout and leaf-capped silver loop handle,	Lyle Silver Review 1982 p115
1754/55	IM in a rectangle James McKenzie I or James Mitchelson	Edinburgh	Teapot, inverted pear body, chased at the shoulders with foliage, flowers and scrolls, leaf-capped silver loop handle with later fillets, bud finial to the domed flush-hinged lid, on spreading foot engraved "KF", body with the later engraved initial "R", 6 ½" ht, 21oz	Sotheby's Gleneagles August 29, 1994 #132
1754/55	Alexander Gardner	Edinburgh	Teapot, inverted pear shape, chased with fruit, flowers and scrolls, original insulated silver handle, engraved with coat of arms, crest and motto, Arms (worn) - quarterly first, lion rampant, 2nd forearm fess-ways holding a cross, 3rd cross, crosslets, 4th illegible, crest – a mailed forearm clasping a dagger, motto "PER MARE PER TERRAM"	Private Collection
1754/55	Thomas Leslie	Edinburgh	Teapot, near spherical, chased in low relief with flower clusters, scrolls and cartouches, one later engraved with initials, curved fluted spout, lid with applied hinge, silver bun finial, probably wrong date, Thomas Leslie possibly as a retailer if date is correct, 5 ¾" ht, 22oz all	Sotheby's Gleneagles August 29, 1974 #128
1755 ca	David Warnock	Glasgow	Teapot, spherical, silver handle, 5 ½" ht, 21.6oz	Nicholas Shaw Catalog 1999 p63
1755/56	Ker & Dempster	Edinburgh	Teapot, inverted pear shape, bud finial, upper body chased with flowers and scrolls, leaf capped silver loop handle, partly fluted curved spout, domed cover, 20z	Christie's February 23, 1983 #206
1755/56	IM in a rectangle James Mitchelson or James McKenzie I	Edinburgh	Teapot, The Harry Lauder Teapot, inverted pear shape, chased at the shoulder with asymmetrical scroll cartouches, one enclosing a crest, motto and initials, flanked by flowers and foliage, domed lid with bud finial, part fluted curved spout, capped wooden loop handle, spreading foot, later inscribed on the underside "To Sir Harry and Lady Lauder from Lord & Lady Forteviot, a remembrance of a happy evening, June 3rd 1927", 7" ht, 18.3oz all	Lauder Sale May 1966 Sotheby's Hopetoun House March 27, 1984 #125 Bonhams The Scottish Sale August 21, 2003 #13
1756/57	Alexander Gardner	Edinburgh	Teapot, in a case, crest and motto, part of a service, date also given as 1758/59 for the service	Christie's London October 1988 #154
1756/57	John Clark	Edinburgh	Teapot, unusual design, plain tapering cylindrical body on tucked in base, simple rim foot, straight tapering spout with hinged flap, domed lid, urn finial, short uninsulated plain capped loop handle, crest and motto, 9 ½" ht	Sotheby's NY USA April 12, 1994 #291
1756/57	Ker & Dempster	Edinburgh	Teapot, inverted pear shaped body, chased on shoulder with flowers, foliage, fruit, shell and scroll cartouches, curved fluted spout, hinged lid, foliate finial,	Sotheby's October 23, 1958 #91

YEAR	MAKER (continued)	LOCATION	DESCRIPTION	SOURCE
			molded rim foot, 21.6oz	Shrubsole, NY USA 1981 EM999
1757/58	Robert Gordon	Edinburgh	Teapot, inverted pear shape, chased floral and scroll decoration around lip, round molded foot, 5 ½"ht, 12.3oz	Finlay 1991 #93
1758/59	Lothian & Robertson	Edinburgh	Teapot, inverted pear shape, shoulder with heavy chasing, silver acanthus capped loop handle, curved spout	*Jackson Marks p548*
1758/59	*Lothian & Robertson*	*Edinburgh*	*Teapot, no details*	Finlay 1991 #81 Private Collection
1758/59	Robert Gordon	Edinburgh	Teapot, plain, cylindrical drum shape, slightly curved spout, wooden handle, flat lid, button finial, crest and motto	Phillips Edinburgh May 18, 1990 #49
1758/59	Alexander Gardner	Edinburgh	Teapot, inverted pear shape, upper part chased with floral, fruit and foliate decoration, scroll handle, molded circular foot, one vacant cartouche, other with 2 crests for Robertson and McDonald, sold with a cream jug by same maker 1763/64, 24.7oz probably both	Scottish Art Review 1955 vol IV #4 Bell of Aberdeen advertisement
1758/59	William Dempster or William Davie	Edinburgh	Teapot, part of a 3 piece service of different dates, inverted pear shape, chased shoulders, silver handle	Bell of Aberdeen 1961 #18
1758/59	Daniel Ker	Edinburgh	Teapot, inverted pear shape, decorated with scroll, flowers and foliage in the rococo style, domed lid with flush hinge and silver finial, fluted spout, silver handle	P G Dodd & Son, Ltd, London UK 1951 Christie's NY USA 1999 #279 Christie's East NY USA 2000 #340
1759/60	Lothian & Robertson	Edinburgh	Teapot, inverted pyri form on a circular base, shoulder flat chased with birds, garlands, and scrolls, leaf capped spout, ivory insulated handle, lid with bud finial, 6 ¾" ht, 22.5oz gross	Hyman Collection - Colonial Williamsburg Antiques Magazine June 1996 p842 #6
1759/60	Lothian & Robertson	Edinburgh	Teapot, square, heavily chased, crest and motto of Dunlop, pelican finial, ornate cast spout and handle, 6 ¼" ht	*Jackson Marks p548*
1759/60	*Lothian & Robertson*	*Edinburgh*	*Teapot, no details*	Christie's September 28, 1994, #40
1759/60	Not available	Edinburgh	Teapot, spherical, on spreading circular foot, partly fluted spout, hinged domed lid, bud finial, leaf capped silver loop handle, engraved coat of arms in a rococo cartouche, arm of Hope of Hopetoun, 6 ¼" ht, 25oz	

541

YEAR	MAKER	LOCATION	DESCRIPTION	SOURCE
1759/60	Lothian & Robertson	Edinburgh	Teapot, part of a tea service, no details	National Museums of Scotland MEQ 604 1961.1674
1759/60	Ker & Dempster	Edinburgh	Teapot, plain inverted pear shape, on spreading circular foot, fluted curved spout, *flame finial*, flush hinged domed lid, leaf capped plain loop handle, 6 2/3"ht, 22oz	Christie's June 24, 1986 #161
1760ca	David Warnock	Glasgow	Teapot, near-spherical body, domed lid, lightly engraved with a narrow band round the mouth, leaf-capped silver loop handle, half-scroll curved spout, baluster silver knop, 5 ½" ht, 21.5oz	Bonhams The Scottish Sale August 21, 2003 #76 National Museums of Scotland K.2003.1084
1760 ca	David Warnock	Glasgow	Teapot, spherical on spreading circular foot, partly fluted curved spout, leaf capped silver handle, ball finial, interior of the cover engraved with initials "R.C.L.B", 6", 21oz gross	Christie's London UK 1997 #130
1760 ca	G Roger & J Gordon over striking another	Aberdeen	Teapot, no details	Sotheby's London June 1988 #180
1760 ca	Bayne & Napier	Glasgow	Teapot, inverted pear shape, chased, cone finial, crest, 23oz 2d	Christie's July 31, 1962 #189
1760/61	William Davie or William Dempster	Edinburgh	Teapot, no details	Antiques Magazine vol 39 p54 Shreve advertisement
1761/62	Not available		Teapot, *no details*	Antiques Magazine vol 98 1st
1761/62	Lothian and Robertson	Edinburgh	Teapot, cylindrical body, upper and lower parts repoussed and chased with floral festoons, partly-fluted spout with duck's head terminal, flat hinged lid, lead-capped C-scroll handle 4 ¼" ht, 25oz	Sotheby's June 29, 1967 #218 de Havilland Antiques
1761/62	Not available	Edinburgh	Teapot, oval baluster body, chased with foliage and scrolls, vacant cartouche, domed chased cover, pineapple finial, *handle London 1835ca* 7" ht, 26.5oz	Sotheby's June 20, 1968 3150 Simon Kaye Antiques
1761/62	I O possibly James Oliphant	Edinburgh	Teapot, inverted pear shaped body, chased band of scrolls, leafage and flowers, curved fluted spout, bird finial, initialed, 6 ½" ht, 24.5oz	Sotheby's April 17, 1969 #? JH Bourdon-Smith, London
1761/62	William Dempster or William Davie	Edinburgh	Teapot, drum shaped, chased with fruit swags, curved spout, leaf capped scroll handle, flat lid, initial "B" below a baron's coronet, 5" ht, 19.8oz	Sotheby's Gleneagles August 29, 1978 #433
1762/63	Lothian and Robertson	Edinburgh	Teapot, bombe form, sides chased with floral festoons, curved spout, hinged flush lid, ball finial, crest and motto, 22oz	Christie's January 26, 1972 #101 Christie's November 22, 1972 #188

YEAR	MAKER	LOCATION	DESCRIPTION	SOURCE
1763/64	Ker & Dempster	Edinburgh	Teapot, circular, on molded foot, upper body chased with flowers, foliage and scrolls, partly fluted curved spout, slightly domed cover, bud finial, engraved with an initial	Christie's May 4, 1977 #157
1764/65	Gilliland & Ker	Edinburgh	Teapot, inverted pear shape, chased, 29oz 14d	Christie's November 11, 1955 #146 Christie's February 22, 1957 #116
1764/65	Gilliland & Ker	Edinburgh	Teapot, with stand	Apollo November 1980 vol 92 p2
1764/65	Gilliland & Ker	Edinburgh	Teapot, early acquisition, no details	National Museums of Scotland MEQ 53
1765 ca	William Dempster or William Davie	Edinburgh	Teapot, inverted pear shaped	Lyle Silver Review 1982 p116
1765 ca	Ebenezer Oliphant	Edinburgh	Teapot, 20oz	Lyle Annual Review 1983 p626 Sotheby's Sale
1765ca	Adam Graham	Glasgow	Teapot, inverted pear shape, scroll and floral sprays, curved fluted spout, bud finial, spreading base, 6 ¾"ht, 24.1oz	Sotheby's June 20, 1974 #189 Sotheby's March 3, 1975 #143
1765ca	Adam Graham	Glasgow	Teapot, inverted pear shape, body flat chased with flowerheads below rim, leaf-capped loop handle, lobed and fluted curved spout, domed decorated lid, bud finial, armorials 6 ½" ht, 21.4oz	Sotheby's ?? #195 Christie's May 24, 1972 #155
1765ca	Adam Graham	Glasgow	Teapot, no details	National Museums of Scotland MEQ 53
1765ca	David Warnock	Glasgow	Teapot, spherical form, curved spout, lead-capped handle, lid with bird finial, rim foot 6 ½"ht, 22.7oz	Sotheby's June, 1959 #7 Simon Kaye Antiques
1765ca	Adam Graham	Glasgow	Teapot, inverted pear shape, plain, domed lid, leaf wrapped bud finial, silver loop handle, curved fluted spout, 7 ¾" ht, 23oz	Sotheby's November 29, 1984 #250
1765 ca	*Adam Graham*	*Glasgow*	*Teapot, inverted pear shape, 7 ¾" ht, 23oz 18d*	*Sotheby's November 29, 1983 #250*
1765 ca	James Wildgoose	Aberdeen	Teapot, inverted pear shape, silver handle, curved handle, pineapple finial, 25oz	Apollo July 1940 vol 32 p29 #10
1765 ca	James Wildgoose	Aberdeen	Teapot, on 3 feet, with wooden handle	National Museums of Scotland MEQ 1185

YEAR	MAKER	LOCATION	DESCRIPTION	SOURCE
1765/66	James Gilliland	Edinburgh	Teapot, straight, tapered, cylindrical form, flat separate cover, curved spout, 5" ht, 21oz	Sotheby's NY USA October 28, 1980 #525
1765/66	Ker & Dempster	Edinburgh	Teapot, inverted pear shape, spreading foot, scroll handle and spout, cover with bud finial, part chased with fruit, foliage, 2 vacant rococo cartouches, 6 ¼" di, 22oz	Christie's London February 22, 2005 Sale #5839, #333
1765/66	Gilliland and Ker	Edinburgh	Teapot, with stand, inverted pear shape, circular molded foot, fluted curved spout, chased decoration 29.8oz for both items	Christie's February 27, 1957 #?
1765/66	James Oliphant	Edinburgh	Teapot, drum shaped teapot, with pull off cover, bright cut decoration, 25oz	JH Bourdon-Smith Catalog 2002 p22 #44
1765/66	Gilliland & Ker	Edinburgh	Teapot, plain cylindrical drum form, lid with flush hinge, engraved with four sections of floral decorations, plain C-form ivory insulated handle, ivory disc finial (old damage), one side with crest and motto of Gordon, earl's coronet over, 4 ½" ht, 21oz	Christie's London UK 2002 #16
1766ca	James Gordon and George Roper	Aberdeen	Teapot, silver and fruit wood, no details, base marked IG, 3 crosses, ABD, GR	Aberdeen Museums and Galleries ABDAG008656
1766/67	Alexander Gardner	Edinburgh	Teapot, inverted pear shaped body, chased at shoulders with fruit and flower clusters, scrolls and foliage, domed lid, bird finial, leaf capped fluted spout, possibly ivory insulators, 7 ½" ht, 24oz 14d	Sotheby's Gleneagles August 29, 1974 #89 Muirhead Moffat Antiques
1766/67	John Welsh	Edinburgh	Teapot, on molded foot, partly fluted curved spout, upper part of body chased with flowers, shells and rococo cartouches, one engraved with monogram, cover with cone finial, 23oz 16d	Christie's June 3, 1959 #142
1766/67	Ker & Dempster	Edinburgh	Teapot, pear shaped body, engraved with crest and motto, shoulders chased with fruit, flowers and foliage, domed lid, bud finial, leaf capped silver scroll handle, 6 ½" ht, 20oz 6d	Sotheby's April 10, 1975 #158
1766/67	William Taylor	Edinburgh	Teapot, pear shaped, on molded circular base, body with vacant oval cartouche, wriggle work border to each side, partly fluted leaf capped spout, dome cover, bud finial, scroll handle with spur thumbpiece, 6 1/8" ht, 19.5oz	Christie's Glasgow November 21, 1989 #52
1767/68	James Gillliland	Edinburgh	Teapot, barrel shaped, wooden handle, straight spout, 5 ¼" ht, 18oz 14d	Private Collection
1767/68	James Weems	Edinburgh	Teapot, 27oz	Lyle Annual Review 1984 p753 Christie's Sale
1767/68	James Welsh	Edinburgh	Teapot, oval foot, shaped curved spout, 26oz	Christie's June 13, 1934 #29

YEAR	MAKER	LOCATION	DESCRIPTION	SOURCE
1767/68	James Welsh	Edinburgh	Teapot, oval	*Connoisseur Magazine* 1934 vol 94 p138
1767/68	Patrick Robertson	Edinburgh	Teapot, drum shaped, 6 ½" di	Scotland Art Academy Exhibition #896 Stirling-Maxwell Collection
1767/68	Alexander Gardner	Edinburgh	Teapot, inverted pear shape, shoulder chased with scrolls, flowers and foliage, domed lid with bud finial, silver loop handle, 25oz	Scottish Art Review, 1958 vol VI p41 #4 Bell of Aberdeen advertisement
1768/69	Patrick Robertson	Edinburgh	Teapot, no details	Antiques Magazine vol 100
1768/69	Alexander Gardner	Edinburgh	Teapot, plain, cylindrical, curved spout, engraved, 24oz	Christie's March 31, 1965 #91
1768/69	William Dempster or William Davie	Edinburgh	Teapot, drum shaped, chased with fruit swags below the rim, part fluted curved spout, loop handle, lid with initial "B" below a baron's coronet, 5" ht, 19.8oz all	Sotheby's Blair Castle September 12, 1980 #10 Sotheby's Gleneagles August 29, 1983 #501
1769/70	James Hewitt	Edinburgh	Teapot, inverted pear shape, wood finial	William Walter Antiques London February 1994
1770ca	Patrick Robertson	Edinburgh	Teapot, with a stand, no details, no date provided	Dundee Museum and Art Galleries 1986-73
1770ca	James Wildgoose	Aberdeen	Teapot, small size, silver and dark wood, no details, base marked – JW, ABD	Aberdeen Museums and Galleries ABDAG001353 (acquired 1984)
1770 ca	Adam Graham	Glasgow	Teapot, spherical shape, engraved at shoulder and on the lid with lattice and foliate scroll motifs, on a conforming foot, leaf capped ivory insulated handle, engraved coat-of-arms, 9 ¾" long, 21oz gross	Christie's London UK 2002 #230
1770 ca	Adam Graham	Glasgow	Teapot, vase-shaped on circular foot, beaded borders, acanthus capped scroll handle, knop finial, 27.4oz	Bonhams Sale 15120 Aug 22, 2007 #112
1770/71	William Dempster or William Davie	Edinburgh	Teapot, oval inverted pear, upper body restrainedly chased with irregular band of blossoms, scrolls, and rococo work, 2 cartouches, one with a faint crest and motto, 6 ½" ht, 24.8oz	Sotheby's Scone Palace April 14, 1980 #103
1770 ca	Milne & Campbell	Glasgow	Teapot, not pictured	Sotheby's Gleneagles August 1990 #32

545

YEAR	MAKER	LOCATION	DESCRIPTION	SOURCE
1770 ca	Milne & Campbell	Glasgow	Teapot, spherical, curved spout, silver handle, 21oz	Sotheby's Scone April 19, 1977 #55
1770 ca	Adam Graham	Glasgow	Teapot, with a mixed service	Christie's May 23, 1962 #18
1770 ca	James Wildgoose	Aberdeen	Teapot, inverted pear shape, on 3 feet, floral sprays 7 ½" ht	Scotland Art Academy Exhibition 1939 #978 Noble Collection
1770 ca	*James Wildgoose*	*Aberdeen*	*Teapot, no details*	*Clayton Christie's Book #208*
1770 ca	Milne & Campbell	Glasgow	Teapot, inverted pear shape	National Museums of Scotland MEQ L1980.3
1770 ca	Adam Graham	Glasgow	Teapot, urn shape, beaded edge, pedestal foot, curved spout, domed cover, 8 ¾" ht, 27.5oz	Nicholas Shaw Catalog 2005 p91
1770/71	William Dempster or William Davie	Edinburgh	Teapot, inverted pear shape, on corresponding foot, upper body embossed with a band of floral garlands, hinged lid with flat gadrooned border, wooden scroll handle and finial, 16oz	Bonhams Sale 15120 Aug 22, 2007 #10
1770/71	William Dempster or William Davie	Edinburgh	Teapot, oval, chased with flowers and scrolls, gadrooned, finial, 26oz 2d	Christie's February 20, 1935 #107
1770/71	William Dempster or William Davie	Edinburgh	Teapot, oval bombe form, chased, rococo decoration, domed cover, swan necked spout, repaired rim, oval pedestal foot, later finial, 6 1/3" ht, 25 oz	Sotheby's NY USA October 5, 1979 #343
1770/71	William Dempster or William Davie	Edinburgh	Teapot, inverted pear shape, on corresponding foot, upper body embossed with a band of floral garlands, hinged lid with flat gadrooned border, wooden scroll handle and finial, 16oz	Bonhams Sale 15120 Aug 22, 2007 #10
1770/71	William Dempster or William Davie	Edinburgh	Teapot, oval, chased with flowers and scrolls, gadrooned, finial, 26oz 2d	Christie's February 20, 1935 #107
1771/72	William & John Taylor	Edinburgh	Teapot, no details	Jackson Marks p549
1771/72	William Taylor	Edinburgh	Teapot, inverted pear shape, shoulder chased with scrolls, flowers, and foliage with vacant cartouches, domed lid with bud finial, silver leaf capped loop handle, curved half fluted spout, 22oz	Scottish Art Review, 1956 vol VI, p41 #1 Bell of Aberdeen advertisement
1771/72	Gilliland and Ker	Edinburgh	Teapot, Inverted pear shape, domed hinged lid, 7 ½"ht, 9 ¾" long	Metropolitan Museum of Art, NY USA 38.21.14
1771/72	David Edmond	Edinburgh	Teapot, no details	Jackson Marks p549

546

YEAR	MAKER	LOCATION	DESCRIPTION	SOURCE
1771/72	WD William Davie or William Dempster	Edinburgh	Teapot, spherical, circa 1730 form, said to be made by William Drummond but probably made by either William Dempster or William Davie	JH Bourdon-Smith London 1993
1771/72	James Dempster	Edinburgh	Teapot, spherical, curved spout, light chasing, 6 ½" ht, 20oz 16d	Sotheby's NY USA October 13, 1981 #243
1772/73	William Dempster or William Davie	Edinburgh	Teapot, drum shape, 5 ½" ht, 19oz 19d	Sotheby's Hopetoun House May 1990 #95 Bell of Aberdeen 1961 #21
1772/73	*William Dempster or William Davie*	*Edinburgh*	*Teapot, drum shape, 4 ½" ht, 19oz 16d*	Sotheby's February 28, 1991 #214
1772/73	*William Dempster or William Davie*	*Edinburgh*	*Teapot, drum shape, wood handle, 20oz*	*Apollo July 1940 vol 32 p29 #11*
1773/74	Alexander Ziegler	Edinburgh	Teapot, inverted pear shape, domed foot, chased with fruit and flowers, acanthus capped scroll handle, bird finial, 7 1/8" ht, 22oz	Bonhams Sale 10814 #3
1773/74	Alexander Gardner	Edinburgh	Teapot, plain urn shaped body, on a pedestal foot, with bead mounts, ivory insulated handle (repaired), knop finial, 9", 28oz	Christie's London UK 2004 #122
1773/74	William Dempster or William Davie	Edinburgh	Teapot, oval, straight sided, with a tapering faceted spout, hinged lid chased with leaf and flower motifs, centering a cartouche engraved with a crest and motto, later ivory insulated handle, 11" long, 22oz gross	Christie's London UK 2002 #177
1774/75	Alexander Aitchison & Son	Edinburgh	Teapot, spherical, curved spout, early style, 28oz 3d	Christie's June 6, 1965 #5 Christie's Scottish Picture Files
1774/75	*Alexander Aitchison & Son*	*Edinburgh*	*Teapot, spherical, ivory handle possibly replaced, mushroom finial, on molded spreading foot, 6 ¾" ht, 28oz 3d*	*Sotheby's June 16, 1995 #5* Garrards, London
1774/75	William Dempster or William Davie	Edinburgh	Teapot, oval form, engraved swags, later crest, flat cover, straight tapered spout, scrolled wood handle, 5 ¾" ht, 17oz	Sotheby's NY USA June 16, 1981 #467
1774/75	*William Dempster or William Davie*	*Edinburgh*	*Teapot, no details*	*Holland p21*
1774/75	James Welsh	Edinburgh	Teapot, no details	Jackson Marks p549
1774/75	Patrick Robertson	Edinburgh	Teapot, drum shaped, no further details	National Museums of Scotland MEQ 1133a-b
1775ca	James McEwan	Glasgow	Teapot, part of a 3 piece service, oval inverted pear form	Private Collection

YEAR	MAKER	LOCATION	DESCRIPTION	SOURCE
1775/76	William Davie or William Dempster	Edinburgh	Teapot, Drum shaped, straight spout, 4 ¾" ht, 20oz 10d	Sotheby's Gleneagles August 27, 1980 #12 Private Collection
1775/76	Alexander Gardner	Edinburgh	Teapot, oval base, squared body, wood finial	JH Bourdon-Smith 1994
1775/76	Alexander Gardner	Edinburgh	Teapot, neo-classical, oval engraved body, flattened cover, large	Hyman Collection-Colonial Williamsburg G1994-133
1775/76	Patrick Robertson	Edinburgh	Teapot, oval, crest, engraved with festoons and flowers, 25oz	Christie's April 26, 1966 #101 Lt. Col. Hay Collection
1775 ca	Milne & Campbell	Glasgow	Teapot, rectangular body, with stand, chased bands, 6" ht	Sotheby's October 31, 1974 #38
1776ca	Milne and Campbell	Glasgow	Teapot, baluster body, shoulder chased with floral scrolling, 23.8oz	Breadalbane Collection sale, 1935, #126
1776/77	James Gilliland	Edinburgh	Teapot, inverted pear shape, upper body chased with swags of foliage and flowers, curved spout, wooden handle and finial	Finlay 1991 #97
1776/77	*James Gilliland*	*Edinburgh*	*Teapot, inverted pear shape*	*National Museums of Scotland MEQ 902 1968.3464*
1776/77	James Gilliland	Edinburgh	Teapot, with stand	Apollo July 1940 vol 32 p30 #15
1777/78	Patrick Robertson	Edinburgh	Teapot, drum shape, straight spout, black wooden handle, 5 ½" ht, 9 3/8"long	Huntley House Museum, Edinburgh HH 3186/68
1777/78	William Dempster or William Davie	Edinburgh	Teapot, inverted pear shaped body, with rocaille and scroll motif cartouches connected by leaf and flower scrolls, carved wood handle, fruiting finial, 23oz gross	Christie's London UK 2001 #117
1777/78	Archibald Ochiltree	Edinburgh	Teapot, oval with beaded borders, straight spout, wood handle, wood finial, hinged lid engraved with scrolls and a shell, 10" long over handles, 22oz gross	Christie's NY USA 1999 #282
1777/78	AC	Edinburgh	Teapot, oval, with foliate engraved lid, wood handle, 5 ¼" ht, 23oz gross	Sotheby's Chicago IL, USA 1998 #314
1778/79	James Welsh	Edinburgh	Teapot, cylindrical, with festoons and foliage, 21oz 5d	Christie's July 16, 1919 #207
1779/80	William Davie or William Dempster	Edinburgh	Teapot, no details	Antiques Magazine vol 36, p210 Shreve advertisement

YEAR	MAKER	LOCATION	DESCRIPTION	SOURCE
1780ca	Milne and Campbell	Glasgow	Teapot, with stand, drum shaped body, upper half decorated with chased swags, fluted shaped spout, ivory finial, 28.6oz both pieces	How of Edinburgh, 1937, #103
1780 ca	Not available	Edinburgh	Teapot vase form, beaded borders, engraved festoons, domed cover, knop finial, 24oz	Woolley & Wallis January 26, 2005 #380
1780 ca	Adam Graham	Glasgow	Teapot, repaired 9 ½" ht, 27oz	Sotheby's NY USA October 1991 #365
1780/81	James Hewitt	Edinburgh	Teapot, inverted pear shape, on a spreading foot, bright cut, partly domed cover, leaf capped silver looped handle, 7 ½" ht, 22oz 10d	Sotheby's NY USA February 18-19, 1981 #555
1780/81	James Hewitt	Edinburgh	Teapot, inverted pear shape, 7" ht	Sotheby's Picture Files
1780/81	Taylor & Hamilton	Glasgow	Teapot, vase shaped, beaded circular base, chased with a band of foliage, ribbon tied husk festoons in neo-classical style, domed lid with baluster finial, silver leaf capped scroll handle, condition not too good, appears to have been dropped, 8 ½" ht, 25oz	Christie's Edinburgh April 29, 1992 Private Collection
1782/83	James Hewitt	Edinburgh	Teapot, classical vase shape, bird's head to spout and handle, body with neoclassical ribbon tied floral garlands, crest of Thompson, motto, initials "MWT" for Thompson, odd shaped wood finial topped by a silver foliate ferule, 8 1/8" ht, 21.7oz	Nicholas Shaw Catalog 2000 p74 Bonhams the Scottish Sale August 21, 2003 #8
1782/83	James Hewitt	Edinburgh	Teapot, vase-shaped on spreading circular base, bird's head spout, pineapple finial, crest, motto and initials, part of a mixed service, 9" ht	Christie's Lanarkshire UK 1998 #61
1782/83	Patrick Robertson	Edinburgh	Teapot, vase shaped, beaded borders, engraved with festoons of flowers and an initialed oval, curved spout, on oval pedestal base, 8 ½" ht, 23.2oz	Sotheby's Gleneagles August 29, 1978 #399
1782/83	Robert Bowman	Edinburgh	Teapot, silver gilt teapot, swag and bow chasing, dolphin head handle, animal head spout	Finlay 1991 pl 101 National Museums of Scotland MEQ 1334
1782/83	William Dempster or William Davie	Edinburgh	Teapot, fluted with scroll handle and straight spout, lid with wood finial, engraved with scrolls and flowers, Greek key cypher below Greek Royal crown for King George I of the Hellenes, Prince of Denmark (1845/1913), 10" long, 11oz	Christie's London UK 2007 #149
1783ca	James McEwan	Glasgow	Teapot, inverted pear form, silver finial, leaf-capped scroll to the plain loop handle, teapot marked for Edinburgh 1760ca and marks over struck for retailing in Glasgow, 23.3oz	How of Edinburgh, 1937, #104

YEAR	MAKER	LOCATION	DESCRIPTION	SOURCE
1783 ca	James McEwan	Glasgow	Teapot, inverted pear shape, wooden handle and finial, curved spout, 6 ¾" ht, 24.2oz	Nicholas Shaw Catalog 2005 p96
1783/84	William Davie or William Dempster	Edinburgh	Teapot, part of a service	Lyle Annual Review 1983 #733 Sotheby's Gleneagles August 25, 1997 #149
1783/84	*William Davie or William Dempster*	*Edinburgh*	*Teapot, part of a service*	*Country Life May or June 1968*
1783/84	William Davie or William Dempster	Edinburgh	Teapot, with stand, no details	The Maple Swan Collection
1784/85	William Davie or William Dempster	Edinburgh	Teapot, oval, on paw and bracketed feet, wooden handle, coat of arms, with fitted stand, 2/3 fluted spout, 29oz 19d	Christie's July 31, 1963 Clayton Dictionary p307 #647
1784/85	Alexander Gardner	Edinburgh	Teapot, with stand, oval, bright cut engraved with floral swags, each side engraved with an urn over a wreath, one with a crest and motto, with laurel leaf and bead borders, straights spout, wood scroll handle, flat lid, wood finial, 11" long over handle, 26oz gross	Crichton Bros London UK 1953 Christie's NY USA 1999 #281
1784/85	Alexander Edmonstoun	Edinburgh	Teapot, no details	Jackson Marks p550
1785ca	James McEwan	Glasgow	Teapot, neo-classical, oval chased body, rococo spout, flattened lid	Hyman Collection-Colonial Williamsburg G2003-87
1785ca	Robert Gray	Glasgow	Teapot, with stand, no details	National Museums of Scotland MEQ 55
1786/87	James Dempster or James Douglas	Edinburgh	Teapot, no details	National Museums of Scotland MEQ 1117
1788/89	William Dempster	Edinburgh	Teapot, oval, floral swags, ribbons, tassels and festoons, straight spout, domed lid, original fruit wood handle, (Note: William Davie was deceased by this date), 6 ½" ht, 15oz	William Walter Antiques, London Private Collection
1789/90	Patrick Robertson	Edinburgh	Teapot, straight sided octagonal, each panel engraved with a classical figure in a circle, straight spout, loop wooden handle	Finlay 1991 #98
1789/90	Patrick Robertson	Edinburgh	Teapot, wooden handle, with a 3 piece service	National Museums of Scotland MEQ 671

YEAR	MAKER	LOCATION	DESCRIPTION	SOURCE
1789/90	James McKay	Edinburgh	Teapot, with stand	Antiques Magazine vol 99 p316 Firestone advertisement
1789ca	Not available	Edinburgh	Punch pot, Arms of Stuart, no mm, 11 1/4" ht, 52oz	Christie's London May 13, 1992 #144
1790 ca	W & P Cunningham I	Edinburgh	Teapot, vase shaped with draped swags and festoons	Lorentz Antiques Toronto Canada 1992
1790/91	W & P Cunningham I	Edinburgh	Teapot, part of a 4 piece service, Arms of Christie of Bedlay Larkshire	Christie's Edinburgh May 1-2, 1992 #236
1790/91	William Dempster	Edinburgh	Teapot, oval, bright cut, given to Alexander Campbell of Ballochyle, (Note: William Davie was deceased by this date), 12" across, 27oz	JH Bourdon-Smith Catalog 1997 p34 #39
1791/92	William Robertson	Edinburgh	Teapot, with 4 piece service, straight spout, wooden handle and finial	Country Life February 13, 1964 vol 135 #31
1792/93	W & P Cunningham I	Edinburgh	Teapot, oval vase shaped body, on spreading navette shaped pedestal foot, body with 2 vacant oval cartouches, a frieze of drapery festoons, 8" ht, 21.3oz	Woolley & Wallis April 20, 2005, #794
1792/93	Alexander Ziegler	Edinburgh	Teapot, no details	Jackson Marks p 550
1793/94	James Douglas	Edinburgh	Teapot, part of a service	William Walter Antiques, London 1994
1793/94	William Cunningham I	Edinburgh	Teapot, no details	The Maple Swan Collection
1793/94	Thomas Sempill	Edinburgh	Teapot, with stand, shaped oval, bright cut engraved borders, further engraved to either side with initials "P.Y.E.W.", straight tapering spout, wood pineapple finial, scroll handle, 12' wide	Christie's Lanarkshire UK 1997 #52
1794/95	Alexander Gardner	Edinburgh	Teapot, with stand, oval section with engraved foliate bands and an ebonized handle, 12 ¼" across, 20oz both	Christie's London UK 2005 #429
1794/95	Alexander Gardner & Co	Edinburgh	Teapot, no details, indicated in ad as Alexander Graham & Co	Antiques Magazine vol 7 p130 Shreve advertisement
1794/95	Alexander Gardner	Edinburgh	Teapot, part of a 4 piece service, no details	Dundee Museum and Art Galleries 1978-2059-1
1794/95	Alexander Spence	Edinburgh	Teapot, engraved with vacant drapery cartouche within bright cut leaves and wiggle work bands, initial "N" underneath, part of a 4 piece tea service	Sotheby's Gleneagles September 1, 1998 #542

YEAR	MAKER	LOCATION	DESCRIPTION	SOURCE
1795 ca	Edward Livingstone	Dundee	Teapot, with stand	Finlay 1991 #111
1796 ca	W & P Cunningham I	Edinburgh	Teapot, not pictured	Sotheby's London November 1987 #114
1796/97	William Robertson	Edinburgh	Teapot, with tray	Antiques Magazine vol 92 p168
1796/97	*William Robertson*	*Edinburgh*	*Teapot, with stand, no details*	*National Museums of Scotland MEQ 1945.37*
1796/97	Graham & McLean	Edinburgh	Teapot, oval outline, concave fluting, bright cut engraving, initials "JB" in cartouche, part of a 4 piece tea service	N & I Franklin Private Collection
1796/97	William Robertson	Edinburgh	Teapot, with stand, rectangular with cut corners, engraved with a crest and motto, "HAVE AT YOU", straight spout, wood handle, foliate decoration, 11' wide, 23.5oz gross	Christie's East NY USA 1999 #200
1798/99	McHattie and Fenwick	Edinburgh	Teapot, with stand, oval shape, straight spout, wooden handle, 5 5/8' ht	Huntley House Museum, Edinburgh HH 3187/68
1798/99	John Leslie	Aberdeen	Teapot, oval body, straight spout, wooden handle and finial, with stand, 6 ¼" ht	JH Bourdon-Smith Catalog 2005 p36 #46
1799/1800	W & P Cunningham I	Edinburgh	Teapot, oval, bright cut with 2 wreaths enclosing initials on one side and a crest and motto on the other, decorated matted band of foliage below the everted shoulder, straight spout, domed lid with button finial, 6 ½" ht, 15.3oz	Sotheby's Gleneagles September 1, 1981 #457
1799/1800	W & P Cunningham I	Edinburgh	Teapot, oval vase-shaped body, beaded edges, engraved with floral festoons, curved spout, wooden loop handle and finial, with a stand, 9 1/8" ht, 32 oz with stand	Woolley & Wallis April 24, 2002 #314
1800ca	Edward Livingstone	Dundee	Teapot, part of a 3 piece service, no details	Dundee Museum and Art Galleries 1986-136-1
1800ca	Nathaniel Gillet	Aberdeen	Teapot, silver, wood and ivory, crest hunting horn and stag's head in a shield shaped cartouche, base marked NG, Abd	Aberdeen Museums and Galleries ABDAG000061 (acquired 1978)
1800ca	Nathaniel Gillet	Aberdeen	Teapot, silver and fruit wood, no details, base marked floral motif, NG, floral motif, NG, floral motif	Aberdeen Museums and Galleries ABDAG001033
1800ca	Nathaniel Gillet	Aberdeen	Teapot, (with stand), oval shape, decorated with engraved bands, hinged domed lid, silver finial, coat of arms,	Bell of Aberdeen Collection, 1961, #28a

YEAR	MAKER	LOCATION	DESCRIPTION	SOURCE
1800ca	Nathaniel Gillet	Aberdeen	Teapot, urn shaped, with delicate engraving, beaded borders, spreading foot, straight spout, wooden handle, crest of Johnstone, 9 ½"ht	Bell of Aberdeen Collection, 1961, #30
1800ca	James Erskine	Aberdeen	Teapot, with stand, large oval concave fluted body, band of engraving round the mouth and base, plain shaped spout, wooden handle, 6½'ht	Bell of Aberdeen Collection, 1961, #32
1800 ca	Thomas Davie	Greenock	Teapot, oval form, straight sided, bright cut borders, straight tapering spout, domed lid with integral hinge, fruitwood oval finial, scroll handle, with crest, motto, and initials, 6" ht, 19oz gross	Christie's London UK 1999 #60
1800ca date?	Newlands and Grierson	Glasgow	Teapot, part of a three piece service, modified oval rectangular form, engraved bands of acorns and flowers below reeded bands at the shoulders,	Sotheby's Gleneagles August 25, 1997 #122
1800/01	Edward Livingstone	Dundee	Teapot, octagonal, with conforming stand, 19oz 2d all in	Finlay 1991 #111 Sotheby's Gleneagles August 31, 1999 Private Collection
1800/01	McHattie & Fenwick	Edinburgh	Teapot, part of a 3 piece service, 7 ½" ht, 28oz	Christie's NY USA April 18, 1990 #93
1800/01	W & P Cunningham I	Edinburgh	Teapot, oval shape, wooden handle, initials "MJB", 6 ¼"ht, 18.1oz	Nicholas Shaw Catalog 1999 p58
1800/01	W & P Cunningham I	Edinburgh	Teapot, with stand, with bright cut engraved foliate decoration, 18oz both	Gorringes LLP, East Sussex UK 2006 #1531
1800/01	W & P Cunningham I	Edinburgh	Teapot, with stand, shaped oval and faceted sides, bright cut borders of scrolling foliage, scroll spout, wood handle, oval wood finial, cartouche enclosing a monogram, on four bracket feet, 11 ¾" long over handle, 18oz both	Christie's London UK 2000 #176
1802/03	Alexander Spence	Edinburgh	Teapot, part of a 3 piece service	Apollo March 1951 vol 53 p5 Bracher & Sydenham advertisement
1802/03	John McDonald	Edinburgh	Teapot, with stand	Park-Bernet 46 p61 Rudkin Collection
1802/03	W & P Cunningham I	Edinburgh	Teapot, 14.5oz	Lyle Annual Review 1981 p625 Phillips
1802/03	W & P Cunningham I	Edinburgh	Teapot, oval shape, part fluted foot, Greek key shoulder motif, below a gadrooned rim, ebonized handle, silver mounted finial, with a crest, motto and initials, part of a service	Christie's London UK 2000 #369

YEAR	MAKER	LOCATION	DESCRIPTION	SOURCE
1802/03	John McDonald	Edinburgh	Teapot, oval with a curved spout, wood squared loop handle, lightly engraved, cartouche both sides, domed lid with Key fret design, sold with a creamer, 7" ht	Christie's East NY USA 2000 #342
1805/06	Francis Howden	Edinburgh	Teapot, part of a service	Lyle Annual Review 1984 p743 Sotheby's
1806/07	Francis Howden	Edinburgh	Teapot, with stand, oblong, curved spout, bright cut engraved with a floral band, initial "W", 27oz both	Gorringes LLP, East Sussex UK 2006 #1479
1806/07	Dick & McPherson	Edinburgh	Teapot, oval pot, straight spout, wood handle, full arms, crest and motto on one side, crest on the reverse, also engraved with a name, date 1806	N Horowitz Inc, NY USA 1996
1806/07	R Keay	Perth Edinburgh assay	Teapot, low rise, 4 ½" ht, 24oz	Kovel's 1995 p624 Christie's Sale
1806/07	W & P Cunningham I	Edinburgh	Teapot, part of a 3 piece service, Arms of Kincragie	Sotheby's Hopetoun House April 26, 1988 #76
1806/07	W & P Cunningham I	Edinburgh	Teapot, no details	National Museums of Scotland MEQ 1271
1808/09	Not available	Edinburgh assay	Teapot, with stand	Connoisseur Magazine 1927 p50 #305 Advertisement
1808/09	James McKay	Edinburgh	Teapot, part of a 4 piece coffee set	Sotheby's April 27, 1927 #174
1808/09	George McHattie	Edinburgh	Teapot, no details	National Museums of Scotland MEQ 851
1808/09	Dick & McPherson	Edinburgh assay	Teapot, bright cut, engraved, on 4 ball feet	Nicholas Shaw Catalog 2002/03 p88
1809/10	George Fenwick	Edinburgh	Teapot, oblong bellied body, angular handle, curved spout, part of a service	Pook & Pook, Downingtown, PA USA 2004 #624
1809/10	George Fenwick	Edinburgh	Teapot, part of a 3 piece set, with initial "H"	Sotheby's February 26, 1976 #38
1810/12	*George Fenwick*	*Edinburgh*	*Teapot, part of a 3 piece set, bombe form, Crest of Hay, with initial "H"*	*Christie's Edinburgh May 1-2, 1991 #246*
1810/11	Patrick Cunningham & Sons	Edinburgh	Teapot, compressed circular, later chased with flowers, scrolls and fruit, 28oz 6d	Sotheby's London Oct 22, 1998 #411

YEAR	MAKER	LOCATION	DESCRIPTION	SOURCE
1811/12	George Fenwick	Edinburgh	Teapot, part of a service	Lyle Annual Review 1983 p729 Christie's Sale
1813/14	James McKay	Edinburgh	Teapot, no details	National Museums of Scotland MEQ 687
1814/15	James McKay	Edinburgh	Teapot, part of a 3 piece set	Apollo 1934 vol 19, p4 Bell of Aberdeen advertisement
1814/15	George Fenwick	Edinburgh	Teapot, oblong bellied form, with tongue and dart border, bright cut engraved band of foliage, angular handle, on ball feet, part of a service	Bonhams London UK 2006 #291
1814/15	Robert Gray & Son	Glasgow Edinburgh assay	Teapot, squat circular form, on gadrooned circular foot, ivory handle, snake-head joints, hinged lid, button finial, shoulder with anthemion band, part of a service, 10 ½" long	Christie's NY USA 2005 #172
1814/15	Robert Gray & Son	Glasgow Edinburgh assay	Teapot, circular form, Greek revival manner, chased and embossed with bands of anthemion and stylized foliage with fluted borders, part of a service, 6" ht	Christie's London UK 1999 #80
1815/16	Robert Gray & Son	Glasgow Edinburgh assay	Teapot, urn form, fluted short circular base, shoulder chased with decoration, angular handle, anthemion topped and acanthus clad partly covered spout, partly raised chased lid, beaded ball finial, 5" ht, 32 oz gross	Christie's East NY USA 1997 #78
1815/16	George McHattie	Edinburgh	Teapot, rounded rectangular form, egg and dart borders, molded reeded girdle, part of a service, 5 1/8" ht	Lyon & Turnbull Edinburgh UK 2003 #233
1815/16	James McKay	Edinburgh	Teapot, spherical form with engraved foliate scroll motifs on the shoulder, central coat-of-arms, on a pedestal foot, sold with a cream jug	Christie's London UK 2001 #107
1815/16	James McKay	Edinburgh	Teapot, not pictured	Sotheby's NY USA February 1985 #160
1815/16	R Green or R Grierson	Edinburgh assay	Teapot, not pictured	Sotheby's Gleneagles August 1988 #480
1815/16	John McDonald	Edinburgh	Teapot, no details	National Museums of Scotland MEQ 812
1818 ca	Thomas Davie	Greenock	Teapot, multi-sided drum shaped pot, silver handle, ivory inserts, pineapple finial, bright cut, crest and motto of Rankin in rectangular cartouche, vacant cartouche on the reverse side	Sakiel Inc NY USA 1996

YEAR	MAKER	LOCATION	DESCRIPTION	SOURCE
1818/19	William and Patrick Cunningham II	Edinburgh	Teapot, part of 3 piece service, fluted body, scrolled cartouche, curved fluted spout, leaf-capped silver handle, mushroom finial, 6"ht, 12"long	Fogg Art Museum, Harvard University, 1948.47 (Leverett House)
1818/19	James McKay	Edinburgh	Teapot, compressed form, with part fluting and a shell and leaf motif border, crested, part of a service	Christie's London UK 2001 #183
1819/20	George McHattie	Edinburgh	Teapot, no details	National Museums of Scotland MEQ 1067
1820ca	George Booth	Aberdeen	Teapot, silver and ivory, on body near handle - GB, AB, AB, unclear	Aberdeen Museums and Galleries ABDAG000060 (acquired 1977)
1820ca	Alexander Cameron	Dundee	Teapot, part of a 3 piece service, squat regency teapot, circular shaped body and fluting around the outside of the lower half, handle decorated with acanthus leaf at the top and has two bone inserts as insulators, on 4 bun feet	Dundee Museums and Art Galleries 1994-307-1
1820 ca	James McKay	Edinburgh	Teapot, no details	National Museums of Scotland MEQ 1310
1820/21	CB	Edinburgh	Teapot, partly fluted compressed circular, partly reeded foliated capped loop handle, scroll spout, fluted lid topped by fluted button finial, 7" ht, part of a service	Christie's East NY USA 1998 #52
1820/21	Robert Gray	Glasgow	Teapot, part of a 3 piece service	Apollo May 1940 p7 Bell of Aberdeen advertisement
1820/21	Alexander Edmonstoun	Edinburgh	Teapot, part of a 3 piece service	Sotheby's Picture File "AE"
1823/24	James McKay	Edinburgh	Teapot, not pictured	Lyle Annual Review 1993 p619
1823/24	James McKay	Edinburgh	Teapot, squat circular form, spreading rim foot, richly chased with foliate motifs, flower head finial, part of a service, 12" wide	Christie's Lanarkshire UK 1997 #91
1824/25	John McDonald	Edinburgh	Teapot, inverted pear form, spreading foot, upper body and lid chased with scrolls, floral sprays and rocaille on a matted ground, lid with fixed cast finial, handle with later insulators, 6" ht, 14.5oz	Christie's London UK 2002 #233
1824/25	Js H	Edinburgh	Teapot, spherical form, with a band of floral and scroll motifs on a granulated ground, on four leaf and scroll capped paw feet, leaf capped ivory insulated handle, domed lid with a flower finial, engraved with a crest and motto, 11" ht,	Christie's London UK 2001 #185

YEAR	MAKER (continued)	LOCATION	DESCRIPTION	SOURCE
	James Howden	Edinburgh	21oz gross	
1824/25	James Howden	Edinburgh	Teapot, inverted pear shape, on rising circular foot, chased and embossed with foliate motifs, entered cartouches, partly fluted spout, acanthus capped handle, domed lid, finial formed as a goose, part of a service	Christie's Lanarkshire UK 1997 #135
1825 ca	William Jamieson	Aberdeen	Teapot, bachelor's, no details	National Museums of Scotland MEQ 1201
1826/27	Alexander Edmonstoun	Edinburgh	Teapot, part of a 3 piece service	Sotheby's April 26, 1988 #91
1827/28	James McKay	Edinburgh	Teapot, flattened sphere on a pedestal base, knopped leaf wrapped berry finial, body chased with rocaille, cartouche on either side, one engraved with a monogram, replacement base, 6 ½" ht, 27oz 10d	Butterfields Auctioneers Corp, San Francisco CA USA 1991 #1111
1827/28	*James McKay*	*Edinburgh*	*Teapot, no details*	*Lyle Annual Review 1993 p621*
1827/28	James McKay	Edinburgh	Teapot, engraved, no details	National Museums of Scotland MEQ 813
1827/28	Robert Gray and Son	Glasgow	Teapot, Ardrossan Coursing Prize	National Museums of Scotland MEQ 744
1828/29	Robert Keay II (continued)	Perth Edinburgh assay	Teapot, part of a 3 piece service, no details	National Museums of Scotland MEQ one of 949-51 1969
1829/30	Leonard Urquhart	Edinburgh	Teapot, no details	National Museums of Scotland K2000.378
1830/31	James McKay	Edinburgh	Teapot, compressed spherical form, with a foliate scroll motif rim, on a spreading foot, ivory insulated handle, part of a service, 11 3/8" ht	Christie's London UK 2001 #107
1832/33	Elder & Co	Edinburgh	Teapot, part of a 3 piece service	Sotheby's Gleneagles August 27, 1977
1832/33	James McKay	Edinburgh	Teapot, plain circular compressed form, on four shell and scroll tab feet, leaf capped handle, part of a mixed service, 6 ½" ht	Christie's London UK 2002 #226
1833-36	James McKay	Edinburgh	Teapot, part of a service	Lyle Annual Review 1984 Sotheby's Sale

YEAR	MAKER	LOCATION	DESCRIPTION	SOURCE
1834/35	TAF	Edinburgh	Teapot, pheasant finial, 8" ht	Lunds Auction, December 11, 2000 #14
1834/35	Elder & Co	Edinburgh	Teapot, part of a 3 piece service	Sotheby's Gleneagles August 28, 1990 #101
1834-36	Elder & Co	Edinburgh	Teapot, not pictured	Lyle Annual Review 1982 p618 Sotheby's Sale
1835/36	Elder & Co	Edinburgh	Teapot, part of a 4 piece coffee service	Christie's April 23, 1983 #92
1836/37	Marshall & Sons	Edinburgh	Teapot, inverted pear form, chased scroll floral decoration, leaf capped scroll handle, domed flush lid, knopped melon finial, 6 7/8" ht, 24oz	Lyon & Turnbull Edinburgh UK 2003 #358
1837/38	Leonard Urquhart	Edinburgh	Teapot, with repossed floral boughs, initial "B", part of a service	DuMouchelles Detroit MI USA 2002 #1025
1837/38	Leonard Urquhart	Edinburgh	Teapot, fluted inverted pear shape, with foliage and scroll borders, body chased with upright acanthus foliage, flower finial, engraved with a crest, part of a service	Christie's London UK 1999 #57
1837/38	James McKay	Edinburgh	Teapot, baluster shape on shaped circular foot, decorated with swirling flutes, scrolling foliage and flowers, engraved with a monogram, ivory insulated handle, part of a service	Christie's London UK 2005 #331
1837/38	James McKay	Edinburgh	Teapot, spherical, chased with bands of foliated scrolls, bud finial, acanthus clad scroll handle, part of a service	Christie's Lanarkshire UK 1998 #540
1837/38	Marshall & Sons	Edinburgh	Teapot, tapering bullet shape, on a rim foot, straight spout, loop handle, acanthus thumbpiece, hinged lid with bud finial, engraved about the shoulders, lid, handle and spout with foliate motifs, 47oz	Christie's Lanarkshire UK 1997 #133
1837/38	Marshall & Sons	Edinburgh	Teapot, formed as a realistic curling stone, cylindrical handle, lid engraved with presentation inscription "to Edward Hoggan from the Duddington Curling Society", 7" across, 42oz 10d	Christie's NY USA 1997 #245
1837/38	James McKay	Edinburgh	Teapot, vase shape on spreading circular base and square foot, chased foliage to the corners, corded girdle, chasing to lower body and spout, bud finial, contemporary initial "C", part of a service, 9 ¼" ht	Christie's Lanarkshire UK 1998 #62
1838/39	Leonard Urquhart	Edinburgh	Teapot, semi-fluted inverted pear form, on a spreading circular foot, body chased with scrolls and foliage, with vacant scroll cartouches, wood scroll handle, part of a service, 7" ht	Christie's London UK 2004 #119

YEAR	MAKER	LOCATION	DESCRIPTION	SOURCE
1839/40	James McKay	Edinburgh	Teapot, baluster shaped on circular foot, repossed body with a cartouche, scroll spout, handle with ivory insulators, part of a service, 7 ¾" ht	Christie's NY USA 2004 #984
1839/40	James McKay	Edinburgh	Teapot, tapering spherical form with flat hinged lid, top section of body and lid with engraved floral and scroll details, with semi-fluted swan neck, 6 1/8" ht, 18oz	Lyon & Turnbull Edinburgh UK 2007 #259
1839/40	Robert Keay II	Perth Edinburgh assay	Teapot, with stand, no details	National Museums of Scotland 1972/3 MEQ 1074a,b
1839/40	Elder & Co	Edinburgh	Teapot, part of a service	Lyle Annual Review 1979 p593
1839/40	James McKay	Edinburgh	Teapot, part of a service	Lyle Annual Review 1979 p 593 Sotheby's Sale
1839/40	James McKay	Edinburgh	Teapot, 6 ¾" ht, 22oz 12d	Lyle Annual Review 1980 p639 Sotheby's Sale
1839/40	Robb & Whittet	Edinburgh	Teapot, no details	National Museums of Scotland MEQ 1216
1840/41	C & C Also Robb & Whittet	Edinburgh	Teapot, on foliate feet, sides with scroll and floral flanked cartouches, one with initials, ivory insulators to handle, flared rim and foliate chased dome lid with foliate knop finial, 25.3oz	Christie's London UK 2007 #772
1840/41	Robb & Whittet	Edinburgh	Teapot, circular waisted form, body chased on embossed with band of scrolls, rocaille, and floral sprays, on four tab feet, 8 ½" ht, part of a service	Christie's London UK 2003 #406
1841/42	W & C	Edinburgh	Teapot, no details	Bonhams London UK 2000 #809
1842/43	McKay & Chisolm	Edinburgh	Teapot, part of a service	Lyle Annual Review 1983 p728
1842ca	Robert Keay II	Perth Edinburgh assay	Teapot, part of a 3 piece service, no details	National Museums of Scotland MEQ 736-38 964
1844/45	James McKay	Edinburgh	Teapot, part of a service	Lyle Annual Review 1983 p729
1846/47	James Howden & Co	Edinburgh	Teapot, part of a service	Lyle Annual Review 1982 p619 Sotheby's Sale
1846/47	Marshall & Son	Edinburgh	Teapot, fully hallmarked, nicely decorated, curved spout, lid with finial, 6 ¾" ht, 10 ¼" long from spout to handle, 22oz	eBay listing #6511177247, February 10, 2005

YEAR	MAKER	LOCATION	DESCRIPTION	SOURCE
1846/47	William Marshall & Sons	Edinburgh	Teapot, part of a 4 piece service, octagonal, butterfly decoration, 7"ht, 10"long	Huntley House Museum, Edinburgh HH 2809/65
1847/48	James & William Marshall	Edinburgh	Teapot, designed by David Ramsay Hay	National Museums of Scotland 1986.150
1847/48	WC	Edinburgh	Teapot, spherical, on stepped domed foot, acanthus capped partly fluted curved spout, double scroll silver handle, lid and upper body with chased decoration, 6 1/8" ht, 15.8oz	Bonhams Sale 15120 Aug 22, 2007 #4
1848/49	MacKay & Chisholm	Edinburgh	Teapot, fluted sides with floral chased panels, floral borders, acanthus capped scroll handle and game bird finial, cartouches either side engraved with respectively a huntsman with hound and a stag, 30.8oz	Christie's London UK 2007 #54
1849/50	Walker Crichton	Edinburgh	Teapot, globular on a spreading foot, body chased with C-scrolls and foliage, part of a service	Christie's London UK 2006 #1682
1849/50	AGW	Edinburgh	Teapot, engraved with foliage, an armorial and motto, with another item	Christie's London UK 2005 #670
1857/58	Walker Crichton	Edinburgh	Teapot, round body, silver handle, ball finial	National Museums of Scotland MEQ 811
1859/60	MacKay & Chisholm	Edinburgh	Teapot, spherical with flat lid, double scrolled handle, spreading foot, curved spout, 6" ht	Bonhams London UK 2001 #952
1862/63	Crichton	Edinburgh	Teapot, heavily decorated, curved spout, winged animal on handle, engraved script initial "B", in cartouche	National Museums of Scotland MEQ 954
1865/66	William Marshall	Edinburgh	Teapot, no details	National Museums of Scotland MEQ 942
1866/67	EM	Edinburgh	Teapot, globular form, heavily embossed floral and scroll decorated, leaf capped scroll handle, sold with a coffeepot	Lyon & Turnbull Edinburgh UK 2003 #232
1867/68	James McKay	Edinburgh	Teapot, ivory insulated handle, curved spout, hemispherical shape, part of a service	Christie's London UK 2005 #578
1873/74	Marshall & Sons	Edinburgh	Teapot, oval drum form with engraved initials, ivory insulated handle, hinged lid with an ebonized wood finial, 9 7/8" long, 18oz gross	Christie's London UK 2001 #130
1873/74	Marshall & Sons	Edinburgh	Teapot, oval drum form with engraved initials, ivory insulated handle, hinged lid with an ebonized wood finial, 9 7/8" ht, 18oz gross	Christie's London UK 2001 #103

YEAR	MAKER	LOCATION	DESCRIPTION	SOURCE
1874/75	Pollack & Meldrum	Edinburgh	Teapot, part of a 3 piece service, chased cartouche, 8 ½" ht, 8 5/8" long	Huntley House Museum Edinburgh part of LF 36/60
1876/77	John Crichton	Edinburgh	Teapot, in aesthetic taste, faceted oblong, serpent handles, beaded rim, bodies repoussed and chased with animals and foliage, straight spout, also with a French import mark, part of a service, 5"ht, 22oz 10d	Christie's NY USA 1998 #292
1888/89	Marshall & Sons	Edinburgh	Teapot, spherical on a spreading foot as in a mid-18th century manner, shoulder chased with escallop shells and scrolling foliage, 5" ht, 9oz gross	Christie's Lanarkshire UK 1998 #220
1891/92	Brook & Son	Edinburgh	Teapot, spherical, part gadrooned, upper body chased with flower heads amidst scrolling foliage, low foot, knop finial, 14.6oz	Bonhams Sale 15120 Aug 22, 2007 #46
1896/97	Not available	Glasgow	Teapot, part of a 3 piece service, chased with a scene from Sir Walter Scott's "Lay of the Last Minstrel", 8 ½" ht, 9" long	Dundee Museum and Art Galleries 1986-88
1899-1904	James Ramsay	Dundee	Teapot, part of a 4 piece service, no details	Dundee Museum and Art Galleries 1986-88
1994/95	Malcolm Appleby	Edinburgh	Teapot, The Cressbrooke Teapot, silver and wood	Aberdeen Museum and Galleries ABDAG 008855, 1995

Tea Service

Plate 50. An Assembled Edinburgh Tea Service.
Sugar Bowl 1730/31, Cream Boat 1735/36, Salver 1740/41 all by William Aytoun.
Teapot 1734/35 by Hugh Penman.
Courtesy of The Phoenix Collection. Photograph by Janice M Dietert.

YEAR	MAKER TEA SERVICE	LOCATION	DESCRIPTION	SOURCE
1723/24	James Ker	Edinburgh	Tea service, 3 piece, probably later separated, teapot – wavy border, molded rim sugar bowl, helmet cream jug	Wilson & Sharp Glasgow Exhibition 1911 vol I p108 #22
1725 ca	George Robertson and another	Aberdeen	Tea service, matching 3 piece set, bullet shaped teapot with spreading base and semi fluted curved spout 6 ½" ht, baluster milk jug with leaf capped double scroll handles on 3 hoof feet 4 ½" ht, almost spherical sugar bowl by George Cooper on spreading foot 4 ¼" di, each piece identically initialed, 35oz 11d all	Sotheby's July 4, 1968 #133
1727/28	James Ker	Edinburgh	Tea service, The Ford Service, also called the Johnson Tea Service, 4 pieces, spherical teapot, helmet cream jug with girdle, wavy border molded edge sugar bowl, stand from 1729/30 by Henry Bethune, all with the Arms of Johnson	Apollo 1934 vol 20 p21 Wilson & Sharp advertisement How's Notes on Antique Silver 1941 vol I, p23 Finlay 1991 p126 Antique Silver 1941, vol I, p23
1728 -37	Henry Bethune Archibald Ure Edward Lothian	Edinburgh	Tea service, mixed set with 1730 teapot and 1728 sugar Henry Bethune, stand 1733 by Archibald Ure, and cream boat 1737 by Edward Lothian	Christie's Picture File Neg #25239 Christie's Auction Lots 374-377
1730 ca	George Cooper	Aberdeen	Tea service, The Kirkhill Tea Service, 5 pieces, apple shaped teapot, covered sugar bowl, cream jug and pair of oblong tea caddies, crest, motto and the initial "D", 50.8 oz all	Connoisseur Magazine 1955 vol 135, p90 Sotheby's November 20, 1986 #108 How of Edinburgh advertisement Aberdeen Museums and Galleries ABDAG008510-008505
1733/34	William Aytoun	Edinburgh	Tea service, The Girdwood Tea Service, spherical teapot, covered hot milk jug, wavy border molded lip sugar bowl and matching stand	Connoisseur Magazine 1934 vol 91, p342 Finlay 1991 #74 John Girdwood Collection Christie's December 13, 1933 #36 Christie's December 13, 1967 #22 Partridge Ltd London Christie's May 22, 1991#85
1734/35	James Ker	Edinburgh	Tea service, The Hopetoun Tea Service, 6 pieces, tea kettle with stand, covered milk jug (5 5/8" ht), oval sugar bowl on 4 feet, oval spoon tray on 4 feet, shaped square stand (8" long, 9 3/8" wide), Arms of Hope	Clayton Dictionary p 419 #650 Christie's June 15, 1977 #121 National Museums of Scotland 1207-1211

YEAR	MAKER	LOCATION	DESCRIPTION	SOURCE
1739/40-43/44	James Mitchelson and William Dempster or William Davie	Edinburgh	Tea service, 3 piece service, teapot by Mitchelson, sugar bowl and dolphin-handled cream boat by WD	Apollo July 1972 vol 96 p94 Spink Ltd, London Asprey, London
1739/40	James Ker	Edinburgh	Tea service, 4 piece, pot with part fluted curved spout, flush hinged lid, ball and button finial, silver capped loop handle, flat chased near mouth; circular stand similarly chased; sugar bowl larger than average size, on 3 feet, issuing from trefoil scrolls; cream boat on 3 similar feet, capped scroll handle, 48.5oz all	Christie's London April 27, 1949 #81 Christie's Negative #157597 or #157592 Country Life December 2, 1976 How of Edinburgh advertisement
1739/40	James Ker, David Mitchell, Archibald Ure	Edinburgh	Tea service, 4 piece, David Mitchell was the assayer and not the maker	Connoisseur Magazine 1934 vol 91 p342
1742/43	James Campbell I	Edinburgh	Tea service, 3 piece, originally attributed to James Clark, teapot - spherical on molded foot, partly fluted curved spout and ball finial, flush hinged lid, chased around the mouth with bunches of flowers and fruit in shells and scrollwork, circular sugar bowl – flat scalloped rim chased with flowers and shells, cream boat – on 3 hoof feet, acanthus capped double scroll handle and everted rim similar to that of the bowl, prominent lip chased with scrolls and diaper work, 37oz all	Sotheby's July 18, 1963 #297 Christie's July 5, 1967 #172 Apollo October 1968 vol 88 p54 De Havilland Antiques
1743/44	James Ker	Edinburgh	Tea service, The Erskine Tea Service, 3 pieces, near spherical teapot – chased on the shoulder with a broad band of scrolls, flowers and foliage, half fluted spout, silver leaf capped loop handle, slightly domed lid with flush hinge, silver ball finial, jug and sugar bowl with chased and shaped everted rims, each on 3 volute cabriole legs with paw feet, each piece engraved with the initials "AE" for a member of the Erskine family, ancestors of the seller in 1960, sold also with 6 Scots fiddle pattern teaspoons also by James Ker, 36.7oz with the spoons	Christie's June 22, 1960 #101 Antiques Magazine 1960 vol 78 Shrubsole Inc Clayton Dictionary 1985 p421, #651
1750 ca	Colin Allan	Aberdeen	Tea service, 3 piece, no details	Christie's London July 1992 #100
1758/1770	William Dempster	Edinburgh	Tea service, inverted pear shaped teapot, sugar bowl, cream jug with flying scroll handle	Scottish Art Review 1953 vol IV #4 Bell of Aberdeen advertisement
1765/66	Ker & Dempster	Edinburgh	Tea service, probably a 3 piece service, no details	Antiques Magazine 1956 vol 69
1767 ca	Not Available	Edinburgh	Tea service, 3-4 piece service, no details	Antiques Magazine 1951 vol 60 Bell of Aberdeen advertisement

YEAR	MAKER	LOCATION	DESCRIPTION	SOURCE
1775 ca	James McEwan	Glasgow	Tea service, 3 piece, no details	Private Collection
1783/84	William Dempster or William Davie	Edinburgh	Tea service, 3 piece, teapot with no mm and perhaps 1773, jug and sugar bowl fully marked, bowl in inverted pear form, jug helmet shaped, teapot with curved spout, insulated silver loop handle and silver flower finial	Sotheby's Gleneagles August 25, 1997 #149
1789/90	Patrick Robertson	Edinburgh	Tea service, 3 piece, no details	National Museums of Scotland MEQ 671-674
1790 ca	Alexander Stewart Jr	Inverness	Tea service, no details	Connoisseur Magazine 1934, vol 93 p347
1790/91 and 92/93	WR probably William Robertson	Edinburgh	Tea service 4 piece, teapot, stand, sugar basket, and cream jug, pot in plain oval style, others to match pot 6 ¼" ht, stand 8 3/8" X 6 1/8", 40.6oz all	Sotheby's Gleneagles August 1992 #147 Private Collection
1791/92	William Robertson	Edinburgh	Tea service, 3 piece, all with classical 6 sided diamond shape outline, coat of arms	Finlay 1991 #98
1791/92	Patrick Robertson	Edinburgh	Tea service, 4 piece, no details	National Museums of Scotland MEQ 667-870
1794/95	Alexander Gardner	Edinburgh	Tea service, 4 piece, no details	Dundee Museum and Art Galleries 1978-1550-1-4
1794/95	Alexander Spence	Edinburgh	Tea service, 4 piece, teapot, stand, cream jug and sugar basket, bright cut leaves and wriggle work bands, vacant cartouche, initial "N" on underside	Sotheby's Gleneagles September 1, 1998 #542
1795/96	Not available	Edinburgh	Tea service, 3 piece, no details	Antiques Magazine vol 38 p50
1795/96 and 96/97	Alexander Gardner and Graham & McLean	Edinburgh	Tea service, 4 piece, no details	Private Collection
1797/98	George Christie	Edinburgh	Tea service, 3 piece, no details	The Lipton Collection #101
1800/01	W & P Cunningham I	Edinburgh	Tea service, no details	Antiques Magazine 1957 vol 71
1800 ca	Edward Livingstone	Dundee	Tea service, 3 piece, no details	Dundee Museum and Art Galleries 1986-136-1=3
1801/02	W & P Cunningham I	Edinburgh	Tea service, 4 piece, no details	National Museums of Scotland MEQ 833

YEAR	MAKER	LOCATION	DESCRIPTION	SOURCE
1802/03	W & P Cunningham I	Edinburgh	Tea service, 3 piece, oval section, part fluted foot, Greek key motif on shoulder, crest, motto and initials, 29.5oz gross	Christie's London 2000 #369
1804/05	Alexander Spence	Edinburgh	Tea service, 3 piece, no details	Antiques Magazine vol 41 p295 Bell of Aberdeen advertisement
1807/08	James McKay	Edinburgh	Tea service, 4 piece, teapot, stand, bowl, cream no details	Apollo September 1974 vol 100 p17 Holmes advertisement
1807/08	Dick & McPherson	Edinburgh	Tea service, 3 piece, no details	National Museums of Scotland MEQ 629-631
1808/09	Francis Howden	Edinburgh	Tea service, 3 piece, no details	Antiques Magazine vol 46, p120
1808/09	Robert Keay I	Perth Edinburgh assay	Tea service, 3 piece, RK over striking another's mark, no details	Sotheby's Hopetoun House April 1989 #42
1809/10	George McHattie	Edinburgh	Tea service, 3 pieces, 41 oz	Pook & Pook Downingtown PA USA 2004 #624
1809/10	James McKay	Edinburgh	Tea and coffee service, no details	Apollo 1967 vol 85 p87
1810 ca	Newlands & Grierson	Glasgow	Tea service, 3 piece, teapot, ovalled rectangular form, with engraved bands of flowers below, reeded bands at the shoulders, the jug and basin with gilt interiors, each piece on applied rim base with 4 ball supports, 39.6oz	Sotheby's Gleneagles August 25, 1997 #122
1811/12	George Fenwick	Edinburgh	Tea service, 3 piece, no details	Lyle Annual Review 1983 p615 Christie's auction
1811/12	James McKay	Edinburgh	Tea service, 3 piece, no details	Sotheby's Hopetoun House March 1990 #86
1812/13	James McKay	Edinburgh	Tea service, no details	Antiques Magazine vol 115 p1328 Shreve Inc Boston USA advertisement
1814/15	Robert Gray & Son	Glasgow Edinburgh assay	Tea service, 3 pieces and plated hot water jug, Greek revival manner, 56oz	Christie's London UK 1999 #80
1814/15	Robert Gray & Son	Glasgow Edinburgh	Tea service, 3 pieces, squat circular form, 50 oz gross	Christie's NY USA 2005 #172

YEAR	MAKER (continued)	LOCATION assay	DESCRIPTION	SOURCE
1815/16	George McHattie	Edinburgh	Tea service, 3 pieces, rounded rectangular form, on ball feet, 33oz	Lyon & Turnbull Edinburgh UK 2003 #233
1816-19	James McDonald	Edinburgh	Tea service, no details	Antiques Magazine vol 76 Shreve Inc Boston USA advertisement
1817/18	James McKay	Edinburgh	Tea service, 4 piece, no details	National Museums of Scotland MEQ 632-635
1818/19	James McKay	Edinburgh	Tea service, 3 piece, no details	Sotheby's Gleneagles 1990 p29
1818/19	James McKay	Edinburgh	Tea service, 3 piece, partly fluted compressed form, crested, 47.5oz	Christie's London UK 2001 #183
1819/20	W & P Cunningham I	Edinburgh	Tea service, 3 piece, teapot – fluted body, curved fluted spout, mushroom finial, scrolled cartouche, sugar bowl – fluted body, 2 handled gadrooned rim, scrolled cartouche, cream jug – oval fluted body, leaf capped scroll handle, scrolled cartouche	Fogg Art Museum, Harvard University 1948.47-49
1819/20	James McKay	Edinburgh	Tea service, 3 piece plus a tray	Sotheby's Gleneagles 1990 p29
1820 ca	James McKay	Edinburgh	Tea service, 3 piece, no details	National Museums of Scotland MEQ 1310-13112
1820/21 and 22/23	James McKay	Edinburgh	Tea service, 3 piece, bottom half gadrooned, heavily chased with script initials "AE"	National Museums of Scotland K.2004.117
1820/21	Not available	Edinburgh assay	Tea service, 3 piece, said to be Scottish, no details	Connoisseur Magazine 1952 vol 130 p24
1820/21	Edward Livingstone	Dundee	Tea service, 3 piece, no details	Finlay 1991 #111
1820/21	CB	Edinburgh	Tea service, 4 pieces, teapot – partly fluted compressed spherical form, elaborate shell and foliate scroll rim, partly reeded, foliate capped loop handle, scroll spout, lid partly raised and fluted, fluted button finial, 3 footed circular stand, 2 handled open sugar, cream jug, 57oz all	Christie's East NY USA 1998 #52
1823/24	James McKay	Edinburgh	Tea service, 3 piece, no details	Apollo April-June 1968 vol 87 p106 Sotheby's

YEAR	MAKER	LOCATION	DESCRIPTION	SOURCE
1823/24	James McKay	Edinburgh	Tea service, 3 pieces, squat circular forms, 54oz	Christie's Lanarkshire UK 1997 #91
1824/25	James McKay	Edinburgh	Tea service, 3 piece, no details	Sotheby's Gleneagles August 1987 #305
1824/25	James Howden	Edinburgh	Tea service, 3 pieces, inverted pear form, 52oz	Christie's Lanarkshire UK 1997 #135
1825/26	James McKay	Edinburgh	Tea service, 3 piece, no details	Sotheby's Hopetoun House April 1988 #77
1825/27	Not available	Edinburgh assay	Tea and coffee service, 4 pieces, said to be Scottish, no details	Apollo August 1967 vol 86 #2
1826/27	Alexander Edmonstoun	Edinburgh	Tea service, 3 pieces, no details	Sotheby's Hopetoun House April 1988 #81
1828/29	Robert Keay & Son	Perth Edinburgh assay	Tea service, 3 piece, no details	National Museums of Scotland MEQ 949-951 1969.685-687
1829/30	James McKay	Edinburgh	Tea service, 3 piece, no details	Sotheby's Hopetoun House April 1988 #83
1830/31	James McKay	Edinburgh	Tea service, 3 pieces, compressed globular form, gilt interiors, 49oz gross	Christie's London UK 2001 #107
1832/33	James McKay and William Whitcross	Edinburgh and Aberdeen	Tea service, 3 pieces, mixed service, teapot by McKay, 53.5oz	Christie's London UK 2002 #226
1832/34	William Marshall	Edinburgh	Tea service, 3 piece, no details	Sotheby's Gleneagles August 1988 #483
1835/36 and 1839/40	James McKay	Edinburgh	Tea service, 3 pieces, inverted pear shape, 48oz	Christie's London UK 1999 #14
1837/38	Leonard Urquhart	Edinburgh	Tea service, 3 pieces, initial "B", 50.1oz	DuMouchelles Detroit, MI USA 2002 #1025
1837/38	Leonard Urquhart	Edinburgh	Tea service, 3 pieces, fluted inverted pear shape, foliage and scroll borders, bodies chased with upright acanthus foliage, crested, 48oz	Christie's London UK 1999 #57
1837/38	James McKay	Edinburgh	Tea service, 3 piece, no details	National Museums of Scotland MEQ 641

YEAR	MAKER	LOCATION	DESCRIPTION	SOURCE
1838/39	James McKay	Edinburgh	Tea service, 3 pieces, baluster shape, 50 oz 10d	Christie's NY USA 2004 #984
1838/39	Leonard Urquhart	Edinburgh	Tea service, semi-fluted, inverted pear form, 3 pieces, 47oz gross	Christie's London UK 2004 #119
1840/41	Robb & Whittet	Edinburgh	Tea service, 3 pieces, circular waisted form, 46.5oz	Christie's London UK 2003 #406
1842/43	McKay & Chisolm	Edinburgh	Tea service, 3 piece, no details	Lyle Annual Review 1983 Sotheby's Sale
1842/43	Robert Keay II	Perth Edinburgh assay	Tea service, 3 piece, no details	National Museums of Scotland MEQ 736-738 1965.1809-09
1844/45	James McKay	Edinburgh	Tea service, 3 piece, no details	Lyle Annual Review 1983 Sotheby's Sale
1844/45	Leonard Urquhart	Edinburgh	Tea service, 4 pieces, bombe form, with a kettle	Christie's Amsterdam NE 1997 #92
1846/47	William Cunningham	Edinburgh	Tea service, 3 piece, teapot – with domed cover and urn finial , cream jug and sugar bowl – with pierced scroll border, all are of lobed melon form on octagonal bases, chased panels, scrolling foliage, 55oz all	Bonhams Sale 10914 #1
1849/50	Walker Crichton	Edinburgh	Tea service, 3 pieces, spherical, gilt-lined interiors, 44 oz gross	Christie's London 2006 #1687
1852/53	WCS	Edinburgh	Tea service, 4 pieces, with coffeepot, kettle, cream jug, sugar bowl, in baluster form, 84oz	Christie's NY USA 2005 #249
1867/68	James McKay	Edinburgh	Tea service, 3 pieces, crested	Christie's London UK 2005 #578
1871/72	D C Rait & Son	Glasgow	Tea service, 5 piece, with crest and motto "TRY", Kettle 20" ht, all highly decorated	A Pash & Sons London 2006 #e5406/8013
1876/77	John Crichton	Edinburgh	Tea service, 3 pieces, aesthetic taste, serpent handles, panel scenes, 22oz 10d	Christie's NY USA 1998 #292
1885/86	JR	Glasgow	Tea service, 3 pieces, bombe form, 41oz	Christie's London UK 2001 #114
1900/01	Hamilton & Inches	Edinburgh	Tea service, 4 piece set, no details	The Maple Swan Collection
1911/12 and 1917/18	Edward & Sons	Glasgow	Tea service, 5 pieces, 101 oz	Christie's London UK 1999 #58

Toast & Bannock Racks

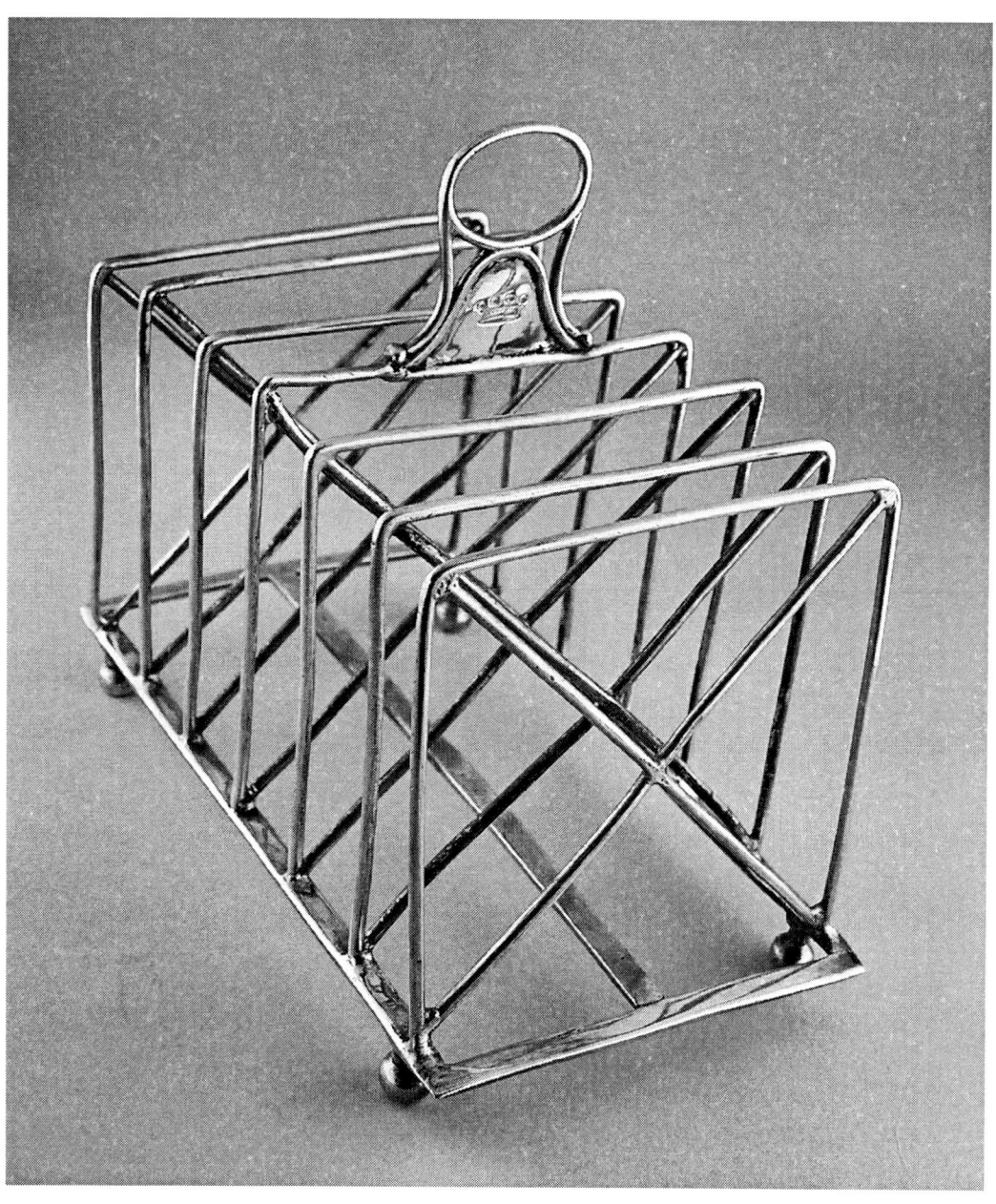

Plate 51. A Toast Rack 1825/26, maker's mark obscured.
Courtesy of The Phoenix Collection. Photograph by Janice M Dietert.

TOAST AND BANNOCK RACKS

YEAR	MAKER	LOCATION	DESCRIPTION	SOURCE
1773/74	Patrick Robertson	Edinburgh	Bannock rack, probably mate to Shaw collection example	National Museums of Scotland 1955.62
1773/74	Patrick Robertson	Edinburgh	Bannock rack, wide 10 bar toast rack from with central loop handle, the crumb tray with gadrooned edge, probably mate to National Museums of Scotland 1955.62 example, 9 7/8"	Shaw Collection Christie's Glasgow March 29, 1983 #66
1785/86	Francis Howden	Edinburgh	Toast rack, no details	National Museums of Scotland MEQ 682 1968.1820
1789/90	Not available	Edinburgh	Toast rack, no mm, oval base crested in the center within pierced foliate motifs, leafy scroll grips, on 4 panel feet, screw on 9 bar frame, 10 ½" wide, 12oz	Sotheby's Scone Palace April 10, 1978 #39
1793/94	Not available	Edinburgh	Toast rack, pair, one lion crested, ovoid with 6 arched sections, ring handle, bun feet, 8" long, 14oz all	Sotheby's Gleneagles August 25, 1997 #137
1800 ca	McHattie & Fenwick	Edinburgh	Toast rack, no details	National Museums of Scotland MEQ 798
1800/01	Not available	Edinburgh	Toast rack, mm rubbed, with 9 bars of double arched wire work and central handle, on 4 bun feet	Sotheby's Scone Palace April 19, 1977 #28
1802/03	RL ? Possibly Robert Keay	Perth Edinburgh assay	Toast rack, oval section frame incurving at either end, with 9 wire supports and a central loop handle, 9 ¼' long, 8oz	Christie's London UK 2001 #106
1810 ca	Peter Lambert	Aberdeen	Bannock rack, on 4 ball feet, with 9 double loop wire work divisions and a central ring handle, engraved initials "JMB" and a stag's head crest, 6 ¾" wide	Christie's Lanarkshire UK 1997 #120
1810 ca	Peter Lambert	Montrose	Bannock rack, no details	Aberdeen Museums and Galleries ABDAG011098
1819/20	Robert Gray & Son	Glasgow	Toast rack, no details	National Museums of Scotland MEQ 63
1820ca	William Jamieson & Co	Aberdeen	Toast rack, no details	National Museums of Scotland MEQ 1054
1825/26	Not available	Edinburgh	Toast rack, mm indistinct, with 7 bars and X internal supports for each bar, ring handle, resting on bell shaped connection to central bar, support with the crest and motto "PRO REGE, LEGE, GREGE", for Henry Brougham, Baron of	The Phoenix Collection

YEAR	MAKER (continued)	LOCATION	DESCRIPTION	SOURCE
			Brougham and Vaux and Lord High Chancellor for Great Britain, 6" long, 3 ¼" wide, 5 " to top of handle	
1826/27	Not available	Edinburgh	Toast rack, no details	The Maple Swan Collection
1830 ca	George Booth	Aberdeen	Toast rack, marked - GB, ABD, GB, no details	Aberdeen Museums and Galleries ABDAG001032
1830 ca	William Jamieson	Aberdeen	Toast rack, marked - WGJ, ABD, no details	Aberdeen Museums and Galleries ABDAG001333
1835 ca	GP	Edinburgh	Toast rack, engraved boar's head and drawn bow with arrow	Aberdeen Museums and Galleries ABDAG0010351

Urns

Plate 52. An ovoid shaped Urn with snake handles 1738/39 by James Weems, Edinburgh. Courtesy of a private collector. Photograph by Janice M Dietert.

URNS AND URNSTANDS

YEAR	MAKER	LOCATION	DESCRIPTION	SOURCE
1723/24	William Aytoun	Edinburgh	Urn, tea, oviform, with snake handles	National Museums of Scotland MEQ 1983.13
1724/25	James Mitchelson	Edinburgh	Urn, tea, oviform with snake handles	Connoisseur Magazine 1948 p899 Private Collection UK
1725 ca	Not available	Edinburgh	Urn, oviform with detachable domed cover, spout at front with wooden handle to the spigot, snake handles, on 3 double scroll legs terminating in wooden paw shaped feet, 11 ½" ht, 43.5oz	Sotheby's Gleneagles August 29, 1978 #427 Sotheby's Gleneagles September 1, 1998 #559
1729/30	Hugh Gordon	Edinburgh	Urn, egg shaped, silver spigot, snake handles, banner between 3 legs on wooden mounts, coat of arms	Holland p222 Noble Collection Finlay 1991 #83 Shrubsole NY USA 2004
1732/33	James Mitchelson	Edinburgh	Urn, oviform, with snake handles	Holland p222 Country Life April 1959 p130-33 National Museums of Scotland 1956.368
1733/34	Archibald Ure	Edinburgh	Urn, tea, no details	Connoisseur Magazine 1939 vol 103 p74
1735 ca	James Ker	Edinburgh	Urn, tea, with snake handles, with tray, see listing below for the later reunited stand	Scottish Art Review 1984 vol XVI #1 back cover How of Edinburgh advertisement National Museums of Scotland MEQ 1573
1735/36	James Ker	Edinburgh	Urn stand, urn it belongs with is previous listing, quatrefoil shape, plain center bounded by an engraved shell, scroll and hatched border, on 4 stump supports, later reunited with its urn, 14 ½" long, 36.1oz	Phillips Edinburgh July 22, 1983 #245 How of Edinburgh National Museums of Scotland
1735/36	John Rollo	Edinburgh	Urn, oviform for tea, with snake handles	National Museums of Scotland L.1983.14
1736/37	William Aytoun	Edinburgh	Urn, egg shaped, for tea, with snake handles, Arms of McKenzie impaling Gordon, 12 ¾" ht, 56oz 10d	Brett, p 194 #815 Hyman Collection - Colonial Williamsburg G1995-187

YEAR	MAKER (continued)	LOCATION	DESCRIPTION	SOURCE
1736/37	James Ker	Edinburgh	Urn, tea, acanthus capped knees to legs, hoof feet, 62.1oz	Antiques Magazine June 1996 p848 Sotheby's NY USA October 28, 1980
1738/39	James Weems	Edinburgh	Urn, oviform, on 3 plain cabriole legs with shell feet, snake handles, eyes with foliage tufts on a scale work background, flat chased around the mouth and on the domed cover with shells and scrolling foliage, the cover with girdled orb and button finial, the spigot with wooden handle, 45oz	Connoisseur Magazine 1939 p197-99 How's Notes on Antique Silver 1941 vol I p12
1742/43	James Ker	Edinburgh	Urn, egg shaped body, snake handles, leaf capped cabriole legs with shell terminals and paw feet, spigot with wood handle, finial part wood, crest – deer's head, motto "SI JE PUIS", arms and motto on opposite side "CNOCK ELA CHAN", a comparable urn is in the Folger's collection, illustrated in their catalog on p62, mm not clear	Scottish Art Review 1967 vol XI #1 back cover How of Edinburgh advertisement Bell of Aberdeen Grantully Castle Antiques Private Collection
1746/47	James Ker	Edinburgh	Urn, oviform with snake handles with shell capped heads, no plumes at the eyes, on 3 leaf capped cabriole legs with paw feet, chased around the shoulder and on the lid/cover with scrolls and foliage, armorials, wooden handled spigot, silver mounted wooden finial,	Baltimore Museum of Art 1981.106
1746/47	James Ker	Edinburgh	Urn, no details	Burlington Magazine May 1960 Clayton Dictionary p426 #660
1750 ca	Assayer Hugh Gordon	Edinburgh	Urn, on leaf capped shell and paw cabriole supports, the upper part of the shouldered pear shaped body richly chased with flowers, foliage and masks, flat domed hinged lid with similar decoration, ebony bun finial, snake handles, 11" ht, 53oz	Jackson Marks p547
1759/60	Alexander Gardner	Edinburgh	Urn, tea, snake handles, chased body, hoof feet	Christie's Scotland November 11, 1987 #58 Christie's Glasgow April 25, 1990
1767/68	Not available	Edinburgh	Urn, egg shaped for tea, on stand with tall legs, chased heavily , snake handles, Arms of the McLachlan family, 11 ½" ht, 44oz	National Museums of Scotland MEQ 1190 0976.37
1767/68	Benjamin Tait	Edinburgh	Urn, oviform, on 3 cabriole legs, chased with foliage, paw feet, body chased with rococo cartouche engraved with coat of arms, festoons of flowers, snake	Antiques Magazine October 1963 vol 84 Bell of Aberdeen advertisement Christie's November 30, 1960

YEAR	MAKER (continued)	LOCATION	DESCRIPTION	SOURCE
			handles, surmounted by figure of a swan, 11 ½" ht, 44oz 13d	
1767/68	Alexander Aitchison I	Edinburgh	Urn, no details	Dundee Museum and Art Galleries 1978-2065
1770/71	Patrick Robertson	Edinburgh	Urn, heart shaped body on flat base with grill work skirt rising in bell stem to the body, lid/cover also shaped like a bell, all heavily chased, loop handles with bead work	Apollo 1934 vol 20 p137 Freeman advertisement
1775/76	Patrick Robertson	Edinburgh	Urn, large cup shaped body with fluting at the base, standing on flat base on 4 ball feet, snake coiled handles, also wrapped around the body coat of arms, flat stepped lid/cover	Christie's Auction #293
1776/77	Patrick Robertson	Edinburgh	Urn, large tea, classical vase shaped body	Private Collection UK
1778/79	Patrick Robertson	Edinburgh	Urn, large classical form, fluted body, tall loop handles, 19 ½" ht, 160oz	Jackson Marks p549 Apollo 1947 p69 Finlay 1991 #96 Antiques Magazine vol 56 p273 National Museums of Scotland 1899.391
1781/82	William Davie or William Dempster	Edinburgh	Urn, tea, 14 1/3" ht	Sotheby's Photo file
1781/82	*William Davie or William Dempster*	*Edinburgh*	*Urn, no details*	*Antiques Magazine 1953 vol 63*
1784/85	William Rhind or William Robertson	Edinburgh	Urn, vase form, tall loop handle, square base on 4 ball feet, internal heating chamber engraved behind spigot with initials "AMD", crest of sinking ship, motto "DISCE PATI", 15 ½" ht, 54oz	Private Collection
1786/87	W & P Cunningham I	Edinburgh	Urn, pair,	Antiques Magazine vol 98 p960
1786/87	*William Davie or William Dempster*	*Edinburgh*	Urn, no details	Antiques Magazine 1954 vol 66
1786/87	*William Davie or William Dempster*	Edinburgh	*Urn, vase shaped, inscription, 139oz 9d*	Sotheby's November 8, 1973 #20
1788/89	WM William McKenzie	Edinburgh	Urn, silver and ivory, 15 ½" X 7 ¾" X 7 ½"	Musee des Beaux Arts, Montreal Canada 1950/51.Ds.5a-b

YEAR	MAKER	LOCATION	DESCRIPTION	SOURCE
1789/90	Patrick Robertson	Edinburgh	Urn, tea, vase shaped, square base with 3 ball feet, bright cut engraved with garland and scroll borders, applied with 2 reeded handles, 23 ¼" ht, 92oz	Bonhams Sale 10914 #11
1789/90	William Robertson	Edinburgh	Urn, fluted and paneled body, bright cut engraving, applied oak leaves on the cover, acorn finial, 20 ¾" ht	Firestone and Parsons, Boston, USA
1790/91	William Robertson	Edinburgh	Urn, tea, no details	Litchfield CT USA Auction 1992
1791/92	William Robertson	Edinburgh	Urn, marked on base and cover, 15" ht, 57oz 10d	Christie's NY USA October 30, 1990 #296
1792/93	William Robertson	Edinburgh	Urn, 16" ht	Sotheby's Picture File
1793/94	William Robertson	Edinburgh	Urn, tea, no details	National Museums of Scotland MEQ 706
1794/95	William Robertson	Edinburgh	Urn, hemispherical, on reeded cushion shaped stand, with egg cup lamp, engraved behind spigot with arms of Simpson, inscription on reverse side "Part of Silver Plate, value One Hundred Guineas, voted to William Simpson Esq., in Augt 1794 by the Paper Manufacturers Near Edinr.", 12" ht, 55oz 10d	Private Collection
1800 ca	Alexander Edmonstoun	Edinburgh	Urn, no details	Antiques Magazine vol 128 #113 Wakefield advertisement
1801 ca	McHattie & Fenwick	Edinburgh	Urn, tea, no details	National Museums of Scotland MEQ 663
1802/03	McHattie & Fenwick	Edinburgh	Urn, tea, no details	National Museums of Scotland MEQ 1062
1802/03	Not available	Edinburgh	Urn, tea or coffee, no details	Apollo April – June 1968 vol 87 p106 Sotheby's Sale
1802/03	James McKay	Edinburgh	Urn vase shaped, covered, inscribed, 17 ¼" ht, 93oz	Sotheby's Gleneagles August 23, 1976 #119
1806/07	George Fenwick	Edinburgh	Urn, tea, ball shaped body, 2 ring handles attached by lion's masks, unicorn finial, on flat base and 4 ball feet, 4 reeded looped supports connecting body to base, 21 ½" ht,	Clayton Christie's Book p426 #662
1822/23	James McKay	Edinburgh	Urn, coat of arms, 17 ½" ht, 163oz	Sotheby's June 18, 1981 #96

YEAR	MAKER	LOCATION	DESCRIPTION	SOURCE
1827/28	James McKay	Edinburgh	Urn, presentation tea urn 170oz	Lyle Silver Review 1982 p239
1860 ca	Elder & Co	Edinburgh	Urn, Georgian style tea urn, 21 ½" ht, 9" di	Dayton Art Institute, Dayton, OH USA 33.7
1894/95	Hamilton & Inches	Edinburgh	Urn, tea, vase-shaped, circular base on 3 foliate scroll and rocaille feet, with pierced apron of scrolling foliage between, dolphin spout, leaf capped flying scroll handles, high domed cover with flame finial, body chased, with heating cylinder, 128oz	Christie's Lanarkshire, UK 1007 #104

Wine

Plate 53. Items Used With Wine Service.
Wine Label 1825/26 by JH, Edinburgh, Wine Funnel 1790 ca no maker's mark,
Wine Funnel Stand 1810 ca by James McKay, Edinburgh
Courtesy of The Phoenix Collection. Photograph by Janice M Dietert.

YEAR	MAKER	LOCATION	DESCRIPTION	SOURCE
	WINE COASTERS		**WINE**	
1781/82	William Davie or William Dempster	Edinburgh	Wine coasters, pair, circular, pierced sides with navette pattern, crest, wood bases and ivory initial disks, 4 ½" di	Nicholas Shaw Catalog Autumn 1999 p50
1784/85	Not available	Edinburgh assay	Wine coasters, pair, beaded edge, 4 pierced cartouches between swags of ferns and one cartouche with a crest of a bird and a motto, 5" di, 1 ½" ht	William Walter Antiques, London April 2006 #SA174X4
1790 ca	Alexander Spence	Edinburgh	Wine coasters, pair, straight side engraved with initials below reeded rims, with turned wooden bases	Sotheby's Scone Palace April 10, 1978 #90
1790/91	W & P Cunningham I	Edinburgh	Wine coasters, pair, pierced double bands near top and bottom, bright cut or pierced fans in between	Antiques Magazine vol 90 p728 Bell of Aberdeen advertisement
1793/94	Alexander Spence	Edinburgh	Wine coaster, decanter stand, no details	National Museums of Scotland MEQ 817 1965.1888
1797/98	Not available	Edinburgh	Wine coasters, pair, pierced with volutes, the waved rims threaded, probably en suite with next pair, maker not stated but possibly James Douglas	Breadalbane Collection Sale 1935 #91
1797/98	Not available	Edinburgh	Wine coasters, pair, pierced with volutes, the waved rims threaded, probably en suite with the previous pair, maker not stated but possibly James Douglas	Breadalbane Collection Sale 1935 #92
1801/02	I D James Douglas	Edinburgh	Wine coasters, set of 4	The Maple Swan Collection
1802/03	John McDonald	Edinburgh	Wine coasters, pair, plain, 5 ½" across, 1 ¼" deep	Goodwins, Edinburgh 1991
1808/09	James McKay	Edinburgh	Wine coasters, set of 4, circular shape, double gadroon border, wood bases, presented to Captain John Drysdale, 1809, 6" di	Nicholas Shaw Catalog 2004 p104 J H Bourden-Smith Catalog #47 Spring 2007 p29
1810 ca	James Erskine	Aberdeen	Wine coaster, silver, wood, felt, marked - "E", hand with dagger, Aberdeen town mark	Aberdeen Museums and Galleries, ABDAG011172, acquired 2003
1810/11	Patrick Cunningham & Sons	Edinburgh	Wine coasters, pair, fluted circular form, with wood bases and silver bosses engraved with the armorials of the royal Lanark Militia, sold with others, 6 ¾" di	Christie's London UK 2002 #135
1810/11	Patrick Cunningham & Sons	Edinburgh	Wine coasters, pair, circular shape, gadroon borders, lobed sides, wood bases, 6 ¾" di	Nicholas Shaw Catalog 2004 p105

YEAR	MAKER	LOCATION	DESCRIPTION	SOURCE
1818/19	Jonathan Millidge	Edinburgh	Wine coasters, pair, with floral rims, wood bases, with central bosses and a crest of a cornucopia of fruit, 6 ½" di	Christie's London UK 2006 #668
1819/20	Not available	Edinburgh	Wine coasters, pair, with molded foot, straight sides, everted foliate scroll and shell rims, turned wood bases with engraved crest to boss, 6 2/3" di	Dreweatt Neate Bristol Jan 31, 2006 #52
1824/25	CC	Edinburgh assay	Wine coasters, pair, baluster sides, band of chased leaf, scroll and flower decoration, center button with initial "R"	Shrubsole, NY USA 1981 E4739
1825/26	Robert Gray & Son	Glasgow	Wine coasters, pair, circular, the sides with embossed grape and leaf decoration, egg and dart molded base, gadrooned rim with an inner leaf tip border, crested central boss, fruitwood base, 6" di, 29oz gross	Joel Auctions, South Yarra AU 2007 #811
1826/27	Robert Gray & Son	Glasgow	Wine coasters, pair, sides decorated with grave vines above a gadroon bottom band, gadroon top rim, inside border leaf tip, matched on central crested silver bosses, 6 ½" di	Ragamont House Antiques Salisbury, CT USA 2006 #03159
1826/27	Robert Gray & Son	Glasgow	Wine coasters, circular, gadrooned borders, sides with grapevine on a matted ground, boss engraved with a crest, 6 ¼" di	Christie's NY USA 2005 #316
1830/31	George Paton	Edinburgh	Wine coasters, pair of wine slides, made from dog collars	National Museums of Scotland MEQ 1064
1838/39	Robert Gray & Son	Glasgow	Wine coasters, pair, in the form of wire work baskets, rim decorated with pendant grapevines, fluted interiors centered by engraved arms	Sotheby's NY USA April 1993 #146
1863/64	James McKay	Edinburgh	Wine coasters, no details	The Maple Swan Collection
1905/06	Hamilton & Inches	Edinburgh	Wine coasters, pair, plain with flared sides and molded rims, 5" id, 10oz	Christie's London UK 2004 #609

YEAR	MAKER WINE FUNNELS	LOCATION	DESCRIPTION	SOURCE
1640 ca	Adam Lamb	Edinburgh	Wine funnel, no details	Finlay 1991 #34 National Museums of Scotland MEQ 686 1964.1824
1780 ca	WD William Dempster or William Davie	Edinburgh	Wine funnel, circular form with a reeded rim, mm only 3 ½" di	Christie's London UK 2000 #11
1790 ca	Patrick Robertson	Edinburgh	Wine funnel, spirally fluted, sold with other items	Sotheby's NY USA 1995 #46
1790 ca	George McHattie	Edinburgh	Wine funnel, no details	JH Bourdon-Smith London 1993
1790 ca	Not available	Edinburgh	Wine funnel, in 2 sections, griffin crest on base, no mm	The Phoenix Collection
1790 ca	Charles Fowler	Elgin	Wine funnel, no details	Aberdeen Museums and Galleries ABDAG001345
1790 ca	James Hewitt	Edinburgh	Wine funnel, top of spout with ribbed girdle joining bowl, shallow bowl with thumbpiece, crest and motto, 2.5oz	Bonhams London UK 2006 #264
1790 ca	William Auld	Edinburgh	Wine funnel, with reeded rim, of conventional form	Lyon & Turnbull Edinburgh UK 2004 #180
1795 ca	William Robertson	Edinburgh	Wine funnel, with reeded rim, engraved with a crest and motto, sold with another,	Bonhams London UK 2004 #352
1795 ca	James Erskine	Aberdeen	Wine funnel, engraved initials, pronounced ribs, detachable inner bowl, marked - 'E', 3 castles, and mailed fist, 6" ht, 3" di, 7oz	Mary Cooke Antiques London 1996
1795/96	Archibald Ochiltree	Edinburgh	Wine funnel, in 2 sections, 5" long, 2oz 8d	Private Collection
1800 ca	W & P Cunningham I	Edinburgh	Wine funnel, no details	National Museums of Scotland MEQ 703
1800 ca	W & P Cunningham I	Edinburgh	Wine funnel, with three applied ribs and reeded border, the pierced detachable strainer with plain clip, 5" long 2.5oz	Christie's London UK 1999 #31
1800 ca	McHattie & Fenwick	Edinburgh	Wine funnel, applied with three short reeds, lacking pierced strainer, 4 ½" long	Christie's Lanarkshire UK 1998 #452
1800 ca	Robert Gray	Glasgow Edinburgh assay	Wine funnel, plain reeded, 5 ½" long	JH Bourdon-Smith Catalog Autumn 2001 p46 #43

YEAR	MAKER	LOCATION	DESCRIPTION	SOURCE
1800 ca	Robert Gray	Glasgow Edinburgh assay	Wine funnel, reeded girdle and rim, sold with other items	Bonhams London UK 2003 #560
1800 ca	John Keith	Banff	Wine funnel, plain, initials "J.M.C.", with stand, 5 ½" long	Noble Collection Nicholas Shaw Catalog 2005 p103
1800 ca	Charles Jamieson	Inverness	Wine funnel, with stand, no details	National Museums of Scotland MEQ 836
1800 ca	Edward Livingstone	Dundee	Wine funnel, no details	Dundee Museums and Art Galleries 1987-153
1800 ca	Robert Gray	Glasgow Edinburgh assay	Wine funnel, with 3 narrow straps applied to the spout, lacks thumbpiece, 4.3oz	Christie's London UK 2004 #380
1800 ca	Edward Livingstone	Dundee	Wine funnel, no details	Dundee Museums and Art Galleries 1965-190
1800 ca	Robert Keay	Perth	Wine funnel, with stand, 3 3/8" ht, 5 3/8" di	Huntley House Museum, Edinburgh HH3226/68
1800 ca	John Ziegler	Edinburgh	Wine funnel, with three applied staves to the plain spout, and reeded lower edge, 5 1/8" ht, 3oz	Lyon & Turnbull Edinburgh UK 2006 #265
1800 ca	A McLeod	Inverness	Wine funnel, plain, 5 ½" long	Lyon & Turnbull Edinburgh UK 2004 #306
1805 ca	Charles Jamieson	Inverness	Wine funnel, plain campana style edge with reeded border, 5 ½" long, 2.5oz	Nicholas Shaw Catalog Winter 2001 p74
1810 ca	George Fenwick	Edinburgh	Wine funnel, with gadrooned rim and fluted stem, 5 ½" ht	Gorringes LLP Lewes 2007 #1480
1810 ca	Robert Keay I	Perth	Wine funnel, no details	Argentum Antiques San Francisco, CA USA 1993
1810 ca	G & M	Edinburgh assay	Wine funnel, oval, with crest, 3oz	JH Bourdon-Smith Catalog Autumn 1997 p31 #31
1810 ca	G & M	Edinburgh or Provincial	Wine funnel, with reeded gilt oval bowl and plain cup, 3oz	Christie's London UK 2004 #596

YEAR	MAKER	LOCATION	DESCRIPTION	SOURCE
1810 ca	William Jamieson	Aberdeen	Wine funnel, plain circular form with a tapering spout, reeded rim, lacking detachable strainer, 5 ¾" long, 2.8oz	Christie's London UK 1999 #93
1816/17	David Manson	Dundee Edinburgh assay	Wine funnel, conventional form, detachable strainer, with monogrammed clip, 4 7/8" long	Lyon & Turnbull Edinburgh UK 2003 #289
1817/18	James McKay	Edinburgh	Wine funnel, cup-shaped bowl, engraved with sunburst crest, curved spout, fitted pierced strainer with a gadrooned border and clip on one side, 5 ½" long 5oz	Christie's East NY USA 2000 #224
1819/20	IH	Edinburgh	Wine funnel, of usual form, with reeded borders and stylized floral thumbpiece, 5 ¼" ht, 3.5oz	Lyon & Turnbull Edinburgh UK 2006 #116
1820/21	W & P Cunningham II	Edinburgh	Wine funnel, all in one piece, 4 5/8" tall, 1oz 18d	Private Collection
1821/22	Luke F Newlands	Glasgow	Wine funnel, plain strainer with a gadrooned edge and bud shaped clip, funnel with reeded edge, 5 ¾" ht, 5.3oz	Cheffins Grain & Comins Cambridge UK 2007 #320
1821/22	James McKay	Edinburgh	Wine funnel, traditional shape, the body well chased with fruiting vine decoration spout engraved with crest and motto, 5 1/3" ht, 3oz	Lyon & Turnbull Edinburgh UK 2006 #395
1823/24	George McHattie	Edinburgh	Wine funnel, acanthus leaves decorated, presented to Rev'd Innes Thomson on 3rd July 1821, either presentation date is wrong, or maker's date is wrong, 5" long, 3.5oz	Christie's London 2001 #105 Nicholas Shaw Catalog Winter 2001 p78
1824/25	W & P Cunningham II	Edinburgh	Wine funnel, gadroon border, crest of Nisbet, 3.8oz	JH Bourdon-Smith Catalog Autumn 1997 p31 #39
1824/25	Robert Gray & Son	Edinburgh	Wine funnel, circular with egg and dart borders, 5 ½" long	JH Bourdon-Smith Catalog Autumn 1997 p49 #39
1825/26	W & P Cunningham II	Edinburgh	Wine funnel, no details	National Museums of Scotland MEQ 903
1825/26	P Grierson	Glasgow	Wine funnel, campana shaped, chased with vines and grapes, crest of a cockerel, 6 3/8" long, 4.9oz	Christie's London UK 1999 #272 Nicholas Shaw Catalog Winter 2001 p74
1827/28	Alexander Edmonstoun	Edinburgh	Wine funnel, no details	The Maple Swan Collection
1829/30	GP	Edinburgh	Wine funnel, double domed detachable pierced strainer with chased foliage border and shell clip funnel with three applied short reeds, 5 ¼" long	Christie's Lanarkshire UK 1997 #117

YEAR	MAKER	LOCATION	DESCRIPTION	SOURCE
1830 ca	Alexander McLeod	Inverness	Wine funnel, of conventional form, marks AML, INS, 6" ht, 3.5oz	Bonhams Sale 15120 Aug 22, 2007 #236
1830/31	Alexander Edmonstoun	Edinburgh	Wine funnel, circular base, gadroon border, shell thumbpiece, 5 5/8" long, 4.6oz	Nicholas Shaw Catalog 2004 p108
1837/38	Robert Gray & Son	Glasgow	Wine funnel, gadrooned borders, plain arched thumbpiece, crested with a leaping stag within a wreath, 5 ½" ht, 6.3oz	Christie's London UK 2005 #419
1838/39	James McKay	Edinburgh	Wine funnel, with shell thumbpiece, initial "D", 5 ½" ht, 4.7oz	Bonhams Sale 15120 Aug 22, 2007 #23
1840/41	Alexander Wilkie	Edinburgh	Wine funnel, with stand	The Maple Swan Collection
1844/45	WRC	Edinburgh	Wine funnel, vase shaped, circular, 3.3oz	JH Bourdon-Smith Catalog Autumn 1997 p31 #39

WINE FUNNEL STANDS

YEAR	MAKER	LOCATION	DESCRIPTION	SOURCE
1760 ca	James Welsh	Edinburgh	Wine funnel stand, reeded edge, 3 ½" di, 1.1oz	Nicholas Shaw Catalog Winter 2000 p74
1760 ca	*James Welsh*	*Edinburgh*	*Wine funnel stand, plain, circular, reeded border, 3 ½" di*	*Phillip Edinburgh November 27, 2000 #308*
1760 ca	Lothian & Robertson	Edinburgh	Wine funnel stand, circular, reeded rim, engraved with a monogram, mm only, sold with another item	Christie's March 31, 1971 #68
1782/83	William Davie or William Dempster	Edinburgh	Wine funnel stand, circular with beaded border	J H Tee Antiques, Vancouver Canada 2006 #00958
1782/83	James Hewitt	Edinburgh	Wine funnel stand, plain circular form with a reeded rim and domed center, 3" di, sold with other items	Christie's London UK 1999 #24
1800 ca	James McKay	Edinburgh	Wine funnel stand, circular, plain, beaded edge	The Phoenix Collection
1800 ca	W & P Cunningham I	Edinburgh	Wine funnel tray, no details	National Museums of Scotland MEQ 703
1800 ca	John Keith	Banff	Wine funnel stand, plain, circular, with funnel, engraved initials "J.M.C.", 4 ¼" di	Christie's London UK 1999 #65 Nicholas Shaw Catalog 2005

YEAR	MAKER (continued)	LOCATION	DESCRIPTION	SOURCE p103 Noble Collection
1800 ca	Charles Jamieson	Inverness	Wine funnel stand, with funnel, no details	National Museums of Scotland MEQ 836
1800 ca	Edward Livingstone	Dundee	Wine funnel stand, plain	Private Collection
1800 ca	Robert Keay I	Perth	Wine funnel stand, with funnel 3 5/8" di	Huntley House Museum, Edinburgh HH3226/68
1808/09	Matthew Craw	Edinburgh	Wine funnel stand, circular form, beaded border, 4 1/8" di, 1.6oz	Bonhams Sale 15120 Aug 22, 2007 #21
1810 ca	William Constable	Dundee	Wine funnel stand, simple design, patterned edge	Dundee Museums and Art Galleries, 1998-133
1816/17	JH James Howden	Edinburgh	Wine funnel stand, no details	The Maple Swan Collection
1817/18	James McKay	Edinburgh	Wine funnel stand, flat, gadrooned border, domed center, engraved with crest – a wild cat courrant, below the motto "Touch not the Cat but a Glove" probably for Mackintosh, 4" di, 1oz 19d	Private Collection
1820 ca	Peter Ross	Aberdeen	Wine funnel stand, plain circular, reeded border, domed center, with a crest and motto	Morris Collection Christie's Scotland UK July 3, 1984 #108 Christie's Lanarkshire UK 1998 #82
1820 ca	David Gray	Dumfries	Wine funnel stand, with reeded border, initials "RMcC", with funnel, 3 ½" di, 1.6oz	Nicholas Shaw Catalog Autumn 1999 p50
1820/21	James McKay	Edinburgh	Wine funnel stand, circular form with domed center, with a border of repousse scrolls, 3 ½" di, 1.5oz	Bonhams Sale 15120 Aug 22, 2007 #20
1821/22	George McHattie	Edinburgh	Wine funnel stand, plain, circular, with acanthus border around rim, 4 3/8" di, 2.4oz	Nicholas Shaw Catalog Winter 2000 p80
1823/24	George McHattie	Edinburgh	Wine funnel stand, acanthus leaf decoration on rim, with funnel, 4 ½" di, 2.6oz	Nicholas Shaw Catalog Winter 2001 p78
1840/41	Alexander Wilkie	Edinburgh	Wine funnel stand, with funnel	The Maple Swan Collection

Wine Cups & Goblets

Plate 54. A Wine Goblet 1807/08 by Robert Gray & Son, Glasgow (Edinburgh assay)
Courtesy of J H Bourdon-Smith, London.

YEAR	MAKER	LOCATION	DESCRIPTION	SOURCE
	WINE GOBLETS, CUPS & TASTERS			
1630 ca	Thomas Cleghorne I	Edinburgh	Wine cup, no details	Finlay 1991 #32
1646-48	Thomas Cleghorne I Deacon John Scott	Edinburgh	Wine taster, engraved "AC" on one handle, "MWG" on the other, 6 pedal flowers in the center	Shaw Collection National Museums of Scotland MEQ 1567
1660 ca	Robert Gairdyne	Dundee	Wine cups, pair, virtually identical to the Kilspindie Communion cups, engraved with the arms of Sir James Mercer of Aldie and Meiklour impaling those of Jean Stewart, daughter of Sir Thomas Stewart of Grantully, Kt, their marriage occurred in 1656.	Finlay 1991 #35
1680 ca	Thomas Cleghorne II	Edinburgh	Wine cup, on spreading reeded trumpet stem and foot, mm only on lip mound	Scottish Art Review 1973 vol XIV #2 back cover How of Edinburgh advertisement
1685/86	James Penman	Edinburgh	Wine goblets, pair, slightly tapering bowls with slightly flaring lips on baluster stems, 8 ¾" ht, 34.2oz	Sotheby's November 6, 1969 #191 Christie's NY USA April 16, 1999 #335
1720 ca	George Walker	Aberdeen	Wine taster, small, on rim foot, shallow circular bow, engraved with simulated staves, flat handle, engraved with initials "AS", 1oz	Christie's July 3, 1984 #128
1720ca	*George Walker*	*Aberdeen*	*Small wine taster, no details*	*Aberdeen Museums and Galleries ABDAG001360*
1720 ca	WA Probably William Aytoun	Edinburgh	Miniature wine taster, low bowl, round tapering to a flat bottom, punched outside with dots and dashes, a central beaded flower, 2 7/8" across handles	Royal Ontario Museum Toronto Canada 988.33.147
1724/25	James Mitchelson	Edinburgh	Wine cups, pair, standing cups, decoration similar to 17th century communion cups, 9" ht, 8 ½" di of bowls, 52oz both	Asprey Antiques Catalog June 1990 p26
1730/31	William Aytoun	Edinburgh	Wine chalice, on stepped high domed foot, broad trumpet stem, applied reeded girdle, plain bell shaped bowl, slightly everted rim, engraved "DEO DICAVIT DOROTHEA SANDFORD DOMINA DE FERNY", foot renewed, 6 1/3", 7.3oz	Bonhams The Scottish Sale August 24, 2005 ##
1763/64	Alexander Gardner	Edinburgh	Wine cups, pair, tulip shaped bowls, baluster stems, on molded and domed bases, 37.9oz both	Sotheby's Scone Palace April 23-24, 1979 #89
1767/68	William Davie or William Dempster	Edinburgh	Wine goblet, reel shaped base with bead edged border, bell shaped bowl, engraved with festoons of flowers below a thin band of bright cut work,	Nicholas Shaw Catalog 2001 #74

YEAR	MAKER (continued)	LOCATION	DESCRIPTION	SOURCE
1773/74	Alexander Gardner	Edinburgh	Wine goblets, pair, no details 6 ¼" ht, 7.1oz	Antiques Magazine vol 91 #570 Mannheim advertisement
1775/76	Alexander Gardner	Edinburgh	Wine goblets, pair, silver gilt, round foot 6 ½" ht, 5.5oz each	Dallas Museum of Art 1987.173.1,2
1775/76	Patrick Robertson	Edinburgh	Wine goblets, pair, each stem with gadroon edge knop, on spreading foot with fluting, the cups engraved with a crest and motto "FIRM", initials "JD", gilt interiors, 5 ¾" ht, 14oz	Lyon & Turnbull The Murray Collection August 20, 2003 #187
1776/77	Patrick Robertson	Edinburgh	Wine goblet, no details	Christie's Edinburgh November 21, 1990 #123
1776/77	*Patrick Robertson*	*Edinburgh*	*Wine goblet, knopped stem on spreading foot, with fluting, cup with crest – a lion's head, initials "WFC", other side crest and motto of Strother, 5 7/8" ht, 8oz*	*Lyon & Turnbull The Murray Collection August 20, 2003 #188*
1785/86	Francis Howden	Edinburgh	Wine goblets, pair, bright cut, engraved, crest and motto of Walker, "CURA ET INSDUSTRIA", 6 ¾" ht, 18.6oz	Nicholas Shaw Catalog 2005 p97
1788/89	George Fenwick	Edinburgh	Wine goblet, 7 ½" ht	Antiques Magazine vol 121 669 James Robinson NY, advertisement
1789/90	Patrick Robertson	Edinburgh	Wine cups, pair, plain vase shaped bowls, engraved with crest – goat's head beneath the motto "SPARE NOUGHT" for Hay, gilt interiors, resting on trumpet bases, 6 ¼" ht, 16.4oz	Sotheby's Gleneagles August 28, 1975 #55
1791/92	Francis Howden	Edinburgh	Wine goblet, pair, circular pedestal foot, slender ovoid bowls, gilt interiors, arms of Kellock, 7 1/8" ht, 14oz	Bonhams The Scottish Sale August 21, 2003 #43
1801/02	John McDonald	Edinburgh	Wine goblets, pair, presented by the NC-officers and privates of the Aberdour Volunteer to Capt. Hugh Coventry, 6 ¾" ht, 30.2oz both	Nicholas Shaw Catalog 2005 p97 Bonhams Sale 15120 Aug 22, 2007 #9
1804/05	Robert Gray & Son	Glasgow Edinburgh assay	Wine goblet, with plain bowl and reeded foot, 5 ¾" ht, 6.3oz	Waddington, McLean & Co Ltd, Toronto CA 1995 #135

YEAR	MAKER	LOCATION	DESCRIPTION	SOURCE
1805/06	Robert Gray & Son	Glasgow Edinburgh assay	Wine cups, pair, inscribed "to Captain Alexander Hamilton", 7" ht, 22oz 16d	Sotheby's Gleneagles August 29, 1977 #178
1805/06	Robert Gray & Son	Glasgow Edinburgh assay	Wine goblets, pair, no details	The Maple Swan Collection
1805/06	Robert Gray & Son	Glasgow Edinburgh assay	Wine goblets, pair, reel shaped bases, crest and motto of Strother, 4 ¾" ht, 12.1oz	Nicholas Shaw Catalog 2004 p105
1806/07	George Fenwick	Edinburgh	Wine goblets, pair, gilt interior, crest, 8" ht, 30.2oz	Nicholas Shaw Catalog 2005 p98
1806/07	Robert Gray & Son	Glasgow Edinburgh assay	Wine goblets, pair, no details	Shrubsole NY
1807/08	James Gordon Over striking another	Aberdeen	Wine goblets, no details	Sotheby's Gleneagles August 1986 #469
1807/08	Robert Gray & Son	Glasgow Edinburgh assay	Wine goblet, see photo	JH Bourdon-Smith London March 2006
1810 ca	William Jamieson	Aberdeen	Wine goblets, pair	Finlay 1991 #114
1810 ca	William Jamieson	Aberdeen	Wine goblets, pair, gilt, marked WJ, ABD, WJ	Aberdeen Museums and Galleries ABDAG008808
1810/11	James McDonald	Edinburgh	Wine goblets, no details	Antiques Magazine vol 78 p525
1812/13	James McKay	Edinburgh	Wine cups, no details	Sotheby's Hopetoun House April 1988 373
1814/15	Not available	Edinburgh assay	Wine goblet, said to be Scottish, no details	Antiques Magazine vol 117 p309 Argent Antiques advertisement
1815/16	W & P Cunningham II	Edinburgh	Wine goblet, globular bowl with a flaring rim, supported on a trumpet foot, 5 1/8" ht, 6.5oz	Christie's London UK 2002 #234
1820/21	John Hay	Leith	Wine goblet, no details	Finlay 1991 #102

YEAR	MAKER	LOCATION	DESCRIPTION	SOURCE
1820/21	*John Hay*	*Leith*	*Wine cup, presentation date 1821*	*National Museums of Scotland MEQ 1332 1980.61*
1821/22	Not available	Edinburgh	Wine presentation goblet, in bowl later embossed with a rural setting depicting a farmhand and animals, the trumpet stem terminating in a circular base, presented to "Mr. George Norrington", sold with another, 7 ½" ht, 17.5oz	Bonhams London UK 2005 #515
1825 ca	George & Alexander Booth	Aberdeen	Wine goblet, vase shaped on spreading circular foot with lobed border, short stem with compressed knop, partly lobed body with everted lip, engraved crest, motto and initials of Lumsden, gilt interior, 6" ht	Christie's Lanarkshire UK 1997 #55
1827 ca	Not available	Edinburgh	Wine cup, standing cup, mm indistinct, said to be Scottish	Sotheby's Hopetoun House April 1989 #47
1830 ca	William Jamieson	Aberdeen	Wine goblets, pair, no details	Aberdeen Museums and Galleries, ABDAG008655, acquired 1988
1830/31	Alexander Edmonstoun	Edinburgh	Wine goblet, no details	Sotheby's Hopetoun House April 1988 #80
1832/33	D C Rait	Glasgow	Wine goblet, plain form, on circular stepped pedestal foot, gilt interior, 6 3/8" ht, 7.4oz	Nicholas Shaw Catalog 2005 p98
WINE LABELS				
1775 ca	DK possibly Daniel Ker	Edinburgh	Wine label, CLARET, shaped rectangular with incurved sides and domed top, narrow gadrooned borders, trio of beads at each corner	Bonhams London UK 2005 #434
1780 ca	William Scott	Dundee	Wine label, circular, bright cut, "Port"	Nicholas Shaw Catalog 2005 p103
1790 ca	Edward Livingstone	Dundee	Wine label, RUM, crescent shaped with a feather edge	Bonhams London UK 2006 #224
1795 ca	Robert Keay I	Perth	Wine label, mm only, LISBON, plain narrow rectangular with rounded ends	Bonhams London UK 2005 #433
1795 ca	Robert Gray	Glasgow Edinburgh assay	Wine label, bright cut, curved, "Madeira"	Nicholas Shaw Catalog 2005 p103
1797 ca	JH	Edinburgh	Wine label, "Whiskey"	California Dealer Corning Museum Antiques Show NY USA

YEAR	MAKER	LOCATION	DESCRIPTION	SOURCE
1797 ca	JH	Edinburgh	Wine label, foliage border, "Gin"	Asprey Catalog 1990
1800 ca	Alexander Ziegler	Edinburgh	Wine label, no details	The Maple Swan Collection
1800 ca	George McHattie	Edinburgh	Wine label, escutcheon shaped, with vines and Bacchic figures, "Port"	Private Collection
1800 ca	James Erskine	Aberdeen	Wine label, marked "E" incuse, hand with dagger, "GIN"	Aberdeen Museums and Galleries ABDAG008797
1800 ca	James Erskine	Aberdeen	Wine label, mm 2 X's, "MADEIRA"	Aberdeen Museums and Galleries ABDAG8798
1800 ca	Robert Gray	Glasgow Edinburgh assay	Wine label, MADEIRA, bright cut engraved and with foliate ends, curved rectangular form with cut out Prince of Wales feathers surmount	Bonhams London UK 2005 #429
1800 ca	W & P Cunningham I	Edinburgh	Wine label, PORT, with rounded reeded border	Woolley & Wallis Salisbury US 2007 #800
1800 ca	James McKay	Edinburgh	Wine labels, set of 4, CLARET, LISBON, PORT and MADEIRA, oblong with a suspension chain, 2oz	Christie's London UK 2005 #25
1800 ca	James Erskine	Aberdeen	Wine label, BRANDY, shaped and pierced curved form, with bright cut twist borders and leafage, 1 5/8" long	Sotheby's NY USA 1997 #149
1800 ca	James Erskine	Aberdeen	Wine label, GIN, navette shaped, wigglework border	Sotheby's NY USA 1997 #133
1800 ca	James Erskine	Aberdeen	Wine label, NOYAU marked IE, IE	Aberdeen Museums and Galleries ABDAG008854
1800 ca	William Jamieson	Aberdeen	Wine label, mm 2X's, "MARSALA"	Aberdeen Museums and Galleries ABDAG008799
1800 ca	Edward Livingstone	Dundee	Wine label, crescent form, with feather edge, "PORT"	Dundee Museums and Art Galleries 1995-269
1800 ca	Edward Livingstone	Dundee	Wine label, set of 4, no details	Dundee Museums and Art Galleries 1986-119
1800 ca	James Douglas	Dundee	Wine label, no details	Dundee Museums and Art Galleries 1995-269
1800 ca	W & P Cunningham I	Edinburgh	Wine label, oblong, reeded border, "Sherry", 1 ¾" X 7/8"	eBay #6614660984 March 2006 UK

YEAR	MAKER	LOCATION	DESCRIPTION	SOURCE
1800 ca	James Erskine	Aberdeen	Wine labels, 2 eye shaped labels for "Whiskey" and "Rum", marked – JE - with a 3rd "Brandy" unmarked	Schredds Antiques London #9526
1802 ca	John McDonald	Edinburgh	Wine label, no details	The Maple Swan Collection
1805 ca	James Erskine	Aberdeen	Wine label, cut corner, rectangular, 3 labels, "Gin", "Port", "Whiskey"	Nicholas Shaw Catalog 2005 p103
1805 ca	Robert Gray & Son	Glasgow Edinburgh assay	Wine label, curved, each end formed and engraved as a vine leaf, "PORT"	Private Collection
1805 ca	Robert Gray & Son	Glasgow Edinburgh assay	Wine labels, two, SHERRY and PORT, crescent shaped, sold with others	Christie's London UK 2006 #175
1806/07	George Fenwick	Edinburgh	Wine label, set of 6, no details	The Maple Swan Collection
1810 ca	George McHattie	Edinburgh	Wine label, square with round corners, "Whiskey"	Asprey Catalog 1990
1810 ca	William Constable	Dundee	Wine label, "CURRANT"	Dundee Museums and Art Galleries 1964-29-2
1810 ca	RG	Edinburgh assay	Wine label, "Madeira", no details	National Museums of Scotland MEQ 787 1965.1858
1810 ca	Alexander Stewart	Inverness	Wine label, rectangular, "Brandy"	Nicholas Shaw Catalog 2005 p103
1810 ca	Alexander Stewart	Inverness	Wine label, rectangular, "Gin"	Nicholas Shaw Catalog 2005 p103
1810 ca	W & P Cunningham II	Edinburgh	Wine label, shaped shield, "Brandy", "Whiskey"	Nicholas Shaw Catalog 2005 p103
1810 ca	Robert Naughton	Inverness	Wine label, WHISKEY, curved scroll form with vacant cartouche surmount, ends engraved with flowers, borders bright cut engraved with zig-zag chevrons	Bonhams London UK 2006 #406
1810 ca	David Manson	Dundee	Wine label, SWEET WINE, plain oval, 1 ½" long	Sotheby's NY USA 1997 #155
1810 ca	WC	Greenock	Wine label, BRANDY, plain shaped crescent, 1 5/8" long	Sotheby's NY USA 1997 #147

YEAR	MAKER	LOCATION	DESCRIPTION	SOURCE
1810 ca	William Jamieson	Aberdeen	Wine labels, set of 4, cut corner rectangular form, with reeded borders, for WHISKEY, BRANDY, RUM and GIN, 1 ¾" long	Bonhams Sale 15120 Aug 22, 2007 #157
1814/15	Mitchell & Russell	Glasgow	Wine label, rounded rectangular, thread edge, "Gin"	JH Bourdon-Smith Catalog Autumn 2002 p28 #44
1814/15	Robert Gray & Son	Glasgow Edinburgh assay	Wine label, MADEIRA, plain crescent shape, sold with another	Bonhams London UK 2004 #366
1815 ca	William Ritchie	Perth	Wine label, plain, rectangular, "Whiskey"	Nicholas Shaw Catalog 2005 p103
1815 ca	James McKay	Edinburgh	Wine label, "PORT	Dundee Museums and Art Galleries 1978-964
1815 ca	George McHattie	Edinburgh	Wine labels, matched set of 4 oval labels for GIN, HOLLAND, RUM, and WHISKEY, with gadrooned borders, 1 ½" long	Gorringes LLP, East Sussex UK 2006 #1598
1815 ca	John Ziegler	Edinburgh	Wine label, WHISKEY, scroll and shell stamped shaped, oblong, sold with others	Sotheby's NY USA 1998 #506
1815 ca	Alexander Ziegler	Edinburgh	Wine label, RUM, curved form with beaded borders, sold with another	Christie's Lanarkshire UK 1998 #588
1815 ca	Joseph Pearson	Dumfries	Wine label, MADEIRA, plain curved oblong, 2 ¼" wide	Sotheby's NU USA 1997 #132
1815/16	James McKay	Edinburgh	Wine label, cartouche shaped, MADEIRA, sold with another, 2 ¼" long	Gorringes LLP, East Sussex UK 2006 #1591
1816/17	James McKay	Edinburgh	Wine label, broad rectangular, "MADEIRA", 1" X 1 13/16"	Cincinnati Museum of Art 1936.414
1817/18	James McKay	Edinburgh	Wine label, plain center, shell edge, "MADEIRA"	Museum of Fine Art, Boston MA USA 1917.1971
1817/18	Francis Howden	Edinburgh	Wine label, incised "G", oblong form, double thread border, sold with others	Bonhams London UK 2002 #473
1817/18	James McKay	Edinburgh	Wine label, cartouche shaped, HOLLANDS, sold with another, 2 ½" long	Gorringes LLP, East Sussex UK 2006 #1591
1818 ca	Alexander Cameron	Dundee	Wine label, "Sherry"	Antiques Magazine vol 35, p20
1818/19	Robert Gray & Son	Glasgow Edinburgh	Wine label, SHERRY, canted oblong with a thread border and a surmount of grapes, vine leaves on an anthemion	Woolley & Wallis 2007 #798B

YEAR	MAKER (continued)	LOCATION assay	DESCRIPTION	SOURCE
1818/19	James Howden or John Hay Leith	Edinburgh	Wine label, rectangular, "Sherry"	National Museums of Scotland MEQ 719 1964.1879
1819/20	James McKay	Edinburgh	Wine label, oblong, "PORT", 1 7/8" long, 7/8" wide	Huntley House Museum Edinburgh HH3227/68
1820 ca	George McHattie	Edinburgh	Wine label, rectangular, rounded corners, "Lisbon"	National Museums of Scotland 1964.254
1820 ca	William Marshall	Edinburgh	Wine label, rectangular, no details	National Museums of Scotland 1964.255
1820 ca	Alexander Cameron	Dundee	Wine label, "WHISKEY"	Dundee Museum and Art Galleries 1962-743-1
1820 ca	Alexander Cameron	Dundee	Wine label, ornate border, "MADEIRA"	Dundee Museum and Art Galleries 2005-59
1820 ca	William Jamieson	Aberdeen	Wine label, "BRANDY"	Aberdeen Museums and Galleries ABDAG001015
1820 ca	George Booth	Aberdeen	Wine label, "WINE"	Aberdeen Museums and Galleries ABDAG00016
1820 ca	George Booth	Aberdeen	Wine label, "WINE"	Aberdeen Museums and Galleries ABDAG001084
1820 ca	Not available		Wine label, "GINGER", presumably Scottish	Aberdeen Museums and Galleries ABDAG001085
1820 ca	A McLeod	Glasgow	Wine label, "S"	Dundee Museum and Art Galleries 1978-695
1820 ca	George McHattie	Edinburgh	Wine label, "Brandy"	National Museums of Scotland MEQ 1030
1820 ca	James McKay	Edinburgh	Wine label, "Shrub"	National Museums of Scotland MEQ 724
1820 ca	William Law	Dundee	Wine label, rectangular, "Geneva"	Nicholas Shaw Catalog 2005 p103

YEAR	MAKER	LOCATION	DESCRIPTION	SOURCE
1820 ca	David Gray	Dumfries	Wine label, pair, rectangular, "Port", "Sherry"	Nicholas Shaw Catalog 2005 p103
1820 ca	George McHattie	Edinburgh	Wine label, set of 3, rectangular, plain "Port", "Claret," "Madeira"	Schredds Antiques London #9474
1820 ca	GE	St. Andrews	Wine label, broad rectangular shape, with reeded edge, "Port", marks – GE, fouled anchor, St. Andrew's Cross, TL	Schredds Antiques London #9624
1820 ca	George McHattie	Edinburgh	Wine labels, set of 3, PORT, SHERRY and MADEIRA, of symmetrical form with shell and scroll border, sold with others	Bonhams London UK 2004 #371
1820 ca	WL	Dundee	Wine labels, set of 3, GIN, BRANDY, and RUM, with lobes and shells at the angles, 2" wide	Sotheby's NY USA 1996 #50
1820 ca	George McHattie	Edinburgh	Wine labels, set of 3 in two sizes, CURRANT, HOLLANDS and RUM, oblong with gadrooned borders	Christie's Lanarkshire UK 1997 #8
1820 ca	William Mill	Montrose	Wine label, RUM, cut cornered rectangular shape, 2" wide	Sotheby's NY USA 1997 #124
1820/21	PG	Glasgow	Wine label, "R", incised, sold with others	Bonhams London UK 2006 #409
1821 ca	Not available	Edinburgh assay	Wine label, retailed by Forrests, no details	M Getz, Washington DC USA 1992
1822/23	George McHattie	Edinburgh	Wine labels, pair, PORT and CLARET, within gadrooned borders, engraved crests, sold with others, 2" long	Christie's London UK 2002 #146
1824 ca	J Austin	Dundee	Wine label, cut corner, rectangular, "Sherry"	Nicholas Shaw Catalog 2005 p103
1824 ca	J Austin	Dundee	Wine label, cut corners, rectangular, "Port"	Nicholas Shaw Catalog 2005 p103
1824	JH	Edinburgh	Wine label, RUM, die stamped with borders of scrolls and flowers, sold with others	Bonhams London UK 2004 #393
1824/25	Robert Gray & Son	Glasgow	Wine label, CLARET, plain festoon form, 1 ¾" long	Bonhams London UK 2006 #235
1825 ca	J Millidge	Edinburgh	Wine label, rounded corners, rectangular, floral border, "Islay"	Nicholas Shaw Catalog 2005 p103
1825 ca	James Howden	Edinburgh	Wine label, shaped oval, with shells and scrolls and leaves around border, "Port"	Alexandria, VA Antique Center, 1995 The Phoenix Collection

YEAR	MAKER	LOCATION	DESCRIPTION	SOURCE
1825 ca	Peter Gill	Aberdeen	Wine label, TENERIFF, with fruiting vine leaves at each end, curved form	Woolley & Wallis Salisbury UK 2007 #812
1825 ca	James & William Marshall	Edinburgh	Wine label, SHERRY, die stamped shaped oval, border with scrolls, flowers and bunches of grapes, sold with others	Bonhams London UK 2004 #393
1826/27	CB	Edinburgh	Wine label, CLARET, shaped oval with C-scroll top with fruiting vines, lower rim with thistle leafage centered by a vase, lacking a chain, sold with others, 2 ½" long	Bonhams London UK 2003 #09
1828 ca	James Howden	Edinburgh	Wine label, no details	Hyde Park Center, NY USA 1992
1828/29	Robert Gray & Son	Glasgow	Wine label, pair, reeded cut cornered oblong stippled and applied rope initials "L" and "C", 2" wide	Sotheby's NY USA 1997 #131
1829 ca	Robert Keay & Son	Perth	Wine label, oblong, presentation dated 1829	National Museums of Scotland MEQ 147 1953.1329
1830 ca	William Cunningham	Edinburgh	Wine label, MADEIRA, die stamped sold with others	Bonhams London UK 2004 #386
1830 ca	David Greig	Perth	Wine label, PORT, plain shield shaped, engraved, 1 ¾" wide	Sotheby's NY USA 1997 #143
1830 ca	James Holliday Overstriking Joseph Pearson	Dumfries	Wine label, RUM, plain curved oblong, engraved, 1 7/8" wide	Sotheby's NY USA 1997 #145
1830 ca	Robert Naughton	Inverness	Wine label, GIN, gadrooned oblong, 1 ½" long	Sotheby's NY USA 1997 #150
1833/34	Alexander Mitchell	Glasgow	Wine labels, set of 3, large labels, cut out "P", "S", and "M", 2-2 1/8" ht	Bonhams London UK 2003 #238
1839/40	Robert Gray	Glasgow	Wine label, cut out "P" with foliate decoration to front, sold with others	Bonhams London UK 2003 #338
1840 ca	Robert Keay II	Perth	Wine label, BRANDY, cut cornered oblong, engrave within an incised border, 1 ¼" wide	Sotheby's NY USA 1997 #122
1840 ca	Andrew Davidson	Arbroath	Wine label, capital initial "M" engraved within a gadroon cast and chased border, with shells at the angles of a shaped oblong label, 2" wide	Sotheby's NY USA 1997 #141
1840 ca	Robert Naughton	Inverness	Wine label, rectangular, cross hatched border, "Sherry"	Nicholas Shaw Catalog 2005 p103
1840 ca	J L	Cupar	Wine label, rounded corners, rectangular, floral border, "Port"	Nicholas Shaw Catalog 2005 p103

YEAR	MAKER	LOCATION	DESCRIPTION	SOURCE
1847/48	J & W Mitchell	Glasgow	Wine label, block "P" for Port	JH Bourdon-Smith Catalog Autumn 2001 p60 #43
1850 ca	MacKay & Chisholm	Edinburgh	Wine (sauce) label, HOCK, with gadrooned and shell border	Woolley & Wallis Salisbury UK 2007 #793
1890 ca	Fergusson & McBean	Inverness	Wine label, engraved BRANDY, shield shaped, running pellet border, 2" wide	Sotheby's NY USA 1997 #136

BRIEF GLOSSARY AND EXPLANATIONS

To aid the reader, a brief glossary of terms found in the compendium and related sources are provided along with explanations for some maker assignments within this book. For a far more comprehensive definition of terms, we would refer the reader to Michael Clayton's <u>Dictionary of the Silver and Gold of Great Britain and North America</u>. (see Works Cited).

Acanthus = a leafy plant used as a model for some stylized decoration

Adam-style = following the architectural designs of Robert Adam, the important 18th century Scottish architect.

Argyll = a container with a heat preserving component (hot water jacket or a heated bar of iron) to enable gravy to stay warm.

Assay master = the goldsmith entrusted by the Incorporation with certifying the standard of wares wrought by the freemen. Prior to 1681, the elected deacon in Edinburgh also performed the function of assay master. The elected posts were separated in 1681 but the assay master continued to use his maker's mark punch for certification until the advent of the thistle mark in 1759. The Scottish standard for silver was not the same as English sterling for much of the 18th century and earlier.

Ashet = an oval meat dish; the term is frequently used in Scotland and is derived from French.

Bale (or bail) = a swing handle as on a bucket

Baluster = a column or stem of small size with a shaped outline.

Bannock Rack = a variant on the toast rack but with fewer especially wide dividers to accommodate Scottish bannock bread.

Beaker = a tall cylindrical cup, usually of tapering-cylindrical form, without handles.

Blackjack = a leather tankard or bottle, sometimes with silver mounts

Bleeding Bowl = in this book a form of shallow dish or cup with a single handle (also called a porringer in some countries).

Bobeche = from the French, a collar on a candlestick nozzle used to catch wax drippings

Bogie box = a container for holding and sometimes burning tubular, coiled wax

Bombe = curving or bulging outward. Based on French and used extensively in furniture designs. This form would contrast with the inverted pear or baluster descriptions in that the bulge is usually dramatic but following a smooth line.

Cabriole = resembling the leg of a capering (e.g. goat) animal. It is a leg that curves outward at the knee and then narrows downward ending is an ornamental foot. The term and use was prominent in Thomas Chippendale's furniture designs.

Campana = the shape of a bell.

Canted corners = corners having slanted or oblique surfaces.

Canteen = a container usually with cutlery, spice containers and a cup or beaker for use when traveling.

Capped = sitting atop, as in a stylized leaf sitting atop a handle on a mug, (i.e. leaf-capped.)

Capstan = the shape of a vertical spool-shaped cylinder used on docks for securing boats

Caryatid = usually a supporting column that takes the form of a draped female figure.

Cartouche = an oval shaped decorated element usually engraved or as an applied plaque. Its function was usually to permit owner designations. It is either vacant or containing heraldic elements or initials.

Caster = a tall, narrow covered container for sugar and spices. They may have pierced covers or be blind (not pierced, but sometimes engraved to match the pierced design on others).

Casting = made involving a mold usually created in wood, metal or wax. Examples of casting would include spouts on teapots and some candlesticks. Exceptional Scottish casting required a different set of expertise from that of raising spoons, etc. Therefore, examples of cast Scottish candlesticks are found for only an expert subset of all Scottish goldsmiths.

CD letters in a heart-shaped shield, Edinburgh maker's mark = Originally early 18th century (1719-1738ca) CD marks were attributed solely to Charles Dickson I, a goldsmith in both Edinburgh and Dundee. However, the recent appearance of items carrying the mark in question prior to Dickson becoming free suggests that Charles Duncan is the more likely attribution for the mark presented
in Jackson. In this compendium, both names are listed in many cases where the source had attributed the piece to Dickson. This current confusion over this specific mark for Duncan *vs.*
Dickson should be sorted out in favor of Duncan in the near future.

Chamfered corners = corners given a smooth rounded or beveled shape.

Chasing = the pushing of the silver surface with no removal of silver to create decorative patterns or designs. Flat chasing is performed from the front and is in low relief. In contrast, repousse chasing is done from the back where silver is pushed into raised patterns and then finished on the front

Chocolate Pot = of similar form to a coffee pot but with a finial either hinged or sliding to permit ready use of a stirrer for suspending the sediment before serving

Cinquefoil = an architectural design having five sides consisting of converging arcs. The origin is derived from five petaled flowers or the plant of the same name.

Cipher = a design of interweaving letters of a monogram in an intricate manner. With many cipher engravings the letters are virtually indecipherable or coded. Hence the derivation of the term

Citrine = a pale yellow type of crystallized quartz

Cover = a fully detachable lift-off top usually to a two-handled cup, sugar bowl or occasionally a few teapots.

Coconut Cup = a coconut shell usually mounted with silver.

Coronets = coronets on Scottish silver have different distinctions depending upon its exact form. This explains references made in the descriptions to the coronet of a duke, an earl, etc. Sometimes, a specific coronet and an initial (of the last name) are sufficient to suggest a likely family of prior ownership. Coronets are of five types distinguishing the ranks of duke, marquess, earl, viscount and lord in descending order. In the peerage of Scotland "lord" is the correct title for the equivalent English rank of "baron".

Cowrie Box = a box, in this case-silver mounted, using the shell of a specific tropical marine gastropod

Cruet = a low stand with rings to hold casters, casters and bottles, bottles alone or egg cups

Cut-Card Work = a late 17th early 18th century decorative procedure involving pieces of silver, sometimes decorated itself, which were then applied to the body or cover of an item via solder. In Scottish silver, the most frequently seen examples are the lobes found on thistle mugs arranged in such a way as to suggest stylized leaves.

Deacon = the Deacon of the Incorporation of Goldsmiths in Edinburgh was the highest elected position and the post was most usually held for two years in duration. Until 1681, the deacon also served as the assay master and his maker's mark was used for certifying that the appropriate silver standard had been used in making an item. Once a goldsmith had served as Deacon he continued to be referred to as Deacon in subsequent minutes, notes and correspondence of the Incorporation. This is a practice that can lead to some confusion in the present day.

Diaper-Work = a decorated usually engraved area consisting of a network of shaped geometric elements usually boxes or lozenges (sometimes with a dot in the center of each)

Dirk = a particular type of Highland dagger with a long straight blade. The dirk is at least twice the length of a skene dhu, slung from a belt at the waist when wearing the kilt.

Dish Cross = an X-shaped stand having a combination of four arms (usually adjustable in length) used to support a dish for serving and/or warming. Scottish examples may or may not be equipped with a central burner.

Dish Ring = In Scotland, a circular open ring or shallow cone on a stand used to accommodate a circular food container such as a serving dish. It serves the same function as a dish cross. It sometimes has a fitting for a spirit burner.

Disk-end spoons = among the earliest form of Scottish spoon. The terminal is an almost complete circle joining the stem. The disk may carry decoration and/or engraving of initials or arms.

Dog-nose flatware/spoons = a modification of the trefid without any notches. The center of the terminal is rounded and projecting while the shoulders are also slightly rounded. The terminal is angled upward slightly from the plane of the stem (in contrast with wavy-end flatware). The pattern was found mainly between 1690-1715 in Scotland

Dolphin-handle = the famous dolphin handles applied to select Scottish cream boats, etc. of the 1740s and 50s were used by only a small cadre of Scottish goldsmiths. From close inspection of several cast forms, the figure does not resemble an actual dolphin but rather is a heraldic dolphin or stylized sea creature with mixed features derived from dolphins, eels and fish. The earliest use recorded to date is 1743/44 WD mm for either William Dempster or William Davie.

Double-scroll = two connected scrolls, as used in forming a handle, with the second curved at a different angle from the first.

Dredger = a container with a perforated cover for sifting through flour or other materials.

Edinburgh Silver post 1783 = Since Scottish silver was supposed to be assayed in Edinburgh and duty paid from 1784-, many provincial goldsmiths made work carrying Edinburgh marks, particularly between 1784 and the opening of the Glasgow assay office in 1819. Therefore, any pieces falling in this interval should be viewed as potentially crafted by goldsmiths based anywhere in Scotland and not necessarily the output of an Edinburgh goldsmith.

Engraving = design created by removing silver from the surface. Engraving was used in Scotland for including armorials, initials and also for other decorations. Bright cut-engraving is seen from about 1775 on and is created by using contrasting depths and angles of the cut.

Epergne = usually a centerpiece with a large central bowl and several smaller bowls distributed around the circumference: a French term

Everted = turned outward

Ewer = a pitcher of various shapes accompanying a basin, both were used for hand washing during meals (particularly necessary preceding the use of utensils).

Faceted = having multiple flat surfaces oriented at different angles as on a cut gemstone.

Fiddle pattern flatware/spoons (English) = this is the traditional flatware with the terminal half of the stem forming a slightly rounded rectangle. Slight projections can occur where this rectangle thins to the profile of the stem.

Flagon = frequently these were made for secular use but then later presented by donors to churches. These usually take the form of tall, slender tankards/pitchers, often they are cylindrical and on a spreading foot

Flange = a protruding rim or collar

Festoon = a draped arrangement of flowers and fruit tied at either end and sometimes secured in the middle as well

Filigree = openwork metal formed into geometric design or foliage-like ornament

Finial = an element, usually architecturally-derived, placed atop covers, lids and some spoons

Fluting = a series of long usually rounded grooves incised into otherwise flat surfaces, the effects resemble that of a pleated ruffle of cloth.

Foliate = resembling foliage

Freedom = as in Freedom Boxes. Freedom was the term used when of the right to become a burgess of a burgh or alternatively a freeman of an Incorporation or Guild was granted to an individual. It could be given by town councils in gratitude or earned though apprenticeship and successful essays. Freedom Boxes were designed to hold the documents.

Gadroons = probably referring to gathered-rounds, in this case decorative raised arcs of silver used in the borders of tazzas, sauceboats, and on the bases of various pieces.

Girdle = in this case an applied band of silver, sometimes decorated, placed surrounding the body and used to strengthen the piece while providing decoration.

Hanoverian flatware/spoons = This is a pattern common across the UK and the earliest use in Scotland was 1702/03. The pattern has an upturned mostly rounded terminal on a stem sometimes with an upper midrib. Contemporary engraving was always placed on the terminal reverse.

Hash Spoon = here a large serving spoon greater than 13" in length

IB Glasgow 1707-50 mark = In this book, these marks are designated as by Johann Got-helf-Bilsings as according to Jackson. However, this maker assignment seems tenuous and is likely to be revised in the near future. The reader should approach this with caution. James Boyd became a freeman in 1707 and the earlier IB marks possibly pertain to him.

IM maker's marks 1707-57, Edinburgh = Based on the most recent information at press time, designation for the mark IM with a figure between has been given to James Mitchell. Pieces previously attributed to John Main have been assigned to James Mitchelson in this compendium. Pieces carrying the mark, IM in an engrailed rectangle, are listed as by either James McKenzie I or James Mitchelson. (see Silver Studies 2006 for more detail).

Knop = a decorative knob such as those found on the stems of some communion cups and candlesticks or on the tops of handles of some early Scottish two-handled cups.

Lattice (or Trellis) work = a framework of regularly overlaid lines.

Leith Race Prizes = The Leith Race was an annual horserace where prizes were awarded. The contract for producing the prize usually went to the Deacon of the Edinburgh Incorporation of Goldsmiths. The gold teapots by James Ker are examples of Leith prizes. Additional forms were produced such as Monteith bowls, handled cups and kettles. Regrettably, only a small proportion of those that were made have survived.

Lid = a top to items such as a teapot, tankard or jug, that is not designed to detach completely and is hinged either via a flush hinge or through an applied hinge.

Lozenge = a heraldic device in a diamond-like shape.

Lug = literally "ear", the Scottish word for a small handle as on a quaich, piggin, etc.

Maker vs. Deacon = For pre-1681 Edinburgh silver where the elected deacon served as the assay master, it is not always possible to determine with certainty which punch is that of the maker of a piece and which is by the deacon at the time of assay. Because of this, the same piece may appear to have different makers as described in different catalogs. A famous example is the set of trefid spoons carrying the marks of Edward Cleghorne I and Alexander Reid. We have attempted to use the most recent designations based on style and other considerations. But these still lack complete certainty. Usually the maker's mark is on the left of the castle and the deacon's mark on the right, but this method of identification breaks down when marks are struck vertically on spoons, etc.

Marrow Spoon = a spoon that has the stem incorporating a marrow scoop

Mazer = a shallow, broad bowl, often wooden, on a single foot that can range from a low rim to a taller pedestal (for "standing mazers")

Monteith = a bowl, usually a punch bowl, with a notched rim (sometimes detachable), named after a Scotsman whose cloaks were notched at the bottom.

Muffineer = a container with a perforated cover for applying sugar to breads, etc.

Nozzle = also called a socket. The top part of the candlestick into which the candle is inserted. Sometimes these are made to be detachable.

Octagonal hollowware = silver items with eight-sided finished surfaces   Employed in the early 18th century by only the more expert Scottish goldsmiths.

Old English flatware/spoons = a modification of the Hanoverian pattern where the terminal curves downwards and usually with a smooth stem and no mid-rib. See pointed Old English for a common Scottish variant.

Pap Boat = a shallow bowl used for feeding. It is shaped like the top of a Scottish cream boat but without a foot or handle.

Paten = a cover for a communion cup. Sometimes it is not easily distinguishable from a small tazza. Communion cups of the Church of Scotland never have patens. Patens go with chalices and are used by the Catholic Church but they have no foot. Patens in the Episcopal Church of Scotland might occasionally have a foot like a tazza but are normally just a shallow dish without a foot. Scottish patens, if any Scottish-made ones really exist before the later 19th century, are extraordinarily rare.

Piggin = A piggin is a miniature stave-built pail, with one of the staves rising above the rest to form a single vertical lug. This shape was occasionally copied in silver.

Pointed Old English = the variant derived from the Old English flatware (i.e. a down-turned rounded end on spoon terminals) pattern using a pointed rather than a rounded terminal. It was made mainly in Scotland, Ireland and by Scottish or Irish craftsman in the colonies. It has been called by a variety of names over the years. It has nothing whatsoever to do with being Celtic.

Points = repeating projections within the wavy borders of bowls, salvers and teapot stands. These may be enumerated as one means of distinguishing among otherwise identical pieces. The number of "points" on a stand is usually 2-6 more than the number of points on a sugar bowl within the same set.

Porringers = In this compendium, a form of two handled cups that are usually shallow, wide and bulbous near the base. Here it is distinguished from a bleeding bowl that has only one handle.

Punch Bowl = in this book, a bowl of 8 1/2" or larger in diameter

Puritan spoons = modified from earlier slip-top spoons. The stem is not flat but rather largely square like a plank of wood. These spoons have essentially no special terminal beyond a cut made at right angles.

Quaich = a two-lugged shallow bowl. The earliest were originally made of wood. Many silver examples (1650-1730) attempt to simulate the wooden sections by engraving stave lines.

Reeded = having a series of parallel incised lines.

Repousse = a technique of hammering designs in relief from the reverse side of metal.

Reticulated = a series of lines forming a net, mesh or network.

Riband = a ribbon used for decoration or to contain a motto.

Rocaille = decorative rococo work emphasizing shells and scrolls. Originally it meant artificial rock-work and this gradually slid into scrollwork. In contrast with rococo work, rocaille does not necessarily have to be asymmetrical.

Rococo = an ornate decorative style with intricate work of flowers, shells and scrolls. The defining element of rococo is that it is asymmetrical.

Roundels = a series of round panels.

Saltire = A St. Andrew's Cross in the shape of an X.

Salver = in this book, a tray on three or more feet of greater than 6 ½" in diameter

Sander = a container, usually part of the 18th century writing implements set, with perforations in the cover to apply drying sand to documents just completed using ink. The sand aided in the drying process by stabilizing the ink on the document.

Sauceboats = this term for a handled sauce container of boat shape is somewhat confused with cream boats in 18th century Scotland. We have reserved the "sauceboat" term generally for early double-lipped handled boats and for later boats of larger size and deeper shape than those used for cream. Many boats of the 1740s and early 50s termed sauceboats in catalogs were of a form described as cream boats in contemporary accounts.

Scalloped = having curved projections forming an ornamental border. Derived from the marine mollusk shell patterns. In this book, it is also used to describe the pie-crust-like borders on salts, etc.

Sconce = protruding top part of a candlestick (sometimes detachable), used to prevent wax from dripping on surfaces below.

Scots Fiddle pattern flatware/spoons = different from the tradition English fiddle pattern. Scots fiddle is a pattern found mainly from 18th century Scotland. It is a modified Hanoverian where the stem has two pronounced bulges with the outline resembling the body of a fiddle or violin. These items were usually with maker's mark only. The design overlaps with styles seen in Denmark and the Norse countries. Scots fiddles usually date from 1730ca-1790ca.

Scottish crests and mottos = unlike families in England and Ireland where the mottos were placed beneath the crest, Scottish family mottos are usually seen on ribbons draped across the top of crests. As a result, the vast majority of armorial silver in this listing would exhibit mottos placed above the crest. This helps readily identify pieces as previously Scottish owned. However, the maker of Scottish owned pieces may or may not be a Scottish goldsmith. London made silver was also purchased by Scottish patrons. Scottish mottos are most frequently seen in Latin or English but some examples of French and Scots mottos also exist. The combination of a specific crest (usually shared by only a few families) and motto (usually shared by a small and overlapping subset of families) is a powerful tool in identifying the single Scottish family that previously owned a piece of silver. Provenance for many of the silver items in this listing have been narrowed to a single family. An example of a motto in Scots is *Quhidder will zie*, with a unicorn's head, pertaining to several families of the Stewarts of Appin.

Scratch weight = the weight of an object as designated through usually light "scratched" engraving by the goldsmith. Scratch weights are usually placed in inconspicuous places most frequently applied to the bottom of more significant items of silver. Modern weights of old pieces should be slightly lower than the scratch weight given the loss of silver over time through cleaning and wear. Scratch weights can be useful to determine if an item has been altered from its original form at some time in the past.

Scrolls = decorative ornaments on silver and furniture that resemble, in form, partially unrolled rolls of paper

Seal = a die or signet having a raised or impressed symbol used to stamp the impression in wax, etc. In this case used to seal and effectively sign correspondence. Seals were frequently made with handles of silver or gold. Seal Boxes were designed to protect wax seals associated with important documents.

Seal-top spoons = very rare in Scotland and from the late 16th century. Unlike English seals with balustoid elements as the terminal Scottish seals may consist of a terminal formed as a simple tapering rectangular section attached to the stem.

Serving Spoon = in this book, a large spoon usually between 9 1/2-13" in length

Silver Handles = It should be noted that silver handles on tea service items were not common in England or Ireland but were prominent in Scotland from 1720-50. Therefore, the descriptions indicate silver or wooden handles when the information was available.

Skene Dhu = meaning "black knife". About half the length of a dirk, a skene dhu is a small sheathed knife worn in the top of the right stocking when wearing the kilt.

Slip-top spoons = 17th century spoons similar to Puritan except that the end is cut at a severe angle (said to be slipped) rather than at a right angle.

Slop Bowl = a bowl used for disposal of used tea leaves or coffee sediment, usually broad and shallow compared with a sugar bowl. However, the distinction between slop and sugar bowls is not always clear.

Snuff Mull = a vertical snuff container usually of baluster form rather than a horizontal box. They may be all silver or simply silver-mounted.

Snuffer = usually a bell or cup shaped implement on a handle used to cover and extinguish the flame on a lighted candle or spirit lamp.

Socket = also called nozzle. The hollow upper part of a candlestick into which the candle is fitted. Sometimes sockets are made to be detachable.

Spherical = round, important in describing shapes of some teapots, milk jugs, covered sugars, etc. It is used here in place of the less-precise terms such as a globular and bullet.

Spool = of general cylindrical shape, slightly waisted.

Sporran = a Highland dress version of a leather or fur pouch worn at the front of the kilt and hung via a chain and leather strap. Frequently mounted with silver.

Spume = foam on a liquid as in breaking ocean waves at the shoreline.

Stands = early teapot and urn stands are usually supported on a simple rim foot contrasting with tazzas on one pedestal foot or salvers on three or more feet. After about 1735 specialized stands became less frequent and salvers served the purpose.

Stippled = having a group of dots or flecks applied via short strokes.

Stirrup Cup = designed to be taken on foxhunts. It is a slender drinking cup shaped frequently like a fox's or hound's head.

Swags = ornamental draperies resembling draped curtains.

Tazza = a salver or shallow dish on a raised pedestal foot

Thistle Mug = also called thistle cup. A relatively small mug of bell-shape with a flared rim similar to the shape of a thistle flower, usually with one or more applied girdles and frequently with several applied vertical lobes at the base simulating leaves. It may have a scrolled bead-decorated handle or a simple strap handle. It is uncommon outside of Scotland.

Toilet Service = equipment needed for the dressing table usually including a mirror, comb boxes, scent bottles, pin cushion, whisk, and sometimes candlesticks or ewers and basins.

Traprain silver (e.g. salts) = early 20th century reproductions of items from an ancient Roman silver hoard found on Traprain Law (hill), Scotland during quarrying activity in 1919. The firm of Brook and Son, Edinburgh, meticulously reproduced some items. The salts have a characteristic triangular shape.

Tray = In this book, it usually refers to a large salver with handles.

Trefid flatware/spoons = referring to a three lobed attachment or terminal as on a spoon. On a spoon this is created by flattening the upper part of the stem and using two notches two divide the terminal into three sections. When as attachments to bowls, etc the two side members are frequently described as commas. The trefid spoon terminal usually angles slightly upward form the plane of the stem. The trefid pattern was produced in Scotland mainly between 1670ca and 1710.

Trefoils = decorative elements of a leaf with three parts. Taken from the *Trifolium* genus.

Tumbler Cup = a cup without handles that tended to be broad but not deep. Sometimes these were nested when as sets. Scottish examples sometimes have slightly flared rims.

Two-Handled Cups = self explanatory except that they are distinguished from porringers by being more vertical compared with the diameter.

Unmarked Covers = Note that in 18th century Scotland and in contrast with London silver, the marking of covers was not common. Therefore, the descriptions lack a reference to this.

Vinaigrette = a small container (sometimes worn) designed to hold a sponge soaked in perfume or alternatively vinegar for use as smelling salts. It may be of small box form or take numerous other shapes.

Volute = a spiraled ornament resembling the designs found on gastropod mollusk (*Volutidae* family) shells (also used on Ionic capitals)

Waiter = in this book, used for a tray resting on three or more feet and 6 1/2" or less in diameter.

Warwick Cruet = a form of the cruet having the base designed with five rings. The earliest English example held five casters, however, many later examples hold two bottles and three casters.

Wavy-end flatware/spoons = similar to dog-nose in that it has a rounded center projection, like a dog's snout and two slightly rounded shoulders on the terminal. However, in this case, the end of the terminal of the spoon or fork is flat and in line with the stem. This is a largely early 18th century pattern in Scotland

Wax jack = an item used to distribute sealing wax from a reel to be melted and used in sealing correspondence. The molten wax was then stamped with the sender's seal.

WD maker's marks, 1740-92 Edinburgh = At press time for Compendium II, there remained considerable confusion surrounding Edinburgh WD marks. William Drummond is not included in the compendium because he made little if any silver in Edinburgh. Numerous variants of WD marks were employed between William Dempster and William Davie. The designations originally in Jackson are now viewed as uncertain at best. In many cases, a description of the letters (block vs. script) is provided where possible and both makers' names are listed in most cases. Hopefully, this will be resolved in the near future.

Widow's Lozenge = a heraldic rhombus-shaped geometric device for displaying the arms of a woman, usually a widow

William Jamieson – the maker's mark shown in Jackson marks is really James Mitchelson's mark turned upside down. Therefore, it is probably not Jamieson's mark at all, but rather Mitchelson's punch. Instead, a WI or IM in a plain oval seems likely to be the mark for either William Jamieson or possibly John Main. This quandary should be resolved in the near future.

Wine Label = also called wine tag, or bottle ticket, usually indicating the type of wine on a shaped shield or rectangle suspended around a bottle or decanter via a silver chain.

Wire and Wire work = Wire is created by drawing malleable silver through a series of smaller and smaller holes in a draw plate thereby reducing the gauge after each new pass and also strengthening the silver with each hardening. The resulting string may be round, square or multi-sided and can be used as a mouth wire to fortify a bowl, etc. rim or it may be twisted for use in decorative filigree work.

Works Cited

ARTICLES

Fell, H. G. "Scottish Silver at Stratton Street" [Messr. How of Edinburgh], in <u>Connoisseur</u> Vol CIII February 1939 pp107, 109.
[How of Edinburgh 1939]

Jones, Alfred E. "Some Old Scottish and English Plate of the Marquess of Linlithgow, K T" in <u>Apollo</u> vol XVIII September 1933 pp153-161.
[Linlithgow Collection]

.... "Binning Collection of Old English and Scottish Plate," in <u>Burlington Magazine</u>, vol LXVIII March 1936 pp199-225.
[Binning Collection]

...................."Collection of Plate of Sir John Stirling Maxwell, Bart. K T" in <u>Apollo</u> Vol XXIII April 1936 pp99-104, 207-214.
[Stirling Maxwell Collection]

...................."Silver at the Exhibition of Scottish Art" in <u>Burlington Magazine</u> Vol LXXIV 1939 pp71-72.
[Scottish Art Exhibition 1939]

Oman, Charles C. "Scottish Silver at the Royal Academy" in <u>Connoisseur</u> vol CIII, February 1939 pp70-75.
[Scottish Art Exhibition 1939]

BOOKS

Alcorn, Ellenor M. <u>English Silver at the Museum of Fine Arts in Boston Volume II.</u> MFA Publications: Boston 2000
[Alcorn, Museum of Fine Arts]

Bannister, Judith. <u>Collecting Antique Silver</u>. Galahad Books: NY 1972.
[Bannister]

Brett, Vanessa. The Sotheby's Directory of Silver 1600-1940. Sotheby's Publications: London 1986.
[Brett]

Burns, Thomas. <u>Old Scottish Communion Plate</u>. R & R Clarke: Edinburgh 1892.
[Burns]

Clayton, Michael. <u>The collector's Dictionary of the Silver and Gold of Great Britain and North America 2nd edition.</u> Antique Collector's Club: Suffolk 1985.
[Clayton Dictionary]

....................<u>Christie's Pictorial History of English and American Silver</u>. Phaidon-Christie's Ltd: Oxford 1985.
[Clayton Christie's Book]

<u>Connoisseur Art Sales Annual</u>, Connoisseur London.

[Connoisseur]

Cripps, Wilfred Joseph. <u>Old English Plate: Ecclesiastical, Decorative and Domestic: Its Makers and Marks</u>. J Murray: London 1906
[Cripps]

Curtis, Tony ed. <u>The Lyle Official Antique Review 1979</u>. Lyle Publication's: London 1978
[Lyle Annual Review 1979]

................<u>The Lyle Official Antique Review 1980</u>. Lyle Publication's: London 1979
[Lyle Annual Review 1980]

................<u>The Lyle Official Antique Review 1981</u>. Lyle Publication's: London 1980
[Lyle Annual Review 1981]

................<u>The Lyle Official Antique Review 1982.</u> Lyle Publication's: London 1981
[Lyle Annual Review 1982]

................<u>The Lyle Official Antique Review 1983</u>. Lyle Publication's: London 1982
[Lyle Annual Review 1983]

................<u>The Lyle Official Antique Review 1984</u>. Lyle Publication's: London 1983
[Lyle Annual Review 1984]

................<u>The Lyle Official Antique Review 1994</u>. Perigee 1993
[Lyle Annual Review 1994]

................<u>The Lyle Antiques and Their Value: Silver</u>. Voor Hoede Publications B. V.: NY 1982
[Lyle Silver Review]

Dalgleish, George and Stuart Maxwell. The Lovable Craft: 1687-1987. Pinpoint Direct Marketing: Edinburgh
[Dalgleish and Maxwell]

Davis, John D. <u>English Silver at Williamsburg</u>. Colonial Williamsburg Foundation and University Press of Virginia: Charlottesville 1976.
[English Silver at Williamsburg, Davis]

Delieb, Eric. <u>Investing in Silver</u>. Clarkson N Potter: NY 1967
[Delieb]

Finlay, Ian. <u>Scottish Gold and Silver Work.</u> Pelican Publishing Co: Gretna, LA 1991.
[Finlay 1991]

Grimwade, Arthur. <u>The Queen's Silver: A Survey of Her Majesty's Personal Collection</u>. The Connoisseur: London 1953
[Grimwade, The Queen's Silver]

Guthrie, Dr. William. <u>Dundee Silver 1750-1850</u>. W Guthrie Publisher: 1995.

Harkenbroch, Yvonne. <u>English and Other Silver in the Irwin Untermeyer Collection</u>. NY Metropolitan Museum of Art 1963
[Untermeyer Collection]

Hayden, Arthur. Chats on Old Silver. Dover Publications Inc: NY 1969
[Hayden]

Holland, Margaret. Silver: An Illustrated Guide to Collecting Silver. Octopus Books Ltd: Hong Kong 1983.
[Holland]

Houart, Victor. Miniature Silver Toys. Alpine Fine Arts: NY 1989.
[Houart]

How, G.E.P and Jane P How. English and Scottish Silver Spoons 3 volumes. 1952-1957
[How Spoons]

Hughes, George Bernard and Therle Hughes. Three Centuries of English Domestic Silver: 1-1820. W Funk: NY 1952
[Hughes]

Jackson, Charles James. An Illustrated History of English Plate 2 volumes. Country Life Ltd And B T Batsford: London 1911
[Jackson 2 vol]

Jackson, Charles. Jackson's Silver and Gold Marks. ed. Ian Pickford Antique Collector's Club: Suffolk 1987
[Jackson Marks]

Jones, E. A. Old English Gold Plate. Bemrose & Sons Ltd: London 1907
[Jones]

Kovel, Ralph and Terry Kovel. Kovel's Antiques and Collectible's Price List for the 1992 Market 24th edition. Crown Publishers: NY 1991
[Kovels 1992]

.................................Kovel's Antiques and Collectibles Price List for the 1995 Market. Crown Publishers: NY 1994
[Kovels 1994]

Lee, Georgiana and Ronald A Lee. British Silver Monteith Bowls Including American and European Examples. Manor House Press: Surry 1978.
[Lee Monteiths]

Luddington, John. Starting to Collect Silver. Antique Collector's Club: Suffolk 1984
[Luddington]

Pickford, Ian. Silver Flatware: English, Irish and Scottish 1660-1980. Antique Collector's Club: Suffolk 1988.
[Pickford Spoons]

Rabinovitch, Benton Seymour. Antique Silver Servers for the Dining Table: Style, Function, Food and Social History. Joslin Hall Publishing: Concord, MA 1991
[Rabinovitch]

Rinker, Harry L. ed. Warman's Antiques and Their Prices 27th edition. Krause Publications:

Iola, WI 1993
[Warmans]

Ticher, Kurt. Irish Silver in the Rococo Period. Irish University Press: Shannon 1972
[Ticher Irish Silver]

Walden, Maurgherita Howard de. Queen Charlotte's Loan Exhibition of Old Silver May 1st- June 8th Seaford House, Belgrave Square London. The Saint Catherine Press Royal: London 1929
[Queen's Exhibition]

Waldron, Peter. The Price Guide to Antique Silver 2nd edition. Antique Collector's Club: Suffolk 1988
[Waldron]

Wark, Robert R. British Silver in the Huntington Collection. Huntington Library & Art Gallery, San Marino, CA 1978.
[Wark]

Wees, Beth Carver. English, Irish and Scottish Silver at the Stirling and Francine Clark Art Institute. Hudson Hills Press: NY 1997
[Wees, Clark Art Institute]

Wills, Geoffrey. Candlesticks. C N Potter: NY 1974
[Wills, Candlesticks]

CATALOGS

Bonhams Sales Catalogs
[Bonhams]

Breadalbane Collection of Silversmith's Work. The Dowell, Ltd Sale Catalog May 30-31 1935. Edinburgh
[Breadalbane Collection Sale]

Catalog of Exhibition of Scottish Silver, Royal Scottish Museum, August – September 1948
[Royal Scottish Museum Exhibition]

Catalog of Highly Important English, Scottish and Continental Silver, the Property of His Grace The Duke of Buccleuch…and the Hopetoun Estates Company. Sotheby's Sales Catalog

25 July 1953
[Hopetoun Silver]

Christie's Art Treasures Exhibition Catalog 1932
[Art Treasures Exhibition]

Christie's International Sales Catalogs
[Christie's]

Exhibition of Scottish Silver from the Collection of John Noble, Chairman of the Scottish Craft Center, 24 August – 12 September 1959
[Noble Collection]

Glasgow Empire Exhibition May-October 1938 Old Scottish Silver. Catalogue of Loan
  Collection in Scottish Historical Pavilion. The Scottish Committee 1938
  [Glasgow Empire Exhibition]

How of Edinburgh Ltd, Silver Exhibition at 15 Stratton Street, London W1 1936
  [How of Edinburgh 1936]

How of Edinburgh Ltd, Silver Exhibition at 15 Stratton Street, London W1 1937
  [How of Edinburgh 1937]

J H Bourdon-Smith Catalogs London
  [JH Bourdon-Smith Catalog]

Loan Exhibition of Old English Plate 1929 Park Lane, London
  [Park London Exhibition]

Nicholas Shaw Catalogs
  [Nicholas Shaw Catalog]

Palace of History: Scottish Exhibition of Natural History, Arts & Industry, Glasgow (1911)
  2 volumes
  [Glasgow Exhibition of 1911]

Phillip's Auction House Catalogs
  [Phillips]

Scottish Provincial Silver from the David Morris Collection 3 July 1984 and 9 October 1984
  Christie's Scotland Sale Catalogs
  [The Morris Collection]

Shaw Collection of Important Scottish Silver and Pistols, the 29th March 1983 Christie's Sale
  Catalog
  [Shaw Collection]

Silver Teapots from the John Bell of Aberdeen Collection, 20th November – 16th December at the
  Ceylon Tea Center, Glasgow Exhibition Catalog 1961
  [Bell of Aberdeen]

Sotheby's Sales Catalogs
  [Sotheby's]

JOURNALS

Antiques Atwood: Boston 1922-1971.
  [Antiques Magazine]

The Magazine Antiques Straight Enterprises: NY 1971-present.
  [Antiques Magazine]

Apollo Apollo: London 1925-present.
  [Apollo]

Burlington Magazine Burlington Magazine Publications Ltd: London 1903-present.
   [Burlington Magazine]

The Connoisseur National Magazine Company: London 1901-present.
   [Connoisseur Magazine]

Country Life Country Life: London 1897-present.
   [Country Life]

The Scottish Art Review. Glasgow Art Gallery and Museums Associations: Glasgow 1948 -
   present
   [Scottish Art Review]

Silver Studies. Journal of the Silver Society ed. Vanessa Brett
   [Silver Studies]

MEDIA

Christie's Negative File, identification numbers for images housed at Christie's London

Christie's Picture Files, photographs stored at Christie's International London

Sotheby's Picture Files, photographs stored at Sotheby's London

MUSEUMS

Aberdeen Museums and Galleries

Art Institute of Chicago IL USA

Baltimore Museum of Art MD USA

Berkshire Museum Pittsfield, MA USA

Birmingham Museum of Art, Birmingham AL USA

Boston Museum of Fine Art MA USA

Campbell Museum Camden NJ USA

Carnegie Institute Museum of Art, Pittsburgh PA USA

Cincinnati Art Museum OH USA

Clark Art Institute

Brooklyn Museum Brooklyn NY USA

Dallas Museum of Art TX USA

Dayton Art Institute OH USA

Detroit Institute of Art MI USA

Dewitt Gallery, Hyman Collection - Colonial Williamsburg, Williamsburg VA USA
    [Hyman Collection - Colonial Williamsburg, VA USA

Dundee Museums and Art Galleries

Fogg Art Museum, Harvard University, Cambridge MA USA

Glasgow Museums Glasgow Scotland

High Museum of Art, Atlanta GA USA

Huntington Library San Mateo CA USA

Huntley House, The City of Edinburgh Museum, Edinburgh Scotland UK

Indianapolis Museum of Art IN USA

J B Speed Museum Louisville KT USA

Los Angeles County Museum CA USA

Lyman Allyn Art Museum New London CT USA

McKissick Museum University of SC Columbus SC USA

Metropolitan Museum of Art NY USA

Milwaukee Art Museum WI USA

Minneapolis Institute of Art MN USA

Musee de Beaux Arts Montreal Canada

National Museums of Scotland, Edinburgh Scotland

National Museum of Wales Cardiff Wales

Nova Scotia Museum Halifax Nova Scotia Canada

Perth City Art Gallery and Museum Perth Scotland

Philadelphia Museum of Art PA USA

Portland Art Museum OR USA

Rhode Island School of Museum Providence, RI USA

Royal Ontario Museum Toronto Canada

St Louis City Art Museum LA USA

San Diego Museum of Art CA USA

San Francisco, Fine Arts Museums of CA USA

Toledo Museum of Art OH USA

Victoria and Albert Museum London UK

Virginia Museum of Fine Arts Richmond VA USA

Yale University Art Gallery New Haven CT USA